Moral Enhancement: Critical Perspectives

ROYAL INSTITUTE OF PHILOSOPHY SUPPLEMENT: 83

EDITED BY

Hauskeller and Coyne

CAMBRIDGE
UNIVERSITY PRESS

PUBLISHED BY THE PRESS SYNDICATE OF THE UNIVERSITY OF CAMBRIDGE
The Pitt Building, Trumpington Street, Cambridge, CB2 1RP,
United Kingdom

CAMBRIDGE UNIVERSITY PRESS
UPH, Shaftesbury Road, Cambridge CB2 8BS, United Kingdom
32 Avenue of the Americas, New York, NY 10013–2473, USA
477 Williamstown Road, Port Melbourne, VIC 3207, Australia
C/Orense, 4, planta 13, 28020 Madrid, Spain
Lower Ground Floor, Nautica Building, The Water Club, Beach Road,
Granger Bay, 8005 Cape Town, South Africa

Printed in the United Kingdom at Bell and Bain Ltd.
Typeset by Techset Composition Ltd, Salisbury, UK

A catalogue record for this book is available from the British Library

ISBN 9781108717342
ISSN 1358-2461

Contents

Notes on Contributors

Robbie Arrell is International Research Fellow in the School of Philosophy at Wuhan University (China). He previously held positions at the University of Melbourne and Monash University (Australia). His main research interests are political philosophy and ethics (both normative and applied).

Lewis Coyne received his Ph.D. from the University of Exeter (UK) in 2018, where he also obtained an M.Res. in Science and Technology Studies. His principal research interests are practical ethics, the philosophy of nature, and philosophical anthropology. His monograph, *Hans Jonas: Life, Technology, and the Horizons of Responsibility*, is forthcoming with Bloomsbury.

John Danaher is a lecturer in the School of Law at NUI Galway (Ireland). His research interests lie, broadly, in the areas of ethics, the philosophy of law, and emerging technologies. He has published numerous articles on human enhancement, brain-based lie detection, the philosophy of punishment, and artificial intelligence. He writes the blog *Philosophical Disquisitions*, and is an affiliate scholar at the Institute for Ethics and Emerging Technologies.

Brian D. Earp is Associate Director of the Yale-Hastings Program in Ethics and Health Policy at Yale University and The Hastings Center (USA). His work is interdisciplinary, combining philosophy, psychology, and bioethics. He holds degrees from the universities of Yale, Oxford, and Cambridge.

Kathryn B. Francis is currently Postdoctoral Research Fellow in the Department of Philosophy and School of Psychology at the University of Reading (UK). Prior to starting her postdoctoral position, Kathryn completed her Ph.D. in moral psychology at the University of Plymouth (UK).

Lily Eva Frank received her Ph.D. from the Graduate Center of the City University of New York (USA) in 2014. She is Assistant Professor in the Department of Philosophy and Ethics at the Eindhoven University of Technology (The Netherlands). Her research focusses on the ethics of technology, biomedical ethics, and moral psychology.

doi:10.1017/S1358246118000504   © The Royal Institute of Philosophy and the contributors 2018
Royal Institute of Philosophy Supplement **83** 2018   v

Notes on Contributors

Walter Glannon is Professor of Philosophy at the University of Calgary (Canada). He is the author of *Bioethics and the Brain* (2007), *Brain, Body, and Mind: Neuroethics with a Human Face* (2011), and editor of *Free Will and the Brain: Neuroscientific, Philosophical and Legal Perspectives* (2015).

Valerie Gray Hardcastle is St. Elizabeth Healthcare Executive Director of the Institute for Health Innovation, and Vice President for Health Innovation at Northern Kentucky University (USA).

Michael Hauskeller is Head of the Department of Philosophy at the University of Liverpool (UK), and author of *Better Humans? Understanding the Enhancement Project* (2013), *Sex and the Posthuman Condition* (2014), and *Mythologies of Transhumanism* (2016).

Pei-Hua Huang is a Ph.D. candidate in the Department of Philosophy at Monash University (Australia). Her project focusses on how moral enhancement may impact on both personal and political autonomy. She is also interested in conceptions of disease, just health care, and moral responsibility.

Michał Klincewicz is Assistant Professor in the Department of Cognitive Science, Institute of Philosophy at Jagiellonian University, Kraków (Poland) and was a postdoctoral researcher at the Berlin School of Mind and Brain. He received his Ph.D. in philosophy at the Graduate Center of the City University of New York in 2013. His research focusses on temporal aspects of cognition and ethical problems connected to artificial intelligence.

Aleksandra Kulawska is a Ph.D. student at the University of Birmingham, where she researches the prospective impact of climate change on temperate forests. She obtained her M.Sc. in Environmental Protection and Management from the University of Edinburgh, and her Batchelor's degree in Philosophy from the University of Exeter (UK). Her research interests include ecosystem science, plant ecology, and environmental philosophy.

Teodora Manea studied philosophy in Romania and Germany. Since 2010 she has been working for the University of Exeter (UK), teaching medical humanities and medical sociology. She also works as an ethics expert for the European Commission and does further research in the areas of ethics of care and medical sociolinguistics.

Inmaculada de Melo-Martín is Professor of Medical Ethics at Weill Cornell Medicine, Cornell University (USA). She holds a Ph.D. in Philosophy and an M.S. in Biology. Her research focusses on ethical and epistemological issues related to biomedical sciences and technologies. She has published extensively on those topics in both philosophy and science journals. Her most recent book is *Rethinking Reprogenetics* (2017).

Norbert Paulo is a lecturer in practical philosophy at the University of Graz and the University of Salzburg (Austria). He holds a Ph.D. in Philosophy from the University of Hamburg (Germany), where he studied both philosophy and law. His research concerns applied ethics, ethical theory, the philosophy of law, and empirical ethics. His monograph *The Confluence of Philosophy and Law in Applied Ethics* was published in 2016. He is also co-editor (with Christoph Bublitz) of a forthcoming special issue of *Neuroethics* on moral enhancement.

Nigel Pleasants is Senior Lecturer in Philosophy and Sociology at the University of Exeter (UK). He works and has published on Wittgenstein and ethics (particularly the idea of moral certainty and its application to the wrongness of killing and to progressive moral change), institutional wrongdoing, philosophical issues arising from the Holocaust, genocide and slavery, and animal ethics.

Mark Rowlands (D.Phil., Oxon.) is Professor of Philosophy at the University of Miami (USA). He is the author of eighteen books, translated into more than twenty languages, and over a hundred journal articles, book chapters, and reviews. His primary areas of research are the philosophy of mind and ethics.

Elizabeth Shaw is a lecturer in criminal law and criminology at the University of Aberdeen (UK), and a director of the *Justice Without Retribution Network*. Her primary research interests are criminal responsibility, penal theory, and moral uncertainty. She has written on the moral enhancement of offenders, psychopathy, and free will.

John R. Shook is Research Associate in Philosophy, University at Buffalo, New York, and also Lecturer in Philosophy, Bowie State University, Maryland (USA). His research areas include philosophical psychology, moral neuroscience, and neuroethics. He co-edited *Neuroscience, Neurophilosophy, and Pragmatism* (2014), and his articles have appeared in *Neuroethics, AJOB-Neuroscience*, and the *Cambridge Quarterly of Healthcare Ethics*.

Edward Skidelsky teaches philosophy at the University of Exeter (UK). His previous books include *Ernst Cassirer* (2008) and *How Much is Enough?* (with Robert Skidelsky; 2012). He is currently writing a history of virtue and vice.

Marta Sokólska graduated from Jagiellonian University (Poland) with a Batchelor's degree in Sociology and a Master's degree in Cognitive Science. She has a particular interest in the issue of moral education and moral development, focussing on global education and its methods.

Sylvia Terbeck is a social psychologist and lecturer at the University of Plymouth (UK). Her research involves group processes and morality using interdisciplinary methods, such as psychopharmacology and immersive virtual reality. She has published numerous scientific papers and a book about the social neuroscience of intergroup relations.

Peter Shiu-Hwa Tsu received his Ph.D. from the Australian National University in 2011 and is currently an associate professor in Chung Cheng University in Taiwan. His research interests include particularism in ethics and aesthetics, bioethics, and free will. His articles have appeared in the journals *Philosophical Studies* and *Erkenntnis*, amongst others. He was recently commissioned to write an entry on particularism for *Oxford Bibliographies Online*.

Giuseppe Turchi is Collaborator for Teaching and Research Activities (Cultore della Materia) in the Department of Humanities, Social Sciences, and Cultural Industries at the Università degli Studi di Parma (Italy). His research interests include pragmatism, neuroethics, and naturalism.

Anna Frammartino Wilks received her Ph.D. from the University of Toronto and is currently Senior Instructor in Philosophy at Acadia University (Canada). Her research interests are metaphysics, epistemology, and ethics in Kant and Early Modern Philosophy; causality, substance, and the self; and the application of Kant's thought to problems in the philosophy of biology, mind, and artificial intelligence.

Harris Wiseman is a fellow of the International Society for Science and Religion. He gained his Ph.D. in Divinity from the University of Cambridge (UK), where he worked as a research associate. He is author of *The Myth of the Moral Brain: The Limits of Moral Enhancement* (2016).

Introduction

MICHAEL HAUSKELLER AND LEWIS COYNE

In 2016 the annual Royal Institute of Philosophy conference was held at the University of Exeter on the topic of moral enhancement, or, more precisely, moral *bio*enhancement. While we can understand and describe moral enhancement as any intervention that improves, or intends to improve, somebody's morality (which would include, for instance, teaching about right and wrong, character-building exercises, or leading by example), moral *bio*enhancement seeks to achieve said improvement directly through the manipulation of people's biological constitution, using pharmacological, neuroscientific, or genetic means of modification.[1]

Whether that is possible or indeed desirable has proven controversial. The debate began ten years ago with Ingmar Persson and Julian Savulescu's first paper on the subject, warning against the dangers of cognitive enhancement and urging us to explore the possibility of moral bioenhancement to counter those dangers.[2] It was followed by many other articles by the same authors, all insisting that we have good reason to think that moral bioenhancement is not only possible – or likely to become possible very soon – but also something we simply cannot afford *not* to pursue. As Persson and Savulescu argued in their 2012 monograph *Unfit for the Future: The Need for Moral Enhancement*, our very survival as a species may well depend on it: without moral bioenhancement humanity is doomed to perish, defeated by our own technological might and constitutional inability to wield it responsibly.[3]

Naturally, not everyone agreed with Persson and Savulescu's assessment. Various issues have been raised with their proposal,

---

[1]   Throughout the remainder of this introduction – and in most of the contributions, unless otherwise stated – "moral enhancement" and "moral bioenhancement" are used interchangeably.

[2]   Ingmar Persson and Julian Savulescu, 'The Perils of Cognitive Enhancement and the Urgent Imperative to Enhance the Moral Character of Humanity', *Journal of Applied Philosophy* **25**:3 (2008), 162–77.

[3]   Ingmar Persson and Julian Savulescu, *Unfit for the Future: The Need for Moral Enhancement*, Oxford: Oxford University Press, 2012.

doi:10.1017/S1358246118000255

which, if nothing else, has stimulated a lively and fruitful debate on what can and should be done regarding the moral character of humanity, the effectiveness of the suggested means, and the desirability of the suggested ends. The debate, however, has so far been largely confined to those who have a strong research interest in the ethics of human enhancement *per se*.[4] But just as the human enhancement debate ultimately revolves around the question of what it means to be *human*, the debate about moral enhancement ultimately revolves around the question of what it means to be *moral*, and that question, as John Harris has rightly pointed out, should be of interest to all moral philosophers and ethicists.[5] Moreover, precisely because the fundamental question at the heart of the debate is what it means to be moral, it would seem pertinent to seek the advice of those who have studied the nature of morality from a variety of perspectives, and ask them what they think of the idea of moral enhancement. Hence those we invited to contribute to the conference and subsequently to the present volume are not the usual suspects, but rather philosophers, psychologists, cognitive scientists, and other scholars who may not have written on moral enhancement before, but whose expertise and perspective appeared nonetheless highly relevant for a comprehensive assessment of the proposal.

Consequently, the focus of the volume is the question: What *is* morality? After all, how we answer this question determines whether it *can* be enhanced, and if so, *how*. Does morality consist in having the right emotions, or in being rational, or in a combination of the two? Does something called "morality" exist as such, or can there only ever be certain moral belief systems and different moral frameworks, so that before we can enhance someone morally we need to determine *which* morality we would like to see enhanced?

There are, however, various other crucial questions that will be addressed along the way, among them the following:

Are we really "unfit for the future", as Persson and Savulescu have claimed? Is our moral psychology – with its anti-utilitarian adherence to the act-omission doctrine, and lack of concern about events that occur at a distance – no longer fit for purpose?

Are we constitutionally incapable of refraining from the things that imperil our own existence (climate change, nuclear war, and

---

[4]   Cf. Michael Hauskeller, *Better Humans? Understanding the Human Enhancement Project*, London: Routledge, 2013.

[5]   John Harris, *How to Be Good: The Possibility of Moral Enhancement*, Oxford: Oxford University Press, 2016, 117: '[a]ll moral philosophers, and indeed all ethicists, must have an interest in moral enhancement'.

aggression)? Are the problems that moral enhancement is supposed to solve even caused by a lack of morality?

Is it sufficiently obvious what is right and wrong, good and bad – what is just, fair, or altruistic? Are justice, fairness, and altruism *always* good or *always* commendable?

Would the new moral enhancement envisioned compromise our moral autonomy? Would it matter if it did? What about "traditional" moral enhancement – i.e., education? Does that work, and if so, how?

How likely is it *in practice* that we can morally enhance people, and do so in time? How then would it be implemented? Would we want a (regulated) market for moral enhancement drugs, or instead to make their usage compulsory?

And finally: Who makes the decisions? Who guards the guardians? Who enhances the enhancers?

It is clear, then, that the apparently straightforward prospect of moral enhancement in fact raises many problems. Some of these are of a practical nature and might be answered empirically, while others are questions of principle, permitting less certainty. Both kinds, however, must be satisfactorily addressed if we are to determine the value of the moral enhancement proposal. We hope that the present volume goes some way towards doing so.

University of Liverpool
M.Hauskeller@liverpool.ac.uk
University of Exeter
lc453@exeter.ac.uk

What is Moral Enhancement?

MARK ROWLANDS

Abstract
The idea of moral enhancement has no clear meaning. This is because the idea of being moral has no clear meaning. There are numerous ways in which one might go astray, morally speaking, and each of these ways, in turn, fragments on further analysis. The concept of moral enhancement is as broad, messy, and mottled as the reasons why people behave badly. This mottled character of moral failure calls into question the feasibility of (non-traditional) programmes of moral enhancement.

1. Introduction

If there is a case for our moral enhancement – if such enhancement is thought desirable – it is presumably based on the idea that, while we humans are not as bad as we might be, neither are we as good as we could be. And if we are not as good as we might be this is, again presumably, because we do things that are (i) various shades of bad, and (ii) at least to some extent avoidable. Human history is littered with bad but seemingly avoidable episodes. And so too, barring the occasional moral saint or savant, are the lives of each one of us. The purpose of moral enhancement would be to get us to stop doing these bad, avoidable things. But if this is the purpose of moral enhancement then the *concept* of moral enhancement is likely to be as broad and mottled as the reasons why people do bad but avoidable things. The messy, mottled character of the concept of moral enhancement, I shall argue, is not merely of academic interest. On the contrary, it has implications for the practical feasibility of such enhancement.

2. Dumb and Dumber: Enhancing Doxastic Health

A fact so obvious that it is frequently overlooked is that many – perhaps most – of the bad, avoidable things we humans do are the result of us holding stupid, stupid beliefs.[1] The belief that one

[1] See Mark Rowlands, *The Philosopher and the Wolf* (London: Granta, 2008) and also 'The Structure of Evil', in A. Linzey (ed.), *The Link Between*

doi:10.1017/S1358246118000267   ©The Royal Institute of Philosophy and the contributors 2018
Royal Institute of Philosophy Supplement **83** 2018

belongs to a master race; that one is the victim of a worldwide Jewish conspiracy; that one can attain heaven, not to mention the ministrations of seventy-two virgins, simply by murdering a few non-believers; that there is no such thing as climate change, or if there is it does not have an anthropogenic source; and so on and so forth. These days, it might not be politically correct to characterise the sincerely held worldviews of people as stupid. But the belief that we can't or shouldn't do this is, as far as I can see, just another stupid belief from which misery ensues. And, anyway, these examples are just off the top of my head. We all have our favourite examples of gross human stupidity and the misery that results. Without taking a stand on just how stupid each belief is and just how much misery results from it, one thing is clear: there are more than enough stupid beliefs to go around, and more than enough misery that results from them. This misery is entirely avoidable ... if only we could find a way of foregoing the stupid beliefs.

This type of moral failing, then, yields a corresponding form of moral enhancement: enhance people so they are less likely to hold stupid beliefs. How does one do this? Is there a pill that will do this? Can we achieve it by snipping a few genes here and there? Perhaps we can, or one day will. But there is no obvious reason why such a strategy would be preferable to, for example, a better education system – one that, say, more effectively enhances the ability to think critically about issues, and emphasises the importance of such trifles as logic and evidence and even that old chestnut: truth.

I wouldn't want to unfairly rule out a potential role for cognitive enhancing drugs. Stupidity is, after all, a cognitive deficit. So, why not try to mitigate it through the use of cognitive enhancers – *nootropics*? We can overlook the fact that the current generation of such enhancers still looks rather primitive – with effects that are highly variable between individuals, often highly dependent on base-line cognitive functioning, and which seem to unevenly target long term memory rather than intelligence *per se*. I have in mind something a little better than this. Not a stimulant – that won't be much use. And not something that primarily targets memory – that probably won't be much use either. But perhaps some sort of positive allosteric modulator of AMPA receptors – some suitably developed version of the *racetam* family, for example – might do the trick. Suppose, in short, we did have a proven, reliable cognitive enhancer

Animals Abuse and Human Violence (Brighton: Sussex Academic Press), 201–5.

at our disposal. If we did, it would likely make us intelligent enough to realise that this is not what we need. There is something about the appeal to cognitive enhancement as a route to moral enhancement that misses the mark – by a rather spectacularly wide margin. We might put matters thus: it's not rocket science! It's not rocket science that views that have no evidence supporting them, or are illogical, should not be trusted – not enough to base a life and a consistent policy upon them. This is not an idea lying just beyond the limits of our cognitive powers – limits that we might be able to transcend with the right chemical stimulation. We don't need a *racetam* to work that out. It is a fact that belongs to the realm of the *bleeding obvious*.

This suggests that the stupidity that is at the root of many moral problems is not, in fact, a cognitive phenomenon – certainly not a *purely* cognitive phenomenon. The sort of stupid beliefs that can engender moral problems arise from an exercise of the will as much as of a lack of exercise of the intellect. When a belief is really, really, stupid, and one nevertheless has it, this can only be because one really, really wants to have it. This might be because one has a significant stake in the belief being true. Perhaps the status of the group with which one identifies depends on the belief being true. Perhaps one's status within that group depends on it. There can be a variety of reasons for one having a stake in the truth of such a belief. But none of these involves a deficit of the intellect. We are talking about *affect*, not intellect. This brings us to the next possible form of moral enhancement.

3. Enhance Critical Scrutiny

There is a tradition of thinking of moral action as dependent on our scrutiny, or at least the ability to scrutinise, our motivations. The tradition in question is, of course, the Kantian tradition. Christine Korsgaard puts the idea very nicely:

> As rational beings we are conscious of the principles on which we are inclined to act. Because of this, we have the ability to ask ourselves whether we should act in the way we are instinctively inclined to. We can say to ourselves: "I am inclined to do act-A for the sake of end-E. But should I?"[2]

---

[2]   Christine Korsgaard, 'Fellow Creatures: Kantian Ethics and Our Duties to Animals', in G. Peterson (ed.), *Tanner Lectures on Human Values* (Salt Like City: University of Utah Press, 2004).

It is this ability, according to Kant, that separates us from the rest of creation: this is what elevates us to the kingdom of *ends* rather than that of mere *means*. We do not simply have motivations; in addition we can scrutinise them. That is, we can interrogate our motives and try to work out if they are motives we should endorse or ones we should reject. I have motive M, I can think to myself. Is this a motive I should embrace or one I should resist? We can ask ourselves these sorts of questions. Nothing else can. Kant's view of how we should go about answering such questions is well known. In a nutshell, we must identify if our motivation is one such that we can consistently will that it be adopted by all members of the kingdom of ends – i.e., rational beings. If we can consistently will this, then the motivation is one that we should embrace.

We can, however, take this *general* Kantian picture of moral motivation and divorce it from Kant's *specific* conception of in what the critical scrutiny of motivations consists. Instead of asking whether our motivation is universalisable, we might instead ask whether it *maximises utility*; or whether it is a motivation that would be agreed to by *rational contractors under appropriate conditions of ignorance*; or whether it is a motivation that would be embraced by a *virtuous person*, and so on. These are all possible forms that critical scrutiny of one's motivations might take – and there are, of course, others. My interest here is with the general idea of critical scrutiny rather than the specific forms such scrutiny might take.

If being a moral actor requires the ability to critically scrutinise one's motivations, then the corresponding form of enhancement seems clear: enhance the ability of people to critically scrutinise their motivations. Simple! Yet the sheen of simplicity quickly dissipates – fragmenting into several quite different ideas. A failure to critically scrutinise one's motivations can be the result of more than one type of cause. It might simply be that one can't be bothered. One is perfectly capable of scrutinising one's motivations but, for one reason or another, one would rather not. One is *unwilling* to scrutinise one's motivations. Perhaps it seems like a lot of trouble? Perhaps one has other things one would rather be doing? Whatever the reason, this is an *affective* deficit. One has the ability to critically scrutinise one's motivations. But one does not *care* enough to exercise this ability. If this is the problem, then the corresponding form of moral enhancement will have to target an affective deficit of this sort. It will have to instill a concern for, and desire to engage in, the scrutinising of one's motivations.

On the other hand, it may be that a person's failure to scrutinise her motivations does not stem from a lack of desire but from lack of *ability*.

She does not critically scrutinise her motivations because she is *unable*, rather than unwilling, to do so. This would be a *cognitive* rather than affective deficit. The corresponding form of moral enhancement would, therefore, involve augmenting one's cognitive – specifically one's meta-cognitive – powers. This, however, is only the beginning of the story. There are at least *two* distinct cognitive deficiencies that might be at the root of her problem.

First, a person might be hopeless at identifying her motivations. We know this is a problem for all of us to some degree. We commonly, for example, attribute to ourselves judgements that we never really made. In a classic study, Nisbett and Wilson convinced various test subjects that they were taking part in a market survey. The unwitting subjects were presented with four pairs of identical pantyhose and asked which they preferred.[3] The majority of subjects strongly preferred the pantyhose placed on the right. When asked to explain this, they confidently – but wrongly – declared that their preferred pantyhose were superior because they were softer, had the nicest colour, etc. In fact, they chose the pantyhose on the right because of a quirk of our brain: we have a strong right-preference. It was the location of the pantyhose that was the basis of their judgement.

A common refrain emerging from the "new unconscious" research is that we have far from infallible access to the workings of our minds and the causes of our behaviour.[4] Confabulation is the norm, not the exception. Even if this overstates matters, a healthy scepticism regarding one's ability to identify one's real motivation in any given circumstance is certainly justified. One form moral enhancement might take, therefore, is augmenting our ability to identify our motivations – to make confabulation a rare exception rather than depressingly common.

On the other hand, even if a person is exceptionally good at identifying his motivations, he might suffer from another deficiency: he is absolutely hopeless at bringing moral principles – universalisability, utility maximisation, impartiality, etc. – to bear on them. He has a motivation, and has correctly identified this motivation, but is hopeless at working out whether it will maximise utility, or whether it is universalisable, or would be agreed to by rational contractors under appropriate conditions of ignorance. Like the person who is useless at identifying her motivations, this person suffers

[3]   R. Nisbett and T. Wilson, 'Telling More Than We Can Know: Verbal Reports on Mental Processes', *Psychological Review* **84**:3 (1977), 231–59.
[4]   D. Wegner, *The Illusion of Conscious Will* (Cambridge, MA: MIT Press, 2002).

from a cognitive deficiency. But it is a *different* cognitive deficiency. Each deficiency would require a corresponding form of enhancement. The enhancement would aim to instill or improve a certain meta-cognitive skill, but this would be a different skill in each case.

Even if we could work out which meta-cognitive skill we must try to enhance in any given case of scrutiny-deficiency, there is a further problem. Someone may be superb at identifying their motivations, and faultless in the bringing to bear of ethical or meta-ethical principles on them. But this would hardly qualify as moral enhancement if the principles thus brought to bear were hopelessly warped – for example, murderous or xenophobic. Enhancing a person's ability to critically scrutinise his motivations only counts as moral enhancement if the ethical/meta-ethical principles brought to bear in such scrutiny are morally *good* or *right* ones. Now we have some real problems, of course, since what counts as morally good or right will vary between theories. Whether universalisability, and the good will that seeks and acts on this, is the paramount moral consideration depends on whether you are a Kantian or a utilitarian. So, it seems, to properly pursue the idea of moral enhancement as enhancement of the ability to critically scrutinise one's motivations, we would have to enhance the ability to identify correct moral theories. This, as millennia of internecine strife amongst moral philosophers seems to demonstrate, is a bit of a tall order (to put it mildly).

4. Enhance Virtue

Never mind. Never mind. We've crossed off critical scrutiny, but never mind. There are plenty of other traditions in moral psychology we might work with. There is the Aristotelian, virtue-ethical tradition, for example. Perhaps moral enhancement should be understood as enhancement of one's moral *virtues*. Of course, there are disagreements as to what counts as a moral virtue. As Michael Slote has pointed out, kindness and compassion did not feature highly on Aristotle's list of virtues, but contemporary theorists such as Philippa Foot, John McDowell, and Rosalind Hursthouse assume they are virtues.[5]

---

[5] Michael Slote, 'Virtue Ethics', in J. Skorupski (ed.), *The Routledge Companion to Ethics* (London: Routledge, 2010) 478–89; Philippa Foot, *Virtues and Vices and Other Essays in Moral Philosophy* (Oxford: Oxford University Press, 1978); John McDowell, 'Virtue and Reason', *The Monist* **62**:3 1979, 331–50; Rosalind Hursthouse, *On Virtue Ethics* (Oxford: Oxford University Press, 1999).

But that doesn't really matter. We can decide which things are moral virtues, and then go about enhancing them – or so the idea goes.

The first problem with this is that virtues do not exist in a vacuum: they exist only in a surrounding cognitive and emotional milieu. This is so for several reasons. First, consider this famous passage from the *Nicomachean Ethics*. Aristotle writes:

> But for actions in accord with the virtues to be done transparently or justly it does not suffice that they themselves have the right qualities. Rather, the agent must also be in the right state when he does them. First he must know that he is doing virtuous actions; second, he must decide on them, and decide on them for themselves; and, third, he must also do them from a firm and unchanging state.[6]

The expression, 'decide on them and decide on them for themselves' is commonly taken to mean that the agent must perform an action because it is the virtuous thing to do. Thus, Aristotle's first two conditions place what we might call a reflection condition on virtuous action. Roughly:

> For any action φ, performed by agent A, for φ to be an instance of virtuous behaviour, it is necessary that A (1) understands that φ exemplifies virtue V, and (2) performs φ because he wishes to be virtuous.

Therefore, contained in this account of what is required to engage in virtuous behaviour are two possible forms of moral enhancement. First, one might enhance: the ability to *understand* which actions exemplify or instantiate virtues. Second, one might enhance the *desire* to be virtuous. Once again, we find the enhancement proposal straddling both cognitive and affective elements. The notion of enhancement breaks down into two kinds – one cognitive and one affective – just as it did with the scrutiny-based model of enhancement.

There is, however, more to the complexity of the virtue-based model of enhancement than this. The third condition Aristotle places on an action counting as virtuous invokes the notion of a 'firm and unchanging state'. This firm and unchanging state is far more than a mere behavioural disposition. The following definition of a virtue, inspired by Hursthouse, is typical:

[6] Aristotle, *Nicomachean Ethics*, trans. by T. Irwin (Indianapolis: Hackett, 1999), II.4.

A virtue is (i) a good, admirable, or otherwise praiseworthy character trait, where (ii) a character trait consists in a relatively stable set of behavioural dispositions that are embedded in an appropriate surrounding milieu of judgments and emotions, broadly understood.[7]

To possess a virtue is not just to act but also to *judge* and *feel*. To have the virtue of honesty, for example, is not just to behave in an honest way. A person might behave honestly because he was terrified of being caught and punished. To have the virtue of honesty – to be an honest person – one must also judge dishonesty to be wrong and to deplore cases of dishonesty whenever one encounters them, whether this dishonesty is exhibited by others or yourself, and so on.

Therefore, a virtue-based programme of moral enhancement would require us not only to modify behaviour, but also enhance dispositions to feel and judge. As in the case of the Kantian approach to moral enhancement, any moral augmentation pursued here would have to be multifactorial: targeting a variety of quite different psychological systems, some of which are cognitive, and some of which are affective. It is not immediately clear what sort of genetic manipulation or chemical modifier would be able to hit these sorts of diverse targets.

Judgement enters the virtue-ethical picture in another, even more important way. Virtue-ethical accounts typically accord a central role to what is known, following Aristotle, as *phronesis* or practical wisdom. In another famous passage from the *Nicomachean Ethics*, Aristotle writes:

Getting angry, or giving and spending money, is easy and everyone can do it; but doing it to the right person, in the right amount, at the right time, for the right end, and in the right way is no longer easy, nor can everyone do it. Hence doing these things well is rare, praiseworthy, and fine.[8]

To have a virtue requires the ability to judge what a particular situation calls for. To lie in order to spare a person's feelings may be required in some situations. But in other situations the truth, though painful, may be something that a person really needs to hear. According to Aristotle, this sort of wisdom – the ability to judge what a particular situation does and does not call for – is acquired only through years of experience and consistent practice. It is not

7   Hursthouse, *On Virtue Ethics*.
8   Aristotle, *Nicomachean Ethics*, II.9.

immediately clear how genetic tweaking or chemical infiltration is going to be able to supply this or otherwise make up for it.

5. Enhancing Sentiment

It might be thought that, if moral enhancement is our game, the most promising ethical theory would be some or other form of *sentimentalism*. The guiding idea is a simple one: if only we could get people to be a little *nicer*. If only we could get them to commiserate more with the sufferings of others. If only we could get them to rejoice more in others' happiness. If only, that is, we could get them to be more *sympathetic*.

The centrality of sympathy to morality is an idea strongly associated with David Hume, Adam Smith, and others.[9] Sympathy is, on this view, the primary moral sentiment, and is essentially connected to moral good and bad. There are, however, two distinct ways in which the centrality of sympathy to moral good and bad might be developed. According to the first, emotional reactions, such as sympathy, allow us to *detect* the good- and bad-making features of situations. This is an objective form of sentimentalism. Moral good and bad exist independently of our emotional reactions. It is just that these reactions give us an especially reliable – perhaps uniquely reliable – insight into which things are good and which are bad.[10] Our emotional reactions allow us to identify the features of situations that make them either good or bad. They provide us with *sensitivity* to such features.

It is more usual, however, for moral sentimentalism to be understood in another way. According to this more usual understanding, moral good and bad are *constituted* by our emotional reactions. This is the subjective version of sentimentalism – the form of sentimentalism that Hume and Smith had in mind. It is not clear where, precisely, this subjective form of sentimentalism leaves the idea of moral enhancement. The desirability of enhancement is based on the idea that human behaviour is not as good as it might be. But if good and bad are simply constituted by our emotional reactions then this idea of our behaviour not being as good as it might be is

[9] David Hume, *A Treatise of Human Nature,* ed. by P. Nidditch (Oxford: Oxford University Press, 1975); Adam Smith, *The Theory of Moral Sentiments*, ed. by D. Raphael and A. Macfie (Oxford: Oxford University Press, 1976).

[10] Mark Rowlands, *Can Animals Be Moral?* (New York: Oxford University Press, 2012).

quite difficult to understand. By what standard of good does our behaviour fall short? There seems to be no independent standard with
which to measure the alterations to emotional response that are enhancing and those that are not. This is, probably, not fatal to the
idea that we can use the subjective version of sentimentalism to
explain the idea of moral enhancement. Subjectivist ethical theories
have long been faced with this problem and developed a variety of
ways of dealing with it. But it is worth pointing out that we can't
just assume that subjective versions of sentimentalism are compatible
with moral enhancement. A not inconsiderable amount of work will
have to be done to make them compatible. I shall ignore this compli-
cation, and assume that either objective or subjective versions of sentimentalism are available for understanding the idea of moral
enhancement.

The idea that we can understand moral enhancement in sentimentalist terms also fragments into several distinct possible views. When
discussing the moral sentiments, it is orthodox to draw a distinction
between *empathy* and *sympathy*. Very roughly – it is sometimes said
that there are as many definitions of empathy as there are people
working on empathy – empathy is the ability to understand what
another is feeling or thinking. Sympathy, on the other hand, is the
ability, indeed willingness, to care about what you find when you
do this. Empathy is the ability to understand something. Sympathy
is the ability to have an affective response to this understanding.
So, the first question arises for the moral enhancement project understood in sentimentalist terms: do we enhance empathy (a form of understanding) or sympathy (an affective response)?

Suppose we decide to try to augment empathy. The problem is that
the notion of empathy breaks down into two different sorts.[11] On the
one hand there is *projective* empathy. This is the ability to put oneself
in the shoes of the other and imagine what they must be feeling in
their current circumstances. Projective empathy is an *imaginative*
ability. On the other hand, there is *receptive* empathy. This is the
ability to respond to the mental condition of another by producing,
in oneself, a condition of the same sort, or of a similar sort. There
is nothing imaginative about this. It is a form of *sensitivity*.
Imagination will involve significant contribution from the cortex.
But the amygdala will be centrally involved in receptive empathy.
Genetic manipulation or chemical intervention will, somehow, have
to target two distinct brain regions – sometimes simultaneously,

[11] Michael Slote, *Moral Sentimentalism* (Oxford: Oxford University
Press, 2010).

and always in the right way. It is not clear how we are going to get it to do this.

Even if we can sort out the issue of what, precisely, we are trying to enhance, there is a further problem. We can enhance neither empathy nor sympathy in a vacuum. Enhancement of empathy and/or sympathy will be useful only if it is located in a complex cognitive/intellectual milieu. We can't avoid the necessity of *phronesis* here any more than we could when our focus was on virtue. Following Nussbaum, we might distinguish between *thick* and *thin* versions of sympathy.[12] A sympathetic response is thick if it is embedded in a surrounding milieu of judgements of the sort constituted by *phronesis*. A sympathetic response is *thin*, on the other hand, if it is not thus embedded.

In the absence of *phronesis* our sympathetic responses are likely to go awry in one of three different ways. First they are susceptible to problems of *size*. Without *phronesis*, we are likely to misrepresent the size or significance of another's suffering. Let us suppose that a friend, a multimillionaire best-selling author, is devastated by the critical reaction to his latest offering, and hasn't left his huge mansion in the Hamptons for days, so upset is he. If we had a little practical wisdom we would realise that he should just "cop on" and that, all things considered, he is one of the most fortunate of people. Without this wisdom, and the perspective it provides, we are likely to be swayed by his outpouring of grief and, consequently, to be sucked in to his orgy of despair.

Another friend insists on making the same mistake over and over again. You've told her, you really have. But still she persists. Practical wisdom tells you that any sympathy you feel for this person should at least be tempered by their persistent recidivism and refusal to take your advice. Without it, you may fall victim to their overt displays of grief.

Sometimes the truth can be painful, but at the same time something a person really needs to hear. Sparing them the truth may temporarily save them unhappiness, but will only increase their unhappiness in the long term. The long term/short term distinction is the most obvious version of the distinction between local and global interests. A person needs to give up smoking – for the sake of their health, a global interest. Doing so will cause them anguish now – a local interest. Local interests typically receive more vivid experiential expressions than global interests. Without practical wisdom we are likely to unacceptably emphasise local over global interests.

[12]   Martha Nussbaum, *Upheavals of Thought: The Intelligence of the Emotions* (New York: Cambridge University Press, 2003).

The sympathy we feel is one thing. The sympathy we should feel is quite another. Practical wisdom is what allows us to identify, and appropriately emphasise, the latter.

6. Moral Education and Moral Enhancement

Nothing I have said entails moral enhancement cannot work. Indeed, moral enhancement clearly does work. Traditional moral education is a form of moral enhancement, and moral education works – not all of the time, of course, but at least sometimes. There are, however, significant differences between traditional moral education and technological approaches to moral enhancement. If the arguments developed in this essay for the messy, variegated character of moral enhancement are correct, these differences are likely to be crucial.

Certain environmental contingencies, with which I shall not bore you, have caused me to think it instructive to think of moral education by analogy with football (or, as the locals on this side of the pond insist on calling it, soccer) education. That is, it is instructive to think of the development of moral skills as analogous, in some ways, with the development of football skills. If you are coaching an Under-11 football team – don't ever do it, you're essentially wrangling cats for hours every week – the most important thing to realise is that, with regard to skills, different players need different things. Some will have developed bad habits – trying to control the ball with their preferred foot, when the situation requires they use the other foot, for example – and these will have to be expunged. So you devise drills to target that. Others make poor decisions – for example, they run when they should pass, or pass when they should run – and this sort of decision-making is also something you can target with the appropriate drills. Others are highly skilled, but not sufficiently aggressive. There are drills you can use to target that. The development of soccer skills requires this sort of targeted programme and approach. There is no one method for the improvement of soccer skills. There are different methods that are sensitive to what the developing player already has and, crucially, what he/she does not have.

It is this directed and flexible nature of targeting that is also a crucial feature of traditional moral education. A developing moral person can go awry in many ways – some cognitive, some meta-cognitive, some affective – and which specific aspect requires targeting depends on the kind of moral truancy in question. Perhaps the most obvious component of traditional moral education involves simply talking, and in particular questioning. But this sort of questioning can target several quite different brain structures and aspects of functioning – sometimes individually, at other times all at once. We can talk to a child in a variety of ways – depending on what we, their moral educator, think they need. "How do you think Johnny felt when you did that?" This sort of question targets *projective* empathy: the child is being asked to imaginatively put herself in the shoes of another. "How do you think you would feel if someone did that to you?" This functions in a similar way: the child is being asked to imaginatively project itself into a counterfactual situation. The same is true of "Remember when so-and-so did that to you?" Other questions target different systems. For example, the target of "You have a toy but Johnny doesn't. Does that seem fair?" seems to be the child's sense of fairness. This is also true of the far more advanced, Kantian inspired, question: "What would happen if everyone did that?" Notice that nothing in this sort of approach assumes that the deficit in question is a persisting one. It is not necessary that a child suffer from, for example, a persisting projective empathy deficit. Rather, all that is required for the above approach to be legitimate is that, in the judgement of the moral educator, this sort of deficit is evident at the present time.

By the time the question-and-answer form of moral education is likely to be efficacious, much stage setting – to use an expression of Wittgenstein's – must already have been put in place. Prior to that one must not overlook the importance of a distinctly Aristotelian component of moral education – *habit*. One becomes virtuous by doing virtuous things – repeatedly, habitually. Excellence – moral excellence included – is not an act, but a habit. Moral habits can be established in children in several ways but, again, the analogy with football education is quite useful. In the latter, you first demonstrate a skill you wish the players to acquire, explain why this skill is a desirable one to have, and then you let them practice it – at length – taking care to immediately correct mistakes. In moral education, a virtue, and its desirability, is often explained by way of a story in which a character exhibits it (or, sometimes, the lack thereof). Then the child's deviations from this virtue are corrected as expeditiously as possible.

Even habit, however, is not the earliest stage of traditional moral education. Before habit, there is the setting of an example. The tears of a sibling, for example, are met with the hugs and soothing voice of a parent. This is, to the other sibling, both a lesson in behaviour and an *axiological* lesson – a lesson about what has value or what

17

should be valued. If those tears were met by the parent's indifference or annoyance, then a very different lesson would have been imparted.

This, of course, only scratches the surface of the forms traditional moral education may take. The crucial point, however, is that traditional moral education can, and often does, target very different capacities and deficiencies of a developing moral person – both cognitive and affective. The targeting is not indiscriminate but intelligent and based on an assessment of what a particular individual, at a particular time, *needs*, and with no assumption that these needs will stay the same over time. In a nutshell, traditional moral education addresses the person as a whole, and not some neurochemical or genetic aspect of that person. That is why it has been so successful.

A *vehicle-content confusion* is the mistake of supposing that structures and distinctions appropriate to one level of analysis will transpose seamlessly to another level, merely because the former supervenes or is otherwise dependent on the latter.[13] It may be that the idea of moral enhancement, as a neurochemical or genetic enterprise is guilty of this sort of confusion. We are moral beings, ultimately, because of our brains and our genes. However, being a moral person does not depend on this or that specific feature, whether neurochemical or genetic. It depends, rather, on a multiplicity of distinct features, each interacting with and dependent on the others. Traditional moral education – being capable of intelligent, flexible targeting of deficiencies as and when the need arises, is well suited to dealing with such an arrangement of factors. But the idea that neurochemical or genetic targeting will achieve the same sort of – or even better – outcome rests, I suspect, on a grossly oversimplified way of understanding what it is to be a moral being. This is not to say that such technological intervention could never be successful. But it is to say that, as yet, we have no clear idea of how it is supposed to work.

University of Miami
mrowlands@miami.edu

---

[13] Susan Hurley, *Consciousness in Action* (Cambridge, MA: Harvard University Press, 1998).

The Trouble With Moral Enhancement

INMACULADA DE MELO-MARTÍN

Abstract
Proponents of moral enhancement believe that we should pursue and apply biotechnological means to morally enhance human beings, as failing to do so is likely to lead
to humanity's demise. Unsurprisingly, these proposals have generated a substantial
amount of debate about the moral permissibility of using such interventions. Here I
put aside concerns about the permissibility of moral enhancement and focus on the
conceptual and evidentiary grounds for the moral enhancement project. I argue that
such grounds are quite precarious.

1. Introduction

At a time when racist, sexist, and xenophobic attitudes are again becoming normalised, falsehoods are publicly presented as reality, the
US – one of the most polluting countries in the world – is rolling
back on initiatives aimed at mitigating climate change and promoting
the use of fossil fuels, and wars all over the world are prematurely
ending the lives of thousands of people and displacing thousands
more, the idea of finding some quick technological fix to morally
enhance human beings appears more appealing than ever. Alas, the
moral enhancement project,[1] the latest fad in the bioethics literature,
betrays, like most technological fixes, a problematic understanding of
the nature of the problems it ostensibly attempts to solve. Part of the
overall process to remake humanity by various technological means,
the moral enhancement project calls for the use of biomedical technologies, from drugs to genetic interventions, to make human
beings more moral.[2] Its proponents warn that a failure to pursue
this project will likely bring about the annihilation of the planet

---

[1] Proponents and critics of using various biomedical technologies to
enhance humanity's moral sense use "enhancement" and "bioenhancement"
interchangeably. I use here simply the term "enhancement".

[2] See for instance, T. Douglas, 'Moral Enhancement', *J Appl Philos.*
25:3 (2008), 228–45; I. Persson and J. Savulescu, 'The Perils of Cognitive
Enhancement and the Urgent Imperative to Enhance the Moral Character
of Humanity', *Journal of Applied Philosophy*, **25**:3 (2008), 162–67;
I. Persson and J. Savulescu, *Unfit for the Future: The Need for Moral
Enhancement* (Oxford: Oxford University Press, 2012); D. DeGrazia,

doi:10.1017/S1358246118000279   © The Royal Institute of Philosophy and the contributors 2018
Royal Institute of Philosophy Supplement **83** 2018   19

Inmaculada de Melo-Martín

and of the human species with it.[3] Noticeably, the fact that human beings find themselves in this precarious situation is, according to proponents of moral enhancement, the result not only of our less than reliable moral sense, but also of our increased technological power. This makes all the more puzzling the insistence that yet more technology can save us from our folly.

This perplexing fascination with technological solutions, particularly biomedical interventions, as a way to solve complex social, political, and ethical problems is not the only concern that the moral enhancement project raises. Indeed, proposals for human enhancement in general and moral enhancement in particular, are actually quite confusing. Its most staunch proponents have upheld inconsistent claims. For example, they defend both the necessity of moral enhancement as the only way to avoid our planet's demise,[4] and its simple advisability alongside other, more traditional, means of improving people's moral sense and addressing complex social problems.[5] They similarly have defended the claim that biomedical interventions able to enhance people's moral capacities are within reach,[6] and that their development is in its infancy.[7] They repeatedly remind us that evolutionary processes have led to the development of a human moral sense that is less than stellar,[8] but nonetheless trust the human ability to develop the right kind of moral bioenhancements.[9] The fact that proponents often misunderstand and misinterpret the criticisms presented against the

---

'Moral Enhancement, Freedom, and What We (Should) Value in Moral Behaviour', *J Med Ethics* **40**:6 (2014), 361–68.

[3] For the most forceful defense of this claim see Persson and Savulescu, 'The Perils of Cognitive Enhancement'.

[4] Persson and Savulescu, 'The Perils of Cognitive Enhancement'; I. Persson and J. Savulescu, 'The Turn for Ultimate Harm: A Reply to Fenton', *J Med Ethics* **37**:7 (2011), 441–444; I. Persson and J. Savulescu, 'Getting Moral Enhancement Right: The Desirability of Moral Bioenhancement', *Bioethics* **27**:3 (2013), 124–31.

[5] Persson and Savulescu, *Unfit for the Future*; I. Persson and J. Savulescu, 'The Art of Misunderstanding Moral Bioenhancement', *Cambridge Quarterly of Healthcare Ethics* **24**:1 (2015), 48–57.

[6] Persson and Savulescu, 'The Perils of Cognitive Enhancement'.

[7] Persson and Savulescu, *Unfit for the Future*.

[8] Persson and Savulescu, 'The Perils of Cognitive Enhancement'; J. Savulescu and I. Persson, 'Moral Enhancement, Freedom and the God Machine', *Monist* **95**:3 (2012), 399–421.

[9] Persson and Savulescu, *Unfit for the Future*; Persson and Savulescu, 'The Art of Misunderstanding Moral Bioenhancement'.

moral enhancement project also contributes to this confusion.[10] But, as I show below, moral enhancement proposals are also confused: plagued by conceptual problems, beset by category mistakes, and packed with conclusions that rarely follow from the arguments presented. Equally troubling, such proposals are scientifically uninformed and often misleading. As I will discuss later, the misuse of the so-called "scientific evidence" purportedly supporting various claims about moral enhancement is staggering. Moreover, moral enhancement proposals, particularly when situated in the context of human enhancement in general are alarming. Although presented under the guise of liberalism and progressivism, there is an implicit – and sometimes not so implicit – embracing of the status quo and of a simplistic notion of choice that serves to perpetuate current injustices. The same authors who support the need for moral enhancement are all too happy to defend a moral obligation to enhance future offspring with physical and character traits suspiciously consistent with the ideologies of sexists, racists, and ableists.[11] Similarly, they regularly present technological advances as value-neutral, and thus ignore the role that social, political, and ethical values have in the development of biomedical technologies as well as their effect on what we can choose, what we might think is morally permissible, and what we value.[12] Moreover, they uncritically sanction technological interventions even if doing so contributes to and furthers social injustices.[13]

In spite of all of these problems, the enhancement project has commanded an astounding amount of attention.[14] This is a tribute to its

[10]   For arguments about such misinterpretation see Michael Hauskeller, 'The Art of Misunderstanding Critics: The Case of Ingmar Persson and Julian Savulescu's Defense of Moral Bioenhancement', *Cambridge Quarterly of Healthcare Ethics* **25**:1 (2016), 152–60.

[11]   J. Savulescu and G. Kahane, 'The Moral Obligation to Create Children with the Best Chance of the Best Life', *Bioethics* **23**:5 (2009), 274–90; J. Savulescu, 'New Breeds of Humans: The Moral Obligation to Enhance', *Reproductive Biomedicine Online* **10**:1 (2005), 36–39.

[12]   I. de Melo-Martín, *Rethinking Reprogenetics: Enhancing Ethical Analyses of Reprogenetic Technologies* (New York: Oxford University Press, 2017).

[13]   J. Savulescu and G. Kahane, 'The Moral Obligation to Create Children with the Best Chance of the Best Life'; J. Savulescu, 'New Breeds of Humans'. For others also calling attention to this disturbing tendency see, for instance, R. Sparrow, 'Egalitarianism and Moral Bioenhancement,' *Am J Bioeth.* **14**:4 (2014), 20–28.

[14]   The attention is not just the result of the significant amount of criticism that is has received, but also due to a surprising amount of support.

proponents' ability to frame their proposals in ways that makes them appear, on the one hand, business as usual – we have been morally enhancing ourselves all along – and, on the other hand, absolutely indispensable – the only way to save humanity from the destructive technologies we have developed, a cognitive capacity too great for our own good, and a moral brain best suited to the Paleolithic jungle. If to this we add a context where many people embrace scientism and welcome the use of technological fixes to address complex social problems, we have all one needs to make discussions on moral enhancement appear consequential and enhancement proposals to look as if they were desirable.

Is it possible to improve current proposals for moral enhancement, to make them more meaningful, informed, and intelligible? That depends. It is, of course, conceivable that someone could offer new proposals that lack all the problems the present ones have. I confess, however, that I am sceptical of such a possibility. It seems to me that any talk about "morally enhancing human beings" has to rest on some mistake or another: conceptual errors, ambiguities and vagueness, problematic background assumptions, and the like. No doubt, a better understanding of moral philosophy, philosophy of science, and philosophy of technology, as well as attention to feminist perspectives in all of these areas would serve proponents of moral enhancement well, not just regarding moral enhancement, but human enhancement in general. In any case, given the very confusing and confused state of moral enhancement proposals, it seems to me that the best way – perhaps the only way – to make such proposals more meaningful and intelligible is to point out the many problems they have. Space prevents me from attending to all such problems – which will require a book. Thus, in what follows I discuss just some of those problems – and for the most part, I will be able to only scratch their surface.

2. What is Wrong With Moral Enhancement Proposals?

Although a significant amount of the debate over moral enhancement has focussed on whether biomedical interventions to enhance humanity's moral capacities are or are not permissible, such a question presupposes that talk of moral enhancement is meaningful. Alas, it is not clear that such is the case.[15] So, how do proponents

---

[15] For arguments about the meaningless of moral enhancement proposals see I. de Melo-Martín and A. Salles, 'Moral Bioenhancement: Much Ado About Nothing?', *Bioethics* **29**:4 (2015), 223–32.

understand "moral enhancement"? They do not all agree on what exactly constitutes moral enhancement and different authors have given diverse definitions of it. For example, Douglas takes moral enhancements to refer to interventions that will expectably leave an individual with more moral motives or behaviour than the person would otherwise have.[16] Persson and Savulescu understand moral enhancements as improvements, by genetic or other biological means, to moral dispositions, such as altruism and a sense of justice, in ways that make it more likely that one will arrive at the correct judgement regarding what is right and more likely to act on that judgement.[17] DeGrazia sees them as interventions that aim at either boosting or selecting an existing moral capacity to act in a particular way, or at creating such a capacity when nonexistent.

None of these definitions is particularly clear, but in any case the *moral* part of the moral enhancement equation is equated with motives, behaviours, or some type of primitive disposition such as altruism and a sense of justice. But as many have pointed out – indeed, as even proponents have recognised[18] – none of these things by themselves would uncontroversially result in a moral person or a moral action. People can do the right thing for the wrong reasons, appropriate motivations can be disregarded, and primitive dispositions are hardly sufficient – and perhaps even necessary – to produce people who are unproblematically more *moral*.[19] Of course, if the biointerventions in question worked – a very big if indeed – we might want to say that the person has been motivationally, behaviourally, or dispositionally enhanced. But that is a far cry from creating a more *moral* person. Indeed, Douglas himself, for instance, explicitly states 'I will not claim that the morally enhanced person is more moral, has a more

[16]   Douglas, 'Moral Enhancement'.
[17]   Persson and Savulescu, 'The Perils of Cognitive Enhancement'; Persson and Savulescu, 'Getting Moral Enhancement Right: The Desirability of Moral Bioenhancement'; Savulescu and Persson, 'Moral Enhancement, Freedom and the God Machine'.
[18]   Persson and Savulescu, *Unfit for the Future*.
[19]   See, for instance, H. Maibom, 'Feeling for Others: Empathy, Sympathy, and Morality', *Inquiry* **52**:5 (2009), 483–499; S. Nichols, *Sentimental Rules: On the Natural Foundations of Moral Judgment* (Oxford: Oxford University Press, 2004); S. Darwall, *The Second-Person Standpoint: Morality, Respect, and Accountability* (Cambridge, MA: Harvard University Press, 2006); B. Herman, *The Practice of Moral Judgment* (Cambridge, MA: Harvard University Press, 1993); M. Weber, 'The Motive of Duty and the Nature of Emotions: Kantian Reflections on Moral Worth', *Can J Philos.* **33**:2 (2003), 183–202.

moral character, or will necessarily act more morally than her earlier, unenhanced self'. This makes it all the more puzzling that nonetheless he insists in talking about *moral* enhancement. But if enhancing dispositions, behaviour, or motivations cannot be said – not, at least, without various problematic assumptions – to make people more moral, then the so-called *moral* enhancement proposals do nothing of the sort.

But can the interventions proposed actually *enhance* relevant behaviour, dispositions, or motivations? That also seems questionable. Consider for instance moral dispositions of interest to proponents of moral enhancement, such as altruism or empathy, which are conceptualised in fragmentary and disconnected ways. They take these dispositions to be the result of evolutionary pressures, and interventions, such as oxytocin, are aimed at altering the dispositions in question independently of the context in which they will be activated. But, as mentioned earlier, dispositions such as altruism or empathy are not always morally appropriate – imagine, for instance, someone feeling empathy towards a distraught thief who has become incapable of stealing as much as he wants. Thus, even if the interventions were to work, it is not clear that they would actually be enhancing; that is, it is not clear that they would reliably produce a dispositional change that would be judged to be morally better. This is so because the various traits of interest can be used for good or evil. Indeed, Savulescu and Persson explicitly call attention to the problems with altruism[20] – it is, they say, one of those pesky traits that evolved in a context where it paid to be concerned with the in-group and not particularly sympathetic to the out-group.[21]

But if bio-intervening in particular dispositions, motivations, or behaviours cannot reliably produce a change that by itself could be judged to be morally better, then it is not clear that such interventions can result in an *enhancement*. "Enhancement" after all, connotes *improvement*. If using a particular bio-intervention affecting altruistic dispositions does not necessarily result in an appropriately altruistic person – rather than in a person who is unduly concerned with the interest of in-group members – then one wonders in what sense they have been enhanced. Thus, one can agree that bio-interventions might produce modifications in people's dispositions, motivations,

---

[20] See, for instance, Persson and Savulescu, *Unfit for the Future*.

[21] In another contradictory statement, Persson and Savulescu also claim that altruism is *essentially* a moral disposition, unlike the courage or strength of will that they contend can characterise criminals. See Persson and Savulescu, 'The Perils of Cognitive Enhancement', 72.

or behaviours, but such modifications need not result – and often will not, as proponents acknowledge – in an *enhanced*, i.e., improved, bettered, person.

Now, talk of motivational, dispositional, or behavioural modifications seems significantly less radical than "moral enhancement" would suggest. More importantly, insofar as the purported goal of the moral enhancement project is to protect humanity from "ultimate harm", talking about motivational, dispositional, or behavioural alterations would call into question the effectiveness of that project – terrorists, for instance, could have their empathy "enhanced" with not particularly good results. In fact, the belief that reliably producing the right kind of modifications – making people more appropriately altruistic, less aggressive, or more suitably empathetic – would constitute any protection against "ultimately harm" is patently absurd. Those determined to obliterate the planet are, after all, unlikely to believe that their moral self is in need of fixing, and thus unlikely to voluntarily use any enhancing interventions. Even if one could make such interventions compulsory, the loners likely to cause such ultimate harm will be somewhat difficult to find. And, of course, none of the bio-interventions proposed are powerful enough to deter someone who is completely committed to destroying the planet.

It seems then that by the proponents' own lights the moral enhancement project fails to constitute *enhancement* and fails to enhance *morality*. Indeed, recognition of these problems has led proponents of moral enhancement to talk about "modulation" and using bio-interventions to enhance second-order moral capacities. It is true that at least some possible conceptualisations of the new types of targets can reasonably be understood as involving morality. However, to the extent that such is the case – that is, to the extent that the bio-interventions in question attempt to create individuals who *are* good (have the right kind of dispositions and motivations) and *do* what is right, for the *right* reasons – the notion that any of the candidates suggested for these interventions (SSRIs, oxytocin, propranolol) would achieve any such thing betrays an astounding lack of understanding of the complexities of human biology, the nature of normativity, and the relevance of language.[22]

Note that the problems mentioned – fatal ones, in my opinion – do not involve appeals to disagreements regarding whether particular

[22] For arguments about some of these complexities see Harris Wiseman, *The Myth of the Moral Brain: The Limits of Moral Enhancement* (Cambridge, Massachusetts: MIT Press, 2016).

motives, dispositions, or behaviours are or not in fact morally right. We can all agree that having certain altruistic or empathetic dispositions or less biased motives is a good thing. Nonetheless we can still contest the belief that enhancing those traits would make anyone more *moral*. Of course, the fact that morality is context-dependent and that legitimate disagreements can exist about whether particular actions, motivations, or dispositions are right or wrong, permissible or impermissible, makes the whole project even more hopeless.

Proponents of the moral enhancement project might object that education, or what they insist on calling "traditional means of enhancement", involves just this same piecemeal modification of people's motives, dispositions, and behaviours. But this is simply false. When we educate children to become moral agents we do not – or not usually – target a particular motivation or disposition, but rather target a *person*, situated in a particular context, using a particular language, and bringing with us particular assumptions about what is right and wrong, what we think might be best for them, directed at them, and attending to their particularities. It is the whole package that concerns us when we practice moral education, not a specific motivation or disposition – even if we are trying to modify some motivation or disposition. The development of moral agency requires engagement with other human beings who live in certain social and political contexts, and it is in that way that – hopefully – we help children to become morally competent adults.[23]

Denying that education is not a "traditional means of enhancement" is not simply a matter of semantics. In contesting such an analogy I want to call attention to the fact that the goal of bioenhancement and the goal of moral education are similar only in appearance. It is not just that the means are obviously different, it is that the *ends* are different also. Indeed, this is why the proponents' strategy of equating the ends of moral bioenhancement with those of moral education are so rhetorically powerful. Once we agree that the end is worth pursuing – and who would not want to have people who are more moral? – then the discussion can proceed to focus on the *means* to achieve that goal. And an emphasis on the means leads effortlessly to a concern with the usual inventory of risks and benefits.[24]

---

[23] Or what, in another rhetorical move, proponents call "morally enhanced individuals with respect to children".

[24] And it is indeed talk of risks, rather than uncertainties and ignorance, that abounds in the enhancement debate. The language of risks reduces issues of uncertainty, ambiguity, and ignorance to the more controllable and deterministic processes usually associated with risk evaluations, and

Proponents believe, of course, that the benefits are unquestionably good, while they take the risks to be either not that serious, or, insofar as they do present some serious risks, they have confidence that we will be able to manage them.[25] In fact, when one has framed the need for moral enhancement as the only way to avoid humanity's demise, there will not be many risks that appear not worth taking. Unsurprisingly, given this framing, criticisms of interventions aimed at enhancing human beings – morally or otherwise – are met with accusations of conservativism and delaying progress. Those who frame the debate have the power to direct the discussion.[26]

So far, I have argued that conceptual problems reveal the moral enhancement project to be nothing of the sort: insofar as the targets of biomedical interventions are particular dispositions, motivations, or behaviours, it is incorrect to talk about *moral* enhancement rather than dispositional, motivational, or behavioural enhancement. And insofar as these are understood as piecemeal characteristics or properties, it is mistaken to talk about *enhancement* rather than simply modifications or alterations.

But the moral enhancement project also rests on shaky scientific grounds. In fact, there are so many problems related to the misuse of scientific evidence that it would be difficult to even mention all of them here. I will thus focus on two that are particularly problematic: the use of scientific claims that proponents present as uncontroversial and the weakness of the scientific evidence purporting to show that moral enhancement is plausible.

Moral enhancement supporters attempt to buttress their proposals by appealing to various sources of scientific evidence.[27] In doing so,

---

obscures the multiple uncertainties in the development and implementation of biomedical interventions.

[25] Such confidence in humanity's ability to manage even serious risks confronting the development and use of bioenhancements constitutes another inconsistency present in moral enhancement proposals. Why – it seems imperative to ask – would we trust members of a species that is on the brink of destroying the planet and everything in it to appropriately manage such risks?

[26] For a discussion of the importance of the framing of the moral enhancement project, see de Melo-Martín and Salles, 'Moral Bioenhancement: Much Ado About Nothing?'.

[27] See, for instance, Douglas, 'Moral Enhancement'; Persson and Savulescu, 'Getting Moral Enhancement Right'; Persson and Savulescu, 'The Perils of Cognitive Enhancement'; Savulescu and Persson, 'Moral

they not uncommonly present some such scientific evidence as un-controversially accepted. In fact, however, many of the scientific claims they present are not only highly contentious but by many accounts simply false. This is the case, for instance, regarding many of the evolutionary psychological claims proponents use to support the moral enhancement project. Many such claims have been discredited for multiple reasons, from problematic assumptions, to incorrect interpretations of the evidence, to inadequate conclusions.[28] Some of the claims proponents make in this regard are plainly ridiculous. For instance, trying to argue that altruism and a sense of justice have a genetic basis, Persson and Savulescu offer the following evidence: '[i]t is plausible to think that in general women have a greater capacity for altruism than men. If this psychological difference tracks gender, this is surely good evidence that it is biologically based'.[29]

Another area of research often cited to support their claims regarding the plausibility of using bio-interventions to enhance people morally involves twin studies. Proponents use such studies to defend their claim that the human sense of fairness and altruism have a genetic basis. This is proven, they argue, because identical twins present striking correlations in what they consider fair and unfair in ultimatum games, while such correlations are lacking in the case of fraternal twins. Identical twins apparently also present striking correlation in respect to altruism.[30] As with evolutionary psychology, many people have criticised twin studies on both methodological and

---

Enhancement, Freedom and the God Machine'; Persson and Savulescu, *Unfit for the Future*; T. Douglas, 'Moral Enhancement Via Direct Emotion Modulation: A Reply to John Harris', *Bioethics* **27**:3 (2013), 160–68; DeGrazia, 'Moral Enhancement, Freedom, and What We (Should) Value in Moral Behaviour'.

[28] For some work criticising many of the claims made in evolutionary psychology see, for instance, Hilary Rose and Steven P. R. Rose, *Alas, Poor Darwin: Arguments Against Evolutionary Psychology* (New York: Harmony Books, 2000); John Dupré, *Human Nature and the Limits of Science* (New York: Oxford University Press, 2001); Cordelia Fine, *Delusions of Gender: How Our Minds, Society, and Neurosexism Create Difference* (New York: W. W. Norton, 2010).

[29] Persson and Savulescu, 'Getting Moral Enhancement Right', 130.

[30] Persson and Savulescu, 'Getting Moral Enhancement Right', 130; Persson and Savulescu, 'The Perils of Cognitive Enhancement', 171; Savulescu and Persson, 'Moral Enhancement, Freedom and the God Machine'.

substantive grounds.[31] To present results from such studies as accepted evidence of the genetic basis of moral dispositions and emotions is therefore highly problematic.

I hasten to note that questioning such evidence in no way means that no biological basis for moral dispositions or emotions exist. It is, of course, unlikely that such a basis is genetic, if this is understood as proponents seem to: that is, as one that would allow us to tinker with some genes so as to reliably produce particular effects. There is, of course, no such thing as a gene for altruism or for a sense of justice. But one need not deny that modifications of, say, neurotransmitters – which are clearly biological – can produce emotional and dispositional changes. Nonetheless, to interpret evidence for such modifications as evidence for the plausibility of moral enhancement – or more precisely, for the plausibility that some morally relevant aspects can be biomedically modified – involves more than just looking into people's brains or making them play some lab game or another.

Proponents of moral enhancement use different sources of evidence as proof that biomedical interventions can affect various aspects of people's moral life. For instance, they defend their claims by citing, among others, experiments that purport to show the effect of propranolol on implicit bias,[32] neuroimaging studies showing that the amygdala plays a role in race aversion,[33] and experiments attempting to assess the effect that selective serotonin reuptake inhibitors (SSRIs) have on harm aversion.[34]

Let us accept, if only momentarily, that the results of some of these scientific studies regarding enhancement interventions are correct, that

---

[31] See, for instance, J. Joseph, 'Twin Studies in Psychiatry and Psychology: Science or Pseudoscience?', *Psychiatric Quarterly* **73**:1 (2002), 71–82; P. V. Tishler and V. J. Carey, 'Can Comparison of Mz- and Dz-Twin Concordance Rates Be Used Invariably to Estimate Heritability?', *Twin Res Hum Genet.* **10**:5 (2007), 712–717; K. Richardson and S. Norgate, 'The Equal Environments Assumption of Classical Twin Studies May Not Hold', *Br J Educ Psychol.* **75**:3 (2005), 339–350.

[32] See Douglas, 'Moral Enhancement'; T. Douglas, 'Moral Enhancement via Direct Emotion Modulation'; Savulescu and Persson, 'Moral Enhancement, Freedom and the God Machine'; DeGrazia, 'Moral Enhancement, Freedom, and What We (Should) Value in Moral Behaviour'.

[33] Douglas, 'Moral Enhancement'.

[34] Savulescu and Persson, 'Moral Enhancement, Freedom and the God Machine'; DeGrazia, 'Moral Enhancement, Freedom, and What We (Should) Value in Moral Behaviour'.

is, that they show what they purport to show about the effects of propranolol, SSRIs, and so on. Consider, for instance, proponents'
claims that implicit racial biases are indeed attenuated with the use of
propranolol. Such results can be taken to constitute evidence for the
plausibility of moral enhancement only if one presupposes various contested assumptions, among them that implicit biases express some
negative appraisal or attitude, that they have some negative effect on
the treatment of racial minorities, and that people who hold implicit
biases are somehow morally deficient.[35] That implicit biases express
some negative attitude and are thus morally suspect might seem
obvious to many, as "bias" is often used normatively. If indeed those
biases express aversive or hostile attitudes, as proponents of moral enhancement appear to believe, it would make sense to attempt to correct
them and to take such corrections as an indication that at least some
morally relevant attitudes can be bettered. But some evidence indicates
that implicit bias might be the outcome of anxiety or discomfort rather
than hostility.[36] Some research also suggests that sympathy, rather than
hostility, might underlie the responses to outgroup faces, and that implicit biases result from anxiety about past oppression and mistreatment associated with some racial groups.[37] Thus, it is not
uncontested that implicit biases express some morally negative attitude.
Furthermore, the evidence that implicit biases, at least as measured by
the Implicit Association Test (IAT), correlate with negative behaviour
towards racial minorities is similarly disputed.[38] Moreover, even assuming that implicit biases express negative attitudes, whether
people who have such biases are morally deficient – and thus whether
they can plausibly be understood as improving some aspect of their

[35] For a more detailed discussion of these assumptions see de Melo-
Martín and Salles, 'Moral Bioenhancement: Much Ado About Nothing?'.
[36] C. Frantz, A. Cuddy, M. Burnett, H. Ray, and A. Hart, 'A Threat in
the Computer: The Race Implicit Association Test as a Stereotype Threat
Experience', *Pers Soc Psychol Bull*. **30**:12 (2004), 1611–24.
[37] E. Uhlmann, V. Brescoll, and E. Paluck, 'Are Members of Low
Status Groups Perceived as Bad, or Badly Off? Egalitarian Negative
Associations and Automatic Prejudice', *J Exp Soc Psychol*. **42**:4 (2006),
491–99; M. Andreychik and M. Gill, 'Do Negative Implicit Associations
Indicate Negative Attitudes? Social Explanations Moderate Whether
Ostensible "Negative" Associations are Prejudice-Based or Empathy-
Based', *J Exp Soc Psychol*. **48**:5 (2012), 1082–93.
[38] F. Oswald, G. Mitchell, H. Blanton, J. Jaccard, and P. Tetlock,
'Predicting Ethnic and Racial Discrimination: A Meta-Analysis of IAT
Criterion Studies', *Journal of Personality and Social Psychology Studies*,
105:2 (2013), 171–192.

morality when using particular biomedical interventions such as propranolol – depends not on determining that such implicit biases are
indeed reduced, but on complex normative judgements about,
among other things, the causative role of unconscious motivation and
our moral responsibility for unconscious beliefs.

It is true that to the extent that implicit biases have negative implications for the treatment of various racial groups, their elimination or reduction would be a very desirable thing regardless of whether the
source of the bias is morally unproblematic or whether people are
morally responsible for them. If implicit biases do result in discriminatory practices against out-groups particularly, the world would surely
be a better place if people did not have such biases. However, if as mentioned earlier, implicit biases are the result, for instance, of recognising
that some groups have been unjustly treated and that they are owed
compensation for such injustices, it is at least not obvious that eliminating the source of the implicit biases would constitute a betterment of
the individuals in question. Similarly, the issue of whether or not
people are responsible for implicit bias is very much of relevance to
whether we can say that someone's attitudes have been improved
when such biases are eliminated or reduced. Thus, maintaining that,
regardless of people's responsibility for, or the source of, implicit
biases, those who have them are necessarily morally deficient – as proponents must assume if they want to use evidence that such biases are
reduced as support for their project – presupposes substantive normative judgements that need to be defended and critically assessed.

It is thus not clear at all that experiments showing that propranolol
reduces implicit bias constitute evidence that peoples' moral attitudes
can be improved in some morally relevant sense, and thus that such
experiments constitute evidence for the plausibility of moral enhancement interventions. But there are still more problems with
the evidence presented by moral enhancement proponents. Why
should we take the results of such experiments to be showing that propranolol, for instance, does eliminate or reduce implicit biases, that
the ultimatum game provides us with relevant information about
some evolved sense of fairness, or that use of SSRIs sheds any light
on how human beings appraise harm? In fact, we have very good
reasons to be sceptical of putting too much stock in these and
similar results. This is for several reasons. First, the experiments
involve only a handful of people.[39] Second, the conclusions of these

[39]   M. J. Crockett, L. Clark, G. Tabibnia, M. D. Lieberman, and
T. W. Robbins, 'Serotonin Modulates Behavioral Reactions to
Unfairness', *Science* **320**:5884 (2008), 1739; M. J. Crockett, L. Clark,

studies are grounded on results that come from the highly artificial conditions involve in laboratory experiments. Third, the tests used, i.e., the IAT to measure implicit bias, the ultimatum game, etc., have been tested overwhelmingly on similar populations – the so-called WEIRD (Western, Educated, Industrialised, Rich, and Democratic) populations. Indeed, evidence shows that within the field of psychology, 96% of psychological samples come from countries with only 12% of the world's population.[40] Similarly, within the field of human neuroimaging, 90% of peer-reviewed neuroimaging studies come from Western countries.[41]

But why would these factors be relevant to the conclusions of the studies discussed? First, insofar as the number of people participating in these studies is limited, it calls for caution in the interpretation of the results. After all, small numbers of research subjects make statistical analyses difficult.[42] Second, the fact that these are laboratory studies assessing extremely complex aspects of human psychology and neurobiology, and that the tests have been validated in a very particular population, calls for restraint regarding the generalisation of these results. Indeed, the fact that the overwhelming majority of studies in psychology and neuroimaging use WEIRD people as test subjects and that the tests used in such experiments have been primarily validated with WEIRD people would not be a significant problem if it were the case that human psychology and neurobiology are unaffected by cultural and social factors. But it turns out that when researchers have taken the time to test other populations, these other populations do not respond as the WEIRD populations do.[43] Some studies have shown that differences exists even in brain activation based on socio-economic status and that therefore not even brain imaging studies

---

M. D. Hauser, and T. W. Robbins, 'Serotonin Selectively Influences Moral Judgment and Behavior through Effects on Harm Aversion', *Proceedings of the National Academy of Sciences of the United States of America* **107**:40 (2010): 17433–17438; S. Terbeck, G. Kahane, S. McTavish, J. Savulescu, P. J. Cowen, and M. Hewstone, 'Propranolol Reduces Implicit Negative Racial Bias', *Psychopharmacology* **222**:3 (2012): 419–24.

[40] J. Henrich, S. J. Heine, A. Norenzayan, 'The Weirdest People in the World?' *Behav Brain Sci.* **33**:2/3 (2010), 61–83.

[41] J. Y. Chiao, 'Cultural Neuroscience: A Once and Future Discipline', *Progress in Brain Research* **178** (2009), 287–304.

[42] See, on this point, J. Ioannidis, 'Why Most Published Research Findings Are False', *PLoS Medicine* **2**:8 (2005), e124.

[43] Henrich, Heine, and Norenzayan, 'The Weirdest People in the World?'.

can ignore population-level variations. In fact, the much touted high heritability of IQ, for instance, has been concluded from studies done overwhelmingly with children of high socioeconomic status (SES). But some evidence indicates that for high-SES children, where environmental variability is negligible, the genetic differences account for 70–80% of the variation, with shared environment contributing less than 10%. However, for low-SES children, where there is far more variability in environmental contributions to intelligence, genetic differences account for 0–10% of the variance, with shared environment contributing about 60%.[44] In fact, the findings of studies done with diverse populations suggest that members of WEIRD societies, including young children, are among the least representative populations one could find for generalising about human beings' psychology or neurobiology.[45] Many of these findings involve domains that are associated with fundamental aspects of psychology, motivation, and behaviour, and, if this is so, we have very good reasons to be sceptical about claims that a particular behavioural phenomenon is universal based on sampling from a single subpopulation.

Where do all of these problems leave the moral enhancement project? I believe that it leaves it in a not so good place. As the arguments presented here show, both the conceptual and the evidentiary grounds for moral enhancement are shaky. Let me, however, end this contribution by noting that the fact that biomedical interventions fail to constitute enhancements or that, insofar as they do, they fail to enhance morality, means neither that such interventions could have no effect on various aspects of our moral life, nor that the likely-scarce efficacy of these interventions would prevent their development and implementation. Surely, however, claims about the necessity of these interventions to prevent our demise are not going to be particularly helpful in promoting an informed and critical dialogue.

Weill Cornell Medicine, Cornell University
imd2001@med.cornell.edu

---

[44] E. Turkheimer, A. Haley, M. Waldron, B. D'Onofrio, and I. I. Gottesman, 'Socioeconomic Status Modifies Heritability of IQ in Young Children', *Psychological Science* **14**:6 (2003), 623–28.
[45] Henrich, Heine, and Norenzayan, 'The Weirdest People in the World?'.

The Sins of Moral Enhancement Discourse

HARRIS WISEMAN

Abstract

The chapter will argue that the way current enthusiasm for moral enhancement is articulated in the extant literature is itself morally problematic. The moral evaluation (and ultimately disapproval) of the discourse will proceed through three stages. First, we shall look at the chequered history of various societies' attempts to cast evil, character, and generally undesirable behaviour, as biological problems. As will be argued, this is the larger context in which moral enhancement discourse should be understood, and abuses in the recent past and present should therefore be highlighted. Second, it will be argued that, given moral functioning's profoundly contextual and responsive qualities, any notion of a fine-grained, powerfully efficacious moral enhancement is both unrealistic and, actually, incoherent. Since enthusiasts' hopes are unrealistic and incoherent, such enhancement would not even be capable of providing the transformative ends that supposedly justify the sometimes extreme prescriptions set forward. Finally, the chapter concludes with the claim that moral enhancement enthusiasm actually serves to trivialise the evils of this world, and not only to trivialise the hard-won efforts required to diminish and overcome such evils, but to misdirect attention away from the real hard work that needs to be done in facing such evils.

1. Introduction

The aim of this chapter is to argue that there is something morally dubious about the way current enthusiasm for moral enhancement is articulated in the extant literature. The goal is to show that there are numerous intellectual sins committed in the discourse, and that much enthusiasm for moral enhancement is itself morally problematic – despite, or perhaps because of, its good intentions. Moral enhancement discourse is replete with moral pronouncements regarding interventions that *should* be actualised. As such, the discourse of moral enhancement enthusiasm itself should be subjected to moral evaluation.

This moral evaluation (and ultimately disapproval) of the discourse will proceed through three stages. First, we shall look at the chequered history of various societies' attempts to cast evil, character, and generally undesirable behaviour, as biological problems. The term

doi:10.1017/S1358246118000280   © The Royal Institute of Philosophy and the contributors 2018
Royal Institute of Philosophy Supplement **83** 2018

"history" is somewhat misleading. As we shall see, such tendencies continue unabated into the present (if anything, they have accelerated in light of recent pop-neuroscience, and tabloid misrepresentation of genetic science). Providing this historical context is particularly important. Given the profound continuity of this tendency to biologise morality, the litany of abuses committed in the process (not just by totalitarian states, but primarily by our own) needs to be made starkly clear.

Second, it will be argued that, given moral functioning's profoundly contextual and responsive qualities, any notion of a fine-grained, powerfully efficacious moral enhancement is both unrealistic and, actually, incoherent. Since enthusiasts' hopes are unrealistic and incoherent, such enhancement would not even be capable of providing the transformative ends that supposedly justify the sometimes extreme prescriptions set forward.

Finally, the chapter concludes with the claim that moral enhancement enthusiasm, given the unjustified optimism surrounding its potential efficacy, actually serves to trivialise the evils of this world, and not only to trivialise the hard-won efforts required to diminish and overcome such evils, but to misdirect attention away from the real hard work that needs to be done in facing such evils. The focus lies, instead, on advocating for unrealistic techno-fixes and easy answers that cannot be forthcoming.

2. Biologising Morality

2.1. From History to the Present

> Perhaps evil is a disease – one we can treat. [Then] you could start to define and describe the basic flaw in the human condition. "Just as a constellation of symptoms such as fever and a cough may signify pneumonia, defining the constellation of symptoms that signify this syndrome may mean that you could recognise it in the early stages". [And] if evil really is a pathology, then society ought to try to diagnose susceptible individuals and reduce contagion.[1]

As can be seen from Izhak Fried's proposal quoted above, the desire to biologise morality, to predict bad behaviour and to pre-emptively

---

[1] Izhak Fried, quoted in Laura Spinney, 'Is Evil a Disease? ISIS and the Nueroscience of Morality', *New Scientist* **3047**, 14th November 2015: https://www.newscientist.com/article/mg22830471-000-syndrome-e-can-neuro-science-explain-the-executioners-of-isis/.

"treat" it remains strong. Such a desire manifests in numerous forms. One can still observe discourse and policy pointing to heredity as the cause of crime; one can see tabloid headlines warning us about so-called "psychopath genes", "nefarious amygdalae", and "addictive brains" – evocative terms which very poorly describe the actual science surrounding these matters. With Fried we observe the latest mainstream academic attempt to describe evil itself as a literal neurological disorder, the so-called 'Syndrome E',[2] which articulates genocide in terms of faulty neurological machinery. Terms like "chemical imbalance", though shown to be without empirical foundation, pervade the public lectionary, used by psychotherapeutic professionals and public alike for explaining the root cause of persons' inability to conform, to behave desirably, and to be happy whilst doing so. Deceptive misconstruals of empirical research have seduced (and continue to seduce) various interested parties into clothing what are, all too often, cultural mores and social deviance in apparently objective, genetically, neurologically, or psychologically defective terminology.

Not least amongst those deceived by misapplications of medical metaphors in describing moral functioning are the enthusiasts for moral enhancement, who rarely bring into question the rather large gap between the colourful, though misleading language used in the dissemination of science to the general public, and the much more hesitant and limited claims made by most of the empirical researchers themselves. A critical inspection of the various empirical work on moral functioning reveals a much more ambiguous and conflicting picture, one which does very little to justify the sorts of excessive optimism that pervades the enthusiasts' discourse.

The misapplication of medical metaphors and psychotherapeutic labels when describing moral functioning, and the simplifications involved in such language-use (both illuminating and misleading in different ways), are hardly represented only in a small fringe of enthusiasts. Hans Eysenck, the personality theorist giant, in his 1964 book *Crime and Personality* was adamant that 'criminality' could be attributed to 'levels of extroversion and anxiety causing a failure in conditioning' – failures that 'could be remedied by early childhood administration of appropriate drugs'.[3] Eysenck's proposal is one example of a whole body of work constituting an entire movement

---

[2] Spinney, 'Is Evil a Disease?'.

[3] Hans Eysenck, *Crime and Personality* (London: Routledge & Kegan Paul, 1964), quoted in A. J. W. Taylor, 'Eysenck – "Aloof, Dismissive", *The Psychologist* **29**:7 (2016), 490–499.

(one well-funded by both state institutions and pharmaceutical in-
dustry research grants), taking what is considered to be problematic
behaviour and attempting to squeeze it into a too narrow box of psychological disorders, so that it might be "treated" through medical
means.

Long before the discourse of moral enhancement, therefore, the
notion of testing, profiling, and pre-emptively drugging children to
prevent "criminality" was enthusiastically forwarded by many influential names offering simple reductive remedies to profound social
problems. And the fact is that pharmaceutical treatments for bad
behaviour, now re-labelled "personality disorders", are multiplying
in the present. This testing, profiling, and pre-emptive recommenda-
tion of pharmaceutical intervention, given the increasing prevalence
of so-called behavioural modification, data aggregation, and algorith-
mic analysis, represents a trajectory that is only continuing to gain
momentum and funding as time goes on. This is moral enhancement's
broader real-world context, and if the former is not described with
respect to the latter, then it risks being profoundly misunderstood.

So, there is nothing new at all in the biologisation of morality and
character. States throughout the world have used, and continue to
use, whatever means available (previously, psychiatry and genetics
were the primary tools, and in many ways remain so),[4] for taking
judgements about right and wrong, behaviours that were desirable
and undesirable, matters of superior and inferior character, and
articulating them in biological and medical terms. In this way, deviance and undesirable behaviour can be given the visage of objectivity
and construed as physiological issues that can be, likewise, remedied
through biological modes of control.

Evil and criminality, in this view, is not a person's fault, but an
epiphenomenon, or phenotypic expression of a deeper biological
malfunction (though the question of what precisely constitutes
"normal" or "well-functioning" biology in the moral context is
rarely raised). Above all, evil, when described as a physiological
breakdown, brings with it the implication that deviant behaviour
can be *controlled*, not by the agents themselves, who are no longer regarded as agents, but by medical professionals who alone comprehend the biological or psychological mechanisms at hand. Evil and
deviance, rather than being construed as largely socially-located phenomena, can then be thought of like any other disease, which can be

---

[4]   D. R. Alexander and R. L. Numbers (eds), *Biology and Ideology: From
Descartes to Dawkins* (Chicago: The University of Chicago Press, 2010),
1, 10.

alternatively cured or sectioned, subjected to palliative care, so to speak, so that the effects of the "disease" do as little harm to society and the "infected" individual as humanly possible. We have already found in moral enhancement literature calls to segregate and monitor those with the very poorly named 'psychopath gene'.[5]

The consequence of this way of understanding bad behaviour – for whatever germ of truth it may contain – is surrounded by the sad reality of abuse. *Any* behaviour or group that is considered undesirable can be, and in many cases has been, subjected to the label of biological degeneracy, of one form or another. One need not look to the Nazis and Soviets for examples, and one must be suspicious of the likes of John Harris when he makes claims to the effect that, well, it was just the Nazis that really abused science, and since we are not Nazis we have nothing to worry about.[6] Our own Western states have been prolific, and continue to be prolific, in engaging in such a tendency. Political dissidents have been labelled schizophrenics; the "feral lower classes" considered the product of poor breeding; homosexuals considered subjects of a mental illness (and still are, in many Fundamentalist circles); and all sorts of undesirable behavioural problems were to be solved by fusing the temporal lobes of deviant individuals. Less famous examples include the relatively recent involuntary sterilisation of Native American women, and institutionalised psychiatric patients sterilised as part of a social beneficence project in the 1960s and 1970s.[7] The list of such abuses is,

---

[5]   What is in a name? The same mutation called "the psychopath gene" has also been called "the warrior gene", and though neither are really appropriate descriptors, notice how the latter term is less pejorative than the former. Had the mutation only been labelled "the warrior gene" I wonder if it would have stirred the imaginations of moral enhancement enthusiasts quite so readily. Poor labels, in short, have led commentators far astray.

[6]   R. Sparrow, 'A Not-So-New Eugenics: Harris and Savulescu on Human Enhancement', *Hastings Center Report* **41**:1 (2011), 32–42, 40. And, one might add that it is primarily Anglo-American scientistic philosophers coming from John Harris' own tradition that have been most vocal in extolling the virtues of the worst forms of moral eugenics, and the pseudoscience it was based upon – of whom the Nazis were but their most prolific students. A look at the history of eugenics in the UK and USA based on such philosophy and "science" very much disabuses us of the notion that the Nazis were the only culprits of inhuman abuses of science.

[7]   G. Rutecki, *Forced Sterilization of Native Americans: Late Twentieth Century Physician Cooperation with National Eugenic Policies*, 2010: https://cbhd.org/content/forced-sterilization-native-americans-late-twentieth-century-physician-cooperation-national-.

unfortunately, extremely long and stretches consistently into the present in various forms.

The primary thing to be observed is that most, if not all, of these projects were carried out under the sincere belief on the part of the policy-makers that *they were doing something morally good* – that they were improving the moral stock of humanity. We find precisely the same sincere talk of 'beneficence', of moral obligations to enhance, coming from our moral enhancement enthusiasts.[8] This pattern is something that needs to be remarked upon. For, the above "biologise, predict, and treat" practices continue into the present most visibly under the mantle of profiling and pre-emptive pharmacological interventions for children and populations of inner-city locations most "at risk" of violence and crime in later life.

The underlying discourse can be found everywhere at present, from popular discourse, to academic discourse, clinical discourse, and even in the court systems. The pop-neuroscience discourse regarding the illusory nature of the self and conscious choice – the supposedly false image of conscious control over one's actions[9] – encounters and welcomes the neuro-legal discourse in which terrible crimes are dealt with in terms of neurochemistry, and parts of the brain are described as literally malfunctioning, as broken machinery, indicating a diminished or entirely lacking capacity for agency on the part of the accused. These narratives play into TV fiction and real life court proceedings in equal measure.

Whatever the truth of agency, of conscious control and choice (and surely no simple answer can be given), the important point for present purposes is to get very clearly in focus the extant trend which takes the locus of control for moral action, evil, undesirable behaviour and deviance, away from any given agent and relocates it into the biological domain. Moral enhancement discourse, rather than offering something fundamentally new, is itself a symptom of this overarching trend and needs to be understood as part of that larger context. Claims regarding the beneficence of moral enhancement, or its neutrality, completely neglect the historical and social context out of which moral enhancement discourse arises, and into which it would be implemented. The same old attempts at control are simply reworded in the "new" terms of the current discourse, value-judgements are then presented as objective scientific truths

[8]   J. Savulescu, *Unfit for Life: Genetically Enhance Humanity or Face Extinction*, 2009: http://humanityplus.org/2009/11/genetically-enhance-humanity-or-face-extinction/.

[9]   E. Valentine, *Philosophy & History of Psychology: Selected Works of Elizabeth Valentine* (New York: Psychology Press, 2014), 61.

or psychological disorders, and the process can continue unabated as if it is something completely fresh and new. Moral enhancement discourse enters in right here. Yet the same old intuition is always at play: if morality can be defined as a physiological issue *then it can be controlled*. And then it *should* be controlled. This is precisely what we find the moral enhancement enthusiasts advocating – either by means of the individual making the responsible choice to enhance, or by the state enforcing such enhancement, or incentivising it in various as yet undetermined ways.[10]

But this *"if"* regarding whether morality can be defined as a physiological issue has never been demonstrated. Worse, despite concerted efforts to do, attempts to pin morality down to biological precursors continue to fail – except under the broadest and most superficial experimental conditions. There have never been, and perhaps will never be (more on this presently), any sophisticated mapping of moral behaviour onto biological substrates. So, not only does the project of control apply morally dubious means to achieve its ends, but no-one has come close to providing a non-superficial way of describing the complexities of moral living in biological terms to begin with.

The suffering caused by such policies is felt by some groups more than by others. The overwhelming majority of interventions for social control of undesirable behaviour (which is the real moral enhancement as far as we have seen it), have been directed at the disenfranchised, the marginalised and the impoverished. When we see, for example, policies like the NHS's recent denial of non-emergency surgery to the obese (as explicit behavioural incentives to alter persons' life-choices),[11] we see that such measures are aimed specifically at those that are not wealthy. In this case, wealthy persons have private medical insurance and are utterly immune to such measures. And, of course, the larger social issues are ignored.

This observation is particularly relevant when one takes the claim made in enhancement discourse that the voluntary public uptake of moral enhancements be motivated by means of various politically-enacted schemes of social incentives and disincentives.[12] This

---

[10]   Savulescu, *Unfit for Life*; V. Rakić, 'Voluntary Moral Enhancement and the Survival-at-Any-Cost Bias', *Journal of Medical Ethics* **40**:4 (2014), 246–250.

[11]   BBC News, 'Harrogate Obesity and Smoking "Surgery Ban" Move', 7th October 2016: http://www.bbc.co.uk/news/uk-england-york-north-yorkshire-37583399.

[12]   Rakić, 'Voluntary Moral Enhancement and the Survival-at-Any-Cost Bias', 246–250.

suggestion suffers from the same family problem as noted above. Such measures are socially stratified, and disincentives and incentives alike, those aimed at the finances of the populace at least, have not the least impact on the wealthy, whilst being unavoidable, and having sometimes life-altering consequences, for the impoverished. What have the wealthy to fear from so-called "sugar taxes", recently brought into the UK, aimed at disincentivising unhealthy eating? Marie Antoinette's pronouncement 'let them eat cake' will ring hollow in the ears, and stomachs, of lower income families who have up till now (because of the very low price of sugary and fatty foods) been forced to take her at her word. But, to what extent is obesity amongst the lower classes a matter of weakness of will, and to what extent is it a somewhat understandable decision given the exorbitant prices of good food? The larger issues are never addressed. Because of the excessive price of healthy foods, all too often, the choice for many impoverished families has been between bad food or going hungry – when the behavioural disincentives are put in place, what is the choice then?

The notion of dealing with the social causes of such problems is given lip service in moral enhancement discourse (as if to say: "well of course we should tackle social issues"), and then decisively bracketed from view, never to be mentioned again, with no reflection on how any supposed moral enhancement is to be integrated with these larger social and political realities, nor how they are to work alongside the social change that this most cursory of lip-service is paid to. Indeed, it is neither insignificant nor coincidental that no research at all into the profiling and pre-emptive "treatment" of white-collar criminality exists. The medicalisation of morality extends not much further than "diagnosing" and "treating" the sorts of crimes predominantly carried out by those of low income status. Since the overwhelming majority of incarcerated criminals are of lower class status, these persons present the most opportune group upon which moral enhancement will, in practice, be applied.

A recent example of precisely this can be observed in the New Hampshire prison system's decision to offer Vivitrol, an opioid inhibitor, to addicted inmates. The rationale is given as cost-cutting (Vivitrol costs $1000 per month, rehabilitation costs more than twice that – though how administrators expect the former to be effective, and thus cheaper, over the long-term without recourse to the latter is another question).[13] However, as one paper observed:

[13] K. Blessing, 'N.H. Prison System to Start Using Vivitrol — 'Wonder Drug' for Addicts Already Given in Mass.', *Eagle Tribune*, 8th May 2016:

'[m]any experts view prisons – where addiction's human toll can be seen most clearly – as a natural place to discover what works'.[14] Opinions differ however, with some experts suggesting that Vivitrol has saved lives, and others noting that '[w]hen the injections stopped, many in the study relapsed. A year later, relapse rates looked the same in the two groups'.[15]

Moral enhancement enthusiasts too often refuse to recognise the realities in which any moral enhancement, if applied, would become manifest, or the sorts of interests that would profit from co-opting moral enhancement discourse. Our extant system is already replete with modes of socially stratified behavioural control, with many more being developed. This is the concrete context which will define and co-opt instantiations of moral enhancement. And, to the extent that moral enhancement would be, *de facto* (and regardless of good intentions), an extension of social control,[16] then given such social control extends above all to the marginalised, advocating moral enhancement implicitly involves advocating morally dubious modes of socially stratified biological control over the least protected subjects in the general population.

Understood in this way, one can see that the words "moral enhancement" themselves have a mystique that conceal something less illustrious. If one were to ask: "what is moral enhancement, really?" – breaking the term down into its practical instantiations suggests that "moral enhancement" is really little more than a euphemism for prescribing drugs, profiling, monitoring, therapy, and perhaps surgery. Then one sees that such enhancement would not involve anything fundamentally new, but rather be a simple extension of current social practice, for better or worse, and a further entrenchment

---

http://www.eagletribune.com/news/new_hampshire/nh-school-bus-driv ers-to-vote-on-possible-strike-tonight/article_2dd6d086-aa99-11e6-a77f-d 3e0eb9053dc.html.

[14]   C. K. Johnson, 'Prisons Fight Opioids With $1000 Injection: Does it Work?', *Associated Press*, 14th November 2016: http://www.dailymail.co. uk/wires/ap/article-3933514/Prisons-fight-opioids-1-000-injection-Does-work.html.

[15]   Johnson, 'Prisons Fight Opioids With $1000 Injection'.

[16]   A deconstruction of the notion that individual choice and social control are so sharply distinct. Even voluntary moral enhancement would have its social context and imply social obligations to "voluntarily" take up such enhancement. See H. Wiseman, 'SSRIs and Moral Enhancement: Looking Deeper', *American Journal of Bioethics Neuroscience* 5:4 (2014), 1–7.

of the goods and evils thereof. This larger context, bringing moral enhancement back to earth, as it were, diminishes the seductive qualities of the beneficence claims made about its salvatory power, or its power to drive forward the moral evolution of mankind.

2.2. Morality and the Mechanistic Metaphor

This misuse of medical metaphors is only part of the problem here. For the objectification of matters of character and morality are combined with the overwhelmingly biomechanical thought-world applied by philosophical moral enhancement enthusiasts, which still envisages, consciously or not, the human person as a *bête machine*. This has fostered a kind of reasoning which proceeds as follows:

a) humans are biological mechanisms, problems with which can be understood as mechanical breakdowns, and thus every human problem merely needs to be located somewhere in his biology;

b) the biological, mechanical part responsible for the human or social ill in question can be isolated from the whole, as a cog or piston can be isolated from other elements in a mechanism; and

c) that problem can then be rectified by simply repairing the malfunctioning biomechanical piston or cog responsible for the bad character and general misbehaviour of the person or group in question (examples below).

In combination, these two processes, the medicalisation of values discussed above, and the mechanistic thought-world, are extremely destructive. On its own, mechanistic metaphors provide a helpful, though provisional, way for scientists to approach their problems. Scientists simplify their problems so as to find better ways of modelling and grasping reality. But metaphors, illuminating and necessary as they are in the scientific process, can be just as misleading if one does not grasp the basic science through which the metaphors make sense. A recent example of the havoc that comes from talking in simplified metaphors can be found in the physics discourse surrounding "the holographic universe". While there is a sense in which the universe can be understood broadly as functioning in some of the same ways that a hologram works – it is a helpful metaphor for physicists who understand the maths of it all – the metaphor then runs wild amongst the public, and one finds senseless discussions about the implications of 'the unreality of reality' even in philosophical

44

discourse.[17] This is a helpful example, for one can readily see the problem in this instance: commentators have simply taken a colourful metaphor too literally, and got carried away in their speculations because of it. *But biological metaphors are more deceptive.* What happens when one starts talking about "psychopath genes", or "the moral molecule", or "neurological machinery"? What happens when medical metaphors and psychotherapeutic labels proliferate? They are taken literally, and philosophers and the public alike are misled by them. The simplifications that scientists rely upon, and understand, run wild and philosophers and public alike, not grasping the nature of the science, start making unfortunate claims on the basis of a misunderstood set of shorthand labels. Moral enhancement enthusiasm is constituted almost entirely on the basis of such misunderstandings.

So many examples of misleading mechanistic metaphors can be found in the relevant literature. Joshua Greene has been quoted talking about impulsive criminality as 'faulty machinery', then discussing the implications for the legal system given the lack of responsibility on the part of such apparently helpless, brain-defective subjects;[18] "optogenetic" treatments for addiction are presented as if addiction were a literally an engineering problem, a "neurological disease", relating to the transmission of dopamine through synaptic pipework; whilst aggression is talked about, *vis-à-vis* serotonin, in much the same way one talks about putting oil into the engine of a car – too little serotonin and the engine starts to growl and fume, whilst just enough serotonin lubricates the mood, making persons less punishing and less liable to erupt into a violent rage.[19] The list of such bio-reductive, mechanistic simplifications continues to increase.

Despite everything we continue to learn about the complexity of genomic and neuron interactions with other complexities such as epigenomic and neuronal plasticity, development, and social-environmental interactions,[20] the optimism that the moral character of humankind might eventually be perfected through genetic selection,

[17] N. Bostrom, 'Are We Living in a Computer Simulation?', *Philosophical Quarterly* **53**:211 (2003), 243–55.

[18] C. Goldberg, *Beyond Good and Evil: New Science Casts Light on Morality in the Brain*, 2014: www.commonhealth.wbur.org/2014/08/brain-matters-morality.

[19] M. Crockett, L. Clark, M. Hauser, and T. Robbins, 'Serotonin Selectively Influences Moral Judgement and Behavior Through Effects on Harm Aversion', *Psychology and Cognitive Sciences* **107**:40 (2010), 17433–17438.

[20] I. Gadjev, 'Nature and Nurture: Lamarck's Legacy', *Biological Journal of the Linnean Society* **112**:1 (2015), 242–47.

pharmacological intervention, and neurosurgery, remains unsinkable. But, once one has taken on board the fact that contemporary biological research, on the whole, is increasingly coming to view biological causality as an immensely convoluted web of innumerable interactions across numerous scales (and constituted precisely as the *interaction* of such parts), the prospect that there might be a clear and identifiable "biological cause" for a given moral trait becomes more and more unrealistic.

By extension, the idea that fine-grained enhancement of something so sophisticated as human moral functioning might be developed, has to dissipate with the notion of the identifiable "biological cause" for morality that it is constructed upon. No such mechanical cogs and levers exist. Altering biology in systemic, multiscale wholes – such as human beings in their social contexts – proffers no reliably clear improvements with respect to complex behaviours which rely, instead, on the interactions of innumerable biological factors taken in relation to their environmental whole.

So, the key reality that serves to deflate the idea of finely-grained moral enhancement is that biological factors are but one element in a long recursive chain of causal inputs, and so it makes no sense to either talk of biology in isolation or to think of biology as a primary cause of sophisticated moral functioning. When one starts to understand things in this way, realising that biology plays but a partial, and essentially unclear role in moral functioning – a role that manifests precisely as interactive, rather than as being based in "biological causes" – the widespread optimism regarding moral enhancement has to be overwhelmingly drawn back.

In reality, the very same biology that contributes to one's ability to reason morally contributes to our ability to reason immorally, the same biology that contributes to human empathy also contributes to human aggression. The two cannot be disentangled. All of the powers required for moral functioning are spread out over innumerable biological interactions, a web of interactions whose synergistic operations make possible both moral and immoral behaviour alike. It is precisely because moral functioning is so sophisticated that it relies as its bedrock upon such an immensely convoluted biological foundation of powers and capabilities. It relies upon an integrated base of cognitive and affective, imaginative, somatic, and responsive powers that are not readily separated, nor manipulated in any sophisticated way that would allow for a specifically moral enhancement.

Simply put, enthusiasts' hopes here are based on a basic misunderstanding of human biology. Whatever moral enhancement might be possible, it must be broad-scope and very limited in nature. With that, we have returned to the sledgehammer approach that is already available, so-called because such interventions can only be effective, at best, by making tremendously broad changes to the organism's biology as a whole, creating numerous side-effects that might just as well diminish other moral powers (for example, SSRIs for reducing explosive aggression have, in some cases, resulted in an increase in pre-meditated aggression).[21]

In any case, even with moral bio-intervention, the overwhelming morally generative work would still remain on the side of individual cultivation, combined with social-environmental, political, developmental, and psychological encouragement of "desirable" behaviour. For these remain the dominating factors in giving conceptual shape to the enactment of particular behaviours that are deemed moral or immoral. As such, bio-intervention offers little by way of resolving the larger context of humankind's moral difficulties. Cultivation of fine-grained moral functioning will continue to require, as it has always required, the shape that can be given only by social scaffolding, personal reflection, and clear intent. If social change is the dominating factor regarding the "grand scale" of moral functioning, attention needs to be directed first and foremost towards those ends. And, when one recognises that sophisticated moral functioning simply is not appropriately understood in biological terms, *that biology was the wrong place to be seeking answers to begin with*, then the entire bottom falls out of the hope for some sophisticated bioenhancement of moral functioning, and the "grand" project simply falls apart.

3. Context, Responsiveness, and the Challenge to Fine-Grained Moral Enhancement

Apart from these biological realities, one sees the notion of fine-grained moral enhancement is conceptually incoherent on its own terms. Whenever one is talking about fine-grained moral enhancement one must always be mindful of the manner in which contextual factors modulate how moral acts are to be expressed *in situ*. Moral living is

---

[21]   See H. Wiseman, 'SSRIs as Moral Enhancement Interventions: A Practical Dead End', *American Journal of Bioethics Neuroscience* **5**:3 (2014), 1–10. *But why this privileging of the biological mode at all?* Humans are biological beings, of course, but we are also social beings, and we are also psychological beings, and responsible beings, and we have innumerable dimensions besides. So what would even make one think that biology should hold the keys to moral improvement anyway?

always responsive to context and most moral activity must be shaped in relation to the situation in which one's actions are expressed. Even the most simplistic forms of moral absolutism face this problem. For example, if one abides by the strict rule "be kind unto others", one is still faced with having to figure out how to express appropriately that kindness in any new situation that one finds oneself in.

Context is a thorny issue for commentators here. It is almost universally acknowledged that context is significant with respect to moral enhancement, yet few seem to bring the notion to bear as part of any extended exploration of the matter. At the very least, moral enhancement enthusiasts seem to think that universally extolled moral virtues like "empathy" or "kindness" can somehow be enhanced in an abstract, all-encompassing sense. Such thinking is problematic because the situation is always in part constitutive of the moral good in question. Moral goods are underdetermined with respect to form and shape. They can be applied, or misapplied, in as numerous a set of ways as the range of potential situations in which the moral good in question might be called for. When empathy, or kindness, or generosity, or trust (to take but a few examples mentioned in the literature), can take so many different potential forms, the notion that any of them can be simply enhanced in a generic or abstract way cannot be made sense of.

So, it should be no surprise that any links between a given moral good and biological substrates have proven themselves impossible to reliably pin down – the underdetermined nature of moral goods gives them an ephemeral and shifting quality that is challenging enough to articulate in conceptual terms (and it is no small matter that no-one can even agree upon how to conceptually define particular moral goods like empathy in the first place), let alone finding specific biological substrates that map onto these multiform goods which take their sense at least in part through instantiation in concrete contexts.

Moreover, any moral power or trait that one can think of will always require some degree of practice by which the person involved gains some embodied sense (to varying degrees conceptual, intuitive, and practical) of how that moral power is to be instantiated across the given range of contexts appropriate to it. This is one reason why focussing on the cognitive prospects for moral enhancement can in no way be adequate: the cognitive aspects of moral living are but one part of a larger integrative, embodied whole, and so too with affective moral enhancement.[22] This responsive, practical, embodied

---

[22] And "embodied" is meant to indicate that moral activity is not something done solely "in the brain", but rather relies on the faculties of a whole

dimension of moral living is, as I have argued elsewhere,[23] impervious to biomedical enhancement.

Though it is a well-rehearsed point, it is important to note that situationality also throws up problems for enhancement here simply because all moral goods can be harmful in the wrong context. Being primed to act compassionately, for example, might not be morally helpful in situations that call for some tough policies. The political problem of so-called "dirty hands" articulates the sad reality that sometimes the greater good is only obtained by doing bad things. A nation's security services, for example, might be disabled if prohibited from certain immoral activities. Likewise the journalistic press, insofar as they are acting in the public interest, might be forced to engage in dubious activities to obtain the truth (as the adage goes, "good journalist, bad person"). So, even if a particular moral good could be enhanced in some generic sense, this would not necessarily lead to improved outcomes over all – and one's enhanced motives, though well-intentioned, could find themselves being inappropriate to the given situation.

Moreover, different situations demand flexibility with respect to different, and often contrary, moral powers. There are times when one needs to be co-operative to achieve one's moral aims, and there are times when one must stand one's ground, or times when one must stand alone. Moral living requires a practiced ability to discern moral salience and selectively modulate moral impulses as necessary – how would a moral enhancement technology know which to motivate and when? It is of little use saying that one could enhance a person's ability to know what is morally required in different circumstances. Again, the faculty of moral discernment is not a cog of which one can point to the bit of biology involved and say: "there, let us enhance this thing". Enhancing some elements of cognitive responsiveness is certainly possible. But even then, this would not be a *moral* enhancement, for that would mean enhancing a person's

---

person embedded in a situation, comprehending that situation as "ready-to-hand", as phenomenologically situated within that situation, as opposed to thinking of moral activity as nothing but a set of neural processes applied abstractly. For an account of how comprehension and reflection involve embodied, that is, not purely neurological activity, see N. Murphy and W. S. Brown, *Did My Neurons Make Me Do It? Philosophical and Neurobiological Perspectives on Moral Responsibility and Free Will* (New York: Oxford University Press, 2007), 240.

[23] H. Wiseman, *The Myth of the Moral Brain: The Limits of Moral Enhancement* (Cambridge: The MIT Press, 2016).

capacity to see and exploit the evil potential of a situation every bit as much as the good – and the fundamentally ambiguous relation between biology and morality is thereby further underlined.

It is also worth considering that moral enhancements do not have an "on/off switch". It would be a strange thing indeed if one could devise some contraption wherein one could press a button to say "enhance my ability to discern what is morally appropriate", and then press another button to say "empathy is required now", or to press another button which can say "empathy is not appropriate here, diminish my empathic impulses accordingly". The prospect seems somewhat farcical, and, again, based on a rather basic misunderstanding of how human biology works.

The contextual problems are yet more manifold. Say an enhancement did exist to enhance one's moral discernment of which virtue to apply, and could even stimulate the will to apply that virtue (even to the appropriate amplitude), such technologies would not be of much use in moral dilemmas, or in situations in which there are conflicting groups all making legitimate claims on one's empathy. Say an enhancement increased one's empathy, could it differentiate between different parties, weighing moral claims, such that one particularly deserving group was empathised with but not others? For *whom* exactly is one to have empathy, and what are the reasons for this in the particular context one is in? Moreover, it is worth considering that increasing empathy might lead to avoidance of moral situations. Sometimes the sensation of empathy is experienced as an unpleasant state, which can be responded to by means of aversion. Who does not occasionally turn their eyes away from the suffering and misfortune of others? This is not because one feels no empathy, but precisely because one does feel empathy.

In short, sophisticated moral functioning seems to defy the sort of generic approach that is assumed by moral enhancement enthusiasts. This need for responsiveness in determining timing and intensity of so-called "moral emotions" is particularly problematic for advocates of so-called "affective moral enhancement", who seem to think that unreflective impulses, urges, emotions, and affect generally have some manner of intrinsic moral status in and of themselves. The idea seems to be that emotions can be biologically dissociated from one another, that undesirable behaviours can be isolated in terms of their base affective impulses, and that these Lego-like dissociable impulses can then be selectively removed or enhanced at will. But emotions are not like this. And, in the real world, moral situations are often obscure, emotions are often conflicting and messy, and equally compelling reasons push one in multiple directions. Too often, as far as real life moral living goes, there are numerous moral paths, or sometimes no "right answer", and sometimes there are simply "no win" moral scenarios wherein someone has to lose out somewhere. It is hard to imagine how some technology could help resolve the emotional messiness of moral living.

Even a computational machine with unclouded moral motivation and judgement would fail to reach moral perfection, following this logic, because that robot would still face precisely the same real world problems we do. Namely, having to respond to competing claims, coping with competing visions of the good, dealing with "no-win situations", balancing near and far-sightedness, weighing interests, making trade-offs and defending them against those who think differently, knowing when to break the moral rules, then discerning and enacting the appropriate extent to which any moral good should be amplified or diminished to provide the most morally appropriate response given one's situation.

All of these context-based considerations, I suggest, make a mockery of the notion of fine-grained moral enhancement – which, in this light, presents itself as both unrealistic and conceptually incoherent. It is understandable, then, that the profoundly contextual nature of moral functioning gets roundly ignored by moral enhancement enthusiasts. Context presents a range of obstacles to fine-grained moral enhancement that cannot be plausibly overcome. One might suggest, therefore, that the failings of moral enhancement are not merely failures of present technology such that they might be overcome "in the future". Rather, such failings might be inevitable and necessary in light of the contextual responsiveness that moral living demands, combined with the indirect and ambiguous relationships between biology and moral functioning. These will always be the limits to what moral enhancement can achieve. In which case, moral enhancement might have, more or less, already reached its technological zenith.

4. Trivialising the Hard-Won Conquest of the Good

Who can be blamed for wanting a magic wand for dealing with the evils of the world? Every day one is confronted with war and the inordinate profiteering from it. Gangs, human trafficking, drugs, money laundering, and all manner of human exploitation flourish at the international level. Honour killings are reported nearly every day. Drone strikes kill civilians indiscriminately, and such deaths are covered up by the states perpetrating them. Spree killings occur frequently. Child soldiery, social injustice, poverty, and environmental destruction are rife. The logic of mutually assured destruction represents the victory of rationality over good sense. We face gun crime, knife crime; domestic violence and torture; at home and abroad. The pervasiveness of human evil and weakness seems to be everywhere one cares to look.

So again, the wish for some magical technology that might deal with such corruptions is understandable. But it is precisely because of the severity of such evils that one should be adamant in resisting the retreat into easy answers. No-one is denying that evil can be seen in almost every facet of human activity, and no-one is denying that mankind is on the precipice of technological self-destruction. The suggestion, instead, is that moral enhancement will not, and *cannot* offer the least bulwark against these realities. Moral enhancement simply is not capable of being potent enough, nor fine-grained enough, to make the needed changes.

Moreover, I would suggest that it is morally blameworthy to place one's hopes in such fantasia, when real work needs to be done elsewhere. Such retreats are cheap and easy, and since they have no workable basis in reality, the diversion of attention and discussion towards hopes of techno-fixes of this order actually threatens to trivialise the suffering in this world, as well as the all-too-real sacrifices made by persons throughout the globe in attempting to confront such evils. The severity of such realities makes it all the more important that lazy proposals regarding completely unrealistic bio-interventions not be allowed to take up the centre ground.

Calling moral enhancement enthusiasm intellectually lazy may sound strong, but the moral disapprobation is just. There is no short supply of examples of enthusiasts that refuse to look in the eye the practical, political, historical, and biological realities that severely undermine their proposals. A brief survey will suffice to indicate how enthusiasm here has led contributors to skirt what are fairly obvious, and severe, impediments to their future enhancement designs.

For example, we hear Nick Bostrom talking of humans beings potentially being provided with genetically-engineered oxytocin receptors for our brains to make us more compassionate.[24] But, oxytocin does not operate in nearly this kind of way, and can in some instances make persons more aggressive to members of out-groups.[25] Again,

---

[24] In J. Hughes, *Virtue Engineering*, 2016: http://ieet.org/.

[25] C. De Dreu, L. Greer, M. Handgraaf, S. Shalvi, G. Van Kleef, M. Baas, F. Ten Velden, E. Van Dijk, and S. Feith, 'The Neuropeptide Oxytocin Regulates Parochial Altruism in Intergroup Conflict Among Humans', *Science* **328**:5984 (2010), 1408–1411.

empathy and aggression are conjoined twins – sedating aggressive persons lessens their capacities to care, and increasing their empathy can produce violent indignation against those considered to be outside their own group, whether such indignation is merited or not. There is no one without the other.

Then we hear that technologies should be generated to directly feed glucose into the brain in order to enhance willpower.[26] Traditional methods of increasing brain glucose, like drinking a sugary beverage, or proper diet, are not adequate it seems, instead we need "technology" to feed this apparently morally efficacious carbohydrate directly to the brain. Yet, the nuances of something so multifaceted and diverse in form as willpower are not the sort of thing that can be sufficiently well reduced to brain glucose levels in the first place, such that neuro-devices (and presumably the surgery required to implant such devices) could be justified. Are there no better ways of improving will-power than by neuro-surgically implanting glucose feeders into the brain? And just how much benefit is this likely to yield? The whole prospect is based on a misreading of pop-science – for, while it is true that exhausted persons find it harder to motivate themselves (an obvious truth, they are exhausted after all), I fail to see why directly implanting glucose into the brain is going to have any more beneficial effects than, say, drinking orange juice, or taking a brief nap – all of which have the advantage of not requiring complex neurosurgery to be efficacious. Common sense does seem to be lacking here.

Then we hear that mankind is on the verge of self-destruction and therefore needs to be compelled to use "technologies" in order to save us from very present techno-oblivion.[27] But, the authors of such proposals themselves note that such nondescript "technologies" neither exist, nor are they even on the horizon with respect to the time-frame in which we are so endangered (i.e., now). Present dangers, which are real, are used as a vehicle to justify future undevised technologies, which, as yet, have no shape, form, or content about which moral evaluation might be carried through. Then, very real crimes, and very real suffering (like the Virginia Tech massacre) – with living members of the public still coping with the consequences of these tragedies – are used to justify the need for these as-yet fantastical modes of compulsory moral enhancement. It seems insensitive, to

---

[26] Wiseman, 'SSRIs as Moral Enhancement Interventions', 9.
[27] Savulescu, 'Unfit for Life', 2009: http://humanityplus.org/2009/11/genetically-enhance-humanity-or-face-extinction/.

say the least, to exploit real suffering to make such extreme and ill-formed proposals.

Next, we hear proposals that marriages might be saved by putting together some "love" philtre composed of oxytocin, drugs, and other hormones[28] – as if the nuances of human relationships and human disagreements can be resolved through drug use and such quick fixes. Note that my central claim throughout has been, not just that such proposals are weak, but that they are actually morally blameworthy. Would it really be a step forward in the responsible management of human difficulties (of which marital strife might be considered one form) to suggest that the parties be put on drugs that produce the effect of making them like each other more? This sort of proposal is a microcosm for moral enhancement enthusiasm. I would suggest that the intrinsic higher motives of most persons would be profoundly dissatisfied with such easy techno-fixes on the existential level, and that the public would ultimately reject such practices even if they were made available (I would like to think that medical professionals themselves would eschew such shallow proposals before they became policy to begin with).

A few more illustrations will suffice. We hear proposals for the moral enhancement of judges, justified on the grounds that their judgements should become more reliably Rawlsian.[29] We hear talk of an oxytocin-fuelled world of hugs, and warmth, generosity, and economic prosperity.[30] We hear talk of genetically enhancing serotonin receptivity in order to make persons more politically liberal-leaning.[31] The list continues seemingly without end. And, the simple fact is that I have listed here but a partial catalogue of the fantastical, bizarre, poorly thought through, and often patently ridiculous claims that have been made by leading philosophers at the highest scholarly level. Is it really morally appropriate to place sincere hopes in such things when one is confronted with the present reality of suffering and evil?

---

[28] K. Hookem-Smith, 'Experts Recommend a "Love Pill" to Save Marriages', *Yahoo News*, 3rd May 2012: https://in.news.yahoo.com/love-pill-save-marraiges-relationships-couples.html.

[29] G. O. Schaefer and J. Savulescu, 'Procedural Moral Enhancement', *Neuroethics* (2016), 1–12.

[30] P. Zak, *The Moral Molecule: The New Science of What Makes Us Good or Evil* (London: Bantam Press, 2012).

[31] J. Hughes, *The Benefits and Risks of Virtue Engineering,* 2012: http://bioethics.as.nyu.edu/object/bioethics.events.20120330.conference.

And what of the idea, variously discussed in the enhancement literature, regarding prospects for indiscriminate, society-wide implementation of moral enhancement?[32] In terms of political and practical realities, this prospect is untenable. One might consider two forms of moral enhancement – pharmaceutical or neuro-surgical. The logistical problems here are overwhelmingly decisive in negating such society-wide prospects. Consider that, just in the UK there are 65 million persons, and in the USA there are 324 million persons. Are we to think the NHS or Medicare could cover mandated neurosurgery for the entire nation? Neurosurgery is, and will continue to be, an incredibly risky business (problems of post-operative infection, allergies and rejection, technological breakdown, malfunction, and decay, cannot be avoided). Such surgery is fraught with dangers and a recourse of last resort, a real world practicality seemingly forgotten by enhancement enthusiasts. Or, what about the costs of ongoing prescriptions for nootropic morally improving pharmaceuticals for every man, woman, and child, into perpetuity, so that they might have some limited increase in their powers of appreciating moral salience? Just how many moral enhancement drugs are the general population expected to consume – a drug for empathy, a drug for trust, a drug to increase charitable donations, a drug to increase moral discernment, a drug to enhance moral imagination, a drug to overcome moral cynicism? That is a lot of drugs.

So, is the prospect of encouraging medical intervention for the entire population even desirable? Scrutinising the logistics of such a proposal helps indicate that it is neither desirable nor feasible to instantiate moral enhancement on this level. How would persons be tested to ensure they are taking these moral enhancement drugs? Blood testing kits at voting booths? And, would the drugs' side-effects (there is no drug that is without side-effects, or that does not perpetrate some manner of long-term damage through on-going use), given through life-long use, justify the cost of having a nation of life-long drug users? How many decades of safety testing would such drugs require to ensure they are safe for life-long use? What populace would stand for mandated neurosurgery or drug-use being imposed upon them?

---

[32]   It is possible to have selective society-wide moral enhancement. This would be directed at members of given categories, say, those perpetrating crimes on the basis of their addictions to drugs or alcohol. It is current practice in the UK to place drug addicts in rehab as part of their sentence. See H. Wiseman, 'Moral Enhancement: "Hard" and "Soft" Forms', *American Journal of Bioethics* **14**:4 (2014), 48–49.

And, why would a pharmaceutical company devote billions in research for compounds to enhance various moral traits?

Therefore, the prospect of state-wide moral enhancement is not only convoluted and wholly impractical, it is financially unprofitable, and so undesired by all parties involved,[33] that one can reasonably conclude that state-wide moral enhancement of the sort proposed in the literature is not something that we are likely to witness any time soon. Here again, such enthusiasm represents the triumph of logic over good sense, of dislocated rationality over any kind of reasonableness.

But what really gets lost in all this is the "hands on" element of those trying – in the real world – politically, socially, institutionally, journalistically, and through creative media, to bring awareness and change to regions of the world where evils are pervasive. Moral enhancement can never realistically hope to impact a society in which, for example, a brutal "honour code" is woven into its fabric. Yet, through media focus on such evils as, say, the caste system in India, genuine change seems, slowly, to be occurring.[34] The sacrifices and suffering of those bringing such crimes to light is truly heroic, and, in contrast to this, diverting one's attention towards incoherent techno-fixes should indeed be subjected to sharp moral critique.

Instead, the severity of such threats demand of our philosophical commentators much greater care and sensitivity with respect to the claims that they put forward. If there is any moral obligation that the presence of such evils puts upon us, it is to take such matters seriously, to be responsible towards them, and not to exploit them by making the sorts of outlandish (and dare I say, morally offensive) proposals that we have been exploring above.

---

[33] A cynical eye might also observe that Western affluence is continually premised on exploitation of the developing world, and that our citizens benefit from not looking too deeply at any potential moral obligations implied to resolve such exploitation.

[34] It is interesting to note that the caste system is illegal in India, yet it prevails, particularly in rural areas. Changing laws is one helpful step, but changing attitudes towards systems that have been in operation for so many generations is a big challenge. It is hard to imagine how some technology or drug would contribute in any way towards changing such attitudes towards social stratification, and the terrible discrimination against such 'untouchables'. See Ravi Agrawal, 'India's Caste System: Outlawed Yet Omnipresent', *CNN*, 24th February 2016: http://edition.cnn.com/2016/02/23/asia/india-caste-system/index.html.

5. The Sins of the Discourse

To conclude, then, I would like to point out the irony of an enthusiasm for moral enhancement that is itself lacking in so many intellectual virtues. The enthusiasts' discourse, I suggest, sins against the standards of excellence demanded of rigorous intellectual conversation in what I consider to be morally problematic ways. Such enthusiasm has rejected historical and sociological analysis, and has ignored the larger present context which embraces it. By extension, such enthusiasm has not seen that it is a symptom and extension of larger, and often disturbing set of attempts to biologise and control human behaviour. Enthusiasm has not adequately confronted the extent to which moral enhancement would inevitably be implemented (as such interventions have been, and continue to be) as socially stratified modes of behavioural control levelled primarily against the least protected amongst us.

Such embracing social and historical trajectories must surely make us rethink the beneficence claims behind moral enhancement projects (innocent enough as such claims may be on the part of the philosophers), and re-envision moral enhancement as simply another branch of the perennial project of social control. In such a case, moral enhancement would itself produce various forms of morally problematic phenomena. Or, put differently, moral enhancement would itself be an open invitation for various immoral applications given in an existing social context already primed for such abuse.

We see that there are many other intellectual sins committed in the discourse. Enthusiasts have made excessive use of pop-science that they do not understand. Nor have they taken the time to investigate, evaluate, or think at all critically about such science either. Even the wildly effusive Paul Zak is careful when wearing his academic apparel to state clearly how tentative and limited his actual findings have been. The use of metaphor in science, which is a necessary device in coming to generate novel understandings of the natural world, is a dangerous thing when transmitted through media that like buzzwords and exciting headlines. Enthusiasts have not been careful enough regarding their reception of such science to differentiate between the metaphors and colourful buzzwords, on the one hand, and the more subtle and limited science on the other. Even then, such empirical work has not been subjected to the least critical scrutiny, and some of the science upon which moral enhancement claims rest is superficial and dubious in the extreme.

Worse, enthusiasts for moral enhancement have not taken adequate care to ensure that their concepts are coherent, even at face value. We

Harris Wiseman

have argued that the most cursory analysis of how context shapes moral living gives us powerful reasons for thinking that any kind of fine-grained moral enhancement is impossible on its own terms. Enthusiasts have simply bought in, wholesale, to the current trend of attempting to medicalise all facets of human existence, without even subjecting that tendency to moral evaluation, or recognising the moral dubiousness of the consequences of attempting to characterise all human activity in biological terms above all. The greed for biotechnological solutions to what are, in the end, non-biological problems, has been gluttonous – certainly at the expense of more meaningful ways of thinking about how the very real evil in the world might be better managed (namely, institutional and political exchange; creating wise leaders and inspiring persons; forging international legislation; the use of investigative journalism and various media for bringing light to the invisible suffering of those around the world; mentors, modelling, exemplars; and so on).

The worst sin of all, because it refers to real suffering and justifies itself on the backs of real persons that have to cope with the consequences of terrible crimes, is the trivialisation of the evils of this world by misdirecting attention away from much needed real activity towards unrealistic hopes for easy answers and techno-fixes to our moral problems. Perhaps if moral enhancement enthusiasts shifted their focus away from the standard terms of present discussion, and refocussed on considering present forms of moral enhancement *qua* social-paternalistic influence (which are increasingly rife and prolific with respect to the scope of the interventions used), and the pathologisation of social deviance into objective medical terminology (which is proving itself increasingly profitable and likewise prolific), enthusiasm might move more quickly in a positive, serious, and worthwhile direction.

Acknowledgements

Thanks go to The MIT Press for publishing the author's book on moral enhancement *The Myth of the Moral Brain* and for allowing reference to that book to be made. Thanks must also go to Michael Hauskeller for inviting me to contribute to this volume, and for his patience throughout.

University College London
harriswiseman@gmail.com

Moral Enhancement as a Collective Action Problem

WALTER GLANNON

Abstract
In light of the magnitude of interpersonal harm and the risk of greater harm in the future, Ingmar Persson and Julian Savulescu have argued for pharmacological enhancement of moral behaviour. I discuss moral bioenhancement as a set of collective action problems. Psychotropic drugs or other forms of neuromodulation designed to enhance moral sensitivity would have to produce the same or similar effects in the brains of a majority of people. Also, a significant number of healthy subjects would have to participate in clinical trials testing the safety and efficacy of these drugs, which may expose them to unreasonable risk. Even if the drugs were safe and effective, a majority of people would have to co-operate in a moral enhancement programme for such a project to succeed. This goal would be thwarted if enough people opted out and decided not to enhance. To avoid this scenario, Persson and Savulescu argue that moral enhancement should be compulsory rather than voluntary. But the collective interest in harm reduction through compulsory enhancement would come at the cost of a loss of individual freedom. In general, there are many theoretical and practical reasons for scepticism about the concept and goal of moral enhancement.

1. Introduction

Neuroscientist Donald Pfaff claims that altruistic behaviour is hard-wired into our brains.[1] Neurobiological mechanisms draw us out of self-interest and into the sphere of others by blurring the lines of identity. Cognitive psychologist Steven Pinker attributes the decline of violence over the centuries to a particular conception of morality, which 'is a consequence of the interchangeability of perspectives and the opportunity the world provides for positive-sum games'.[2] The ability to consider different perspectives is a function of our capacity to reason. Yet something clearly has gone awry in our altruistic brains and rationality when considering the magnitude

---

[1]   Donald Pfaff, *The Altruistic Brain: How We Are Naturally Good* (New York: Oxford University Press, 2015).
[2]   Steven Pinker, *The Better Angels of Our Nature: Why Violence Has Declined* (New York: Penguin, 2011), 182.

doi:10.1017/S1358246118000292

of harm among humankind. Another comment from Pinker provides some insight into the apparent loss of human pro-sociality:

> The indispensability of reason does not imply that individual people are always rational or are unswayed by passion and illusion. It only means that people are *capable* of reason, and that a community of people who choose this faculty and *exercise* it openly and fairly can collectively reason their way to sound conclusions in the long run.[3]

Pinker's second comment suggests that reason itself has motivating power and that 'passion' and 'illusion' prevent people from acting on it. The tendency of certain emotions and irrational beliefs to interfere with reason may be part of an explanation for why individuals and groups harm others at local and global levels.

Interpersonal harm is not so much the result of a failure to recognise moral reasons as a failure to be motivated to act on them. Since the question at issue is how to reduce harm by improving moral behaviour, one would expect moral philosophers to offer guidance and provide the impetus for the action necessary to achieve this end. With arguably a few exceptions, however, they have not been successful in this regard.[4] Philosophical arguments are generally ineffective in moving people and governments to act morally in respecting the rights, needs, and interests of all people. Some of these arguments rely on objective moral truths that presumably exist independently of our beliefs and attitudes.[5] Many moral philosophers focus primarily on showing why one moral theory is superior to others in purportedly establishing these truths and often use implausible thought-experiments to defend their positions.[6] The overemphasis on theoretical aspects of morality leaves their arguments motivationally inert.

Educational and political institutions have also failed to instill the motivation for moral behaviour. Noting this failure, Ingmar Persson

---

[3] Pinker, *The Better Angels of Our Nature*, 183. Second emphasis added.

[4] Peter Singer, 'Famine, Affluence and Morality', *Philosophy & Public Affairs* **1**:3 (1972), 229–243, and *The Most Good You Can Do: How Effective Altruism is Changing Ideas About Living Ethically* (New Haven: Yale University Press, 2015).

[5] T. M. Scanlon, *Being Realistic About Reasons* (Oxford: Oxford University Press, 2014).

[6] Derek Parfit, *On What Matters*, Volumes I and II (Oxford: Oxford University Press, 2011).

and Julian Savulescu emphasise the need to enhance our moral sensitivity and agency through biological means:

> Our knowledge of human biology, in particular of genetics and neurobiology, is now beginning to supply us with the means of directly affecting the biological or physiological bases of human motivation [...]. We shall suggest that there are in principle no philosophical or moral objections to the use of such biomedical means of moral enhancement – moral bioenhancement, as we shall call it – and that the current predicament of humankind is so serious that it is imperative that scientific research explore every possibility of developing effective means of moral bioenhancement, as a complement to traditional means.[7]

As the last part of this passage indicates, Persson and Savulescu do not believe that moral bioenhancement (henceforth MB) alone will move us to engage in the type of moral behaviour necessary to meet the challenges of the 'predicament of humankind'. Still, they suggest that MB would be the most critical intervention in addressing and ideally resolving this predicament. While they focus mainly on the threat from weapons of mass destruction (WMDs) and the effects of climate change, the problem also includes the harm resulting from genocide, civil wars, economic inequality, and smaller-scale criminal behaviour.

The concept of MB is fraught with scientific, ethical, and political challenges. I discuss MB as a set of collective action problems. Psychoactive drugs or other forms of neuromodulation designed to enhance moral sensitivity would have to produce the same or similar effects in the brains of a majority of people. This is a questionable hypothesis, given structural and functional differences in people's brains and differences in how their neural networks mediate behaviour. A significant number of healthy subjects would have to participate in clinical trials testing the safety and efficacy of the drugs, which may expose them to unreasonable risk. Concerns about the ethical justification of the research alone may prevent such a project from getting off the ground. Even if research demonstrated that the drugs were safe and effective in improving moral motivation, a majority of the population would have to co-operate in a moral enhancement programme for such a project to succeed. This goal could be thwarted if enough people opted out and refused to enhance. It could also be thwarted if a minority who cause much of the world's harm not only refused to enhance but

---

[7]   Ingmar Persson and Julian Savulescu, *Unfit for the Future: The Need for Moral Enhancement* (Oxford: Oxford University Press, 2012), 2.

also took advantage of the co-operation of others. To avoid either of these outcomes, Persson and Savulescu argue that moral enhancement should be compulsory rather than voluntary. But the collective interest in harm reduction through compulsory enhancement would come at the cost of a loss of individual freedom.

After analysing and discussing these issues, I conclude on a sceptical note. Although there is an urgent need to promote moral behaviour and reduce harm among humans, there would be too many problems with implementing and enforcing a programme of moral enhancement on a grand scale. Traditional indirect methods of moral enhancement, such as education, parenting, and political institutions, have fallen far short of this goal and at best can only approximate it. Yet even if these methods are limited in what they can achieve, they may be more viable and defensible alternatives to voluntary or compulsory alteration of thought and behaviour by manipulating the brain through pharmacological or other means.

2. The Neurobiology of Moral Decision-Making

The goal of any programme of moral enhancement would be to provide the motivation to act and facilitate the execution of this motivation in action. Although John Martin Fischer and Mark Ravizza develop and defend their theory of reasons-responsiveness to account for moral responsibility, it can be applied to moral enhancement. Reasons-responsiveness consists in the capacity to *recognise* reasons for or against actions and the capacity to *react* to these reasons in morally appropriate behaviour.[8] Reasons-responsiveness involves not only the cognitive capacity to recognise moral reasons but also the emotional and volitional capacity to translate these reasons into right actions. These actions ideally would balance deontological considerations of treating individuals as ends in themselves and not merely as means[9] with consequentialist considerations of bringing about outcomes that reduce or prevent harm and increase human welfare.[10] Unlike the Kantian view, however, the crucial issue is

---

[8] John Martin Fischer and Mark Ravizza, *Responsibility and Control: A Theory of Moral Responsibility* (New York: Cambridge University Press, 1998), 62–91.

[9] Immanuel Kant, *Groundwork of the Metaphysics of Morals* (1785), trans. and ed. by M. Gregor (New York: Cambridge University Press, 1998).

[10] John Stuart Mill, *Utilitarianism and Other Essays* (1863), ed. by A. Ryan (London: Penguin, 1987).

not whether one acts from duty or inclination in treating others as ends in themselves, but that one treats them in this way. It is the action itself that matters. The moral worth of the action depends more on how it affects others than the mental states behind it.

There has been disagreement in the debate on moral enhancement as to whether its goal would more likely be achieved by focussing on cognitive or on emotional processing. In a seminal paper on this topic, Thomas Douglas identifies what he calls 'counter-moral emotions' as targets for neuromodulation and a more general programme of moral enhancement.[11] These emotions include 'a strong aversion to certain racial groups' and 'the impulse towards violent aggression'.[12] Douglas argues that the most promising way to correct these tendencies would be 'an enhancement that will expectably leave the enhanced person with morally better motives than she had previously'.[13] Emphasising the emotional aspect of behaviour, Douglas says that 'the distinctive feature of emotional moral enhancement is that, once the enhancement has been initiated, there is no further need for cognition: emotions are modified directly'.[14] In contrast, John Harris argues that moral enhancement is an extension of cognitive enhancement and that 'emotional moral enhancement is simply ethically otiose'.[15] Harris claims that 'it is to rationality and its evolutionary origins, rather than to the emotions that we should look'.[16] He further claims that 'it is human imagination that is one of the most potent of cognitive faculties that enables us to put ourselves into, if not the shoes of relevant others, at least into an understanding of the nature and consequences of our acts and decisions, and of the effects of those decisions on others and the world'.[17]

Douglas' and Harris' analyses of moral behaviour in terms of separate cognitive and emotional faculties are symptomatic of a discredited dualistic model of explaining this behaviour. This model offers at best an incomplete explanation of moral reasoning and action and thus fails to include all the capacities that need to be targeted for moral enhancement. Increased imagination and decreased

[11] Thomas Douglas, 'Moral Enhancement', *Journal of Applied Philosophy* **25**:3 (2008), 228–245.

[12] Douglas, 'Moral Enhancement', 231.

[13] Douglas, 'Moral Enhancement', 231.

[14] Thomas Douglas, 'Moral Enhancement via Direct Emotion Modulation: A Reply to Harris', *Bioethics* **27**:3 (2013), 160–168, at 162–163.

[15] John Harris, *How to Be Good: The Possibility of Moral Enhancement* (Oxford: Oxford University Press, 2016), 115.

[16] Harris, *How to Be Good*, 125.

[17] Harris, *How to Be Good*, 131.

counter-moral emotions would strengthen the recognitional component of reasons-responsiveness. But they would not automatically strengthen the reactive component of responsiveness and move one to perform the right actions in different circumstances.

Cognition and emotion are not segregated but integrated processes whose interaction enables moral sensitivity and rational and moral decision-making.[18] These normative capacities are mediated by a distributed network of neural circuits. The prefrontal cortex (PFC) is particularly important in regulating the capacity to reason. It also has a critical role in emotion regulation. This is not only because of its projections to and connectivity with the amygdala and other limbic structures such as the cingulate cortex, but also because reason and emotion are both partly processed within the PFC itself. The complex function of the PFC shows that it is oversimplified and inaccurate to divide the brain into distinct regions mediating separate cognitive and emotional processing at the mental level.

Psychopathy is instructive in this regard. This is a behavioural disorder characterised by impaired capacity for empathy, impaired responsiveness to fear-inducing stimuli, and failure to conform to social norms. Because of these impairments, many psychopaths cause a substantial amount of harm to others. They have difficulty representing outcomes of actions. This can preclude or weaken their moral judgement by precluding or weakening their ability to foresee how their actions can adversely affect others.[19] Functional imaging studies of psychopaths' brains have shown dysregulation in PFC-amygdala pathways, and this finding is part of an explanation of their behaviour. It is the result of dysfunction of not only cognitive or emotional processes but of dysfunctional interaction between

---

[18] Antoine Bechara, Hanna Damasio, and Antonio Damasio, 'Emotion, Decision-Making and the Orbitofrontal Cortex', *Cerebral Cortex* **10**:3 (2000), 295–307. See also Antonio Damasio, *Descartes' Error: Emotion, Reason and the Human Brain* (New York: Grosset/Putnam, 1994), Jean Decety, Kalina Michalska, and Katherine Kinzler, 'The Contribution of Emotion and Cognition to Moral Sensitivity: A Neurodevelopmental Study', *Cerebral Cortex* **22**:1 (2012), 209–220, and Luiz Pessoa, *The Cognitive-Emotional Brain: From Interactions to Integration* (Cambridge, MA: MIT Press, 2013), 107–134.

[19] R. J. R. Blair, 'Neurobiological Basis of Psychopathy', *British Journal of Psychiatry* **182**:5–7 (2003), 5–7, and R. J. R. Blair, 'Psychopathy: Cognitive and Neural Dysfunction', *Dialogues in Clinical Neuroscience* **15**:2 (2013), 181–190. See also Andre Glenn and Adrian Raine, *Psychopathy: An Introduction to Biological Findings and Their Implications* (New York: New York University Press, 2014).

them. Any improvement in a psychopath's behaviour would require enhancing his cognitive-emotional processing by enhancing how his neural circuits generate and sustain this processing. Still, it is not clear to what extent psychopaths' brain abnormalities influence their wrongful and harmful behaviour. One must be cautious in drawing inferences from their brain abnormalities to their impaired moral reasoning and immoral behaviour because the first is not necessarily the cause of the second. Claims about the power of structural MRI and functional PET and fMRI scans to validate these inferences warrant caution as well. Scans of people's brains are only indirect measures of brain activity. They are visualisations of statistical analyses based on averaging large numbers of images. Brain scans are more appropriately described as scientific constructs than direct "real-time" pictures of the brain.

Empathy is a critical component of moral sensitivity. Harris' comment about moral enhancement depending on the cognitive capacity for imagination in 'putting ourselves into the shoes of relevant others' reflects a narrow conception of empathy. While imagination may promote concern for others that extends spatially and temporally beyond local interpersonal bonds held together by emotion, empathy is not a purely cognitive disposition. Nor is empathy separable from reason but can influence it in guiding action. Jean Decety and Jason Cowell explain:

> Empathy [...] is not always a direct avenue to moral behavior. Indeed, at times it can interfere with morality by introducing partiality, for instance by favoring in-group members. But empathy can provide the motivational fire and push toward seeing a victim's suffering end, irrespective of group membership and culturally determined dominance hierarchies, preventing rationalization of injustice and derogation.[20]

Decety and Cowell further state that empathy consists of cognitive, affective, and motivational components. The cognitive component enables one 'to consciously put oneself into the mind of another and imagine what that person is thinking or feeling'.[21] The affective component enables one to become emotionally aroused by others'

---

[20]   Jean Decety and Jason Cowell, 'The Equivocal Relationship Between Morality and Empathy', in Jean Decety and Thalia Wheatley (eds), *The Moral Brain: A Multidisciplinary Perspective* (Cambridge, MA: MIT Press, 2015), 297–302, at 279.
[21]   Decety and Cowell, 'The Equivocal Relationship Between Morality and Empathy', 284–285.

condition. The motivational component involves the urge to care for another's welfare. These mental capacities and their neural underpinning are not domain-specific but domain-general and involve an interconnected network of circuits distributed throughout cortical and limbic brain regions. This network comprises the 'moral brain'.[22] It is similar to what Andrea Glenn, Adrian Raine, and Robert Schug describe as the 'moral neural circuit', which they point out is dysfunctional in psychopaths and may at least partly explain the failure to align their behaviour with moral and legal norms.[23] This circuit would have to be modulated in order to generate or improve moral sensitivity in the psychopath or others who lack this disposition. MB involving neuromodulation would have to influence not just one but all or most of the components in the moral neural circuit and how they interact with each other in regulating behaviour. Still, what Decety and Cowell describe as the 'urge' to care for another's welfare by itself is not sufficient to act in a way that exemplifies this care. One must translate this urge into morally appropriate behaviour. Any form of moral bioenhancement would have to facilitate the exercise of this motivational capacity in action.

Three hypothetical drug interventions have been proposed as possible ways of modulating neural networks associated with moral reasoning. Theoretically, they would enhance the capacity to translate the urge to care for others into action and thereby enhance moral behaviour. But there are neurobiological, psychological, and social reasons to be sceptical of the idea that taking a psychotropic drug targeting these networks would have this effect.

One study conducted by Molly Crockett and co-investigators showed that the selective serotonin reuptake inhibitor (SSRI) citalopram increased harm aversion in healthy subjects.[24] They claimed that 'these findings have implications for the use of serotonergic agents in the treatment of antisocial and aggressive behaviour' in promoting pro-social behaviour.[25] Crockett is more circumspect about

[22]   Decety and Cowell, 'The Equivocal Relationship Between Morality and Empathy', 283.

[23]   Andrea Glenn, Adrian Raine, and Robert Schug, 'The Neural Correlates of Moral Decision-Making in Psychopathy', *Molecular Psychiatry* **14** (2009), 5–6.

[24]   Molly Crockett, Luke Clark, Marc Hauser, and Trevor Robbins, 'Serotonin Selectively Influences Moral Judgment and Behavior Through Effects on Harm Aversion', *Proceedings of the National Academy of Sciences* **107**:40 (2010), 17433–17438.

[25]   Crockett, Clark, Hauser, and Robbins, 'Serotonin Selectively Influences Moral Judgment', 17437.

the behaviour-modifying potential of these drugs in a more recent contribution to a symposium on moral enhancement:

> Most neurotransmitters serve multiple functions and are found in many different brain regions [...] serotonin plays a role in a variety of other processes [than harm aversion] including (but not limited to) learning, emotion, vision, sexual behavior, sleep, pain and memory, and there are at least 17 different types of serotonin receptors that produce distinct effects on neurotransmission. Thus, interventions [...] may have undesirable side effects, and these should be considered when weighing the costs and benefits of the intervention.[26]

Differences in how neurotransmitters influence the activity of neural circuits, and how increasing levels of neurotransmitters might also influence this activity, suggest that there would be different effects on the behaviour of healthy people taking SSRIs, including no effects at all. It is unclear whether or how these drugs would influence cognitive-emotional processing. Variable responses to psychotropic drugs could mean that there would not be the uniformity of effects on neural circuitry necessary to reach a threshold of enhanced moral behaviour among a majority of the population. Also, while neurotransmitters have a critical role in regulating the activity of these circuits and the mental processes they sustain, these are not a function of these substances alone but of the influence of genetic, endocrine, immune, and environmental factors on neural circuitry as well. The capacity for moral sensitivity and moral reasoning, and impairments in these capacities, depend on more than the function or dysfunction of a particular neurotransmitter. It is not known how increasing levels of serotonin would affect all of the serotonergic receptors in all of the circuitry of the distributed neural network that partly regulates moral reasoning. So it is unclear whether or to what extent increasing levels of serotonin would make one more responsive to moral reasons when acting. Increasing harm aversion would not imply a corresponding increase in moral sensitivity and make one

---

[26] Molly Crockett, 'Moral Bioenhancement: A Neuroscientific Perspective', *Journal of Medical Ethics* **40**:6 (2014), 370–371, at 370. See also Molly Crockett, 'Morphing Morals: Neurochemical Modulations of Moral Judgment and Behavior', and Ricardo de Oliveira-Souza, Roland Zahn, and Jorge Moll, 'The Neuropsychiatry of Moral Cognition and Social Conduct', both in S. Matthew Liao (ed.), *Moral Brains: The Neuroscience of Morality* (Oxford: Oxford University Press, 2016), 237–245, 203–236.

more attentive to the needs of others. It would not necessarily enhance the motivation to act in response to these needs. A small number of people with enhanced moral behaviour could have some positive effects on interpersonal relations. But unless a majority did this, the effects on reducing collective harm and increasing collective welfare would likely be negligible. Regarding the neurobiological basis of moral behaviour, because no two people's brains are alike and probably would not respond to the drugs in the same way, it is unlikely that broad use of an SSRI such as citalopram would move people to act morally and reduce harm.

The beta-adrenergic receptor antagonist propranolol has been used as an indirect means of cognitive enhancement. The drug inhibits the release of the stress hormones adrenaline and noradrenaline in response to perceived threatening stimuli. This in turn dampens the autonomic response to stress in the form of increased heart rate, palpitations, sweating and other symptoms. By dampening this response, the drug may enable one to avoid being distracted by these symptoms and remain focussed on a demanding cognitive task such as surgery, musical performance, or public speaking. The drug could also be used as one component of moral bioenhancement. One study has shown that propranolol can reduce implicit negative racial bias.[27] As with drugs used to raise levels of serotonin, however, one cannot infer that a reduction in a fearful or negative perception of groups and harm aversion will result in an increase in morally justifiable actions. Reducing bias would not necessarily translate into pro-social behaviour. The cognitive and affective capacities necessary for co-operation require much more than harm aversion or an absence of bias. Racial bias detected in lab experiments is not predictive of immoral behaviour in real life. In addition, like other pharmacological agents used for moral enhancement, trade-offs between positive and negative effects of propranolol in the body and brain would have to be considered.

Some neuroscientists have claimed that the neuromodulating effects of the neuropeptide oxytocin may have the greatest potential as a morality-enhancing agent. Oxytocin plays a critical role in social cognition.[28] Its highest levels are found in the hypothalamus,

[27] Sylvia Terbeck, Guy Kahane, and Sarah McTavish, 'Propranolol Reduces Implicit Negative Racial Bias', *Psychopharmacology* **222**:3 (2012), 419–424.

[28] Heather Ross and Larry Young, 'Oxytocin and the Neural Mechanisms Regulating Social Cognition and Affiliative Behavior', *Frontiers in Neuroendocrinology* **30**:4 (2009), 534–547. See also, Jennifer

and it influences activity in the hypothalamic-pituitary-adrenal (HPA) axis by inhibiting the fear response to social stimuli in the amygdala. Increasing levels of oxytocin in the brain through intra-nasal administration could reduce fear and increase trust and social co-operation. Yet any positive social effects of oxytocin may be more local than global and limited to particular groups, with negative effects more likely to occur outside the compass of these groups. Studies show that this neuropeptide facilitates social bonding but also produces non-prosocial effects that may have evolved to promote off-spring survival.[29] Oxytocin may promote antisocial rather than pro-social behaviour on a broad scale by strengthening a person's bonding and identification with an in-group and the perception of those in out-groups as competitors or threats. It could promote rather than prevent or reduce aggression between groups and individuals.[30]

It would be an oversimplification to claim that increasing the level of a psychoactive substance would make one less self-regarding and more other-regarding. Moral behaviour is a function of multiple biological, psychological, and environment factors, not just neural chemicals and circuits. It is a disposition that depends on factors both inside and outside of the brain. The idea that pharmacological neuromodulation alone could enhance moral behaviour fails to appreciate the complexity of human moral psychology.[31]

Research in the form of randomised placebo-controlled clinical trials would be the only empirically verifiable way to determine the effects of psychotropic drugs or other brain- and mind-altering inter-ventions on the neural networks mediating moral reasoning. These trials would be necessary to determine whether or to what extent the drugs could enhance moral behaviour. The trials would be

---

Bartz, Jamil Zaki, Niall Bolger, and Kevin Ochsner, 'Social Effects of Oxytocin in Humans: Context and Person Matter', *Trends in Cognitive Sciences* **15**:7 (2011), 301–309, and Patricia Churchland, *Braintrust: What Neuroscience Tells us About Morality* (Princeton: Princeton University Press, 2011), 63–94.

[29] Rene Hurlemann and Dirk Scheele, 'Dissecting the Role of Oxytocin in the Formation and Loss of Social Relationships', *Biological Psychiatry* **79**:3 (2016), 185–193.

[30] Andreas Bartels, 'Oxytocin and the Social Brain: Beware the Complexity', *Neuropsychopharmacology* **37**:8 (2012), 1795–1796.

[31] Among those who make this point are Nicholas Agar, 'A Question about Defining Moral Bioenhancement', *Journal of Medical Ethics* **40**:6 (2014), 369–370, and Harris Wiseman, *The Myth of the Moral Brain: The Limits of Moral Enhancement* (Cambridge, MA: MIT Press, 2016).

necessary to establish a ratio of potential benefits to risks for research subjects taking these drugs. But there would be methodological and ethical problems with conducting this research.

3. Research Challenges

There are two questions about research into MB that are especially ethically fraught. The first question is whether any risk to which human subjects participating in clinical trials testing the drugs would be exposed could be ethically acceptable. Would the potential of the drugs to produce toxic levels of the relevant neurotransmitters or cause other adverse effects influence the permissibility of conducting these trials? The second question is how the outcome would be assessed with regard to the research question driving the trial. How would we know whether a drug actually enhanced moral behaviour?

In medical research, clinical trials are necessary to determine the safety and efficacy of any potential drug therapy. The aim of a Phase I trial for a drug is to determine its safety by determining its toxicity in human subjects following tests in animal models. Toxicity is measured in terms of the highest dose a human can tolerate without serious side effects. This is necessary in order to move to Phase II and III trials testing the efficacy of a drug or procedure in treating a disease or condition. In an MB trial, the main concern about safety would arise when researchers increased normal levels of a neurotransmitter with a drug to determine whether this could increase moral sensitivity. What the research would have to determine is how much of an increase in the relevant neurotransmitter would be optimal for achieving this effect. Again, though, not all people's brains are alike. Different people have different optimal levels of serotonin and other substances in their brains regulating mood, motivation, and behaviour. When researchers tried to determine the dose of a drug necessary to increase harm aversion, some subjects could be harmed by an excess of the neurotransmitter in their brains, which could rise to a toxic level. For example, increasing normal levels of serotonin in the brain has resulted in the serotonin syndrome, which can be caused by the adverse interaction of two or more drugs, one of which is an SSRI. This syndrome occurs in approximately 14–16% of persons who overdose on a drug in this class.[32] Its symptoms may include euphoria, rapid muscle

---

[32] Edward Boyer and Michael Shannon, 'The Serotonin Syndrome', *New England Journal of Medicine* **352**:11 (2005), 1112–1120.

contractions, hyperthermia, and in severe cases coma and death. Similarly, in an attempt to determine the optimal level of oxytocin to promote trust and pro-social behaviour, it is possible that some researchers would unwittingly administer a dose of this neuropeptide that would raise its level above what the brain could tolerate. Like the serotonin syndrome, this could result in deleterious effects in the brain.

In response to the concern about risk of drug toxicity in an MB trial, some might point out that healthy subjects participating in drug trials for medical treatments are also exposed to risk. But the second type of trial is necessary to test drugs for treating disease. Healthy subjects in an MB trial would be exposed to risk in testing a drug for a condition that is not a disease in the generic medical sense of mental or physical dysfunction. The medical or non-medical purpose of the trial could influence the acceptability of risk. There would be no grounds for medicalising immoral or amoral behaviour because such behaviour is not simply a manifestation of dysfunction in the brain, mind, or body. Immorality is not a disease in the medical sense relevant to the ethical criteria necessary to conduct clinical trials. More precisely, while some types of neurophysiological dysfunction may correlate with some types of immoral behaviour, many factors in addition to processes in the body and brain are needed to explain this behaviour. Others might object that it would be paternalistic to deny healthy subjects the opportunity to participate in an experiment testing the effects of drugs intended to improve behaviour. But investigators conducting the trial would have a duty of nonmaleficence not to expose healthy subjects to unreasonable risk. The potential for positive behaviour modification would probably not be enough to justify exposing these subjects to any risk of neurobiological sequelae. These considerations of risk underscore the difficulty investigators would have in obtaining ethics approval from the appropriate regulatory body to conduct the trials.[33] The categorical difference between the physiological risk and potential behavioural benefit would make it difficult to calculate a risk-benefit ratio and judge that the risk was justifiable. Assuming that the risk of adverse neuropsychiatric outcomes from drugs increasing neurotransmitter levels was low, it would still be difficult to justify exposing subjects to *any* risk in testing the effects of a drug used for a condition that was not a disease.

[33] Ezekiel Emanuel, Christine Grady, Robert Crouch, Reidar Lie, Franklin Miller, and David Wendler, *The Oxford Textbook of Clinical Research Ethics* (New York: Oxford University Press, 2008).

Walter Glannon

Many people would argue that any improvement in moral behaviour would not offset the risk of neuropsychiatric sequelae from psychoactive drugs used in an MB trial. This would limit voluntary enrolment. Altruistic individuals might agree to be included in the earliest phase of the trial testing drug safety. They would already have a high level of moral sensitivity and would not need moral enhancement. In these respects, they would be exposing themselves to some risk of harm without any compensatory benefit. Self-interested individuals with less moral sensitivity might agree to be included in a later phase of a trial testing drug efficacy. They might benefit from an increase in their moral disposition if the drugs were deemed effective. This could generate unfair inequality between altruistic and self-interested subjects in the distribution of risks to benefits. Such an unequal distribution of potential negative and positive effects from the drugs is an additional reason why research necessary to make MB available to all would have difficulty meeting ethics standards.

Pharmaceutical companies have decreased development of new antidepressant and antipsychotic drugs and funding the research necessary to market them.[34] The estimated profit from developing and testing these drugs may not be enough of a return on their investment to fund the studies. This may limit the development of new therapies that could treat psychiatric diseases more effectively. These companies would be even more reluctant to underwrite drug trials for moral enhancement because the outcomes of the trials could not be measured by the standard quantitative and qualitative methods used in research designed to control or prevent diseases. Lack of funding from pharmaceutical companies or other private sources would mean that much if not all of the funding for MB research would have to come from publicly funded health care institutions such as the US National Institute of Mental Health (NIMH). In addition to the challenge of recruiting enough subjects for enough trials to determine the drugs' safety and efficacy, the research would be costly. With limited public resources to conduct research, this would raise the question of whether research into drugs that could enhance moral behaviour should be treated on a par with research aimed at developing safer and more effective treatments for and prevention of neuropsychiatric and other disorders. Some might argue that the harm resulting from behaviour symptomatic of our limited moral

---

[34]   Steven Hyman, 'Psychiatric Drug Development: Diagnosing a Crisis,' *Cerebrum*, April 2013: http://www.dana.org/Cerebrum/2-13/Psychiatric_Drug_Development_Diagnosing a Crisis/.

outlook is as significant as the harm resulting from disease. But the salience and global burden of neurological, psychiatric, and other diseases, as documented by empirical data, give priority to treating or preventing these diseases over trying to improve moral behaviour.

In her discussion of the 'urgency of moral enhancement', Elizabeth Fenton points out that 'if we do not continue scientific research into enhancement, if we halt it out of concern for the consequences, then we have no hope of achieving the great moral progress that will ensure the survival of our species'.[35] This comment raises three issues. First, it is questionable whether scientifically sound clinical trials testing drugs for moral bioenhancement have begun or could begin, much less whether they should continue. These trials would be fundamentally different from studies of harm aversion and racial bias because the research question driving them would be different. Second, if the consequences of the research included significant neurological and psychiatric risks, then these risks could make the research ethically unacceptable. Third, we cannot assume that any evidence of the drugs enhancing moral behaviour would be evidence of moral progress.

Among the problems in trying to compare research into treating disease with research into moral enhancement is that the outcomes in the first type are measured *empirically* while outcomes in the second type would be measured *normatively*. The outcome of an MB study would be assessed in terms of social expectations and whether people's actions met these expectations and displayed respect for others. This is part of a broader problem of defining what constitutes moral and immoral behaviour and how public consensus on a definition of "moral behaviour" could be reached. Research into MB would involve very crude measures that may not tell us much or anything about whether it actually increased or improved people's moral sensitivity. Most medical research relies on quantitative measures of outcomes, such as the five-year survival rate of subjects receiving a new oncology drug for cancer. Some of the research relies on qualitative measures, such as reports from subjects about symptom relief in a psychiatric disorder or chronic pain. Whether a drug improves people's moral behaviour cannot be measured by these models. The lack of empirical measures of outcomes of a prospective MB study would leave uncertainty about how to assess the efficacy of the intervention. It is not clear how we could judge the success or

---

[35]   Elizabeth Fenton, 'The Perils of Failing to Enhance: A Response to Persson and Savulescu', *Journal of Medical Ethics* **36**:3 (2010), 148–151, at 148.

failure of research other than observing people's behaviour after they had taken a drug for moral enhancement. But which criteria would we use to judge what we observe and whether the behaviour displayed greater moral sensitivity than before and led to a reduction in harm?

One proposed way of confirming whether the drugs enhanced moral behaviour would be to present hypothetical cases or thought experiments of moral conflict to subjects and assess their responses to them. The Trolley Problem is the most well-known of these methods. Philosopher Philippa Foot introduced this problem as a way of distinguishing what we owe to people in the form of aid from what we owe to them in the form of non-interference.[36] Psychologists and cognitive neuroscientists have adopted this problem in attempting to gain a better understanding of the neuro-biological basis of moral judgement.[37] In a number of studies, subjects have been presented with two scenarios. In the first scenario, an out-of-control trolley is headed toward five workers on a track. The driver could turn the trolley onto another track on which there is one worker. Turning the trolley would save the five on the first track but would kill the one on the second. Subjects are asked whether it would be permissible to turn the trolley and kill the one worker rather than the five. In a variant of this case, subjects are asked if it would be permissible to push a fat man off a bridge and onto the track to stop the trolley. This action would stop the trolley

[36] Philippa Foot, 'The Problem of Abortion and the Doctrine of the Double Effect', in Foot, *Virtues and Vices* (Oxford: Oxford University Press, 2002), 19–32. This problem has been discussed by many other philosophers, most notably Judith Jarvis Thomson, 'Killing, Letting Die and the Trolley Problem', *The Monist* **59**:2 (1976), 204–217, and F. M. Kamm, Judith Jarvis Thomson, Thomas Hurka, and Shelly Kagan, *The Trolley Problem Mysteries* (New York: Oxford University Press, 2016).

[37] Joshua Greene, Leigh Nystrom, Andrew Engell, John Darley, and Jonathan Cohen, 'The Neural Bases of Cognitive Conflict and Control in Moral Judgment', *Neuron* **44**:2 (2004), 389–400; Joshua Greene, 'Why Are VMPFC Patients More Utilitarian? A Dual-Process Theory of Moral Judgment Explains', *Trends in Cognitive Sciences* **11**:8 (2007), 322–333; Michael Koenigs, Liane Young, Ralph Adolphs, Daniel Tranel, Fiery Cushman, Marc Hauser, and Antonio Damasio, 'Damage to the Prefrontal Cortex Increases Utilitarian Moral Judgments', *Nature* **446**:7138 (2007), 908–911; and Carla Harenski, Olga Antonenko, Matthew Shane and Kent Kiehl, 'A Functional Imaging Investigation of Moral Deliberation and Moral Intuition', *NeuroImage* **49**:3 (2009), 2707–2716.

from killing the five workers but would kill the fat man. Whereas most subjects responded that it would be permissible to turn the trolley in the first case, there was disagreement about whether it would be permissible to push the fat man off the bridge to stop the trolley in the second case. Some investigators have claimed that the impermissibility of pushing the man reflects a deontological judgement, while the permissibility of pushing him reflects a consequentialist judgement.[38] Some of these subjects have been put through fMRI scanners when presented with the question about what to do with the trolley or fat man. Recorded differences in neural activity in different brain regions during their responses presumably correspond to deontological or consequentialist judgements about the right action in these hypothetical cases.

These judgements are not accurate reflections of moral reasoning because they involve only quick intuitive responses that fall short of the consideration and argumentation necessary to justify an action or policy.[39] This, combined with the fact that fMRI images are scientific constructs rather than actual pictures of brain activity, provides a good reason to be sceptical of combining brain imaging and thought-experiments to assess moral reasoning and moral judgement after taking a psychotropic drug. "Trolley cases" involve unavoidable harm and the question of whether it is permissible to cause a lesser harm to prevent a greater harm. Most of the harm committed by humans is not the result of actions they perform or fail to perform in times of moral conflict but from the more general failure to recognise and react to reasons for performing certain actions. Thought-experiments like trolley cases are generated in artificial settings and tell us nothing about how people act in the real world. There is often a gap between moral judgement and action. One may judge that A is the right thing to do in a situation but choose B when they are actually in that situation. Whether a drug effectively enhanced moral behaviour could not be determined by

---

[38]   Greene, 'Why are VMPFC Patients More Utilitarian?', and Koenigs, Young, Adolphs, Tranel, Cushman, Hauser, and Damasio, 'Damage to the Prefrontal Cortex Increases Utilitarian Moral Judgments'.

[39]   For criticism of these experiments and what they presumably tell us about moral judgement, see Kwame Anthony Appiah, *Experiments in Ethics* (Cambridge, MA: Harvard University Press, 2008), Selim Berker, 'The Normative Insignificance of Neuroscience', *Philosophy & Public Affairs* **37**:4 (2009), 293–325, and F. M. Kamm, 'Neuroscience and Moral Reasoning: A Note on Recent Research', *Philosophy & Public Affairs* **37**:4 (2009), 330–345.

asking questions about what one would do in hypothetical cases but by observing people's actual behaviour.

Unlike the outcome of a clinical trial in medical research, whether a psychotropic drug enhanced moral sensitivity would not be amenable to assessment by quantitative or qualitative methods. The end-point of an MB trial would be open to varying interpretations of whether people displayed greater attention to and respect for others after taking a drug. There would be considerable variability in the behaviour of subjects after taking a brain-altering substance because of the complex interaction between and among biological, psychological, and environmental factors and the unique effects these factors have in each person's brain. It is thus unlikely that there could be a definitive answer to the research question of whether a psychopharmacological intervention enhanced moral behaviour. The outcome would likely be too crude to measure by any scientific model of research.

4. Co-operate or Defect?

Although particular philosophical arguments fail to provide the motivation to act morally, we need a general moral theory to serve as a framework in which to spell out the goal of moral enhancement and the process by which it might be achieved. This would require public consensus on which theory to adopt, a theory that ideally would accurately reflect human moral psychology. It would be overly simplistic to expect one theory to be sufficient for this purpose. Insofar as the goal of moral enhancement is to reduce harm, some form of consequentialism would be needed. Some form of deontology would also be necessary to recognise people's rights, especially the negative right to non-interference. Still, given that most people are mainly self-interested, something more than recognition of others' rights and the value of preventing or reducing harmful outcomes of actions or omissions would be needed to move people to act appropriately. An additional theory would have to complement consequentialism and deontology to ground the requisite motivational force. Most people are not naturally altruistic and do not typically act from other-regarding reasons. Some of us act altruistically at times, but not often enough and not to the extent necessary to have sustained beneficial effects on other people and their lives. The most realistic theory would be one consistent with a lower common behavioural denominator – rational self-interest. Accordingly, some version of social contract theory would be the most plausible moral complement to consequentialism and

Moral Enhancement as a Collective Action Problem

deontology as a theoretical basis for a moral enhancement programme.[40] It would be based on rational choice and promote social co-operation for mutual benefit. Each person would give up some of her self-interest by co-operating; but all would be better off by doing this. Such a model would be imperfect. In particular, future people who would be more adversely affected by the consequences of our present policies and actions or omissions could not participate in such a contract. A more demanding moral theory would be necessary to respect their claims. Given our limited moral compass and tendency to discount the future, though, a social contract model of moral enhancement, agreed upon by the present generation, would probably have the best chance of achieving a reasonably modest goal.

A social contract model of moral bioenhancement to promote co-operation would involve another collective action problem. A critical number of people would have to agree to take psychotropic drugs enhancing their moral disposition to produce the collective effect of reducing harm and promoting general welfare. Many would rely on this reasoning and assume that others would reason in the same way in deciding to enhance. They would calculate that the threshold effect of a large number of individuals co-operating in an enhancement programme would make co-operating and sacrificing some self-interest mutually beneficial and better for them than if they chose not to enhance. The psychology of this reasoning is similar in some respects to what is involved in the classic prisoner's dilemma. Each of two prisoners accused of a crime must decide whether they will co-operate by confessing or defect by remaining silent or testifying against the other. Defecting would be the most rational decision for each independently of how the other reasons and decides what to do. But each knows that the outcome is a function of what both decide, and that they would have a worse outcome if both defected. Each chooses the second best but all-things-considered most rational option of co-operating.[41]

This game-theoretic strategy would be of limited value in a programme of moral enhancement, however. The number of players is too large to be accommodated by these strategies, which involve

[40] Thomas Hobbes, *Leviathan*, ed. by M. Oakeshott (Oxford: Blackwell, 1987/1651); David Gauthier, *Morals by Agreement* (New York: Oxford University Press, 1986); T. M. Scanlon, *What We Owe to Each Other* (Cambridge, MA: Harvard University Press, 1998); and Harris, *How to Be Good*, 156–171.
[41] Richard Dawkins, *The Selfish Gene*, 30th Anniversary Edition (Oxford: Oxford University Press, 2006), 202–233.

cooperation 'in cozy little local enclaves'.[42] While these enclaves may evolve into larger entities, they would still be local or relatively small in scale. The collective action problem of MB would be more difficult to resolve because it would be global and involve a very large number of people. The main problems in these scenarios would be having enough people enhancing to produce a positive collective effect and preventing some from free riding on the co-operation of others.[43] If less than a critical mass of people decided to cooperate, then the goal of reducing harm would not be achieved. Even if a drug could safely and effectively enhance moral behaviour, some would refuse to enhance. They might not trust others to voluntarily enhance and might not want to sacrifice any self-interest for fear of becoming worse off than they would be if they pursued self-interest in an unconstrained way. In a scenario where many people enhanced and a threshold of co-operation had been reached, some would calculate that they could refuse to enhance and benefit from the cooperation of others without sacrificing any self-interest. A few of these who engaged in the most harmful behaviour and needed MB the most would not only refuse to co-operate but would also take advantage of the co-operation of others for their own malevolent ends. In these scenarios, defectors would be making a rational choice. Given the sheer number of people involved, it would be difficult to prevent free riding or manipulation and implement and enforce measures that would punish people who did this.

The number of people and the behaviour that would thwart the realisation of the goals of MB may depend on which moral problem one focussed. Climate change would involve the largest number of players, and the harmful outcome would result from many individual omissions as much as from many individual actions. Civil wars and ethnic conflicts typically involve a smaller number of decision-makers and their more numerous followers adversely impacting the lives of others. The threat of WMDs lies primarily with a few agents or even one individual. An irrational decision by what Martin Rees calls one 'village idiot' controlling these weapons could have catastrophic consequences.[44] In the second and third scenarios, even if a majority of people chose MB, a small number or even one person who refused to co-operate in a project to prevent or reduce the threat of harm could be enough to doom it.

---

[42]   Dawkins, *The Selfish Gene*, 219.

[43]   Mancur Olson, *The Logic of Collective Action: Public Goods and the Theory of Groups* (Cambridge, MA: Harvard University Press, 1965).

[44]   Martin Rees, *Our Final Century* (London: Arrow Books, 2004), 61.

To prevent the idiot's irrational decision and its consequences in Rees' hypothetical scenario, Harris would argue that what we need is not moral but cognitive enhancement aimed at improving rationality. Yet because reasons to prevent outcomes adversely affecting other people are moral reasons, and because moral reasoning involves cognitive and emotional processing, preventing catastrophic outcomes would depend not only on enhanced cognition but also on enhanced cognitive and emotional capacities.

Harris says that '[e]thics is for bad guys! The good don't need ethics'.[45] Further, he claims that 'ethics is for those occasions in which compassion, altruism, and basic decency fail'.[46] MB is Persson and Savulescu's way of providing the ethics we need. But too many of the bad guys among us would choose not to enhance. In light of this and the likely general failure of voluntary MB to achieve its normative goal, Persson and Savulescu state: '[i]f safe moral enhancements are ever developed, there are strong reasons to believe that their use should be obligatory [...]. That is, safe, effective moral enhancement would be compulsory'.[47] The argument for compulsory MB should not just be to get the bad guys on Harris' interpretation to improve their behaviour. It should be aimed not only at those whose actions and omissions incrementally contribute to climate change, for example, but also and indeed more so at the "worst guys", those whose actions directly cause substantial harm to others. On an ideal reading of the prisoner's dilemma and the standard collective action problem, "nice guys finish first" if they reason that co-operating is in their all-things-considered best interests and do in fact co-operate.[48] Yet the likely scenario of morally deficient persons taking advantage of those who voluntarily enhanced their moral sensitivity would mean that the worst guys who produced most of the world's harm would "finish first" in achieving their own self-serving ends. Incentives to nudge those with the greatest need of moral enhancement would do little to motivate them to act in accord with

---

[45]   Harris, *How to Be Good*, 112.

[46]   Harris, *How to Be Good*, 112.

[47]   Persson and Savulescu, 'The Perils of Cognitive Enhancement and the Urgent Imperative to Enhance the Moral Character of Humanity', *Journal of Applied Philosophy* **25**:3 (2008), 162–177, at 173. Also, Persson and Savulescu, 'Moral Enhancement, Freedom and the God Machine', *The Monist* **95**:3 (2012), 399–421, *Unfit for the Future*, and 'Getting Moral Enhancement Right: The Desirability of Moral Bioenhancement', *Bioethics* **27**:3 (2013), 124–131.

[48]   Dawkins, *The Selfish Gene*, 219, and Olson, *The Logic of Collective Action*.

moral norms.[49] Because of the extent of their moral deficiency, changing their behaviour would take much more than incentives or nudges. The refusal of the worst perpetrators of wrongdoing to do this voluntarily could make state-sponsored compulsory enhancement necessary to reduce interpersonal harm. Could this be justified?

5. Compulsory Moral Enhancement: The Cost to Freedom

Compulsory MB would depend on research demonstrating the safety and efficacy of the drugs used to enhance. If MB were compulsory, then would participation in this research also be compulsory? Any action regarding MB could in principle be obligatory only if it was proven safe and effective, which the research itself is designed to determine. Since the research would be necessary to determine the safety and efficacy of the drug for public administration and consumption, compulsory participation in the research itself would be unjustifiable. This would be significantly different from military conscription or jury duty, which are compulsory but based on established social and legal institutions that protect people's rights and liberties. It would also be different from requiring young adults to purchase health insurance to ensure a fair distribution of risk across populations.

Harris has argued elsewhere that we have a moral duty to participate in medical research.[50] This obligation is generated by the fact that people in the present generation have benefited from medical treatments resulting from the sacrifices of people in the past who participated in medical research. These subjects exposed themselves to some risk without any direct therapeutic benefit. We in the present generation have benefited from the actions of those in the past in the form of better treatment and prevention of many diseases. Because of this, we have an obligation to participate in medical research that could benefit future people. This argument about a fair intergenerational distribution of burdens and benefits does not apply to MB, for three reasons. First, morally deficient behaviour is not a disease in the sense of physical or mental dysfunction and thus involves a different assessment of risk of psychotropic drugs intended to improve it. Second, none of us in the present generation has benefited from the results of previous research into MB, since there was no such research. Third, having a duty to participate in research

[49] Cf. Wiseman, *The Myth of the Moral Brain*, 8–9, 253ff.
[50] John Harris, 'Scientific Research is a Moral Duty', *Journal of Medical Ethics* **31**:4 (2005), 242–248.

is different from being compelled to participate in it. One can voluntarily fail to discharge a duty, which is not an option in compulsory action. The potential harm from being exposed to any risk of tinkering with neurotransmitters, hormones, or neuropeptides in the brain for the purpose of possibly improving moral behaviour undermines any claim for an obligation to participate in moral bioenhancement research. Harris does not extend his argument about an obligation to participate in medical research to research into MB because of his rejection of the idea of compulsory MB.

Even if one believed that safe and effective MB should be compulsory for all citizens in a liberal democratic society, there would remain the daunting task of enforcing compliance. This would require different levels of co-ordinated social and political action. It would also assume the moral integrity and public acceptance of those empowered with overseeing these tasks. This may assume too much. Harris appropriately asks, '[w]ho guards the guardians?'.[51] More fundamentally, even if compulsory MB significantly reduced harm, it could come at an unacceptable cost: it would leave no space for freedom.[52] For some, the magnitude of the actual and potential harm resulting from voluntary action might be significant enough to justify imposing limits on action. For others, no amount of harm from our actions could justify such limits. Compulsory MB would undermine the free choice necessary for moral responsibility, praise, blame, and other normative concepts and practices on which our social and political institutions are based and which define us as human agents. By ensuring that everyone always acted in a certain way, MB would eliminate the capacity to choose between different courses of action – good and bad, beneficial and harmful.[53] Without this capacity, we would no longer be moral agents. As Harris puts it: '[a]gents are quintessentially actors: to be an agent is to be capable of action. Without agency in this sense, decision-making is [...] morally and indeed practically barren'.[54] The

---

[51]   Harris, *How to Be Good*, 105.
[52]   Harris, *How to Be Good*, 92. Also, Harris, 'Moral Enhancement and Freedom', *Bioethics* **25**:2 (2011), 102–111, and Harris, 'Moral Progress and Moral Enhancement', *Bioethics* **27**:5 (2013), 285–290. Cf. David DeGrazia, 'Moral Enhancement, Freedom and What We (Should) Value in Moral Behaviour', *Journal of Medical Ethics* **40**:6 (2014), 361–368.
[53]   For discussion, see Michael Hauskeller, *Better Humans? Understanding the Enhancement Project* (Durham: Acumen, 2013), 35–54, and Hauskeller, 'Is it Desirable to Be Able to Do the Undesirable? Moral Bioenhancement and the Little Alex Problem', *Cambridge Quarterly of Healthcare Ethics* **26**:3 (2017), 365–376.
[54]   Harris, *How to Be Good*, 94.

collective interest in preventing or reducing harm could never justify violating what is inviolable. Harris adds, 'I, like so many others, would not wish to sacrifice freedom for survival'.[55]

What he calls the 'freedom to fall' has its limits, however.[56] Free actions often have consequences that adversely affect other people. We should have the freedom to fall provided that we do not cause others to fall along with us. This is consistent with John Stuart Mill's principle of liberty. Mill states that 'over himself, over his own body and mind, the individual is sovereign'.[57] He qualifies this statement in saying that 'the only purpose for which power can be rightfully exercised over any member of a civilized society, against his will, is to prevent harm to others'.[58] The question for MB is whether and in which circumstances the freedom to fall could be overridden by the collective interest in preventing harm. At one end of the harm spectrum, it would take only one "village idiot" to cause or initiate a process resulting in the extinction of the human species through the use of nuclear weapons. At the other end of the harm spectrum, extinction could also eventually be our fate from the collective effects of individual actions and omissions causing climate change. If none of us survived, then freedom to fall would have no value because there would no longer *be* any human agents, free or unfree.

Some might equate moral progress with moral enhancement insofar as enhancement resulted in a reduction of harm among humankind. But harm reduction alone would not be sufficient for a robust conception of moral progress. Indeed, depriving people of their autonomous agency through compulsory MB would eliminate the "moral" in moral progress. If being a moral agent presupposes the ability to choose between alternative courses of action, and if there were no choice under compulsory MB, then there would be no moral agents. Our actions would not be our own but the products of brain-altering interventions. There is something paradoxical about the idea of moral progress achieved though the elimination of or limitations on moral agency. Any plausible concept of moral progress presupposes responsibility, praise, blame, and other normative concepts, as well as the associated psychological properties of conscientiousness, remorse, and regret. These depend on the capacity to decide and act on our own

---

[55]   Harris, *How to Be Good*, 74–75.
[56]   Harris, *How to Be Good*, 74, 81.
[57]   John Stuart Mill, *On Liberty*, ed. by G. Himmelfarb (London: Penguin, 1974/1859), 119.
[58]   Mill, *On Liberty*, 119.

considered desires, beliefs and reasons, to overcome weakness of will through our own efforts and to learn from our mistakes. These capacities are anathema to the idea of forcibly taking or undergoing a neuro-modulating drug or technique to prevent us from performing actions with potentially harmful consequences. Still, the value of reducing harm in promoting the survival of the human species cannot be mini-mised. Having choice is necessary for moral agency and responsibility. At the same time, reducing or preventing harm resulting from bad or evil choices is necessary for us and especially future generations to have the space for agency. There may be an intractable conflict between individual liberty and collective interest, between the freedom to fall and compulsory MB to reduce or prevent harm.

6. Conclusion

Moral bioenhancement would be a way of increasing people's moral sensitivity in motivating them to act in ways that respected the rights, needs, and interests of others. The aim would be to reduce actual harm and prevent future harm caused by humans at individual and collective levels. Persson and Savulescu's argument for MB as a response to the magnitude of global harm is well-motivated. But it is fraught with scientific, ethical, social, and political problems that would probably doom it as a viable normative project. Voluntary MB would likely fail to reach a critical level to have a positive collect-ive effect because a significant number of people would refuse to enhance. Among those refusing to enhance would be individuals who contributed most to global harm and with respect to whom there would be the most compelling reasons for enhancement. Yet making it compulsory would threaten to undermine freedom of choice and cognitive liberty. While there is an urgent need to protect the collective interest in avoiding harm and promoting the sur-vival of the species, it is doubtful that compulsory MB eliminating free choice would be justifiable. Questions about voluntary or com-pulsory MB also depend on the scientific question of whether research could determine that drugs designed to enhance moral behaviour were safe and effective. Yet clinical trials designed to test these drugs for this purpose would likely fail to meet standard ethical criteria for an acceptable risk-benefit ratio in medical research. There are also ques-tions about whether drugs intended to modulate brain circuits and networks mediating moral reasoning and decision-making alone would strengthen moral motivation and enhance moral behaviour.

Allen Buchanan claims that 'biomedical intervention might be one aspect of a multifaceted effort to extend concern and respect to all human beings, not just those who are like us'.[59] This is consistent with what Persson and Savulescu say about MB 'as a complement to traditional means'.[60] The other aspects of the effort Buchanan describes would be psychological and social. Yet even if biomedical interventions were proven to be safe and effective, it is unclear how all three aspects of a bio-psycho-social model would be integrated and how such a model would be implemented and enforced. Acknowledging the hypothetical nature of MB and the obstacles that such a programme would face, Persson and Savulescu state that the development and perfection of moral enhancement is 'not likely to be possible in the near future'.[61] Harris makes a stronger claim against MB, stating 'I believe it will never be possible to the extent the Persson/Savulescu thesis requires, or indeed that Tom Douglas believes [...] because moral enhancement has little prospect of preventing idiocy – but of course I could be wrong'.[62] Perhaps the strongest claim among sceptics of moral bioenhancement is from Harris Wiseman, who says that 'an explicit project of state-sponsored moral improvement of the general public is *unthinkable* in liberal states'.[63] This is in reference to what he calls 'hard, fine-grained, moral enhancement' of the compulsory type defended by Persson and Savulescu.[64] Yet what Wiseman calls a 'soft, coarse-grained, moral enhancement' project consisting of nudging and incentives would also likely fail.[65] These strategies would not provide the necessary motivational force for enough people to co-operate in a moral enhancement project. Nor would they prevent some from taking advantage of this co-operation for their own selfish ends. Education aimed at improving moral behaviour might reduce interpersonal harm to some extent but would not eradicate it. Moreover, not all states and their guardians would be interested in such a plan, much less implement and enforce it.

---

[59] Allen Buchanan, *Better Than Human: The Promise and Perils of Enhancing Ourselves* (New York: Oxford University Press, 2011), 170. See also Wiseman, *The Myth of the Moral Brain*, 280.

[60] Persson and Savulescu, *Unfit for the Future*, 2.

[61] Persson and Savulescu, 'The Perils of Cognitive Enhancement', 175.

[62] Harris, *How to Be Good*, 75.

[63] Wiseman, *The Myth of the Moral Brain*, 79.

[64] Wiseman, *The Myth of the Moral Brain*, 12. 129.

[65] Wiseman, *The Myth of the Moral Brain*, 129.

Moral Enhancement as a Collective Action Problem

Derek Parfit expresses a positive view on the possibility of moral progress: '[l]ife can be wonderful as well as terrible, and we shall increasingly have the power to make life good. Since human history may be only just beginning, we can expect that future humans, or supra-humans, may achieve some great goods that we cannot now even imagine'.[66] The goods of which Parfit writes cannot be separated from or achieved without an increase in the level of our moral sensitivity. They would be contingent on preventing or reducing harm. Moral progress requires enhanced moral sensitivity. The key issue is whether this sensitivity and progress can be made through any means. There are indeed many theoretical and practical reasons for scepticism about the concept and goal of moral enhancement. If there is no viable alternative project that could move people to act morally and resolve the most pressing issues of current and future generations, then a bad end may be in store for us all.[*]

University of Calgary
wglannon@ucalgary.ca

[66]   *On What Matters,* Volume II, 618. I do not take human existence as such to have intrinsic value. What makes nuclear catastrophe and global warming harmful is not that they would extinguish the human species but that they would cause suffering in people who exist now and will exist in the future.
[*]   I am grateful to the other participants in the University of Exeter conference on moral enhancement for discussion of these issues, and especially to Michael Hauskeller for very helpful comments on an earlier version of this essay.

Would Aristotle Have Seen the Wrongness of Slavery If He Had Undergone a Course of Moral Enhancement?

NIGEL PLEASANTS

Abstract
I agree with those proponents of bio-medical moral enhancement who claim that we face large-scale global moral problems which are currently un-recognised or un-acted upon. But I argue that the proposed bio-medical means for tackling them is miscon-ceived. I show that both bio-medical and "traditional" conceptions of moral enhancement share a misleading picture of the relation between the moral psych-ology of individuals and the socially structured moral problems with which they are faced. The argument unfolds in three stages. First I reflect on prominent histor-ical cases of large-scale progressive moral change to assess the role of the agents' moral psychology in bringing that about and sustaining it. Second, I identify some current cases of people recognising one or more of (what I call) the "new moral problems" that we face but not acting in accordance with that recognition. Third, I adumbrate an alternative stance to the idea of both traditional and bio-medical moral enhancement.

> The sickness of a time is cured by an alteration in the mode of life of human beings, and it was possible for the sickness of philosophical problems to get cured only through a changed mode of thought and life, not a medicine invented by an individual. (Ludwig Wittgenstein, *Remarks on the Foundations of Mathematics* [Oxford: Blackwell, 1978], II.§23)

1. The Idea and Aim of Moral Enhancement

The idea of moral enhancement is surely a good and important one. We all *ought* to be in favour of it. In his 'A Lecture on Ethics' Wittgenstein imagines someone observing him playing tennis and of-fering the judgement 'you play pretty badly'.[1] Wittgenstein says it would be unexceptionable for him to reply 'I know... but I don't

---

[1] Ludwig Wittgenstein, 'A Lecture on Ethics', *Philosophical Review* **74**:1 (1965), 3–12, 5.

doi:10.1017/S1358246118000309

Royal Institute of Philosophy Supplement **83** 2018

want to play any better'. The observer would then have to concede 'Ah, then that's all right'. Contrast this with Wittgenstein telling someone 'a preposterous lie', the recipient telling him 'You're behaving like a beast', and Wittgenstein replying 'I know… but then I don't want to behave any better'. The recipient of the lie would not want to say 'Ah, then that's all right'; rather, she would object: 'Well, you ought to want to behave better'.

Wittgenstein is not advocating that people generally ought to want to make themselves morally better than they are – he is just noting that no-one should be content with being morally bad or behaving morally badly. Most people probably think that they already are morally (just about) good enough. And whilst we all admire people that are *exceptionally* morally good, there is no requirement to be exceptionally morally good oneself. This is why we have the concept *supererogation*. Thus it would seem that the only people that need moral enhancement are egregiously bad ones.

However, in making their call for moral enhancement, some of its more prominent proponents justify it by reference to large-scale global moral problems the responsibility for which implicates very large numbers of people, such as the effects of humanly-caused climate change[2] and world poverty.[3] It is argued by radical critics such as Peter Singer[4] and Thomas Pogge[5] that virtually every citizen in modern society is responsible for the amelioration or eradication of the conditions that condemn a quarter of the world's population to life-debilitating and life-threatening poverty.[6] Environmentalists

---

[2]   Julian Savulescu and Ingmar Persson, 'Moral Enhancement, Freedom and the God Machine', *The Monist* **95**:3 (2012), 399–421; Thomas Douglas, 'Moral Enhancement', *Journal of Applied Philosophy* **25**:3 (2008), 228–45; David DeGrazia, 'Moral Improvement, Freedom, and What We (Should) Value in Moral Behaviour', *Journal of Medical Ethics* **40**:6 (2014), 361–368.

[3]   Douglas, 'Moral Enhancement'; DeGrazia, 'Moral Improvement'.

[4]   'Famine, Affluence and Morality', *Philosophy and Public Affairs* **1**:3, (1972), 229–43.

[5]   'Real World Justice', *The Journal of Ethics* **9**:1/2 (2005), 29–53.

[6]   Pogge, in 'Real World Justice', argues that we are actively complicit in sustaining these conditions (we are, he says, 'participants in the largest, though not the gravest, crime against humanity ever committed') and that therefore we have a moral duty to stop causing the harm. Singer, in 'Famine, Affluence', famously argues that whether or not we are responsible for the conditions that make people suffer 'absolute poverty', we are responsible for trying to help as many as we can, up to the point at which to do more would entail sacrificing something of 'moral significance' to ourselves.

argue that the citizens of modern western society are required to shrink the size of their "carbon footprint" by drastically reducing their consumption of energy-intensive goods in order to try to prevent the impending calamitous effects of climate change, which will be disproportionately suffered by poor people in the near- to medium-term future. In addition to these massive global moral problems, the same constituencies of moral agents are tasked with finding humane and just solutions to the crises presented by unprecedentedly large numbers of refugees, economic migrants, and other displaced persons desperately seeking sanctuary and a peaceable place to live. I also think, along with other "animal liberationists",[7] that we are morally required to cease the vast amount of killing and suffering that we impose on non-human animals through industrialised food production and scientific and medical experimentation. I call these states of affairs "new moral problems". They are "new" because we have barely even begun to address them, and because they are not widely recognised *as* moral problems regarding which every citizen bears responsibility for trying to solve.[8]

If the radical critics are right about where responsibility for causing and resolving these new moral problems lies, then most people's belief that they are a morally good enough person will look complacent and ill-founded, because nearly all of us are in fact behaving very badly. Such harsh judgement would no doubt be received with widespread incredulity. Hence the ostensible need for moral enhancement, of some kind. The kind proposed by recent proponents of "moral enhancement" is to enhance individuals' moral psychology through bio-medical intervention. The aim is to stimulate, augment, or create 'morally relevant traits', capacities, and dispositions such as trust, co-operation, empathy, and altruism,[9]

---

[7]   DeGrazia, in 'Moral Improvement', includes 'other sentient beings', as well as human beings, as deserving beneficiaries of human moral enhancement.

[8]   Cf. Judith Lichtenberg, 'Negative Duties, Positive Duties, and the "New Harms"', *Ethics* **120**:3 (2010), 557–78. I realise that some, probably most, readers would not accept that these are all genuine moral problems. I accept that this is a matter of "reasonable disagreement". But I do not think it plausible that someone might reasonably deny that any of the aforementioned is a genuine moral problem, still less that that there *are* any moral problems of this scope, scale, and weight. Nevertheless, I do not here engage in first-order advocacy for any particular putative moral problem. My focus, rather, is on what it would take for these to be widely recognised *as* moral problems and for the recognisers to act in accordance with that recognition.

[9]   Savulescu and Persson, 'Moral Enhancement', 401.

'morally better motives',[10] and to foster *'improved insight*: better understanding [...] of what is right'.[11]

Proponents of bio-medical moral enhancement seem simply to assume that once in possession of morally relevant traits and cognitive awareness of the moral problems faced, agents would thereby be sufficiently motivated to do what is morally required. But this is a very big assumption, and it needs interrogation. What exactly has to occur for people to accept the moral demands emanating from the new moral problems to which I have adverted and to take appropriate action directed at solving or ameliorating them?

Recognising and accepting a moral problem, and taking appropriate action, involves both cognitive and emotive (motivational) dimensions. First of all, there needs to be an accurate perception of the group of existentially imperilled victims and an understanding of the nature of the harm that they suffer. Second, the harm that the victims suffer has to be seen as *morally unjust* harm, with the entailment that it is someone's (some people's) responsibility to cease causing the harm and/or to help the victims. Third, the responsible agents have to see and accept that it is *their* responsibility to take appropriate action. Fourth, they then have to devise what the appropriate action would be. Finally, they have to actually take the required action.[12]

In the cases of life-threatening poverty and the international refugee crises there is probably widespread perception and awareness in general terms of the suffering and loss of life, and this is probably quite widely seen to be *unjust* suffering. But evidently, few people see it as *their* responsibility to take the appropriate action and to devise and set about doing what is required. In the case of climate change there is probably little clear understanding and acknowledgement of the suffering that will be caused and at most a vague conception of the future victims that will come to bear it. It is surely quite clear what needs to be done (consume far less and change lifestyle) but still there is very little embracing of personal responsibility and effective action taken. In the case of animal exploitation, there is some perception of the suffering involved, but scant belief in it being *unjust* suffering and therefore little incidence of people

---

[10]   Douglas, 'Moral Enhancement', 229.
[11]   DeGrazia, 'Moral Improvement', 363.
[12]   The foregoing mirrors Latané and Darley's five-stage model of the process of transition from bystander to helper in their classic situationist social psychology of 'the bystander effect', *The Unresponsive Bystander: Why Doesn't He Help?* (New York: Appleton-Century Crofts, 1970).

holding themselves personally responsible for opposing the institutionalised practices.

The foregoing is obviously a very rough sketch of the prevailing structure of attitudes towards the new moral problems that I have identified. In general terms, the obstacles to the communities of responsible moral agents taking effective action directed at addressing and resolving these moral problems are, variably: not seeing a group of victims as *bona fide* moral patients of the same moral status as themselves, and not seeing themselves as personally responsible for tackling and ending, or preventing, the suffering. It is surely highly likely that the major cause of these obstacles to moral action resides in the perceived self-interest of responsible moral agents.[13] The personal costs of taking the action seemingly required to solve the new moral problems are perceived to be very large indeed, such that it would incur large and painful changes in lifestyle. In a word, the (perceived) sheer demandingness of the action needed to solve these problems is the principal cause of, or reason for, moral agents failing to see the situations and scenarios that I have called "new moral problems" *as* moral problems, or failing to take responsibility for tackling them. How, then, is bio-medical intervention envisioned to deliver the moral enhancement needed to transform un-seeing, passive, and unmotivated moral agents into seeing, active, motivated ones?

A couple of quite obvious concerns over the idea of bio-medically induced moral enhancement, were it to be possible, are that it would be either too dangerous if compulsory, or otiose if voluntary. However confident were the medical experts that an enhancement therapy was totally safe, the possibility of unanticipated disastrous side effects on some patients renders the idea of involuntary administration untenable (cf. the experience of Thalidomide, a supposedly straightforward medicine to relieve morning sickness in pregnancy). The obvious problem with voluntary consumption of an *ex hypothesi* effective enhancement therapy is the motivation to take it. If one has

---

[13] On this see Michele Moody-Adams, 'Culture, Responsibility, and Affected Ignorance', *Ethics* **104**:2 (1994), 291–309, who convincingly argues that self-interest in terms of material benefit and personal conservatism motivates people to remain ignorant of the wrongness of wrongful institutionalised practices in their society. She argues that this ignorance is culpable because it is *affected*, but I think the ignorance is largely caused by social and cultural influences and that therefore it is often genuine and for this reason excusable to a significant degree (see Nigel Pleasants, 'Institutional Wrongdoing and Moral Perception', *Journal of Social Philosophy* **39**:1 [2008], 96–115).

sufficient motivation to undergo a therapy that would make one perform what one perceives to be highly costly (to oneself) moral actions, then one has sufficient motivation to perform the actions without therapeutic intervention, making the idea of voluntary enhancement otiose. I will expand on this point later.

The objections to bio-medical moral enhancement most prominent in the literature are that it is morally impermissible (because it would diminish the agent's freedom of action or freedom of will),[14] or misconceived (because actions of this provenance would not count as moral actions).[15] I do not regard these as strong objections. Even if it is the case that moral enhancement would diminish (some of) the responsible agents' freedom,[16] I think the benefits for the currently suffering victims would justify this comparatively trivial loss to the agents. And if actions performed by morally enhanced agents should not count as moral action (because not motivated by their autonomous identification with appropriate reasons for their action), this really does not matter very much.[17]

My argument against the idea of bio-medical moral enhancement will be that both it and "traditional" conceptions of "moral enhancement" share a misleading picture of the relation between the moral psychology of individuals and the moral problems with which they are faced. I will develop the argument in three stages. First I reflect on prominent historical cases of large-scale progressive moral change to assess the role of the agents' moral psychology in bringing it about and sustaining it. Second, I identify some current cases of people recognising one or more of the new moral problems but not acting in accordance with that recognition. Third, I adumbrate an alternative stance to the idea of (traditional and bio-medical) moral enhancement.

[14] John Harris, 'Moral Enhancement and Freedom', *Bioethics* **25**:2 (2011), 102–111; Christoph Bublitz, 'Moral Enhancement and Mental Freedom', *Journal of Applied Philosophy* **33**:1 (2016), 88–106.

[15] Robert Sparrow 'Better Living Through Chemistry? A Reply to Savulescu and Persson on "Moral Enhancement"', *Journal of Applied Philosophy* **31**:1 (2014), 23–32, 25; cf. Bublitz, 'Moral Enhancement', 103.

[16] I return to this point in section 4 below.

[17] It does matter to those that hold a virtue-ethical conception of the moral agent, which many participants in the enhancement debate do seem to hold. But I think that what matters morally has more to do with the beneficiaries of agents' action than the moral character of the agent themselves. The latter is primarily a good for the agent, and I find virtue-ethical fixation on the agent's character somewhat narcissistic. This issue is further explored in section 4 below.

Would Aristotle Have Seen the Wrongness of Slavery

2. Historical Reflections on Progressive Moral Change

Institutionalised slavery existed in all parts of the world for millennia. For most of its existence it was seen to be a natural, necessary, and inevitable status and practice in the societies that hosted it. It was not until quite late in the eighteenth century that substantial moral criticism of it began to emerge.[18] By the end of the nineteenth century it had been abolished, that is, rendered 'illegal throughout the Western Hemisphere'.[19] The British abolition movement and the British parliament and government were at the vanguard of moral criticism and effective legislative action against it. Their endeavours were characterised by the nineteenth century historian William Lecky as 'among the three or four perfectly virtuous acts recorded in the history of nations'.[20]

It is generally believed that abolition was brought about by moral agents blessed with the acuteness of moral perception to see through conventional justifications and rationalisations of slavery, and the moral virtue to act against it. If this was so, then the moral psychology of these agents must have been significantly superior to that of all those preceding agents that either failed to see the wrongness of slavery or did not care enough to do anything about it. In a word, the moral psychology of the abolitionists would have been an *enhanced* version of what their predecessors – and many of their contemporaries – possessed. One could imagine a philosophical debate conducted by maverick radicals shortly before the advent of the abolition movement, wherein they might have pondered what it would take to get people to see the wrongness of, and to act against, slavery. They might well have concluded that nothing would change without an enhancement of those people's moral psychology. They would have been wrong, though.

Leading historians of slavery and its abolition tell us that there is no reason to think that it was enhanced moral psychology that enabled the abolitionists to do what their predecessors had failed to do. The foremost historian of slavery, David Davis, conjectures that 'men of

---

[18]   'Before the eighteenth century practically no one, no matter how compassionate or scrupulous, regarded slavery as an intolerable evil', Thomas Haskell, 'Convention and Hegemonic Interest in the Debate over Antislavery', *The American Historical Review* **92**:4 (1987), 829–78, 848.

[19]   David Brion Davis, 'The Universal Attractions of Slavery', *The New York Review of Books*, 17th December 2009.

[20]   Quoted in David Brion Davis, *The Problem of Slavery in the Age of Revolution* (Ithaca, NY: Cornell University Press, 1975), 453.

the mid-eighteenth century were no more virtuous than men of earlier times'.[21] Thomas Haskell, arch-critic of Davis's theory of the causes and conditions of abolition, concurs with him: 'people who lived before the eighteenth century were about as insightful and capable of moral choice as people are today'.[22] The idea that people prior to the advent of eighteenth century abolitionism were 'morally primitive' in their acceptance of slavery emanates from what Bernard Williams calls the myth of 'progressivism'.[23] I do not need to go into details here,[24] but Haskell, Davis, and Williams argue and cite evidence that the pivotal variable was significant changes in the socio-economic conditions in which the abolitionists were embedded that enabled them to recognise and acknowledge the wrongness of slavery and to take up arms against it, not newfound moral powers.

Over the course of the twentieth century there have been a range of other revolutionary moral changes to societal practice and social status, all of which, like the abolition of slavery, are about recognising and institutionalising the basic moral equality of all human beings. The most prominent changes are those that established women's suffrage and those that promote racial, gender, sex, and sexual orientation equality. These changes are grounded in the formal legal right to, and enforcement of, non-discrimination, and fair, equal, and inclusive treatment of all individuals regardless of gender, sex, sexuality, and racial categorisation.

But, as with the abolition of slavery, there are good reasons for thinking that these moral changes were not brought about, and are not sustained, by an enhanced moral psychology. If it *was* the case that such progressive change requires an enhanced moral psychology that brings autonomous moral insight and motivation to the majority of responsible moral agents, we would undoubtedly still be waiting for change. I aver that it is self-evident, via direct personal reflection, that we citizens who are now enculturated into a social life that upholds principles of gender, sex, sexuality, and racial equality do not denounce and eschew sexism, homophobia, and racism (to the

---

[21] Davis, *The Problem of Slavery*, 41–42.

[22] Haskell, 'Convention and Hegemonic Interest', 858.

[23] Bernard Williams, *Shame and Necessity* (Berkeley: University of California Press, 1993).

[24] See Nigel Pleasants, 'Moral Argument is Not Enough: The Persistence of Slavery and the Emergence of Abolition', *Philosophical Topics* **38**:1 (2010), 139–160.

extent that we do)[25] because we have an enhanced moral psychology. We can surely see that recognising the wrongness of, and complying with the legal prohibitions on, slavery, racism, sexism, and homophobia involves no specially enhanced or refined sense of trust, co-operation, empathy, altruism, or "morally better motives" on our part. Recognition and compliance is, rather, just palpably obvious and effortless. To put it bluntly, we have simply learned, through basic instruction in and experience of our society's way of life, which kinds of attitude, belief, values, and behaviour are required and appropriate. Is there any reason to think that people today have more or greater powers of empathy, altruism, compassion, and critical moral insight than people (most of whom were blatantly sexist, homophobic, and racist) in the 1950s? In a word, No;[26] our appropriately non-sexist, non-homophobic, and non-racist attitudes, beliefs, values, and behaviour are grounded in our institutional, social, and cultural life, not an enhanced individual moral psychology.

It is noteworthy that those radical critics that agitate for recognition of and action on the new moral problems typically do not do so via sophisticated concepts and arguments, and presuppose only averagely motivated agents of merely ordinary moral decency. Singer's famous argument for there being a moral duty to aid distant destitute peoples requires only that the agent acknowledge that they would unhesitatingly incur a minor cost or inconvenience in the course of

---

[25]   This is an important qualification – I do not, implausibly, maintain that contemporary society is now (even largely) free of racism, sexism, and homophobia. There is still much to be done to achieve justice on these fronts. Arguably the main remaining recalcitrant barrier to justice is "implicit bias". This phenomenon is claimed to be very widespread and its effect is most dramatically seen in those whose *explicit* beliefs, values, and attitudes are resolutely opposed to racism, sexism, and homophobia. Countless psychological studies have shown that many, perhaps most, individuals unknowingly harbour, and sometimes act upon, implicit (unconscious) biases that contradict and subvert their explicit (conscious) beliefs, values, and attitudes. There is a burgeoning philosophical literature on implicit bias – see, for a recent overview, Neil Levy, 'Implicit Bias and Moral Responsibility: Probing the Data', *Philosophy and Phenomenological Research* **93**:3 (2017), 3–26. The phenomenon of implicit bias coheres very well with my claim that we modern citizens who denounce the evils of racism, sexism, and homophobia do not possess an enhanced moral psychology *vis-à-vis* our overtly racist, sexist, and homophobic predecessors.

[26]   This judgement coheres with Haskell's, Davis', and Williams' broader claim that the moral capacities of modern, early, and pre-modern peoples are about the same as ours.

rescuing a drowning child from a pond that they are passing. Singer is insistent that the duty to aid the destitute is no more supererogatory than this readily acknowledged duty. Likewise, moral arguments for vegetarianism and anti-vivisection require only that the agent extend their natural moral sympathies for pet-animals to food-animals and laboratory-animals. The only sacrifice that vegetarianism involves is said to be that of foregoing trivial gustatory pleasures and reconfiguration of dietary habits and routine.

Still, it might be objected that enhanced moral psychology was necessary for the radical critics, campaigners, and reformers that were instrumental in promoting and forging institutional change on gender, sex, sexuality, and racial equality (as opposed to the masses that simply acquiesced to the changes that reformers inspired). But as discussed above, there is strong reason and evidence for thinking that it was not a feature of the monumental achievement of the abolition movement, and this suggests that it was not a feature of the more mundane campaigns on gender, sex, sexuality, and racial equality either. The history of moral change around these morally arbitrary features of persons exhibits a protracted process of incremental, piecemeal, institutional, and legislative reforms, with each change creating a new context for reformers to respond to. There is also good reason to think that, as with the abolition of slavery, the requirements of a modern, increasingly sophisticated economic structure encouraged institutional and legislative reform. This is perhaps most easily and clearly seen in the case of labour supply and employment practice, where discrimination, disqualification, and restriction on the grounds of gender, sexuality, and race places irrational restrictions on the availability of talent and hinders the flexible working practices needed for a modern economy.

It is true of course that individual, and organised groups of, critics and campaigners played an important role in agitating for institutional and legislative reform. But their activities are ineffective on their own and only become effective when wedded to government-led, societal-wide imposed change to which the masses acquiesce. There are currently vociferous critics that campaign for recognition of, and action towards, the new moral problems to which I am adverting in this essay. But without the support of the government legislature, and a foothold in substantial public moral consensus, their claims are easily dismissed as the ravings of eccentric lunatics and dangerous fanatics (think of the popular image of the animal liberation movement, for example). The claims of earlier campaigners for racial, sexual, and gender justice were initially, and for a considerable time, similarly dismissed. Without the affordances of propitious social and economic conditions their claims would have continued to be dismissed on these grounds by political and epistemic authorities and the wider public.

I concede that many people, both inside and outside of moral philosophy, believe that enhanced moral psychology was and is a necessary factor in revolutionary moral change of the kind discussed above. But there are good explanations for this propensity; one emanates from classical Marxism and the other from contemporary social psychology. Both of these explanations diagnose a commonplace, almost inveterate, tendency to mistake the effect for the cause and to be taken in by the "surface" appearance of things. One of the central propositions of Marx's "historical materialism" is that "social being determines individual consciousness", not the other way round, as inevitably seems to us to be the case. In social psychology, the 'fundamental attributional error' diagnoses a congenital tendency to attribute the principal causes of peoples' behaviour to their character and psychology, when it is their social environment that plays the larger, and determining, causal role.[27]

3. Contemporary Observations on Radical Moral Criticism

If my analysis of the conditions of already-achieved progressive moral change is along the right lines then an enhanced moral psychology of the individuals that enacted it was not a driving factor. And if the new moral problems that I have identified are of a broadly similar kind to these historical ones (abolishing slavery, establishing the equal value, rights, and treatment of people whatever their gender, sex, sexuality, and racial classification), then the latter provide strong inductive evidence for the enhancement of moral psychology not being needed to tackle the former. But I think there is also more direct suggestive evidence that enhanced moral psychology is neither necessary nor sufficient for tackling the contemporary new moral problems.

It is not hard to find examples of outspoken critics recognising a large-scale injustice and accepting responsibility for tackling it, yet failing to act accordingly. A neat demonstration of the phenomenon is revealed by G. A. Cohen's irreverently probing question: "If

---

[27] See Gilbert Harman, 'Moral Philosophy Meets Social Psychology: Virtue Ethics and the Fundamental Attribution Error', *Proceedings of the Aristotelian Society* **99** (1999), 315–31, and John Doris, *Lack of Character: Personality and Moral Behavior* (Cambridge: Cambridge University Press, 2005).

you're an egalitarian, how come you're so rich?", which he addresses largely to fellow left-wing political philosophers, though the reader immediately recognises quite a large category of kindred candidates.[28] It is directed at anyone who enjoys much greater personal wealth than they would were their society to be organised according to a principle of distributive justice which they themselves profess sincerely to believe in. The conversational implicature of Cohen's question is: "Why don't you redirect to poor people, or to egalitarian causes, a substantial part of that portion of your wealth that exceeds what you yourself believe you would have in the just society that you say you fervently desire?" We have here, then, people with a vivid moral perception of the plight of the poor, a penetrating cognitive grasp of the injustice of that plight, recognition and acceptance of (socially shared) responsibility for ending that injustice, and even a realistic idea of what kind of remedial action is required (channelling their excess wealth to egalitarian causes). Only the actual action of setting about materially helping those whose suffering they recognise is missing from the rich egalitarian's response to the moral problem that they perceive.

One could say that in virtue of their perception and cognitive grasp of the moral problem, rich egalitarians have an enhanced moral psychology compared to those that are not (economic) egalitarians at all. Rich egalitarians that are political philosophers do exhibit prodigious cognitive power in their ability to comprehend and formulate elaborate conceptual analysis of, and formal justifications for, the egalitarianism that they uphold (the moral desirability and justness of significantly diminished economic inequality). But this cognitive power is not correlated with any moral action that substantially accords with their espoused egalitarianism. This being so is what motivates Cohen's enquiry into the comportment of the rich egalitarian in the first place. So whilst one might concede that the rich egalitarian possesses enhanced perceptual and cognitive power *vis-à-vis* most of the rest of the (non-egalitarian) population, this does not amount to *moral* enhancement as such. Indeed, it can be called into question whether the rich egalitarian really does believe what they purport to believe. Cohen does not share my scepticism on this. He says his question 'does not ask how the people under inspection can credibly claim to *believe* in equality'; 'I *know* they believe in it', he proclaims.[29] I think I am following Wittgenstein in suggesting that, with some

---

[28] G. A. Cohen, *If You're an Egalitarian, How Come You're So Rich?* (Cambridge, MA: Harvard University Press, 2000).
[29] Cohen, *If You're an Egalitarian*, 157.

beliefs at least, a person's mere avowal of the belief does not *ipso facto* make it a genuine belief, and it may be impugned by their sharply discordant (in)action. The crux of Wittgenstein's dismissal of Cartesian doubt is that one *cannot* – as Descartes purported to do – doubt that X simply by announcing the words 'I doubt that X'.[30] This holds for certain beliefs too, I think, namely, those such as the one in question that seems to commit the holder to some kind of accordant action.[31]

Consider another example of intellectual recognition of a moral problem in conjunction with an absence of ameliorative action that would accord with that recognition. In a recent interview John Searle says:

> I think there is a very good case to be made for saying that if you grant the validity of universal human rights, then it looks like it would be some kind of special pleading if you said there's no such thing as universal animal rights. I think there are animal rights.

Even so, he 'confesses' that 'I try not to think about animal rights because I fear I'd have to become a vegetarian if I worked it out consistently'.[32] The unmistakeable implication is that for Searle, becoming a vegetarian would incur a higher cost in personal sacrifice than he is currently prepared to pay.

Searle is not particularly unusual on this. I have quite often encountered students, philosophers, and non-academics who admit that whilst they are intellectually persuaded by the moral arguments for vegetarianism, they have no intention of becoming vegetarian, or say they would like to but lack the resolve.[33]

I hasten to record that my intention is not to criticise Searle (on the contrary, I admire his honesty and forthrightness), or rich egalitarians for that matter. Even the peerlessly virtuous Peter Singer is not immune to a glaring discrepancy (by his own lights) between

---

[30] Ludwig Wittgenstein, On *Certainty* (Oxford: Blackwell, 1979).

[31] Cf. Wittgenstein, *Philosophical Investigations* (Oxford: Blackwell, 1968): 'an "inner process" stands in need of outward criteria', §580.

[32] Tim Crane, 'An Interview with John Searle' (2014): http://www. crassh.cam.ac.uk/blog/post/an-interview-with-john-searle.

[33] It is interesting that whilst there is something *prima facie* peculiar, or questionable, about the comportment of rich egalitarians, the very idea of a meat-eating vegetarian is patently preposterous. In the former case one may wonder how the egalitarian reconciles their (relative) wealth with their egalitarian belief; in the latter it hardly even makes sense for someone that eats meat, even just occasionally, to say that they are, or think of themselves as, a vegetarian (witness such expressions as "I am *nearly* vegetarian", or "I am vegetarian *most* of the time").

his moral belief and his action. Singer argues that the very least one should be doing to help the world's destitute people is to give aid up to the point at which to give more one would be sacrificing something of 'moral significance' to oneself.[34] Yet he himself apparently gives 'only' 20% of his income.[35] This is still evidently a much higher proportion than nearly everyone else, and one might think that to give more than 20% of one's income *would* be to sacrifice something of moral importance to oneself, but it is evident from what Singer says[36] that *he* does not think so.[37] I should add my own confession too: I think Singer's basic argument for our duty to help the world's destitute people is unanswerable. Yet I give only a tiny fraction of Singer's 20%, i.e., much less than 1%, an amount which I know falls out of sight of the line of 'moral importance'.

It might be thought that in the foregoing examples we have people that *would* act in accordance with their moral beliefs were it not that their moral will is too weak (they suffer from the classically recognised condition of *akrasia*). Then, if there were a bio-medical intervention capable of fortifying the moral will of these "weak-willed" people it would enable them to do what they ostensibly believe they should, but cannot currently bring themselves to, do. But I do not think that it is a weak moral will that prevents (most of) these actors from acting in accord with their avowed beliefs.

Cohen seems to diagnose *akrasia* in those rich egalitarians that acknowledge a troubling discrepancy between their belief and their action (though his chief interest is in rich egalitarians that think there is no discrepancy, and that therefore they do not need the "*akrasia*" excuse). This is in line with standard definitions of *akrasia*, according to which the akratic agent is one that both 'believes that he ought (all things considered) to do X' and 'does not intend to do X'.[38] By this definition, rich egalitarians that acknowledge a discrepancy between their belief and their action are indeed akratic.

---

[34] 'Famine, Affluence and Morality', 234.

[35] Howard Darmstadter, 'Peter Singer Says You Are a Bad Person', *Philosophy Now* **89** (2012): https://philosophynow.org/issues/89/Peter_Singer_Says_You_Are_a_Bad_Person.

[36] 'Famine, Affluence and Morality', 241.

[37] Cohen admits to fitting the description 'rich egalitarian' himself: 'I am, like most professors, much richer than the average person in my society', and he confesses to giving to egalitarian causes 'only a fraction of the money that I earn (by which I don't mean that I give away something like, for example, three quarters of it; I mean a different, more fractional, sort of fraction)', *If You're an Egalitarian*, 150.

[38] Cohen, *If You're an Egalitarian*, 155.

However, it seems to me that someone who believes that they are morally required to do X but have no intention of doing or trying to do X does not thereby have a weak *will* in relation to X. I would say that they have a weak will only if they *want* to do X but fail to. If there is no kind of attempt to exercise the will against the resistant object (the doing of X), this is not a *weak* attempt at willing but no willing at all.

Thus to put it bluntly, the rich egalitarian, the meat eater that intellectually accepts a moral argument for vegetarianism, the typical believer in environmentalist arguments, and those like myself who accept that there is a duty to do what one reasonably can to help the world's destitute and those in need of refuge, really do not *want* to do what they purportedly believe they should do.[39] They do not want to because they believe that doing so would be extremely demanding and costly to themselves, to an extent that would sharply diminish their quality of life. If demandingness and costliness is the principal reason for the inaction of those that recognise the new moral problems yet fail to act amelioratively towards them, it is likely also to be a determining factor in the perception and judgement of those (the large majority of the population) that do not even recognise them as genuine moral problems.

Another principal reason for non-recognition of the putative new moral problems to which I advert is the normative force that emanates from the routineness and non-controversialism of believing and acting in line with the large majority of people, especially when this majority includes those of impeccable epistemic authority and moral standing, and most of one's family, friends and acquaintances. Consider the following illustration of this phenomenon, which features morally risky behaviour that occurs chronically in every modern society, the putative wrongness of which is, *ex hypothesi*, recognised by *virtually no-one*. The behaviour in question is car-driving.[40] We all know that the consequences of driving a car, when it goes wrong, can be devastating to human life and limb. The frequency with which it goes wrong is dramatically framed by Douglass Husak: 'more Americans were killed in car accidents in the month of September 2001 than died in the terrorist attacks of

---

[39]   I do not deny that there may be a rare few that fail to act only on account of a weak will.

[40]   The purpose of this example is not to argue that car-driving *is*, in itself, morally wrong. I am interested here only in the fact that hardly anyone has even *considered* whether it might be, despite, as I will show, there being strong *prima facie* reasons at least to pose that question.

September 11. Motor vehicle crashes are the leading cause of death for persons of *every* age from 4 through 33 years old'.[41]

Husak contends that driving a car is wrong (because it risks causing death or serious injury to other people) when done under two conditions conjointly. These are, when the vehicle is a SUV or truck that is constructed in such a way that it causes much greater damage to other types of car upon impact than it suffers from them (due to its disproportionate weight and strength), and when the purpose of driving it is what Husak categorises as 'frivolous'. Driving under these conditions is to engage in activities that are not necessary, and which risk killing and injuring other people (often those that have not consented to be party to the activity, and in the case of children, those that lack the capacity to consent). There are reasons for thinking that by his own lights Husak is too lenient in only designating as wrongful driving that occurs under both conditions conjointly rather than under each of them. And one might also note that even when driving is done for non-frivolous purposes it might still be morally questionable – the claim of putative "economic necessity" is often rejected as a justification or excuse for slavery.[42] But the essential point is that a lot of deaths and injuries are being inflicted on innocents as the result of routine activity that hardly anyone, not even moral philosophers, thinks is morally questionable, never mind actually wrongful.[43] The reason why almost no-one sees fit to question the morality of car driving (aside from the indirect and aggregative environmental harm it causes) is of course that nearly everyone participates in and benefits from it.

The conclusion of this section is that where progressive changes to an established practice or way of life would seem to entail substantial costs to its responsible agents, no enhancement of their moral psychology would bring them to see the status quo as a moral problem, or motivate them to take the required action if they do see it. How, then, can the new moral problems be addressed if the idea of moral enhancement is otiose, as I have argued it to be?

4. How is "Moral Enhancement" to Be Achieved?

In essence, there are two main problems with the idea of moral enhancement: it is overly individualistic, focussing too much attention

---

[41] Douglas Husak, 'Vehicles and Crashes: Why is this Moral Issue Overlooked?', *Social Theory and Practice* **30**:3 (2004), 351–70, 354.

[42] See for example, Moody-Adams, 'Culture, Responsibility'.

[43] Husak, 'Vehicles and Crashes', 364.

on individuals and their personal moral psychology, and too much is asked of it *vis-à-vis* the scale and magnitude of the moral problems we face. I readily concede that it is easier to identify what is wrong with the idea of moral enhancement than it is to diagnose how the new moral problems should instead be conceived and tackled. I offer a number of observations.

Let us first remind ourselves of the nature and basic structure of the new moral problems themselves. They share a number of core features, principally: their scale and the difficulty of solving them; the perceived costliness to the responsible agent of attempting to solve them; the pervasive taken-for-granted permissibility and normality of acting in ways that perpetuate the harm suffered by victims, or of being unconcerned with aiding victims that one could aid. In sum, the new moral problems are embedded in socially structured, institutionalised, and highly normalised ways of living that are impervious to the putative moral demands raised by the plight of the victims. Because of these features, the measures required to address the new moral problems must be of a fundamentally *collective* nature, and this is why modes of moral enhancement directed at individuals' moral psychology are bound to be ineffectual.

The historical examples canvassed in section 2 show that there has been substantial moral progress in addressing and rectifying unjust forms of oppression, exploitation, disregard, contempt, and discriminatory treatment of whole groups of people. Indeed, one could say that this is moral enhancement, albeit moral enhancement of the *ways of life* shared by the victims and the morally responsible agents – but not, as I argued previously, moral enhancement of the character or psychology of the responsible agents themselves.

I contend that our new moral problems are closely analogous to these historical ones in terms of the aforementioned dimensions of magnitude and institutionalisation of the way of life that sustains them. If the analogy is justified it provides optimistic inductive support for the new moral problems being soluble in ways that the "old" ones were/are. The new moral problems are just like the old ones (at the latter's early stage of evolvement) in being recognised *as* moral problems only by what I call 'dissident critics'.[44] Dissident critics are those isolated radicals that publicly object to an institutionalised and normalised practice, and the behaviour, beliefs, and attitudes entwined with it, on the grounds of its alleged cruelty, disrespectfulness, and injustice to victims. In taking this stance, such critics attract bewilderment and ridicule from the

[44]   Pleasants, 'Institutional Wrongdoing'.

incredulous and indignant majority, who either (especially in the early stages of critique) find the criticism too absurd to take seriously, or react with hostility to what they take to be an attack on something constitutive of their way of life.

Dissident criticism has played a vital role in stimulating and promoting progressive societal moral change. Without dissident criticism – thus no criticism at all – there is not even a *prima facie* case for anyone to consider the justness of an institutionalised practice in their society.[45] But as the examples of now-acknowledged unjust institutionalised practices such as slavery, racism, sexism, and homophobia show, such criticism on its own, without widespread support from persons of respected epistemic, moral, and political authority, and the wider public, is utterly ineffective. The new moral problems that I have identified already have dissident critics advocating their victims' cause, which is what constitutes the behaviour and practices in question *as* putative moral problems. So the question is, how might this merely dissident, isolated criticism be converted into a respectable popular moral crusade?

I argued in section 2 above that there is no reason to think that enhancement of individual moral psychology was involved in the transition from isolated dissident criticism to popular moral crusade in the historical cases, and section 3 presented further reasons why it would not be efficacious in advancing the contemporary new moral problems. I suspect that there is very little of substance that can be said on how to promote the transition from merely dissident criticism to popular moral crusade. There simply is no "magic bullet" that would show how this is best pursued in all cases. I think the best strategy, therefore, is to seek to learn from what *has* been achieved with other moral problems.

The main lesson that I derive from our historical experience is that too much emphasis on the need for responsible agents to become morally better persons, through enhancement of their moral psychology, is likely only to hinder moral progress. Telling the responsible agents that they need to undergo moral enhancement to face up to the moral problems confronting them[46] just reinforces the main barrier to them not recognising, or acting on, these moral problems in the first place, namely, the ostensible demandingness

---

[45] Notwithstanding Husak's maverick, but outlandish, critique, this is currently the situation regarding car-driving as such, as discussed above.

[46] As do Savulescu and Persson, in 'Moral Enhancement': '[a] willingness to sacrifice one's own interests is [...] a feature of even undemanding moralities', 407.

and costliness of doing so. The very idea of moral enhancement, in this context at least, evokes an alienating and demoralising utopianism. Conversely, though, it is cause for optimism that the (relatively) successful historical cases show that enhancement of individual moral psychology is not necessary for progressive moral change. In this light, the prospect of making progress with the new moral problems is less utopian than it first appears.

In an environment where norms of racial, gender, and sexual equality and respect have not been established it is hard and costly for individuals to stand up for those principles because to do so incurs ridicule, disapproval, and hostility, both from the wider public and from family and friends. But in an environment where these norms have become entrenched, adhering to and acting in accord with them is easy, effortless, and routine. Adhering to these norms does involve a change in living compared to how people lived in societies where they were not established, but whilst the prospective changes may have looked onerous and costly then, experience now shows this perception to have been illusory. Likewise, in order to tackle effectively the new moral problems there would have to be changes to the way people currently live. But if the changes were spread across the whole collective of responsible agents, guided and supported by new institutionalised norms of appropriate behaviour and comportment (as occurred with the old moral problems), they need not be as burdensome as they currently appear to be.[47] When the costs are spread across the whole group, the cost to each individual is minimal, and *ex hypothesi*, the object of progressive change was not really good for the responsible agents anyway (e.g., the consumption of animal products, and energy-intensive and consumerist lifestyles, are deleterious to health and well-being).[48]

One final observation may be worth registering. Proponents of biomedical moral enhancement have been charged with being prepared to embrace as a consequence of enhancement the suppression of a

---

[47] See Robert Goodin, 'Duties of Charity, Duties of Justice', *Political Studies* **65**:2 (2017), 268–283, for an argument on how the moral duty to aid the world's poorest people should be institutionalised and thereby transformed from isolated acts of supererogatory charity to a strict (perfect) duty of justice for all liable citizens.

[48] Kate Pickett and Richard Wilkinson present arresting empirical evidence in their bestselling *The Spirit Level: Why Equality is Better for Everyone* (London: Penguin, 2010), that fundamental inequality, disrespect, exploitation, and injustice is bad for *everyone*, perpetrators as well as victims.

central human freedom, namely, what John Harris describes as the 'precious' 'freedom to fall', morally speaking.[49] The objection is that proponents of moral enhancement want to change people biologically such that 'the freedom to do immoral things [becomes] impossible',[50] and taking away this freedom removes something that is intrinsically morally valuable (more valuable than the good that morally enhanced individuals would bring to others). My argument that historical moral progress is not the product of an enhanced individual moral psychology and that it is now effortless and routine for people not to engage in manifestly racist, sexist, or homophobic behaviour also entails that people no longer have the freedom to act thus – and therefore deserve no moral credit for forbearance. Those particular freedoms have been just as much supressed, by social and institutional means, as they would be by the vaunted biomedical means. Of course, to remove people's freedom to behave in overtly racist, sexist, or homophobic ways by social and institutional reconfiguration is not to remove their freedom to "act immorally" at all; there are countless other ways of acting immorally.

5. Conclusion

I share with advocates of moral enhancement the view that we currently face urgent, large-scale moral problems and that we are obliged to search for the most effective ways of addressing them. But I find the idea of the (biomedical) means they propose for addressing these problems fundamentally misconceived. Moreover, I think that the underlying individualist conception of moral agency that these advocates share with most of their critics is flawed in ways that hinder our understanding of what is required to overcome the moral problems. Rather than pinning our hopes on a soon-to-be-available technological fix that will transform our moral nature from that of Kant's 'rational devils' into "moral angels", I suggest we look *back* to what has already been achieved with other moral problems. And rather than aiming at achieving a non-specific, general moral enhancement *per se*, we should attend to the issues raised by the particular moral problems that we face. Being fixated on our own moral improvement through moral enhancement looks to me potentially dangerously narcissistic (there is much evidence that many, probably most, of the large-scale atrocities of the twentieth and

---

[49]   Quoted in Savulescu and Persson, 'Moral Enhancement', 406.

[50]   Savulescu and Persson, 'Moral Enhancement', 409, quoting Harris.

twenty-first century have been perpetrated by people obsessed with their own moral rightness). Societal moral problems, I have argued, are much more tractable when we focus attention on the practicalities of what can be done right now, with the resources we already have, rather than fantasising over a utopian programme of mass enhancement of personal moral psychology.

Acknowledgement

I would like to thank the editors, Michael Hauskeller and Lewis Coyne, for staging the marvellously congenial and convivial conference on Moral Enhancement at Exeter in July 2016, and for their very helpful and sharp comments and suggestions on earlier drafts of this essay.

University of Exeter
n.j.pleasants@ex.ac.uk

Moral Enhancement and the Human Condition

EDWARD SKIDELSKY

Abstract

I argue that the project of moral enhancement is incipiently contradictory. All our judgements of human excellence and deficiency rest on what I call the human "form of life", meaning that a radical transformation of this form of life, such as is envisioned by advocates of moral enhancement, would undermine the basis of those judgements. It follows that the project of moral enhancement is self-defeating: its fulfilment would spell the abolition of the very conditions that allow us to describe it as an "enhancement".

1. Introduction

"Moral enhancement" refers to the project (still purely notional) of enhancing the moral capacities of humanity through drugs, genomic editing, and other such technologies. Its supporters present it as expedient, necessary even, to avert the potentially catastrophic misuse of nuclear and biological weaponry and to revive our slackening enthusiasm for the fight against global warming. Technology, they say, has brought us to the brink of disaster; so now we need a new technology, a technology of the self, to reel us back again.[1]

Critics of moral enhancement have generally focussed on its consequences for the enhanced, arguing that they would be robbed of autonomy or placed on an unequal footing *vis-à-vis* the non-enhanced. My own critique of the enhancement project is different, though not necessarily contradictory, to this. Its focus is not men but Man, not individual humans but the human "form of life". This form of life is (I suggest) the foundation on which all judgements of human goodness and badness ultimately rest; hence its dissolution through enhancement technologies would rob such judgements of their point

---

[1] This, in very brief outline, is the argument of 'The Perils of Cognitive Enhancement and the Urgent Imperative to Enhance the Moral Character of Humanity', the article in which Ingmar Persson and Julian Savulescu first launched the concept of moral enhancement. See Ingmar Persson and Julian Savulescu, 'The Perils of Cognitive Enhancement and the Urgent Imperative to Enhance the Moral Character of Humanity', *Journal of Applied Philosophy* **25**:3 (2008), 162–177.

doi:10.1017/S1358246118000310   ©The Royal Institute of Philosophy and the contributors 2018
Royal Institute of Philosophy Supplement **83** 2018

and purpose. Moral enhancement is thus revealed as a self-defeating project: its fulfilment would mean the disappearance of the very conditions that could permit us to describe it as an "enhancement". We risk finding ourselves in a situation in which humanity has been not so much enhanced as *replaced* by an altogether different form of life, with different standards of excellence and deficiency.

2. Meta-Ethical Assumptions

The following reflections are based on meta-ethical assumptions which are broadly Aristotelian and naturalistic. I will not argue for those assumptions directly, but the chapter as a whole can be seen as a kind of abductive demonstration of them: insofar as the prospect of a "morally enhanced" humanity repels us, and insofar as Aristotelian naturalism explains and justifies that repulsion better than rival theories, we have reason to be Aristotelian naturalists. So readers with a prior commitment to Aristotle can find in here an argument against moral enhancement, and readers with a prior aversion to moral enhancement can find in here a vindication of Aristotle. And readers with no brief for Aristotle and no aversion to moral enhancement can give up now: this chapter is not for you.

Aristotelian naturalism is the view, roughly speaking, that judgements of goodness and badness are not absolute but relative to particular forms of life. When I point at a thing and describe it as "good" I tell you next to nothing about it until you know what form of life it embodies, or what role it might play in a form of life. Everything that is good or bad is good or bad "as" or "for" one or another form of life. There is no goodness or badness on barren Mars, except insofar as we think of it as the potential environment of some living thing.[2]

What is true of goodness and badness in general is true also of the various species of goodness and badness. Strength, swiftness, intelligence, and health are all relative to one or another form of life: a swift bear would make a very slow cheetah, and a clever lion would make a rather stupid chimp. *Moral* goodness, though unique to us (we being the only creatures capable of acting on reasons), is no different in principle: it too is a requirement of a particular form of life, dependent on that form of life for its specific shape and colour. Were human life to be radically other than what it is, human morality would be too. Philippa Foot gives the example of trustworthiness:

[2]   See Philippa Foot, *Natural Goodness* (Oxford: Clarendon Press, 2001), 27. I have borrowed this example from her.

Moral Enhancement and the Human Condition

It is easy to see how much good hangs on trustworthiness if one thinks, for instance, of the long dependency of the human young and what it means to parents to be able to rely on a promise securing the future of their children in the case of their death. It would be different if human beings were different, and could bind the wills of others through some kind of future-related mind-control device. But we have not got such powers, any more than animals who depend on cooperative hunting have the power to catch their prey as tigers do, by solitary stalk and pounce.[3]

These remarks can easily be construed in a utilitarian sense, as implying that trustworthiness is good only as a means to some independently desirable end. That is not what Foot means, however. She regards trustworthiness as good in itself, but only *because* of its role in the economy of human life. This is not the paradox it might at first seem. All goods require a setting, a place in an accustomed form of life. The value of an icon, though not in any sense instrumental, is nonetheless dependent that icon's role in the liturgical life of the church. Detach it from that role, put it behind glass in a museum, and it becomes just a pretty piece of painted wood. The moral virtues are no different in principle. They too depend for their value on their role in the human form of life.

Utilitarians and Kantians both reject any notion of specifically human goodness. For utilitarians, goodness is well-being, which is fundamentally the same for all sentient beings, though some of its dimensions may be available to some and not others. For Kantians, goodness is goodness of the will, which is identical in all rational agents. But as I said, I will not argue the case against utilitarianism and Kantianism here, but rather note the disagreement and move on.

I use the expression "form of life" rather than the scientific "species" in recognition of the unique malleability of human existence, which means that biology cannot by itself determine our standards of weal and woe. It must be supplemented by those perennial features of our lived environment which together with our biology make up what Hannah Arendt called 'the human condition' or what I am calling the human "form of life".[4] Consider again the quotation from Philippa Foot. If humans ever did succeed in creating some 'future-directed mind-control device' then trustworthiness as

---

[3]   Foot, *Natural Goodness,* 45.
[4]   See Hannah Arendt, *The Human Condition* (Chicago: The University of Chicago Press, 1958), 1–6.

we understand it would no longer be a virtue. This means that the lack of such a device, though not implicit in our species nature, must nonetheless be considered as part of our "form of life".

Which other features of our lived environment should be included in our form of life? Aristotelians will presumably not want to cast the net too wide, or they risk endorsing a cultural relativism they usually reject. But I think the following would be on most people's lists:

- The fact that our innate constitution is the product of chance, not design.
- The fact that we live on the surface of the earth, not scattered across the galaxy.
- The fact that we cannot expect to live much past three score years and ten.

These three features of our condition could all be abolished without transforming us into a different species in the biological sense, but their abolition would, I take it, transform us into a radically different "form of life", with different possibilities of flourishing and foundering. (Just imagine the qualities of character required to endure 300 years of conscious existence, or to find fulfilment on alien planets.) It is no accident that post-humanists have pressed for the abolition of these three limitations in particular, for they seem more than others to define our "creaturely" condition, our dependence on circumstances not of our making.

3. Strong, Stronger, Strongest

Before turning to our chief subject of moral enhancement, it will be useful to linger for a moment on a purely physical enhancement. The argument in both cases is similar in structure.

Strength, like other excellences, is relative to particular forms of life. A strong man suffers nothing by comparison with a gorilla, for his is a specifically *human* strength, perfectly adequate to the tasks that humans are called on to perform: cycling to work, carrying children and furniture, and so forth. Of course, there is a good deal of cultural and historical variety here. Some ways of life demand more in the way of physical strength than others. But this is a variety within limits. No human society calls on its members to pluck trees out by their roots or to kill buffalo barehanded. These are not "normal" human activities.

Now let us suppose that an advance in genetics, or pharmaceuticals, or some combination of the two – it does not matter for present purposes – allows human beings to become progressively stronger, year after year. To be clear, I am not imagining a situation in which all humans are brought asymptotically up to a limit of strength, but one in which this limit is itself progressively extended. Over the decades, humans metamorphose into creatures resembling the Incredible Hulk, or even more fantastic monsters.

In such a world, we could no longer describe an individual as "strong", at least not in the familiar sense, for the background conditions that give determinate content to such a statement would have disappeared. At best, we might say things like "he's strong for someone born in 2020, but of course, things have come on a long way since then", or "she's strong for someone from India, but the technology over there is still quite rudimentary". In short, the content of "strong" would be indexed not to a form of life but to contingent features of a given individual's historical and social situation. Everyone would be becoming progressively stronger, yet no-one could be described as simply *strong.*

It is worth pondering for a moment the likely psychological effects of this transformation. In our world, people generally want to be stronger, or at least not weaker, so as to be able to discharge the normal human functions. But this could not be their motive in the world I have described, for in this world there would be no such thing as "the normal human functions" but only a range of functions expanding progressively in tandem with our strength. In this world, the only possible motive for wanting to be stronger would be to become stronger *than other people,* or at least not weaker than other people. In other words, opening up the limits of human strength would have the effect of making the desire for strength a competitive one, rather like the desire for money.[5] We can see the beginnings of this dynamic already. Bodybuilders, using advanced machinery and (often) powerful drugs, are able to develop their muscles far beyond the limits of what is required in the normal course of life. Their motive for engaging in this strange behaviour is purely competitive: they want to keep up with, or stay ahead of, other bodybuilders. An enhanced future would see us all in this unhappy situation.

---

[5]   Mainstream economics assumes that people want money simply in order to acquire the goods that they want, regardless of what others have. But this ignores the way in which consumer wants are themselves shaped by social expectations. See Robert H. Frank, *Luxury Fever: Weighing the Cost of Excess* (Princeton: Princeton University Press, 2010).

Edward Skidelsky

4. Moral Enhancement

Let us turn to the question of moral enhancement. "Moral enhancement" will of course mean different things to people with different moral views. The originators of the concept, Julian Savulescu and Ingmar Persson, are sensibly unspecific on the matter. They identify the core moral dispositions as *altruism*, defined as 'the sacrifice of one's own interests for the welfare of others', and *justice*, identified with what game theorists call a "tit-for-tat" strategy.[6] This may seem rather simplistic, but let that pass. My argument against moral enhancement is consistent with any view of the content of morality.

Moral enhancement refers, then, to the strengthening of our moral dispositions (whatever these might be) through drugs, surgery, and other biomedical procedures. Alleged examples include the use of serotonin reuptake inhibitors like Prozac 'to make subjects more fair-minded and willing to cooperate' and the use of deep-brain stimulation to modify addictive behaviours.[7] The implied moral psychology is Humean: moral conduct is not the product of some "will" distinct from our natural inclinations but of those inclinations themselves. To have a moral disposition is simply to *want* to do the right thing, in the same sense that we *want* to eat or make love. Again, there may be plenty to object to here, but let that pass; my target is elsewhere.

Savulescu and Persson appear, then, to be committed to the following two theses, though they do not state them explicitly:

> Thesis 1: A morally ideal agent is one who is inclined to act only morally, never immorally.
>
> Thesis 2: A morally ideal world is one in which all agents are morally ideal, in the sense given above.

Thesis 1 is a straightforward consequence of Savulescu and Persson's moral psychology. And Thesis 2 seems to follow from Thesis 1 together with some simple and plausible assumptions about aggregation: if it is better for any particular agent to be morally ideal, it must be best for *all* agents to be morally ideal.

Critics of Savulescu and Persson have tended to focus on Thesis 1. John Harris, in particular, has argued that moral enhancement,

[6]   See Julian Savulescu and Ingmar Persson, 'Moral Enhancement, Freedom and the God Machine', *The Monist* **95**:3 (2012), 399–421, 407–8.
[7]   Savulescu and Persson 'Moral Enhancement, Freedom and the God Machine', 400–405.

by making it impossible for us to act immorally, would destroy the 'freedom to fall' that is, for Harris, a condition of genuine moral worth.[8] Savulescu and Persson are (rightly in my view) unpersuaded by this objection. They point out that the morally enhanced would be 'unfree' to act badly only in the familiar, uncontroversial sense of being motivationally incapable of it.[9] Aristotle's crown of virtue is also "unfree" to do the bad thing, meaning simply that it is psychologically out of the question for him; and while one might doubt the empirical plausibility of such a figure, it is hard to deny that he represents an ideal. At any rate, it is bizarre to suppose that perfect virtue requires a continual struggle against our baser impulses.

A modified version of Harris' objection might run as follows: even if the morally ideal agent feels no inclination to act immorally *now*, he must have a) felt some such inclination at some point in his past and b) overcome it through his own efforts. In other words, his good character must be a product of his own volition, not a gift of fortune or technology. I am not so sure. The roots of character are deeply buried in early longings and traumas, which age can moderate to a degree but never entirely overcome. 'At 50, everyone has the face he deserves', wrote Orwell, memorably but falsely. Does anyone have the character he deserves, at 50 or at any other age? And if not, can we withhold the highest praise from someone whose character is blatantly *un*deserved? Apart from anything else, this would rule out those saints who swore that they were nothing except through God's grace.

I do not have answers to these questions myself. But I shall leave the point moot, since my target is not Thesis 1 but Thesis 2. Even if we concede, for the sake of argument, that an agent who feels no inclination and has never felt an inclination to act immorally might be morally ideal, it does not follow that a world of such agents would be morally ideal. Why not?

I have said that our virtues depend on our form of life; were this form of life different, those virtues would also be different. One aspect of this dependency was highlighted by Aristotle when he said the virtues are about what is difficult for men.[10] Maternal love is not usually regarded as a virtue, though it is certainly necessary for the flourishing of human life, because with rare exceptions it

---

[8]   John Harris, 'Moral Enhancement and Freedom', *Bioethics* **25**:2 (2011), 102–111.
[9]   Savulescu and Persson, 'Moral Enhancement, Freedom and the God Machine', 409.
[10]   *Nicomachean Ethics* II.9.

comes easily and spontaneously. By contrast, filial piety can and has been reckoned a virtue precisely because it does *not* come easily or spontaneously; it requires deliberate cultivation. The virtues, explains Philippa Foot, 'are corrective, each one standing at a point at which there is some temptation to be resisted or deficiency of motivation to be made good'.[11] This statement can be misunderstood as implying that only those who feel the tug of vice can be called virtuous – a view often (though probably falsely) attributed to Kant. That is not what Foot means, though. The perfectly just person feels no temptation *at all* to do the unjust thing, but it remains the case that justice is a virtue only because human beings in general are often tempted to be unjust. If we felt no inclination to be unjust, there would be no need for a virtue of justice, any more than there is need for a virtue of maternal love. Such a virtue would have no functional role in our lives.

With this in mind, let us return to Thesis 2. It states that a morally ideal world is one in which all agents are morally ideal, in the sense that they feel no inclination at all to act immorally. In such a world, the motives of justice, benevolence, etc. would require no cultivation; they would operate as strongly and spontaneously as does the motive of self-preservation in our actual world. We would all love our neighbours as we love ourselves, without any effort or struggle. This is (I take it) Savulescu and Persson's ideal. But my question now is this: in what sense is this a *morally enhanced* world as opposed to one in which morality, as we understand it, has no place or purpose? For it seems that once the shortcomings and defects that our moral virtues serve to correct have been eradicated those virtues themselves must fall away as superfluous. There will then be no need for justice or benevolence, any more than there is now for a virtue of maternal love. Other virtues might still be relevant, of course. Morally enhanced humans would presumably still have use for notions such as "clever", "competent", "inquisitive", and so forth. But the specifically moral virtues would have no foothold in their lives.

Three responses might be made on behalf of the moral enhancers. First, it will be said that Thesis 2 follows mathematically from Thesis 1, whose truth I have already conceded. It does not, however. This is a version of the "fallacy of composition", familiar to economists. I can view the match better standing up, but it does not follow that everyone can view the match better standing up. I am wise to save, but it does not follow that everyone would be wise to save. Linguistics

[11]   Philippa Foot, *Virtues and Vices* (University of California Press, 1978), 8.

offers an even closer analogy. If some people use "who" to mean "whom", they are breaking the rules of English; if all people use "who" to mean "whom", the rules of English have changed. Grammatical error cannot be universalised. Neither can moral perfection.

Second, it might seem that traditional moral education, insofar as it too aims at universal perfection, is pregnant with the same contradiction I have discerned in moral enhancement. But this is a misconception. Plato and Christ never aspired to make sages or saints of more than a small minority. Material conditions, as well as the inherent mediocrity of our kind, did not permit them to hope for more. Even in our democratic age, no-one really supposes that education alone can change the frame of human nature. Moral enhancement, by contrast, is an avowedly universalist project, whose goal is the transformation of humanity as such. This goal is implicit in the project's original rationale as expounded by Savulescu and Persson: to protect the world from our collective greed, or from the threat posed by a single rogue agent. Enhancement *has* to be universal, or it will not save us.

Finally, it will be retorted that my argument, even if sound, is ludicrously beside the point. The abolition of morality is a small price to pay for averting global catastrophe. One might point out that someone who argues like this is not really concerned with *moral* enhancement at all but with the avoidance of certain undesirable states of affairs, but that would be quibbling. The substantive point at issue is this: is the eradication of the suffering flowing from our evil natures worth the abolition of morality? A question this big can only be answered personally. It seems to me (to paraphrase something Dr Johnson said about marriage) that although our current world is full of evil, a morally enhanced world would be devoid of good. The entire *interest* of human life lies in the struggle between good and evil; abolish that struggle, and human life would be transformed into something utterly flat and without incident, like the life of ants or bees. 'What excites and interests the looker-on at life', wrote William James, 'what the romances and the statues celebrate and the grim civic monuments remind us of, is the everlasting battle of the powers of light with those of darkness; with heroism, reduced to its bare chance, yet ever and anon snatching victory from the jaws of death'.[12] But of course, one cannot expect a utilitarian to agree with James and I about this.

[12] William James, 'What Makes Life Significant?', in John McDermott (ed.), *The Writings of William James* (Chicago: University of Chicago Press, 1977), 647.

Edward Skidelsky

5. The Invasion

It is hard to imagine a transformation of the human form of life of the kind envisaged here. This is where film can help out. *The Invasion* (Oliver Hirschbiegel, 2007) is a remake of the old sci-fi classic, *The Invasion of the Body-Snatchers*. Although not entirely successful as a movie, it has the merit, from my point of view, of bringing out the philosophical issue that interests me clearly, somewhat obtrusively even.

The film depicts the colonisation of human life by an alien virus, borne to earth on the debris of a crashed space shuttle. The virus' effect on its hosts is immediate and dramatic. Physical appearance, memory, and intellect are left intact, but all personal emotion is extinguished and replaced with one overriding drive: to spread the virus as widely as possible. Infected individuals are recognisable by their calm, impassive tone of voice and by the uncanny synchrony of their movements, as if they were radio-controlled by some central intelligence. They can put on a show of human feeling when talking to the uninfected, but left to themselves they are usually silent, presumably because they understand each other perfectly without words. In sum, they are moral zombies.[13]

These creatures are not just out to spook us, however. They have (or claim to have) a high moral mission: to replace the bloody conflicts of human life with perpetual peace and harmony. The movie comes to a climax with the following dialogue between the recently infected Ben (Daniel Craig) and his still uninfected girlfriend, Carole (Nicole Kidman):

Ben: You were wrong to fight them. Do you remember our trip up to Colorado? Do you remember the aspen grove? How beautiful and peaceful it was? You remember what you said to me?

Carole: I didn't say anything to *you*.

Ben: You wondered what it would be like if people could live more like those trees, completely connected with each other, in harmony, as one.

Carole: You're not Ben. I know you're not Ben!

---

[13]   A "moral zombie" possesses consciousness and reason but lacks personality. I owe this useful concept to philosopher Rodion Garshin (private conversation).

Ben: I'm not just Ben. I'm more than Ben. [Opens door to let
            others in.]

Carole: [Waving gun] Stop! Don't open that door!

Ben: Have you seen the television? Have you read the news-
            papers? Have you seen what's happening here and what
            we're offering? A world without war, without poverty,
            without murder, without rape. A world without suffer-
            ing. Because in our world, no-one can hurt each other or
            exploit each other or try to destroy each other. Because
            in our world, there is no other. You know it's right,
            Carole. Deep down inside, you know that fighting us
            is fighting for all the wrong things. Carole, you know
            it's true. Our world is a better world.[14]

Can we describe these alien beings as "morally enhanced"? They certainly seem to possess many of the standard virtues. They are selfless
and impartial. They are unhesitatingly self-sacrificing: they will walk
into gunfire or in front of moving cars at the drop of a hat. In fact, they
seem to have no personal attachments whatever, even to their own
lives. In this sense, they are rather like Stoic sages. On the other
hand, their complete lack of love or joy makes it hard for us to
think of them as morally ideal, since (for most of us) morality has
to do with affections as well as actions. So perhaps we can sharpen
our dilemma by imagining these alien creatures as capable of
certain affections. Of course, these would have to be affections consistent with their strict impersonality, so romantic or familial bliss
is out of the question. Christian *agape* and "joy in the Lord" might
come closer.

Taken individually, such creatures might be described as morally
ideal. However, their *world*, so far from being morally ideal, is one
in which morality as we conceive it has no place at all. Saintly behaviour is admirable in humans precisely because it is rare and (for most
of us) difficult. Make it universal and instinctive, and it becomes a
matter of mere zoological interest, like lactation. The alien world is
depressingly devoid of moral *drama*. We feel that nothing of deep significance could ever happen in this world, though it might be full of
enjoyable experiences and technical discoveries.

Take the particular case of courage. In a scene towards the end of
the film, the aliens are shown clinging threateningly onto Carole's
moving car as she tries to shake them off. The image evoked –

---

[14]   *The Invasion* (Oliver Hirschbiegel, 2007).

deliberately, I think – is one of swarming bees. In human beings, such behaviour might be called courageous, but one hesitates to call these creatures courageous. On the contrary, there is something disgusting about the sight of humans (as they appear) throwing away their lives like insects. It is not that we expect courageous people always to manifest signs of inner struggle. Perhaps, as Aristotle claims, the perfectly courageous man feels no fear at all except where fear is due. Nonetheless, what makes his action courageous is that fact that most people in his situation *would* feel fear. Here, as elsewhere, the individual act receives its significance from its place in a form of life.

6. Conclusion

I suggested near the beginning of this chapter that my argument as a whole could be considered as a kind of abductive demonstration of Aristotelian naturalism. I hope it is now clear what I meant by that. Most of us would, like Carole, reject Ben's offer of a 'better world'. That world instinctively revolts us, and would continue to do so even if we imagined away its more overtly B-movie features – the cold, staring eyes, the mechanical gestures, etc. Reflection on this revulsion reveals its intellectual basis: the alien world offers no foothold for judgements of moral excellence and deficiency, for those judgements are grounded in our specifically *human* form of life. In other words, our response to Ben's offer shows us to be Aristotelian naturalists, conscious or otherwise.

Of course, not everyone will be revolted by Ben's offer, just as not everyone is revolted by the analogous prospect of moral enhancement. To such people, I have offered an argument, based on the assumption that Aristotelian naturalism is indeed a correct account of moral judgement. But those who are neither revolted by moral enhancement nor convinced of the truth of Aristotelian naturalism will find nothing here to ruffle their certainties. Such is the nature of philosophical argument.

University of Exeter
E.B.H.Skidelsky@exeter.ac.uk

Kantian Challenges for the Bioenhancement of Moral Autonomy

ANNA FRAMMARTINO WILKS

Abstract

In the debate over moral bioenhancement, some object that biochemical, genetic, and neurological interventions aiming at enhancing moral agency threaten the autonomy of persons, as they compromise moral deliberation and motivation. Opponents of this view argue that such interventions may actually enhance autonomy itself, thereby increasing a person's capacity for moral agency. My aim is to explore the various senses of autonomy commonly appealed to in such controversies and to expose their limitations in resolving the central disputed issues. I propose that a Kantian conception of autonomy is more effective in addressing these issues, as it specifies the key features that inform an intelligible account of moral worth and moral law. A consideration of these features is typically lacking in the arguments advanced by contenders in these debates. Guided by a Kantian framework, I argue that moral bioenhancement projects directed at affecting moral autonomy are not as promising as they appear, for both metaphysical and empirical reasons.

1. Introduction

Among the central issues in debates over moral bioenhancement is the threat this type of enhancement poses to human autonomy. Bioenhancement may take a variety of forms including biochemical, genetic, neurological, and bio-technological interventions. While some maintain that moral bioenhancement, if possible, would surely threaten the autonomy of persons and consequently the authenticity of moral agency, others argue that such interventions may actually enhance autonomy itself, thereby increasing a person's capacity for moral agency.[1] My interest in this chapter is to explore the various senses of autonomy commonly appealed to in such controversies, which I do not think fully address the complexity of the

---

[1] Jona Specker, Farah Focquaert, Kasper Raus, Sigrid Sterckx, and Maartje Schermer, in 'The Ethical Desirability of Moral Bioenhancement: A Review of Reasons', *BMC Medical Ethics* **15**:67 (2014): https://doi.org/10.1186/1472-6939-15-67, offer a helpful summary of the various positions in the debate.

doi:10.1017/S1358246118000322

Anna Frammartino Wilks

issues involved.[2] I then show how a properly construed Kantian conception of *autonomy* is more effective in identifying the relevant target in moral bioenhancement endeavours. Specifically, I argue that it is more than just the capacity for *instrumental reasoning* that is operative in the kind of autonomy necessary for moral agency. It is the typically overlooked notion of "acting from the *motive* of the moral law". Thus, if biological enhancement is to facilitate genuine *moral enhancement*, it must focus its efforts on affecting the agent's *motive* for moral action, which is rooted in the absolute worth of the agent's personal autonomy. The highest form of an agent's personal autonomy is their *moral autonomy*. I argue, however, that the strategies thus far advanced for enhancing moral autonomy are both metaphysically unintelligible and empirically implausible.

On a motive-based account of moral agency, a genuine form of moral bioenhancement is one that targets the *motives* of moral agents. In the sections that follow, I examine a few key issues that arise concerning the possibility of bioenhancement directed at rendering the *motives* of moral agents more morally worthy. Specifically, I show how enhancing the *motives* of moral agents, and not just their behaviour, is inextricably linked with enhancing their moral autonomy. I then present some puzzles that arise from the conception of a bioenhanced moral autonomy, which I think ought to inform our considerations about the possibility of genuine moral bioenhancement.

2. Defending Motive-Based Moral Bioenhancement

Over the past few decades, scholars and researchers have defended different forms of moral bioenhancement varying from mild to radical. Ingmar Persson and Julian Savulescu occupy the radical end of the spectrum, defending extreme forms of bioenhancement, which they usually justify on utilitarian grounds. We need to engage in the widespread, obligatory, moral bioenhancement of human beings, they claim, in order to avoid the dangers that the development of other forms of technology pose for the well-being of the human species.[3]

---

[2]   See Joel Feinberg, 'Autonomy', in John Philip Christman (ed.), *The Inner Citadel: Essays on Individual Autonomy* (Oxford: Oxford University Press, 1989), 27–53.
[3]   See Ingmar Persson and Julian Savulescu, 'The Perils of Cognitive Enhancement and the Urgent Imperative to Enhance the Moral Character of Humanity', *Journal of Applied Philosophy* **25**:3 (2008), 162–177, and

They maintain, moreover, that this goal even justifies our depriving human beings of their autonomy, as would be the case in an obligatory, programmatic system of moral bioenhancement. Their position rests on the view that autonomy is just one of many values and that we should not consider it to be *the* most valuable. They assert that 'the value of human well-being and respect for the most basic rights outweighs the value of autonomy'.[4] What is lacking in Persson and Savulescu's account, however, is a reason *why* human well-being is of such fundamental value. This reason, I maintain, can only be provided by a deontological moral framework.[5]

Specifically, this reason may be found at the basis of Kantian moral theory, which acknowledges that human beings are not merely things but *persons*, i.e., beings possessing rationality and a will. As persons, they possess a dignity that no other things possess. They have this dignity by virtue of being capable of legislating to themselves the moral law of reason.[6] This capacity constitutes their *moral* autonomy. It is this autonomy that grants human beings their unconditional worth. It is, therefore, the autonomy of human beings that morality serves. This is precisely what Kant's moral law, in the form of the categorical imperative, commands: always treat humanity as an end in itself, never as a means only to some other end. Kant explains, however, that we treat humanity merely as a means precisely when we fail to respect a person's autonomy. Thus, given that valuing humanity consists exactly in valuing human autonomy, it is logically impossible to value persons as ends in themselves if our actions *threaten* their autonomy. Apparently, however, Persson and Savulescu think this *is* possible, and legitimate. Clearly, the reason for the discrepancy between Kant's view and that of Persson and Savulescu derives from their use of two distinct senses of *autonomy*.

Ingmar Persson and Julian Savulescu, *Unfit for the Future: The Need for Moral Enhancement* (Oxford: Oxford University Press, 2012).

[4] Julian Savulescu and Ingmar Persson, 'Moral Enhancement, Freedom and the God Machine', *The Monist* **95**:3 (2012), 399–421, 416.

[5] Robert Sparrow, 'Better Living Through Chemistry? A Reply to Savulescu and Persson on "Moral Enhancement"', *Journal of Applied Philosophy* **31**:1 (2014), 23–32, 25, also draws attention to deontological considerations in these debates.

[6] Immanuel Kant, *Groundwork of the Metaphysics of Morals*, trans. and ed. by Mary J. Gregor, in *Practical Philosophy: The Cambridge Edition of the Works of Immanuel Kant* (Cambridge: Cambridge University Press, 1996), 37–108, 86–88 (4: 437–440 in the *Akademie* edition of Kant's works [hereafter AA]).

Anna Frammartino Wilks

According to Kant, the kind of autonomy required for morality is not merely the agent's personal autonomy, i.e., their capacity to choose between alternatives. Rather, it is the kind of autonomy that enables a rational being a) to choose their subjective moral principles in accordance with the constraints issuing from reason, in the form of universal moral law, and b) to have their will guided in its choice and motivation by this law.[7] This is *moral autonomy*. I do not mean to suggest that moral autonomy is, for Kant, distinct in kind from general personal autonomy, but rather that moral autonomy is the highest expression of personal autonomy.[8] As Kant states, 'autonomy of the will is the property of the will by which it is a law to itself'.[9] Kant contrasts *autonomy* to *heteronomy*, which is the condition of the will's seeking its law in the spurious *objects of volition*, i.e., inclination, as opposed to *reason*.[10] Heteronomy gives rise to merely instrumental reasoning while autonomy generates moral reasoning. Through moral reasoning, the moral law does not *necessitate* the will of rational agents but merely *constrains* it. This constraint takes the form of self-imposed *duties*, i.e., moral obligations. In this way, rational beings are *self-legislating* beings. The capacity of persons to legislate to themselves the moral law of reason is what Kant means by *autonomy* – the feature that gives persons their absolute moral worth and dignity.[11] On this view, any moral bioenhancement programme that aims to achieve some moral end at the cost of threatening or devaluing human autonomy would be morally incoherent.

Oddly, the general approach that Persson and Savulescu propose acknowledges the importance of enhancing the agent's *moral motivation*.[12] In this respect, their position echoes that of Kant, which requires not only that the agent act *in accordance with* the moral law but also *from the motive of* the moral law. In a moral context, the sole motive of the agent must be 'respect for the moral law', as opposed

---

[7]   Kant, *Groundwork of the Metaphysics of Morals*, 88–90 (AA 4: 439–441).
[8]   For further discussion of this point see Anna Frammartino Wilks, 'Kantian Foundations for a Cosmocentric Ethic', in James S. J. Schwartz and Tony Milligan (eds), *The Ethics of Space Exploration* (Cham: Springer, 2016), 181–194.
[9]   Kant, *Groundwork of the Metaphysics of Morals*, 88–89 (AA 4: 440).
[10]   Kant, *Groundwork of the Metaphysics of Morals*, 88–90 (AA 4: 440–441).
[11]   Kant, *Groundwork of the Metaphysics of Morals*, 86–90 (AA 4: 437–441).
[12]   Persson and Savulescu, 'The Perils of Cognitive Enhancement and the Urgent Imperative to Enhance the Moral Character of Humanity', 167.

to material desires, personal goals, sentiments, etc.[13] Given that respecting the moral law essentially amounts to respecting the autonomy of persons, it is difficult to see how moral action could be properly motivated if the autonomy of persons is subordinated to some other end. This, however, is precisely what Persson and Savulescu ultimately advocate. While recognising the value of autonomy for moral motivation, Persson and Savulescu defend obligatory, moral bioenhancement programmes, even if they have the effect of diminishing the agent's autonomy. The reason they offer for this is that autonomy is merely *one* among many crucial values in morality, such as the virtues of altruism and justice.[14] But it is not clear *why* altruism and justice should be fostered, if not to respect the autonomy of persons. The problem is this. Given that the will of the agent must be autonomous in its choice to be guided by the moral law, how can it be possible to biochemically *enhance* the agent's autonomy without negating that autonomy, and thereby rendering the agent *determined*? How can moral motivation be enhanced without rendering the motivation mechanical, artificial, or inauthentic, and thereby compromising the person's moral agency and worth?

This problem is further complicated by the fact that moral motivation is challenged by weakness of will, which Aristotle refers to as *akrasia*.[15] The will is often impeded in its moral intentions. In such cases we recognise what the morally correct action is, but we nonetheless fail to perform that action because of competing, influential factors such as emotions, material goals, ambitions, and desires. Kant also acknowledges the reality of this problem, arguing that as rational beings (rather than divine beings) we need to be constrained by moral law through the duties it entails. The key point here is that our will be merely *constrained* by this law, not *necessitated* by it, otherwise we would not be truly autonomous. Given this limiting condition, how is the problem of *akrasia* to be addressed through moral bioenhancement? Owen Schaefer indicates that two possible approaches

---

[13] Immanuel Kant, *Critique of Practical Reason*, trans. and ed. by Mary J. Gregor, in *Practical Philosophy* (Cambridge: Cambridge University Press, 1996), 133–272, 198–207 (AA 5: 72–83). Kant acknowledges, however, that not every context is a moral one, and thus not every instance of personal autonomy involves the exercise of moral autonomy.

[14] Persson and Savulescu, 'The Perils of Cognitive Enhancement and the Urgent Imperative to Enhance the Moral Character of Humanity', 167–168.

[15] Aristotle, *Nicomachean Ethics*, VI.

are open to us: the *direct approach* and the *indirect approach*. He distinguishes these in the following way. Direct moral enhancement 'is designed to bring someone's beliefs, motives, and/or actions in line with what the enhancer believes are the correct moral beliefs, motives, and/or actions'.[16] Indirect moral enhancement, by contrast, 'is designed to make people more reliably produce the morally correct ideas, motives, and/or actions'.[17] Schaefer defends only indirect moral bioenhancement and rejects direct forms, such as the widespread, compulsory programmes that aim to affect large groups or whole societies. I agree with Schaefer's general position, but for reasons different from those Schaefer offers.

Schaefer's main objection to direct moral enhancement is another instance of a utilitarian approach. He argues that direct moral enhancement compromises the moral deliberation of people in that it deprives them of their freedom to think for themselves, to engage in genuine reasoning processes, and to form their own opinions, including dissenting opinions from those of the enhancers – who are themselves morally fallible. He stresses that 'moral fallibility will entail a strong instrumental reason to preserve moral disagreement in a society, while moral reasoning and individuality are values threatened by the absence of moral disagreement'.[18] Although I agree with this precept, I do not think it is the most pertinent reason for refraining from direct forms of moral bioenhancement. The most critical threat that such interventions pose is not to one's freedom to think and do as one pleases (although this is certainly important). More serious is the threat they pose to one's ability to be guided and motivated by the moral law. The reason, again, why this motive is so important is that when one operates on this motive, one recognises fully the reason why the moral law is sovereign – *because it respects the autonomy of rational beings*. Thus, the kind of reasoning that is crucial in morality is not the *instrumental reasoning* that Schaefer, in the tradition of Mill and Hume, places at the centre of moral deliberation. If this were so, then *cognitive* enhancement alone would suffice to achieve this end. Rather, the kind of reasoning specific to, and necessary for, morality is that which is grounded in the moral law, which the agent self-legislates when their will operates autonomously, i.e., in a way unaffected by ulterior forces, motives, or purposes – regardless of their utility. It is the capacity to choose and act, unimpeded, in

---

[16]   G. Owen Schaefer, 'Direct vs. Indirect Moral Enhancement', *Kennedy Institute of Ethics Journal* **25**:3 (2015), 261–289, 262.
[17]   Schaefer, 'Direct vs. Indirect Moral Enhancement', 262.
[18]   Schaefer, 'Direct vs. Indirect Moral Enhancement', 264.

accordance with one's better judgement, i.e., one's *rational* judgement. This is the kind of reasoning that may ward off *akrasia*. This is *moral* reasoning, and it proceeds from *moral* autonomy.[19]

3. The Possibility of Direct Forms of Moral Bioenhancement

If the goal of bioenhancement is to enhance *moral* reasoning, as characterised above, it is not clear how direct forms of bioenhancement could bring this about, since moral reasoning must originate autonomously in the rational agents themselves, not in some external "enhancer". Persson and Savulescu also acknowledge this limitation of direct approaches to moral bioenhancement. Thus, while they still think such interventions are justified, they do not consider them to be genuine instances of *moral* bioenhancement, since these procedures fail to enhance the *moral motivation* of the agent. Their concern is that what is lacking for this motivation is the actual act of *deliberation* on the part of the agent, in their decision to perform the morally right action. Deliberation of this sort, they say, requires effort and learning, and heightened cognitive capacities. However, their account only captures the *instrumental reasoning* involved in moral deliberation. It fails to appreciate the Kantian sense of moral deliberation, which stresses that the correct *motive* for moral action must be *respect for the moral law* that commands the acknowledgement of the absolute worth of autonomous beings. No other motive, regardless of its degree of utility, counts as an incentive to genuinely *moral* action, not even the appeal to *altruism* and *justice* – as in Persson and Savulescu's view. Their utilitarian position seems to invest *morality* itself with absolute worth, rather than the persons in service of whom morality exists.

This view, as Michael Hauskeller aptly points out, turns rational beings into mere means rather than ends in themselves. Hauskeller argues that 'if people have become mere means to the end of morality and are no longer ends in themselves, what then is the point of morality, of being moral in the way we treat each other?'.[20] The absolute worth of self-legislating beings is what gives force and substance to

---

[19] See Allen W. Wood, *Kantian Ethics* (Cambridge: Cambridge University Press, 2008), 106–142, for further discussion of Kant's notions of autonomy and freedom.
[20] Michael Hauskeller, *Better Humans? Understanding the Enhancement Project* (Durham: Acumen, 2013), 52.

the moral law. This is why respect for the moral law should be the guiding motive for moral action. From a thoroughgoing deonto- logical perspective, the notion of "direct moral bioenhancement" turns out to be self-contradicting, since moral reasoning must be au- tonomous reasoning, and "direct" here actually indicates that the "reasoning" is imposed on the agent by another source, i.e., an exter- nal agent – the enhancer. I maintain, therefore, that we should refrain from engaging in direct forms of widespread, obligatory, and exter- nally imposed moral bioenhancement, and that the deontological reasons for refraining from it are more compelling than the utilitarian reasons that are typically offered.

Nonetheless, the impermissibility of direct forms of widespread, obligatory, and involuntary moral bioenhancement does not auto- matically rule out special instances of such interventions. Thomas Douglas forcefully defends this position.[21] Instances of these cases would be those involving subjects who had already performed serious immoral acts. Their consequent loss of freedom is the price to be paid for their moral misconduct, i.e., for their failure to respect the autonomy of other persons. I think Kant would agree with this general position. Unlike Douglas, however, Kant would not consider such intervention "moral enhancement", as it fails to enhance the agent's moral motivation.[22] The use of such interven- tions simply amounts to an *act of justice*, in the form of punishment for wrong-doing, though perhaps a more enhanced form of moral punishment in comparison with those in current use.

A possible objection to this position might take the following form. Although direct forms of intervention do not constitute genuine *en- hancement*, they may constitute genuine *treatment* – as opposed to mere punishment. In the case of treatment, the consequence is not the improvement of a trait or capacity *beyond* the norm but merely to a degree that *meets* the norm for that species. However, the validity of the distinction between enhancement and treatment has been con- tested. David DeGrazia, for example, contends that these concepts are, in fact, indistinct. Consequently, DeGrazia defines *human en- hancement* in a more neutral way, as 'any deliberate intervention that aims to improve an existing capacity, select for a desired capacity,

---

[21] Thomas Douglas, 'Moral Enhancement', *Journal of Applied Philosophy* **25**:3 (2008), 228–245, 239–240.
[22] William Simkulet, 'Intention and Moral Enhancement', *Bioethics* **30**:9 (2016), 714–720, maintains that a crucial missing element here is 'inten- tion', which is also required for moral motivation.

or create a new capacity in a human being'.[23] This definition deliberately blurs the treatment/enhancement distinction, as DeGrazia does not think that *treatment* differs from the aforementioned goals in any substantive sense. In contrast, Nicholas Agar defends the distinction by appealing to the difference between *achieving* and *exceeding* a norm.[24] It may be questioned, however, whether these categories are actually dichotomous. In fact, Raus, et al. identify a third type of intervention, whereby the individual or group being enhanced begins at a lower than average level of moral capacity, and is brought to a higher than average level. This form of intervention, they argue, is partly treatment and partly enhancement, posing further challenges for demarcating the boundary between moral treatment and moral enhancement. They suggest acknowledging 'a continuum that ranges from below average functioning of moral capacities through to above average functioning'.[25] I find Raus, et al.'s position compelling. What this continuum account of treatment and enhancement entails, I maintain, is that the same basic conditions that hold for the one may also hold for the other – though perhaps to a lesser degree, or in a different way. The fundamental condition required for *both* enhancement and treatment is some elevation or increase in efficacy of the agent's moral motivation, which requires affecting their *autonomy*. This requirement, however, fails to be met both for enhancement and treatment in *direct* forms of moral bioenhancement. The reason is that such direct procedures do not at all affect the agent's autonomy in a manner that enables them to engage more effectively in the full range of *moral reasoning* that grounds moral deliberation and motivation; that is, it does not affect their *moral* autonomy. Given that direct forms of intervention are inefficacious in achieving this end, regardless of whether the goal is to achieve or exceed the moral norm, such interventions constitute neither enhancement nor treatment. Thus, a "directly enhanced" individual has neither been *morally enhanced* nor *morally treated* at all. Rather, they have merely been *punished* for failing to exercise effectively their autonomy as moral agents.

[23] David DeGrazia, 'Moral Enhancement, Freedom, and What We (Should) Value in Moral Behaviour', *J Med Ethics* **40**:6 (2014), 361–368, 361.
[24] Nicholas Agar, 'A Question About Defining Moral Bioenhancement', *J Med Ethics* **40**:6 (2014), 369–370.
[25] Kaspar Raus, Farah Focquaert, Maartje Schermer, Jona Specker, and Sigrid Sterckx, 'On Defining Moral Enhancement: A Clarificatory Taxonomy', *Neuroethics* **7**:3 (2014), 263–273, 267.

A cautionary note is called for here. The implementation of bioenhancements to punish individuals for radical cases of moral misconduct does *not* imply that their moral worth is completely determined by their biology. Some purely reductionist accounts of morality, however, might entail this view. Philip Robichaud draws attention to this feature of naturalistic accounts of moral character. He says that 'to write [certain] agents off as morally bad or vicious simply because of their biological features is to commit a blatant naturalistic fallacy'.[26] This insight informs Robichaud's view that we ought not to expect moral enhancement projects to be able to affect that dimension of persons that determines their value as moral beings.[27] In section 5 of this chapter, I show that there are also serious problems with a purely naturalistic account of *moral autonomy*. Before turning to that, however, I consider, in the following section, whether indirect forms of moral bioenhancement offer more promise than direct forms.

4. The Possibility of Indirect Forms of Moral Bioenhancement

I now address the question of whether *indirect* moral bioenhancement avoids the serious problems entailed by direct moral bioenhancement. An appropriate springboard, I think, is the *minimal moral commonsensism* advocated by John Shook, as it convincingly exemplifies the advantages of the indirect approach. On Shook's view, there are certain essential objectives that it is reasonable for moral enhancement projects to strive to achieve. These include improving moral sensitivity and thoughtfulness, moral judgement and motivation, and moral intention and will power.[28] Shook thinks a considerable advantage of these objectives is that they are scientifically identifiable. It is of particular importance that moral enhancement projects set for themselves such scientifically identifiable objectives, Shook maintains, in the absence of a scientifically identifiable *unified*

---

[26] Philip Robichaud, 'Moral Capacity Enhancement Does Not Entail Moral Worth Enhancement', *The American Journal of Bioethics* **14**:4 (2014), 33–34.

[27] Moreover, Allen Buchanan, 'Moral Status and Human Enhancement', *Philosophy and Public Affairs* **37**:4 (2009), 346–381, worries that the enhanced might be considered to have greater moral status than the unenhanced, giving rise to moral inequality between them.

[28] John R. Shook, 'Neuroethics and the Possible Types of Moral Enhancement', *AJOB Neuroscience* **3**:4 (2012), 3–14, 5–6.

cognitive system responsible for morality. 'It already appears', Shook explains, 'that there is no unified cognitive system responsible for the formation and enaction of moral judgments, because separable factors are more heavily utilized for some kinds of moral judgments rather than others'.[29] The objectives Shook specifies are also exemplified in Douglas' account of what human enhancement should involve. According to Douglas, enhancement works by enabling the individual to resist the influence of their *brute self*, and increase the influence of their *true self,* and in this way granting their true self greater freedom to run the show. Thus, in contrast to those who claim that bioenhancement *threatens* freedom, Douglas construes enhancement as *increasing* the enhanced subject's 'freedom to have and to act upon good motives', as opposed to diminishing their 'freedom to have and to act upon bad ones'.[30] What Douglas offers here is a means of addressing the problem of *akrasia*. He acknowledges, with Schaefer, that '*akrasia* reduction' is the primary goal of moral enhancement, and best achieved by indirect approaches.

Schaefer's distinction between direct and indirect moral enhancement is closely related to the distinction between *behaviour-oriented* and *capacity-oriented* moral enhancement.[31] As Raus, et al. note, contenders in the moral enhancement debate tend to characterise moral enhancement in one of two ways, as interventions that bring about either a) a real or intended effect on the enhanced individual's *behaviour,* or b) a real or intended effect on the enhanced individual's *capacities for moral reflection.*[32] The capacities-oriented conception of moral enhancement is analogous to what some refer to as the *functional-augmentative approach to enhancement.* According to this view, enhancements in general are interventions that 'improve some capacity or function (such as cognition, vision, hearing, alertness) by increasing the ability of the function to do what it normally does'.[33] In the case of moral enhancement, the relevant capacities are typically considered to be the capacities for sympathy or

[29] Shook, 'Neuroethics and the Possible Types of Moral Enhancement', 5–6.
[30] Douglas, 'Moral Enhancement', 240.
[31] Raus, et al., in 'On Defining Moral Enhancement: A Clarificatory Taxonomy', 267, discuss a related distinction between *active involvement* and *passive receiving*, analogous to the distinction between indirect and direct approaches.
[32] Raus, et al., 'On Defining Moral Enhancement: A Clarificatory Taxonomy', 268.
[33] Brian D. Earp, Anders Sandberg, Guy Kahane, and Julian Savulescu, 'When is Diminishment a Form of Enhancement? Rethinking

empathy, justice or fairness, altruism, righteous anger, etc., commonly referred to as *first-order capacities*. Against the capacities-oriented approach, Douglas has argued that it is not the case that an increase in certain capacities is desirable in all situations. Whether or not an increase is desirable in a given situation depends on a variety of factors, such as the agent's baseline moral motives and dispositions, the agent's role in a specific social context, etc.[34] Brian Earp, et al. maintain, in fact, that in some circumstances it may be more desirable to *diminish* a particular function or capacity to bring about moral enhancement. For example, to achieve the requisite partiality for justice, sometimes it is necessary to diminish one's sympathy for the victim. Thus, the goal should be not to increase, e.g., sympathy *simpliciter*, but rather to improve 'second-order empathic control'.[35] This approach, I think, represents a refinement of both Schafer and Shook's approach.

Endorsing the need for moral bioenhancement to augment the agent's *second-order* or *higher-order capacity*, Earp, et al. defend what they call an *agential* approach to moral enhancement. Their position resembles an Aristotelian-type virtue ethics, with its emphasis on the development of the moral *character* of the agent, rather than the performance of certain kinds of actions, or the observance of certain principles. Earp, et al. characterise this higher order capacity as the capacity to 'respond flexibly to different situations, and to employ or tap into different cognitive and emotional resources as necessary to arrive at the motives, decisions, and behaviors that are morally desirable given the context'.[36] Augmenting in the agent this capacity to modulate their moral responses in a reason-sensitive and context-dependent manner is what Earp, et al. think would constitute a more reliable strategy for moral bioenhancement. Because this approach does not aim at directly modifying particular moral traits, functions, or sentiments, but rather at affecting the higher-order capacity to regulate them, Earp, et al. think this form of moral enhancement amounts to *facilitation* rather than *determination*

---

the Enhancement Debate in Biomedical Ethics', *Frontiers in Systems Neuroscience* **8**:12 (2014), 2.

[34] Douglas, 'Moral Enhancement', 228–245, and, from the same author, see 'Moral Enhancement via Direct Emotion Modulation: A Reply to John Harris', *Bioethics* **27**:3 (2013), 160–168.

[35] Brian D. Earp, Thomas Douglas, and Julian Savulescu, 'Moral Neuroenhancement', in S. Johnson and K. Rommelfanger (eds), *Routledge Handbook of Neuroethics* (New York: Routledge, 2017), 166–184, 170.

[36] Earp, et al., 'Moral Neuroenhancement', 169.

of the agent's moral actions. This, they argue, permits the development of a genuine moral understanding, as opposed to generating a merely mechanical form of moral behaviour. As John Harris and Robert Sparrow argue, this moral understanding is impeded by *direct* approaches to moral enhancement.[37] In contrast, the agential approach fosters the agent's critical reflection on moral values, and augments their ability to deliberate, in a rational manner, on the relevant moral content.

The agential approach that Earp, et al. advocate goes a long way in addressing some of the weaknesses of the positions I examined earlier in this essay. In line with this *agential* indirect form of moral bioenhancement, the approach that Owen Schaefer, et al. propose specifies even further the target to be aimed at to achieve the desired ends. They propose that the particular higher order capacity that would enable an individual to function more effectively as a moral agent is the capacity for *autonomy*. If enhancing moral motivation is the goal, then the requisite intervention is one that motivates the enhanced individual to *choose* to be moral rather than immoral, as opposed to merely compelling them to do so. Clearly, this would involve targeting the individual's *will*. Because the exercise of one's will is, generally speaking, what is conceived of as *autonomy*, it seems that enhancing moral motivation necessitates enhancing autonomy.

With respect to the possibility of this endeavour, however, many have expressed serious concerns and scepticism. Among the strongest of the sceptics is Harris.[38] Contrary to the view that moral bioenhancement necessarily diminishes autonomy, Schaefer, et al. propose that certain forms of bioenhancement may enhance autonomy itself. They maintain that the common feature pertaining to the various mainstream accounts of autonomy is *reasoning ability*. They argue that, since reasoning ability is a cognitive function, its improvement may be achieved through *cognitive* enhancement, which, in turn, would enhance autonomy. Schaefer, et al. specify several influential conceptions of autonomy which they think indicate the

---

[37]   See John Harris, 'Moral Enhancement and Freedom', *Bioethics* **25**:2 (2011), 104, and Sparrow, 'Better Living Through Chemistry?', 23–32.
[38]   John Harris, 'Moral Enhancement and Freedom', 102–111, and John Harris, *How to Be Good: The Possibility of Moral Enhancement* (Oxford: Oxford University Press, 2016), 56–109. Although in the latter work Harris appears to have moved closer to Persson and Savulescu on many points, he still seems resolute in his claim that moral bioenhancement is bound to threaten human freedom.

strong relationship between cognitive capacity and self-determination. On Harry Frankfurt's view, autonomy consists in the coherence between one's higher order and lower order desires; Tom Beauchamp and James Childress take autonomy to involve understanding and intentionality, as well as psychological integration and the resistance to manipulative and deceptive influences; Bernard Berofsky locates autonomy in competence and individuality.[39] All of these, and many other conceptions of autonomy, they assert, incorporate fundamental cognitive capacities, which foster the instrumental reasoning and deliberation that characterise self-determination. Enhanced autonomy, they conclude, would be a likely by-product of the enhancement of those cognitive capacities.

While Schaefer, et al. recognise that instrumental rationality is not *identical* to autonomy, nor even sufficient for it, they maintain that, nonetheless, 'cognition and reasoning capacity can significantly contribute to agents' autonomy'.[40] They conclude by 'encouraging people to voluntarily undergo [bioenhancements] themselves, as a way to live more autonomous lives'.[41] I have briefly offered my general assessment of the *indirect* approach to moral bioenhancement throughout this section. In the section that follows, I offer a more detailed assessment, focussing on the bioenhancement of *autonomy* – especially in light of the proposals of Schaefer, et al. just presented.

5. Assessing Claims to the Bioenhancement of Autonomy

My assessment of the claim that it may be possible to bioenhance autonomy appeals to two types of argument: one based on metaphysical grounds, the other on empirical grounds. These arguments, however, are intertwined, as we shall see. My general concern about the claim that "autonomy itself could be enhanced" is that it is very misleading. The difference between the claims: "(a) facilitates autonomy" and "(a) enhances autonomy" can be very great, depending on how one understands not only the notion of *autonomy* but also the notion of *enhancement*. My view is that improving the relevant cognitive capacities – specifically, reasoning ability – does *not* amount to enhancing autonomy – even though it may render the autonomy of agents more *efficacious*. While bioenhancements that are biochemically-based,

---

[39]   These views are cited in G. Owen Schaefer, Guy Kahane and Julian Savulescu, 'Autonomy and Enhancement', *Neuroethics* **7**:2 (2014), 123–136.
[40]   Schaefer, et al., 'Autonomy and Enhancement', 123.
[41]   Schaefer, et al., 'Autonomy and Enhancement', 135.

genetically engineered, or neurologically facilitated may have an effect on the agent's ability to *respond* to the commands of its autonomous will, this is not equivalent to an alteration in the will's capacity to *be* autonomous. The difference is a profoundly metaphysical one.

The view that the will of a rational agent could be affected as a consequence of the bioenhancement of cognitive capacities, in a manner that would augment or diminish their *autonomy,* presupposes a reductionist account of the will. Such an account, however, has not yet been supplied by any of the natural sciences. At most, it may be argued that the bioenhancement of cognitive capacities may promote the agent's ability to be less affected by objects of volition that may otherwise inhibit the agent from acting in accordance with their autonomous will. This is not identical, however, to affecting the *will* itself, and motivating *it* to choose the moral law more effectively. In the Kantian framework, only the biological/psychological workings of the cognitive faculties, corresponding to the phenomenal self, can be affected by natural causes. The will, a function of the noumenal self, is independent of natural causes, as it is *self-determined.*[42] Jotterand voices a similar objection in his remark that 'the emphasis on the control of moral emotions appears reductive and one-sided in the sense that it conflates moral reasoning (as practical reasoning) with moral psychology (how moral reasoning acts on one's motivational/emotional states)'.[43] Even on a particular type of compatibilist view, which some, such as Allen Wood, ascribe to Kant, bioenhancements are more reasonably viewed as affecting the material body of the agent, not their will.[44] Bioenhanced cognitive capacities might also promote the agent's *instrumental reasoning,* which could improve their ability to determine the most effective means for carrying out the will's resolve, but not to *determine* its resolve. To be sure, the above argument does not entail that all efforts towards the bioenhancement of cognitive capacities are, therefore, ill-directed, illegitimate, or lacking in utility. The argument is only intended to expose the weakness of the claim that cognitive bioenhancement, which may promote an individual's capacity for instrumental reasoning, may thereby have an effect on the will itself and its moral motivation.

[42] Kant, *Critique of Practical Reason*, 185–187 (AA 5: 57–58).
[43] Fabrice Jotterand, '"Virtue Engineering" and Moral Agency: Will Post-Humans Still Need the Virtues?', *AJOB Neuroscience* **2**:4 (2011), 5.
[44] See Allen W. Wood, 'Kant's Compatibilism', in Allen W. Wood (ed.), *Self and Nature in Kant's Philosophy* (Ithaca: Cornell Press, 1984), 73–101, for an account of this type of compatibilism.

In principle, if it *were* possible to devise a complete set of natural-istic criteria that could serve as the conditions for bioenhancing moral motivation, the argument Schaefer, et al. propose would be more cogent. However, scepticism on this point is occasioned by recent empirical findings. In a report concerning the current use of non-in-vasive brain stimulation for moral enhancement, Darby and Pascual-Leone confirm that 'the actual physiological effects of specific brain stimulation parameters remain unknown'.[45] We may know that a par-ticular form of brain stimulation modifies moral behaviour in some way, without necessarily knowing whether the modification was the result of a modification in brain activity of a specific region or whether it was due to a more complex pattern of brain activity modi-fication.[46] Darby and Pascual-Leone echo the view expressed by many that 'rather than improving one single moral capacity, brain stimulation alters specific neuropsychological processes contributing to moral behavior. Enhancement of these processes can lead to morally enhanced behaviour in some situations, but less morally de-sirable behavior in other circumstances'.[47] Clearly, these conse-quences are less than optimal.[48] Molly Crockett warns about misleading laboratory studies purported to demonstrate that selective serotonin reuptake inhibitors have been shown to be somewhat effect-ive in the treatment of aggressive behaviour. These studies neglect to mention that this is true only for certain types of individuals. Specifically, 'serotonin appears to be involved more in reactive, im-pulsive aggression (e.g., personality disorders) than in premeditated aggression (e.g., psychopathy)'.[49] Furthermore, Crockett draws at-tention to inadequate sample sizes of studies indicating that single genes considerably predispose individuals towards particular virtues. She also stresses that most neurotransmitters perform

---

[45]   R. Ryan Darby and Alvaro Pascual-Leone, 'Moral Enhancement Using Non-Invasive Brain Stimulation', *Frontiers in Human Neuroscience* **11**:77 (2017), 2.

[46]   For further discussion of related issues see Patricia S. Churchland, *Braintrust: What Neuroscience Tells Us About Morality* (Princeton and Oxford: Princeton University Press, 2011).

[47]   Darby, et al., 'Moral Enhancement Using Non-Invasive Brain Stimulation', 8.

[48]   Hauskeller points out that there are also less than optimal cultural and sociological consequences to human enhancement projects in general; see Michael Hauskeller, *Mythologies of Transhumanism* (London: Palgrave Macmillan, 2016).

[49]   Molly J. Crockett, 'Moral Bioenhancement: A Neuroscientific Perspective', *Journal of Medical Ethics* **40**:6 (2014), 370–371, 370.

multiple functions and are located in numerous regions scattered throughout the brain, rendering them difficult to track and control; the attempt to manipulate them may give rise to unintended and undesirable effects.[50]

Moreover, while acknowledging that significant progress may certainly be forthcoming that could reduce the undesirable effects of these kinds of interventions, Crockett remarks that, by targeting very specific receptor types in particular neural locations, other problems ensue from this precision. Crockett agrees with DeGrazia, who asserts that 'highly selective and targeted forms of moral bioenhancement may pose a greater threat to freedom'.[51] The reason is that, the more focussed the target, the more *direct* the effect on the agent's behaviour, which entails less control of the agent over their deliberation. This problem is particularly pertinent, I think, to attempts at moral bioenhancement via gene editing, especially in its most current form – using CRISPR-Cas9. This molecular technology may modify any segment of an individual's genome, sometimes by the mere modification of 'single incorrect letters of DNA out of the 3.2 billion letters that make up the human genome'.[52] Jennifer Doudna, one of the founders of the CRISPR technology, cautions that there is no reason to think this technology will stop at treatment: 'once it becomes feasible to transform an embryo's mutated genes into "normal" ones, there will certainly be temptations to upgrade normal genes to supposedly superior versions', even for the germline.[53] Though some, for example Hauskeller, remain unconvinced of the *need* for human enhancement in general, others advocate a moral obligation to implement such technology to address the unfairness of 'the genetic lottery'.[54]

[50]   See, however, Nick Bostrom and Anders Sandberg, 'The Wisdom of Nature: An Evolutionary Heuristic for Human Enhancement', in Julian Savulescu and Nick Bostrom (eds), *Human Enhancement* (Oxford: Oxford University Press, 2009), 375–416, for suggestions on developing bioenhancements that minimise risk and increase benefits.

[51]   Crockett, 'Moral Bioenhancement: A Neuroscientific Perspective', 371.

[52]   Jennifer A. Doudna and Samuel H. Sternberg, *A Crack in Creation: Gene Editing and the Unthinkable Power to Control Evolution* (Boston and New York: Houghton Mifflin Harcourt, 2017), xiii–xvii.

[53]   Doudna and Sternberg, *A Crack in Creation*, xvi.

[54]   For Hauskeller's response to the "genetic lottery" argument, see Michael Hauskeller, 'Levelling the Playing Field: On the Alleged Unfairness of the Genetic Lottery', in Steve Clarke, Julian Savulescu, C. A. J. Coady, Alberto Giubilini, and Sagar Sanyal (eds), *The Ethics of Human*

Anna Frammartino Wilks

The capacity of such exacting forms of technology to avoid affecting non-targeted genes and minimise unwanted side-effects entails that the more precise the editing of such genetic material, the more *direct*, and thus less autonomous, the moral bioenhancement of the individual will be. These complicating factors are further accentuated in embryonic genetic manipulation and germline modification, since these interventions bypass completely the autonomy of *future* individuals.[55] Even the most concerted attempts to target moral motivation, which, as we have seen, essentially involve the attempt to enhance *autonomy*, fail to accomplish what is demanded. The main obstacle, in my view, is that usually these attempts are directed at a notion of autonomy that reflects the philosophical tradition Henry Allison refers to as the 'liberty of indifference', which essentially consists in the freedom to choose between alternatives.[56] This notion of autonomy constitutes the basis of the various positions Schaefer, et al. consider in their treatment of the issue, despite their claim that their strategy adopts a neutral stance towards the concept of autonomy. Neutrality on the very definition of autonomy, however, cannot be had, especially when there exist concepts of autonomy directly opposed to that on which Schaefer, et al. establish their claims. One of these is Kant's.

Even though Schaefer, et al. seem to suggest that their position may also accommodate a Kantian conception of autonomy (though the extent to which they think so is left rather ambiguous), I think the evidence for this is slim. They characterise Kant's notion of autonomy as 'an aspect of the will [that] does not just cause one to act, but is also itself uncaused; it moreover involves attending to substantive normative principles that give rise to reasons for action'.[57] They correctly point out that, on the Kantian scheme, 'autonomous judgment amounts to attending to normative reasons, which in turn ground obligation'.[58] Understood in this way, however, it is not clear how autonomy may be enhanced via the enhancement of cognitive

---

Enhancement: Understanding the Debate (Oxford: Oxford University Press, 2016), 202–204.

[55] Dena Davis, 'The Parental Investment Factor and the Child's Right to an Open Future', *The Hastings Centre Report* **39**:2 (2009), 24–27, for example, has expressed this worry. Others, however, do not think this is a valid concern; see, for example, Schaefer, et al., 'Autonomy and Enhancement', 130.

[56] Henry E. Allison, 'Morality and Freedom: Kant's Reciprocity Thesis', *The Philosophical Review* **95**:3 (1986), 393–425, 400.

[57] Schaefer, et al., 'Autonomy and Enhancement', 124.

[58] Schaefer, et al., 'Autonomy and Enhancement', 124.

138

capacities, as suggested by Schaefer, et al., except in an extremely tenuous way. The problem is that the bioenhancement of cognitive capacities is achieved through natural causes. However, the *will*, on Kant's terms, is not a faculty that is determined by natural causes, i.e., natural laws. This, however, does not render the will completely undetermined by *any* laws. Rather, the will is governed by the *moral law* of reason, which the will *legislates to itself*. Kant asserts that

> *will* is a kind of causality of living things insofar as they are rational, and *freedom* would be that property of such causality that it can be efficient independently of alien causes *determining* it. [...] Freedom, although it is not a property of the will in accordance with natural laws, is not for that reason lawless but must instead be a causality in accordance with immutable laws but of a special kind; for otherwise a free will would be an absurdity. [...] What, then, can freedom of the will be other than autonomy, that is, the will's property of being a law to itself?[59]

On this conception of autonomy, it is difficult to see how the bioenhancement of an individual's cognitive or other capacities may be *transferred* to the individual's *will*, thereby enhancing its autonomy. On Kant's view, this transference cannot happen, not even by the most indirect and remote means. The reason is that the will is *free*, i.e., is able to act autonomously, precisely in so far as it is *not* affected by the efficient causality operative in nature; it operates only in accordance with the law of practical reason, i.e., the moral law, which the will legislates to itself. The autonomy of the will cannot be accessed via natural means either to augment or diminish it.

Savulescu and Persson seem to acknowledge that, on a non-reductive, incompatibilist view of free will, autonomy is immune to *direct* effects of moral bioenhancement.[60] They fail to recognise, however, that this conception of autonomy is also immune to effects of *indirect* moral bioenhancement, insofar as those means are *naturalistic*. No bioenhancement of any single capacity, or combination of capacities, could generate the kind of effect on the agent's moral motivation that a Kantian view of moral agency entails. Only reason, through its own practical laws, may motivate the will – though in varying degrees of strength. Thus, even though biological interventions could not

---

[59] Kant, *Groundwork of the Metaphysics of Morals*, 94–95 (AA 4: 446–447).
[60] This point receives extended treatment in Ingmar Persson and Julian Savulescu, 'Moral Bioenhancement, Freedom and Reason', *Neuroethics* **9**:3 (2016), 263–268.

inhibit human autonomy, as Kaebnick and others have argued, there are no grounds for thinking that they could *enhance* it either.[61] Given that the Kantian conception of autonomy is not equivalent to a mere cognitive capacity rooted in a purely neurological phenomenon, it withstands access via natural causes of any kind. Even the more moderate claim that autonomy may be bioenhanced *indirectly*, and as a by-product of the bioenhancement of a complex combination of cognitive capacities, turns out, on this view, to be unjustifiable. Moreover, while some type of compatibilist position might appear to obviate these consequences, it poses the equally weighty challenge of specifying a conception of autonomy robust enough to ground a genuine form of moral agency.

The objective of bioenhancing autonomy through the bioenhancement of cognitive capacities confronts difficulties analogous to those featured in certain theories of consciousness. The difficulty is explaining how conscious experience can arise from the mere combination of purely material, non-conscious elements. The claim that consciousness simply arises from the functional organisation or configuration of completely non-conscious material factors is conceived, by some, as an implausible and inexplicable *brute emergence*.[62] I think the claim that the bioenhancement of moral autonomy could arise from the bioenhancement of cognitive capacities – which are claimed to be neither identical nor equivalent to autonomy – faces a similar problem. The bottom line is that this view requires us to accept some radical form of emergence of an enhanced autonomy from the enhancement of capacities that are merely cognitive in nature. I have no doubt that the enhancement of such capacities may very well increase an individual's general capacity to control their behaviour in some moral contexts, and perhaps considerably

[61] For further discussion of Kantian autonomy, reductionism, and compatibilism in connection with moral bioenhancement see Gregory E. Kaebnick, 'Moral Enhancement, Enhancement, and Sentiment', in Steve Clarke, Julian Savulescu, C. A. J. Coady, Alberto Giubilini, and Sagar Sanyal (eds), *The Ethics of Human Enhancement: Understanding the Debate* (Oxford: Oxford University Press, 2016), 225–238, 228–230. See also Gregory E. Kaebnick, 'Behavioral Genetics and Moral Responsibility', in Erik Parens, Audrey R. Chapman, and Nancy Press (eds), *Wrestling With Behavioral Genetics: Science, Ethics, and Public Conversation* (Baltimore: Johns Hopkins University Press, 2006), 220–234.
[62] David J. Chalmers, in *The Conscious Mind: In Search of a Fundamental Theory* (Oxford and New York: Oxford University Press, 1996), offers a comprehensive treatment of these issues in theories of consciousness.

so. I do not think, however, that this warrants referring to this kind of enhancement as an enhancement of their *autonomy* – at least not on any sense of autonomy that is substantive enough to ground an intelligible account of moral motivation. The kind of autonomy that is essential for moral motivation is neither reducible to, nor emergent from, merely cognitive capacities.

On Kant's non-reductionist and non-emergent account of moral agency, *will* is conceived of as 'a kind of causality belonging to rational beings so far as they are rational'.[63] Kant's notion of *rationality* is construed as 'the capacity to form and act upon general principles'.[64] Kant calls such principles 'maxims', indicating an 'idea of law'. Allison aptly notes that 'a maxim has a purposeful component built into it', either explicitly or implicitly.[65] This purposeful component – some goal, end, or interest – may be either *pure* or *material*. It is pure when the motive of the agent is simply respect for the moral law itself. It is material when the motive of the agent is a sensuous desire for some object of volition. On these terms, the problem of *akrasia*, i.e., weakness of will, consists in the agent's interest in, and pursuit of, some material object. It does not consist in the will's being *determined by* material, i.e., natural, causes. In fact, it is precisely in its inability to be so determined that the will is *free*. Thus, even the phenomenon of *weakness of will* admits of a possible non-naturalistic account. On this view, it is not the *cause* of the will that is material in nature, but rather the *object* that the will chooses to pursue.[66] Thus, the will is still *free*, even when it is *akratic*; it is just not directing its freedom towards the pursuit of the appropriate object, and thus not operating in accordance with maximal autonomy, i.e., moral autonomy.

This account accommodates the view that autonomy admits of degrees, i.e., an agent may be more or less autonomous – as Schaefer, et al. also propose. On a Kantian notion of autonomy, however, what diminishes the degree of the agent's autonomy is not the effect of natural causes acting on it, such as sensuous desires, etc., but rather the *objects* that the will chooses to make the purposeful components of its maxims. The more appropriately the will chooses the objects of its maxims, the more autonomous it will be. In this framework, however, there does not appear to be any way in which autonomy may be bioenhanced – not even indirectly – through the

---

[63]   Allison, *Morality and Freedom: Kant's Reciprocity Thesis*, 400.
[64]   Allison, *Morality and Freedom: Kant's Reciprocity Thesis*, 401.
[65]   Allison, *Morality and Freedom: Kant's Reciprocity Thesis*.
[66]   Kant, *Critique of Practical Reason*, 185–188 (AA 5: 57–59).

bioenhancement of some fundamental cognitive capacities, since any form of bioenhancement involves natural causation, which is completely inefficacious on the will of rational agents.[67]

6. Conclusion

On the analysis I have offered, even the most promising approaches to moral bioenhancement that have been proposed thus far do not, in the end, amount to anything that may properly be considered *moral* enhancement. On the increasingly popular view that moral motivation is central to genuine moral deliberation and agency, and that the autonomy of the moral agent is the fundamental condition for such motivation, enhancing autonomy becomes the ultimate goal in moral bioenhancement projects. In pursuit of this goal, however, both direct and indirect forms of moral bioenhancement seem unviable. The reason is that the various forms both these approaches may take do not affect the agent's autonomy in the relevant manner. Rather, they simply morph into mere punishment, or they amount to enhancement or treatment of a kind other than moral. Inadequate accounts of the biotechnological interventions examined throughout this chapter result in the misidentification of these procedures. As I have argued, such interventions would more accurately be described as either a) cognitive or psychological enhancement, or b) cognitive or psychological treatment – if, indeed, these may be adequately distinguished. In either case, and contrary to what some claim, the chances of mis-firing are, I think, extremely high.[68] More fundamentally, however, if moral agency requires a non-naturalistic type of moral autonomy, as Kant contends, such autonomy is not able to be influenced by naturalistic interventions of any kind. Thus proposals for the possibility of bioenhancing autonomy turn out to be uncompelling, for both metaphysical and empirical reasons.

---

[67] It should be noted that, on this view, even traditional forms of moral enhancement (for example, through moral education) are limited in their effect on the will, as others have also remarked.

[68] One further difficulty, not treated here, is that if genuine voluntary moral bioenhancement were possible, it would give rise to the problem of *free-riders*. The enhanced would be rendered more vulnerable to the actions of unenhanced individuals. Moreover, those individuals who would be most willing to undergo moral enhancement would not necessarily be those in greatest need of it.

This misidentification problem is not merely a verbal dispute. Acknowledging these forms of intervention for what they are, as opposed to what they are not, urges us to exercise greater caution in their use. Conceiving of such interventions and advertising them as autonomy enhancing measures that facilitate moral agency may have the effect of enticing people to avail themselves of these procedures with unreasonable expectations. I conclude, therefore, that once we recognise the real target of moral bioenhancement, we also recognise that we are bound to miss it. This is not to say, however, that I think we should, for these reasons, refrain from any and all such interventions, and that it is inconceivable that they could genuinely "enhance" in some important respects the lives of numerous individuals, and even human society in general. I think they may very well do so, especially with the ever-increasing precision and scope in the advancements of science and technology. I contend, however, that we should refrain from conceiving of such interventions as forms of *moral* bioenhancement, at least until we have a more rational basis for doing so.

Acadia University
anna.wilks@acadiau.ca

Enhancing Care

TEODORA MANEA

> In the sense in which a man can be ever said to be at home
> in the world, he is at home not through dominating,
> or explaining, or appreciating, but through caring and
> being cared for. (M. Mayeroff, *On Caring*).[1]

Abstract
If moral enhancement is possible, the caring capacity of human beings should be
considered one of the first and most important traits for augmentation. To assess
the plausibility of enhancing care, I will explore how the concept and its associated
human dispositions are socially constructed, and identify some of the critical
points and complexities. Scientific advances regarding neuro-enhancing substances
that allegedly make humans more caring will be considered and assessed against the
main principles that govern the ethics of care approach. I argue that given the rela-
tional and contextual nature of care, its enhancement, if targeted at the individual
level, can be more disadvantageous than helpful, by overlooking the "webs of
care" people are situated in, and the role of social institutions in shaping behaviours,
duties, attitudes, and principles.

1. Care as a Moral Category: Semantics, Discourse, Principles, and Webs of Care

The philosophical discourse promoting moral enhancement is
difficult to align with the ethics of care perspective. The former
tries to match technological developments with individuals' interests,
insisting on the necessity of embracing and creating better humans.
After the extensive debate around cognitive enhancement,[2] and the
various critiques stating that more intelligence does not necessarily
make humans better,[3] the field of neuroethics and the possibilities
of moral enhancement have attracted increased attention. Moral
enhancement arguments are constructed around individuals and

---

[1] M. Mayeroff, *On Caring* (New York: Harper Collins, 1971), 2–3.
[2] I. Persson and J. Savulescu, 'The Perils of Cognitive Enhancement
and the Urgent Imperative to Enhance the Moral Character of Humanity',
Journal of Applied Philosophy **25**:3 (2008), 162–176.
[3] M. Hauskeller, *Better Humans? Understanding the Enhancement
Project* (Durham: Acumen, 2013).

doi:10.1017/S1358246118000334   ©The Royal Institute of Philosophy and the contributors 2018
Royal Institute of Philosophy Supplement **83** 2018   145

their brains, infused with elements of evolutionary biology[4] and abstract ethical scenarios – like the ultimatum game[5] or the trolley experiment – and highly simplified models of moral decision making.[6]

The ethics of care, by contrast, adopts a 'different voice' to offer an alternative to the ethical discourse of rights and abstract principles.[7] This perspective focusses on contexts and relationships, and looks closer at social realities in a sustained attempt to make marginal voices heard and to reveal existing vulnerabilities. The obvious question is then how and why these two perspectives – the ethics of care and moral enhancement – intersect. I would argue that although they approach morality from different points of view, both discourses offer a central role to values like *trust* and *altruism*, and so their object of reflection seems to be similar. For this reason, the ethics of care might be able to shed light on any social complexities that are over-looked in the current moral enhancement debate. Looked at from the other angle, one might ask whether the ethics of care would benefit from engaging with the moral enhancement perspective. Although we might be sceptical that it could generate a direct methodological benefit, the idea of enhancing care is *prima facie* worthy of consideration.

The necessity of enhancement has been a constant cultural and philosophical problem. In Greek mythology, human beings came

---

[4] J. Savulescu, 'Unfit for Life: Genetically Enhance Humanity or Face Extinction', 2009: https://vimeo.com/7515623. Savulescu presented an argument about deficient human nature by invoking *love*. He deplored the rate of divorce in contemporary societies, and used evolutionary theories to provide an explanation for our failed monogamy, thereby ignoring socio-economic factors that have empowered women to exit no longer wanted marital relationships.

[5] P. J. Zak, R. Kurzban, S. Ahmadi, R. S. Swerdloff, J. Park, L. Efremidze, K. Redwine, K. Morgan, and W. Matzner, 'Testosterone Administration Decreases Generosity in the Ultimatum Game', *PLoS One* **4**:12 (2009), 1–7.

[6] According to Molly Crockett, an influential neuroscientist, '[t]he science of moral bioenhancement is in its infancy. Laboratory studies of human morality usually employ highly simplified models aimed at measuring just one facet of a cognitive process that is relevant for morality'. M. Crockett, 'Moral Bioenhancement: A Neuroscientific Perspective', *Journal of Medical Ethics* **40**:6 (2014), 370–371, 370.

[7] C. Gilligan, *In a Different Voice: Psychological Theory and Women's Development* (Cambridge, MA: Harvard University Press, 1984).

into existence in a somewhat imperfect condition. Their survival and flourishing was made possible only by a constant enhancement in the form of learning and the acquisition of different arts and crafts, which enabled humans to protect a feeble body, to fight, to better organise, and to keep away all kinds of danger.[8] From this perspective, *enhancement* and humanity are inseparable.

Let us imagine for a moment that there were either a good god or a brave Prometheus to give us a last gift, a last *enhancement* to humans. If there were the possibility to choose one and only one type of enhancement, I would want to make a case for enhancing the human capacity of *care*. Humans are, generally speaking, intelligent enough for all human purposes and have created technologies that assist memory and expand knowledge, from writing to computers. However, we could certainly do with more *care*, in the form of better healthcare, better education, better programmes for the most vulnerable members of society, and greater concern for animals and the environment. At the global level, we should be able to extend our moral feelings and redefine the scope of our responsibilities to accommodate both people in distant countries and ecosystems affected by technological developments and our current lifestyle. At the domestic level, the *relocation of care* in contemporary societies[9] – from the private to the public realm – has generated new structural problems. Institutions entrusted to care often fail in their task: fields of care like health and education are increasingly commodified and marketised as goods designed for economic profit (e.g., universities, private schools).[10]

At the same time as public care is becoming so precarious, often undermined by right-wing governments, private care retains a low social status (e.g., cleaning, nursing the elderly) traditionally associated with women and their domestic "duties". Finally, not only have contemporary societies and globalisation created new types of vulnerability and injustice[11] – like refugees, migrants, or homeless people that cannot afford medical care or education – but, in

[8]   Plato, *Protagoras*, 320b–323a, in B. Jowett (ed.), *The Dialogues of Plato in Five Volumes*, 3rd edn (Oxford: Oxford University Press, 1892).
[9]   S. Sevenhuijsen, 'The Place of Care: The Relevance of the Ethics of Care for Social Policy', in S. Sevenhuijsen and A. Svab (eds), *Labyrinth of Care: The Relevance of the Ethics of Care Perspective for Social Policy* (Ljubljana: Mirovni Institut, 2003), 14–20.
[10]   M. Barnes, *Care in Everyday Life: An Ethic of Care in Practice* (Bristol: Policy Press, 2012).
[11]   V. Held, *The Ethics of Care: Personal, Political and Global* (New York and Oxford: Oxford University Press, 2006).

tandem with this, it is possible that our capacity to care is affected by a type of 'moral myopia' restricting our feeling of responsibility to very small groups or communities.[12]

Clearly, then, it looks as though societies stand to benefit, both nationally and internationally, from programmes aiming to enhance care. Enhancements, however, are not gifts from God, or from science. They are complex processes of negotiation, trial and error, and sacrifice, and many achievements so far – such as improvements to health, sanitation, education, and human rights – have been brought about through institutions created to protect them. Furthermore, there is a methodological question to be considered: should we enhance care by aiming to change individual *dispositions* or *traits*, or should we create better institutional frameworks that encourage and sustain caring *actions*? The answer to this question depends on how care is best understood, and therefore some conceptual analysis courtesy of the ethics of care literature is required.

1.1. Semantic Considerations

Care is a broad notion, starting with the *existential* understanding of care as a fundamental human disposition to engage with others and the world.[13] Accordingly, care is more than a practice between a care giver and a care receiver; it is a way of *understanding* and *positioning* ourselves within relationships.[14] Secondly, from a *sociological* point of view care characterises social relationships, and defines different roles and interactions between individuals, as carer and cared for. These roles, however, are in a constant state of change, and societal understandings of care duties are constantly renegotiated at the individual and institutional levels. If an institution cannot foster caring relationships, the practice of care is compromised. Thirdly, at a *political* level care reflects policy that defines social vulnerability and designs interventions to diminish or end poverty, inequality, or discrimination. With the advent of neoliberalism as an ideological force, care has been *relocated*[15] from the private to the public

---

[12] I. Persson and J. Savulescu, *Unfit for the Future: The Need for Moral Enhancement*, (Oxford: Oxford University Press, 2012), 100–134.

[13] M. Heidegger, *Being and Time*, trans. by J. Stambaugh (New York: SUNY Press, 2010), 174–221.

[14] Barnes, *Care in Everyday Life*.

[15] S. Sevenhuijsen, 'The Place of Care'.

sector, *marketised*[16] – increasing social inequalities – and *dislocated*, in the case of migrants and asylum seekers.[17]

These three levels capture the main dimensions of care. They show at the same time that care as an individual virtue is intrinsically connected and defined by relationships and socio-political context. We care *for* and *about* people and the environment, and we care *about* human rights. Every activity or being that captures our attention and enters our world can benefit from our care; as a fundamental human disposition we identify and recognise things, ideas, or beings in *need* of care. But this very broad definition can lead us into error: sometimes words containing "care" make us rashly assume the existence of it, as, for example, in institutionalised care – health*care*, or *care* homes. Even though those institutions were designed in accordance with what we felt to be right at a certain point, they require constant analysis and evaluation.[18] Money "saved" on social care can compromise meaningful care practices and negatively affect the vulnerable. At the same time, those measures put more pressure on carers, generating wide social discussions about doctors and nurses having to work long shifts, teachers with overcrowded classes, and care workers who are abused and underpaid.[19]

The precise meaning of "enhancing care" also needs to be clarified. For the purpose of this chapter – namely, to engage with the moral enhancement debate – my focus will be more on what happens when we enhance care at an individual level. There are at least two ways to enhance care in this sense: by 1) making more acute our capacity to *recognise* and *assess* vulnerabilities or care needs, or by 2) improving our present ability to *perform* care (e.g., continuing to care without sleep, or having an increased physical and emotional strength to cope with difficult situations). Regarding the latter, such enhancement already exists: targeting the ability to focus on a task for a long time is used by pilots and the military. Although this form of

---

[16] Held, *The Ethics of Care*.

[17] T. Manea, 'Medical Bribery and the Ethics of Trust: The Romanian Case', *Journal of Medicine and Philosophy* **40**:1 (2015), 26–43.

[18] M. Barnes, *Care in Everyday Life*, and J. C. Tronto, *Caring Democracy: Markets, Equality, and Justice* (New York and London: New York University Press, 2013).

[19] Alexandra Ricard-Guay and Thanos Maroukis, 'Human Trafficking in Domestic Work in the EU: A Special Case or a Learning Ground for the Anti-Trafficking Field?', *Journal of Immigrant & Refugee Studies* **15**:2 (2017), 109–121.

enhancing care seems to be desirable (in the health service for example), often it can lead to the exploitation of people, making them work long hours and damaging their well-being.[20]

For the purpose of this chapter I will focus more on care as an *activity*, although it is hard to separate it from the *dispositions* that make people care for others. I understand care as a personal capability that can be expressed and realised only as part of a complex *life-sustaining web* that maintains, repairs, and consolidates our *world*.[21] My central point is that in isolation care has no meaning. It is an interpersonal activity, needing the other for its existence. It is worth mentioning that although care presupposes a certain degree of altruism – especially at the dispositional level – altruism and care as activities can be different. Altruism, even if is done with the other in mind, does not necessarily depend on the feedback of another person. Someone can offer money to a charity, or build a school for a poor village from an altruistic disposition. Their action is deeply moral, no doubt. But care would entail direct engagement by teaching the children, or by implementing the charity programme into the community. Care involves a personal engagement, whereas altruism can be remote and impersonal.

My overall argument is that aiming to enhance care at the individual level, and ignoring the web of care a person is in, can be detrimental for society and for individuals. A meaningful enhancement of care should rather aim at revealing the webs, examining them so that we could better understand which social practices are able to generate and sustain care.

1.2. The Ethics of Care Discourse

Care and caring have received a lot of attention from feminist philosophy, starting with Nell Noddings and Carol Gilligan and continuing in the present with writers like Joan Tronto, Virginia Held, Marian Barnes, and others. Generally, this field focusses on relationships, emotions, contexts, vulnerabilities, and needs. A common criticism is that the contextual character of this perspective compromises the

---

[20] John Temple, 'Resident Duty Hours Around the Globe: Where Are We Now?', *BMC Medical Education* **14**:Suppl. 1 (2014).

[21] J. C. Tronto, *Moral Boundaries: A Political Argument for an Ethic of Care* (London and New York: Routledge, 1993), 103; B. Fisher and J. C. Tronto, 'Toward a Feminist Theory of Caring', in E. K. Abel and M. Nelson (eds), *Circles of Care* (Albany: SUNY Press, 1990) 35–62.

universality and applicability of ethics.[22] However, it is by no means clear whether the aim of ethics is to prescribe general rules for the decontextualised individual, or rather to bind together local communities. The recognition of contextual problems, beliefs, attitudes, and specificities is attuned to postmodern thought,[23] and can generate a flexible framework that should be adapted to the needs of different communities. Only the rejection of a totalising metaphysics can ensure that we avoid othering and the danger of what Rorty calls *final vocabularies*.[24] General ideas and principles of action – often being the content of dangerous ideologies – can lead to overlooking individual suffering or minority interests. Ethics should instead be understood as embedded and analysed together with societal constructions that regulate particular social interactions. An Inuit community and a Central African village function in different ways: there are correspondingly different models of care and relationships. It is hard to say from the comfort of a Western office what problems and vulnerabilities people there face. Thus, the focus on context is more than legitimate and presupposes a general recognition of human diversity, because 'morality does not come in one homogeneous and internally consistent chunk, but in various bits and pieces. It is, in one word, multidimensional'.[25]

Caring is also a personal virtue and a normative concept: for example, when a relationship is classified as being or not being *caring*. Is there something that we can say *a priori* about care, abstracted from all empirical content? What do caring relationships have in common – caring for a child, an elderly parent, or a patient? Is there an "Idea of care"? Certainly, we can trace our representations of care back to our memory and to previous experiences: we learn to care very early, as part of our socialisation, but care might also have an instinctive basis, something that we share with non-human animals.[26] Then again, some authors think that there is 'no recipe for good

[22] J. Rachels, *The Elements of Moral Philosophy* (San Francisco: McGraw-Hill, 1999).
[23] R. Rorty, *Contingency, Irony, and Solidarity* (Cambridge: Cambridge University Press, 1989).
[24] Rorty, *Contingency, Irony, and Solidarity*, 70–75.
[25] M. Hauskeller, 'The Art of Misunderstanding Critics: The Case of Persson and Savulescu's Defence of Moral Bioenhancement', *Cambridge Quarterly of Healthcare Ethics* **24**:1 (2015), 48–57.
[26] J. Donovan and C. J. Adams, *Beyond Animal Rights: A Feminist Caring Ethic for the Treatment of Animals* (New York: Colombia University Press, 1996).

care'.[27] Arthur W. Frank, for instance, emphasises the subtle character of care and the fact that a proper 'job description' of care is impossible to give. Care surrounds humans and other animals throughout their life in a silent and unobtrusive way: only its failure is noticeable. The concept is not only broad, but it is also quite diffuse, informed by traditions, a multiplicity of associated practices, and the ambiguity of perceptions. Care has always been subtle, diffuse, disseminated between other activities, and somewhat elusive. It reflects and reproduces the characteristics and quiet voices of people involved in care practices.

1.3. On the Principles of Care

Let us imagine that we have deciphered all complicated hormonal codes in our brains and bodies, and can harness their potential. There would, then, be the possibility of moral enhancement, so that we might even be able to create more caring individuals. If there is a kind of recipe for creating *caring persons*, the main ingredients of it should accord with the following principles.

Joan Tronto identifies six principles[28] of care that reflect not only characteristics of actions, but also personal attributes: *attentiveness, responsibility, competence, responsiveness, trust,* and *respect.*[29] To this list I would add *commitment*. It is immediately clear that these involve our cognitive *and* emotional capacities, so that a respective moral enhancement would have to consider modifications in both senses.[30] I will describe these principles and examine whether some "moral molecules" (like oxytocine) can play a role in their enhancement.

Attentiveness is the practice of *caring about* ideas and beings. It is defined by Marion Barnes as: the *awareness* and *recognition* of the need for care.[31] Tronto emphasised that in order to recognise and be attentive to others, we should be able to *suspend* our own

[27]   A. W. Frank, *At the Will of the Body: Reflections on Illness* (Chicago: University of Chicago Press, 1995), 42–50.
[28]   The term "principle" is not entirely adequate here, but it is present in the care literature. As I have mentioned before, the ethics of care – with its focus on context and relationships – differs from principlism. A better term would be "characteristics".
[29]   Tronto, *Moral Boundaries.*
[30]   For the debate regarding the primacy of cognitive enhancement for enhancing morality, see: J. Harris, *How to Be Good* (Oxford: Oxford University Press, 2016).
[31]   Barnes, *Care in Everyday Life,* 20; Sevenhuijsen, 'The Place of Care', 20.

ambitions, life plans, and concerns.[32] Ethicists of care point out that our duty of care does not encompass only a private concern for known others, but also a broad recognition of social and cultural factors or circumstances that affect people that we do not know personally.[33]

From the ties of friendship, kinship, and other specific contexts, attentiveness for others has been progressively – but so far incompletely – implemented in international politics aiming towards global justice and responsibility. Global warming, refugee crises, and migration in general are just a few cases that show the efforts and the failure of our present caring activities. A capitalist and individualistic model of thinking might question the extent of our responsibility for the socio-economic disparities of the world. Recent political developments, including the denial of environmental responsibility[34] and halting of child refugee programmes,[35] remind us that decades of moral effort invested in caring about others are easily reversed. It is incontestable that the measure of our moral behaviour is given by the scope of our self-defined responsibility, but the two examples above have less to do with individual dispositions; they instead reflect questionable governmental policies. The role of democratic institutions – from parliament to the judiciary and a free press – is to react to those policies and eventually to inform them.

Responsibility means *taking care* of things, having the *willingness* and the *capacity* to address an identified need.[36] How can we make people more responsible? A traditional answer is through *education*. The more we know about the past, the deeper we understand the complexity of social and international relationships, and the more

---

[32] Tronto, *Moral Boundaries*, 128.

[33] Barnes *Care in Everyday Life*; Held, *The Ethics of Care*.

[34] In the USA the *Climate Action Plan* (2013) is set to be replaced by the *America First Energy Plan*: 'President Trump is committed to eliminating harmful and unnecessary policies such as the Climate Action Plan and the Waters of the U.S. rule. Lifting these restrictions will greatly help American workers, increasing wages by more than $30 billion over the next 7 years' (White House, 2017).

[35] E. Addley, 'Why Has the UK Ended its "Dubs" Child Refugee Scheme?', *The Guardian*, 10th February 2017: https://www.theguardian.com/uk-news/2017/feb/10/why-has-the-uk-ended-its-dubs-child-refugee-scheme.

[36] Sevenhuijsen, 'The Place of Care', 21.

we might comprehend our position and role in the present historical moment.

It is hard to imagine a drug that increases responsibility, because responsibility deals with different types of emotions, sometimes even with contradictory feelings. Responsibility can take the form of providing constant care for someone, or it can drive people who suddenly identify with a cause or an acute need to take drastic action. Should we, therefore, enhance our *willingness* to take risks with testosterone? For instance, Suffragettes, or animal or human rights activists, put themselves in a great deal of danger trying to take care of the vulnerable beings they choose to speak for and to protect. But equally, responsibility can involve quiet and supportive love. The delicate balance of those two is decided predominantly by external circumstances and not so much by individual hormones. Some might suggest that the use of cognitive enhancement[37] represents a solution – however, intelligence alone is not a sufficient and sometimes not even a necessary condition of caring.[38]

Competence is an essential ingredient of *care giving*. It is not enough to provide care, but care should have a certain *quality*; it should properly address relevant needs. Examples from care homes, hospitals, and schools illustrate the necessity of this principle. The way competence is assessed directs the discourse towards what society designs as *caring institutions*.[39] They can be analysed from the community level (schools, hospitals) to the national (judiciary systems and national protection systems for workers or the disabled) and at the international level (international organisations, forums, unions). *Caring* institutions incorporate certain suppositions about needs, vulnerability, power, and responsibility. Even if the individual competence of a mother to take care of her baby seems to be regulated by oxytocin, creating *institutional competence* is a meta-individual, abstract, and bureaucratic procedure. Democratic institutions, for example, can be enhanced by having dedicated politicians, but those institutions will have to pass the Popperian test, meaning that they preserve their principles even if corrupt or bad politicians are in office.[40] Applying this to the present topic, caring institutions should be built in a way that careless individuals who might be

---

[37] Harris, *How to Be Good.*
[38] Tronto, *Caring Democracy*, 54–63.
[39] Tronto, *Moral Boundaries.*
[40] Karl R. Popper, *The Open Society and Its Enemies* (London: Routledge, 1945).

employed there will not have any chance to derail the caring processes. Hospital and care home abuses revealed in recent years prove that there is still space for improving these institutions and thereby care competence.

Responsiveness pertains to *care-receiving*. There is a subtle dialectic between the care-giver and the receiver of care that is reflected in successful or unsuccessful caring processes. For one thing, we cannot force someone to accept care. The relationship between a care-giver and a care-receiver typically reflects an inequality of power.[41] The problem with this is that vulnerability is sometimes shameful and people are not always happy to recognise or accept it. We have to remember that every one of us can be and will be at certain times in a vulnerable position. By accepting the position of care-recipient, one submits to the power of the care-giver, responsiveness to which ideally takes the form of positive feedback to something both parties understand as care and caring. But sometimes being in the position of a care-receiver can be damaging to people who have constructed their identity (only) as independent and autonomous individuals. One suspects that the prevalence and pervasiveness of neoliberal ideology has encouraged people to think about themselves in this way. Regardless, to properly enhance care in this context means to change the present understanding of what we are. The phase of our lives marked by youth, as active, successful individuals, is for most of us a short one: illness, disability, age, and familial commitments have to be incorporated into our self-understanding, and with them an acceptance of care practices.

Trust was one of the principles of care underlined by Selma Sevenhuijsen,[42] and seems to be where oxytocin promises great things.[43] What is trust? Starting with the basic interpersonal level, we trust different people with different things, or even the same person to different degrees depending on the action or opinion in question. For example, someone can trust a friend to take care of their dog, but not trust their political judgement. A partner can be trusted with essential things – from fidelity, to children's education, finances, and provision for the family – but distrusted for other

---

[41] Barnes, *Care in Everyday Life*; Tronto, *Moral Boundaries*, 136.
[42] S. Sevenhuijsen, *Citizenship and the Ethics of Care*, trans. by L. Savage (London and New York: Routledge, 1998).
[43] H. Wiseman, *The Myth of Moral Brain: The Limits of Moral Enhancement* (Cambridge, MA: MIT Press, 2016), 88–93.

activities such as cooking, choosing the right wine, or caring for plants. Relationships compartmentalise roles and responsibilities; negotiate permanently areas of "excellence". A successful relationship is not based on an *average* trust for *all* domains, but a *total* trust in *some* of those areas. Each partner might have a particular idea about priorities, or what necessary and sufficient care is. Should we use cognitive enhancement to change their epistemological capacity,[44] or should we use oxytocin ourselves to accept them unconditionally and enjoy a happier relationship? Some may argue that if we had the same degree of intelligence and knowledge – helped possibly by enhanced cognition (about politics, wine, and plants) – trusting someone might be easier. But still people have different interests and different past experiences, situations, and other ingredients that make them what they are. Trying to change someone implies a paternalistic attitude, a lack of *respect* for who and what that person is.[45]

Respect was added to the definition of care by Daniel Engster.[46] In caring, respect should be a reciprocal value. People in vulnerable situations need it and caring people usually deserve it as well. However, respect is shaped by different and complex factors, from early education to general societal attitudes. Respect for a patient, a child, or a homeless person cannot be taken for granted: there is a difference between the type of respect imposed by law, regarding individual rights, and the type of respect experienced even in situations when there are no rights to compel our attitudes. If the first type of respect can be connected with a certain type of authority, and even fear of being punished,[47] the second type relies on empathy, openness, and understanding. For example, there is no law that compels people to respect their pets. There are regulations regarding animal welfare and prohibiting cruelty, but not for respecting a dog's autonomy. I understand autonomy here not as an abstract ethical value, but a contextual manifestation of free will.[48] What I mean is that relationships are the condition of possibility for the manifestation of free will:

---

[44]   As John Harris would presumably suggest.
[45]   M. Hauskeller, *Better Humans?*
[46]   D. Engster, *The Heart of Justice: Care Ethics and Political Theory* (Oxford: Oxford University Press, 2007).
[47]   For example, when someone respects the speed limit in an area because of speed cameras, although accelerating will not put anybody immediately in danger because the road at this exact time is empty.
[48]   M.A. Fineman, *The Autonomy Myth: A Theory of Dependency* (New York: The New Press, 2004).

others are co-creators of our sense of liberty and entitlement. Regarding the dog example, the fact that an owner stops to allow her dog to sniff a wall or to eat a particular blade of grass leads the dog to have expect that her owner will support this particular preference. If a dog, or a human being, is consistently prevented in their relationships from realising certain interests, their behaviour and sense of liberty might well change. In other words, respect is a condition of liberty. But there are two different types of respect: respect for laws and rights, and respect for the other in a relationship. To chemically manipulate respect, we would most likely have to target totally different groups of "moral molecules" and it is questionable if science currently allows for this, or ever will.[49]

Commitment has so far not been theorised as a principle of care, but in analysing different types of moral enhancement interventions it becomes clear that they target generally moral *traits* or dispositions, and *actions*.[50] Discussing the structure of morality in order to identify at which level Persson and Savulescu's moral enhancement project is aiming, Nicholas Agar has drawn attention to the difference between moral *motivation*, moral *cognition* – knowing what is good – and moral *action*.[51] Reflection on the complexity of moral action involved in care reveals the necessity of adding to this structure another key element: moral *commitment*, which is a kind of "temporal test" for our moral actions.

Regarding climate change, Persson and Savulescu's key concern, it is clear that care for the future of the planet is insufficient if only ephemeral: it is not enough to now and then refrain from using the car. The disposition and the impulse to act – or not act – is necessary, but not sufficient for changing moral behaviour that has distant or unclear consequences. While commitment is generally recognised as an ethical value, it is pointless to demand commitment if society does not offer an institutional framework to harness and reward meaningful actions.

2. The Relevance of Care for Moral Enhancement

On the basis of the preceding, I shall summarise the main points where the ethics of care can contribute to the moral enhancement

[49] Crockett, 'Moral Bioenhancement', 370–371.

[50] M. Hauskeller, 'The Art of Misunderstanding Critics', 48–50.

[51] N. Agar, 'Moral Bioenhancement is Dangerous', *Journal of Medical Ethics* **41**:4 (2013), 343–354.

debate. Firstly, it demonstrates the need to emphasise the role of *relationships* and *context*.[52] Secondly, the main characteristics of care illustrate that the idea of *autonomous individuals* needs to be fundamentally revised. With its revision, the whole project of targeting individuals with moral enhancement – for example by giving them the option to take it or not – becomes moot. Wider contexts, interests, relationships, family, and community structures need to be considered, and in doing so concerns about liberty gain a new immediacy. Thirdly, the ethics of care brings forward the relevance of *commitment* as an additional element to be considered alongside moral traits and actions. The final point I would like to make regards the distinction between *therapy* and *enhancement* in the case of care. The reason for invoking this somewhat "classic" distinction is that a lot of examples used in the moral enhancement debates which relate to caring, or contain components of care, are in fact therapy cases.

The distinction between therapy and enhancement is a pivotal one for the enhancement debate; it is better to keep it in place[53] than to replace it with that between soft and hard enhancement as Wiseman has suggested.[54] When applying this distinction to care some characteristics of care are made more prominent. The "therapy of care" should aim to restore care to a socially acceptable level. I specify a "socially acceptable level" and not "species normal-functioning" because for the moral domain biological standards are less relevant than in the question of enhancing physical traits. Socially acceptable standards of care differ from one society to the other. I will illustrate this with a straightforward and basic activity of care, the one of a mother for her baby. Even if there is a strong presence of biological factors in this case, what is expected from a mother as "acceptable care" differs between societies. Written and unwritten social norms define the optimal body shape of the mothers (e.g., how acceptable it is to be fat or not during pregnancy), whether breastfeeding is a must or not, the amount of maternity paid leave (determining for how long a mother should be home with her baby), the possibility of paternity leave, room and home arrange-

---

[52]   Ideas already developed by other ethicists (e.g. R. Sparrow and M. Hauskeller), albeit from different perspectives.
[53]   R. Sparrow, 'Better Living Through Chemistry? A Reply to Savulescu and Persson on "Moral Enhancement"', *Journal of Applied Philosophy* **31**:1 (2014), 23–32.
[54]   H. Wiseman, *The Myth of the Moral Brain*, 8–9.

ments, etc. A basic engagement between the mother and the baby is expected to happen: when it is absent, mental health issues, like postpartum depression, are explored and tackled (in the UK, at least). This is a case of "therapy of care". An *enhancement* of care would be to bring care *above* the socially-expected capacity: for example, creating "super-mums" that breastfeed their children for the exactly right amount of time – a topic which is still controversial across Western cultures – and never get tired, stressed, or depressed. Branching out from mothers, we can imagine creating housewives that are caring and loving, like Ira Levin's *Stepford Wives:*[55] perfect women 'without the flaws', 'perfectly usable, obedient and ready to serve'.[56] With the last example, it is easy to see how crossing the line between therapy and enhancement immediately causes alarms to ring regarding freedom, autonomy, and respect.

In the context of a care home, "enhanced carers" could mean: physically stronger, more perceptive, sleepless, and even immune to smells and disgust. For doctors, we can imagine enhancing their ability to perform long operations or long shifts without being tired or distracted. For teachers, perhaps more empathetic capacities, attention, and other cognitive abilities allowing them to understand and know every individual child – even in state schools with overcrowded classrooms! – and to find the best ways to motivate them. In all of these examples, regarding possible "care enhancements", the focus is on individuals. My main criticism is that this approach is not only hard to implement – why would anyone wish for it? – but also dangerous for individuals and for the social fabric. The social danger comes from keeping poor structures in place: overcrowded classrooms, long hospital shifts, low status and badly paid care work, gender inequalities, and asymmetries in parental obligations and duties. To agree that enhancing care at the individual level is the solution for our society's needs entails an acceptance of common social practices as morally just and to stop any social critique of or change in our present day institutions. It means stopping our efforts to recognise dysfunctional activities, abuses, and inequalities. On this basis, I suggest that our "natural" moral progress over time – perhaps the only consistent and safe "moral enhancement" – would cease. Chemical solutions targeting individual enhancements might lead to even more

[55] I. Levin, *The Stepford Wives* (London: Constable and Robinson, 2011).
[56] M. Hauskeller, *Sex and the Posthuman Condition* (Basingstoke: Palgrave Macmillan, 2014), 28, 40.

inequalities, abuses, and further ignorance of the complexity of caring relationships and contexts.

3. Limitations and Worries

One might argue that care is just one aspect of our moral behaviour. This is true, but it is also true that early experiences of care might affect the way people develop and act later in life.[57] An analysis of care can only enrich the moral enhancement debate.

Another limitation follows from the very nature of care practices: long term commitment to care can lead to a feeling of overwhelming obligation at the expense of freedom. Taking care of children or elderly parents, no matter with how much love, dedication, or attentiveness, can be frustrating at times. Without institutions of care in place, and without social recognition of these practices, dedicated people can be at risk of abuse. Similarly, morally enhanced people can be subjects of abuse at the hands of other people or socio-political institutions. This shows that without pre-existing social structures for morality that are practically proven to be just and responsible, individual moral enhancement could even be dangerous.

Another concern is that moral enhancement conforms to 'the magic bullet syndrome'[58] of present Western societies: namely, where pharmaceutical companies and a broader paradigm characterised by 'biological materialism'[59] contribute to the 'magic solution' of problems themselves caused by certain lifestyles and social influences. These problems were quickly medicalised, pathologised, and associated with certain 'chemical deficiencies'.[60] For example, depression has been connected with low levels of serotonin, and schizophrenia

---

[57] J. A. Bartz, J. Zaki, K. N. Ochsner, N. Bolger, A. Kolevzon, N. Ludwig, J. E. Lydon, and S. E. Taylor, 'Effects of Oxytocin on Recollections of Maternal Care and Closeness', *Proceedings of the National Academy of Sciences of the United States of America*, **107**:50 (2010), 21371–21375.

[58] P. J. Zak, *The Moral Molecule: The New Science of What Makes Us Good or Evil* (London: Bantam Press 2012); P. J. Zak and A. Fakhar, 'Neuroactive Hormones and Interpersonal Trust: International Evidence', *Economics and Human Biology* **4**:3 (2006), 412–429.

[59] E. Martin, *Bipolar Expeditions: Mania and Depression in American Culture* (Princeton and Oxford: Princeton University Press, 2007).

[60] C. Elliott, *Better Than Well: American Medicine Meets the American Dream* (New York: W. W. Norton & Co., 2004).

with dopamine malfunctions. Moncrieff's analysis showed that instead of addressing the socio-economic causes of depression, medicine was given as a quick fix.[61] Similarly, if the presence of *care* or trust are connected with increased levels of oxytocin, focussing on the connection between morality and bio-chemistry, then wider social contexts that determine the quality and quantity of care will be overlooked.[62]

4. Conclusion: Webs of Care

The complexity of the brain's networks and connections are mirrored in the complexity of our relationships. In *Unfit for the Future*, Persson and Savulescu argued for the urgent necessity of moral enhancement, given that our *technological power*, together with *liberal democratic* freedom and *moral myopia*, imperil human existence. Their observation is correct, at least at first glance. But as Hauskeller notes, humans have already considerably expanded their circles of moral concern, so that they do not relate only with their own 'kin and a small circle of acquaintances', but also with people from different countries, societies and races.[63]

With a full acknowledgment of people as situated in their webs of care, or by making visible the webs of care that surround us, we can no longer maintain an ethical concept of "individuals" as autonomous, independent, and abstract agents. Human life builds up in *clusters* of people and not in isolation.[64] Moral decisions are influenced by others, directly or indirectly, and the morality of an action has significance only with the other in mind. The tensions, relationships, and dynamics of those clusters go beyond biological or evolutionary explanations. Biological factors are present, of course, and the

---

[61] J. Moncrieff, *The Myth of the Chemical Cure: A Critique of Psychiatric Drug Treatment* (Basingstoke and New York: Palgrave Macmillan, 2008); and J. Moncrieff, *The Bitterest Pill* (Basingstoke and New York: Palgrave Macmillan, 2013).

[62] S. Vreko, 'Folk Neurology and the Remaking of Identity', *Molecular Interventions* 6:6 (2006), 300–303.

[63] M. Hauskeller, 'Is it Desirable to Be Able to Do the Undesirable? Moral Bioenhancement and the Little Alex Problem', *Cambridge Quarterly of Healthcare Ethics* 26:3 (2017), 365–375.

[64] T. Manea, 'Care for Carers: Care Issues in the Context of Medical Migration', in Marian Barnes, Tula Brannelly, Lizzie Ward, and Nicki Ward (eds), *Ethics of Care: Critical International Perspectives* (Bristol: Policy Press, 2015), 207–219.

Teodora Manea

neurosciences can reveal and help us understand these aspects of morality. But seeing the complexity and the interconnectivity of our moral actions, it is clearly difficult, if not impossible, to isolate certain moral traits and declare them to be "good" or "bad" in themselves.[65] Ambition can be good and bad; aggression can sometimes be a lifesaver, or used to start a political protest against a pernicious law, or to fight against discrimination. Excessive care, too, can be damaging for a child who needs space to experiment in taking risks and in life in general. There are no optimal levels of alertness, aggression, love, care, or bonding. Rather, all are produced by subtle and constant feedback processes involving moral feelings and the actions triggered, defined, and provoked by our web of care.

Regarding our alleged "moral myopia", another question arises: why and how do we extend our web of care? Modern technology entails that our social networks extend far beyond the physical space that once defined a community. People have "friends" around the globe with whom they share common interests, affinities, and parts of their life. To connect with someone presupposes the acknowledgement of some sort of commonalities that can generate empathy, love, or other feelings. Those commonalities – the knots of the web – can be totally contingent, like past life events, similar cases, people that resemble other people we cared about, or even a certain type of atmospheric situation brought about by a book, a film, or some other experience. It will be hard to explain the hormonal changes triggered by *Guernica* or the *Moonlight Sonata*, partly because different people will have different reactions. Yet those differences make us what we are.

In order to be more caring, at least in the sense of cultivating our attentiveness, there is a need to extend our particular group in order to connect with people that are not normally part of it. Can we artificially create or trigger commonalities and make new *web knots*? The picture of a dead child washed to the shore changed Europe's attitude towards war refugees. What was it in the picture that made us care? Perhaps the response was based on the fact that most of us have children. But what made the knot stronger was the realisation of our cruelty, the same cruelty analysed by Rorty, which is not in a particular action or disposition, but rather the absence of both, the indifference. We begin to step out of our cruel indifference when we learn to recognise possible commonalities and train our attentiveness. Commonalities are strengthened by

---

[65]   M. Hauskeller, 'Being Good Enough to Prevent the Worst', *Journal of Medical Ethics* **41**:4 (2014), 289–290.

recognising the insecurity of our world, and a possible reversibility of our historical *situatedness*. The way we perceive refugees is different, because perception and understanding is designed by personal experience, history, memory, events, or even capacity of understanding. Analysing the *situatedness* of each of us and the situatedness of our *clusters of care*, though complicated, could be achieved through the better cultivation of moral sensitivity. Finding a neurochemical equivalent of it seems at best a very remote possibility. To conclude, if we could hope for a possibility to enhance care, the answer is not juggling hormones at the individual level, but revealing and mending our social webs of care.

University of Exeter
etm205@exeter.ac.uk

Moral-Epistemic Enhancement

NORBERT PAULO

Abstract

The idea of using biomedical means to make people more likely to behave morally may have a certain appeal. However, it is very hard to find two persons – let alone two moral philosophers – who agree on what it means to be moral or to act morally. After discussing some of the proposals for moral enhancements that all ethicists could agree on, I engage more closely with the recent idea of "procedural moral enhancement" that aims at improving deliberative processes instead of particular moral views, motivations, or dispositions. I argue that it is better understood as a contribution to moral epistemology and should thus be labeled "moral-epistemic enhancement". I then defend perspective-taking as a moral epistemic capacity which can be enhanced by both traditional and non-traditional biomedical means; a capacity which almost always contributes to the epistemic value of moral decision-making. Perspective-taking seems to be an uncontroversial non-trivial capacity for moral decision-making reasonably widely shared by proponents of ethical beliefs within the academic community. The enhancement of this capacity is thus a good candidate for an uncontroversial non-trivial moral enhancement.

1. Introduction: Moral Bioenhancement Without Uncontroversial Presuppositions?

The idea of using biomedical means to make people more likely to behave morally may have a certain appeal. Who would be against a world with more moral behaviour? However, it is very hard to find two persons – let alone two moral philosophers – who agree on what it means to be moral or to act morally. Some proponents of the idea of moral bioenhancement (roughly, the use of biomedical means to enhance people's moral dispositions)[1] try to circumvent the problem of determining what it is to be moral by invoking changes in humans that seem relatively uncontroversial, such as enhanced empathy. Unfortunately, there do not seem to be any *non-trivial substantial*

---

[1] For puzzles concerning the precise definition of moral enhancement, see Kasper Raus, et al., 'On Defining Moral Enhancement: A Clarificatory Taxonomy', *Neuroethics* **7**:3 (2014), 263–273; Brian D. Earp, Thomas Douglas, and Julian Savulescu, 'Moral Neuroenhancement', in L. Syd, M. Johnson, and Karen S. Rommelfanger (eds), *Routledge Handbook of Neuroethics* (New York: Routledge, 2017) 166–184.

doi:10.1017/S1358246118000346

moral dispositions of which it would be uncontroversial to say that to act on them is morally good in all circumstances. Empathy, to stick with this example, might be a good disposition to have in many (if not most) circumstances. Similarly, being more empathic would be morally better than being less empathic in most circumstances. But empathy can also yield immoral behaviour, for instance if it makes people unreasonably favourable to the members of their particular in-group and unreasonably hostile to members of out-groups;[2] it might also lead to or deepen morally questionable forms of partiality.[3] As far as I can see, an uncontroversial non-trivial moral disposition has not yet been found. Also, some authors doubt that the empirical findings are promising for the idea of moral enhancement.[4]

However, one might argue that the need to find moral dispositions that are uncontroversial would not necessarily pose a problem for more restrained understandings of moral bioenhancement. Suppose you are a proponent of effective altruism. As such you could argue that it would be morally good if everyone were to have enhanced dispositions to act more altruistically. This would be a restrained understanding of moral bioenhancement – *moral bioenhancement for effective altruists*, say – as opposed to moral bioenhancement *for all ethicists**, i.e., an enhancement of which moral philosophers of all stripes would agree that it truly enhances morality.[5]

Another possibility to make sense of the idea of moral bioenhancement is to argue that even if there is no uncontroversial non-trivial moral disposition, some moral dispositions seem to be so widely

[2] Cf. Jesse Prinz, 'Against Empathy', *The Southern Journal of Philosophy* **49**:1 (2011), 214–33; Paul Bloom, *Against Empathy: The Case for Rational Compassion* (New York: Ecco, 2016).

[3] See Brian Feltham and John Cottingham (eds), *Partiality and Impartiality: Morality, Special Relationships, and the Wider World* (Oxford; New York: Oxford University Press, 2010).

[4] For instance, Veljko Dubljević and Eric Racine, 'Moral Enhancement Meets Normative and Empirical Reality: Assessing the Practical Feasibility of Moral Enhancement Neurotechnologies', *Bioethics* **31**:5 (2017), 338–48; Harris Wiseman, *The Myth of the Moral Brain: The Limits of Moral Enhancement* (Cambridge, MA: MIT Press, 2016), chap. 4 and 5.

[5] I hasten to add that the demand to find a disposition about which literally all ethicists agree that it enhances morality is arguably too high; there are always outliers defending views almost no peers find persuasive. I use "all ethicists" here and in what follows as a short way to express a more qualified demand – something like "all proponents of ethical beliefs reasonably widely shared within the current academic community". I indicate this use with an asterisk.

accepted that they can be used as a guideline for what we might want to enhance biomedically if we wish to enhance moral behaviour. After all, the world religions would appear to share a moral core; and even most nation states apparently share some form of common-sense morality. Without such a core, we would not be able to agree on what should be considered criminal conduct, which human rights to adopt, whether or not to combat climate change, how to regulate global trade, and even which morals our children should be taught at school,[6] or so the argument goes.[7]

But what exactly is that moral core? Is there any non-trivial moral disposition that is universally accepted, one that is not relative to a certain culture or historical period? One might reject the idea of such a moral core out of hand, given the seemingly widespread moral relativity within any given modern-day plural society, let alone across the world and across the centuries. However, moral relativity of views publicly articulated does not necessarily imply that an underlying moral core cannot be reconstructed. In fact, some philosophers have argued for a *universal common-sense morality* that is not relative to culture or historical period, in contrast to the many particular moralities, which consist of relatively concrete

[6] In Austria, teaching empathy is one explicit aim of ethics classes in school, although as we have seen, it is said to not always be conducive to moral behaviour. So proponents of moral bioenhancement might want to argue we should not be asking more of moral bioenhancement than of traditional forms of moral education. After all, when we accept empathy as a proper aim of *moral* education in schools, we should also be willing to call biomedical enhancements of empathy *moral* enhancement. However, the fact that higher levels of empathy are regarded as being sufficiently morally valuable to be included in the school curriculum does not answer the philosophical question of whether enhanced empathy would be *moral* enhancement. After all, school policy can err; the mere fact that in some school districts creationism is taught should not in itself count as evidence for the belief that creationism is scientifically credible. Similarly, biomedical enhancements of empathy might count as moral enhancements for Austrian ethics teachers, but certainly not for all ethicists*.

[7] This line of argument can be found in Ingmar Persson and Julian Savulescu, 'The Art of Misunderstanding Moral Bioenhancement: Two Cases', *Cambridge Quarterly of Healthcare Ethics* **24**:1 (2015), 48–57. For the somewhat similar idea of an 'overlapping consensus' see David DeGrazia, 'Moral Enhancement, Freedom, and What We (Should) Value in Moral Behaviour', *Journal of Medical Ethics* **40**:6 (2014): 361–368; and the critique in Norbert Paulo and Jan Christoph Bublitz, 'How (Not) to Argue For Moral Enhancement: Reflections on a Decade of Debate', *Topoi* (2017), doi:10.1007/s11245-017-9492-6.

norms that are not universal, such as (some) religious or legal norms. The concept of a common (or common-sense) morality owes much to Alan Donagan,[8] whose natural-law and Kant-inspired ethics was very influential in North American philosophy in the late 1970s. It is no coincidence that two widely discussed moral theories by American ethicists developed in the 1970s – Bernard Gert's ten moral rules and Tom Beauchamp and James Childress's principlism in medical ethics – draw on Donagan's ideas and ground their respective theories on common morality. In the words of Beauchamp and Childress, the idea is that '[a]ll persons living a moral life grasp the core dimensions of morality. They know not to lie, not to steal others' property, to keep promises, to respect the rights of others, not to kill or cause harm to innocent persons, and the like. All persons committed to morality do not doubt the relevance and importance of these rules. [...] [We] rightly judge all human conduct by its standards'.[9]

This idea of a universal common morality also faces some more or less obvious criticism.[10] The most obvious line of criticism is that a universal morality, which is said not to be relative to culture or historical period, is profoundly counterintuitive given the changes of moral practices over time – just think about the relatively recent changes in attitudes towards discrimination on grounds of race or gender, or about the quite recent moral concern for animals and the environment. The argument for a universal common morality would need to be substantiated with empirical support from cross-cultural field observations, which will be hard to conduct.[11] This is ultimately an

---

[8]   Alan Donagan, *Theory of Morality* (Chicago: University of Chicago Press, 1977).

[9]   Tom L. Beauchamp and James F. Childress, *Principles of Biomedical Ethics*, 7th edn (New York: Oxford University Press, 2013), 3. The tradition of common morality or common sense morality of course also includes philosophers of earlier periods, such as Thomas Reid, Richard Price, or W. D. Ross.

[10]   For a fuller discussion, see Katarzyna de Lazari-Radek and Peter Singer, *The Point of View of the Universe: Sidgwick and Contemporary Ethics* (New York: Oxford University Press, 2016), 82 ff.; Norbert Paulo, *The Confluence of Philosophy and Law in Applied Ethics* (Basingstoke: Palgrave Macmillan, 2016), 116 ff.

[11]   Leigh Turner, 'Zones of Consensus and Zones of Conflict: Questioning the "Common Morality" Presumption in Bioethics', *Kennedy Institute of Ethics Journal* **13**:3 (2003), 193–218; Peter Herissone-Kelly, 'Determining the Common Morality's Norms in the Sixth Edition of Principles of Biomedical Ethics', *Journal of Medical Ethics* **37**:10 (2011), 584–87.

empirical question. But as long as there is no empirical support of this kind, it seems plausible to assume that there is no universal common morality, but rather particular moralities only (that are more or less overlapping). Note, however, that this way to flesh out the idea of moral bioenhancement in terms of a common morality is just as conceivable as other restricted forms of moral bioenhancement. It would be a *moral bioenhancement for common-sense philosophers*; it would not be moral bioenhancement *for all ethicists**.

Closely related to common (or common-sense) morality is the idea of *prima facie* moral norms. W. D. Ross famously developed the idea of *prima facie* norms; and it has been fruitfully used by proponents of a common morality such as Beauchamp and Childress. The idea is, roughly, that moral norms 'are binding other things being equal, but each can be outweighed in a particular context by another principle or rule. However, the principles' different weights cannot be assigned in advance; they can only be determined in particular contexts in addressing cases or policies'.[12] The idea is also widely used in basic rights and human rights adjudication.[13] This understanding of moral norms as binding *prima facie* only might also be a way to solve the problem and to explain what a moral bioenhancement *for all ethicists** could look like. One could claim that certain moral dispositions hold *prima facie* universally without necessarily trumping other moral considerations or dispositions in all circumstances. And this seems to be the strategy of Ingmar Persson and Julian Savulescu in a recent paper defending moral bioenhancement. They argue that one of their critics, Michael Hauskeller, the co-editor of this volume,

> seems to assume that effective moral bioenhancement requires knowing what is the morally right thing to do in every situation. So he objects that "it seems that there is hardly any action that is always wrong, or always right, independent of the context and the individual circumstances in which every concrete action is embedded". However, because we take moral bioenhancement to consist in enhancing the motivation to act on reasons, it is

---

[12]   James F. Childress, 'Methods in Bioethics', in Bonnie Steinbock (ed.), *The Oxford Handbook of Bioethics* (Oxford; New York: Oxford University Press, 2007), 22.

[13]   T. Alexander Aleinikoff, 'Constitutional Law in the Age of Balancing', *The Yale Law Journal* **96**:5 (1987), 943–1005; Kai Möller, 'Balancing and the Structure of Constitutional Rights', *International Journal of Constitutional Law* **5**:3 (2007), 453–68; Stavros Tsakyrakis, 'Proportionality: An Assault on Human Rights?', *International Journal of Constitutional Law* **7**:3 (2009), 468–93.

enough that we can identify considerations that are always moral reasons. And we can do this: for instance, the fact that an action is causing someone else considerable pain is always a moral reason (of beneficence or nonmaleficence) against doing it, or the fact that someone has done you a favor is always a moral reason (of justice) to return the favor. Certainly, in particular situations, these reasons can be outweighed by other reasons, so ensuring that people are more motivated by them [...] is not to ensure that they act in any specific way in the particular situations.[14]

Persson and Savulescu now seem to defend a version of moral bioenhancement that aims at enhancing the disposition to be motivated to act on certain reasons that are universally accepted as *prima facie* moral reasons, i.e., reasons that always count for or against something without necessarily determining the moral verdict all things considered. This version of moral enhancement escapes some of the problems mentioned above. For instance, being empathetic with another person might always be *prima facie* morally good, although one will need to have to override empathy with other considerations in rare circumstances all things considered. Take the example of a judge in court feeling empathy with one of the parties involved in the case. She has moral reasons not to be moved by these feelings if, in fact, the law demands action against that person. Enhanced empathy might, in such cases, make it more likely that judges will act immorally when they find it harder to override their empathetic feelings. Persson and Savulescu would argue that these empathetic feelings still have some moral weight, but they should be outweighed by for example, the considerations of impartiality.

Such a proposal not only requires a thoroughly fine-tuned – although theoretically conceivable – form of moral bioenhancement (that makes you more likely to act on moral reasons – just not too much so); it also faces a deeper and more theoretical objection. The objection is that not even the idea of *prima facie* norms (or *prima facie* moral dispositions) makes for a moral bioenhancement for all ethicists*. Just consider moral particularists such as Jonathan Dancy. He defends what he calls holism in the theory of reasons, according to which 'a feature that is a reason in one case may be no

---

[14]   Persson and Savulescu, 'The Art of Misunderstanding Moral Bioenhancement', 52. The authors' reference to three of the four principles of biomedical ethics proposed by Beauchamp and Childress (autonomy, nonmaleficence, beneficence, and justice) underlines the similarity, mentioned earlier, to theories of common morality coupled with *prima facie* norms.

reason at all, or an opposite reason, in another', as opposed to atomism in the theory of reasons, according to which 'a feature that is a reason in one case must remain a reason, and retain the same polarity, in any other. The atomist holds that features carry their practical relevance around from place to place; the holist thinks that context can affect the ability of a feature to make a difference in a new case'.[15]

Thus Dancy and other particularists would argue that when one should not act out of empathy all things considered, then empathy does not provide *any reason* to act. For particularists, the picture is not one of empathy providing *prima facie* reasons that are outweighed by other considerations. It is rather that empathy does not provide any moral reasons in this situation – but it might well provide moral reasons in other cases. To be sure, the particularism camp in ethics is relatively small; but the main claims of this group are, I assume, shared reasonably widely and taken seriously within the academic community in order to conclude that not even the idea of *prima facie* moral norms (or dispositions) makes for a moral bioenhancement *for all ethicists**.

That being said, however, fleshing out the idea of moral bioenhancement in terms of widely-shared *prima facie* moral norms (or dispositions) is – similarly to the other restricted forms mentioned above – yet another conceivable restricted form of moral bioenhancement. It would be a *moral bioenhancement for atomists in the theory of reasons* or, if you prefer, *for generalists in ethics*.[16] Note that this version of moral bioenhancement is likely to find more support among moral philosophers than the other restricted forms of moral bioenhancement discussed above; and it is possible that at some point, all particularists (and proponents of related theories such as ethical casuistry) will become convinced of atomism or generalism and abandon their theories. But as of now, it seems that proponents of moral bioenhancement do not have a concept of moral enhancement that all ethicists* would subscribe to.

I have just argued that different ways in which proponents of moral bioenhancement have tried to determine what counts as *moral*

---

[15] Jonathan Dancy, *Ethics Without Principles* (Oxford; New York: Oxford University Press, 2004), 7; see also Shelly Kagan, 'The Additive Fallacy', *Ethics* **99**:1 (1988), 5–31.

[16] On generalism vs particularism in ethics, see Sean McKeever and Michael Ridge, *Principled Ethics: Generalism as a Regulative Ideal* (Oxford; New York: Oxford University Press, 2006); and Jan Gertken, *Prinzipien in der Ethik* (Paderborn: Mentis, 2014).

enhancement hinge on controversial substantial or metaethical presuppositions, i.e., presuppositions not shared by all ethicists*. Although different versions of moral bioenhancement seem to be conceivable as restricted forms of moral enhancement, proponents of moral enhancement continue searching for a version that is not thus restricted – albeit with a surprising shift. They have recently defended a kind of moral enhancement – called "procedural moral enhancement" – that improves deliberative processes instead of particular moral views, motivations, or dispositions. In what follows I will outline and discuss this shift towards a procedural form of moral enhancement (sec. 2) and argue that what is at stake is better described as "moral-epistemic enhancement" (sec. 3). I will defend the view that moral-epistemic (bio-)enhancement in the form of perspective-taking can count as a moral enhancement for all ethicists*.

2. Procedural Moral Enhancement

The main idea behind "procedural moral enhancement" is pretty straightforward. Instead of enhancing views, motivations, or dispositions about which there is no agreement if they would constitute *moral* enhancements, it might be uncontroversial to say that the enhancement of certain deliberative processes makes people more morally reliable. Drawing on the characteristics John Rawls famously proposed for 'competent judges' in his 'Decision Procedure for Ethics' and, later, in *A Theory of Justice*,[17] Owen Schaefer and Julian Savulescu suggest that the following capacities contribute to reliable moral decisions: logical competence, conceptual understanding, empirical competence, empathetic understanding, openness to revision, and bias avoidance.[18] Schaefer and Savulescu argue that biomedical enhancements of such capacities are conducive to reliable moral decision-making in a variety of normative settings, thus avoiding the critique of other forms of moral bioenhancement mentioned above.[19]

[17] John Rawls, 'Outline of a Decision Procedure for Ethics', *Philosophical Review* **60**:2 (1951), 177–197; John Rawls, *A Theory of Justice* (Cambridge, MA: Belknap Press, 2005).
[18] Owen Schaefer and Julian Savulescu, 'Procedural Moral Enhancement', *Neuroethics* (2016), doi:10.1007/s12152-016-9258-7.
[19] In Owen Schaefer and Julian Savulescu, 'Better Minds, Better Morals: A Procedural Guide to Better Judgment', *Journal of Posthuman Studies* **1**:1, 26–43, the authors further develop these ideas; some of which are already to be found in Will Jefferson, et al., 'Enhancement and Civic Virtue', *Social Theory and Practice* **40**:3 (2014), 499–527.

Logical competence, conceptual understanding, and empirical competence can be described as cognitive capacities.[20] For instance, logical competence might help in coming closer to the moral truth in that one can recognise the implications of one's views and identify inconsistencies between them. One reason for being logically consistent is that consistency is a minimal condition for truth. Of any two inconsistent moral beliefs, at least one does not track the moral truth. It is in this sense that inconsistencies can be problematic when they lead to the revision of one's beliefs.[21] Logical competence alone does not tell you how to revise your beliefs, but it helps you to recognise the need for revision. Similarly, having a better understanding of moral concepts does not magically give you the "right" moral concepts. It rather helps to avoid confusion and misapprehension of such concepts, because one is better able to clearly formulate moral ideas and to distinguish between different ideas. And so on for the other competences, some of which will be described in more detail below.

As is widely known, the aim of Rawls' decision procedure sets out to provide an answer to this question: 'what is the test of whether a judgment in a particular case is rational?' His 'answer is that a judgment in a particular case is evidenced to be rational by showing that, given the facts and the conflicting interests of the case, the judgment is capable of being explicated by a justifiable principle'.[22] The decision procedure has roughly two parts, the first of which determines the relevant judgements about cases to be taken into account; the second part is the justification of the principles invoked in rationalising these judgements. The first part begins with relatively stable and certain intuitive judgements about particular cases. Already here Rawls names idealising narrowing conditions which pave the way for the rationality judgement. He is not interested in all judgements, but in considered judgements by competent judges. In the procedure's second part, the preselected judgements get rationalised by various means. For instance, the judgements must be explicable by simple moral rules, which are the result of 'moral insight', determined without 'strong emotional or physical duress'.[23] The rules must in turn justify the judgements; they must further be action-guiding in

---

[20]   Schaefer and Savulescu, 'Better Minds, Better Morals: A Procedural Guide to Better Judgment'. In what follows, I am drawing on this paper.

[21]   On how to do this, see Richmond Campbell and Victor Kumar, 'Moral Reasoning on the Ground', *Ethics* **122**:2 (2012), 273–312.

[22]   Rawls, 'Outline of a Decision Procedure for Ethics', 187.

[23]   Rawls, 'Outline of a Decision Procedure for Ethics', 187.

non-trivial future cases and stand trial against alternative rules and other judgements.

As mentioned, Rawls only takes into account *considered judgements* by *competent judges*. One requirement for a judgement to count as considered is that the competent judge is not herself affected by the case.[24] This impartiality constraint might make sense in many circumstances, but also has a tendency to render the procedure under-inclusive.[25] We have already seen some criteria for competent moral judges. They are supposed to have 'a certain requisite degree of intelligence, which may be thought of as that ability which intelligence tests are designed to measure. [...] I am inclined to say that a competent moral judge need not be more than normally intelligent'. They are also 'required to know those things concerning the world about him and those consequences of frequently performed actions, which it is reasonable to expect the average intelligent man to know. Further, a competent judge is expected to know, in all cases whereupon he is called to express his opinion, the peculiar facts of those cases'. Moreover, a competent moral judge is required to be a 'reasonable man', who 'shows a willingness, if not a desire, to use the criteria of inductive logic in order to determine what is proper for him to believe'; who 'whenever he is confronted with a moral question, shows a disposition to find reasons for and against the possible lines of conduct which are open to him'; who 'exhibits a desire to consider questions with an open mind'; and who 'knows, or tries to know, his own emotional, intellectual, and moral predilections and makes a conscientious effort to take them into account in weighing the merits of any question. He is not unaware of the influences of prejudice and bias even in his most sincere efforts to annul them'. Finally, to be a competent judge, one is further required to have 'sympathetic knowledge of those human interests which, by conflicting in particular cases, give rise to the need to make a moral decision'.[26]

The procedure thus described is meant to identify what Guy Kahane calls 'non-accidental patterns in non-accidental intuitions',[27] i.e., moral intuitions that survive various steps of epistemic screening, which in turn justify decisions in particular moral cases. Or, in Rawls' words, '[i]f competent judges are those persons most likely to make

---

[24] Rawls, 'Outline of a Decision Procedure for Ethics', 181 f.
[25] Thomas Kelly and Sarah McGrath, 'Is Reflective Equilibrium Enough?', *Philosophical Perspectives* **24**:1 (2010), 325–359.
[26] Rawls, 'Outline of a Decision Procedure for Ethics', 178 f.
[27] Guy Kahane, 'The Armchair and the Trolley: An Argument for Experimental Ethics', *Philosophical Studies* **162**:2 (2013), 421–445, 430.

correct decisions, then we should take care to abstract those judgments of theirs which, from the conditions and circumstances under which they are made, are most likely to be correct'.[28] I believe it is fair to say that Rawls' decision procedure is an extremely demanding thought exercise: one is (individually) to imagine a (social) process in which one abstracts from hypothetical judgements of hypothetical competent judges, which are moreover understood as being extremely gifted and conscious about their own psychological dispositions and patterns of (actual) reasoning.

What is more important for the purpose of this essay, however, is to emphasise that Rawls really proposed a *procedure*; it takes various steps before one can tell 'whether a judgment in a particular case is rational'. What Schaefer and Savulescu take from Rawls is only one element, namely the features defining competent judges. Just as Rawls holds that 'competent judges are those persons most likely to make correct decisions', so Schaefer and Savulescu claim that competent judges are all the more morally reliable the better their logical competence, conceptual understanding, empirical competence, empathetic understanding, openness to revision, and bias avoidance. All of these features of competent judges are said to contribute to reliable moral decisions and thus do not assess moral decision-making in terms of certain outputs. But even though the contribution to moral decision-making has to do with how people come to a certain decision, the enhancement of logical competence, conceptual understanding, etc. has nothing to do with a procedure that describes several consecutive steps that must be followed.

3. Moral-Epistemic Enhancement

Schaefer and Savulescu argue that certain capacities are always conducive to more reliable moral decision making,[29] and that biomedical enhancements of those capacities are to be understood as moral bioenhancements for all ethicists*. I suggest taking this argumentative goal seriously and to give up the talk of "procedural moral enhancement". The proposal is better described, I suggest, as

---

[28] Rawls, 'Outline of a Decision Procedure for Ethics', 183.
[29] Note that this does not imply persons thus enhanced always reach moral decisions that are better than decisions by the not enhanced. After all, a group of not enhanced persons might employ Rawls' decision procedure, merely imagining the moral deliberation among competent judges, and thus reaching a better moral decision. They might also simply follow their gut feelings, which by chance point them to the better moral decision.

"moral-epistemic enhancement". After all, the proposal does not offer anything like a decision procedure to arrive at correct or reliable moral decisions. It is rather a contribution to moral epistemology, hence the label "moral-epistemic enhancement".

I take it that Schaefer and Savulescu offer a plausible way to think about moral-epistemic enhancements. One could at least conceive biomedical means to make people more likely to avoid biases, to be more open to revisions, to be more open to empirical evidence, and so on, even if the two authors do not offer more precise ideas concerning what these biomedical means to bring about the desired enhancements might look like. In what follows, I will further pursue the idea of moral-epistemic enhancement, but I will focus on another capacity, namely perspective-taking. I assume that perspective-taking is generally epistemically valuable in moral decision-making. By this I mean that it contributes to the epistemic value of moral decision-making when one is able to put oneself in someone else's shoes, to take the point of view of other persons, to imagine what a decision would mean for other persons, etc. For now I take this to be uncontroversial, but I will consider some objections later in the chapter.

3.1. Perspective-Taking as Moral-Epistemic Enhancement

Let me begin my argument for moral-epistemic enhancement in the form of perspective-taking by motivating the idea that we, as humans, are always influenced by certain biochemical states. This is probably most obvious when untypical biochemical states lead to unusual choices or behaviour. Simply consider the typical cravings for certain foods caused by hormones during pregnancy, or impatience caused by low blood sugar levels. Blood sugar levels are even said to significantly influence the rulings of experienced judges.[30] There are many more biochemical influences that seem to play a role in moral decision-making, although we do not recognise them when making decisions. For instance, the neurotransmitter serotonin not only seems to have an effect on impulsivity; it also seems to influence decisions regarding whether to co-operate with others, and especially how to react to unfair behaviour.[31] I am not saying that such

---

[30] Shai Danziger, Jonathan Levav, and Liora Avnaim-Pesso, 'Extraneous Factors in Judicial Decisions', *Proceedings of the National Academy of Sciences* **108**:17 (2011), 6889–92.
[31] Molly J. Crockett, et al., 'Serotonin Modulates Behavioral Reactions to Unfairness', *Science* **320**:5884 (2008), 1739.

influences fully determine how people act. What I am saying is that they can have some influence on how we feel, think, and act.

To make this point one does not even need to invoke scientific research on such influences. Just recall your first serious crush as a teenager, or the last time you fell in love with another person. Many will remember that falling in love deeply changed how they perceived the world around them; that they were suddenly more optimistic, more open and friendly to others; that they began to care less about school or their job; and that they became interested in things they had never cared about previously. Many will also remember the feeling of lovesickness; how jealousy made them think and act in ways they knew to be completely silly. Or remember severe headaches and migraines and how they affect the way you feel, think, and act. Some will also be familiar with more drastic biochemical influences on feelings, motivation, and behaviour. You might know a person who has received hormone therapy; it is often reported that persons change significantly during or after such treatments. You might also know someone who has or had severe depression and received biochemical treatment; the whole point of such treatments is to change the person, sometimes to a degree that makes one wonder if the treatment still treats the person or rather creates a different one. These are all examples for biochemical influences on how people feel, think, and act.[32] They all causally influence people's mind-sets and emotional patterns, such as levels of anxiety, joy, or empathy.

The second step in my argument for moral-epistemic enhancement in the form of perspective-taking is that changing such biochemical states could have epistemically valuable effects. Many people assume that what is natural is generally preferable to what is not natural. But why should our natural biochemical states be any better than a different biochemical state, which one can induce through biomedical means? It is certainly true that there are always worries about possible side-effects. However, our natural biochemical states also have significant effects on almost all aspects of our lives. Some people are more energetic than others and perform much better in competitive tasks; some are more able to sit quietly and follow the teacher in school. Why should the natural lottery that produces biochemical states, which are partly responsible for such differences, be any better than artificially altered or created biochemical states that might have positive effects? This general question is too broad and complex to be answered

---

[32] I am not claiming that these effects referred to in the examples can be reduced to biochemical influences, only that biochemistry plays a (more or less significant) role in them.

in this chapter.[33] But it stands behind my moral-epistemic argument. Changing one's biochemical state can put you in someone else's shoes and thus enable perspective-taking. Imagine the use of already existing forms of talking therapy, which potentially facilitate self-understanding by overcoming ego-defenses. Why not use such therapies to more deeply understand others? And why not couple this with bio-medical means that enhance the ability for perspective-taking? Take, for instance, cannabis. It is a widely used substance, although it is illegal to possess, sell, or consume cannabis in many jurisdictions. Apparently, it has de-stressing and relaxing effects, which is why it is also used for medical and recreational purposes. It is also said to have aggression-reducing effects – it is not by accident that advocates call it "the drug against wars". So if cannabis has such effects, why not give cannabis to overly aggressive people (integrated into therapy and supervised by a doctor in order to control for unwanted side-effects), thereby letting them experience a less aggressive and more laid-back view of the world? This might enable them to understand persons who are more anxious, people who fear aggression and violence, people who are paralysed by dominant behaviour. In other words, cannabis might help them to take the perspective of people with different feelings, of people they never took seriously before. Experiencing their anxieties might lead them to reach very different conclusions about how to act.[34]

[33] But see Neil Levy, *Neuroethics: Challenges for the 21ˢᵗ Century* (Cambridge: Cambridge University Press, 2007), 147 ff.

[34] Some of these ideas have been mentioned in Paulo and Bublitz, 'How (Not) to Argue For Moral Enhancement'. Note that I do not want to commit myself to a substantial view about how precisely to understand perspective-taking, and how to distinguish it from empathising. For instance, one question would be whether perspective-taking is imagining *how another person feels* or rather imagining *how you would feel* in her situation: see C. Daniel Batson, Shannon Early, and Giovanni Salvarani, 'Perspective Taking: Imagining How Another Feels Versus Imaging How You Would Feel', *Personality and Social Psychology Bulletin* **23**:7 (1997), 751–58; Amy Coplan, 'Will the Real Empathy Please Stand Up? A Case for a Narrow Conceptualization', *Southern Journal of Philosophy* **49**:1 (2011), 40–65. I think that, for the purposes of the present essay, both count as epistemically valuable forms of perspective-taking. I am leaving aside the question whether ego-dissolving effects that generate feelings of somehow being one with and intimately connected with the natural world, which certain psychedelic substances are said to possess, should count as valuable forms of perspective-taking; I am limiting my discussion here to the perspectives of other humans.

This proposal has some similarities to traditional forms of enhancing the ability for perspective-taking. It is commonly assumed that being exposed to and spending time with people who look, think, or behave differently (for example, due to ethnicity, nationality, social background, upbringing, religion, cognitive or motoric abilities, etc.) helps to take their interests and feelings seriously and in turn, enhances the chance for better moral decision-making.[35] Similar effects are commonly ascribed to reading novels and seeing great plays in the theatre.[36] All these traditional forms of moral enhancement can be understood as being moral-epistemic enhancements in the sense that they enable or enhance perspective-taking – being exposed to a wide variety of people, getting to know their emotional lives as well as those of notable fictional characters as well as their social circumstances, allows one to take their perspectives seriously, which is always epistemically valuable in moral decision-making. The same holds for biochemical changes that complement (or, perhaps, substitute) such traditional forms of moral enhancement.

It is important to understand that perspective-taking as moral-epistemic enhancement does not imply that certain perspectives are morally or moral-epistemically more valuable than others. So when I said that the moral decision-making of overly aggressive persons could benefit from certain forms of therapy that include the use of cannabis in order to help them to perceive the world from a less aggressive and more mellow perspective, this does not imply that the latter perspective is the right one to take. My argument also applies to a very relaxed and laid-back pothead. For her, it would be epistemically valuable to take the perspective of a stressed or even aggressive person. In fact, the argument does not only apply to extreme personalities, but to all. Everyone has his or her perspective – some more narrow than others – and might very well benefit, epistemically, from enhanced perspective-taking capacities.

So the argument for moral-epistemic enhancement in the form of perspective-taking is altogether very simple. It says that we as humans are always influenced by certain biochemical states which – to some degree at least – determine how we think, feel, and act.

---

[35] See Sylvia Terbeck, *The Social Neuroscience of Intergroup Relations: Prejudice, Can We Cure It?* (Heidelberg and New York: Springer, 2016).
[36] On the use of novels in ethics, see Peter Johnson, *Moral Philosophers and the Novel: A Study of Winch, Nussbaum and Rorty* (Cham: Springer, 2004). See also Michael J. Pardales, "'So, How Did You Arrive at That Decision?' Connecting Moral Imagination and Moral Judgement', *Journal of Moral Education* **31**:4 (2002), 423–437.

Changing such biochemical states could have epistemically valuable effects by helping us to understand how other people with other bio-chemical states, think, feel, and act.

Before I come to objections against this proposal, it is worth adding a few words of caution. First, note that the argument does not say or imply that it is morally desirable to be enhanced moral-epistemically in the way outlined above. The claim is merely hypothetical, i.e., if one wants to make a moral decision that is epistemically valuable, then this kind of enhancement will always conduce to the moral-epistemic value of the decision. Second, note again that the idea is not to use cannabis or other means to change the biochemical states of people in order to make them less (or more) aggressive or more (or less) trusting. The idea is rather to use such means to help people experience the state-of-mind (not) to be aggressive or (not) to be trusting, i.e., to perceive the world through the eyes of a person with a different mind-set. Third, note further that I am not arguing for or against the moral de-sirability of moral-epistemic enhancements – let alone a moral duty to enhance others or to be enhanced, be it voluntarily or compulsory.[37] Such questions are interesting and important. However, they are beyond the scope of the present chapter in which I merely argue that moral-epistemic enhancements in the form of perspective-taking might be a solution to the problem of finding dispositions the enhancement of which is always conducive to better moral decision-making.

3.2. Objections

Let me now discuss some possible objections against moral-epistemic enhancement. I will begin with the objection that the kind of perspec-tive-taking I am advocating is not genuine. Then I will discuss the objection that the claimed effects for moral decision making might vanish too fast to be meaningful, and that one never knows if one really has acquired the precise feeling or mind-set of another person. Only then will I discuss the most serious objection, namely

---

[37] In other work Christoph Bublitz and I have discussed some of the social and political problems society-wide moral enhancements would cause: see our 'Pow(d)er to the People? Voter Manipulation, Legitimacy, and the Relevance of Moral Psychology for Democratic Theory', *Neuroethics* (2016), doi:10.1007/s12152-016-9266-7; and Norbert Paulo, 'Liberal Perspectives on Moral Enhancement', *Ethics & Politics* **XVIII**:3 (2016), 397–421.

that moral-epistemic enhancement might not, in fact, always contribute to better moral decision-making because it could lead to outrageous moral positions and because it might lead people to acquire biases which lower the epistemic value in future moral decisions. Responding to all these objections allows me to clarify the proposal.

Objection 1: One might object that perspective-taking is not genuine when it is merely biochemically triggered. The kind of perspective-taking usually meant in moral discourse is a rational procedure in which one is asked to think about the point of view of another person, not merely to feel it.

Response: This objection presupposes a substantial view about what constitutes perspective-taking. I said above that I do not wish to commit myself to such a substantial view about how precisely to understand perspective-taking, and how to distinguish it from empathising and related notions. I take both imagining how another person feels and imagining how you would feel in her situation, as epistemically valuable forms of perspective-taking. Also, nothing in my proposal excludes the possibility that the effect of rational perspective-taking and perspective-taking through biochemical changes could have the exact same effects. Moreover, it is compatible with my proposal to combine the two ways of perspective-taking.

Objection 2: A related objection is that when the biochemical effects vanish, the effect for moral decision-making also vanishes, simply because one did not achieve the change in perspective rationally, but only emotionally.

Response: Since this objection is related to the first one, my response also mirrors the response to the first objection. First, objection 2 is based on an empirical assumption the credibility of which I feel unable to judge. It might be true, but it might also well be unsubstantiated. So it is at least possible to stipulate that the effects remain for similar periods of time. To motivate the possibility that a relevant kind of memory of the biochemically induced feeling remains cognitively available as plausible, just remember, again, your first crush as teenager, lovesickness or a severe headache. I assume that most of us can easily remember what it felt like being in these situations, and how it affected our perspective on many issues, although these were largely biochemically triggered. Second, as I said before, my proposal does not exclude the possibility of combining the rational and biochemically induced perspective-taking. This would undermine the objection, because it seems plausible to assume that the biochemically induced perspective-taking would support or even strengthen the effect of rational perspective-taking, rather than weaken it.

Objection 3: A third objection is that one never knows if one has acquired the feeling or mind-set of another person. That is, one might end up taking a perspective that no-one actually has.

Response: The obvious response to this objection is that one never knows if one really has acquired the feeling or mind-set of another person. One can surely try to design very specific biochemical means, but the required level of specificity is arguably too high to hope for success. One can also try to reassure oneself through questions or mirroring exercises. But as legions of therapists will testify, one can come very close to an understanding of another's perspective, but complete understanding is probably asking too much. What is important for the purposes of the present essay is that it does not seem to be crucial for moral-epistemic enhancement to acquire the exact feeling or mind-set of another person. There might well be moral decisions where it is important to take a very specific point of view (for instance in some moral problems concerning close personal relationships), which might not be possible to attain through biomedical means. However, this is an empirical question, and in most cases specific perspectives are not what moral epistemology asks for. It is always epistemically valuable to take different perspectives, no matter whether or not these are the precise perspectives of another person. This also answers the second part of the objection, namely whether it might be a problem that one might end up taking a perspective that no-one actually has. I do not see how this could be a problem from the standpoint of moral epistemology, at least as long as the perspective is one that others could have. After all, even when moral philosophers promote moral imagination as a means of achieving better informed moral judgement, they are asking for creativity and not so much for a fixed set of moral options.[38] In this sense, moral-epistemic enhancement in the form of perspective-taking can be understood as a means to facilitate moral imagination.

---

[38] See, for example, Steven Fesmire, *John Dewey and Moral Imagination: Pragmatism in Ethics* (Bloomington: Indiana University Press, 2003); Pardales, 'So, How Did You Arrive at That Decision?'.

Objection 4: What I take to be the most serious objection to the idea of moral-epistemic enhancement is that the proposal would not meet the high standard I set for successful moral enhancement proposals. Following the development of the moral enhancement debate, I described the standard-setting litmus test such that it is fulfilled only by proposals to enhance dispositions that are uncontroversial among all ethicists*. I have outlined moral-epistemic enhancement as a promising attempt to fulfill that litmus test. Now the objection is that moral-epistemic enhancements can lead to both epistemically less valuable moral decisions and to morally worse situations (in a substantial sense). Let me explain.

Imagine a person living in a big city in a western democracy. Let us call him Donald. He has a bunch of loosely connected liberal views, including beliefs about equality, human rights, and fairness; but he also has some nationalist and racist views – some implicit, some explicit – which rarely surface. Now, Donald chooses to undergo a safe and effective form of moral-epistemic enhancement to the effect that he now has a very good ability to take, *inter alia*, the perspective of those of his fellow citizens who lost their industry-related jobs due to globalisation or due to the influx of foreigners who are willing to do the same jobs for lower pay.[39] He now feels his fellow citizens' losses and anxieties very strongly and he comes to understand their hatred of mainstream politics and foreigners. Although he himself is in a very different position, living a life full of opportunities and without worries about future developments, he comes to take the positions of his worse-off fellow citizens far more seriously than before. This might lead Donald to feel more confident in his nationalist and racist views, and less confident in his liberal views. So the enhanced ability for perspective-taking might make Donald more nationalist and racist and less liberal, which can be seen as a morally worse situation – in a substantial sense – than before the enhancement. From a moral-epistemic perspective, being more racist is widely considered a (negatively connotated) bias which might in turn yield epistemically less valuable moral decisions.

And this is only the objection concerning perspective-taking. The possible negative effect can be further strengthened through other moral-epistemic enhancements such as improved conceptual understanding and logical competence. That is, Donald might not only

---

[39]   For rich descriptions of such persons (and of many others), see Arlie Russell Hochschild, *Strangers in Their Own Land: Anger and Mourning on the American Right* (New York; London: New Press, 2016).

become more racist and nationalist in a loose sense. Having better conceptual understanding might help him understand the many implications such views actually have, thus extending his racism and nationalism beyond abstract political views to his everyday life and possibly leading to discrimination against certain neighbours, avoiding shops run by immigrants, or much worse developments. Enhanced logical competence might make him realise how racism and nationalism conflict with his more liberal views, which might in turn lead to the abandonment of the latter, making him even more racist and nationalist. Again, I take it that these developments count – in a substantial, first-order morality sense – as being morally bad. From a moral-epistemic perspective, the now even stronger racial bias might lead to epistemically less valuable moral decisions. So the objection is that moral-epistemic enhancements can lead to both epistemically less valuable moral decisions and to morally worse situations (in a substantial sense). Moral-epistemic enhancement would thus not meet the litmus test for successful moral enhancement proposals.

Response: First of all, in this essay I am not concerned with good moral outcomes in a substantial, first-order morality sense. I am merely concerned with the epistemic value of moral decision-making. This being said, it seems perfectly possible that an epistemically better moral decision-making process leads to a worse decision than a completely unreflected or uninformed one. Take the example of Huckleberry Finn. In Mark Twain's novel, Huck is unsure whether or not to return his friend Jim, a runaway slave, to his master. It has been argued that Huck believes the overriding moral reasons would speak for returning Jim.[40] But Huck nonetheless decides, out of sympathy for Jim, not to return him. Schaefer and Savulescu raise the following point: 'what if Huck was a better reasoner, and more open to revising his judgments on the basis of the weight of reasons? He may well have recognized the force of what he took to be good reasons, excluded the "bias" of friendship from consideration, and turned Jim in'.[41] So, yes, Huck might have made a morally worse decision had he been more rational, or more motivated to act on what he thought were overriding moral reasons. But, as I said before, the possibility that moral-epistemic enhancements might, in some cases, lead to morally worse or even outrageous

---

[40] Jonathan Bennett, 'The Conscience of Huckleberry Finn', *Philosophy* **49**:188 (1974), 123–34.
[41] Schaefer and Savulescu, 'Procedural Moral Enhancement'.

outcomes does not affect the moral-epistemic argument as presented in this essay.[42]

This does not do away with the objection, however, that moral-epistemic enhancement might lead to epistemically less valuable moral decisions, which would undermine my argument. Remember that the objection is that moral-epistemic enhancement might not only lead to racist decisions, but also to epistemically less valuable moral decisions. The enhanced ability for perspective-taking might make Donald more nationalistic and racist and these can be understood as biases, which one might argue, are by definition of negative epistemic value.

As for this latter challenge, I wish to emphasise that perspective-taking, as envisioned here, could in Donald's case also include the victims of racism and nationalism. Perspective-taking differs from empathy, which is known to extend primarily to in-group members, in that it makes it easier to take a whole variety of perspectives and thereby to extend the range of concerns. It should thus extend beyond in-group members. One of the most salient features in perspective-taking is that it allows one to empathise with and understand people one is not close to, or who are not similar to oneself. As I described the case of Donald, he came to feel with his fellow citizens who live a life distinctly different from his own. The same kind of moral-epistemic enhancement could enable him to take the perspectives of those who suffer from racism and nationalism. The point at issue here is that moral-epistemic enhancement in the form of perspective-taking is not likely to yield to biases.

This is at least true when the respective enhancer works in that broader way, enabling Donald to take many more morally relevant perspectives than those that potentially yield racism and nationalism. Recall objection 3, above, that one never knows if one has acquired the precise feeling or mind-set of another person. The idea there was that some situations require taking into account a very specific point of view in order to be able to, for instance, treat another person fairly. Responding to this objection I said it is always epistemically valuable to take different perspectives, whether or not these are the precise perspectives of another person. That is to say, even

[42]   But note that moral-epistemic enhancement is likely to lead to morally better decisions in most, if not almost all cases, *inter alia* because the potentially harmful capacities are likely to be countered by other moral-epistemic capacities, see Schaefer and Savulescu, 'Procedural Moral Enhancement'.

if taking a particular point of view were better, it would still be epistemically valuable to take another perspective. From this standpoint every broadening of the range of perspectives being taken into account is epistemically valuable.

The only epistemically problematic case thus appears to rest on the empirical assumption that the respective enhancer is extremely specific and, for instance, only enables Donald to take the point of view of racists. Having available the point of view of racists in addition to one's own does not sound like an epistemically valuable thing to have. But if the view is correct that every broadening of the range of perspectives being taken into account is epistemically valuable, then this should also hold for the racist-only perspective. And indeed, having taken the enhancer, Donald gained the perspective of some of his fellow citizens, namely the perspective of the racists. Why should this broadening of moral perspectives not be epistemically valuable? Even the perspective of racists, sexists, and religious fanatics would appear to be not entirely without their moral-epistemic value.

First, I am not interested in first-order morality but in moral epistemology; and I do not presuppose any view about which first-order moral views are either good or bad, and this includes the possibility – however slim it might be – that racism, sexism, or any of the fanatic religious views might turn out to be morally right or appropriate. From an epistemic perspective, it would be an odd step to rule out this possibility.

Second, taking another's perspective and taking it seriously once the immediate effect of the enhancer vanishes, does not mean to support everything that person believes or does. One can take someone's perspective and understand her better than before, but still be critical of her views.[43] Even if you are strictly anti-racist, it might inform your self-understanding and your moral-decision making to engage with racists. The same applies for religious fanatics. Two fanatics of different denominations – or one religious fanatic and one fanatic atheist for that matter – will not agree on many things, even after the immediate effect of the enhancer vanishes, but they might learn a lot from taking the other fanatic's perspective. Their views and their moral decision-making will be epistemically richer than they were previously.

Third, the worry behind the objection that moral-epistemic enhancement in the form of perspective-taking might lead to biases

---

[43]   This is, for instance, the idea behind Hochschild's illuminating book, *Strangers in Their Own Land.*

such as racism seems to be a temporal problem for the epistemic value in question. One might distinguish between a moral decision being made now, and other moral decisions being made in the future. As for the former, gaining the point of view of racists counts as epistemically valuable in the ways described above. In this situation it is unlikely that the moral judge already has completely subscribed to the new moral outlook (racism). She will thus still have the moral perspective she started with, plus the racist perspective. As for the latter situation, later on, it is possible that she came to adopt the racist view and abandoned her earlier views, just as Donald did in the example. So she might now have a (racial) bias she might not have had otherwise. This bias reduces, by definition, the epistemic value of the moral decision-making. However, she will still remember her earlier perspective – or at least I see no reason of any kind for assuming this will not be the case. She will thus have more perspectives to take into account in her moral decision-making, which again is epistemically valuable. The difference between the moral decision now and future moral decisions is merely that of which perspective she considers to be her own. I feel unable to say whether, in the future cases where she has adopted the biased perspective as her own, the gained perspective outweighs, in terms of moral-epistemic value, the loss caused by the bias.

I cannot confidently rule out the possibility that in rare cases – remember: when the enhancer is so specific as to allow for very precise perspective-taking only, when the moral judge comes over time to adopt the new perspective as her own and when this new perspective is a bias – the moral-epistemic value will turn out to be lower. Yet I want to emphasise that the argumentative bar for this view is very high. Simply imagine someone objecting to history classes in school for the reason that learning about the Nazis poses the risk that some kids might – at some point in the future – become attracted to antisemitism. I believe it would be very hard to present a good case for the view that history classes should be banned, because the expected epistemic gain from such lessons will in almost all cases by far outweigh the risk of some individuals becoming anti-Semites as a result of what they have learned. Sure, one might argue that in history classes pupils are normally presented with the Nazis as the paradigmatic evil, and not as a neutral moral outlook one is asked to seriously consider for oneself. But when we learn about the Nazis at school, part of what it means to truly understand how all these horrors could happen is to understand the mind-set of fanatic Nazis as well as of the hanger-on who is typical of any totalitarian system.[44] Without that kind of understanding, history classes would arguably lose much of their alleged power to prevent the return of nationalism and antisemitism.

Similarly, it would be very hard to make the case for the view that perspective-taking is not moral-epistemically valuable, because with some very specific enhancer some individuals might acquire biases that outweigh the epistemic gain from the additional perspectives that have been opened to them.

4. Conclusion

In this chapter, I have defended perspective-taking as a capacity which can be enhanced by both traditional and non-traditional bio-medical means; a capacity which arguably always – but at least almost always – contributes to the epistemic value of moral deci-sion-making. Other than the proposals for moral bioenhancement discussed in section 1, perspective-taking seems to be an uncontro-versial, non-trivial capacity for moral decision-making, which all proponents of ethical beliefs that are at present widely and with good reason shared within the academic community can agree upon. That is to say, moral-epistemic (bio)enhancement in the form of perspective-taking can count as a moral enhancement for all ethicists*.

Acknowledgments

I am grateful to an audience at the University of Rijeka, Croatia. Thanks, too, to Richard Arneson, Christoph Bublitz, Tom Douglas, and Owen Schaefer for helpful discussion.

University of Graz & University of Salzburg
norbert.paulo@uni-graz.at

[44] This is precisely what many great books about the Third Reich do: see, for example, Hannah Arendt, *Eichmann in Jerusalem* (New York: Penguin Classics, 2006); Viktor E. Frankl, *Man's Search for Meaning* (Boston: Beacon Press, 2006); Herlinde Pauer-Studer and J. David Velleman, *Konrad Morgen: The Conscience of a Nazi Judge* (Basingstoke; New York: Palgrave Macmillan, 2015).

Biomedical Moral Enhancement in the Face of Moral Particularism

PEI-HUA HUANG AND PETER SHIU-HWA TSU

Abstract

Biomedical moral enhancement, or BME for short, aims to improve people's moral behaviour through augmenting, via biomedical means, their virtuous dispositions such as sympathy, honesty, courage, or generosity. Recently, however, it has been challenged, on particularist grounds, that the manifestations of virtuous dispositions can be morally wrong. For instance, being generous in terrorist financing is one such case. If so, biomedical moral enhancement, by enhancing people's virtues, might turn out to be counterproductive in terms of people's moral behaviour. In this chapter, we argue, via a comparison with moral education, that the case for the practice of biomedical moral enhancement is not weakened by the particularists' stress on the variable moral statuses of the manifestations of our virtues. The real challenge from the particularists, we argue, lies elsewhere. It is that practical wisdom, being essentially context-sensitive, cannot be enhanced via biomedical means. On the basis of this, we further argue that BME ought to be used with great caution, for it may wrongly enhance, for instance, a terrorist financier's generosity, a robber's courage, or an undercover detective's honesty. Finally, we sketch how boundaries can be set on the use of BME, and address some potential objections to our position.

1. Introduction

Biomedical moral enhancement, or BME for short, aims to improve people's moral behaviour through improving, via biomedical means (e.g., drugs or genetic engineering), their virtuous dispositions or positive moral character traits such as honesty, sympathy, courage, or generosity. Supporters of BME have held out the hope that through massive biomedical moral enhancement, human beings' immoral behaviour can be significantly reduced and moral behaviour significantly increased. For instance, Julian Savulescu and Ingmar Persson, the staunchest champions of BME, have repeatedly emphasised that the problem of global warming would be significantly mitigated if we were less selfish and more environmentally friendly. Moreover, the pernicious effects of religious fundamentalism could be significantly weakened if we were more open-minded and less

doi:10.1017/S1358246118000358

dogmatic. Finally, the problem of poverty would also be less severe if we were more caring, benevolent, sympathetic, and generous.[1]

In light of this, the cultivation of human virtues and the improvement of moral behaviour are obviously important catalysts for the creation of a better world. And traditional moral education has, without a doubt, played an indispensable role. However, we human beings often fall well short of what moral education aims to achieve – turning us into morally better people who can live up to our moral obligations. As things currently stand, children die due to lack of clean water and food, wars are waged based on dogmatic ideologies, and the environment is polluted thanks to our greed for economic growth. If our world is not to go from bad to worse, there is an urgent need to morally enhance humans – the major source of all these evils. If traditional moral education does not achieve its aim successfully we cannot afford to give up, but should instead seek the help by every other possible means.

The rapid development of biomedical research seems to provide glimmers of hope where traditional moral education has hit a snag. It is believed that through biomedical means such as drug use, we can greatly boost people's virtuous dispositions and their moral behaviour.[2] For instance, Ritalin, a drug typically used for the treatment of ADHD, is believed to be capable of enhancing self-control.[3] SSRIs (selective serotonin reuptake inhibitors), on the other hand, seem to significantly boost people's willingness to co-operate and reduce their tendency to harm others. Finally, oxytocin is reportedly capable of enhancing people's trust and generosity. In light of these biomedical discoveries, a wide administration of these drugs seems

---

[1]   See Ingmar Persson and Julian Savulescu, 'The Perils of Cognitive Enhancement and the Urgent Imperative to Enhance the Moral Character of Humanity', *Journal of Applied Philosophy* **25**:3 (2008), 162–177; Persson and Savulescu, *Unfit for the Future: The Need for Moral Enhancement* (Oxford: Oxford University Press, 2012); Persson and Savulescu, 'The Duty to be Morally Enhanced', *Topoi* (2017), https://doi.org/10.1007/s11245-017-9475-7.

[2]   For a more detailed review of pharmaceuticals that are known to be effective in modulating moral behaviours, see Neil Levy, et al., 'Are You Morally Modified? The Moral Effects of Widely Used Pharmaceuticals', *Philosophy, Psychiatry, and Psychology* **21**:2 (2014), 111–125.

[3]   It is to be noted that although according to Aristotle self-control is not a virtue, Aristotle certainly would not deny its importance for the production of morally right behaviour on many occasions. For instance, it is certainly required for the ethical behaviour of a man who lusts for his friend's wife.

to stand of a chance of preventing our world from deteriorating. If so, why not give it a try? Indeed, several BME supporters have called on the government and the general public to seriously consider such a measure.[4]

This well-meaning proposal, however, soon encountered numerous objections. To begin with, as the BME supporters themselves readily recognise, whether the drugs can achieve their intended effects of moral enhancement remains controversial.[5] For instance, it is not entirely clear whether oxytocin can really increase people's trust and generosity in general or rather just promote in-group parochialism instead.[6] To make things worse, many of the experiments in support of BME cannot be replicated.[7] And, as with other drugs, there is always the concern about side effects.[8]

On a societal level some also worry that the enforcement of the BME programme may eventually lead to an unequal moral status between the enhanced and the unenhanced. To further elaborate, when compared to the morally enhanced, the unenhanced might well be classified as morally inferior citizens, prevented or even banned from taking part in many political activities such as voting or running for political positions, etc.[9] On top of this, it is also worrying that the executors of the BME programme might abuse it to serve

[4]   Persson and Savulescu, 'The Perils of Cognitive Enhancement and the Urgent Imperative to Enhance the Moral Character of Humanity'; *Unfit for the Future: The Need for Moral Enhancement*; Thomas Douglas, 'Moral Enhancement', *Journal of Applied Philosophy* **25**:3 (2008), 228–245.

[5]   See Persson and Savulescu, 'The Perils of Cognitive Enhancement and the Urgent Imperative to Enhance the Moral Character of Humanity', and *Unfit for the Future: The Need for Moral Enhancement*, for instance.

[6]   See Carsten De Dreu, et al., 'Oxytocin Promotes Human Ethnocentrism', *Proceedings of the National Academy of Sciences* **108**:4 (2011), 1262–66. Recently it has even been argued that tinkering with some dispositions via biomedical means might actually lead to adverse effects on others. See Toby Handfield, Pei-Hua Huang, and Robert Mark Simpson, 'Climate Change, Cooperation, and Moral Bioenhancement', *Journal of Medical Ethics* **42**:11 (2016), 742–747.

[7]   Anthony Lane, et al., 'Failed Replication of Oxytocin Effects on Trust: The Envelope Task Case', *PLoS One* **10**:9 (2015), e0137000.

[8]   See, for example, Peter Ahmann, et al., 'Placebo-Controlled Evaluation of Ritalin Side Effects', *Pediatrics* **91**:6 (1993), 1101–1106.

[9]   Nicholas Agar, 'Why is it Possible to Enhance Moral Status and Why is Doing So Wrong?', *Journal of Medical Ethics* **39**:2 (2013), 67–74; Allen Buchanan, 'Moral Status and Human Enhancement', *Philosophy & Public Affairs* **37**:4 (2009), 346–381.

their own political agenda. SSRIs, for instance, might be misused to make the recipients less critical about issues they would otherwise deem unjust.[10]

Finally, some even suggest that BME will deprive people of their 'freedom to fall',[11] leaving people in a state much like the scenario depicted in Skinner's utopian *Walden Two*, where its citizens are peace-loving farmers that are genetically engineered and behaviourally conditioned to love music and arts.[12] Despite a seemingly pleasant existence there seems to be something demeaning about it; that is, residents of Walden Two do not seem much different from programmed robots.

Whether or not the above-mentioned objections and concerns can be successfully addressed has already received a lot of attention in the literature.[13] Our essay is not particularly concerned with adding to that, except in passing. Instead we focus on a particular line of objection that has been thought to pose a serious threat to BME but has not yet been sufficiently dealt with.[14] According to this objection, the change of behaviour resulting from BME is not necessarily a moral improvement. For instance, being more generous with the help of oxytocin is indeed a good thing most of the time, yet under certain circumstances being generous is not something a moral person should be, especially in the case of dealing with terrorists. To give

---

[10] John Harris, 'Moral Enhancement and Freedom', *Bioethics* **25**:2 (2011), 102–11; Robert Sparrow, 'Better Living through Chemistry? A Reply to Savulescu and Persson on "Moral Enhancement"', *Journal of Applied Philosophy* **31**:1 (2014), 23–32.

[11] A phrase used in John Milton's *Paradise Lost*. See Harris, 'Moral Enhancement and Freedom'.

[12] See Robert Kane, *A Contemporary Introduction to Free Will* (Oxford: Oxford University Press, 2005), 3.

[13] For an in-depth review of moral enhancement see Jona Specker, et al., 'The Ethical Desirability of Moral Bioenhancement: A Review of Reasons', *BMC Medical Ethics* **15**:67 (2014): https://doi.org/10.1186/1472-6939-15-67.

[14] See especially Sparrow, 'Better Living Through Chemistry? A Reply to Savulescu and Persson on "Moral Enhancement"', 5; Robert Sparrow, 'Egalitarianism and Moral Bioenhancement', *American Journal of Bioethics* **14**:4 (2014), 20, 21. See also, Thomas Douglas, 'Moral Enhancement', in Julian Savulescu, Ruud ter Muelen, and Guy Kahane (eds), *Enhancing Human Capacities* (Blackwell: Oxford, 2011), 467–485. It is worth mentioning that although Douglas, a supporter of BME, acknowledges this line of objection, he does not really address it but merely sets it aside.

another example, while it is generally good to be sympathetic, one can wrongly sympathise with someone who does not deserve it. So in enhancing people's virtues such as generosity or sympathy, BME does not necessarily help bring about moral behaviour. We call this style of objection "the objection from particularism", as it stresses the variability of the moral statuses of the manifestations of the virtues and dovetails with the general thrust of moral particularism, which we will explain later.

The plan of this essay is as follows. In section 2, we will introduce the idea of moral particularism in more detail, and further explain how an objection derived from it poses at least a *prima facie* threat to BME. In section 3, we defend BME against this objection via a comparison with moral education. In section 4, we argue that the real lesson to be learned from moral particularism is that practical wisdom, being context-sensitive and essentially concerned with the particulars of moral circumstances, cannot be enhanced via biomedical means. This is because biomedical agents can merely serve to enhance behavioural dispositions to perform certain types of context-insensitive behaviours – behaviours that are insensitive to the morally salient features of particular circumstances. In section 5, we will propose where to set boundaries on the use of BME. Finally, in section 6, we will clarify and defend our position by addressing several potential objections.

2. Moral Particularism and Why it Poses a Threat to BME

Moral particularism has certainly cut much ice with analytic ethicists over at least the past two decades. The basic idea goes all the way back to Aristotle, who claimed that the major function of *phronesis* (i.e., practical wisdom) is to discern moral truths via the particulars of circumstances rather than through universals (i.e., moral principles).[15] More recently the doctrine of moral particularism has been understood differently by different philosophers. But, very roughly, it upholds the view that moral principles of one sort or another do not play any essential role in our moral life.[16] Applied to the area of moral values, it supports the view that the moral

---

[15] Aristotle, *Nicomachean Ethics*, VI.
[16] The passage from the beginning of this section is adapted from Peter Shiu-Hwa Tsu, 'Particularism in Ethics', in Duncan Pritchard (ed.), *Oxford Bibliographies Online* (Oxford: Oxford University Press, 2018): https://www.oxfordbibliographies.com/view/document/obo-9780195396577/obo-9780195396577-0367.xml.

values of things such as properties or actions, by and large, cannot be expressed in terms of moral principles; what is morally good in one context may not be so in another, and may even come to be morally bad.[17] For instance, according to moral particularists, a principled value statement such as "pleasure is good" or "pain is bad" does not always hold true. In fact, there are cases in which these statements seem apparently false. For instance, there does not appear to be anything good about sadistic pleasures. And pain does not seem to be obviously bad when it is well-deserved by a depraved and vicious person.

According to moral particularists, not only can natural properties such as pleasure and pain change their values in different contexts, but so can those "thick" properties of virtues, such as generosity, courage, honesty, and sympathy, etc. For instance, Dutch courage may not be good some of the time, whereas one can be both generous and honest to a fault. Moreover, as mentioned, one can feel sympathy with someone who does not deserve it. Jonathan Dancy, the staunchest champion of moral particularism, illustrates the point with a vivid example where someone is unduly considerate to a torturer who is hell-bent on his job.[18] The lesson to be learned from moral particularism seems to be this: whether the manifestation of a virtuous disposition is good is not a settled matter; rather, it is very much context-dependent.

If moral particularism is right about the variability of the moral value of manifestations of the virtues, then it seems to pose at least a *prima facie* threat to BME. How so? As we have mentioned, BME aims to improve people's moral behaviour through improving, via biomedical means, people's virtuous dispositions. Now, if people's virtuous dispositions can actually lead to morally wrong behaviour, then it would seem that BME, by enhancing people's virtuous dispositions via biomedical means, does not necessarily achieve what it aims at – the improvement of people's moral behaviour. It may even be counterproductive sometimes, which some have taken to constitute a reason against BME.

In the next section we will argue, via a comparison with moral education, that the variability of the moral value of manifestations of the

---

[17]   We use "moral values" broadly to refer to not only goodness and badness but rightness and wrongness as well.
[18]   Jonathan Dancy, "Moral Particularism", in Edward N. Zalta (ed.), *The Stanford Encyclopedia of Philosophy*: http://plato.stanford.edu/archives/fall2013/entries/moral-particularism/.

virtues does not suffice to ground a reason to reject BME. Before we do so, some comments are in order.

First, it should be acknowledged that moral particularism when applied to the realm of moral values is a controversial doctrine. While it attracts some supporters, it also attracts many critics. Some critics have argued, for instance, that some natural properties, when specified in more detail, can have a constant value across different contexts.[19] Torturing a six-year-old merely for fun can never be good, whereas the pleasures derived from harmless activities such as horticulture can never be bad.

Second, it is also controversial whether particularism is true of the moral values of the virtues. It has been contended by many that even if the value of natural properties can change, those of the virtues cannot.[20] This is because the values are in-built elements of the virtues. For instance, if someone calls an action "honest" but regards it as bad for that reason, it seems that he has not fully grasped the meaning of the concept "honesty".

In reply to the first concern particularists have stressed the importance of distinguishing the ground of the value from the enablers of the value.[21] Take the torture case. The particularists might well contend that the property of torture is the ground of the negative value, whereas the property of "doing it to a six-year old merely for fun" is enables the ground to function properly. What the particularists are at pains to emphasise is that the natural property that functions as the ground can come to acquire a different value in a context where the enabler is absent; for instance, the property of torturing

---

[19]   See for instance Brad Hooker, 'Moral Particularism: Wrong and Bad', in Brad Hooker and Margaret Little (eds), *Moral Particularism*, (Oxford: Oxford University Press, 2000), 8.

[20]   Hooker, 'Moral Particularism: Wrong and Bad'; Brad Hooker, 'Moral Particularism and the Real World', in Vojko Strahovnik, Mark Lance, and Matjaž Potrc (eds), *Challenging Moral Particularism* (New York: Routledge, 2008), 12–30; Roger Crisp, 'Particularizing Particularism', in Brad Hooker and Margaret Little (eds), *Moral Particularism* (Oxford: Oxford University Press, 2000), 23–47; David McNaughton and Piers Rawling, 'Unprincipled Ethics', in Brad Hooker and Margaret Little (eds), *Moral Particularism* (Oxford: Oxford University Press, 2000), 256–275; Margaret Little, 'Moral Generalities Revisited', in Brad Hooker and Margaret Little (eds), *Moral Particularism* (Oxford: Oxford University Press, 2000), 276–304.

[21]   Ralf Bader, 'Conditions, Modifiers, and Holism', in Errol Lord and Barry McGuire (eds), *Weighing Reasons* (Oxford: Oxford University Press, 2016), 27–55.

might arguably have a positive rather than negative value in an S&M chamber.[22]

In response to the second concern, many with particularist sympathies have argued that values are not in-built elements of the virtues; rather, they are our psychological projections.[23] With a change in context we might well project properties of opposite value onto the virtues. For instance, we might well contend without incoherence that someone is to be condemned for his kindness to a torturer.

For the purposes of this essay, we will not attempt a further discussion of whether these replies from particularism can allay the above-mentioned concerns. Our strategy is to fully grant the variability of the moral value of manifestations of the virtues, and argue that even if the virtues' values are variable this cannot repudiate BME.

3. BME and Moral Education

Some have taken the objection from moral particularism to constitute a compelling reason against BME. In this section we will argue that it does not, via a comparison with moral education. The main reason for this comparison is that moral education, as a means of moral enhancement, shares with BME the same goal of improving people's moral behaviour through augmenting their virtuous dispositions.

Now, as we have mentioned, some bioethicists with particularist sympathies have argued that BME cannot achieve this goal because manifestations of virtuous dispositions are not always appropriate.[24] If this is correct, then presumably it will be a challenge to moral

---

[22] We say "arguably" because one might feel that what happens in the S&M chamber is consensual and therefore cannot really be torture. On the other hand, it might well be contended that if what is going on in the S&M chamber is not real torture then the masochists in the S&M chamber would not get a kick out of it. The fact that the masochists do get a kick, one might therefore suggest, indicates that what they experience is indeed torture. See Mark Timmons, *Moral Theory* (Maryland: Rowman & Littlefield, 2002), 259.

[23] Simon Blackburn, 'Through Thick and Thin', in *Practical Tortoise Raising and Other Philosophical Essays* (Oxford: Oxford University Press, 2010), ch.7, and 'Disentangling Disentangling', in Simon Kirchin (ed.), *Thick Concepts* (Oxford: Oxford University Press, 2013), 121–135.

[24] See for instance Sparrow, 'Better Living Through Chemistry? A Reply to Savulescu and Persson on "Moral Enhancement"', and 'Egalitarianism and Moral Bioenhancement'.

education too, for since time immemorial moral education has played the role of cultivating virtuous dispositions.

However, we will argue that variability of the moral status of manifestations of the virtues does not constitute a good reason against the practice of moral education. That is, we contend that the particularist objection "proves too much". We will explain why this is so and further contend that for the same reason the particularist objection does not count against moral education, it does not count against BME either.

To begin with, we take it to be a fact that moral education is distinguished from brainwashing or indoctrination by its aim to improve our moral behaviour through cultivating good character or virtuous dispositions. Now, while it might be true that the manifestations of virtuous dispositions in some contexts are morally wrong rather than right, as the particularists claim, this does not seem to provide a good reason against the practice of moral education. Why? We think this is for the mundane reason that moral education's dedication to the cultivation of virtuous dispositions still gives us the best chance of performing morally right actions, and the alternative of giving up on teaching our children virtues such as sympathy, courage, generosity, or honesty just seems patently unpalatable. Swanton has observed, quite correctly in our view, that if the virtues did not characteristically lead to morally right actions in most circumstances, we would not have categorised them as virtues in the first place.[25] So there seems to be a stable connection between our virtuous dispositions and the performance of morally right actions.[26]

---

[25]   Christine Swanton, *Virtue Ethics: A Pluralistic View* (Oxford: Oxford University Press, 2003), 244.

[26]   It should be noted that situationist philosophers, such as John Doris and Gilbert Harman, often take the claim here to be falsified by empirical evidence (such as the Good Samaritan experiment) in social psychology. See John Doris, *Lack of Character: Personality and Moral Behavior* (Cambridge: Cambridge University Press, 2002); Gilbert Harman, 'Moral Philosophy Meets Social Psychology: Virtue Ethics and the Fundamental Attribution Error', *Proceedings of the Aristotelian Society* **99**:1 (1999), 315–332. Situationism is roughly the view that our moral behaviour is very much of a function of the circumstances we are in; the virtues do not have much of a role to play. However, we are of the view that the empirical evidence adduced by the situationists might merely show that most people are not as virtuous as they should be, not that the virtues are usually causally inefficacious with regard to morally right actions. Before this alternative interpretation of the empirical evidence is ruled out, we do not think that situationism has much force against our claim.

Pei-Hua Huang and Peter Shiu-Hwa Tsu

If so, giving up on moral education, or BME, for that matter, merely because the moral statuses of manifestations of the virtues are variable seems unwarranted. For this would only reduce the chances of our performing the morally right actions. As Margaret Little has rightly observed, so long as we are not in a post-apocalyptic world where things are turned completely upside down we can reasonably expect that the virtues would characteristically produce morally right actions.[27] The normality of the background conditions ensures that the virtues are so conducive; honesty is usually the best policy, whereas kindness to people is generally good.

If it turns out that in some contexts, the virtues actually lead to morally wrong actions, this does not suffice, *per se*, as a reason to abandon the practice of moral education. We need to ask how much more likely the virtuous dispositions themselves are to lead to wrongs rather than rights. If it is not very likely (which is our view on the basis of Swanton's perceptive observations), then it is just irrational, on a cost-benefit analysis, to give up on their cultivation.

So there seems to be no reason to reject moral education simply because the virtues cannot *guarantee* moral behaviour.[28] Similarly, this cannot constitute a reason to reject BME either. In our view, so long as the virtuous dispositions brought about by biomedical means can produce morally right actions no less reliably than those brought about by moral education, they are worth having.

4. Practical Wisdom and BME

In the last section we argued that if the variability of the moral statutes of manifestations of the virtues does not suffice as a reason against moral education, then nor does it suffice as a reason against BME. So long as virtuous dispositions can reliably produce morally right actions in most circumstances they are worth cultivating and enhancing. In this section, we will argue, however, that unlike moral education, the dispositions and character traits enhanced through biomedical means are merely what we call "context-insensitive traits" such that they may not reliably produce morally right actions. Whether they deserve to be called "virtues" is thus questionable. If there is any lesson to be learned from moral

[27] Little, 'Moral Generalities Revisited', 296–298.
[28] And after all, moral philosophers since the time of Aristotle have long been aware of moral (bad) luck.

198

particularism we think it is this: practical wisdom, something that can be enhanced through moral education, can never be enhanced through biomedical means. There remains, therefore, an indispensable role for moral education to play insofar as the cultivation of practical wisdom and moral virtues is concerned. Let us elaborate.

To begin with, the idea of practical wisdom can be traced back to Aristotle, whom we regard as the founding father of moral particularism. Three features of practical wisdom are especially relevant for our purposes here. First, its context-sensitive nature. Very roughly, practical wisdom is widely regarded as entailing some sort of moral sensitivity to the morally salient features of particular circumstances.[29] It is concerned with getting things right, and this is done through carefully considering the particulars of the circumstances, rather than applying any universal principles. For universal principles deal in samenesses, which are often too crude to capture the nuances and complexities of moral life.[30] One size cannot fit all. To use an analogy from Aristotle to illustrate, the amount of food that is insufficient for Milo, a wrestler, might be too much for a normal adult.[31] There is no principle that tells us what the correct amount of food is in advance. Sensitivities to the particulars of the circumstances are essential for correct judgement. In the moral domain things are not so very different. A gift that is rightly considered generous to our neighbour's three-year-old child might be rightly considered stingy if we give it to our Oxford academic host. Practical wisdom, according to Aristotle, plays the role of discerning the "mean" in actions, which is contingent on particular circumstances.

Second, another significant feature of practical wisdom, according to Aristotle, is that it is essentially involved in the virtues.[32] To put this slightly differently, virtues are those character traits that are regulated by practical wisdom. Dutch courage, according to this view, is not real courage, for real courage is regulated by practical wisdom, which is concerned to hit the mean without going to extremes.

---

[29] Christine Swanston and John McDowell also interpret practical wisdom along these lines. See Christine Swanton, 'A Virtue Ethical Account of Right Action', *Ethics* **112**:1 (2001), 32–52; John McDowell, 'Virtue and Reason', in *Mind, Value & Reality* (Massachusetts: Harvard University Press, 2002), 50–73. For Aristotle's relevant characterisation of practical wisdom, see *Nicomachean Ethics*, VI.8.

[30] Jonathan Dancy, *Ethics Without Principles* (Oxford: Oxford University Press, 2004), 2.

[31] Aristotle, *Nicomachean Ethics*, VI.6.

[32] Aristotle, *Nicomachean Ethics*, VI.13.

Since Dutch courage might well entail excessive drinking, it is not real courage. Real courage is instead exhibited when one resists peer pressure to drink more than one can handle. Take another example. A disposition to tell the truth, according to the view propounded here, is not to be equated with the virtue of being honest if the disposition is not regulated by practical wisdom. Practical wisdom informs the agent to whom the truth is owed; without it, one might well wrongly tell the truth to Nazi guards when enquired as to the whereabouts of a Jewish girl they wish to capture and send to Auschwitz. And such behaviour does not seem to be what honesty, *qua* virtue, requires. For honesty, when regulated by practical wisdom, is not simply the vulgar disposition to tell the truth, but rather, from an Aristotelian particularist perspective, a more sophisticated disposition to tell the truth to the right person in the right way and for the right reason.[33]

Third, practical wisdom essentially involves life experience. In contrasting morality with mathematics, Aristotle maintains that while there can be whizz-kids in maths, there cannot be whizz-kids in morality, the reason being that maths is essentially concerned with discovering *a priori* universal truths, whereas morality is very much down-to-earth, concerned with the particulars of circumstances.[34] To be able to reliably discern moral truths (or to be practically wise, for that matter), therefore, according to Aristotle, will require one to have abundant experience with various circumstances of life. To use a modern example, while Terence Tao, a mathematical genius, could solve difficult maths puzzles at the age of nine, it seems far-fetched and unrealistic to expect him to tell us at that age what we ought to do when facing life-and-death decisions concerning euthanasia or abortion.

Now, having clarified the nature of practical wisdom as (1) being context-sensitive, (2) essentially involved in the virtues, and (3) essentially involving life experience, we can now proceed to explain why BME does not really improve people's virtuous dispositions. This is essentially because BME is ineffectual in enhancing practical wisdom, due to the first and third features of practical wisdom. And since practical wisdom is essentially involved in all of the virtues, as indicated by (2), it follows that BME is not capable of enhancing the virtues.

Let us elaborate. First of all, why would BME not improve people's practical wisdom? As we have mentioned, practical

---

[33]   Aristotle, *Nicomachean Ethics*, II.3.
[34]   Aristotle, *Nicomachean Ethics*, VI.8.

wisdom essentially involves life experience and thus takes time to cultivate. BME, by contrast, purports to be capable of enhancing people's "virtuous dispositions" once the drugs or biomedical means used have come into effect, without necessarily involving life's seasoned experience and years of cultivation. This being the case, we have little reason to believe that the "virtuous dispositions" enhanced via biomedical means involve practical wisdom. To put things slightly differently, in enhancing people's "virtuous dispositions", BME does not thus improve their practical wisdom.

Second, and more importantly, practical wisdom, as we have elaborated, is context-sensitive in nature; it is concerned with doing the right thing contingent on the morally salient features of the circumstances. However, the "virtues" purportedly enhanced through biomedical means are not really context-sensitive in nature. For instance, in principle a moral agent who has been enhanced in "generosity" through biomedical means can be more "generous", we might say, not just in his way of treating his friends, but in his donations to terrorist organisations. The latter is, however, not what a practically wise person would do and would in fact frown upon.[35] So this shows that the "virtue" of generosity purportedly enhanced by BME does not essentially involve practical wisdom. It is *not* context-sensitive in nature. Or rather, it is context-*insensitive*, in that it merely promotes certain types of general behaviour. Take two more examples to illustrate. It is perfectly imaginable that someone with "courage" enhanced through biomedical means might well utilise it to rob a bank, whereas "loyalty" enhanced through biomedical means might well lead to unflinching support for unethical policies such as racial cleansing advocated by a party to which a person is loyal.

So, on the basis of the two observations mentioned above, we have little reason to believe that BME enhances people's practical wisdom. But as we have argued, real virtues, for Aristotle, essentially involve it. This being the case, the "virtues" BME enhances are to be regarded as merely "quasi-virtues" at best, or dispositions that have some semblance of virtues. The real lesson to be learned from

---

[35] A passage from Elizabeth Telfer's work can illuminate why this is so: 'it seems to be true that we do not call someone "wise" in English unless he is in general a good person, and it may be that the Greek noun "phronesis" carries a similar implication'. See Telfer, 'The Unity of the Moral Virtues in Aristotle's "Nicomachean Ethics"', *Proceedings of the Aristotelian Society* **90**:1 (1990), 35–48.

particularism, we maintain, is that BME, being impotent in enhancing people's practical wisdom, cannot really enhance real virtues.

To forestall a possible misunderstanding, we are *not* claiming that BME cannot enhance people's real virtues in any circumstances. In fact, we leave open the possibility that it may well do so with the aid of practical wisdom. We are merely arguing that contrary to what most BME supporters seem to think, BME *by itself* is impotent in enhancing the virtues.[36]

Now, since the virtues are important for living a moral life, and BME by itself, as we argued above, cannot really contribute to their improvement without the aid of practical wisdom, it is obviously important to elaborate on how to cultivate practical wisdom insofar as we are concerned with enhancing our virtues. With regard to the cultivation of practical wisdom, we think that moral education plays an indispensable role. As for methodology, we side with Martha Nussbaum in thinking that critical reflections on ethically charged novels provide good training in moral sensitivities.[37] For it is the art of a great novelist to vividly represent the nuanced details (i.e., the particulars) of moral situations. Students can be invited to think, for instance, why a gentle lift of eyebrows can reverse our moral judgement about the character of the protagonist, or why a certain wave of the hands indicates aloofness rather than passion. In addition to reflections on great novels, we might also add that a good training in moral philosophy can help too.[38] To carefully think through the pros and cons of a live debate, one has to pay

---

[36] For relevant views of the BME supporters, see, for instance, David DeGrazia, 'Moral Enhancement, Freedom, and What We (Should) Value in Moral Behaviour', *Journal of Medical Ethics* **40**:6 (2014), 361–368; Douglas, 'Moral Enhancement'; Persson and Savulescu, 'The Perils of Cognitive Enhancement and the Urgent Imperative to Enhance the Moral Character of Humanity'; *Unfit for the Future: The Need for Moral Enhancement*; and 'The Duty to be Morally Enhanced'; Will Jefferson, et al., 'Enhancement and Civic Virtue', *Social Theory and Practice* **40**:3 (2014), 499–527.

[37] See Martha Nussbaum, 'Finely Aware and Richly Responsible', *Love's Knowledge* (New York: Oxford University Press, 1990), 148–167.

[38] Although it should be admitted that contemporary moral philosophy often involves a heavy use of thought experiments which are abstracted from the concrete details of the case. We are not against their use, for they can indeed help illuminate difficult cases from time to time. But we should also be careful in their use in that there can be morally relevant differences between them and the real cases we encounter. This is a point the particularists have been wont to emphasise. See Jonathan Dancy, 'The Role of

close attention to the morally salient features of the matter. For instance, in the debate regarding the moral permissibility of active euthanasia, one is sensitised to a great number of factors such as whether the recipient is in a sane mental condition, whether he has come of age, whether he is fully informed of alternatives, and whether he is terminally ill, etc.

5. Setting Boundaries to BME

Since BME, being context-insensitive and not involving seasoned life experience, is impotent in improving practical wisdom, the character traits it enhances are not really "virtues" in any robust sense of the term. A terrorist financier, after the use of BME, can be more "generous" in his donations to the terrorists. A robber might use BME to improve his "courage" before proceeding to rob the bank. Finally, an undercover detective sent to infiltrate a criminal cell, after receiving BME might well become more "honest" (possessing a stronger disposition to tell the truth) and thus undermine his task and endanger his life.

So it is actually very important to set boundaries to the use of BME. Far from making it compulsory, as some supporters of BME seem to suggest,[39] certain people should actually be prevented from its use, especially the following two categories of people: (1) those who do not aim to do the morally right thing, for they might well misuse the "virtues" enhanced via biomedical means, and (2) those who *are* concerned with doing the morally right thing, but have to constantly do the "unvirtuous" thing (e.g., telling a lie) because of the professional roles they play. The undercover detective belongs to the second category, whereas the robber and the terrorist financier the first.

In practice, it is difficult, if not impossible, to identify people in the first category, for the mundane reason that (potential) robbers and terrorist financiers are unlikely to reveal their furtive identities. If so, this is a real concern for mandatory implementation of BME.

Imaginary Cases in Ethics', *Pacific Philosophical Quarterly* **66**:1/2 (1985), 141–153.

[39]   See for instance, Persson and Savulescu, 'The Perils of Cognitive Enhancement and the Urgent Imperative to Enhance the Moral Character of Humanity'; *Unfit for the Future: The Need for Moral Enhancement*; and 'The Duty to be Morally Enhanced'.

BME might well result in unethical behaviour, if used by the people in the first category. And for those in the second category, it is clear that they should be exempted or even actively prevented from certain types of BME. For instance, the undercover detectives should perhaps be actively prevented from using BME to improve their truth-telling dispositions.

For the ordinary folks like most of us who belong to neither of the above-mentioned categories, BME is also to be used with caution. For most of us may fall well short of possessing practical wisdom. We might not be sensitive enough, for instance, to when the truth is to be told, and how best to tell it, or to whom the truth is owed. When our truth-telling disposition is enhanced, due to the lack of practical wisdom, we might well misuse it too. The future of the widespread implementation of BME might not be as rosy as its supporters like to think.

6. Objections and Replies

Let us clarify and defend our position by addressing several possible objections.

Objection 1: In section 4 you argue that BME cannot really contribute to people's virtues without the aid of practical wisdom. That seems to suggest that with the aid of practical wisdom, BME might well contribute to people's virtues.

Reply 1: Our view of BME is not entirely negative. We leave open the possibility that with the progress of science and technology, BME might well contribute to the enhancement of virtues when used on people who have practical wisdom (i.e., people who know how to do the right thing, at the right time, in the right place, for the right reason, etc.).[40] That is, we leave open, though do not insist on, the possibility that people who have practical wisdom, *qua* intellectual virtue, might lack enough motivation to do the right thing. In this scenario people who already have practical wisdom might still need BME to improve their virtuous dispositions or motivations.

---

[40] Something along these lines was suggested by Harris Wiseman, *The Myth of the Moral Brain: The Limit of Moral Enhancement* (Cambridge, MA: MIT Press, 2016), 170. He maintains that working alongside traditional moral education, BME might well serve as a supplementary support mechanism for those who are already morally oriented.

The reason why we merely leave open but do not want to insist on the possibility is because it might well turn out that people who have practical wisdom must already have the virtuous dispositions, as most interpreters of Aristotle have maintained.[41] Then it is not clear whether there is still room with regard to these people's virtuous dispositions for BME to improve.

For our purposes, we only want to insist on the claim that *without* the aid of practical wisdom, BME alone cannot contribute to people's real virtues, for the reasons already articulated in section 4. *With* the aid of practical wisdom, whether BME can contribute to the improvement of people's virtues depends on whether one thinks practical wisdom already essentially entails virtuous dispositions.

Objection 2: In section 4 you said that BME is impotent in contributing to practical wisdom. Recently, it has been suggested, however, that moral education is actually a specific form of BME, on the grounds that moral education, like the use of drugs, also changes one's biological makeup such as the shape of the synapses and the brain activities.[42] If so, would your argument not lead to an implausible conclusion by your own lights – that is, that moral education is impotent in enhancing practical wisdom?

Reply 2: First of all, it is controversial whether moral education should be regarded as a form of BME. For although moral education, like BME, modulates people's moral behaviour through their brain chemistry, moral education focusses, *inter alia*, on the exploration of the meaning of life, the reason why an action is right or wrong, or what it means to respect people from different cultures, all of which are open questions and therefore do not align with BME, which is mainly in the business of enhancing people's "virtues". In addition, as we understand the term "BME", it refers to moral enhancement using drugs or genetic engineering. So it seems somewhat misleading to see moral education, which uses neither of these means, as a form of BME. But even if we broaden the meaning of BME so as to include moral education for the sake of argument, we insist that

---

[41]   Indeed, there is good textual evidence in support of this interpretation in *Nicomachean Ethics*, VI.12, where Aristotle claims that '[m]anifestly, then, one cannot be practically wise without being good'.
[42]   Harris Wiseman, *The Myth of the Moral Brain: The Limit of Moral Enhancement*, 285–286. For a more detailed discussion, see Pei-Hua Huang, 'Authenticity, Autonomy and Enhancement', *Dilemata* **19** (2015), 39–52.

moral education is distinctive, in that it distinguishes itself from other forms of BME by being the sort of BME that can contribute to practical wisdom, due to the emphasis it can place on the nuanced details of the moral circumstances one faces.

By conceding that BME, conducted in the form of moral education, may contribute to practical wisdom, we do not believe that we thereby concede the argument *in toto*. For this is scarcely what the BME supporters themselves will be content with. What counts as true victory for the BME supporters is the substantiation of their claim that practical wisdom can indeed be enhanced via drug use or genetic engineering. Yet, insofar as we know, there is no relevant empirical evidence in support of this claim. Moreover, as we have argued in section 4, it is not entirely clear how practical wisdom, being essentially sensitive to the particulars of situations, can be enhanced through drug use or genetic engineering that can only augment dispositions to perform certain types of (context-insensitive) general behaviour. Here we are in agreement with Christen and Narvaez, who perceptively observe that since practical wisdom is about 'acting skilfully in the right way at the right time with the right feelings', it cannot be 'given in measured dosages with predicable outcomes'.[43] BME's purported capacity to increase practical wisdom is best taken with a pinch of salt.

Objection 3: You claim in sections 2 and 4 that Aristotle is a particularist, but Terence Irwin, a prominent Aristotelian scholar, argues that he is not.[44]

Reply 3: There are just as many interpretations of Aristotle as there are interpretations of particularism. Depending on one's interpretation of particularism and one's interpretation of Aristotle, Aristotle may not be a particular brand of particularist, as Irwin rightly suggests. Our interest in this essay, however, is not exegetical. For even if Aristotle is *not* a particularist, the particularist worry we brought up (i.e., that practical wisdom cannot be enhanced via biomedical means) is still valid.

---

[43] Markus Christen and Darcia Narvaez, 'Moral Development in Early Childhood Is Key for Moral Enhancement', *AJOB Neuroscience* 2:4 (2012), 25.

[44] Terence Irwin, 'Ethics as an Inexact Science: Aristotle's Ambition for Moral Theory', in Brad Hooker and Margaret Little (eds), *Moral Particularism* (Oxford: Oxford University Press, 2000), 100–129.

Objection 4: You claim that biomedical means are impotent in enhancing practical wisdom, but some studies have shown that some drugs can improve people's intelligence or cognitive capacities.[45] If so, would those drugs not also help with the enhancement of practical wisdom, *qua* intellectual capacity?

Reply 4: While it is certainly true that practical wisdom involves intelligence or cleverness, it is not to be equated with them, as Aristotle has famously claimed. An evil person might well be clever or intelligent, but he is never practically wise, according to Aristotle.[46] For it is an essential characteristic of a practically wise person that he aims to do the morally right thing. So while some drugs might improve the intelligence of a person, they still may fall short of improving his practical wisdom. To put it differently, intelligence is merely one of the necessary components of practical wisdom; it is not sufficient. One may be intelligent without being practically wise at all. Far too many intelligent people are not morally sensitive. So it is too quick to infer from the claim that some drugs are effective in enhancing one's intelligence to the conclusion that one's practical wisdom is therefore improved.

Objection 5: In section 6, you argue that people who aim to do the morally right thing but have to constantly do the unvirtuous thing due to their professional roles should be exempted or even banned from certain forms of BME. But what if they are already in full possession of practical wisdom? Take the undercover detective, for instance. If they have already acquired full possession of practical wisdom, that just means that they know, for instance, when to tell the truth, to whom the truth is owed, and for what the truth is needed, etc. They can judge that, for instance, the mafia does not deserve to know the truth about their real identity. In this scenario, using BME to improve their truth-telling disposition does not seem to be harmful.

Reply 5: In the scenario depicted by our objector, using BME may indeed not be harmful. But this is entirely compatible with our central point that BME ought to be used with caution. For if the undercover detective is still lacking in the context-sensitive aspects

---

[45]   Nirit Agay, et al., 'Non-Specific Effects of Methylphenidate (Ritalin) on Cognitive Ability and Decision-Making of ADHD and Healthy Adults', *Psychopharmacology* **210**:4 (2010), 511–519.
[46]   Aristotle, *Nicomachean Ethics*, VI.12.

of practical wisdom, it will certainly be dangerous to use BME to improve their truth-telling disposition.

7. Conclusion

It goes without saying that our world faces serious challenges such as global warming, terrorism, pollution, and poverty. One major source of these evils, as the supporters of BME rightly diagnose, is our moral impoverishment. We human beings do not live up to the demands of morality. In the face of such crises, BME supporters recommend further research on it as a potential solution. Although we welcome such attempts, we also think that we should neither overestimate nor romanticise BME. For, as we have argued on the basis of the insights of Aristotelian moral particularism, BME, by itself, is impotent in promoting practical wisdom and hence the virtues. Traditional moral education would still play a major and indispensable role in their cultivation and improvement.[47]

Monash University
pei-hua.huang@monash.edu

Chung Cheng University
u4079238@gmail.com

[47] This chapter is a work of collaboration; both authors contributed equally to the writing of and research for it. We are immensely grateful to the following people for their helpful feedback: Robert Sparrow, Robert Mark Simpson, Andrew McLoughlin, and Hiroshi Miura. Tsu would also like to thank Taiwan's Ministry of Science and Technology for financial support (MOST-104-2628-H-194-001-MY2; MOST-105-2410-H-194-096-MY4).

Is Moral Enhancement a Right, or a Threat to Rights?

JOHN R. SHOOK

Abstract
Enhancements for morality could become technologically practical at the expense of becoming unethical and uncivil. A mode of moral enhancement intensifying a person's imposition of conformity upon others, labeled here as "moral righteousness", is particularly problematic. Moral energies contrary to expansions of civil rights and liberties can drown out reasoned justifications for equality and freedom, delaying social progress. The technological capacity of moral righteousness in the hands of a majority could impose puritanical conformities and override some rights and liberties. Fortunately, there cannot be a human right or a civil right to access righteous moral enhancement, and governments would be prudent to forbid such technology for moral righteousness. From an enlarged perspective, less righteousness could lead to a more just society. Going further, if a neurological intervention for moral righteousness could be invented, so too could moral de-enhancement, here labeled as "moral toleration". Perhaps moral toleration deserves as much commendation as so-called moral enhancement. Justice with less delay can be justice enhanced.

1. Introduction

The moral conviction demanding respect for a civil right or a civil liberty is often a powerful social and political force. Moral convictions in opposition can be just as powerful. Those threatening a violation of familiar categories, traditional statuses, and regular roles are accused of disrupting the social order, claiming an unearned privilege, or inflicting harms on others. Showing that the social order will adapt well, new equalities can elevate everyone, and sure benefits outweigh exaggerated harms, are all morally relevant ways to supply reasoned responses. Convictions do not promptly yield the floor for that rational debate, though. Instead, shrilly moralistic alarms are sounded, tribalistic sides take defensive postures, and fronts of potent resistance are raised. "Only those in the right should be heard", each side declares. Cultural discourse seizes up with symbolic posturing and then crystallises into slogans. Decades soon pass, and successive generations wait for progress.

Faulting morality itself is understandably counter-intuitive. We write our histories after more rights and more equality have been

doi:10.1017/S135824611800036X

secured, crediting the morally inspired and righteously energised victors. (Conservatives, no less morally energised, are clearly wrong only in hindsight.) Those post-victory narratives are accurate enough, considering the moralistic resistance which had to be repeatedly overcome. Less moralistic grounds for social change are not known for arousing fervent support. But those good grounds do not arouse intense opposition either, so long as inequalities and injustices are not worsened by social change. If the eagerness to impose one's moral stance on the lives of others could be diminished across a population, the overall re-balancing of moral energies with mundane reasonings might shift society towards faster expansions and surer protections of civil rights and liberties. The likelihood of such a shift can appear counter-intuitive, especially to partisan political camps (liberal and conservative alike) who are proud of their devotion to civil rights and liberties. And those camps perennially beg the public to be just as morally passionate about the next struggles to come.

Moral psychologists, thanks in part to neuroscience, are discerning cognitive-affective processes connected to moral conviction and action. Proposals for experimental adjustments to people's moral judgements and energies have been aired. If lack of moral passion and social action from the public is at fault, morality enhancement can look like an appealing remedy. This essay argues to the contrary. The sort of moralistic enhancement conducive to partisan victory is not the right solution; no-one has a right to it, and government would be right to suppress it. Moral enhancement need not be the continuation of culture wars by other means. A society may be wiser for encouraging the opposite of moral enhancement where rights and liberties are concerned.

2. Morality Enhancement and Moral Righteousness

Let morality enhancement be defined as a technological intervention that alters neural functioning which happens to improve one's exhibition of moral conduct. For the purposes of this discussion, in order to be a morality enhancer, of whatever contrivance – pharmacological, modulatory, cybernetic, and so on – the intervention demonstrably works. If it does not work by adjusting actual moral conduct in some positive and objective manner, it is not a morality enhancer. (And if it alters other behaviours too, then it is still a morality enhancer, though of dubious value and potentially immoral character.) By "objective", empirical accessibility to behaviour is meant, not other senses of "valid" or "true".

Is Moral Enhancement a Right, or a Threat to Rights?

A person can truly come to sense or understand moral concerns differently over time, and feel validly enhanced in the process. Moral philosophies consider subjective matters supposedly intrinsic to morality (willful freedom, intending good, empathy, dutifulness, right reasoning, and so on), but moral psychology co-ordinates them with behaviours. Morality enhancement, as defined here, does not target anything purely subjective that leaves behaviour entirely unaltered (if that were even possible). A person who continues to act precisely the same manner as before, but acts for clarified motives, is someone with a fresh ethical perspective, not a new moral capacity. The enhancement of morality will not be delayed by inconclusive ethical theorising about internal criteria essential to morality. Besides, those demanding "ethical enhancement" satisfying internal criteria must explain how any alleged subjective improvement would be confirmable in moral conduct.

An agnostic stance is further recommended in regard to ethical theorising looking for the lone "true" morality, and just as much agnosticism towards abandoning that quest as well. The enhancement of morality will not be dispelled as impossible upon the challenge, "By which morality?" The appropriate answer is obvious: "Our morality". What is relative or multiform can still be naturally real. What people can regard as moral provides the only meaning to morality that any human beings in the real world are capable of discussing. That is why the enhancement of morality, like the improvement of anything we do as humans, can only happen in actual human settings. This must never be forgotten. Anyone speaking of moral enhancement takes the risk of inflating transhumanist optimism, encouraging partisan radicalism, or purveying idiosyncratic moralism. These risks accompany "moral enhancement" in the abstract by ignoring key contexts: (a) the diversity to cultural traditions that instill differing sets of moral norms; (b) the varying social conditions that warrant decisions about moral priorities; and (c) the individual characters that balance moral virtues in distinctive ways. For example, could the enhancement of trust be a moral enhancement? Some cultures emphasise trust as a moral duty, while others do not; some groups should not enjoy dutiful trusting from their members; and generous trust is often unwise for people with naïvely helpful characters. For anything that comes to mind as assuredly moral for anyone, it could be immoral, unjust, and/or harmful when intensified in someone chosen at random from around the world.

Recognising context is one step; acknowledging practicalities is the next. No intervention designed for morality enhancement exists today. Alterations to moral ability will more likely be discovered by accident, while tinkering with one or more entwined functions: interpersonal sensitivity, social cognition, foresight salience, threat management, emotional moderation, impulse inhibition, motivational control, practical inference, and the like.[1] Current science has only modest clues about designing morality enhancement, or any sort of cognitive enhancement, but the many physiological and neurological obstacles to practical enhancement are not discussed here.[2] If a neurological intervention was to somehow influence moral ability, experimental detection and confirmation are further hurdles, but they are not insurmountable. Subjects can be tested for certain moral tendencies and preferences after specific moral contexts have been pre-arranged. So long as no-one imagines that "universal" moral abilities of "the human being" are thereby revealed, moral psychology can objectively measure alterations to moral performance.[3]

This essay has so far been talking about "morality enhancement" rather than "moral enhancement" to call initial attention to the way that any ideal moral enhancer could well be an immoral moral enhancer. "Moral enhancement" cannot automatically be moral just because "moral" was prefixed to "enhancement". An imagined moral enhancer may lose its moral character when situated within a real-world context, it might turn out to be largely immoral in its overall effects, or its usage by many could lead to unjust social consequences. No "moral enhancement" should be tautologically defined as entirely moral or ethical. With that cautionary point in place, the rest of this essay returns to convention, with "moral enhancement" standing in for "morality enhancement".

To demonstrate the efficacy of a putative moral enhancer, moral psychology would apply pre-set standards of moral ability, to

---

[1]   Discussions of morally relevant capacities are offered by Thomas Douglas, 'Moral Enhancement via Direct Emotion Modulation: A Reply to John Harris', *Bioethics* **27**:3 (2013), 160–168; Molly Crockett and Regina Rini, 'Neuromodulators and the (In)stability of Moral Cognition', in J. Decety and T. Wheatley (eds), *The Moral Brain: A Multidisciplinary Perspective* (Cambridge, MA: MIT Press), 221–235; and G. Owen Schaefer, 'Direct vs. Indirect Moral Enhancement', *Kennedy Institute of Ethics Journal* **25**:3 (2015), 261–289.

[2]   Consult John Shook and James Giordano, 'Defining Contexts of Cognitive (Performance) Enhancements', in F. Jotterand and V. Dubljevic (eds), *Cognitive Enhancement: Ethical and Policy Implications in International Perspectives* (Oxford: Oxford University Press, 2016), 76–98.

[3]   John R. Shook, 'Neuroethics and the Possible Types of Moral Enhancement', *AJOB Neuroscience* **3**:4 (2012), 3–14.

Is Moral Enhancement a Right, or a Threat to Rights?

compare against the moral conduct of a subject receiving the intervention.[4] What types of behaviours count as morally relevant, and morally right, must be chosen in advance in order to supply needed contexts. The confirmation that moral behaviour has been measurably altered (in whatever direction) in a subject then further permits researchers to realistically determine whether any novel moral behaviours (and possibly other anomalous behaviours), have been added to this subject's performance.

A "generic" moral enhancer by definition only improves the subject's ability to be the kind of moral person that the subject already tries to be. Let the target of moral enhancement be charity, to supply examples. A subject who believes that donating a large percentage of income to one's church will maintain that belief, and display moral enhancement by fulfilling that felt duty more regularly and/or more generously. By contrast, a "morphic" moral enhancer improves moral conduct by altering a subject's moral views, such as moral values or beliefs. A subject who had not thought that avoiding charity was a moral failing will reverse that belief, displaying this moral enhancement by fulfilling a newly acknowledged duty to give generously to charity. As for a theoretical third category, the "ethical" moral enhancer that adjusts morality towards what is truly moral (not simply what any number of people happen to think is moral), this chapter has nothing to say, because moral philosophy is not driving this essay's enquiry. These three goals for moral enhancement must be kept distinct, although philosophical debates over its merits have exhibited their conflation.

Morphic moral enhancement (if anything approaching that mode became technological feasible) is not this essay's focus, but it deserves two observations. First, few people would voluntarily undergo morphic moral enhancement. "There's nothing about wasting money on charities that seems moral to me – why shouldn't my family enjoy the wealth that I've earned?" "I'm pretty sure that killing someone threatening my home is my right – why should I become a defenseless wimp?" Pro-choice advocates will not accept "enhancement" of their baby-loving ability, and pro-life advocates will not accept "enhancement" of their women-respecting ability. If I do not think that a so-called "enhancement" is all that moral, I must regard its morphic application upon me as immoral, or oddly amoral, or just something to make me congenial to others. In the absence of peer pressure or coercion, a typical person will not

---

[4] John Shook, 'My Brain Made Me Moral: Moral Performance Enhancement for Realists', *Neuroethics* **9**:3 (2016), 199–211.

regard morphic enhancement as obligatory. Second, following from this, a society compelling morphic moral enhancement violates human rights and civil rights unless stringent criteria are satisfied, akin to justifications for mandatory mental treatment or imprisonment.

Another distinction by moral psychology is needed next, to distinguish "judgemental" moral enhancement from "performative" and "corrective" moral enhancement. Confirming one mode in an enhancer is not automatically a confirmation of the others. A judgemental moral enhancer improves the subject's ability to make accurate assessments of moral situations and correctly judge what is right more reliably. Expressing judgements upon hypotheticals without participating in actual problematic situations is one way for a subject to reveal aspects of moral capacity. Participation is a second way. A performative moral enhancer improves the subject's ability to judge what is morally right (it fulfils the judgemental mode) and also the subject's ability to do more morally right actions while participating in real-world situations.[5] Scrutinising the behaviour of others goes well beyond attending to one's own behaviour, providing a third target for moral enhancers. A corrective moral enhancer not only improves the subject's own moral performance (it fulfils the judgemental and performative modes), but additionally improves the subject's corrective efforts against wrongs by others.[6] For example, a subject receiving a moral enhancement against theft will duly regard stealing as more morally wrong and also seek harsher punishment for thieves than the subject had approved before enhancement. Corrective efforts against wrongs could take any number of concrete forms, such as voting, donating money, civic activism, social nonco-operation, public unrest, and the like – amounting to material support for group and third-party activities, and not necessarily personal retribution.

This judgemental-performative-corrective distinction agrees that proven moral enhancers will likely manifest multiple modes simultaneously, since their underlying psychological factors are

[5]   Kathryn Francis, et al., 'Virtual Morality: Transitioning From Moral Judgment to Moral Action?', *PLoS ONE* **11** (2015), e0164374.
[6]   The role for punishing in the development of morality is discussed by Robert Kurzban, Maxwell Burton-Chellew, and Stuart West, 'The Evolution of Altruism in Humans', *Annual Review of Psychology* **66**:3 (2015), 575–599. Determining conditions where people regard harms as moral punishment is the subject of research by Kimmo Eriksson, Pontus Strimling, and Per Andersson, 'Costly Punishment in the Ultimatum Game Evokes Moral Concern, in Particular When Framed as Payoff Reduction', *Journal of Experimental Social Psychology* **69** (2017), 59–64.

interrelated. Enhancers affecting psychological factors in isolation would not be helpful. An enhancer that only improves morality in the judgemental mode would produce subjects sounding like self-assured moralisers who are not more moral themselves. An enhancer that improves moral performance, while leaving subjects unsure why they are so good, would be quite disorienting. Busily correcting the behaviour of others while resting content with one's own morality would expose a subject to the charge of hypocrisy. Moralising, self-doubt, and hypocrisy would render a subject's moral life incoherent and incapacitated. By contrast, a moral enhancer significantly elevating all three modes would make a subject noticeably more "righteous" in attitude and action.

This essay now proceeds by considering a singular type of moral enhancement that improves morality through the final "corrective" mode in the generous "generic" direction. We shall label this type of intervention Moral Righteousness. A morally righteous person, we agree to say, is not merely generous with stern moralistic judgements, but also takes concrete action to exemplify them personally and have those judgements enforced on others. Any partisan side to a controversy over rights would be keenly interested in attracting the energies aroused by moral righteousness.

The invention of corrective moral enhancement, if its neurological mechanisms were understood to some degree, could be paired with its counterpart, moral enhancement reduction. Before examining the possible benefits of preventing and reducing moral righteousness for the purpose of promoting civil rights, the next sections first consider whether moral enhancement holds the moral high ground as a human right or a civil liberty.

3. The Morality of Moral Righteousness

If every sort of moral enhancement were treated (wrongly, in my view) as just a non-therapeutic procedure for beneficial self-improvement, then many questions might be easily answered. Respecting the liberty of people to access such a procedure, absent safety or efficacy concerns, is consistent with modern liberal societies and non-intrusive governments. Governments are nevertheless capable of excessive regulation, especially when something new offers lifestyle alternatives disturbing to conventional opinion, or offends mainstream moral sensibilities.[7] Government should at least respect the liberty

---

[7] Matt Lamkin, 'Regulating Identity: Medical Regulation as Social Control', *BYU Law Review* **2** (2016), 501–573.

of competent adults to refuse a procedure unconnected with public health and safety.[8] If government can refrain from indulging popular prejudices and maintain respect for individual liberties, then moral enhancement would be treated much like an innocuous lifestyle choice, akin to a health regimen. The right of people to accept or decline moral enhancement has secure political grounds if it is classified as non-therapeutic self-improvement.

In truth, morality is not just another option for self-improvement. A right to Moral Righteousness has firmer grounds in morality itself, rendering moral enhancement more obligatory. If morality is the repository for whatever we can understand as worthy and right, then morality itself must truly be worthy and right. As morality directs us to unfailingly pursue what is worthy and right, then people have a moral duty to become more moral. That superior duty is indifferent to individual preferences and lifestyle choices. To leave vital moral virtues and values in an underdeveloped and unappreciated condition is practically as immoral as violating them. A basic argument can be constructed favouring the enhancement of all morality to any extreme.

People have a moral duty to accept safe moral enhancement. (Moral Growth)

Moral Growth is always good for one's self and others. (Moral Beneficence)

So, people always have a moral duty to consent to safe moral enhancement. (Moral Perfectionism)

Moral Perfectionism is not comfortable with people freely accepting or declining moral enhancement: it is only right for people to be morally enhanced, and it is never right to avoid moral enhancement.

As far as morality can see, Moral Perfectionism is compatible with corrective moral enhancement, and it even encourages corrective measures.

Moral Perfectionism strengthens one's commitments to moral values. (by definition)

---

[8] Moral enhancement could be linked to questionable therapeutic goals; see Harris Wiseman, *The Myth of the Moral Brain: The Limits of Moral Enhancement* (Cambridge, MA: MIT Press, 2016), chap. 8; and Sarah Carter, 'Could Moral Enhancement Interventions Be Medically Indicated?' *Health Care Analysis* **25**:4 (2017), 338–353.

Is Moral Enhancement a Right, or a Threat to Rights?

Strong commitment to moral values is consistent with motivations to ensure that others must conform or be corrected. (premised)

Hence, Moral Perfectionism approves motivations to ensure conformity through corrections.

Corrective moral enhancement efficiently heightens motivations to ensure conformity through corrections. (by definition)

Therefore, Moral Perfectionism approves corrective moral enhancement.

Finally, since Moral Perfectionism's approval of corrective moral enhancement practically amounts to an approval of Moral Righteousness, the moral duty of people to consent to moral enhancement extends to a duty to become Morally Righteous. So long as Moral Growth and Moral Beneficence are acceptable, a final conclusion seems to follow: everyone has a moral duty to become more Morally Righteous.

The Morally Righteous themselves would not endorse that general conclusion, because generic moral enhancement is involved here. No Morally Righteous person would approve of the enhancement of values that he or she views as immoral. For a population displaying ample disagreement over moral values and how to prioritise them, generic moral enhancement generously distributed throughout a society would deepen those divides. Each Morally Righteous person would vastly prefer selectively generic moral enhancement for those already in agreement (and morphic moral enhancement for those who are not in agreement). Readers who have been thinking, "Just let people who are right get moral enhancement for righteousness, and forbid that 'enhancement' to those who are wrong", already understand what these Morally Righteous people must think.

The typical Morally Righteous person would in effect be a Moral Puritan, let us say, convinced that others should conform to righteous moral values (which are always this Puritan's own values). "Puritanism" is a term with religious connotations that play no role here; Moral Puritanism for this essay's purposes is simply driven by moral conviction to devote resources to increasing social conformity, irrespective of any association with a religious or secular worldview. No-one wants the label of "Puritan" attached to them, of course. Purveyors of "ethical enhancement" would doubtless inform us how to distinguish the truly Righteous from the misguided Puritan – every Puritan movement has its ethical apologists.

Because this essay takes no stand on moral philosophy, it remains agnostic about where righteous morality can always be found. We shall have to leave the Morally Righteous to their moral cacophony, as they criminalise what they can agree upon, and tolerate what they cannot. Are they so different from us in our societies today? Perhaps not. As we imagine a hypothetical future society in which most people have become Morally Righteous, we could be forgiven for hoping that our society does not become more like theirs. Our world already has plenty of moral disagreement and social fractiousness, convulsing many countries with civic tensions and the occasional civil war.

Morally Righteous people are not insensitive to civil strife. Indeed, a remedying proposal occurs to them. If only more people were morally righteous, they would think, then a majority of morally righteous people would emerge, and the law could enforce conformity with that moral majority. Moral groups in the minority can quarrel with that outcome, of course. Yet they would have no right to complain about the illegality of their way of life, as far as the Morally Righteous can see, since those moral minorities are neither righteous nor right. Where civil strife is due to moral conflict between large sectors of society, a dominant moral majority is a blunt but practical remedy. However, until a Morally Righteous majority is well-established, as far as society as a whole can tell, any would-be moral majority is neither so moral nor a majority.

4. A Right to Righteousness?

Undeterred by their status as a moral majority only in name, a group of common-minded Moral Puritans would encourage people of lesser conviction to join them in Moral Righteousness. Those unsure about a moral issue would not use Moral Righteousness to learn what is right. Still, there may already be enough morally agreeable people who only lack strong commitment. Generic moral enhancement for them would amount to a conversion into Moral Righteousness and membership among the Moral Puritans. Moral Puritans have this argument to advance:

> People have a moral duty to accept safe moral enhancement of their stable moral values. (Moral Growth)

> Moral Growth is always good for one's self and others. (Moral Beneficence)

> People cannot be denied a liberty right to access moral and beneficial resources. (Right to Morality)

Is Moral Enhancement a Right, or a Threat to Rights?

Therefore, People have a right to freely pursue moral enhancement. (Right to Righteousness)

Moral Puritans would vastly prefer that only people who are already morally agreeable take advantage of accessible righteousness. Nevertheless, unable to regulate access to moral enhancement (yet), Moral Puritans could at least support a broad Right to Righteousness, in the hopes that they could eventually win an enhancement race by attaining majority status. With a Right to Righteousness securely recognised, society cannot obstruct the growth of the Morally Righteous towards a hoped-for Puritan Majority.

By this reasoning, a typical Puritan-minded group would approve of a legally recognised right to moral enhancement, especially if that group was already a significant segment of society. As for the rest of society, with Puritanical efforts approaching effective levels, moral enhancement may be a good idea for everyone.

Puritanical moral determination is best countered by determined moral opposition. (Moral Counterpoise)

So, the safeguard against Puritanical social "reform" is general moral enhancement. (Moral Standoff)

Therefore, all people have a right to freely pursue moral enhancement. (Right to Righteousness)

Two arguments now stand favouring a general Right to Righteousness, representing both Puritanical and non-Puritanical interests. This right is general, the moral enhancement is generic, and the degree of enhancement is left indefinite.

Anyone has the right, by these arguments, to enhance any moral stance to any (available) degree. Only efficacious limitations will slow someone's moral ambitions, if wisdom cannot. The neural interventions making moral enhancement possible will not know when to stop working when "good enough" morals have been attained. We may not be able to tell when morality is still being enhanced. The ambiguities to "enhancement" come to the fore as we try to classify conduct transcending familiar normalities.[9] Under which special circumstances would peculiar conduct still count as moral? What "posthumans", *übermensch*, or angels must do will surpass our

---

[9]   John Shook and James Giordano, 'Neuroethics Beyond Normal: Performance Enablement and Self-Transformative Technologies', *Cambridge Quarterly of Health Care Ethics* **25**:1 (2016), 121–140.

understanding. Either improved morals are still answerable to our moral judgement (so those morals cannot advance very far), or we must surrender judgement to whomever claims moral superiority (so our morals cannot be so good). Any sufficiently "advanced" morality may be indistinguishable from indecency or evil.[10]

It seems wiser to rely on what we do understand about morality. Can present-day society figure out where to place boundaries on access to moral enhancement?

Motivations for limiting or denying a right to moral enhancement are not difficult to imagine. Privileged classes of society could not be indifferent about Moral Righteousness for aggrieved classes, to begin with. And Moral Righteousness can alarm the many, as well as the few. The majority of society could deny a right to enhance certain moral views on the grounds that they cause behaviours widely deemed too immoral, perverse, or dangerous. Similarly, if resulting conduct due to enhancing certain moral views (immoral views, for the majority) encourages criminality, denying a right to such enhancement would be expected. The majority could also deny a right to enhance morality on the grounds that resulting conduct would impede or contravene an established right. Furthermore, the majority could deny a right to enhance particular moral views if the righteously enhanced would obstruct or delay the establishment of a new right favoured by many.

Defending a Right to Righteousness from an entrenched majority opinion or established legal system might resort to the strategy of portraying this putative right as a human right. Compared against other rights, what is the measure of the importance for a Right to Righteousness?

Over the past three centuries, declarations and constitutions have offered lists of essential rights. Peter Baehr recounts the culmination of those endeavours:

> The Universal Declaration of Human Rights was adopted by the UN General Assembly as a resolution. Such resolutions have the legal status of recommendation, which means that they are not legally binding. However, it is by now commonly accepted that the so-called "core rights" in the Universal Declaration have acquired the status of (binding) international customary law. Core rights are rights that are indispensable for an existence in

---

[10] This point, familiar to theologians, exposes incoherencies to speculation about creating morally superior beings. Consider Vojin Rakić, 'We Must Create Beings with Moral Standing Superior to Our Own', *Cambridge Quarterly of Health Care Ethics* **24**:1 (2015), 58–65.

human dignity and therefore need absolute protection. They include the right to life and the right to the inviolability of the human person, including the prohibition of slavery, serfdom, and torture, wrongful detention, discrimination and other acts that violate human dignity. In addition, the right to freedom of religion is often mentioned in this list.[11]

A Right to Righteousness cannot rank among these core rights. It is not essential to the freedom of thought and expression of moral views: it is not necessary for living according to one's moral conscience, associating with those in moral agreement, or urging others to agree. The generic enhancement of moral righteousness is not to be confused with the basic ability to be a morally conscientious person. A Right to Righteousness goes far beyond a right to live morally, by affecting the moral lives of others. A right to one's moral conscience is vulnerable to oppression and surely deserves legal protection. Protection from the zealous righteousness of others must not be left to chance. Protecting a Right to Righteousness, which presupposes moral conscience, could not take precedence over the ability of everyone to freely possess a moral conscience.

Describing moral righteousness as a potential threat to moral conscience can sound like a contradiction in terms. If a conscience is truly moral, righteousness would respect it. But what is truly moral?

The Morally Righteous do esteem *moral* conscience in anyone, but they see far less value in anyone's immoral *conscience*. Psychologically, this is true of any of us. A warning against a Puritan majority's inability to respect the consciences of smaller groups serves equally well as a warning against any majority righteously concerned with immorality. Sociologically, that is true of any majority. Pretending that society need only be concerned with criminality while mere immorality falls short of social sanction keeps up the pretense that society's laws are not connected to society's moral views. How is a Puritan majority so different from any social majority? If social majorities have the right to enforce important moral norms by law, so long as human rights remain respected, then a Puritan majority has that right, and its Moral Righteousness only threatens serious immorality. Philosophically, this is true if every morality deserves enforcement. Puritans acquire their distasteful reputations while they are in the minority; they retain that reputation as majorities only from an external standpoint. All the same, no Righteous majority needs a Right to

---

[11]   Peter Baehr, *Human Rights: Universality in Practice* (Berlin: Springer, 2016), 4.

Righteousness to uphold civic morals, and no small Righteous group requires a Right to Righteousness to find moral society for company. Ethically, this is true regardless of whether the Righteous know what is truly moral or not. Whether in the company of the majority or not, each conscience at least counts as something not to be overpowered or overruled without due moral consideration.

All things considered, enhancement for Moral Righteousness does not hold the moral, civic, or political high ground. Society may therefore prohibit access to Moral Righteousness enhancement if it inspires conduct attempting to impede or deny a human right, or any right needed for upholding a human right.

5. Moral Righteousness as a Civil Liberty

The conclusion of the previous section suggests that the freedom of adults to obtain Moral Righteousness should not be infringed, so long as one can conduct oneself civilly. Access to civil Moral Righteousness may amount to a civil liberty, in the sense that it pertains to the civic life of a citizen and it is worthy of protection from government infringement.[12] A government able to prohibit access to civil Moral Righteousness would be a government able to infringe upon access to conventional means of arousing moral indignation, inspiring moral idealism, and activating moral energies. That government is on a collision course with freedom of conscience, freedom of speech, freedom of expression, freedom of association, and freedom of religion. Furthermore, because righteous social action translates easily into the sphere of political action, denying access to civil Moral Righteousness without compelling justification amounts to unequal treatment and a violation of civil rights. There are compelling justifications, however. First and foremost, a government would be justified in scrutinising and regulating neurotechnological moral enhancement to ensure its safety, efficacy, and consistency with civil conduct and civil order.

Second, additional government control over moral righteousness is probably warranted. Imagining a society in which access to civil Moral Righteousness is largely unfettered returns us to that

---

[12] There are analogous civil liberties. Citizens already access ordinary means of moral improvement, to the point of righteous social action and corrective civic activism, and they should have the liberty to do so without obstructive government scrutiny or regulation. Many organisations, secular and religious, offer principled exhortations to recruit people for community activism projects and political action agendas.

hypothetical scenario in which much of society is undergoing moral enhancement to run in a righteousness race that no-one can win. Perhaps moral stalemates and political stand-offs will permit an uneasy but stable equilibrium. But perhaps not. Society as a whole may be the loser in the long run. Two concerns for social welfare and civic life are paramount.

First, morally righteous groups have large incentives to not only assist members with access to moral enhancement, but to additionally pressure members into undergoing moral enhancement. It requires no stretch of the imagination to foresee how the Morally Righteous would be motivated to compel moral enhancement as a condition of membership and eligibility for status within the group. If moral enhancement is always an unadulterated good, where is the clear line to show people where enough is enough? Unable to see anything but the beaconing light of moral perfection, the Morally Righteous might be the least likely to know when or how to stop. The eventual consequences could be deleterious for both in-group members and out-group targets of righteous indignation, as the liberty to morally enhance slowly morphs into the confinement of mental cages. This is not a path towards ethical sensitivity or human enlightenment.

Second, many morally righteous groups, all accelerating their momentum simultaneously, must find themselves on a collision course with each other. The erosion of public discourse and the rise of social tensions can only result from highly energised organisations eager and willing to criminalise each other out of existence. Utopian plans about general moral enhancement leading everyone towards a new ethical age of harmony and peace are entertaining but unrealistic. What that utopian actually wants is plenty of morphic moral enhancement in uniformity with his or her own ethical ideals. Unfettered generic moral enhancement will only strengthen moral antagonisms, and weaken civic bonds in the long run. Civil Moral Righteousness is only civil up to point when it is not anymore, and by then it may be too late. This could not be a civil liberty that is truly worth risking the loss of civic solidarity and security.

Even worse outcomes are foreseeable. A privileged class with sufficient political power could enforce moral righteousness for social behaviours conducive to civic conformity and complacency. A Morally Righteous majority may also look to moral enhancement, both generic and morphic, as useful tools. Generic moral enhancement for those already morally agreeable, and morphic moral enhancement for immoral deviants, will appear on the political agenda. Allowing general moral enhancement will no longer be on the agenda, and that civil liberty may be taken away by a sufficiently Puritanical majority. Indeed, the corresponding civil liberty to refuse moral enhancement may be taken away. After all, that Puritanical majority will think, only a moral degenerate would refuse the opportunity to become more morally normal, and such moral degeneracy deserves no respect or toleration. Avoiding proper moral enhancement could be criminalised by a Morally Righteous majority.

The notion of mandatory moral enhancement seems improbable at present because experimental neurological interventions, medical therapies, and non-therapeutic procedures all require informed consent. But we are contemplating a powerful privileged class, or a puritanically principled regime, wielding proven moral enhancement and ample motivation to use it. It does appear that any government has justifications for severely restricting access to civil Moral Righteousness. The drive for perfection behind Moral Righteousness cannot be as good as they seem.

6. The Wrongs of Righteousness

Moral Perfectionism should be deeply questioned. It observes no distinction between remedying moral deficiencies and surpassing moral normalcy. Moral Perfectionism does not consult society's expectations about sufficiently moral conduct. Furthermore, it overrides a person's own judgement about appropriate devotion to moral matters. For Moral Perfectionism, no matter how moral a person may already be, a duty to undergo more moral enhancement awaits.

If Moral Perfectionism is rejected, then its supporting premises, Moral Growth and Moral Beneficence, must be questioned.

Moral Growth: People have a moral duty to accept safe moral enhancement.

Moral Beneficence: Moral Growth is always good for one's self and others.

It is not easy to question Moral Growth. Common sense says that morality must be a very good thing, surely as good as anything else in life, and probably needed for any genuine good to come from life. All the same, common sense also says that uncommon moral zeal is rarely so pure and beneficent.

There is no duty to pursue any of our moral values to extremes. Wisdom cautions that a moderate and balanced commitment to central virtues and values is more congenial to our enterprises and relationships over the course of a lifetime.[13] Must moral duty compel more and more moral ability? If we are speaking in generalities, perhaps, but no neurological enhancement will demonstrably improve just "moral ability" in general or in the abstract. No "essence" to morality could represent a practical goal, either. Platitudes about caring, sharing, sacrificing, protecting, loving (and so on) are ethical ideals, to which no actual moral enhancer will correspond with any specificity. Saintly figures exemplifying one key virtue must be partly mythical – we are instructed to become more like many of them, not to become one of them.

Cautionary principles apply once again. An actual moral enhancer will at best partially modify one or another aspect of human conduct having certain moral ramifications along with other non-moral implications. For any specific moral capacity, distorting its role to the point of domination over, or distraction from, one's moral life is a course that hardly seems advisable, much less dutiful. Replacing these two idealised premises about moral growth and beneficence yields a realistic aim for moral improvement:

> People have a prevailing duty to attain and maintain social standards for morality, which are (almost) always good for one's self and others. (Moral Adequacy)

Alternatively, one's prevailing duty could aspire to a critically minimal level:

> People have a prevailing duty to attain and maintain respect for core human rights and important corollary rights and liberties. (Moral Decency)

Arguments justifying moral enhancement to the point of satisfying Moral Decency could be advanced at this stage, but this essay will not digress into that issue.[14]

Moral Righteousness is clearly in tension with both Moral Adequacy and Moral Decency. General and generic Moral Righteousness will not closely follow pre-existing social standards, since multifarious moral enhancement will somewhere and somehow exceed whatever counts as moral normalcy in a society. Moral Righteousness can even lead to violations of Moral Decency. Someone's moral convictions, sufficiently

---

[13] William Kabasenche, 'Moral Formation and Moral Enhancement', *AJOB Neuroscience* **7**:2 (2016), 130–131.

[14] See I. Glenn Cohen, 'This Is Your Brain on Human Rights: Moral Enhancement and Human Rights', *Law and Ethics of Human Rights* **9**:1 (2015), 1–41.

exaggerated and energised, can motivate a denial of someone else's human rights, civil rights, or important liberties. History is replete with illustrative examples too numerous to recount. Puritanical determination has accompanied pro and con sides to lengthy and torturous struggles over rights and liberties down to our own times. Shall we be resigned to such slow progress? Perhaps not.

In an earlier section, an argument was offered in favour of permitting Moral Righteousness which was premised on that resignation:

> Puritanical moral determination is best countered by determined moral opposition. (Moral Counterpoise)

> So, the safeguard against Puritanical social "reform" is general moral enhancement. (Moral Standoff)

Yet there is a proactive alternative available to society. Puritanical moral determination can be more effectively countered by preventing its intensification, suggesting that society may resort to denying access to general and generic Moral Enhancement.

There is no right to uncivil Moral Righteousness, and no right to Moral Righteousness conducive to the rise of a Puritanical majority. Why should there be a right to Moral Righteousness for sectors of society enabling them to delay the advancement of human and civil rights and liberties? Holding and expressing moral views, associating with like-minded advocates, and engaging in public protest and civil disobedience, is not at issue. What can be questioned is a right to a technology designed for moral zealotry and aggressive activism, so easily targeted against equal rights and expanded liberties for others.

7. The Righteousness of Conformity

Repressing retrograde Moral Righteousness need not be the first resort. If a majority of society is already persuaded of the urgency to enlarge or equalise a right, swift codification renders the opposition unable to access newly uncivil enhancement. However, if a resolute majority has not yet congealed, which partisan position is in the right to demand that others refrain from intensifying their resolve while righteously enhancing their own side?

The inattentive reader is naturally supposing that whoever is truly in the right must not be denied access to Moral Righteousness. The attentive reader is noticing the argumentative symmetry now threatening our deliberations. Did we already clarify who the morally righteous side will always be? We did say that no Puritanical majority should get the opportunity to righteously congeal and suppress its opposition. Of course, from the standpoint of the rest of society, a Righteous majority is the Puritanical majority. Lacking moral philosophy's final call, that moral standoff has returned in converse form:

Denying access to excessive moral enhancement safeguards against any Puritanical social reform. (Righteousness Prevention)

Righteousness Prevention recognises one argumentative symmetry, but a second symmetry awaits on another axis. We are unable to declare in advance who would have the moral high ground for future contests over new rights, having no finalised ethical theory in hand, and we cannot yet say whose moral improvement encroaches on dangerously righteous enhancement, either. Did we lay down that bright line where moral improvement intensifies beyond the level of Moral Decency and surpasses Moral Adequacy? From one righteous standpoint, an increase in moral ability still falls regrettably short; from another righteous standpoint, such "improvement" is too excessive or even a moral disablement. "Moral enhancement" was not defined from the outset as improvement above Moral Adequacy precisely in order to anticipate this local moral relativity. Nevertheless, a society could decide that promoting Moral Righteousness, up to the level of Moral Adequacy, would helpfully increase the number of satisfactorily moral people, who are also eager to promote the conformity of still more people.

For example, society could promote the prevention of theft with an enticement offered to everyone: if you sincerely believe that theft is immoral, accept an inexpensive procedure for Moral Righteousness with regard to stealing and receive a government incentive in return. Governments already subsidise and incentivise innumerable programmes to alter the public's behaviour for the general welfare. The degree of Moral Righteousness could be scientifically calibrated to ensure stricter conformity with Moral Adequacy without causing overzealous excesses. This voluntary programme seems both morally right (by definition – only what is right is promoted) and consistent with the liberty to accept or decline the programme.

Government can incentivise acceptance of Moral Righteousness to elevate conformity to common moral standards. (Righteousness Conformity)

No government pressure is necessary. "Those avoiding enhancement only confess their immorality", the masses will think.[15] As the

---

[15]   'Ethics is for bad guys!', as John Harris puts it, in *How to Be Good: The Possibility of Moral Enhancement* (Oxford: Oxford University Press, 2016), chap. 7.

number of Righteous Conformers gradually increases, they will apply the usual peer pressures and social coercions in order to grow the number of conformists. Those who refuse enhancement will be understood as either expressing their doubt that theft could ever tempt them, or signaling their preference that stealing remains an option. Either way, trust is easily secured by acceding to enhancement. Proof of righteousness could be attached to housing and loan applications, employment criteria, promotion decisions, and even boardroom appointments.

In the long run, Righteous Conformists could conceivably become a vast majority of the population, enveloping even politicians and bureaucrats. As a permanent Righteous majority, they would enforce the common moral norms so rigidly, generation after generation, that any reform movement urging a novel deviation would be disparaged (if not criminalised). If establishing a moral government enforcing serious morality standards for a highly moral society is the goal, then voluntary Moral Righteousness towards near-total Righteous Conformity sounds like an efficient means. Righteous Conformity could also mean endless moral rigidity, accompanied by overall cultural stagnation. Which society really has the right to imprison future generations with whatever passes for moral adequacy nowadays? If authentic moral progress deserves a chance, then Righteous Conformity is not really right.

> Moral Righteousness to elevate conformity to common moral standards should not have social approval or legal sanction. (Moral Nonconformity)

Moral Nonconformity sounds illicit, but that retention of social flexibility preserves adaptability as well as liberty. There is little reason to allow society's current norms to rigidly set the bar for many people forever, as moral relativists and moral objectivists can agree. And society can agree, too. Ask anyone – disappointment with what passes for public morals is heard from plenty of people.

An appetite for moral improvement, at least for others if not oneself, is not scarce, but it is not uniform, either. Righteous Restraint at most offers a tenuous compromise, since little concrete meaning is assignable to "excessive" moral enhancement. Disagreement over what counts as excessive moral righteousness will only serve as a proxy fight over the underlying moral disagreement. Righteous standoffs again appear to be unavoidable, with access to Moral Righteousness at the center of the struggle.

The value of short-cut moral improvement must be seriously doubted. What seemed like a straight-forward means to moral progress has led straight into a roadblock. What was supposed to be lacking, moral conviction and determination, is what can always erupt in abundance. That explains why titanic struggles over modest progress in the name of rights must be fomented and endured practically every time.

8. The Case of Government v. Righteousness

Righteous crusades conflicting over a right typically delay compromise or resolution by disrupting regular political deliberations and sidelining cooler-headed debates. Previous sections have pointed out how access to Moral Righteousness can only exacerbate those delays. If the sort of moral enhancement permitting Moral Righteousness is invented, there are good reasons to discourage its use.

Prohibiting access to Moral Righteousness mitigates righteous crusades over rights. (Righteousness De-Escalation)

Moral disagreement should not be weeded out of society, but it need not grow to strangle society. Two prior guidelines can also provide assistance here:

Denying access to excessive moral enhancement safeguards against any Puritanical social reform. (Righteousness Prevention)

Moral Righteousness to elevate conformity to common moral standards should not have social approval or legal sanction. (Moral Nonconformity)

Combining all three, there is an imperative to discourage Righteous enhancement:

Access to Moral Righteousness should be tightly regulated and illegal for most people, excepting only for rare therapeutic cases. (Criminalised Righteousness)

Criminalised Righteousness should not be confused with government oppression of civil reform movements. No society could, or should, try to obstruct or crush civil crusades. The moral energies of the oppressed and the outraged propel the advancement of rights and liberties as much as anything.[16] Limited moral enhancement

---

[16] This essay is premised on rejecting liberalism's ideal of public debate proceeding without appeals to devoutly-held values. This essay's concerns

John R. Shook

could be useful. The weaker modes – judgemental and performative enhancement – do not fall under as much suspicion as corrective moral enhancement. No society should be obliged to fracture the civic bonds for which civil rights exist. Countries torn by cultural struggles, or countries making progress on rights, might be interested in de-enhancing Righteousness as well as criminalising Righteousness.

9. The Morality of De-Enhancing Morality

Enhancing the advocacy and enshrinement of civil rights would be materially aided by forbidding Moral Righteousness enhancement. That goal could be pursued through encouraging Moral Righteousness *diminishment* as well. The diminishment of Moral Righteousness would be a technological intervention that alters neural functioning which happens to lessen interest in corrective measures taken against violators of the subject's moral judgements, without affecting those judgements to a significant degree. For a label, let us call a workable intervention "Moral Toleration".

Moral Toleration, as defined, does not alter a person's self-conception of who they are as a person with moral dignity and rights, including the right to one's own moral views and the liberty to express them in one's lifestyle. Moral Toleration, accordingly, only tempers a person's capacity to participate in, or lend support for, the prevention of others from pursuing those same rights and liberties. Nor is this hypothetical technique for tempering moralistic righteousness about weakening morality or inspiring moral relativism. Subjects of this technique, if successfully developed, would maintain the same moral convictions and pass the same moral judgements as before, and their own conduct would be unaffected. Other notions of tolerance, detached from moral psychology, may or may not imply the behavioural adjustment due to Moral Toleration, since the idea of toleration is complex and multifaceted for legal, political, and philosophical purposes. For ethical purposes, moral tolerance is far less worthy than mutual respect or communal solidarity. However, any abstract conception of tolerance should at least embrace the same aim as Moral Toleration to have any practical merit.

Although Moral Tolerance has delimited behavioural aims, could its widespread usage lead to unacceptably unjust results? Like any

---

about righteousness within politics presume an essential role for all citizens and their values.

other sort of "enhancement", it cannot automatically be good or just. We may envision a future reform movement, without resistance from a too-tolerant majority, inflicting undue harms on other social groups, rearranging statuses to the unfair detriment of many, or disrupting the social order beyond repair. However, Moral Tolerance does not diminish anyone's concerns for regular social order, fairly distributed privileges, or harms to public welfare. These concerns, while less moralistically defended, would still matter to people and motivate them to the same degree, so unjust reforms would be criticised and reconsidered on those accounts.

With these provisions in mind, a government could tentatively promote the acceptance of Moral Tolerance in a society to promote the goal of increasing overall justice.

> Government can incentivise acceptance of Moral Tolerance to de-escalate moral righteousness. (Tolerance Conformity)

This promotion of Moral Tolerance does not suffer from the problems inherent to Righteousness Conformity. Tolerance Conformity does not threaten any violation of human rights. Even if broad moral tolerance were to spread throughout a society, neither human rights nor established civil rights and liberties would suffer. Disruptions to the comfortable social order (especially to those feeling quite comfortable with their status and privilege) could ensue, but such discomforts would be more easily ameliorated if moral tolerance prevailed over moral righteousness.

What does the world need now? Lauding moral tolerance must sound as futuristically optimistic as the high hopes bestowed on moral enhancement. Neither will come into practical usage in the forms envisaged even by the most well-informed researchers, but the lures are potent and the ends are beckoning. The pursuit of justice and equality, in the form of enlarged civil rights and expanded civil liberties, has never been easy but need not be so hard. This pursuit might deserve Moral Righteousness, or it might require Moral Toleration. If one can be invented, so can the other – which does the world need more?

Bowie State University
j.shook@pragmatism.org

Moral Enhancement and Moral Freedom: A Critique of the Little Alex Problem

JOHN DANAHER

Abstract
A common objection to moral enhancement is that it would undermine our moral freedom and that this is a bad thing because moral freedom is a great good. Michael Hauskeller has defended this view on a couple of occasions using an arresting thought experiment called the "Little Alex" problem. In this chapter, I reconstruct the argument Hauskeller derives from this thought experiment and subject it to critical scrutiny. I claim that the argument ultimately fails because (a) it assumes that moral freedom is an intrinsic good when, in fact, it is more likely to be an axiological catalyst; and (b) there are reasons to think that moral enhancement does not undermine moral freedom.

1. Introduction

Humanity faces a series of existential challenges over the next century: climate change, malevolent artificial intelligence, and the proliferation of nuclear and bio-weaponry, to name but a few. According to Ingmar Persson and Julian Savulescu one of the reasons why we find ourselves on the existential precipice is because our technological capacities far exceed our moral ones.[1] They argue that moral bioenhancement technologies might be needed to redress the balance and pull us back from the brink.

Their argument has attracted a lot of criticism. One of the most persistent is that using drugs and other biomedical interventions to improve moral behaviour will undermine our "freedom to fall", i.e., our freedom to do good or evil (what I call, from here on, our "moral freedom"). John Harris was the first to launch this criticism[2] and he and Persson and Savulescu have slogged it out on the topic ever since.[3] Others have occasionally entered

---

[1] I. Persson and J. Savulescu, *Unfit for the Future: The Need for Moral Enhancement* (Oxford: Oxford University Press 2012).
[2] J. Harris, 'Moral Enhancement and Freedom', *Bioethics* 25:2 (2011), 102–111.
[3] Harris, *How to Be Good: The Possibility of Moral Enhancement* (Oxford: Oxford University Press, 2016) and J. Harris, 'Moral Blindness –

doi:10.1017/S1358246118000371   © The Royal Institute of Philosophy and the contributors 2018
Royal Institute of Philosophy Supplement **83** 2018

the fray (e.g., Sparrow) to pass judgement and offer new insights.[4]

One of the more interesting contributions to the "freedom to fall" debate has come from Michael Hauskeller.[5] Using an arresting thought experiment derived from Anthony Burgess' novel *A Clockwork Orange*, Hauskeller draws our attention to the axiological intuitions underlying the "freedom to fall" objection, and makes a passionate plea for the view that a world with moral freedom and the occasional bad deed is better than a world in which people do good things but lack the freedom to fall.

In this chapter I carefully reconstruct and evaluate Hauskeller's arguments. I start by discussing his "Little Alex" thought experiment and formalising the argument that he derives from it. I then proceed to critically evaluate the key premises of that argument. I first evaluate the moral intuition that Hauskeller uses to motivate his claim, namely, that a world with good outcomes but no moral freedom would be worse than a world with moral freedom and the occasional bad deed. Drawing upon lessons learned in the debate about the existence of God and the problem of evil, I argue that moral freedom lacks intrinsic value: its mere presence does not make the world better or worse. Instead, moral freedom is an axiological catalyst: something that makes good deeds better and bad deeds worse. I then turn to the question of whether moral enhancement would in fact undermine our moral freedom. Looking at common theories of free will and responsibility, I argue that moral enhancement may not undermine our moral freedom and could even on some occasions increase our moral freedom. Then I look at the more political dimension to freedom, which Hauskeller draws upon in his argument, and suggest that moral enhancement need not undermine political freedom and may, in fact, increase it.

The Gift of the God Machine' **9**:3 (2016), 269–273; I. Persson and J. Savulescu, 'Enharrisment: A Reply to John Harris about Moral Enhancement', *Neuroethics* **9**:3 (2016), 275–77; and I. Persson and J. Savulescu, 'Moral Bioenhancement, Freedom and Reason', *Neuroethics* **9**:3 (2016), 263–268.

[4] R. Sparrow, 'Better Living Through Chemistry? A Reply to Savulescu and Persson on "Moral Enhancement"', *Journal of Applied Philosophy* **31**:1 (2014), 23–32.

[5] M. Hauskeller, 'The "Little Alex" Problem', *The Philosophers' Magazine* **62** (2013), 74–78; and M. Hauskeller, 'Is it Desirable to Be Able to Do the Undesirable? Moral Bioenhancement and the Little Alex Problem', *Cambridge Quarterly of Healthcare Ethics* **26**:3 (2017), 365–376.

Moral Enhancement and Moral Freedom

Before I get underway, I need to say a word or two about the terminology I use in this chapter. As will become clear later on, one of the major disputes in the moral enhancement debate is about what exactly counts as a "moral" enhancement. On one interpretation, a *moral* enhancement would involve improving an individual's moral virtue and moral reasoning. It would involve creating 'people who *are* good and *do* what is right, for the *right* reasons'.[6] On other interpretations, moral enhancement is largely about securing preferred moral outcomes, irrespective of the reasoning or virtues of the people implicated. In other words, it involves ensuring enhanced *conformity* with moral norms, not necessarily enhanced moral virtue and reasoning. In this chapter, I will favour the latter interpretation of moral enhancement. It is more inclusive and fits better with the argument Hauskeller defends.

On top of this, there is always some uncertainty in the enhancement debate as to what interventions count as "enhancements". On a broad interpretation, an enhancement is any intervention that improves the human condition relative to its pre-existing state.[7] On this view, the invention of the wheel, literacy, political reform, and better nutrition would all count as enhancements. On a narrow interpretation, an enhancement is a biomedical or technological intervention that directly targets and tries to improve some function of the human brain or body. On this view, drugs, brain implants, and other therapeutic interventions would count as enhancements. Proponents of enhancement frequently stress the broader interpretation in order to highlight the continuity between new and old forms of enhancement, and to reduce opposition to newer interventions.[8] Opponents typically favour a narrower interpretation, trying to draw principled distinctions between narrow and broad enhancements. In this chapter, I will favour the narrower interpretation. The primary reason for this is that if one is to understand the debate about the freedom to fall objection one must be willing, if only for the sake of argument, to draw a distinction between biomedical forms of moral enhancement and more traditional forms such as moral education.

---

[6]   I. de Melo-Martín and A. Salles, 'Moral Bioenhancement: Much Ado About Nothing?', *Bioethics* **29**:4 (2014), 223–232, 224.
[7]   A. Buchanan, *Beyond Humanity? The Ethics of Biomedical Enhancement* (Oxford: Oxford University Press 2011).
[8]   See, for example, J. Harris, *Enhancing Evolution* (Princeton, NJ: Princeton University Press, 2007) and Buchanan, *Beyond Humanity*.

Finally, I will use the term "moral freedom" in two distinct senses. For the majority of the article, I will use it to refer to our capacity for free will and moral responsibility. In other words, I will assume that in order to have moral freedom we must have the capacity to exercise our free will (whatever that requires) and be held morally responsible for what we do (whatever that requires). In the penultimate section, however, I will adopt a more politicised sense of the term "moral freedom", which focusses on liberal and republican conceptions of freedom.[9] In other words, I will hold that we are morally free if we are free from interference and/or domination by others. There is some overlap between these conceptions of freedom, but they are distinguishable in certain instances.

2. Understanding the Little Alex Problem

Hauskeller uses a thought experiment to introduce his version of the freedom to fall objection. The thought experiment comes from Anthony Burgess' (in)famous novel *A Clockwork Orange*. The novel is set in an unspecified, dystopian future. It tells us the story of "Little" Alex, a young man prone to exuberant acts of ultraviolence. Captured by the authorities, Alex undergoes a form of aversion therapy in an effort to rid him of this tendency towards ultraviolence (the therapy is known as "Ludovico's Technique" in the novel). He is given medication that makes him feel nauseous and then repeatedly exposed to violent imagery. His eyes are held open in order to force him to view the imagery. The therapy works. Once he leaves captivity, he still feels violent urges but these are quickly accompanied by feelings of nausea. As a result, he no longer acts out in violent ways. The therapy has enhanced his moral conformity.

The novel takes an ambivalent attitude towards this conformity (and eventually Alex relapses into his ultraviolent exuberance after a suicide attempt). One of the characters (a prison chaplain) suggests that Alex is not truly good as a result of the therapy. In order to be truly good, Alex would have to *choose* to do the good. But due to the aversion therapy this choice is taken away from him. The induced nausea every time he has a violent thought effectively *compels* him to do the good. Indeed, the chaplain goes further and suggests that Alex's induced goodness is not as valuable as his

---

[9]   C. List and L. Vallentini, 'Freedom as Independence', *Ethics* **126**:4 (2016), 1043–1074.

natural badness. It is better if a person can choose to do the bad than be forced to do the good. This is what Hauskeller calls the "Little Alex" problem. And he describes it like this:

> This is what I call the "Little Alex" problem [...] it invites us to share a certain moral intuition (namely that it is in some unspecified way bad or wrong or inhuman to force people into goodness) and thus to accept the ensuing paradox that under certain conditions the bad is better than the good – because it is not only suggested that it is wrong to force people to be good (which is fairly uncontroversial) but also that *the resulting goodness is somehow tainted and devaluated* by the way it has been produced.[10]

This description of the problem hints at an argument, one that can be expressed in more formal terms. It starts with a premise stating the core moral intuition and uses this to critique the practice of moral enhancement. This is how I would reconstruct that argument:

(1)   It is better to have moral freedom, i.e., the freedom to do the bad (and to occasionally act on that freedom), than to be forced to do the good.

(2)   Moral enhancement takes away our moral freedom.

(3)   Therefore, moral enhancement is, in some sense, a morally inferior way of ensuring moral conformity.

This formulation is a little bit loose (the derivation of the conclusion from the premises is not straightforward or watertight), but I think it captures the gist of Hauskeller's interpretation of the freedom to fall objection. Over the remainder of the chapter I will evaluate the two premises of this argument.

3. Is Moral Freedom Intrinsically Valuable?

The first premise of the argument is the most interesting. It makes a seemingly paradoxical and contentious axiological claim. It states that the freedom to do bad is such an important good that a world without it is worse than a world with it. To be more precise, it states that on some occasions, and under certain conditions, we should prefer it when people do bad things than when they do good things.

One of the more important features of Hauskeller's contribution to the freedom to fall debate is the way in which he draws attention to this

10   Hauskeller, 'The "Little Alex" Problem', 75.

axiological claim. I think that this axiological claim is false and defend my view by first showing that in order to accept premise (1) you probably need to believe moral freedom is an intrinsic good (i.e., that its mere presence adds value to the world), and then by arguing that it is implausible to suppose that moral freedom is an intrinsic good. Instead, I argue that we should view it as an *axiological catalyst*, i.e., something that adds to both the moral value and disvalue of the world and hence something whose value cannot be assessed independently from the way in which it is used.

Why think that the argument presupposes that moral freedom is an intrinsic good? Hauskeller has a particular conception of the value hierarchy of different possible worlds that he uses to explain his view. In his original article on the topic, Hauskeller suggests that any proponent of the "freedom to fall" argument must accept something like the following value hierarchy as between different possible worlds:

> **Best World:** A world in which we are free to do bad but choose to do good (i.e., a world in which there is both moral conformity and moral freedom).

> **2nd Best World:** A world in which we are free to do bad and (sometimes) choose to do bad (i.e., a world in which there is moral freedom but not, necessarily, moral conformity).

> **3rd Best World:** A world in which we always do good but are not free to do bad (i.e., a world in which there is moral conformity but no moral freedom).

> **Worst World:** A world in which we are not free and do bad (i.e., a world in which there is neither moral conformity nor moral freedom).

In a more recent paper, he proposes a similar but more complex hierarchy featuring six different levels (the two extra levels capture differences between "sometimes" and "always" doing good/bad). In that paper he notes that although the proponent of the "freedom to fall" argument must place a world in which there is moral freedom and some bad above a world in which there is no moral freedom, there is no compelling, watertight argument in favour of this hierarchy of value. It is really a matter of moral intuitions and weighing competing values. Hauskeller's intuitions lead him to favour the world with the freedom to (sometimes) do bad over the world of moral conformity.

Can we understand this intuition at a deeper level? It seems that there might be much to learn here from the debate between atheists and theists over the problem of evil. As is well-known, the problem of evil is the most famous atheological argument. It comes in a variety of forms. These are usually broken down into two main families: (i) the logical problem of evil and (ii) the evidential problem of evil.[11] The essence of both versions is that the existence of God is incompatible with the existence of any gratuitous or unnecessary evil. The reasoning is as follows: God is a maximally powerful, morally perfect being. Given his moral perfection, he would not allow for evil to occur unless it was somehow necessary for a greater good. Given his maximal power, it is possible for him to intervene to prevent unnecessary evil from occurring. Atheists then claim that there is evidence (certain or highly probable, depending on how strong they want the argument to be) that gratuitous evils occur. They conclude, therefore, that God must not (or is highly unlikely to) exist.

Theists have a variety of responses. They often highlight our epistemic ignorance about value on a grand, cosmic scale.[12] They then try to construct "theodicies" or "defences" that either justify how God might allow a seemingly gratuitous evil act to occur, or introduce *prima facie* justifications that cannot be easily second-guessed or challenged, given our epistemic limitations. The most popular of these theodicies/defences are those that focus on free will and moral responsibility (i.e., moral freedom). The view shared by proponents of these theodicies is that free will and moral responsibility are great goods and their being great goods is what justifies God in creating a world with some evil in it. According to one of the most influential formulations of this view, it is not logically possible for God to create a universe with the great good of moral freedom without also allowing for the possibility of that freedom sometimes (possibly many times) being used for ill effect.[13] The ingenuity of this is that it allows for theists to remain committed to the view that they live in a universe created by a morally perfect being – i.e., in a universe that is, ultimately, the best of all possible words – while tolerating evil deeds. In essence then, they are ascribing to Hauskeller's

---

[11]   On the different problems of evil, see J. L. Mackie, 'Evil and Omnipotence', *Mind* **64**:254 (1955), 200–212; A. Plantinga, *God, Freedom and Evil* (Grand Rapids, MI: Eerdmans, 1977); and W. Rowe, 'The Problem of Evil and Some Varieties of Atheism', *American Philosophical Association* **16**:4 (1979), 335–341.

[12]   For example M. Bergmann, 'Skeptical Theism and Rowe's New Evidential Argument from Evil', *Nous* **35**:2 (2001), 278–296.

[13]   Plantinga, *God, Freedom and Evil*.

intuition that a world with moral freedom in it is, somehow, better than a world without.

I would suggest that the most plausible way to make sense of this shared intuition is to believe that moral freedom is, somehow, intrinsically valuable, i.e. that its mere presence (irrespective of how it is used) adds to the value of the universe. But why is this the most plausible way to make sense of the intuition? Might it simply be the case that moral freedom is necessary for some other goods? Perhaps, but I think it is difficult for Hauskeller or a theist proponent of the free will theodicy to sustain this view alongside a consistent bias towards worlds with moral freedom. Some theists have tended to view free will as a necessary instrumental good for moral responsibility,[14] but this does not get us away from the notion that moral freedom is an intrinsic good since responsibility is part and parcel of moral freedom. Others tend to be a bit cagey and simply suggest that, for all we know, it might be linked to other goods. But this is a difficult argument to make when you do not know what these other goods are and yet still believe they trump other known goods. If you are going to consistently rank a world in which there is moral freedom (and some evil) over a world in which there is no moral freedom (and much good) – in other words, if you are going to accept that there is some good in a world in which people exercise their moral freedom to do tremendous evil – then it seems like you simply must be committed to the view that there is some intrinsic moral magic to moral freedom: that when it is present it automatically ups the value of the world. To be clear, this does not mean that advocates of moral freedom need to believe that the intrinsic good of moral freedom trumps all other goods, or that there could be no other outweighing intrinsic goods. They might still believe that. But in order to maintain their consistent bias toward worlds in which there is moral freedom, it is most plausible to believe that it is because moral freedom has intrinsic value.

The problem I have with this is that moral freedom does not seem to function like an intrinsic good. There are a couple of ways to get to this conclusion. Some have tried to do so by arguing that it is intrinsically neutral. Derk Pereboom[15] has defended this view in tandem with his general free will scepticism, and Steve Maitzen has defended

---

[14]   R. Swinburne, *The Existence of God*, 2nd edition (Oxford: Oxford University Press, 2004).

[15]   D. Pereboom, 'Free Will, Evil and Divine Providence', in A. Dole and A. Chignell (eds), *God and the Ethics of Belief* (New York: Cambridge University Press, 2005), 77–98.

it specifically in response to free will theodicies.[16] The essence of both claims is that in many cases of moral evaluation, the freedom to do bad does not add to the assessed value of an action. It seems to function, instead, as a *morally weightless* consideration, and not just a morally outweighed one. To give an example, suppose there is a violent criminal who has exercised his moral freedom and savagely murdered ten people. Surely we do not think that the fact that he murdered them freely speaks in his favour? His act is very bad, pure and simple; it is not slightly good and very bad.

There is something to this argument. It definitely feels right to say that the murderer's freedom does not add any intrinsic good to his actions (thereby counterbalancing some of the disvalue). But it also feels wrong to say that it is axiologically neutral. Compare two cases: (i) a murderer savagely kills ten people while exercising his moral freedom; and (ii) a murderer savagely kills ten people without exercising moral freedom (because he had some brain tumour that undermined his moral reasoning, or he was compelled to do so by others at gunpoint). Both outcomes are bad, but which case is worse? I think the answer is obviously (i) because there is no excusing factor present in that case. This suggests something interesting. It suggests that moral freedom makes a bad deed much worse. Thus, moral freedom seems to be making an axiological difference; it is not neutral. We can see this happening in the other direction too. Compare the following: (iii) a multi-millionaire donates 90% of his money to some charity by exercising his moral freedom; and (iv) a multi-millionaire donates 90% of his money to some charity because his accountant made a calculation error. The outcomes are both good (assume this, for the sake of argument), but I am confident in saying that case (iii) is clearly better than (iv). Again, the presence of moral freedom seems to be making the difference.

These thought experiments suggest that moral freedom is neither intrinsically good, nor intrinsically neutral. It is, instead, an *axiological catalyst*: it makes good things better and bad things worse. It amplifies whatever value is already present (positive or negative). This, in turn, leads to the conclusion that premise (1) of the Little Alex Argument is flawed. A world with moral freedom and occasional bad is not *necessarily* better than a world without moral freedom. Because it is an axiological catalyst, we cannot use moral freedom to rank and order worlds relative to one another. The value of moral freedom can only be determined in connection

---

[16]   S. Maitzen, 'Ordinary Morality Implies Atheism', *European Journal for Philosophy of Religion* **1**:2 (2009), 107–126.

with how it is exercised. If it is exercised to good effect, then a world with it is, indeed, a better world; but if it is exercised to ill effect, it makes things worse. This significantly undercuts the "freedom to fall" objection. If moral enhancement techniques work as advertised, they would simply be preventing moral freedom from being exercised in wicked ways. They would, consequently, be making the world a better place, without taking away something that is intrinsically good.

This argument might not be plausible to all. Fortunately, even if you cling to the view that moral freedom is an intrinsic good, it does not follow that you ought to reject all forms of moral enhancement on the grounds that they undermine moral freedom. As mentioned earlier, moral freedom could be an intrinsic good and it could be outweighed or countermanded by other goods/bads in certain cases. This is, again, something that has come to the fore in the debate about the problem of evil. When theists press the line about moral freedom providing some God-justifying excuse for the occurrence of evil, atheists push back by pointing to particularly egregious forms of evil that result from moral freedom. Take the case of a remorseless serial killer who tortures and rapes young innocent children. Are we to suppose that their freedom to do bad outweighs the child's right to live a torture and rape-free life? Is the world in which the serial killer freely does bad really a better world than the one in which he is forced to conform? It seems pretty unlikely. This example highlights the fact that moral freedom might be intrinsically valuable but that in certain "high stakes" cases its intrinsic value is outweighed by other moral considerations, particularly the need to ensure greater moral conformity.

It is perfectly open to the defender of moral enhancement to argue that its application should be limited to those "high stakes" cases. Then it will all depend on how high the stakes are and whether moral enhancement can be applied selectively to address those high stakes cases. The thing that is noticeable about Persson and Savulescu's argument for moral bioenhancement is that it is linked directly to high stakes cases. They argue that the future of the human race could be on the line unless we enhance our moral conformity. If they are right, then the stakes might be high enough to outweigh the putative intrinsic value of moral freedom. That said, the burden they face when making this argument is significant since they are not simply arguing that we occasionally interfere with the moral freedom of specific individuals; they are arguing that we interfere with every agent's moral freedom.

4. Is Moral Enhancement Really Incompatible with Moral Freedom?

What about the second premise of the Little Alex Argument? This premise claims that moral freedom is incompatible with moral enhancement, i.e., that if we ensure someone's conformity through a technological intervention like moral enhancement, then they are not really free. How persuasive is this? It all depends on what you understand by moral freedom and how you think moral enhancement works.

Let us stick with idea that moral freedom is the capacity to exercise free will and to be a responsible moral agent. There are many different theories about what this requires that vary depending on whether they think free will and responsibility are possible in a causally deterministic universe, and whether they think we live in such a universe. We can divide them into two main categories: (i) libertarian theories of free will (which hold that free will is only possible if humans are somehow exempt from causally deterministic laws) and (ii) compatibilist theories of free will (which hold that free will is possible even if humans are not exempt from causally deterministic laws). There is also a position known as "free will scepticism", but we can safely ignore that here since a free will sceptic will have no truck with arguments about the good of moral freedom. Now, it is not going to be possible to review every theory of free will within the two main categories in the space of this chapter, but we can review some of them, and by doing so we can see that moral enhancement may be less likely to undermine moral freedom than one might think.

Let us start with the libertarian accounts of free will. These can be fleshed out in a couple of different ways. One can adopt an *agent causalist* approach, which holds that the way in which *agents* cause something to happen is distinct from the way in which *events* cause other events to happen. Agents are primary, *sui generis* causes of events in the real world. They do not sit directly within the ordinary chain of causation. Human beings are agents and so can cause things to happen without being causally determined to do so. This view obviously faces a number of conceptual and philosophical challenges. It is pretty difficult to reconcile the fact that certain aspects and features of human agency are clearly constituted in an event-causalist network of brain activity with the claim that human agency causes events in a distinctive, *sui generis* manner. Consequently, it is difficult to know exactly what an agent causalist would say about the Little Alex case. They might be inclined to share Hauskeller's view that Alex is

John Danaher

being forced to be free (perhaps because the aversion therapy blocks the pathway to agent causation), but they might be more optimistic. After all, if all forms of moral enhancement will operate on the causal networks inside the human brain, it is possible that the "agent" (who is separable from those networks) is unaffected by the enhancement process.

A similar analysis applies to event-causalist libertarian views, such as those advocated by Kane[17] and Balaguer.[18] These views do not posit a *sui generis* agent who sits outside the ordinary causal flow of the universe. They accept that we are (to a considerable extent) constituted by our brains and that our brains usually follow deterministic patterns of causation. They simply argue that there are occasional moments of indeterminism (what Balaguer calls "torn decisions") and that our status as free and responsible agents is tied to these moments of indeterminism. Balaguer's view, for instance, is that on certain occasions, the causal environment in which the human agent operates (which includes their brain and surrounding context) is in a state of equilibrium at the moment prior to the choice – no ordinary causal factor can "make a difference" to whether one option is chosen over the other. At those moments, the human "will" operates and it is at these moments that we exercise free choice.

Again, this view has certain conceptual and philosophical problems, but let us set those to the side and consider what it means for moral enhancement. On the one hand, a proponent of an event-causalist libertarianism might remain optimistic about moral freedom. Enhancement technologies might intervene in the causal networks of the brain but they may leave open the possibility of there being "torn decisions" and our moral freedom could continue to be grounded in those moments. On the other hand, they might fear that enhancement technologies like Little Alex's aversion therapy *reduce the number* of torn decisions the typical human faces. It could be, for all we know, that before his aversion therapy, every time Little Alex was faced with the option of committing an act of ultraviolence he was facing a torn decision: his brain was perfectly equilibrated between committing the act and not. He was exercising his moral freedom on each such occasion. The aversion therapy then changed the causal equilibrium, tipping the balance decisively in

[17] R. Kane, *The Significance of Free Will* (Oxford: Oxford University Press, 1996).
[18] M. Balaguer, *Free Will as an Open Scientific Problem* (Cambridge, MA: MIT Press, 2010).

favour of not committing violence. This would eliminate free will. Then again, the opposite could also be true. Perhaps before the aversion therapy the causal network within his brain was tipped decisively in favour of committing ultraviolence. The aversion therapy then worked by bringing it back to a more equilibrated state where his will could make the critical difference between doing good and doing evil. In other words, perhaps the enhancement therapy works by opening up more opportunities for torn decisions.

The overall point here is that it is very difficult to say, in the abstract, whether libertarian models of free will are undermined or constrained by moral freedom. Because they hold that the will (or the agent) is somehow separate from the causal mechanisms of the universe, it is possible that they are unaffected by moral enhancement. And, even if they are affected, they might be affected in a positive way. A lot depends on the particularities of the individual case.

Other theories of free will and moral responsibility are compatibilist in nature. They claim that moral freedom is possible within a deterministic causal order. Deterministic causation by itself does not undermine freedom. What matters is whether an agent's actions are produced by the right kind of causal mechanism. There are many different accounts of compatibilist free will, but some of the leading ones argue that an agent can act freely if the causal mechanism producing their moral choices is *reasons-responsive* and/or produces actions that are consistent with their character and higher order preferences.[19]

Moral enhancement *could* undermine compatibilist free will so understood. It may change the causal sequence of action from one that is compatible with moral freedom to one that is not compatible with moral freedom. In the Little Alex case, the aversion therapy causes him to feel nauseous whenever he entertains violent thoughts. This is definitely inconsistent with some versions of compatibilism. From the description, it seems like Alex's character is still a violent one and that he has higher-order preferences for doing bad things, yet he is unable to express those aspects of his character thanks to his nausea. He is thus blocked from acting freely according to higher-order preference accounts of freedom. Similarly, it could be

---

[19] G. Dworkin, *The Theory and Practice of Autonomy* (Cambridge: Cambridge University Press, 1988); J. M. Fischer and M. Ravizza, *Responsibility and Control* (Cambridge: Cambridge University Press, 1998); H. Frankfurt, 'Freedom of the Will and the Concept of a Person', *Journal of Philosophy* **68**:1 (1971), 5–20.

that the aversion therapy makes him less responsive to certain kinds of reasons for action. This might undermine a reasons-responsive account of moral freedom.

But, again, the devil will be in the detail. The modality of the enhancement will be all important. Some modalities might be perfectly consistent with compatibilistic moral freedom: they might change an incompatible causal sequence into a compatible one. In this respect, aversion therapy is hardly the only game in town. Some agents might desire the good at a higher-order level and be thwarted from pursuing it by lower-order impulses. A moral enhancement technology might work by blocking these lower order preferences and thereby enabling moral freedom. If we believe that chemical castration can count as a type of moral enhancement, then this is arguably how it works: by blocking lower-order preferences for sexual misdeeds. Other modalities of moral enhancement might work by changing an agent's ability to appreciate, process, and respond to different reasons for action. This would improve their reasons-responsivity. Although not written with moral enhancement in mind, Maslen, Pugh, and Savulescu's paper on using deep brain stimulation to treat Anorexia Nervosa highlights some of these possibilities, showing how neurointerventions that are directly mediated through higher-order brain functions might be preferable to those that are not.[20]

On top of this, those who claim that moral freedom is undermined by enhancement must deal with the case in which an agent freely decides to undergo an enhancement treatment at T1 that will compromise their moral freedom at T2. Most theories of moral freedom accept this as a case involving genuine moral freedom. They view it as a case involving a pre-commitment to being good. To use the classic example, the individual who chooses to undergo the process is like Odysseus tying himself to the mast of his ship: he is limiting his agency at future moments in time through an act of freedom at an earlier moment in time. The modality of enhancement does not matter then: all that matters is that he is not forced into undergoing the enhancement at T1. Hauskeller acknowledges this possibility in both of his papers, but goes on to suggest that they may involve a dubious form of self-enslavement. At this point, the metaphysical account of moral freedom becomes less important. We must turn, instead, to a more political understanding of freedom.

---

[20] H. Maslen, J. Pugh, and J. Savulescu, 'The Ethics of Deep Brain Stimulation for Anorexia Nervosa', *Neuroethics* **8**:3 (2015), 215–230.

5. Freedom, Domination, and Self-Enslavement

Where metaphysical freedom is about our moral agency and responsibility, political freedom is about how others relate to and express their wills over us. It is about protecting us from interference and domination by others so as to meet the conditions for a just and mutually prosperous political community – one that respects the fundamental moral equality of its citizens (Gaus 2010; Pettit 2014).[21] Consequently, accounts of political freedom are not so much about ensuring free will as they are about ensuring that people can develop and exercise their agency without being manipulated and dominated by others. So, for example, I might argue that I am politically unfree in exercising my vote if the law requires me to vote for a particular party. In that case, others have chosen for me. Their will dominates my own. I am subordinate to them.

Although underexplored in the enhancement debate,[22] this politicised account of freedom might provide a more promising basis for a defence of premise (2). After all, one critical problem with debates about moral enhancement – particularly those that appeal to "high stakes" risks such as those that figure in Persson and Savulescu's account – is that they implicitly or explicitly endorse cases in which others decide for us whether we should undergo moral enhancement therapy. Thus, our parents could genetically manipulate us to be kinder; our governments may insist on us taking a course of moral enhancement drugs to become safer citizens; it may become a conditional requirement for accessing key legal rights and entitlements that we be morally enhanced, and so on. The morally enhanced person would, consequently, be in a politically different position from the naturally good person. That, at least, is how Hauskeller sees it:

> The most conspicuous difference between the naturally good and the morally enhanced is that the latter have been engineered to feel, think, and behave in a certain way. Someone else has decided for them what is evil and what is not, and has programmed them accordingly, which undermines, as Jürgen Habermas has argued, their ability to see themselves as moral agents, equal to those who decided how they were going to be. The point is not so much that they have lost control over how they feel and think (perhaps we never had such control in the first place), but rather

21 G. Gaus, *The Order of Public Reason* (Cambridge: Cambridge University Press, 2010); and P. Pettit, *Just Freedom* (New York: W. W. Norton & Co., 2014).
22 Though see Sparrow, 'Better Living Through Chemistry?'.

that others have gained control over them. They have changed [...] from something that has grown and come to be by nature, unpredictably, uncontrolled, and behind, as it were, a veil of ignorance, into something that has been deliberately made, even manufactured, that is, a product.[23]

There is a lot going on in this quote. But the gist of it is clear. The problem with moral enhancement is that it creates an asymmetry of power. We are supposed to live together as moral equals: no one individual is supposed to be morally superior to another. But moral enhancement allows one individual or group to shape the moral will of another. But this complaint does not quite get at the pre-commitment situation. What if there is no other individual or group making these decisions for you? What if you voluntarily undergo moral enhancement? Hauskeller argues that the same inequality of power argument applies to this case:

[W]e can easily extend [this] argument to cases where we voluntarily choose to submit to a moral enhancement procedure whose ultimate purpose is to deprive us of the very possibility to do wrong. The asymmetry would then persist between our present (and future) self and our previous self, which to our present self is another. The event would be similar to the case where someone voluntarily signed a contract that made them a slave for the rest of their lives.[24]

What should we make of this argument? It privileges the belief that freedom from the yoke of others is what matters to moral agency – that we should be left to *grow* and *develop* into moral agents through natural processes – not be *manipulated* and *manufactured* into moral saints (even if the manipulation and manufacturing is done by ourselves). But I am unsure that we should be swayed by these claims. Three critical points seem apposite to me.

First, I think we should be generally sceptical of the claim that it is better to be free from the manipulation of others than it is to be free from other sorts of manipulation or interference. The reality is that our moral behaviour is the product of many things: our genetic endowment, our social context, our education, our environment, and various contingent accidents of personal history. It is not obvious to me why we should single out causal influences that originate in other agents for particular ire. In other words, the presumption

---

[23] Hauskeller, 'The "Little Alex" Problem', 78–79.
[24] Hauskeller, 'The "Little Alex" Problem', 79.

that it is better that we naturally grow and develop into moral agents seems problematic to me. Our natural development and growth – assuming there is a coherent concept of the "natural" at play here – is not intrinsically good. It is not something that is necessarily worth saving or necessarily better than the alternatives. At the very least, the benefits of moral conformity would weigh (perhaps heavily) against the desirability of natural growth and development.

Second, I do not think that the claim that induced moral enhancement involves problematic asymmetries of power holds up under scrutiny. At the very least, it is not a claim that is generally or unquestionably true. If anything, I think moral enhancement could be used to correct for asymmetries of power. To some extent this will depend on the modality of enhancement and the benefits it reaps, but the point can be made at an abstract level. Think about it this way: the entire educational system rests upon asymmetries of power, particularly the education of young children. This education often involves a moral component. Do we rail against it because of the asymmetries of power? Not really. Indeed, we often deem education necessary because it ultimately helps to correct for asymmetries of power. It allows children to develop the capacities they need to become the true moral equals of others. If moral enhancement works by enhancing our capacities to appreciate and respond to moral reasons, or by altering our desires to do good, then it might help to build the capacities that correct for asymmetries of power. It might actually enable effective self-control and autonomy. Being morally enhanced then does not mean that you are problematically enslaved or beholden to the will of others.

Third, and perhaps most controversially, I am not convinced that self-enslavement is a bad thing. Every decision we make in the present enslaves our future selves in at least some minimal sense. Choosing to go to university in one place, rather than another, enslaves the choices your future self can make about what courses to take and career paths to pursue. Is that a bad thing? If the choices ultimately shape our desires – if they result in us really wanting to pursue a particular future course of action – then I am not sure that I see the problem. Steve Petersen has made this point in relation to the creation of robot slaves.[25] He argues that if a robot is designed in such a way that it really, really wants to do the ironing, then maybe getting it to do the ironing is not so bad *from the perspective*

[25]   S. Petersen, 'Designing People to Serve', in P. Lin, G. Abney, and K. Bekey (eds), *Robot Ethics: The Ethical and Social Implications of Robotics* (Cambridge, MA: MIT Press, 2012), 283–298.

of the robot (this last bit is important – it might be bad from a societal perspective because of how it affects or expresses our attitudes towards others, but that is irrelevant here since we are talking about self-enslavement). Likewise, if by choosing to undergo moral enhancement at one point in time, I turn myself into someone who really, really wants to do morally good things at a later moment in time, I am not convinced that I live an inferior life as a result.

6. Conclusion

To sum up, the "freedom to fall" objection is one of the more popular objections to the moral enhancement project. Hauskeller defends an interesting version of this objection, one that draws our attention to certain key axiological intuitions: that it is better to have moral freedom and do bad than it is to be forced into moral conformity; that it is better to naturally develop and grow into a moral person than it is to be manipulated and molded by others (including yourself). In this chapter, I have called these axiological intuitions into question. I argue that they rest on the implausible belief that moral freedom is an intrinsic good and that manipulation/self-enslavement is an intrinsic bad. Neither of these views is correct or sufficient to justify the argument against moral enhancement. Moral freedom is an axiological catalyst, not an intrinsic good; self-enslavement and manipulation are not obviously inferior to other forms of causal determination or external molding. On top of this, it is not even obvious that moral enhancement undermines moral freedom. It all depends on what you mean by moral freedom and the modality of the moral enhancement, and all the leading theories allow for the possibility that moral enhancement increases, rather than undermines, moral freedom.

National University of Ireland, Galway
john.danaher@nuigalway.ie

Retributivism and the Moral Enhancement of Criminals Through Brain Interventions

ELIZABETH SHAW

Abstract

This chapter will focus on the biomedical moral enhancement of offenders – the idea that we could modify offenders' brains in order to reduce the likelihood that they would engage in immoral, criminal behaviour. Discussions of the permissibility of using biomedical means to address criminal behaviour typically analyse the issues from the perspective of medical ethics, rather than penal theory. However, recently certain theorists have discussed whether brain interventions could be legitimately used for punitive (as opposed to purely therapeutic) purposes. For instance, Jesper Ryberg argues (although he himself is not a retributivist) that there is nothing to prevent retributivists from endorsing brain interventions as a legitimate form of retributive punishment. Legal academics have not yet paid sufficient attention to whether this proposal would be compatible with international human rights law, nor have retributivist philosophers discussed whether their favoured penal theories have the conceptual resources to explain why brain interventions would not be an appropriate method of punishment. This chapter considers whether there is any indication that these interventions are being used at present for punitive purposes and whether this would violate the European Convention on Human Rights. It examines different versions of retributivism and considers which theory is in the best position to challenge the use of brain interventions as a form of punishment. Finally, it considers whether offering these interventions as an alternative to punishment would violate principles of proportionality.

1. Introduction

Currently, research is being undertaken into whether anti-social and criminal behaviour can be addressed through biomedical interventions that modify offenders' brains. Such interventions are already being used within the criminal justice system in order to rehabilitate drug addicts and sex offenders. The use of biomedical interventions to improve impulse control and reduce aggression is also being investigated. These interventions can be viewed as forms of "moral enhancement", as they aim at correcting immoral, criminal behaviour. Although legislators and policy-makers often conceptualise such interventions as "treatments" for mental disorders, the line between treatment and enhancement is increasingly blurred. Some of the interventions that are

doi:10.1017/S1358246118000383 ©The Royal Institute of Philosophy and the contributors 2018

Royal Institute of Philosophy Supplement **83** 2018

currently used and being investigated seem primarily to target behaviour that is 'medically unremarkable, but socially undesirable'.[1]

However, the moral permissibility of such interventions is typically assessed from the perspective of medical ethics, rather than by reference to penal theory.[2] Given that brain interventions can be imposed as a mandatory part of a criminal sentence or (more commonly) offered as an alternative to prison, it is surprising that penal theoretical considerations have not played a greater role in the current debate about the acceptability of these practices. One of the most widely accepted theories of punishment is retributivism – the theory that punishment should aim to cause offenders the suffering that they deserve. Until the 1970s, the rehabiliationist approach – which aimed to modify offenders' criminal tendencies – was highly influential. Retributivists were among the fiercest critics of these programmes and, since the 1970s, retributive thinking has gained the ascendency in the UK and US. It is therefore important to consider whether similar retributivist arguments can be successfully levelled against current proposals to reshape offenders' motivations through biomedical interventions.

Neuroscientific advances may give rise to brain interventions that are much more effective at reducing criminal tendencies than previous rehabilitation techniques. If effective techniques to prevent victimisation were developed, then much suffering could be avoided. Such techniques could also generate large economic savings, given that crime is economically very costly and traditional forms of punishment are both expensive and relatively ineffective at preventing recidivism. So there is good reason to consider whether these interventions are compatible with our most plausible ethical theories and with human rights.

Jesper Ryberg has recently argued that there is nothing to prevent retributivists from *endorsing brain interventions as a legitimate form of retributive punishment*.[3] However, legal academics have not yet paid sufficient attention to whether this proposal would be compatible with international human rights law, nor have retributivist philosophers discussed whether their favoured penal theories have the conceptual resources to explain why brain interventions would not be

---

[1] M. J. Farah, 'Emerging Ethical Issues in Neuroscience', in W. Glannon (ed.), *Defining Right and Wrong in Brain Science* (New York: Dana Press, 2008) 16–36, 26.

[2] See J. Ryberg, 'Is Coercive Treatment of Offenders Morally Acceptable? On the Deficiency of the Debate', *Criminal Law and Philosophy* **9**:4 (2015), 619–631.

[3] J. Ryberg, 'Punishment, Pharmacological Treatment, and Early Release', *International Journal of Applied Philosophy* **26**:2 (2012), 231–244.

an appropriate method of punishment.[4] This chapter will begin by considering whether there is any indication that such interventions are being used at present as a form of retributive punishment, whether this would violate the European Convention on Human Rights, and whether there is a realistic chance that brain interventions might be used in this way in the future. I will then examine different versions of retributivism that give rise to different types of objection against brain interventions. I will argue that the versions of communicative retributivism defended by Antony Duff and Christopher Bennett are in the best position to oppose the idea of using these interventions without the free and informed consent of the recipients (although Duff and Bennett have not yet discussed the implications of their theories of punishment for this question). Finally, I will consider whether offering these interventions as an alternative to punishment would violate principles of proportionality.

2. Are Brain Interventions Currently Being Used as Retributive Punishments?

In a number of US states sex offenders can be sentenced to injections with anti-androgen drugs.[5] This can be viewed as a type of brain intervention, as one of the effects of the drugs is to reduce sexual thoughts by directly acting on brain cells.[6] Tom Douglas and Lisa

---

[4]   The literature on pharmacological treatment of sex offenders and the ECHR generally does not specifically consider the use of such treatments for retributive purposes. An exception is Z. B. Akbaba, *The Permissibility of Pharmacotherapy for Paedophilic Sex Offenders In the Light of the Rights Protected Under the European Convention on Human Rights* (Ph.D. Thesis, University of Leicester, 2015).

[5]   E.g., California (Cal. Pen. Code § 465), Florida (Fla. Stat. § 794.0235 [1997]), and Louisiana (La. Stat. Rev. Ann. § 15.538 [1997]). This is sometimes referred to as "chemical castration", but the neurological effects of these drugs on sex offenders' thought-processes are considered to be at least as important as the effect on sexual functioning. C. Scott and T. Holmberg, in 'Castration of Sex Offenders: Prisoners' Rights Versus Public Safety', *Journal of the American Academy of Psychiatry and the Law* **31**:4 (2003), 502–509, and C. Mancini, J. C. Barnes, and D. P. Mears, 'It Varies from State to State: An Examination of Sex Crime Laws Nationally', *Criminal Justice Policy Review* **24**:2 (2013), 166–198, provide overviews of the relevant statutes.

[6]   J. Money, 'Treatment Guidelines: Antiandrogen and Counseling of Paraphilic Sex Offenders', *Journal of Sex & Marital Therapy* **13**:3 (1987), 219–223, 220.

Elizabeth Shaw

Forsberg have suggested that, in California, the state's aim in imposing this medication 'seems to involve a mixture of retribution and de-
terrence'.[7] They cite a number of factors that indicate that this
practice is punitive rather than therapeutic.[8] Firstly, the legislation
governing the provision of these interventions to offenders is part
of California's penal code.[9] Secondly, the decision to administer
the drug is at the discretion of the judge the first time a criminal
commits a specified sex offence[10] and is mandatory for a second
such offence.[11] If the intention were therapeutic rather than punitive
one would expect the intervention to be conditional on a medical professional's opinion that the offender is likely to benefit from the treatment (since sexual offending has many causes and the simple fact that
someone has committed a particular crime is not enough evidence on
which to base a diagnosis that the offender has a paraphilia that is responsive to anti-androgen drugs). Thirdly, criminal justice officials
decide on the duration of the treatment.[12] If the intervention were
therapeutic, one would expect the cessation of the treatment to be
based on the opinion of medical professionals about whether the
treatment had been successful. Fourthly, there is not even a statutory
requirement for the procedure to be carried out under medical supervision, or for medical professionals to be involved in any way. Fifthly,
the original Bill used the phrase 'punished by chemical castration'
and, although this phrase was removed, the wording of the Act
refers to anti-androgen drugs 'in addition to any other punishment',
which still suggests that the legislators intended such drugs to be a
type of punishment.[13] Sixthly, some of the legislators who supported
the Bill used punitive rhetoric when it was debated.[14]

Similar provisions apply in a few other US states. In Florida, the
court order mandating anti-libidinal drugs must specify the duration
of the intervention in advance – like a traditional punishment, rather
than a treatment that lasts until the patient is 'cured'.[15] Furthermore,
the Florida District Court has held that chemical castration is part of

---

[7]   L. Forsberg and T. Douglas, 'Anti-Libidinal Interventions in Sex
Offenders: Medical or Correctional?', *Medical Law Review* **24**:4 (2017),
453–473, 460.
[8]   Forsberg and Douglas, 'Anti-Libidinal Interventions', 460–465.
[9]   Cal. Pen. Code § 465.
[10]   Cal. Pen. Code § 465(a).
[11]   Cal. Pen. Code § 465(b).
[12]   Cal. Pen. Code § 465(d).
[13]   Assembly Bill 3339 and Cal. Pen. Code § 465.
[14]   Forsberg and Douglas, 'Anti-Libidinal Interventions', 465.
[15]   Fla. Stat. § 794.0235 (1997).

the offender's 'punishment package', as opposed to being a 'pure treatment'.[16] In Louisiana (where the criminal himself must cover the financial costs of being injected with the chemical castration drugs) and Florida, offenders are sentenced to receive anti-libidinal interventions *at the same time as incarceration,* rather than as condition of parole.[17] This may suggest that the administration of these drugs has a retributive purpose, rather than simply being based on the need to protect the public after the offender has been released.

In England and Wales, under the Mental Health Act 1983 (MHA 1983), criminal courts can sentence mentally disordered offenders to detention in hospital, where they may be given compulsory interventions, even if they have the capacity to refuse consent.[18] The term 'mental disorder' is defined widely, covering 'any disorder or disability of the mind'.[19] This is broad enough to include sexual deviance as well as personality disorders, such as antisocial personality and psychopathic personality disorder, even though there is controversy over whether these are genuine mental disorders, as opposed to harmful behaviours and socially undesirable character traits.[20] According to Harrison and Rainey the legislation is 'predicated on social control rather than individual treatment'.[21] Forsberg and Douglas acknowledge that, unlike the Californian legislation, the regime for medicating sex offenders in England and Wales does not seem to have a clearly retributive aim. However, they deny that it has an entirely therapeutic objective either. They claim it has a partly 'correctional purpose' – i.e., it is intended to realise some of the other goals of the criminal justice system, such as crime prevention.[22] They cite the following considerations to support this

[16] Tran v. State, 965 So. 2d 226 (Fla. Dist. Ct. App. 2007).

[17] Fla. Stat. § 794.0235 (1997) and La. Stat. Ann. § 15.538 (1997).

[18] Mental Health Act 1983 (as amended by the Mental Health Act 2007). § 63 permits non-consensual interventions except psychosurgery, hormone implants, electro-convulsive therapy and psychiatric medications lasting more than three months. § 58 permits non-consensual psychiatric medications lasting more than three months, provided that the requirements concerning approval by two medical practitioners are met.

[19] MHA 1983 § 1.

[20] See, e.g., R. E. Kendell, 'The Distinction Between Personality Disorder and Mental Illness', *British Journal of Psychiatry* **180**:2 (2002), 110–115.

[21] K. Harrison and B. Rainey, ' Suppressing Human Rights? A Rights-Based Approach to the Use of Pharmacotherapy with Sex Offenders', *Legal Studies* **29**:1 (2009), 47–74, 62.

[22] Forsberg and Douglas, 'Anti-Libidinal Interventions', 458.

claim.[23] Firstly, offenders can be *sentenced to* hospital detention (and once detained there, capacitous offenders can be given certain brain interventions without their consent). Secondly, the Secretary of State, rather than a Mental Health Professional, makes the decision about when certain offenders may be discharged from hospital. Thirdly, one of the grounds for compulsory treatment is the protection of third parties, rather than the patient's benefit. (However, it should be noted the protection of third parties ground for compulsory treatment of mental disorders applies equally to offenders and non-offenders.)[24]

In Scotland, courts can sentence mentally disordered offenders to treatment.[25] The definition of mental disorder is as broad as the equivalent definition in England and Wales.[26] In Scotland an interesting distinction is drawn between the involuntary treatment of individuals involved in criminal proceedings and individuals who have not been prosecuted, which might reflect retributive thinking. Offenders with mental disorders, who are rational enough to be held criminally responsible and who retain the capacity to give and withhold consent can nevertheless be subjected to involuntary treatment for their mental disorders.[27] In contrast, mentally disordered individuals who are not involved in criminal proceedings can only be given involuntary treatment if their decision-making capacity is substantially impaired.[28] A retributivist might justify this distinction by arguing that offenders, because of their culpable choice to commit crimes, have lost the right to refuse consent to such treatments and so their decision-making capacity can be ignored. It might be objected that this distinction could be based on the need for public protection (rather than retribution) and that offenders are simply considered more dangerous than non-offenders. However, in response, the category of "non-offenders" includes individuals who have committed violent acts, but cannot be prosecuted because they were clearly not rational enough at the time of the act to be held criminally responsible.

Official statistics show that hundreds of offenders in the United Kingdom are sentenced each year to hospital detention and

---

[23] Forsberg and Douglas, 'Anti-Libidinal Interventions', 465–471.

[24] This third factor does not, by itself, clearly support Forsberg and Douglas' claim that the purpose of these interventions is 'correctional' (i.e., pursuing the aims of criminal justice), unless the treatment of dangerous non-offenders is also correctional.

[25] Criminal Procedure (Scotland) Act 1995 § 57a.

[26] Mental Health (Care and Treatment) (Scotland Act) 2003 § 328.

[27] CP(S)A 1995 § 57a.

[28] CP(S)A 1995 § 64 (5) (d).

treatment.[29] However, unfortunately there are no publically available statistics on how many capacitous offenders have been forced to receive treatment against their will.

To summarise: In a number of US states biomedical interventions are already being used as punishments. The legislation governing these interventions suggests they have a partly retributive purpose. Currently, in the UK, brain interventions are being imposed on offenders partly in order to achieve "correctional" objectives, but retributive reasons do not (yet) seem to play a major role.

3. Would the Use of Brain Interventions as Retributive Punishments Violate Article 3 of the European Convention on Human Rights?

Article 3 of the European Convention on Human Rights prohibits 'in absolute terms torture or inhuman or degrading treatment or punishment, irrespective of the victim's conduct'.[30] Even offenders who have committed serious crimes do not forfeit this right. Few theorists would advocate giving offenders brain interventions that would cause such severe suffering as to constitute torture. However, there is a range of possible brain interventions with mild to moderate side effects, such as anti-depressants and anti-libidinal medications. Certain interventions are minimally invasive, e.g., transcranial direct current stimulation, which involves electrically stimulating brain regions by placing a device outside the skull. Some theorists have argued that using brain interventions as punishments can objectify offenders, failing to respect them as persons, even if the interventions do not have particularly severe side effects.[31] On this view the concept of 'degrading treatment' seems most relevant. The European Court of Human Rights (ECtHR) defines 'degrading' to include treatment that 'debases' by showing 'a lack of respect for dignity'.[32]

---

[29] Mental Welfare Commission for Scotland, *Statistical Monitoring: Mental Health Act Monitoring 2015–16*: www.cqc.org.uk/sites/default/files/20161122_mhareport1516_web.pdf; Ministry of Justice, *Statistics of Mentally Disordered Offenders: England and Wales* 2008: https://www.gov.uk/government/statistics/statistics-of-mentally-disordered-offenders-ns.

[30] *Chahal v UK* (1997) 23 EHRR 413, at paragraph 80.

[31] See E. Shaw, 'The Right to Bodily Integrity and the Rehabiliation of Offenders', *Neuroethics*: https://doi.org/10.1007/s12152-016-9277-4, which opposes mandatory interventions.

[32] *Pretty v the United Kingdom* (2002) 35 EHRR 1, at paragraph 52.

For article 3 to be engaged, the treatment must meet a certain threshold of severity. This does not require harm to health. For instance, shaving a prisoner's head constituted degrading treatment.[33] It can be enough that the victim feels humiliated 'only in his eyes', provided he has sound reasons for feeling this.[34] However, surprisingly, in *Grare v France* the Commission decided that the threshold of severity had not been met in the case of a patient whose mental disorder had been treated using antipsychotics with distressing side effects (including trembling, hypertension, and visual disturbances), regardless of whether the patient consented to the treatment.[35]

This decision could be criticised on the basis that the Commission should have placed more weight on the issues of consent, capacity, and violation of mental and bodily integrity. Arguably, forcing a capacitous person to receive mind-altering drugs itself shows lack of respect for dignity, even if the side effects are not severe. It is plausible that this invasion of mental and bodily integrity could also justifiably cause someone to feel humiliated. This is particularly likely if the purpose of the intervention is to address criminal behaviour (which was not the purpose of the treatment in *Grare*), given the stigma surrounding the combination of mental health issues and criminality. In *Tyrer v UK* (which involved punishment by birching a juvenile offender convicted of a violent crime) the Court held that the applicant had been subjected to degrading punishment, partly because that punishment involved 'institutionalised violence' which constituted an 'attack on [...] physical integrity' in addition to possible psychological harm.[36] However, the use of brain interventions as a form of punishment might be distinguished from the corporal punishment in *Tyrer* on the basis that it might not be administered in a "violent" manner and may be given for a combination of retributive and therapeutic purposes (discussed below).

In *Dvořáček v Czech Republic*, the ECtHR held that the administration of anti-libidinal drugs to a sex offender was compatible with article 3, but pointed out that it did meet the relevant threshold of severity and also emphasised the importance of consent in the context

---

[33]   *Yankov v Bulgaria* (2003) 40 EHRR 36.

[34]   *Tyrer v UK* (1979–1980) 2 EHRR 1, at paragraph 23. Regarding the 'sound reasons' qualification see E. Webster, 'Degradation: A Human Rights Perspective', in P. Kaufman, H. Kuch, C. Neuhauser, and E. Webster (eds), *Humiliation, Degradation, Dehumanization: Human Dignity Violated* (London: Springer, 2011), 67–84, 75.

[35]   (1991) 15 EHRR CD 100.

[36]   (1978) 2 EHRR 1, paragraph 33.

of that case.[37] It may be that, in future cases, the Court will regard consent as essential if the intervention addresses criminal behaviour. However, it is hard to predict how the ECtHR's jurisprudence will develop in this area, as the Court has not provided a set of necessary and sufficient conditions for compatibility with article 3.

Retributive punishment is typically imposed on offenders without giving them any choice in the matter. If the ECtHR continues to adopt the consent-based approach adopted in *Dvořáček*, then imposing brain interventions as a *mandatory* form of retributive punishment would appear to violate article 3. However, it is arguably consistent with retributivism to give offenders the choice between different punishments that are of roughly equal severity. The ECtHR stated that the difficult choice that Dvořáček faced between drug therapy and a longer time in hospital did not render his consent invalid. Therefore offering a *hard choice* between brain interventions and a more traditional form of punishment, e.g., incarceration, may not by itself violate article 3.

In cases involving both capacitous and non-capacitous offenders, the ECtHR has emphasised the importance of providing convincing evidence that the intervention is a 'medical necessity'.[38] Bartlett has noted that the idea of 'medical necessity' is vague.[39] For the purposes of this chapter the following questions arise. Firstly, as noted above, some of the interventions that are offered to offenders might be regarded as "moral enhancements" – interventions that aim to increase conformity with moral and legal standards – rather than treatments. Can immoral, antisocial, or criminal behaviour qualify as a "medical" condition? Secondly, can "medical necessity" include conferring a psychological benefit on the individual, e.g., enhancing autonomy, even if the intervention does not, strictly speaking, treat a disorder? Thirdly, if a brain intervention is imposed for the purpose of retributive punishment, does this mean that it has not been given out of medical necessity? Would a dual medical/retributive purpose be compatible with article 3?

---

[37]   In *Herczegfalvy v Austria*, the ECtHR held that 'as a general rule' involuntary medical treatment is compatible with article 3, provided that the medical necessity for the treatment has been convincingly shown to exist. However, this case involved a non-capacitous offender, so it is not clear whether medical necessity is enough for involuntary treatment of competent offenders to be compatible with article 3.

[38]   (1992) 15 EHRR 437.

[39]   Peter Bartlett, 'The Necessity Must Be Convincingly Shown to Exist: Standards for Compulsory Treatment for Mental Disorder Under the Mental Health Act 1983', *Medical Law Review* **19**:4 (2011), 514–547, 525.

Regarding the first issue: when considering which conditions count as "medical", it is important to note that in *Dvořáček* the offender's paraphilia was caused by a genetic disorder called Wilson's disease. The ECtHR accepted that treatment for this condition was a medical necessity. It is not clear whether offending that is caused by undesirable character traits or which supposedly results from a condition whose medical status is controversial (such as anti-social personality disorder) would qualify as "medical" under the ECHR.

If the offender's behaviour is clearly caused by disease or disorder then curing this condition might count as a medical necessity. However, it is uncertain whether enhancing the offender's autonomy would be enough. The intervention might enhance autonomy if it enables him to be less impulsive, or reduces inner conflict, by reducing disturbing thoughts. If the interventions would enhance autonomy, it is uncertain whether this would satisfy the medical necessity requirement. However, an intervention's impact on autonomy will not always be clear. For instance anti-libidinal medication could both increase autonomy, by reducing compulsive urges, and interfere with the offender's sexual autonomy.[40]

Regarding the third issue: retributivists sometimes assert that, to be legitimate, punishment must be inflicted with the *sole* intention of meting out deserved suffering. These retributivists would consider it illegitimate to impose a punishment on the basis that it is a "medical necessity". For example, Michael Moore states that a tension 'exists between crime-prevention and retributive goals [...] due to retributivism's inability to share the stage with any other punishment goal. To achieve retributive justice, the punishment must be inflicted because the offender did the offense. To the extent that someone is punished for reasons other than that he deserves to be punished, retributive justice is not achieved'.[41] According to Kant, 'only the law of retribution (*ius talionis*) [...] can specify definitely the quality and the quantity of punishment; all other principles are fluctuating and unsuited for a sentence of pure and strict justice because extraneous considerations are mixed into them'.[42]

---

[40] For a useful discussion of these issues see: Z. B. Akbaba, *The Permissibility of Pharmacotherapy for Paedophilic Sex Offenders In the Light of the Rights Protected Under the European Convention on Human Rights* (Ph.D. Thesis, University of Leicester, 2015).

[41] M. Moore, *Placing Blame: A Theory of the Criminal Law* (New York: Oxford University Press, 2010), 28.

[42] I. Kant, *The Metaphysics of Morals*, trans. by Mary Gregor (Cambridge: Cambridge University Press, 1991), 141.

If direct brain interventions are intended solely as retribution, then it is hard to see how the ECtHR's medical necessity requirement could be met. According to Bernadette Rainey, '[i]f the use of drug therapy is primarily to ensure public protection, with the medical needs of the offender being secondary, then the ECtHR may find it is not medically necessary'.[43] If brain interventions are intended solely as a form of retributive punishment then this seems even harder to reconcile with the ECHR, bearing in mind that retributive punishment is specifically intended to make the offender suffer. Traditional punishments that are imposed for solely retributive reasons do not violate article 3, provided they do not cause more suffering than is "usual" for punishment. However, if punishment is imposed by *means* of a medical intervention, the Court's reliance on the "medical necessity" principle surely implies that imposing this intervention with a solely retributive purpose would violate article 3.

Some retributivists might be more flexible than Moore and Kant and may be willing to allow rehabilitative motives to play a role in sentencing. If the state took this approach it might use the intervention *partly* in order to cause retributive suffering and partly for therapeutic reasons. It is not certain whether this approach would be compatible with article 3.

To summarise: although the ECtHR has not directly considered whether using brain interventions as a form of retributive punishment is compatible with article 3, this proposal would face some formidable obstacles. Firstly, it seems that (at least in cases where the severity threshold has been met and the offender is capacitous) the ECtHR has stressed the importance of obtaining the offender's consent to receive the intervention. It is likely that this rules out imposing brain interventions as a form of *mandatory* retributive punishment. Secondly, the ECtHR, in the context of treatment that reduces offending behaviour, has emphasised the importance of showing that the intervention is medically necessary. The intervention will probably not be regarded as medically necessary if the offender's behaviour is caused by bad character (rather than a genuine disorder). It is unclear whether enhancing the patient's autonomy would count as a medical necessity. Fourthly, in view of the medical necessity principle, providing these interventions for solely retributive reasons would seem to violate article 3. However, providing these

---

[43]   B. Rainey, 'Human Rights and Sexual Offenders', in K. Harrison and B. Rainey (eds), *The Wiley-Blackwell Handbook of Legal and Ethical Aspects of Sex Offender Treatment and Management* (Oxford: Wiley-Blackwell, 2013), 18–37.

interventions for a mixture of retributive and therapeutic reasons might be compatible with article 3.

4. Public Attitudes

It might be thought that using biomedical interventions as a type of retributive punishment would be generally regarded as brutal and so that adopting/expanding this practice would not be politically feasible. However, research into public attitudes towards offenders suggests that there may well be public support for such a policy. For example, according to one study 'respondents balance a complex mixture of retributive and rehabilitative views in assessing biological interventions for criminal offenders'.[44] On one interpretation of the data from this study, respondents regarded such biological interventions as having a partly retributive justification. Public attitudes have a significant effect on criminal justice policies through the democratic process.[45] In addition, in the United States the views of the public are also taken into account when determining whether laws are constitutional. A punishment will be regarded as unconstitutionally 'cruel and unusual' if it would 'outrage the public conscience'.[46] It has not yet been determined whether the current statutes permitting punishment by chemical castration are constitutional. If further research into public attitudes reveals an acceptance of biological forms of retributive punishment, then these findings could lend support to the argument that this type of punishment is constitutionally permitted. As a result, this form of punishment might become more widespread in the US If there is sufficient public support for this kind of punishment in the United Kingdom, British politicians may still be willing to adopt this policy even if it breaches the European Convention on Human Rights (given that they have already ignored the European Court of Human Rights on certain other criminal justice issues, e.g., the UK's blanket ban on prisoners voting).[47]

---

[44] C. Berryessa, J. Chandler, and P. Reiner, 'Public Attitudes Toward Legally Coerced Biological Treatments of Criminals', *Journal of Law and the Biosciences* **3**:3 (2016), 447–467.

[45] J. Wood and G. Viki, 'Public Attitudes Towards Crime and Punishment', in J. Adler (ed.), *Forensic Psychology: Debates, Concepts and Practice* (Cullompton: Willan, 2004), 16–36.

[46] *R v Smith* 1 S.C.R. 1045 (1987).

[47] *Hirst v the United Kingdom* (No. 2) [2005] ECHR 681.

5. Could Retributivists Regard Brain Interventions as a Legitimate Form of Punishment?

Jesper Ryberg claims that retributivists could view biomedical interventions as a legitimate *form of retributive punishment* (as opposed to an alternative to punishment).[48] Retributivists hold that punishment should inflict on offenders the suffering that they deserve. According to Ryberg, this suffering could consist in the unpleasant side effects induced by the injection of a drug or by some other biomedical intervention.[49] He even suggests that, if a drug were developed that reduced offending behaviour without causing unpleasant side effects, retributive justice could be achieved by adding chemicals to the drug to cause painful symptoms.[50] Many retributivists emphasise punishment's communicative function – it expresses society's condemnation. Ryberg maintains that injecting an offender with such a drug would be just as effective as a prison sentence at sending a condemnatory message.

However, Ryberg's argument assumes that retributivists are not particular about the *kind* of suffering that punishment should induce – any form of mental or physical suffering will do, provided the correct *amount* is inflicted. Ryberg's argument may fit with some versions of retributivism. For instance, Igor Primoratz suggests that retributive suffering should involve a setback to the offender's self-interest. Primoratz also thinks this will send the appropriate message of condemnation. He writes:

[I]f society's condemnation of their misdeeds is really to reach [offenders] […] it will have to be translated into the one language

[48] Ryberg, 'Punishment, Pharmacological Treatment, and Early Release'.

[49] Ryberg, 'Punishment, Pharmacological Treatment, and Early Release', 239.

[50] Ryberg ('Punishment, Pharmacological Treatment, and Early Release', 240) touches on the issue of how retributivists would assess whether offenders had experienced the appropriate *amount* of suffering. A retributivist would not wish to offer an offender a biomedical intervention in exchange for early release if that would inflict too little suffering. In order to work out at what point to grant a prisoner who had accepted treatment early release, the retributivist would need to know how much drug-induced suffering was equivalent to suffering the offender would have experienced during the portion of his prison sentence he would otherwise have served. Ryberg sees no difficulty in making such comparisons, since retributivists already need to compare different kinds of sentences, e.g., prison versus community service.

they are sure to understand: the language of self-interest. This translation is accomplished by punishment.[51]

The thought that something would be lost in this translation might cast doubt on that version of retributivism.

Even if retributivists like Primoratz accepted the legitimacy of biomedically induced retributive suffering, they might object to using such techniques to bring about moral enhancement. The drug Ryberg envisages has two effects: a) causing unpleasant symptoms, e.g., headaches, and b) bringing about moral enhancement (e.g., decreasing aggression). As noted above, Michael Moore thinks that retributivism is the *sole* justification for punishment.[52] He might therefore accept the legitimacy of a) but object to b) on the basis that it is unjustifiable to impose punishment in order to benefit the offender or to promote the general good.[53] However, it should be noted that this objection would not only rule out biomedical moral enhancement, but *all* rehabilitation – a position that many would find implausible. Furthermore, this objection would not rule out the use of drug-induced headaches as a form of retributive punishment.

In any case, there are other versions of retributivism that provide more plausible grounds for objecting to the idea that distressing symptoms of medication should be viewed as a form of punishment. For instance, Antony Duff argues that punishment should aim to impose a very specific type of suffering or burden, consisting in feelings of remorse, the experience of making apologetic reparation and being subject to the moral criticism of one's fellow citizens. Clearly the side effects of medication (such as nausea, or headaches) are not what Duff has in mind. According to Duff, punishment will only communicate the appropriate message of moral censure if it is designed to elicit remorse and to provide an opportunity to make amends. He writes:

The aim is not simply that they should "suffer" or be caused pain [...]. Hard treatment [...] should serve both to assist the process of repentance and reform, by focusing his attention on his crime

---

[51] I. Primoratz, 'Punishment as Language', *Philosophy* **64**:248 (1989), 187–205, 199–200.

[52] See footnote 40 and cited text.

[53] Some retributivists deny that rehabilitation is technically "punishment", but accept that it can be legitimate if it is classified as something else, e.g., "correction". These retributivists could not object on retributive grounds to moral enhancement if imposed as a form of correction.

and its implications, and as a way of making the apologetic reparation that he owes.[54]

On this view, the retributive purpose of prison is not to cause the prisoner distress at having to live in such a harsh environment. Rather, prison may be justified, because it allows the offender to dwell on the seriousness of his crime without being distracted by the competing claims on his attention that he would experience if he was still living in the community, e.g., employment, socialising, and family obligations.[55] Victim-offender mediation programmes and other attempts to bring the offender to recognise the wrongfulness of his conduct may also elicit the 'right kind' of suffering.[56] Community service may facilitate reform and reparation if it is likely to remind the offender of his crime and its consequences for the victim. For instance, an offender who maimed the victim might be trained how to make wheelchairs for the disabled. Experiencing drug-induced nausea and headaches are more likely to interfere with the offender's capacity to engage in moral reasoning about his offence and to impede his ability to make reparation than to help achieve these ends.

Another version of retributivism might focus on the way punishment can temporarily change the relationship between the citizen and the rest of the community. For instance, Christopher Bennett has argued that punishment can be a way in which society symbolically dissociates itself from the offender's crime.[57] This is analogous to the way individuals, in the context of personal relations, might withdraw or distance themselves from others whose conduct they find unacceptable. They might refrain from greeting wrongdoers in a friendly manner, stop inviting them to social occasions, or refuse to be in the same room with them. Bennett points out that such actions *may* cause suffering, but even if they do not they will still serve their function, i.e., dissociation.[58] Similarly, the purpose of prison is not to cause the offender to suffer because he is living in unpleasant surroundings, but to symbolically dissociate the community from the offender's wrongdoing by temporarily excluding him from

[54] R. Duff, 'Legal Punishment', in *The Stanford Encyclopedia of Philosophy* (2008): https://stanford.library.sydney.edu.au/archives/spr2008/entries/legal-punishment/.
[55] R. Duff, *Punishment, Communication, and Community* (New York: Oxford University Press, 2000).
[56] Duff, *Punishment, Communication, and Community*.
[57] C. Bennett, 'Précis of "The Apology Ritual"', *Teorema* **31**:2 (2012), 73–94.
[58] Bennett, 'Précis of "The Apology Ritual"'.

full participation in the life of the community. In contrast, injecting offenders with substances that induce headaches and nausea in order to make offenders suffer would not seem to satisfy the requirements of this version of retributivism. It would be hard to characterise such symptoms merely as society's way of "distancing itself" or "withdrawing" from the offender. Returning to the analogy with personal relationships: an individual who responded to a friend's wrongdoing by shouting insults at her or slapping her across the face could hardly be described as simply distancing himself or withdrawing from the relationship. Bennett's concept of dissociation is meant to be different from the 'problematic notion of retaliation'.[59]

I do not attempt to defend Duff and Bennett's versions of retributivism – a task that would not be possible within the scope of this chapter. My purpose is to argue that, contrary to Ryberg, some of the most plausible versions of retributivism rule out the possibility that the side effects of medication could be viewed as legitimate forms of punishment. However, I will add that the ability to rule out this possibility is a merit of Duff and Bennett's accounts. Opponents of retributivism sometimes claim that it is hard to distinguish retribution from mere vengeance or sadism. Theories that endorsed intentionally injecting offenders with drugs in order to generate painful symptoms would leave themselves open to such criticisms.

Retributivists might of course appeal to a separate prohibition on "cruel and unusual" punishment – a constraint on punishment that does not derive from retributivism itself.[60] This strategy would present its own challenges. It is not clear why the state should be restricted to "traditional" forms of punishment as opposed to "unusual" ones. If new forms of punishment became widely used, after a while they would cease to be unusual. If "cruel" is meant to suggest that they cause an unacceptably high level of distress, it is not clear that this claim is correct. Drugs that cause nausea and headaches for a short period of time could impose much less suffering than a lengthy prison sentence. The level of distress therefore cannot

---

[59] C. Bennett, 'Penal Disenfranchisement', *Criminal Law and Philosophy* **10**:3 (2016), 411–425.

[60] For instance, Kant, after endorsing the death penalty for murder, maintains that the way this punishment is carried out 'must still be freed from any mistreatment that could make the humanity in the person suffering it into something abominable' (*Metaphysics of Morals*, 474). This constraint on the types of acceptable punishment does not seem to follow directly from the essential tenets of retributivism.

provide a reason for ruling out the former intervention and permitting the latter. Describing an intervention as "cruel" might also suggest that the intervention is wrong partly because of the *intentions* of those employing it. It might be thought cruel to intervene *in order* to produce suffering for its own sake. However, this argument would be of no help to those retributivists who think that "traditional" punishment should be imposed in order to inflict suffering for its own sake, as the argument would then imply that their conception of traditional punishment is "cruel". However, Duff and Bennett's accounts would not be vulnerable to that objection, as they do not think punishment should inflict suffering purely for its own sake.

The next question is whether retributivists, such as Duff, might view direct brain interventions as a form of punishment, if these interventions are *not* employed in order to inflict suffering for its own sake. Recall Duff's account of prison's role in enabling offenders to focus on the wrongfulness of their actions without being distracted by competing claims on their attention. A direct brain intervention might operate in a similar way by increasing the offender's *capacity* to concentrate on reasons for trying to reform. Duff stresses the importance of engaging the offender in dialogue which both leaves open the possibility that the offender will remain unpersuaded by the state's arguments that he should change his ways and gives him the opportunity to express his disagreement.[61] He opposes techniques such as brain washing; however, increasing the offender's ability to concentrate does not seem to undermine the offender's right to remain unpersuaded. Enabling the offender to concentrate better would not implant new beliefs in him directly, but would simply make it easier for him to grasp certain reasons for himself. At first glance, this type of brain intervention might seem to be compatible with Duff's communication theory. However, Duff might still insist that imposing such interventions on a mandatory basis would preclude the possibility of genuine moral dialogue between the state and the offender. If the state were forcibly to "trespass" into the offender's mental realm and alter his manner of reasoning (by making him more alert and focussed) this would arguably blur the boundary between the two parties in the dialogue. Dialogue requires two independent parties – two clearly separate minds. If one party not only provides the other party with reasons to engage with, but also directly controls, through brain modification, the manner in which he engages with those reasons (albeit not the end result of the reasoning process), arguably this does not count as

---

[61] Duff, *Punishment, Communication and Community*, 22.

genuine dialogue. Even more problematic from the perspective of communication theory would be an attempt to change the offender's attitudes or values by directly modifying his brain. That type of modification would cause a change in the offender's outlook in a way that bypasses his rational faculties – the state has not given him a reason to change his mind. Ryberg correctly points out that in the context of ordinary medical treatment this is unproblematic. He writes: 'almost all sorts of traditional somatic problems are dealt with by treatment that acts directly on the body without providing any kind of understanding. And it is hard to see why a mind-affecting treatment, which has desirable consequences for the person who is treated, should be regarded as impermissible simply because it is not accompanied by a gain in terms of self-knowledge or understanding'.[62] Now, it may be unproblematic if natural changes in people's neurochemistry or psychiatric treatment (that is voluntarily sought by non-offenders) affect people's attitudes without giving them reasons to change their minds. However, it cannot be concluded from this that altering a person's values without giving them a reason to change their mind is acceptable in the context of retributive punishment. A communication theorist might well argue that in that particular context it is inappropriate for the *state* to attempt to change offender's minds without giving reasons. This would undermine the moral "dialogue" and respect for the offenders' rationality, which is meant to be at the heart of communication theory.

6. Brain Interventions and Proportionate Punishment

Ryberg also argues that retributivists may have a reason for supporting offers of biomedical interventions in exchange for early release, even if biomedical interventions do *not* count as a form of punishment. Retributivists believe that punishment should be proportionate to the desert of the offender. Many retributivists also think that our criminal justice system currently imprisons people for longer than they deserve. If early release of those prisoners who accept interventions would, overall, make sentences more proportionate, Ryberg says, retributivists should favour this policy.

One might worry that this approach (as Ryberg describes it) is not in the spirit of retributivism. Consequentialists believe in *maximising* good consequences. However, retributivism is generally considered

---

[62]   Ryberg, 'Punishment, Pharmacological Treatment, and Early Release', 234.

to be a non-consequentialist theory. Retributivists are more likely to believe that each individual judge/lawmaker should *simply apply* retributive principles rather than trying to maximise certain outcomes (e.g., proportionate sentences) by whatever means possible. Ryberg's suggestion would involve a judge imposing a sentence that he knows to be excessively long – a sentence that nevertheless purports to be the deserved punishment for the crime – and then offering offenders the chance of early release if they accept an intervention that is apparently justified on a non-retributive basis: *rehabilitation*. Retributivists who believe punishment should be a form of moral communication might find this problematic, since the sentence handed down by the judge in this scenario could send out a confusing message. Another problem is that it would create a situation where some offenders (those who refuse treatment) would receive a longer period in prison than they deserve, whereas others (who accept treatment) would serve a prison term that is more in line with what they deserve. True, this proposal would give more prisoners the right *quantum* of suffering than if the option of treatment were unavailable and all prisoners received excessive sentences. However, at the same time, it would appear to violate the principle that like cases should be treated alike. Retributivists typically think that ensuring the punishment reflects the *relative* gravity of each offender's conduct compared with other offenders is at least as important as administering the correct amount of punishment in absolute terms.

Nevertheless, it may be possible to modify Ryberg's approach to make it more acceptable to the retributivist. If the offender's willingness to undergo direct brain interventions indicates his commitment to trying to become a better person, then, from a retributive perspective, this could warrant a reduction in his sentence.[63] If this is the case, then offering direct brain interventions in exchange for early release would not violate the principle that like cases should be treated alike. For this position to be plausible there would have to be a way of telling whether the offender's acceptance of the intervention was genuinely motivated by a desire to reform or whether he was simply motivated by the prospect of early release.

---

[63]   For a discussion of similar considerations, see A. Von Hirsch and A. Ashworth, *Proportionate Sentencing: Exploring the Principles* (Oxford: Oxford University Press, 2005).

Elizabeth Shaw

7. Conclusion

In a number of US states biomedical interventions are already being used as punishments. The legislation governing these interventions suggests they have a partly retributive purpose. Currently, in the UK brain interventions are imposed on offenders partly in order to achieve "correctional" objectives, but retributive reasons do not seem to play a major role. Nevertheless, the influence of retributive public attitudes on legislators may change this. It is therefore important to consider whether the use of brain interventions as a method of retributive punishment would be compatible with international human rights law. Using mandatory brain interventions for the sole purpose of inflicting retributive punishment would probably violate the ECHR. However, voluntary interventions given for a mixture of therapeutic and punitive reasons might not. I have argued that some versions of retributivism do not have the theoretical resources to explain why direct interventions could not be a legitimate form of retributive punishment. However, although Duff and Bennett have not yet examined the implications of their theories for this question, I have argued that their versions of communicative retributivism are in the best position to oppose the idea of using these interventions without the free and informed consent of the recipients. Finally, I have argued that offering these interventions on a voluntary basis, as an alternative to punishment, would not necessarily violate principles of proportionality.

University of Aberdeen
eshaw@abdn.ac.uk

Lone Wolf Terrorists and the Impotence of Moral Enhancement

VALERIE GRAY HARDCASTLE

The most likely scenario that we have to guard against right now ends up being more of a lone wolf operation than a large, well-co-ordinated terrorist attack.

—President Barack Obama[1]

I hope they can […] give me the help I need and allow me to get a second chance. I'm not a terrorist, a criminal or a bad person, I'm just a kid who suffered from problems, that made some bad decisions and stupid mistakes.

—Convicted Lone Wolf Terrorist Christopher Cornell[2]

Abstract

In their recent book *Unfit for the Future*, Persson and Savulescu make a heartfelt plea for the increasing necessity of "moral enhancement", interventions that improve human capacities for moral behaviour.[3] They argue that, with all the technological advances of the 20th and 21st centuries, the sheer scope of horror that humans can now potentially wreak on their neighbours or the world is staggering. Hence, we are morally obliged to use interventions at our disposal to prevent such atrocities. However, as we learn more about human behaviour and decision-making, the argument that we are morally obliged to morally enhance our friends, neighbours, or countrymen starts to fall apart. For us to be more moral requires more than sharpening our reasoning capacities so that we can more effectively recognise what is better or increasing personal motivation so that we are more likely to do what is good. It requires that we all agree on what the good is and how to achieve it, and that there are no social, cultural, physical, or psychological impediments that prevent us from recognising the good or acting on it. To illustrate my position, I use the phenomenon of self-radicalised terrorists as a case study. In particular, I focus on how historians, psychologists, sociologists, criminologists, and political scientists understand the process of self-radicalisation, who self-radicalises, and why, and what all this tells us about it should be "treated". Part of my purpose in working my way

---

[1] A. Levine, 'Obama: Biggest Terror Fear is the Lone Wolf', *CNN*, 16th August 2011: http://security.blogs.cnn.com/2011/08/16/obama-biggest-terror-fear-is-the-lone-wolf/.

[2] K. Grasha, 'Man in Terror Plot Says "Allah's in Control, Not the Judge"', *Cincinnati Enquirer*, 5th December 2016.

[3] I. Persson and J. Savulescu, *Unfit for the Future: The Need for Moral Enhancement* (Oxford: Oxford University Press, 2012).

doi:10.1017/S1358246118000395   ©The Royal Institute of Philosophy and the contributors 2018

Royal Institute of Philosophy Supplement **83** 2018   271

Valerie Gray Hardcastle

through this case study is to demonstrate that many philosophers misunderstand or over-simplify the science behind so-called immoral actions; consequently, their discussions of whether to enhance someone's morality miss their mark.

1. Introduction

The threat presented by terrorism in the Western world is very real. According to the Global Terrorism Database at the University of Maryland there have been over 3,069 incidents in North America and Western Europe from 2000 to 2015.[4] It is no wonder that international conversations are occurring about how best to combat such potentially destructive behaviour.

Philosophers included. In their recent book *Unfit for the Future*, Persson and Savulescu make a heartfelt plea for the increasing necessity of "moral enhancement", interventions that improve human capacities for moral behaviour. They argue that, with all the technological advances of the 20th and 21st centuries, the sheer scope of horror that humans can now potentially wreak on their neighbours or the world is staggering. Hence, we are morally obliged to use interventions at our disposal to prevent such atrocities.

Leaving aside practical questions regarding whether such things might actually work or how we might implement such practices, several questions immediately arise from this position: How should we balance individual liberty against the collective good? Is it better to preserve the freedom to choose, even if the choices might be detrimental to others, or would improving the overall good justify restricting an individual's self-determination? Who or what exactly might have this moral imperative? Doctors, parents, neighbours, nation-states? And then, even more fundamentally: what moral code or system should we be reflecting when we enhance someone's behaviour, and who gets to decide this and why?

This chapter addresses this last question, though it comes at it rather obliquely. In particular, I shall argue that as we learn more about human behaviour and decision-making, the less it is clear that there are universal and objective moral codes that ground our behaviour. Consequently, the argument that we are morally obligated to morally enhance our friends, neighbours, or countrymen falls apart, though not because humans should be free to make terrible choices, but for three different reasons. First, the same action can be judged to

---

[4] Global Terrorism Database: https://www.start.umd.edu/gtd/.

be virtuous or abhorrent, depending on which moral system and the interpretation of relevant events is being used. Second, understanding problematic behaviour from a scientific point of view, which is what you would have to do to develop successful behavioural enhancements, removes that action from the realm of moral judgement and into the realm of clinical treatment. And third, our behaviour is significantly influenced by a whole host of environmental factors. We have to change the surrounding circumstances in order to effect significant behavioural changes; simply changing one's mind is generally not enough.

In short, for us to be more moral requires more than sharpening our reasoning capacities so that we can more effectively recognise what is better or increasing personal motivation so that we are more likely to do what is good. It requires that we all agree on what the good is and how to achieve it, and that there are no social, cultural, physical, or psychological impediments that prevent us from recognising the good or acting on it.

To illustrate my position, I shall use the phenomenon of self-radicalised terrorists as a case study. In particular, I shall focus on how historians, psychologists, sociologists, criminologists, and political scientists understand the process of self-radicalisation, who self-radicalis and why, and what all this tells us about how it should be "treated". Part of my purpose in working my way through this case study is to demonstrate that many philosophers misunderstand or over-simplify the science behind so-called immoral actions; consequently, their discussions of whether to enhance someone's morality miss their mark.

2. Philosophers' Perspectives on Moral Behaviour

In general, philosophers who worry about the morality of moral enhancement think of moral actions as a product of three things: (1) knowing what is good, (2) being motivated to do the good, and then (3) deciding to do what one is motivated to do on the basis of (1) and (2). It is both an internal process and deliberative one. For example, in his reply to Persson and Savulescu,[5] Harris notes that 'morality [is] basically a matter of choosing what is for the best all things considered, not simply being well motivated or pro-social; in short, [...] to be good is not simply happening to do no evil but

---

[5] I. Persson and J. Savulescu, 'Moral Bioenhancement, Freedom and Reason', *Neuroethics* **9**:3 (2016), 263–268.

choosing for a reason, choosing on the basis of evidence and argument, not to do wrong'.[6]

Indeed, the idea of deliberately choosing a course of action is fundamentally important to many philosophers' analyses of morality, for
deliberately choosing is bound up with most philosophers' notions of
freedom, and it is the tension between individual freedom to choose
and the collective good that drives much of their discussion. Harris
writes: '[t]he space between knowing the good and doing the good
is a region entirely inhabited by freedom. Knowledge of the good is
sufficiency to have stood, but freedom to fall is all. Without the
freedom to fall, good cannot be a choice; and freedom disappears
and along with it virtue. There is no virtue in doing what you
must'.[7] DeGrazia agrees with Harris that 'we are free when we determine our actions through our own will or when we are able to do what
we want', and that morality requires choosing freely.[8] Hence, from
their point of view, A engages in moral behaviour X if A believes (correctly) that X is the moral thing to do, A prefers to do X, A has this
disposition because A identifies with this preference and prefers to
have it, and this preference does not result from influences that A
would consider alienating.[9]

Oddly, these philosophers do not engage the question of what to do
when A believes, for well articulated reasons, that X is the moral thing
to do, but B believes just as strongly, for equally well articulated
reasons, that −X is the moral thing to do.[10] They appear to be assuming that what counts as the good is already settled, and so the concerns
regarding moral enhancement turn on potential conflicts with other
presumed goods (like liberty), not on what the good is to begin
with or how we know that.

If they are right, then perhaps all we need in order to engage in
moral conduct is moral motivation combined with moral insight
using the appropriate deliberative process. It would then follow
that to enhance our morality, we should improve either knowledge
of the good, motivation to do what is right, or our reasoning capacity.

----

[6] J. Harris, 'Moral Blindness – The Gift of the God Machine',
Neuroethics **9**:3 (2016), 269–273, 270.

[7] J. Harris, 'Moral Enhancement and Freedom,' *Bioethics* **25**:2 (2011),
102–111, 104; see also 110.

[8] D. DeGrazia, 'Moral Enhancement, Freedom, and What We (Should)
Value in Moral Behaviour,' *Journal of Medical Ethics* **40**:6 (2014), 361–368, 366.

[9] See also D. DeGrazia, *Human Identity and Bioethics* (Cambridge:
Cambridge University Press, 2005).

[10] At least I have found no such discussions in anything I have read by
these philosophers on the topic.

DeGrazia distinguishes three possible types of improvement: improvements in motives and character, improvements in comprehending what is right, and improvements in behaviour, though he later clarifies that behavioural improvements stem from improvements in motivation and insight.[11] Similarly, Shook argues that there are two ways someone may be morally lacking: motivational (she lacks the motivation to do what she thinks is right) and doxastic (she cannot form moral beliefs about what is right).[12] From Shook's point of view, to improve morality would mean improving either one's motivation or one's rational capacity or both. Azevendo, Curtis, and Kabasenche all adumbrate similar perspectives as well.[13]

But all of these perspectives are relying on a false, or at least radically over-simplified, folk psychological account of behaviour – that human action is (fully) explained in terms of beliefs, desires, and rationality. Of course, our behaviour is much more complicated than that. Social anxiety might prevent me from speaking up when I see a wrong. Or paranoia might provide me with unconventional interpretations of the world such that my actions appear inexplicable to others, but are perfectly rational using my assumptions. There could be nothing wrong with my reasoning capacity, my belief-making machine, or my motivational strength, and yet still my behaviour could be socially compromised because psychological context for these cognitive modules is compromised, so to speak. Regrettably, philosophical discussions of the morality of moral enhancement often rely on cartoonish views of what drives human behaviour. Equally importantly, they often presume robust psychological health in the moral decision-makers, a health that few of us, if any, have.[14]

[11] DeGrazia, 'Moral Enhancement, Freedom, and What We (Should) Value in Moral Behaviour', 363.

[12] J. R. Shook, 'Neuroethics and the Possible Types of Moral Enhancement', *AJOB Neuroscience* **3**:4 (2012), 3–14.

[13] M. A. Azevendo, 'The Misfortunes of Moral Enhancement', *Journal of Medicine and Philosophy* **41**:5 (2016), 461–479; B. L. Curtis, 'Moral Enhancement as Rehabilitation?', *AJOB Neuroscience* **3**:4 (2012) 23–24; W. P. Kabasenche, 'Moral Formation and Moral Enhancement', *AJOB Neuroscience* **7**:2 (2016), 130–131.

[14] In 2015, the National Institute of Mental Health in the United States estimated that 18 percent of all adult Americans suffered from a diagnosable mental illness in the previous year; this does not include Substance Use Disorders, which would only make the percentage higher: https://www.nimh.nih.gov/health/statistics/prevalence/any-mental-illness-ami-among-us-adults.shtml. Their study did not include Attention Deficit

Valerie Gray Hardcastle

Different philosophers emphasise different aspects of human psychology as most relevant to moral enhancement. Douglas, for example, claims that moral enhancement 'will expectably leave the enhanced person with morally better motives than she had previously'.[15] In particular, Douglas is focussed on reducing things like an impulse toward violence such that 'a reduction in the degree to which an agent experiences those emotions would, under some circumstances, constitute a moral enhancement'.[16] Persson and Savulescu agree that enhancing moral motivations would enable us to act better.[17] Harris, in contrast, holds that moral enhancement must essentially require cognitive enhancement because morality requires the ability to distinguish right from wrong as well as rational capacity.[18] In response, Rakić suggests that a lot of immoral behaviour comes from weakness of will; hence, cognitive enhancement alone would not be enough.[19]

But in each of these cases, whether one is enhancing motivation or cognition, what is being adjusted is internal to the agent; the way the world is structured around the agent is immaterial to moral improvement. Indeed, Simkulet argues that enticing certain behaviours by arranging the world in particular ways is antithetical to morality itself.[20] If I set an alarm to remind myself to check on my ailing mother, and I believe that checking on my mother is a good and moral thing to do, then, because the alarm does not change my moral intentions, it is not enhancing my morality even if it makes it more likely that I get in touch with my mother. Any inducements that bypass my deliberative process might even undermine my moral behaviour by impinging on the freedom I have to choose what to do. However, if all human behaviour is constrained by environmental factors, then it becomes more challenging to connect improvements

---

Disorder or Autism Spectrum Disorder, both of which can impact upon behaviour and decision-making significantly. It is important to keep in mind that psychological problems have to interfere with daily life in order to be classified as a mental illness.

[15] T. Douglas, 'Moral Enhancement', *Journal of Applied Philosophy* **25**:3 (2008), 228–245, 231.

[16] Douglas, 'Moral Enhancement', 231.

[17] Persson and Savulescu, *Unfit for the Future*.

[18] Harris, 'Moral Enhancement and Freedom'.

[19] B. Rakić, 'Voluntary Moral Enhancement and the Survival-at-Any-Cost Bias', *Journal of Medical Ethics* **40**:4 (2014), 246–250.

[20] W. Simkulet, 'Intention and Moral Enhancement', *Bioethics* **30**:9 (2016), 714–720.

in behaviour to enhancements in morality, as opposed to a milieu that is more conducive to doing the right thing, regardless of intention or motivation.

In this chapter, I am not going to adjudicate the details of where moral enhancements might occur or what exactly comprises moral behaviour. Instead, I am going to focus on a prime example of what drove Persson and Savulescu to adumbrate for the moral imperative to morally enhance in the first place: the increase in terrorism around the world as well as the level of destruction that terrorists can now inflict. I do this to illustrate how my three complaints about philosophers' arguments concerning the putative morality of moral enhancement work to undermine their positions.

3. A Brief Primer on Self-Radicalised Terrorism

In the mid-2000s there were several large-scale terrorist attacks and plots, including the 2004 Madrid train attack, the 2005 7/7 attack in London, the 2005 plots disrupted in Sydney and Melbourne, and the 2006 plot disrupted in Toronto.[21] In each of these cases, overseas organisations were directly linked to the perpetrators. But since the mid-2000s, the pattern of terrorist activity has changed in both the United States and Western Europe. In particular, the number of terrorist incidents as a whole has declined, especially where group-based terrorist attacks co-ordinated from afar are concerned. But, at the same time, "homegrown" terrorism has increased in frequency.[22] That is, the number of attacks carried out by citizens against their own neighbours or country, without co-ordination or training from abroad, has risen significantly in the past decade.

A Hastings Report lists 50 publicly known terrorist plots against United States that have been thwarted since 9/11; of those, 42 were

[21] M. Zekulin, 'Endgames: Improving Our Understanding of Homegrown Terrorism,' *Studies in Conflict and Terrorism* **39**:1 (2016), 46–66.
[22] C. Hewitt, *Understanding Terrorism in America: From the Klan to Al Qaeda* (London: Routledge, 2003); G. LaFree, L. Dugan, and E. Miller, 'Integrated United States Security Database (IUSSD): Terrorism Data on the United States Homeland, 1970 to 2011', *Final Report to Resilient Systems Division, DHS Science and Technology Directorate* (College Park, MD: National Consortium for the Study of Terrorism and Responses to Terrorism, University of Maryland, 2012); R. Spaaij, *Understanding Lone Wolf Terrorism: Global Patterns, Motivations and Prevention* (Dordrecht: Springer, 2012).

homegrown.[23] George Washington University's Program on Extremism reports that post-9/11, 79 people in the United States convicted of jihadist-inspired offenses were completely unconnected to the Islamic State, al-Qaeda, or Al Shabaab. In the vast majority of these cases the perpetrators adhered to jihadist movement ideology in general, but displayed no particular loyalty to a specific group and had no formal links to any terrorist organisation. They were also US citizens.[24]

In theory, the reasons for this change are not mysterious. After the 9/11 attacks the West and its allies demolished many terrorist networks, dismantling their training camps and killing their leaderships. As a result the organisations have become more decentralised, which means they depend more on partners and friends to carry out their missions. At the same time, an increased focus domestically on anti-terrorism measures have upped the ante regarding the capabilities needed for carrying out a successful attack in the Western hemisphere from afar. Consequently, co-opting homegrown terrorists have become more appealing to distal operations, and they are what al-Qaeda and other terrorist organisations have been pushing as an alternative to co-ordinated and fully supported attacks as of late.[25] Why waste the resources implanting a complex operation from afar when locals will do approximately the same thing already?

Importantly, distant terrorist masterminds do not recruit terrorists in the West to use them as "remote-controlled weapons", as it were. They rarely induce converts to affiliate with them as part of some long-term plan to acquire the capacity to carry out a spectacular attack in the convert's home country. Instead, the converts themselves are normally pro-actively looking for access to a militant environment, which the militants can then exploit to their advantage.

---

[23] S. Bucci, J. Caragano, and J. Zuckerman, 'Fifty Terror Plots Foiled since 9/11: The Homegrown Threat and the Long War on Terrorism', *The Heritage Foundation Report* (2012): http://www.heritage.org/terrorism/report/fifty-terror-plots-foiled-911-the-homegrown-threat-and-the-long-war-terrorism.

[24] S. Gilkes, 'Not Just the Caliphate: Non-Islamic State-Related Jihadist Terrorism in America', George Washington University Program on Extremism (2016): https://cchs.gwu.edu/sites/cchs.gwu.edu/files/downloads/Not%20Just%20The%20Caliphate_0.pdf.

[25] Bucci, Caragano, and Zuckerman, 'Fifty Terror Plots Foiled since 9/11: The Homegrown Threat and the Long War on Terrorism'.

From the convert's perspective, becoming affiliated with jihadists is the end goal, rather than a means to something else.[26]

And nowadays, the process of radicalisation usually begins at home and it often ends there as well. For example, in 2009, the United States' Federal Bureau of Investigation (F.B.I.) estimated that there were approximately 15,000 websites and online forums supporting terrorism, and over three-quarters of them were based in the US.[27] Deep connections with well-developed overseas organisations are just not necessary to be a domestic terrorist in the West anymore.

But who are these people? Who become terrorists in their own nation? Recent data collection and analyses reveal not only how common these attacks have become but also commonalities among the backgrounds of the perpetrators.[28] For example, the Chicago Project on Security and Threats (CPOST) has looked in detail at over 100 individuals indicted for Islamic State-related crimes or who died during the commission of such crimes between the beginning of 2014 and the end of 2016.[29] Project leaders found striking and counter-intuitive patterns to the alleged perpetrators. Despite how they might be portrayed in the press, most homegrown terrorists are not poor, young, ignorant, uneducated, unemployed, irresponsible, or have a criminal history. As a group, the individuals look pretty much like average Western males (and the vast majority of

[26] M. Crone and M. Harrow, 'Homegrown Terrorism in the West', *Terrorism and Political Violence* **23**:4 (2011), 521–536.

[27] J. Ryan, P. Thomas, and X. Olivares, 'American-Bred Terrorism Causing Alarm for Law Enforcement', *ANC News.com*, 22nd July 2010.

[28] E.g., P. Gill, J. Horgan, and P. Deckert, 'Bombing Alone: Tracing the Motivations and Antecedent Behaviors of Lone-Actor Terrorists', *Journal of Forensic Sciences* **59**:2 (2014), 425–435; J. Gruenewald, S. Chermak, and J. D. Freilich, 'Distinguishing "Loner" Attacks from Other Domestic Extremist Violence: A Comparison of Far-Right Homicide Incidents and Offender Characteristics', *Criminology and Public Policy* **12**:1 (2013), 65–91; G. Michael, *Lone Wolf Terror and the Rise of Leaderless Resistance* (Nashville: Vanderbilt University Press, 2012); R. Spaaij, 'The Enigma of Lone Wolf Terrorism: An Assessment', *Studies in Conflict and Terrorism* **33**:9 (2010), 854–870; Spaaij, *Understanding Lone Wolf Terrorism: Global Patterns, Motivations and Prevention*; see also J. Kaplan, 'Leaderless Resistance', *Terrorism and Political Violence* **9**:3 (1997), 80–85.

[29] R. Pape, J. Decety, K. Ruby, A.A. Rivas, J. Jessen, and C. Wegner, 'The American Face of ISIS: Analysis of ISIS-Related Terrorism in the United States, March 2014-August 2016', Australian Strategic Policy Institute (2017): https://www.aspi.org.au/publications/the-american-face-of-isis-analysis-of-isis-related-terrorism-in-the-us-march-2014august-2016/ASPI_CPOST_ISIS_Indictees.pdf.

terrorists are men; CPOST identified only one woman in their database). Their average age was 27, with almost a third being over 30. Almost half were in a relationship, and a third were married. Three-quarters had jobs or were in school. In short, they seem just like your and my neighbours, which, of course, they are.

A significant number of those were also self-radicalised; they acted alone without any real connection to any terrorist organisation, so-called *lone wolf terrorists*. However, even though the incidence of lone wolf terrorism is increasing and – as President Obama's comments above testify – lone wolf terrorists are more on people's minds these days, they are not a new phenomenon by any stretch of the imagination. Perhaps the Biblical figure Phineas (*Numbers* 25:1–9) might well be credited as being the first lone wolf terrorist, as he averted God's wrath by deciding to murder an Israelite man and a Midianite woman whose interracial relationship threatened the survival of the Hebrew people.[30] And they have been operating ever since.

The United States especially seemed to provoke lone wolf terrorists. For example, solitary or only very loosely affiliated actors primarily committed the violence wrought by anti-civil rights and anti-Black extremists, right-wing militias, eco-terrorists, and anti-abortion activists in the United States. Indeed, until 2005, the US considered only white supremacists, anti-government militias, eco-terrorists, and anti-abortion radicals "homegrown" because it believed that jihadist terrorists had to be foreign.[31] But terminology aside, fully 40% of terrorism cases in the US from 1968 to 2007 have been "leaderless". In contrast, just over 1% of all terrorism cases worldwide were comprised by "lone wolves" during the same time period.[32] In sum, violent solitary actors have a significant history in the United States, and their numbers have steadily risen since 9/11.[33]

Research has shown that lone wolf terrorists are primarily motivated by a failing sense of identity. Often disempowered, alienated,

---

[30]   J. Kaplan, H. Loow, and L. Malkki, 'Introduction to the Special Issue on Lone Wolf Terrorism and Autonomous Cell Terrorism,' *Terrorism and Political Violence* **26**:1 (2014), 1–12.

[31]   L. Vidino, 'The Homegrown Terrorist Threat to the U.S. Homeland', Real Instituto Elcano (2009): http://www.realinstitutoelcano.org/wps/portal/rielcano_eng.

[32]   Spaaij, 'The Enigma of Lone Wolf Terrorism: An Assessment'.

[33]   M. Becker, 'Explaining Lone Wolf Target Selection in the United States', *Studies in Conflict and Terrorism* **37**:11 (2014), 959–978.

marginalised, and frustrated, they lack meaning in their lives. They wish to belong to something inspiring and significant. Affiliating with (what they believe are) distal terrorist organisations can provide the break from their former lives that they had been seeking, offering a new life of notoriety, starkly different from what they had previously known.[34] And organisations like al-Qaeda and the Islamic State work to provide a strong sense of belonging and purpose. They do so by helping converts to identify with those being hurt or oppressed, fueling a group-based sense of relative deprivation.[35] That is, even though the potential individual lone wolf terrorists are generally not personally deprived in any way, they start to identify with a community that they believe are deprived and, as a result, see themselves as exploited as well.[36] At the same time, many simultaneously withdraw from mainstream society, which prevents them for experiencing any counter-narratives to those they pick up from jihadist propaganda.[37] Constants across lone wolf terrorists are a malleability of self-identity, a religious fervour that legitimises violence against their enemies, and a disdain for their countrymen.[38]

Of course, to become a lone wolf jihadist most effectively requires 21st century technologies. While the Internet is not the sole driver here, it has allowed for smaller, informal, and largely independent networks that promote leaderless jihad to form via social media,

---

[34] J. McCoy, and A. Knight, 'Homegrown Terrorism in Canada: Local Patterns, Global Trends', *Studies in Conflict and Terrorism* **38**:4 (2015), 253–274.

[35] A. Speckhard, *Talking to Terrorists: Understanding the Psycho-Social Motivations of Militant Jihadi Terrorists, Mass Hostage Takers, Suicide Bombers, and 'Martyrs' to Combat Terrorism in Prison and Community Rehabilitation* (McLean, VA: Advances Press, 2012); N. R. Springer, 'Patterns of Radicalization: Identifying the Markers and Warning signs of Domestic Lone Wolf Terrorists in our Midsts', (Naval Postgraduate School: unpublished thesis, 2009).

[36] M. King, and D. M. Taylor, 'The Radicalization of Homegrown Jihadists: A Review of Theoretical Models and Social Psychological Evidence', *Terrorism and Political Violence* **23**:4 (2011), 602–622; see also Canadian Security and Intelligence Service (CSIS), 'Annual Public Report 2010–2011' (Ottawa: Government of Canada, 2013): https://www.csis-scrs.gc.ca/pblctns/nnlrprt/2010/2010-2011PublicReport_English.pdf.

[37] Spaaij, 'The Enigma of Lone Wolf Terrorism: An Assessment'.

[38] P. Bergen and B. Hoffman, 'Assessing the Terrorist Threat', Bipartisan Policy Center (2010): http://ctcitraining.org/docs/BPC_Assess TerroristThreat.pdf.

chat rooms, video archives, and so on. The cumulative effect of exposure to interactive forums and violent multimedia materials is that 'people acquire a skewed sense of reality so that extremist attitudes and violence are no longer taboos but – rather – are seen as positive and desirable'.[39] It is not surprising that lone wolf terrorists have become the greatest security threat to the West.[40]

What is most important for our purposes here, though, is that lone wolf terrorists see their violent actions as moral behaviour.[41] People usually do not engage in what others might take to be reprehensible conduct until they have justified to themselves the morality of their actions.[42] Because lone wolf terrorists look to their new communities to define what constitutes the good, they believe that they are pursuing laudable goals. All humans do this sort of social calibration; we all use our reference groups to mirror good and bad choices for us.[43] The differences, of course, are which reference groups we each use.

This naturally raises the question of how we should justify our moral systems, a question that philosophers writing about moral enhancement pointedly and explicitly do not answer. Persson and Savulescu hold that they do not need to define what a moral system is or morality *per se*, because their focus is on enhancing moral motivation, which is to 'do what you *think* is just and beneficial'.[44] Obviously, I do not think that they really want to give that advice

---

[39]   P. Neumann, 'Options and Strategies for Countering Online Radicalization in the United States,' *Studies in Conflict and Terrorism* **36**:6 (2013), 431–432.

[40]   M. Sageman, *Leaderless Jihad: Terror Networks in the Twenty-first Century* (Philadelphia, PA: University of Pennsylvania Press, 2008).

[41]   B. Beck, 'Conceptual and Practical Problems in Moral Enhancement', *Bioethics* **29**:4 (2015), 223–240.

[42]   A. Bandura, 'Mechanisms of Moral Disengagement', in W. Reich (ed.), *Origins of Terrorism: Psychologies, Ideologies, Theologies, States of Mind* (Cambridge: Cambridge University Press, 1990), 161–191; A. Bandura, 'The Role of Selective Moral Engagement in Terrorism and Counterterrorism', in F. Moghaddam and A. Marsella (eds), *Understanding Terrorism: Psychological Roots, Consequences and Interventions* (Washington, DC: American Psychological Association Press, 2004), 121–150.

[43]   A. Speckhard, 'The Boston Marathon Bombers: The Lethal Cocktail that Turned Troubled Youth to Terrorism', *Perspectives on Terrorism* **7**:3 (2013), 64–78.

[44]   I. Persson and J. Savulescu, 'Moral Hard-Wiring and Moral Enhancement', *Bioethics* **31**:4 (2017), 286–295, 295. To be fair, they also discuss increasing empathy and a sense of justice as ways to improve morality in other publications. However, lone wolf terrorists' activities are often fueled by a strong empathy with the sufferings of their new community

to terrorists. They, like other philosophers who discuss moral enhancement, assume that what counts as moral is fairly obvious, and the challenge is getting some to act on what we all agree is the right thing to do. People fail to be moral either because they reason incorrectly about the good or they lack the motivation to follow through on doing what is good. They do not fail to be moral because their value system differs fundamentally from those around them.

But changes in value systems are exactly what happen in the self-radicalisation process. To see this more clearly, let us take examine the case of one particular lone wolf in detail.

4. Christopher Cornell

In 2015, 20-year old Christopher Lee Cornell, a native-born US citizen, raised in a typical middle-class family in the suburbs of Cincinnati, Ohio, was arrested for planning a massacre that was to occur during President Obama's annual State of the Union address in Washington, D.C. He was arrested in a gun shop parking lot near his home, after he had just purchased two M-15 assault rifles and 600 rounds of ammunition. He admitted to using the Internet to research how to build pipe bombs and to pick targets in the D.C. area, as well as to pledge allegiance to ISIS and celebrate terror attacks online. 'I'm with the Islamic State', he said shortly after his arrest. 'I'm very dedicated to establish the Sharia in America, to wage war on the kafr [an Islamic term for "unbeliever"] and raise the word of Allah above all'.[45] He later pleaded guilty to attempted murder of government officials, attempting to provide material support to a foreign terrorist organisation, and possession of a firearm in furtherance of a crime of violence, and was ultimately sentenced to 30 years in prison.[46]

These are the broad facts of the case. And I will admit that on the surface this appears as a textbook case for what Persson and Savulescu

---

and a sense of needing to right what is perceived as a strong injustice, so I do not believe that these suggestions would help much either.

[45]   As quoted in T. Macke and J. Barr, 'Terror Suspect Christopher Cornell: "I'm So Dedicated That I Risked My Whole Life"', *Cincinnati Fox 19 News*, 19th March 2015.

[46]   D. Ernst, '"Allah Is in Control, Not This Judge!": Capital Terror Plotter Receives 30-Year Sentence', *The Washington Times*, 5th December 2016; see also K. Grasha, 'Court: No Appeal for Green Township Man Who Admitted Terror', *Cincinnati Enquirer*, 12th May 2017.

adumbrate: if we could only somehow change Cornell such that he no longer desired to massacre his fellow citizens, or least no longer thought it was a good idea, then we would all be safer and the world would be a better place. But surface facts do not tell the whole story, and the details matter.

Dovetailing with the discussion in the previous section, Cornell himself believed that he was doing the right thing by orchestrating the massacre: 'Yes, they might say I'm a terrorist, but we see the American troops as terrorists as well, coming to our lands, invading, stealing our resources and killing our people, raping our women. [...] Have you seen the photos and videos of the innocent children being killed, bodies upon bodies, stacked inside the back of a truck? You know, that's what's happening to our kids. America is funding and giving weapons to Israel. Israel is using these weapons to kill our children in Palestine every single day'.[47] He, like other lone wolf terrorists, found a new identity and cause through an international organisation. He talked of foreign soil as being 'our land', associating himself with the parents of Middle Eastern children. If you sincerely believed that your own children were being brutally slain by an outside enemy, then it becomes more difficult to maintain that all that needs to happen to prevent terrorism is to stiffen one's moral fortitude. If anything, the opposite should occur! Obviously, whose morality – and the "facts" that underlie that morality – we should adopt are fundamental questions that must be answered before we start any sort of moral enhancement project.

The history of the West, and much of the world in general, is a history of violent uprising; it is a history of slave rebellions, revolts against colonisation, and pro-civil rights revolutions. In hindsight, we generally see these violent acts as necessary goods. But at the time, there were many white slave owners who believed that rebellious slaves were upsetting the natural moral order of the world, Europeans who believed that native attempts to rid themselves of colonisers were in denial about what was good for them. Even today there remain many who see homosexuality as a moral stain. My point is that often the driver of cultural violence is a deep and fundamental clash in moral perspectives; each tribe is convinced that righteousness is on its side. Jihadist terrorists are no different; they believe that they are in the moral right. It misunderstands Cornell's and other terrorists' world-view to claim that enhancing their morality would remove their propensity for violence. It would not. What has to change is their world-view itself.

---

[47] Macke and Barr, 'Terror Suspect Christopher Cornell: "I'm So Dedicated That I Risked My Whole Life"'.

In addition, Cornell suffers from a variety of psychological disturbances. The forensic psychologist who examined him for the courts diagnosed him with schizotypal personality disorder and noted that he was emotionally and cognitively immature as well as had a 'a propensity to distort reality'. In his memorandum to the court the psychologist indicated that these factors, combined with an unstable home life and a desire to impress others, 'played key [roles] in' Cornell's decision-making and made him susceptible to believing what he was reading online.[48] Indicators of schizotypal personality disorder include having few close relationships, having difficulty understanding how personal behaviours might impact upon others, and often misinterpreting the intentions and actions of those around them. While it is the case that most terrorists tend not to suffer from psychological problems, the same cannot be said of lone wolves. Studies show that they suffer from anxiety, depression, social isolation, and diagnosed mental illnesses at much higher rates than the rest of the population, if not universally.[49]

These diagnoses dovetail with how Cornell's father saw Cornell as well: 'He's more like a 16-year-old kid than a 20-year-old'. He was 'kind of lost, and he was trying to find some kind of direction, and he was really vulnerable'.[50] His lawyer described him as a 'loner'.[51] Cornell, too, started to see some of these things about himself as he engaged with mental health professionals while incarcerated. As he wrote in a letter to his parents from prison: 'I never wanted any of this. This way of life is not fun nor is it cool, but it is stressful and humiliating. At the start of this [...] I thought it was fun and cool because of all the attention I was receiving, but that was until reality set in'.[52]

[48] Grasha, 'Man in Terror Plot Says "Allah's in Control, Not the Judge"'.

[49] M. Crenshaw, 'The Causes of Terrorism', *Comparative Politics* **13**:4 (1981), 379–399; M. S. Hamm, 'Lone Wolf Terrorism in America: Forging a New Way of Looking at an Old Problem' (2012); Hewitt, *Understanding Terrorism in America: From the Klan to Al Qaeda*; M. Sageman, *Understanding Terror Networks* (Philadelphia: University of Pennsylvania Press, 2004); Spaaij, *Understanding Lone Wolf Terrorism: Global Patterns, Motivations and Prevention*.

[50] A. Johnson, and S. Walters, 'Stunned Dad: Capitol Bomb Suspect Christopher Cornell was Coerced by F.B.I. "Snitch"', *NBC News*, 16th January 2015.

[51] Grasha, 'Man in Terror Plot Says "Allah's in Control, Not the Judge"'.

[52] Grasha, 'Man in Terror Plot Says "Allah's in Control, Not the Judge"'.

However, if the violent actions of lone wolf terrorists can be traced to psychological problems, then any work done to change their behaviour should be seen as treatment, not moral enhancement. Once we enter the clinical realm we are looking to reduce symptomatology, enhance everyday functioning in patients, and increase pro-social interactions. In this context questions of morality largely disappear.[53] Or, at the least, "moral enhancement" is the wrong name for something done as part of a medical practice;[54] clinical interventions are "treatments".

It is easy to see how someone with Cornell's psychological profile might get swept up in online propaganda, especially if the messaging were targeted to his or her particular background. It therefore should come as no surprise that videos and recorded lectures made by Western jihadist clerics can have a tremendous impact. For example, Anwar Al-Awlaki, a Yemeni imam and Islamic lecturer born and raised in New Mexico, influenced multiple US lone wolf terrorists, including Omar Mateen (2016 Pulse nightclub shooting in Orlando), Abdul Razak Ali Artan (2016 Ohio State attacker), Ahmed Khan Rahami (2016 New York-New Jersey bomber), Syed Rizwan Farook (2015 San Bernardino massacre), Dhokhar Tsarnaev (2013 Boston Marathon bomber), Minh Quan Pham (2012 thwarted suicide bomber), Faisal Shahzad (2010 Times Square bomber), Nidal Hasan (2009 Fort Hood shooting), Umar Farouk Abdulmutallab (2009 "underwear bomber"), as well as Cornell, among others. (According to the Counter Extremism Project, Al-Awlaki has been tied to 55 homegrown violent extremists in the United States, and at least 34 more in Western Europe).[55]

Al-Awlaki can speak to Americans and Western Europeans using their common cultural background as a bridge to radical terrorist ideals. And in a "digital legacy" that has lived on in the ether years after his death in a US targeted drone strike, he continues to persuade others to join the rebellion. He might even be more persuasive since

---

[53] V. G. Hardcastle, 'The Morality of Moral Enhancement? A Case Study of Traumatic Brain Injury and American Vets' (forthcoming); D. Horstkötter, R. Berghmans, and G. de Wert, 'Moral Enhancement for Antisocial Behavior? An Uneasy Relationship', *AJOB Neuroscience* **3**:4 (2012), 26–28.

[54] H. Wiseman, 'SSRIs and Moral Enhancement: Looking Deeper', *AJOB Neuroscience* **5**:4 (2014) W1-W7.

[55] Counter Extremism Project, *Anwar Al-Awlaki. Part I: Prosecuted Homegrown Radicals with Ties to Anwar Al-Awlaki, and Part II: European Extremists with Ties to Anwar Al-Awlaki* (2016): https://www.counterextremism.com/sites/default/themes/bricktheme/pdfs/Anwar_al-Awlaki_Ties.pdf.

the US hunted him down and killed him, for he has been made into a martyr for the cause.[56]

This brings me to my third point: the development of violent extremism is as much social as it is individual. The CPOST study gathered data on the propaganda consumption patterns of the vast majority of the 112 individuals they tracked, and of those, nearly 85 percent viewed propaganda videos. Clearly such materials play a central role in the radicalization of lone wolf terrorists.[57] As de Melo-Martín and Salles remark:

> The assumption that humanity's moral ills are the result of mainly *individual* moral deficits is highly suspect. The framing of morally complex situations like war, famine, terrorism, lack of access to medicines, or poverty, as the result of certain types of individual moral failings ignores the role played by structural – social, cultural, political, economic – forces in enabling and often promoting these evils.[58]

It is a mistake to focus solely on individual deficits, for it is only with those deficits in combination with a variety of external pressures that one will be moved to commit violence.[59] Whatever individual moral enhancing (or clinical treatment) goes on must be in combination with changes to the social and cultural environment of the individual as well. If we could reduce lone wolves' access to incendiary videos, or if we could counter those videos with alternative but still persuasive narratives, then there may be less violence as a result.

At the same time, it is hard to see these social or cultural "nudges" as moral enhancements.[60] In addition to Simkulet's argument against

[56] S. Shane, 'Dead Reckoning: The Lessons of Anwar al-Awlaki', *The New York Times Magazine*, 27th August 2015, MM56.

[57] Pape, Decety, Ruby, Rivas, Jessen, and Wegner, 'The American Face of ISIS: Analysis of ISIS-related Terrorism in the United States, March 2014-August 2016'.

[58] I. de Melo-Martín and A. Salles, 'Moral Bioenhancement: Much Ado About Nothing?', *Bioethics* 29:4 (2015), 223–232, 228.

[59] H. J. Ehni and D. Aurenque, 'On Moral Enhancement from a Habermasian Perspective', *Cambridge Quarterly of Healthcare Ethics* 21:2 (2012), 223–234; J. Harris, 'Moral Progress and Moral Enhancement', *Bioethics* 27:5 (2013), 285–290; R. Sparrow, 'Better Living Through Chemistry? A Reply to Savulescu and Persson on "Moral Enhancement"', *Journal of Applied Philosophy* 31:1 (2014) 23–32; I. M. Young, *Responsibility for Justice* (New York: Oxford University Press, 2011).

[60] J. Wilkes, 'Mind, Nature and the Emerging Science of Change: An Introduction to Metamorphology', in G. Cornelis, S. Smets, and J. Van

Valerie Gray Hardcastle

environmental structures having the potential to be moral improvements, most of these structural changes do little to alter one's fundamental psychology, which is what moral enhancements are supposed to do.[61] Thaler and Sunstein, two prominent proponents of the science of nudging behaviour, define a nudge as 'any aspect of the choice architecture that alters people's behavior in a predictable way [...] without forbidding any options or significantly changing their economic incentives. To count as a nudge, the intervention must be easy and cheap to avoid [...]. Putting fruit at eye level counts as a nudge'.[62] What they describe has nothing to do with rationally coming to some decision about which action to undertake, as philosophers believe moral actions occur through, though it does have everything to do with why we behave the way we do.

And this fact has dangerous implications, for just as we can manipulate an environment to reduce the chances of a violent response, so too can we manipulate an environment to increase the chances of a violent response. While Christopher Cornell believed he was talking to actual jihadist terrorists online, it turns out that he was primarily interacting with undercover F.B.I. agents. It remains unclear what would have happened in this case if the F.B.I. had taken a different path in its dealings with Cornell, if they had encouraged perhaps more engagement with his actual community instead of offering to help with (and actually financing) his terrorist plot.

Martin Pinales, Cornell's attorney, claims that Cornell was a 'keyboard terrorist', that he would not have done anything violent had he not been persuaded to do so by the undercover F.B.I. informant.[63] Cornell's father agrees, saying, '[t]here's no way he could have come up with something like this' on his own.[64] In her sentencing memorandum, attorney Candace Crouse wrote that he 'lived a fantasy life behind

---

Bendegem (eds), *Einstein Meets Magritte: An Interdisciplinary Reflection on Science, Nature, Art, Human Action and Society*, Volume 6 (Netherlands: Springer, 1999), 71–87.

[61] Simkulet, 'Intention and Moral Enhancement'; S. Van der Linden, 'Reply to Dolan', in A. Oliver (ed.), *Behavioral Public Policy* (Cambridge: Cambridge University Press, 2013), 209–215.

[62] T. Thaler and C. Sunstein, *Nudge: Improving Decisions about Health, Wealth, and Happiness* (New York: Penguin Books, 2008), 6.

[63] E. Heisig, 'Cincinnati-Area Man Pleads Guilty to Plotting Terrorist Attack on U.S. Capitol', *Cleveland.com*, 1st August 2016.

[64] Grasha, 'Man in Terror Plot Says "Allah's in Control, Not the Judge"'.

a computer screen'. She goes on to note that Cornell had never even handled a gun before he bought the rifles that led to his arrest, and he believed that he and the undercover F.B.I. agent would go into hiding after the attack. He wanted to create an Islamic State territory in the US for just the two of them. In short, 'his ideas were not rationally possible nor remotely realistic. Chris created a character, with a different name [he called himself 'Rahell Mahrus Ubaydah'], in a fantasy where this character was somebody in the world'.

It is very important to distinguish between radical thought and radical action.[65] For example, in the United Kingdom, according to a 2005 ICM telephone poll, 5 percent of adult Muslims, or roughly 50,000 of the approximately one million adult Muslims living in the UK, believe that suicide attacks are justified. However, significantly less than a thousand terrorism-related arrests have been made since 9/11, which means that only about 0.1 percent of the Muslim population in the UK have been moved to violent action.[66] We find similar statistics in the United States. According to the 2007 and 2011 polls conducted by the Pew Research Center, about 8 percent of US Muslims reported that suicide attacks are justified 'often' or 'sometimes'. And yet, relatively few terrorism-related arrests have been made in the US since 9/11.[67]

Just as the environment can induce one to violent thoughts, it can also induce one to violent behaviour. Importantly, Cornell's father points out that there is 'no way he had the money to carry out any kind of terrorist attack'. So where did the funds to buy guns and ammunition come from? The undercover F.B.I. agent provided them, as well as friendship and conversations about jihadism. Cornell thought he was making connections with a welcoming community in the Middle East, when in reality he was talking to someone in a federal office. Indeed, as attorney Crouse explained in her memo: Cornell

[65] M. Zekulin, 'Islamic-Inspired Homegrown Terrorism: What We Know and What It Means Moving Forward', Occasional Research Paper No.8 (Calgary: Calgary Center for Military and Strategic Studies, 2013).
[66] As discussed in M. McCauley and S. Moskalenko, 'Toward a Profile of Lone Wolf Terrorists: What Moves an Individual from Radical Opinion to Radical Action', *Terrorism and Political Violence* 26:1 (2014), 69–85.
[67] Pew Research Center, 'Muslim Americans: Middle Class and Mostly Mainstream' (2007): http://www.pewresearch.org/2007/05/22/muslim-americans-middle-class-and-mostly-mainstream/; Pew Research Center, 'Muslim Americans: No Signs of Growth in Alienation or Support for Extremism' (2011): http://www.people-press.org/2011/08/30/muslim-americans-no-signs-of-growth-in-alienation-or-support-for-extremism/.

289

thought what was really the F.B.I. informant was 'his only friend besides his brother and his cat'.[68]

At what point do we move from protecting society from violent extremists to inciting people with violent thoughts to try to do violent things and then arresting them for trying to do them? The 2012 Heritage Report describes the details of 50 foiled terror plots in the United States since 9/11. Of those I count 13 that had F.B.I.-enhanced plots. As Aaronson reports, there have been 150 F.B.I. terrorism stings since 9/11 that have resulted in prosecutions. Over 250 of the 500 federal terrorism cases involved informants. At least 49 of those involved F.B.I. undercover agents taking a lead in the planning.[69] In other words, these plots would not have existed but for the F.B.I. In some cases, the perpetrator clearly had no independent means to commit any act of terrorism, and in others, the alleged plots were completely bizarre or unrealistic. Aside from Cornell's plan to set up a two-person caliphate, there was, for example, a Massachusetts man who believed he was getting ready to destroy the United States Capitol building using a remote-controlled airplane filled with grenades.

I do not have a clear answer to when it is better to nudge in one way rather than the other. I do know that the average timeframe from the initial exploration of extremist ideas to "bang" is just over five years, which gives others plenty of time to interfere with the process in a variety of ways.[70] My central point here is that the circumstances surrounding any moral actor have a lot to do with how that actor ultimately behaves. And often those circumstances are beyond the control of those ensnared in them. Without managing the environment, any sort of moral enhancements engaged in internally bucking one up is probably doomed to fail. It is too little and too small an intervention.

5. Conclusion: The Impotence of Moral Enhancement

I understand completely the desire to manipulate our neighbours such that they would do no harm to us or to our environment.

---

[68] Grasha, 'Man in Terror Plot Says "Allah's in Control, Not the Judge"'.

[69] T. Aaronson, *The Terror Factory: Inside the F.B.I.'s Manufactured War on Terrorism* (Brooklyn, NY: Ig Publishing, 2013).

[70] J. Klausen, S. Campion, N. Needle, G. Nguyen, and R. Libretti, 'Toward a Behavioral Model of "Homegrown" Radicalization Trajectories', *Studies in Conflict and Terrorism* **39**:1 (2015), 67–83.

I even understand why such desires are couched in moral terms. However, once we scratch the surface of what really makes people behave the ways they do, it becomes clear that what philosophers want to do would simply not get this job done. As Schaefer notes: '[a]rguably the entire enterprise of moral philosophy is predicated on such an idea that thinking these matters through can lead to the right moral answers – or at least point us in the right direction'.[71] 'Thinking matters through' is but one aspect of what determines our actions, and it is probably a tiny aspect at that. Our beliefs about what counts as the good, our personal psychological profile, and our surrounding circumstances are all determinates of our actions. We would need to change all of these simultaneously to bring about lasting changes in moral behaviour. And without changing any of them, I am afraid that any moral enhancements geared toward helping us to think more rationally or to increase our motivations will be largely impotent.

Northern Kentucky University
hardcastle@nku.edu

---

[71] G. O. Schaefer, 'Direct vs. Indirect Moral Enhancement', *Kennedy Institute of Ethics Journal* **25**:3 (2015), 261–289.

Moral Enhancement, Instrumentalism, and Integrative Ethical Education

GIUSEPPE TURCHI

Abstract
In this chapter I will discuss some of the arguments presented in *Unfit for the Future*, where the authors stress the necessity of moral enhancement to prevent a global catastrophe. Persson and Savulescu promote a reductionistic view of moral intuitions suggesting that oxytocin, serotonin, and genetic treatments could save humanity from the perils of contemporary liberalism, weapons of mass destruction, and uncontrolled pollution. I will contend that although we need a moral enhancement it cannot be a brute manipulation of our biology but something where human plasticity is seen as paramount. Following the lesson of Dewey's instrumentalism, I advocate a non-reductionistic, pluralistic view where neuroscientific data may be used to develop a more effective moral pedagogy. In my opinion, this prospect is currently much more feasible (and less risky) than a hypothetical mass psycho-civilisation created using drugs and electrodes.

1. Introduction

In 1963, when neuroscientist José Delgado stopped a bull from charging at him by pressing a button on a remote control, the idea of exploiting our knowledge about the brain to manipulate human behaviour suddenly seemed possible. Six years later, Delgado gave an overview of the risks and opportunities concerning brain stimulation in relation to a future "psycho-civilised" society.[1] Shortly afterwards Mark and Ervin argued that the permanent elimination of violence was possible by surgically manipulating the limbic system.[2] Those instruments that were originally meant to treat neurological and mental diseases now seemed to provide an opportunity to address social ills.

Forty years later the psycho-civilisation dream seems far from becoming a reality. Nevertheless, there have been several studies

---

[1] José Delgado, *Physical Control of the Mind: Toward a Psychocivilized Society* (New York: Harper and Row, 1969).
[2] V. H. Mark and F. R. Ervin, *Violence and the Brain* (New York: Harper & Row, 1970).

doi:10.1017/S1358246118000401 ©The Royal Institute of Philosophy and the contributors 2018
Royal Institute of Philosophy Supplement **83** 2018

aimed at testing the relationship between neurophysiology, moral intuitions,[3] and pro-social behaviour, by investigating the involvement
of the limbic system in behavioural responses; for example, by observing the impact of oxytocin on affiliative attitudes.[4] Some feel
that hard science is slowly taking over the study of human behaviour,
and this has exacerbated the conflicts between the humanities and
sciences, reductionism and pluralism.

Although the idea of mass brain-grafting is mostly relegated to
dystopian literature, Persson and Savulescu have raised again the
question of moral enhancement and recently published its mani-
festo: *Unfit for the Future*.[5] The authors argue for the legitimacy
of pharmacological and genetic manipulations to enhance the
moral behaviour of citizens of mass democracies, which is, they
claim, a necessary step towards eco-sustainable liberalism.

The aim of this chapter is to highlight practical and conceptual
issues of those enhancement proposals, shifting from unlikely
moral-pharmacogenetic engineering to an interdisciplinary study
with human plasticity at its core. As such, I will first focus on
Persson and Savulescu's proposal before examining in depth the problems of reductionism, taking into consideration John Dewey's
thoughts on human nature and science. It is my conviction that
Dewey's instrumentalism can be used not only to account for the ir-
reducibility of ethics to the hard sciences, but also to prefigure a kind
of moral enhancement centred on education and childcare. I will conclude this chapter by claiming that Darcia Narvaez's research offers a
good example of how neuroscience should be integrated into a holistic
approach focussed on personal experience and the social context of
the individual.

2. Moral Enhancement According to Persson and Savulescu

Contrary to the psycho-civilisation theorists of the 1970s, what
bothers Persson and Savulescu most is not violence and aggression
but the dangerous synergy between common sense morality, technological advancement, and liberal democracy. For example, modern

---

[3] See for example M. D. Hauser, *Moral Minds: How Nature Designed
Our Universal sense of Right and Wrong* (New York: HarperCollins, 2006).
[4] See for example Paul Zak, *The Moral Molecule: The New Science of
What Makes Us Good or Evil* (London: Bantam Press, 2012).
[5] Ingmar Persson and Julian Savulescu, *Unfit for the Future: The Need
for Moral Enhancement* (Oxford: Oxford University Press, 2012).

weapons of mass destruction give a small number of individuals the power to cause catastrophic damage, and it is not too hard to imagine the threat that weapons would pose if they were to fall into the hands of fundamentalist groups. As if that were not enough, the principles governing Western democracies are proving to be a source of severe problems too: excessive emphasis on values such as individual freedom has allowed citizens and entrepreneurs to build a consumer society that has taken environmental pollution levels well beyond the critical threshold, while the obsession with the right to privacy obstructs the tapping of terrorists.

Persson and Savulescu contend that the abovementioned problems stem primarily from a flaw in our common sense morality, which is mostly genetically determined and makes it difficult for moral pedagogy to be effective. In particular, there are two things wrong with our biological heritage: the tendency to limit our trust and altruism to a small group of people and the so-called 'bias toward the near future'.[6] These characteristics evolved to fulfil the needs of our ancestors, who lived in small groups and could not afford the luxury of making long-term plans. Xenophobia, for example, evolved as a defence mechanism because 'when synchronic cooperation involves innumerable agents, or is of long duration, it is usually harder to detect if someone defects or free-rides'.[7] In other words, limiting altruism and trust to a small group of people was a way to increase the chance of survival. The "bias toward the near future" has a similar justification: the life expectancy of our ancestors was low and that forced them to think of their present needs rather than pondering on any long-term damage they might have caused with their actions or omissions. This is clearly not compatible with our modern globalised society, where citizens of mass democracies keep consuming energy and accumulating waste as if the situation was not that serious, when in fact the consequences of climate change are very real and cannot be undone. We should instead extend our range

---

[6]   Persson and Savulescu also emphasise a third problem: the conception of responsibility as causally-based, according to which we tend to consider ourselves more responsible for harm we physically cause than for harm we let happen by omission. Moreover, causally-based responsibility is 'proportionally diluted when we cause things together with other agents', and this has led to climate change because individuals tend not to worry about how much they pollute as they believe their damage is negligible on global scale. See Persson and Savulescu, *Unfit for the Future*, 22–26.

[7]   Persson and Savulescu, *Unfit for the Future*, 37.

Giuseppe Turchi

of trust and work together to redistribute wealth equally and avoid environmental disaster.

The conclusion is that modern humans, even the most virtuous, must reckon with a serious evolutionary disadvantage: the mechanisms underlying moral intuition and social behaviour are still those that evolution developed for life in ancient hunter-gatherer societies. However, Persson and Savulescu point out that if the problem is bio-evolutionary, then we could intervene to avoid ultimate harm. They cite de Waal's studies on capuchin monkeys and Wallace's on homozygote twins in support of the thesis that a sense of justice is genetically determined, and refer to Kosfeld, Zak, Tse, Bond, and Crockett to show how intervention on oxytocin and serotonin circuits could incentivise pro-social conduct, i.e., greater altruism, generosity, trust, and the sense of fairness.[8] These studies demonstrate that biomedical tools can already intervene in our moral behaviour effectively and, in the future, may be employed to overcome the lack of effectiveness of moral pedagogy.

Persson and Savulescu then explain what moral enhancement should consist of, and in their controversial chapter 'Moral Enhancement as a Possible Way Out' they answer those critics who see in their proposal just another manifestation of scientistic reductionism. The crucial point of this chapter is the attempt to configure bio-enhancement as something that can change moral motivations without transforming the individual into a "mindless robot". Persson and Savulescu write:

> Education or instruction about what is morally good is not sufficient for moral enhancement because to be morally good involves not just knowing what is good, but also being so strongly motivated to do it that this overpowers selfish, nepotistic, xenophobic, etc., biases and impulses.[9]

According to the authors, proper moral enhancement should aim to overcome those biological obstacles that obstruct the 'motivational internalization of moral doctrines'[10] and, therefore, the realisation of good conduct. Therefore, it is not a matter of incorrectly identifying what is right and what is wrong, but of not acting in accordance with what we have identified as the right thing to do because of factors such as our "bias to the near future", selfish disposition,

---

[8] See Persson and Savulescu, *Unfit for the Future*, 110–111, 118–120.
[9] Persson and Savulescu, *Unfit for the Future*, 117.
[10] Persson and Savulescu, *Unfit for the Future*, 107.

and xenophobic tendencies. Persson and Savulescu clarify their position with the following:

> We imagine that the moral motivation of those of us who are less morally motivated be increased so that it becomes as strong as the moral motivation of those of us who are by nature most morally motivated, not that this moral motivation be increased to the point at which it becomes irresistible, like a kleptomaniac's desire to steal.[11]

The authors do not talk about forcing the individual to behave in a certain way, but rather about eliminating those obstacles that prevent an individual from acting on what it is considered the right thing to do: those obstacles are the same as those that cause environmental pollution, the growing impoverishment of the Global South, and the excessive *laissez-faire* economics of Western democracies. Persson and Savulescu are convinced that through bio-enhancement of the empathetic response, the sense of fairness, and the sympathetic concern for the well-being of others, it could be possible to create a less selfish citizen, more forward-thinking, more open to give up certain liberties in order to save the planet and its inhabitants.[12] Towards the end of the book, however, the authors admit:

> [M]oral bioenhancement worthy of the name is practically impossible at present and might remain so for so long that we will not master it, nor succeed in applying it on a sufficient scale, in time to help us to deal with the catastrophic problems that we outlined. But our point is just that the predicament of humankind is so serious that all possible ways out of it should be explored. Therefore, it is important that moral bioenhancement is not written off without good reason.[13]

My central objection is that a catastrophic prediction, while realistic, is not a sufficient condition to justify the desirability of moral enhancement. In fact, there are good reasons for us to doubt the desirability of moral enhancement if a) the complexity of moral phenomena and b) the plasticity of individuals are not taken into consideration.

Let us consider this point: Persson and Savulescu suggest that there are not only dysfunctional traits in human nature, but also good ones (altruism, a sense of justice, empathy, etc.), and that

11   Persson and Savulescu, *Unfit for the Future*, 113.
12   Persson and Savulescu, *Unfit for the Future*, 90.
13   Persson and Savulescu, *Unfit for the Future*, 123.

enhancing the latter would neither compromise our ability to judge nor compromise our freedom:

> [A] judicious use of effective techniques of moral bioenhance-ment to increase a sense of justice and altruism will not reduce our freedom and responsibility; it will simply make it the case that we are more often, perhaps always, causally determined to do what we take to be good. It will do so by amplifying those bio-logical factors that by nature are strong in those of us who are morally better.[14]

However, to characterise virtues and vices as mere biological factors that can be fruitfully manipulated with biomedical tools is to address the problem from a limited perspective. In fact, moral action and its motivations can neither be reduced to the artificial con-ditions of experiments nor explained by greater or lesser concentra-tion of hormones in the blood: the virtues of altruism, generosity, honesty, and self-sacrifice are acquired through practice in a social context and are products of psycho-physical integration. They are a sort of embodied know-how that requires continuous exercise to gain and maintain in a fine attunement of cognition, emotion, and bodily powers.[15] The only integration Persson and Savulescu propose instead is between indoctrination, genes, and neurons, as if intervening on brain chemistry would be enough to internalise values and virtues, an internalisation that, I suggest, would impair the ability to obtain a complete picture of a given situation by limiting our behaviour to certain patterns.

My main concern is that from the moment the subject is psycho-logically and biologically limited to a certain behaviour, that behav-iour becomes routine and less prone to adapt. Even if drugs and genetics could intervene on behaviour in a positive way,[16] they

[14]   Persson and Savulescu, *Unfit for the Future*, 112.
[15]   See Wiseman, *The Myth of The Moral Brain: The Limits of Moral Enhancement* (Cambridge and London: The MIT Press, 2016), 171–173.
[16]   Opinions here are divided. Some studies on oxytocin, for example, show that the strengthening of bonding responses is sensitive to the peer group, so much so that it can even reduce pro-social attitudes towards outside groups if this would bring an advantage to their own circle. See C. de Dreu, et al., 'The Neuropeptide Oxytocin Regulates Parochial Altruism in Intergroup Conflicts Among Humans', *Science* **328**:5984 (2010), 1408–1411. This is not the only case: Wiseman has gathered some conflicting evidence to show that, for example, oxytocin tends not to be par-ticularly efficacious with respect to those persons who lack a pre-existing good disposition. Similarly, serotonin has produced some undesirable

should be used such that enhanced human beings do not become moral automata. Moreover, indiscriminate enhancement of certain abilities may have unwanted side effects. Shook, for example, writes:

> [H]eightened empathy and caring should result in greater generosity, but is there common agreement that generosity should be generically elevated across the entire population? We may say that we wish people were more generous, but what we really mean is that ungenerous people should be more generous, or that other people should be more generous to *us*, or perhaps that people should be more generous to others who *deserve* it. Heightened levels of trustworthiness or truthfulness wouldn't be morally wise either, unless matched by a sound ability to discriminate who really deserves one's trust or confidence. The overall problem here is that the maintenance of human morality requires preparedness to judge, condemn, and appropriately punish; dispositions to caring more, by themselves, can ignore or erode those moral obligations.[17]

This quote offers an example of how our moral dispositions should be integrated in a context that is not restricted to excessively liberal democracies. There are cases when it is better not to collaborate or be generous or else to keep a certain emotional distance. The tools of genetics and neuroscience we have at our disposal today cannot handle the difference between cases, nor can they help the individual in better identifying those differences; rather, neural manipulation of emotions and the input of motivational ties risk compromising one's rational capabilities.[18]

Problems such as these are the reason why authors like Wiseman and, similarly, Specker,[19] believe that speculating on unrealistic scenarios such as pharmaco-genetic engineering of morals is unproductive. According to them, research on moral enhancement should

---

effects like increased premeditated aggression and the emergence of violent suicidal ideation during treatment of various psychiatric disorders. See Wiseman, *The Myth of The Moral Brain: The Limits of Moral Enhancement*, 93–106.

[17] John Shook, 'Neuroethics and the Possible Types of Moral Enhancement', *AJOB Neuroscience* **3**:4 (2012), 11.

[18] A similar criticism can be found in John Harris, *How to Be Good* (Oxford: Oxford University Press, 2016).

[19] See Jona Specker, et al., 'The Ethical Desirability of Moral Bioenhancement: a Review of Reasons', *BMC Medical Ethics* **15**:67 (2014): http://doi.org/10.1186/1472-6939-15-67.

focus on and limit itself to treating mental disorders because 1) we already have means that have been proven effective, and 2) through treatment of disorders such as addiction or illnesses caused by injuries we have an improvement of moral behaviour. Proposals like that of Persson and Savulescu are proven to be sterile science fiction instead, because they are neither practically feasible nor desirable.

3. The Instrumentality of the Hard Sciences in Dewey's Pragmatism

Persson and Savulescu claim human nature to be flawed because of an evolutionary lag: the brain and the genes inherited from our ancestors cause intuitions and moral dispositions that are incompatible with the destructive potential of modern technology. Traditional methods of moral education are not enough for the efficacy of political and social reforms; a biomedical intervention is needed to change those intuitions and dispositions so that we are 'more often, perhaps always, causally determined to do what we take to be good'. Gene alteration and hormone manipulation must provide a certain type of good behaviour.

As I tried to show in the previous section, such an approach poses a series of problems that are typical when we try to manipulate behaviour with hard science. The source of these problems is not recognising that the nature of moral agents is formed on several levels that cannot be broached through biology alone. On the other hand, it is also true that modern society needs better people and we realise this not only from those phenomena listed by Persson and Savulescu, but also from increasing instances of cyber bullying and other examples of intolerance.

Moral pedagogy seems to be outdated, or at least not sufficiently effective to face the struggles of our society; but it is one thing to say that moral pedagogy is ineffective, and quite another to claim that it is ineffective because of our biological nature. Perhaps moral pedagogy should be restructured, and perhaps the neurosciences could be useful in developing a new type of intervention, though not in a reductionist sense. Maybe, if we want to develop an alternative approach that could avoid the collateral effects of moral enhancement, what we need is a different concept of human nature and of the role of science, a concept that is naturalistic but pluralistic at the same time. I believe that Dewey's pragmatism offers such a concept.

Dewey's analysis of human nature starts from categories that refer to the theory of evolution: mutation, transition, instability, contingency, and adjustment. These categories derive from the experience of constant renewal that any living being undergoes to overcome external obstacles; biological functions developed through time, high faculties, and conceptual systems are merely instruments to enhance the adaptability potential. In particular, thought is a function that allows us to 'use things as means to affect other things'[20] and 'occurs only in situations qualified by uncertainty, alternatives, questioning, search, hypotheses, tentative trials or experiments'.[21] The whole process is interactive rather than contemplative, wherein human beings make decisions and explore the unknown; they constantly try to gain a better understanding of the environment around them to adapt themselves to it or *vice versa*. For this reason, the objects of perceptions, emotions, aesthetic experience, scientific research, and social relations are all to be considered as real and natural: they are something we deal with daily and that we need to face problems. Määttänen defines those objects as 'interactionables' by distinguishing them from the 'uninteractionables', objects that for the moment do not fall into operational practice and that are not to be considered as objects of knowledge or of nature.[22]

When outlining his naturalistic ontology Dewey recognises the multiplicity of sources of problems for human life, and because of this he strongly opposes the scientific reductionism that denies the importance of qualitative experience and considers mathematical entities to be the only existing ones. Objects of scientific research are, indeed, 'reached by a method which controls them and which adds greater control to life itself, a method which mitigates accident, turns contingency to account, and releases thought and other forms of endeavour', but this does not mean that these objects are ontologically paramount.[23] The idea that 'science is the grasp of reality in its final self-sufficing form' needs to be abandoned,[24] because the 'objects of science, like the direct objects of the arts, are an order of relations which serve as tools to effect immediate havings and beings'.[25] To treat objects as tools means that 'their value and validity

---

[20] John Dewey, *Experience and Nature* (London: Allen & Unwin, 1925), 158.
[21] Dewey, *Experience and Nature*, 68.
[22] See Pentti Määttänen, *Mind in Action: Experience and Embodied Cognition in Pragmatism* (Cham, Heidelberg, New York, Dordrecht, and London: Springer, 2015), 80.
[23] Dewey, *Experience and Nature*, 70.
[24] Dewey, *Experience and Nature*, 135.
[25] Dewey, *Experience and Nature*, 136.

reside in what proceeds from them; consequences not antecedents supply meaning and verity. Truths already possessed may have practical or moral certainty, but logically they never lose a hypothetic quality'.[26]

In saying this Dewey accomplishes two things: firstly, he outlines a fallibilistic conception of science, because the instrumental character of theories and the transactional contest of life make it impossible for a theory to be in principle immune to revision. Secondly, the principle according to which the value and truth of tools 'reside in what proceeds from them' works against reductionism as a justification of the validity of the humanities. Most of the problems I addressed when talking about Persson and Savulescu's theories originate from consequences we would have in using modern genetics and neuroscience to control moral behaviour, namely the creation of moral automata. Using the hard sciences to manipulate moral conduct is like using a pneumatic drill to sculpt Michelangelo's *Pieta*. Dewey claims that experience does not prescribe reductionism as a method, contrary to what physicalists would want. On the contrary, experience shows that different tools develop to solve different problems. Physics, medicine, economics, politics, ethics, and sociology all have their fields of application and cannot substitute each other, but this does not mean they cannot communicate with each other.[27] Phenomena and objects of human life are not strictly divided into metaphysical categories,[28] but exist within a continuum that can be approached by different perspectives. Disciplines such as modern neuropsychology, for example, try to find correlations between neurological stimulation, cortical injuries, fMRI scans, and behaviour; i.e., they develop new tools that do not reduce the complexity of the phenomenon but add a point of view to be used to obtain a better comprehension.

To sum up, Dewey's instrumentalism offers an answer to the debate that divides scientists and anti-naturalists by considering hard scientific ontology as only part of nature on one hand, and

[26]   Dewey, *Experience and Nature*, 154.
[27]   Similar arguments can be found in Mario De Caro and David Macarthur (eds), *Naturalism in Question* (Cambridge: Harvard University Press, 2004), 21–58.
[28]   'If the general traits of nature existed in water-tight compartments, it might be enough to sort out the objects and interests of experience among them. But they are actually so intimately intermixed that all important issues are concerned with their degrees and the ratios they sustain to one another'. Dewey, *Experience and Nature*, 413.

refusing the supernatural characterisation of rationality, mind, and agency on the other, putting the latter in a biological substrate. These considerations have strong implications for ethics, as they are directed to the natural condition of the human being – a form of life subjected to transition and contingency – and allow us to enrich our concept of moral pedagogy.

4. Ethics, Habit, and Human Nature

Consistent with the assumptions of Dewey's naturalism, the guiding principle of any moral enhancement project should be the transactional relationship between organism and environment. Moral behaviour cannot be reduced to a simple product of neurons and genes, but requires a holistic conception of the person and his or her functioning in a given context. Dewey offers such a conception in *Human Nature and Conduct*, introducing the fundamental notion of "habit":

> [H]abits are ways of using and incorporating the environment in which the latter has its say as surely as the former. [...] They involve skill of sensory and motor organs, cunning or craft, and objective materials. They assimilate objective energies, and eventuate in command of environment. They require order, discipline, and manifest technique. They have a beginning, middle and end. Each stage marks progress in dealing with materials and tools, advance in converting material to active use.[29]

Dewey configures habit as an active model of response to the environment which implies the co-ordinated use of external materials, physical organs, and the mental faculties of the individual. In short, it is a solution that the psychophysical unit has repeatedly adopted to confront necessity and that has been transformed into a stable aspect of character. Such habits 'persist until the environment obstinately rejects them [and] they perpetuate themselves, by acting unremittingly upon the native stock of activities; [they] stimulate, inhibit, intensify, weaken, select, concentrate and organize the latter into their own likeness'.[30] In other words, habits influence our perceptions, our thoughts, and our actions so much as to become unreflective when the environment does not resist them. On the other hand, when a habit

---

[29]   John Dewey, *Human Nature and Conduct: An Introduction to Social Psychology* (New York: Henry Holt & Co., 1922), 15.
[30]   Dewey, *Human Nature and Conduct*, 125.

seems insufficient to solve a problem, the blind force of impulse emerges to signal the need to readapt. At that moment, either the impulse manages to unload, thanks to an immediate solution, or thought emerges and deliberation is necessary.

Dewey describes deliberation as a moment of stasis in which the subject has to assume and assess the consequences of various possible actions. At this juncture, engrained habits and conflicting desires are reconfigured according to external conditions by anticipating possible results until one element prevails over the others. Here it is important to stress the importance of the practice of intelligent thinking and imagination, because 'only thought notes obstructions, invents tools, conceives aims, directs technique, and thus converts impulse into an art which lives in objects'.[31] More specifically, Dewey believes intelligence to be the function that 'converts desire into plans, systematic plans based on assembling facts, reporting events as they happen, keeping tab on them and analyzing them'.[32]

However, this process is not automatic: certain habits, desires, and impulses can be so strong that they make an individual blind to any alternative, leading to routine conduct. As a result, the ability of the mind to explore possible alternatives, to question old ideas, to transform the driving force of impulses into a constructive force, is also a habit that needs to be acquired and strengthened. It is no coincidence that Dewey's educational programme targets the cultivation of a plastic individual, that of a person who is not stuck in old habits but ready to question himself or herself, and to broaden his or her view of the world by communicating with others.[33]

We must now consider how ethics is connected with the nature of habits and our problem-solving ability. First, Dewey underlines that moral principles and moral dispositions are acquired, and not innate. Our biology gives us instincts but it is in the interaction with the social environment that those instincts are reconstructed into moral

[31] Dewey, *Human Nature and Conduct*, 171.
[32] Dewey, *Human Nature and Conduct*, 255.
[33] 'Power to grow depends upon need for others and plasticity. Both of these conditions are at their height in childhood and youth. Plasticity or the power to learn from experience means the formation of habits. Habits give control over the environment, power to utilize it for human purposes. [...] Active habits involve thought, invention, and initiative in applying capacities to new aims. They are opposed to routine which marks an arrest of growth. Since growth is the characteristic of life, education is all one with growing; it has no end beyond itself'. John Dewey, *Democracy and Education: An Introduction to Philosophy of Education* (New York: The Macmillan Company, 1916), 62.

dispositions. When we notice a pattern of those dispositions in different cultures, it is not determined by something innate, but by individuals facing the same situation and reacting in like fashion. The persistency of customs (social habits) is explained as individuals 'forming their personal habits under conditions set by prior customs. An individual usually acquires the morality as he inherits the speech of his social group'.[34] But acquired morality is not a fixed achievement. Morality in the largest sense is a continuing process since contexts and problems always change and we will sooner or later need to find new solutions to them. In Dewey's words, 'morality is education', an 'expansion in meaning which is consequent upon observations of the conditions and outcome of conduct'.[35]

It is not a coincidence that the word "education" has appeared at this point. Dewey is convinced that if 'the standard of morals is low it is because the education given by the interaction of the individual with his social environment is defective',[36] where improving the interaction of the individual with his social environment means to 'correct errors and satisfy deficiencies which are perceived as man deals with social situations, as well as to resolve conflicts which occur among the component elements of society'.[37] Ethics is not concerned with an absolute good to which humanity must adapt. Ethics is the tool addressing problems that arise when the consequences of our actions affect others. Life in a society offers unlimited occasions for conflict between several normative instances, desires, and characters, and the purpose of moral theory is indeed to handle those conflicts. In summary, it comes down to recognising the social sources of normativity and – through critical analysis and experimental practices – finding solutions that encourage mediation and co-ordination of both the individual and the community.

To succeed in such a venture clearly requires integration of several factors. Mental faculties and biological assets need to be guided by intelligent thinking: but intelligent thinking is a habit that needs to be acquired and harmonised with the other habits constituting one's character. Then we have environmental influences, social customs, and institutions which heavily influence the formation of character and conduct, so a huge effort needs to be directed to creating a context that would not interfere with the development of good dispositions.

---

[34] Dewey, *Human Nature and Conduct*, 58.
[35] Dewey, *Human Nature and Conduct*, 280.
[36] Dewey, *Human Nature and Conduct*, 319.
[37] John Dewey, *Lectures in China: 1919–1920* (Honolulu: University Press of Hawaii, 1973), 64.

Giuseppe Turchi

In general, any type of intervention should be directed to the development of plasticity of habits, because thanks to plasticity the individual can give new meaning to what he experiences, create assumptions and new action plans: plasticity is the key to adapting to the environment and, at the same time, to adapting the environment to our needs.

The problem with configuring genetics and neuroscience as tools to induce some kind of moral behaviour lies in not considering the adaptive character of plasticity. Whenever we talk about altering genes or giving hormones, the objective of radical naturalists is often to determine a specific behavioural change through a process of cause and effect. However, this means setting unilateral constraints on conduct that could turn unfavourable in some situations. Oxytocin and serotonin may alter responses in trial subjects, but do not directly create values or enhance our ability to interpret the context. Values and interpretative abilities require a plastic individual that can build up material from his or her lived experience, ponder on the consequences of his actions, and change his or her plans.

5. Neuroscience and Moral Pedagogy

In the light of the above, Persson and Savulescu's moral bio-enhancement does not seem a practicable or a desirable solution, and I cannot consider here further critical issues related to a paternalistic imposition of such enhancement.[38] However, even though I criticise the *pars construens* of *Unfit for the Future*, the relation between humankind and environment is indeed defective. The balance of power on which traditions of political realism and international law rely, the inequities created thanks to a *laissez-faire* economic logic, and the lack of ecologically sustainable consumerism show that the present relationship between humankind and the environment is leading to disaster.

In the past Dewey raised some problems of liberalism[39] and suggested that the solution lay in the education of the citizen and the formation of a 'public'.[40] According to him, the moral development of

[38] See Ingmar Persson and Julian Savulescu, 'Response: Should Moral Bioenhancement Be Compulsory? Reply to Vojin Rakić', *J Med Ethics* **40**:4 (2014), 251–252.

[39] See for example John Dewey, *Liberalism and Social Action* (New York: G.P. Putnam, 1935) and John Dewey, *Lectures in China: 1919–1920*, 107–116.

[40] See John Dewey, *The Public and Its Problems: An Essay in Political Inquiry* (New York: Henry Holt & Co., 1927).

the child had to happen through deeply social education, connected with the needs identified outside the school environment:

> [T]he school must itself be a community life in all which that implies. Social perceptions and interests can be developed only in a genuinely social medium – one where there is give and take in the building up of a common experience. [...] In place of a school set apart from life as a place for learning lessons, we have a miniature social group in which study and growth are incidents of present shared experience. Playgrounds, shops, workrooms, laboratories not only direct the natural active tendencies of youth, but they involve intercourse, communication, and cooperation, – all extending the perception of connections.[41]

Dewey thought moral enhancement to be feasible exclusively in a net of relationships that would allow individuals to improve their 'social perceptions and interests' thanks to the reconstruction of the meaning of personal experience. In other words, Dewey recognised moral issues to be far more than just biological problems. However, he was convinced that progress in 'physiology, biology, and the logic of experimental science supply the specific intellectual instrumentalities' demanded to work out and formulate 'a theory of knowledge which sees in knowledge the method by which one experience is made available in giving direction and meaning to another'.[42]

Inspired by Dewey's instrumentalism and psychology, my proposal refers to the concept of habit and focusses on the possible combination of neuroscience and moral pedagogy. I suggest that we use neuropsychology not to speculate on biomedical intervention, but to consider what type of activities may help us to improve both moral habits and the effectiveness of teaching. This approach – which would go side by side with the cure of "moral pathologies" mentioned by Specker and colleagues – is limited, because it aims to enhance the plasticity of the brain[43] and intelligent conduct and

[41] Dewey, *Democracy and Education*, 416.
[42] Dewey, *Democracy and Education*, 401.
[43] Current research in neuroscience is trying to find the mechanisms underlying so-called experience-dependent plasticity. This concept relies on the Hebbian theory that 'neurons that regularly fire together, wire together' and holds that the grey matter volume of a brain region is influenced by its use. For example, some longitudinal imaging studies show that juggling training leads to increased grey matter concentration in occipital-parietal regions; whereas training of working memory impacts on the structural connectivity of white matter – for a review see Robert J. Zatorre, Douglas R. Fields, and Heidi Johansen-Berg, 'Plasticity in Gray and White:

not to produce specific behaviours. However, contrary to moral enhancement, it can be safely tested and does not have the side effects
I mentioned in section 2.

Such a project is being pursued by Darcia Narvaez, a researcher at
the University of Notre Dame. The starting point of her study is a
clear rejection of genetic determinism and of mind/body dualism,
which are replaced by an epigenetic perspective in which the gene expression and the development of functions are largely modulated by
interaction with the environment. Given this premise, Narvaez's
concern is the context in which a child grows up, since the first
years of life are those that provide 'the foundations for what is to
come in terms of social, intellectual and moral development'.[44]
Some examples? Already during pregnancy, a severely anxious
mother produces cortisol discharges that may affect the extra-pyr-
amidal system and the lower limbic areas. These areas are believed
to be related to threat perception, stress response and the "fight or
flight" type of response mechanism; their dysfunction would have
implications on affiliative abilities and pro-social behaviour, i.e.,
the environment coming to be perceived as a perennial threat.
Moreover, a low level of parental care seems to affect the greater
limbic system and frontal cortices by altering, again, the ability to
forge affiliative links – the oxytocin circuit – as well as abstract reasoning skills which are necessary to imagine behavioural alternatives and
related consequences.

The possibilities of intervention at this primitive level, according
to Narvaez, are varied and do not require medicines, engineering,
or systems: to promote the moral development of the child – regulation
of behaviour and affiliation – breast-feeding is particularly recommended,
as well as administration of positive tactile stimuli by the mother-
play, the presence of several support figures, and shared rest.
Narvaez's model of moral neuro-education also does not require

---

Neuroimaging Changes in Brain Structure During Learning', *Nature
Neuroscience* **15**:4 (2012), 528–531. Regarding moral education, a finding
that would need further exploration is the increased grey matter volume in
the bilateral ventromedial pre-frontal cortex (vmPFC) and subgenual anter-
ior cingulate cortex (sgACC) of those subjects that 'judge moral issues based
on deeper principles and shared ideals' – for the experiment, see Kristin
Prehn, et al., 'Neural Correlates of Post-Conventional Moral Reasoning:
A Voxel-Based Morphometry Study', *PLoS ONE* **10**:6 (2015): https://
doi.org/10.1371/journal.pone.0122914.

[44]   Darcia Narvaez, 'Moral Neuroeducation From Early Life Through
the Lifespan', *Neuroethics* **5**:2 (2012), 145–157, 146.

medication or systems, with the double objective of 1) promoting moral virtue in ourselves and in young people, and 2) modifying a 'malfunctioning brain through a change in activities which modify neuronal functioning'.[45] This model pairs with what Narvaez calls Integrative Ethical Education[46] and proposes to intervene on conduct – and the neural basis involved – through various types of activities. The idea would be to build scenarios where individuals, supervised by a mentor, test their moral intuitions, their skills, and their habits, constantly facing new problems and discussing possible solutions. This practice, designed to stimulate the plasticity of brain and moral reasoning, is integrated with recreational activities (singing, dancing, writing, artistic games) and the technique of 'mindfulness',[47] widely used in psychotherapy nowadays. With the former techniques we try to (re)vitalise the emotional areas of the brain, while the latter focusses its attention on the present moment by increasing the levels of concentration and the ability to analyse the context.

---

[45] Narvaez, 'Moral Neuroeducation From Early Life Through the Lifespan', 149.

[46] This approach aims to combine the advantages of two pedagogical guidelines: one founded on the ethics of virtue – a character ethics approach – and one based on the deontological ethics – a rule ethics approach. The first aims at the formation of a virtuous character through the transmission of a set of values: discipline, self-control, and co-operation to mention just some. The educator does not have an equal relationship with the child and transmits knowledge with a top-down pedagogy. Instead, the pedagogy that refers to deontological ethics emphasises the individual's ability of moral reasoning. Here every norm is validated through the principle of universalisation and the child is guided towards a progressive autonomous judgement. See Darcia Narvaez, 'Integrative Ethical Education', in M. Killen and J. G. Smetana (eds), *Handbook of Moral Development* (Mahwah, NJ: Lawrence Erlbaum Associates, 2006), 703–733.

[47] A study conducted in Massachusetts shows that an eight-week mindfulness-based stress reduction training produced an increase in grey matter concentration within the left hippocampus, in the posterior cingulate cortex (PCC), in the left temporo-parietal junction (TJP), and in the cerebellum. TJP is involved in social cognition and shows great activation during feeling of compassion in meditators. The hippocampus contributes to the regulation of emotion and it is involved in the modulation of cortical arousal and responsiveness; according to researchers, 'the structural changes in this area following mindfulness practice may reflect improved function in regulating emotional responding', see Britta K. Hölzel, et al., 'Mindfulness Practice Leads to Increases in Regional Brain Gray Matter Density', *Psychiatry Research: Neuroimaging* **191**:1 (2011), 36–43, 40.

Giuseppe Turchi

If this model proves to be effective, it would require interventions at a political and social level in order to build a supportive environment. Given the large amount of interdisciplinary data that correlates poor parental care with brain dysfunction and behavioural problems, Narvaez suggests the establishment of policies that take parenting into great consideration: we might think of an education programme for parents, a measure that has been requested for a long time by sociologists and psychologists.[48] We should also contemplate a policy promoting the support of children and families, and reconstruction of societies and institutions to create a safe and less stressful context for pregnant women.

It can be argued that Narvaez's project is not particularly revolutionary, because many of its aspects are already known by common-sense and developmental psychology. One might note, moreover, that I prefer this approach because of an *a priori* objection to more invasive methods. To the first, I would respond by saying that Narvaez's non-reductionist use of neuroscience makes it possible to configure new types of intervention, namely, new kinds of activities that can be tested to influence the biological basis of the cognitive and emotional system more effectively.[49] Common-sense and developmental psychology were probably on the right track, but it is with neuroscience that they gain new strength: the strength to enrich previous knowledge to create new tools; the strength to enhance moral education. But this does not mean that we can solve moral problems once and for all. If we want to respect the contextual, social, and experimental nature of morality, no miraculous revolution can be expected.

Regarding procedures being more or less invasive, it is not the electrode or the drug that is evil; rather, the problem is whether these electrodes and drugs are capable of promoting plasticity of the brain and moral habits. If an implant or a drug enhances my empathy in every situation, this is of no help to practical life and does not produce an increase in meaning, which is useful for deliberations. If a genetic intervention allows me to have the best moral intuitions in a given context, as this context changes I may find myself at a

---

[48] See for example M. W. Berkowitz and J. H. Grych, 'Fostering Goodness: Teaching Parents to Facilitate Children's Moral Development', *Journal of Moral Education* **27**:3 (1998), 371–391.
[49] On the importance of establishing relationships between MRI-based effects, neuroanatomy, and behaviour, see Zatorre, Douglas, and Johansen-Berg, 'Plasticity in Gray and White: Neuroimaging Changes in Brain Structure During Learning', 530.

disadvantage in facing new problems.[50] The biomedical interventions we have at our disposal today are not suitable to create plastic moral disposition, nor can they help us to better understand moral contexts: they often influence behaviour by overlooking practical rationality. Darcia Narvaez's project, on the other hand, uses modern knowledge to experiment on the correlation between certain practices and the development of cerebral areas involved with them. This type of research may represent the most feasible solution, in the short term, to promote a reform in education and society that would ease the growth of a democratic electorate and of a public that is more aware of environmental decline, of weapons of mass destruction, and of lawless liberalism.

Università degli Studi di Parma
gppturchi@gmail.com

---

[50] Interestingly, this is the same problem Persson and Savulescu want to solve with enhancement: the context has changed, but humanity has underdeveloped moral intuitions that must be rewritten.

311

The Experimental Psychology of Moral Enhancement: We Should If We Could, But We Can't

SYLVIA TERBECK AND KATHRYN B. FRANCIS

Abstract
In this chapter we will review experimental evidence related to pharmacological moral enhancement. Firstly, we will present our recent study in which we found that a drug called propranolol could change moral judgements. Further research, which also investigated this, found similar results. Secondly, we will discuss the limitations of such approaches, when it comes to the idea of general "human enhancement". Whilst promising effects on certain moral concepts might be beneficial to the development of theoretical moral psychology, enhancement of human moral behaviour in general – to our current understanding – has more side-effects than intended effects, making it potentially harmful. We give an overview of misconceptions when taking experimental findings beyond the laboratory and discuss the problems and solutions associated with the psychological assessment of moral behaviour. Indeed, how is morality "measured" in psychology, and are those measures reliable?

1. Experimental Studies on Psychopharmacology and Human Morality

Recently, studies have begun to elucidate the neural basis of human moral behaviour, including neural correlates of moral action and decision making.[1] Initial studies used fMRI (functional magnetic resonance imaging) to determine areas of the brain associated with moral reasoning. In their widely-cited study, Greene, Sommerville, Nystrom, Darley, and Cohen used fMRI to determine the underlying neural mechanisms of moral judgements.[2] The study involved participants reading vignettes about moral dilemmas, such as the footbridge and the switch dilemma.[3] The authors categorised

---

[1] S. Terbeck, J. Savulescu, L. P. Chesterman, and P. J. Cowen, 'Noradrenaline Effects on Social Behaviour, Intergroup Relations, and Moral Decisions', *Neurosci Biobehav Rev.* **66** (2016), 54–60.
[2] J. D. Greene, R. B. Sommerville, L. E. Nystrom, J. M. Darley, and J. D. Cohen, 'An fMRI Investigation of Emotional Engagement in Moral Judgment', *Science* **293**:5537 (2001), 2105–2108.
[3] P. Foot, *Virtues and Vices and Other Essays in Moral Philosophy* (New York, USA: Oxford University Press, 1978). See also J. J. Thomson,

doi:10.1017/S1358246118000413
Royal Institute of Philosophy Supplement **83** 2018

dilemmas as either personal or impersonal based on features of the scenario (i.e., up-close versus distant, involving redirected versus direct harm, etc.). They found that personal dilemmas were more strongly associated with activations in brain regions involved in emotional processing (such as the ventromedial prefrontal cortex) whereas impersonal dilemmas activated areas of working memory (such as the dorsolateral prefrontal cortex). In addition, the type of judgement individuals made also led to differences in brain activation patterns. Specifically, when making a utilitarian judgement (compared to a deontological judgement) in personal (but not impersonal) moral dilemmas, areas associated with cognitive control were found to be active, suggesting that individuals had to overcome an initial emotional evaluation in personal dilemmas in order to make a utilitarian decision in such cases. Greene, et al. therefore subsequently proposed a dual process theory of moral judgements in which certain dilemmas recruit immediate emotional reactions which can be in conflict with moral reflective "rational" analysis, and might require extra cognitive resources in order to arrive at a utilitarian decision. Further neuroscientific studies, using fMRI, have elaborated on these initial findings, generally supporting the view that certain features in moral dilemmas can trigger different brain processing areas. We understand that all human processes have their basis in the brain and therefore show correlations to brain activation patterns. As such, the new idea that the interfering effects of drugs on brain activity could manipulate not only basic brain functions but also have profound effects on higher order human processes such as moral decision-making seems only logical.

Drug effects are largely produced by interferences with neuronal transmission. Neurons use neurotransmitters to transfer information from one neuron to the next. At the synaptic cleft, the electric potential is transferred into a chemical signal by triggering the release of neurotransmitters into the synaptic cleft. The neurotransmitter then docks onto receptors of the post-synaptic cell membrane, triggering further intercellular mechanisms in the post-synaptic neuron, which enables the signal to be transferred.[4] Whilst the drug may interfere with multiple sites, one common

---

'Killing, Letting Die, and the Trolley Problem', *Monist* **59**:2 (1976), 204–217.

[4] For a description of the mechanism of chemical neurotransmission see Terbeck, et al., 'Noradrenaline Effects on Social Behaviour, Intergroup Relations, and Moral Decisions', 54–60.

mechanism is the blocking of receptors on the post-synaptic cell membrane which subsequently blocks signal transfer. If it is expected that certain human behaviours are mediated by activity of a neurotransmitter to a great extent, then blocking the activity of this neurotransmitter with a pharmaceutical would reduce such "behaviour".

In our previous study, we had the hypothesis that one key neurotransmitter, namely noradrenaline (NA), might be involved in moral judgement and moral behaviour. NA has previously been suggested to be involved in basic emotion processing and is thought to underlie the fight-or flight response. In fact, early research has already determined that fear responses in animals were associated with elevated levels of NA.[5] NA is transferred via alpha and beta receptors, peripherally and centrally. It has been suggested that emotional arousal should be reduced if NA receptors are blocked with a pharmaceutical.[6] Indeed, beta-blockers (i.e., propranolol, which blocks beta 1 and 2 receptors) have been found to reduce effects of emotional arousal. For instance, reduced heart rate and general reduced activation can be observed after emotional stimuli with propranolol intervention.[7] Therefore, propranolol has been prescribed not only as a first-line treatment for hypertension, but also as a means of reducing the effects of panic and anxiety. For example, propranolol is often prescribed for instances of performance anxiety, and for the prevention of the development of post-traumatic stress disorder (PTSD).

Crucially, if basic emotional arousal is also involved in higher order processes, such as our moral decision-making, then propranolol may also affect human morality.[7] And this is indeed what we found in a recent study. Participants either received a single oral dose of propranolol or a placebo tablet. When the drug action had reached its peak effect, the psychological tests were conducted. Participants' heart rates were measured and a mood assessment was completed, followed by the moral dilemma test. In the morality task, participants judged the moral acceptability of a set of 20 moral

[5] A. F. Ax, 'The Psychological Differentiation Between Fear and Anger in Humans', *Psychosom Med.* **15**:5 (1953), 433–442.

[6] S. R. Chamberlain, U. Mueller, A. D. Blackwell, T. W. Robbins, and B. J. Sahakian, 'Noradrenergic Modulation of Working Memory and Emotional Memory in Humans', *Psychopharmacology* **188**:4 (2006), 397–407.

[7] Greene, et al., 'An fMRI Investigation of Emotional Engagement in Moral Judgment', 2105–2108.

Sylvia Terbeck and Kathryn B. Francis

dilemmas comprising both personal and impersonal scenarios including the footbridge and the switch dilemma. As predicted, we found that propranolol significantly reduced heart rate after the intervention but had no effect on self-reported mood. Importantly, participants in the propranolol group also judged harmful actions described in personal moral dilemmas as less morally acceptable, without changing the rating on impersonal moral dilemmas.[8] This suggests that NA function is involved in the psychological process of moral decision making and that responses to personal moral dilemmas may rely on basic emotional processes. However, contrary to what would be predicted according to Greene's theory, we found an increase in deontological or non-utilitarian judgements. We argue that, since NA is also involved in the processing of aggression, propranolol may have reduced aggression and subsequently increased harm aversion.

This theory regarding harm aversion and its role in moral decision making has also been supported by further psychopharmacological research using the drug citalopram. Citalopram is a selective serotonin re-uptake inhibitor and increases the net brain concentration of serotonin. In previous studies, serotonin has been found to be involved in emotion regulation, and is thus also often used for the treatment of mood or anxiety disorders.[9] In this study, Crockett, Clark, Hauser, and Robbins gave participants a single dose of citalopram in a double-blind placebo controlled study before assessing each participant's moral judgements.[10] Again, the authors found an effect of the drug on moral judgements, but only for personal dilemmas. Specifically, they found that citalopram increased deontological responses in these dilemmas, arguing that serotonin reuptake inhibition may have increased harm aversion.

Apart from psychopharmacological manipulation of theoretical moral judgements, studies have also investigated wider moral behaviour and social attitudes, such as pro-social behaviour, generosity, and

[8] S. Terbeck, G. Kahane, S. McTavish, J. Savulescu, N. Levy, M. Hewstone, and P. J. Cowen, 'Beta Adrenergic Blockade Reduces Utilitarian Judgement', *Biological Psychology* 92:2 (2013), 323–328.

[9] For example see I. Kirsch, B. J. Deacon, T. B. Huedo-Medina, A. Scoboria, T. J. Moore, and B. T. Johnson, 'Initial Severity and Antidepressant Benefits: A Meta-Analysis of Data Submitted to the Food and Drug Administration', *PLoS Med.* 5:2 (2008), 260–268.

[10] M. J. Crockett, L. Clark, M. D. Hauser, and T. W. Robbins, 'Serotonin Selectively Influences Moral Judgment and Behavior Through Effects on Harm Aversion', *Proc Natl Acad Sci USA* **107**:40 (2010), 17433–17438.

fairness judgements, as well as perceptions of out-group members.[11] In numerous studies it has been found that pharmaceuticals produce effects on such human behaviours.[12] For instance, oxytocin, a hormone associated with maternal care and bonding, has been found to also increase fairness judgements, willingness to donate, and to help others[13]. In another recent study, we investigated the effect of propranolol on intergroup attitudes, using behavioural as well as combined fMRI methods.[14] We first investigated racial biases using self-reporting as well as response-time based computer test methods (i.e., the IAT). The IAT measures racial biases by comparing response times between associations of in- and-out-group faces as well as positive and negative words. We found that propranolol reduced racial biases, suggesting that NA might be involved in the processing of social attitudes.[14] More recently we repeated this study, but in addition also examined the effect of propranolol on racial face perception in the brain using fMRI.[14] In this study, Caucasian participants received the pharmacological intervention before undergoing fMRI in which they viewed black and white faces. We found activation differences in the fusiform gyrus (a brain area strongly associated with face perception and social categorisation) with propranolol. This suggests that NA might be involved in basic face processing and immediate social categorisation in the brain. The above studies have illustrated that, besides having an effect on basic physiological processes, drugs can also influence higher order human social processes, such as theoretical moral judgements, judgements of fairness and generosity, as well as pro-social behaviour and social perception.

[11] C. K. W. De Dreu, L. L. Greer, G. A. Van Kleef, S. Shalvi, and M. J. J. Handgraaf, 'Oxytocin Promotes Human Ethnocentrism', *Proc Natl Acad Sci USA* **108**:4 (2011), 1262–1266.

[12] For a review see N. Levy, T. Douglas, G. Kahane, S. Terbeck, P. J. Cowen, M. Hewstone, and J. Savulescu, 'Are You Morally Modified? The Moral Effects of Widely Used Pharmaceuticals', *Philos Psychiatr Psychol.* **21**:2 (2014), 111–125.

[13] For example see P. J. Zak, A. A. Stanton, and S. Ahmadi, 'Oxytocin Increases Generosity in Humans', *PLoS One* **2**:11 (2007), 1–5.

[14] S. Terbeck, G. Kahane, S. McTavish, R. McCutcheon, M. Hewstone, J. Savulescu, and R. Norbury, 'Beta-Adrenoceptor Blockade Modulates Fusiform Gyrus Activity to Black versus White Faces', *Psychopharmacology (Berl.)* **232**:16 (2015), 2951–2958. See also S. Terbeck, G. Kahane, S. McTavish, J. Savulescu, P. J. Cowen, and M. Hewstone, 'Propranolol Reduces Implicit Negative Racial Bias', *Psychopharmacology* **222**:3 (2012), 419–424.

Sylvia Terbeck and Kathryn B. Francis

Does this therefore mean that we can take drugs to enhance our morality?

2. Psychopharmacological Effects "Outside" the Laboratory

In neuroscience, when conducting experiments using pharmaceuticals, the idea is to investigate and learn more about the underlying neural mechanisms of certain concepts. For instance, as determined in our own research, we found that NA seems to play a significant and causal role in moral decision-making and social judgement. As such, these studies are theoretically driven. Attempts to *find* a drug which might be used to *enhance* our morality is less theoretical in nature; indeed, to our understanding, previous studies were not designed to test this latter idea, but rather to understand the neuroscience of higher order human processes. Indeed, whilst conducting these studies, we did not consider the concept of moral enhancement or if it was even possible.

When conducting experimental research, the results reported are almost always average effects. For instance, even though we found that propranolol significantly reduced racial biases on the IAT test, this was only the case for the average of the group, meaning that racial biases were not reduced in every single individual. Secondly, several studies must be carried out before meaningful implications can be inferred. For instance, in a recent review we investigated the potential use of metabotropic glutamate receptor 5 antagonists for the treatment of anxiety.[15] In this review we described that, before its application in humans, more than 800 animal studies were conducted. Indeed, in order to assume reliable pharmacological effects, a large number of experiments are required.

It was also suggested that selective serotonin reuptake inhibitors (SSRIs) might be used to elevate or enhance mood in humans.[16] In comparison to the limited number of pharmacological studies on morality, numerous studies have been conducted on "mood

[15]   S. Terbeck, F. Akkus, L. P. Chesterman, and G. Hasler, 'The Role of Metabotropic Glutamate Receptor 5 in the Pathogenesis of Mood Disorders and Addiction: Combining Preclinical Evidence with Human Positron Emission Tomography (PET) Studies', *Front Neurosci.* **9**:86 (2015), 1–10.

[16]   R. De Jongh, I. Bolt, M. Schermer, and B. Olivier, 'Botox for the Brain: Enhancement of Cognition, Mood and Pro-Social Behavior and Blunting of Unwanted Memories', *Neuroscience & Biobehavioral Reviews* **32**:4 (2008), 760–776.

enhancement". A recent review examined the overall effect of SSRIs on mood.[17] The authors found that SSRIs were only effective in changing mood in severe depression but not in moderate or mild depression, suggesting that mood enhancement is selective and therefore not possible across individuals. Furthermore, it is often assumed that the effects of laboratory experiments can translate to the outside world, which may prove problematic. In particular, with regards to drug effects, the short and long term effects may vary. For instance, with regards to aggression reduction in association with propranolol, it was speculated that the effects of aggression reduction would disappear over time, whilst the 'medical' effect of reduced heart rate remained.[18]

In addition, we would like to emphasise another factor associated with pharmacological intervention, which is the inevitability of side-effects. Previously, in ethics and philosophy, some articles discussing the prospect of pharmacological enhancement suggested that in the near future there may be a drug with no or negligible side effects.[19] Other claims, such as the argument that taking a drug might not be different from other non-medical interventions might indeed be defensible, if the assumption that there will be a drug with no or negligible side effects were justified. For example, if we found a drug that could make you fly and nothing else, we would most likely take it. But it is not that straightforward. In fact, in our recent article we discussed why there is not currently, and likely will never be, a drug with no or negligible side effects.[20] Side effects of most psychoactive substances range from allergic reactions to physical problems, but also to psychological side-effects including reduced sexual drive, increased anxiety, loss of attention, increased tiredness, or loss of motivation. From our current understanding of

[17] I. Kirsch, B. J. Deacon, T. B. Huedo-Medina, A. Scoboria, T. J. Moore, and B. T. Johnson, 'Initial Severity and Antidepressant Benefits: A Meta-Analysis of Data Submitted to the Food and Drug Administration', *PLoS Med.* **5**:2 (2008), 260–268.

[18] J. M. Silver, S. C. Yudofsky, J. A. Slater, R. K. Gold, B. L. Stryer, D. T. Williams, H. Wolland, and J. Endicott, 'Propranolol Treatment of Chronically Hospitalized Aggressive Patients', *J. Neuropsychiatry Clin Neurosci.* **11**:3 (1999), 328–335.

[19] For example, see T. Douglas, 'Moral Enhancement', in J. Savulescu, R. ter Meulen, and G. Kahane (eds), *Enhancing Human Capacities* (Oxford, UK: Wiley-Blackwell, 2011), 467–485.

[20] S. Terbeck and L. P. Chesterman, 'Will There Ever Be a Drug With No or Negligible Side Effects? Evidence From Neuroscience', *Neuroethics* **7**:2 (2014), 189–194.

Sylvia Terbeck and Kathryn B. Francis

the brain, we know that interventions that do simply *one* thing and nothing else are not possible. The brain operates in complex networks. We cannot find one area for morality or one neurotransmitter regulating morality, or one drug that has only one effect on this complex network. In our recent article, we illustrated a case of simple visual edge detection in mice and described the potential side effects that 'enhancing' this seemingly simple function might elicit.[21] The complexity demonstrated here with a process as simple as edge detection only emphasises the challenges of attempting to enhance a multifaceted phenomenon such as morality. Therefore, decisions regarding enhancement must be pragmatic evaluations of effect versus side effect.

Crucially, in this pursuit of moral enhancement, we first need reliable measures of morality to determine whether there has been an effect, and this measure would need to prove meaningful outside of the laboratory. But do we have such reliable measures of morality?

3. The Psychological Assessment of Morality and its Reliability

In order to examine measures of morality, we must first look at the history of assessment within the moral domain. Until recently, morality had been a topic of speculation in philosophy, grounded in theory rather than empirical investigation. It was the emergence of moral psychology that marked the fusion of both theoretical and experimental approaches in investigating the nature of morality, but more specifically, moral judgement.[22]

In line with the hybrid nature of moral psychology and as discussed above, provocative moral dilemmas pitting deontological against utilitarian theories have played a central role in the investigation of moral judgement.[23] Both the footbridge and switch

---

[21]   Terbeck, et al., 'Will There Ever Be a Drug With No or Negligible Side Effects? Evidence From Neuroscience', 189–194.
[22]   J. M. Doris, 'Introduction', in J. M. Doris (ed.), *The Moral Psychology Handbook* (New York, USA: Oxford University Press, 2010), 1–2.
[23]   See D. M. Bartels, C. W. Bauman, F. A. Cushman, D. A. Pizarro, and A. P. McGraw, 'Moral Judgment and Decision Making', in G. Keren and G. Wu (eds), *The Wiley Blackwell Handbook of Judgment and Decision Making* (Chichester, UK: John Wiley & Sons, 2015), 478–515. See also F. Cushman, L. Young, and J. Greene, 'Our Multi-System Moral Psychology: Towards a Consensus View', in J. M. Doris (ed.), *The Moral*

dilemmas,[24] which are versions of the so-called "trolley problem", have become a topic of interest for both moral philosophers and moral psychologists for the reason that individuals tend to endorse the utilitarian outcome in the switch dilemma but refuse to do so in the footbridge alternative.[25]

At the methodological level, moral psychologists tend to present these trolley problems to participants in text-based paradigms that require a subsequent moral judgement. Typically, participants are asked whether the utilitarian act described in the dilemma is "appropriate" or "acceptable". In their conception, these hypothetical moral dilemmas were not intended to reveal insights into real-life decisions but instead, in their experimental simplicity, allow moral scientists to explore the 'foundational psychological processes that underlie human moral cognition'.[26] The level of experimental control available to scientists in incorporating these paradigms is paramount; allowing moral conflicts to arise in artificial contexts with anonymous agents.[27]

Despite the prevalent use of these paradigms, concerns have been raised about the precision with which moral dilemmas have been constructed.[28] Differences in several factors including framing, word count, perspective, situational circumstances, and type of question have been shown to influence moral judgements.[29] For example, research has distinguished judgement questions such as 'is it morally acceptable?' from action-choice questions such as 'would you do it?' Arguably, judgement questions address allocentric evaluations of the utilitarian act, whereas action-choice questions offer an egocen-

---

Psychology Handbook (New York, USA: Oxford University Press, 2010), 47–71.

[24] Thomson, *Killing, Letting Die, and the Trolley Problem*, 204–217. See also Foot, *Virtues and Vices*.

[25] Greene, et al., 'An fMRI Investigation of Emotional Engagement in Moral Judgment', 2105–2108.

[26] J. F. Christensen, and A. Gomila, 'Moral Dilemmas in Cognitive Neuroscience of Moral Decision-Making: A Principled Review', *Neurosci Biobehav Rev.* **36**:4 (2012), 1250.

[27] M. Hauser, F. Cushman, L. Young, R. Kang-Xing Jin, and J. Mikhail, 'A Dissociation Between Moral Judgments and Justifications', *Mind & Language* **22**:1 (2007), 1–21.

[28] Christensen and Gomila, 'Moral Dilemmas in Cognitive Neuroscience of Moral Decision-Making: A Principled Review', 1249–1264.

[29] Bartels, et al., 'Moral Judgment and Decision Making', 154–161.

tric perspective, resulting in distinct moral judgements.[30] In a well-known framing study, participants were found to endorse utilitarian outcomes when the phrasing "save" was used as opposed to "kill".[31]

In addition to disagreement over the formulations of these moral dilemmas, research has also questioned the ability of these paradigms to reflect genuine deontological or utilitarian responses.[32] For example, in the footbridge dilemma we have no clear method for distinguishing the action of pushing the man as (i) a moral decision grounded in the belief that killing one to save the majority is morally required, or as (ii) a decision driven simply by less aversion to harm.[33] Crucially, there is evidence to suggest that people possessing antisocial personality traits are more likely to push the man off the footbridge with their intentions masked as being utilitarian.[34] Further, research has found that even when controlling for this antisocial trait association, so-called utilitarian responses do not always reflect concern for the 'greater good'.[35]

Despite these criticisms, recent attempts to validate moral dilemmas have addressed previous inconsistencies in formulation[36] and

[30] S. Tassy, O. Oullier, J. Mancini, and B. Wicker, 'Discrepancies Between Judgment and Choice of Action in Moral Dilemmas', *Frontiers in Psychology* **4**:250 (2013), 1–8.

[31] L. Petrinovich and P. O'Neill, 'Influence of Wording and Framing Effects on Moral Intuitions', *Ethology and Sociobiology* **17**:3 (1996), 145–171.

[32] G. Kahane, J. A. Everett, B. D. Earp, M. Farias, and P. Savulescu, 'Utilitarian Judgments in Sacrificial Moral Dilemmas Do Not Reflect Impartial Concern for the Greater Good', *Cognition* **134** (2015), 193–209.

[33] For example, see I. Patil, 'Trait Psychopathy and Utilitarian Moral Judgement: The Mediating Role of Action Aversion', *Journal of Cognitive Psychology* **27**:3 (2015), 349–366. See also F. Cushman, K. Gray, A. Gaffey, and W. B. Mendes, 'Simulating Murder: The Aversion to Harmful Action', *Emotion* **12**:1 (2012), 2–7.

[34] See D. M. Bartels and D. A. Pizarro, 'The Mismeasure of Morals: Antisocial Personality Traits Predict Utilitarian Responses to Moral Dilemmas', *Cognition* **121**:1 (2011), 154–161. See also H. Djeriouat and B. Tremoliere, 'The Dark Triad of Personality and Utilitarian Moral Judgment: The Mediating Role of Honesty/Humility and Harm/Care', *Personality and Individual Differences* **67** (2014), 11–16. See also Y. Gao and S. Tang, 'Psychopathic Personality and Utilitarian Moral Judgment in College Students', *Journal of Criminal Justice* **41**:5 (2013), 342–349.

[35] Kahane, et al., 'Utilitarian Judgments in Sacrificial Moral Dilemmas Do Not Reflect Impartial Concern for the Greater Good', 12.

[36] J. F. Christensen, A. Flexas, M. Calabrese, N. K. Gut, and A. Gomila, 'Moral Judgment Reloaded: A Moral Dilemma Validation Study', *Frontiers in Psychology* **5**:607 (2014), 1–18.

previous attempts to label individuals as either utilitarian or deonto-logical have been challenged with research arguing that people instead tend to adopt a 'particularist approach to morals that takes the details of each case into account'.[37] Whilst the methodology is valuable in shedding light on the mechanisms underlying moral jud-gements, there remain gaps in our understanding. How can declara-tions made in response to these text-based paradigms translate into real-world moral behaviour?[38]

Attempts to explicate moral behaviour have largely explored non-harmful actions in economical paradigms and so the investigation of harmful moral actions has made little headway.[39] While text-based moral dilemmas possess an advantage in producing unambigu-ous outputs, these questionnaire-based paradigms 'only offer a very low degree of immersion'.[40] In fact, FeldmanHall, et al. found that these contextually impoverished scenarios elicited moral decisions that were different from those made in real counterparts of the same scenario.[41] Critically, by increasing the amount of contextual information available in the hypothetical scenario, the researchers were able to align hypothetical moral choices with real moral choices. This line of research would suggest that contextual richness alters moral decisions and raises further questions regarding the reli-ance on text-based moral dilemmas in moral psychology. Echoing the age-old saying "do as I say, not as I do",[42] this inconsistency between moral judgement and action is supported in research with

[37]   Christensen, et al., 'Moral Judgment Reloaded', 16.
[38]   T. D. Parsons, 'Virtual Reality for Enhanced Ecological Validity and Experimental Control in the Clinical, Affective and Social Neurosciences', *Front Hum Neurosci*. **9**:660 (2015), 1–14.
[39]   C. D. Navarrete, M. M. McDonald, M. L. Mott, and B. Asher, 'Virtual Morality: Emotion and Action in a Simulated Three-Dimensional "Trolley Problem"', *Emotion* **12**:2 (2012), 364–370.
[40]   A. Skulmowski, A. Bunge, K. Kaspar, and G. Pipa, 'Forced-Choice Decision-Making in Modified Trolley Dilemma Situations: A Virtual Reality and Eye Tracking Study, *Front Behav Neurosci*. **8**:426 (2014), 2.
[41]   O. FeldmanHall, D. Mobbs, D. Evans, L. Hiscox, L. Navrady, and T. Dalgleish, 'What We Say and What We Do: The Relationship Between Real and Hypothetical Moral Choices', *Cognition* **123**:3 (2012), 434–441.
[42]   For an overview of moral hypocrisy see B. Monin and A. Merritt, 'Moral Hypocrisy, Moral Inconsistency, and the Struggle for Moral Integrity', in M. Mikulincer and P. R. Shaver (eds), *The Social Psychology of Morality: Exploring the Causes of Good and Evil: Herzliya Series on Personality and Social Psychology* (Washington, DC: American Psychological Association, 2012), 167–184.

institutionalised psychopaths who display intact understanding of moral norms but exhibit antisocial and sometimes violent behaviours.[43]

Taken together, this evidence of a partial dissociation between moral judgements and moral actions and the potential for contextual information to bridge the gap highlights the need for a contextually rich testing tool. Fortunately, the emergence of contextually salient virtual reality technologies has opened opportunities to explore simulated harmful moral actions in environments free from issues concerning de-contextualisation.[44] Virtual reality systems adopt sensory-tracking, most commonly head-tracking, to immerse participants within life-size simulated environments. In these dynamic environments, researchers can begin to investigate active moral choices: 'would someone [...] actually resort to this course of action when the full repertoire of contextual features comes into play?'[45]

In this virtual domain of moral psychology, attempts to reproduce moral dilemmas in virtual reality have revealed mixed findings regarding the relationship between moral judgement and action. While in virtually constructed versions of trolley-like dilemmas some research has demonstrated consistency between judgements in original text-based paradigms and simulated actions in virtual counterparts,[46] contrasting research has demonstrated a disparity with

[43] M. Cima, F. Tonnaer, and M. D. Hauser, 'Psychopaths Know Right From Wrong But Don't Care', *Soc Cogn Affect Neurosci*. **5**:1 (2010), 59–67. See also K. A. Kiehl, 'Without Morals: The Cognitive Neuroscience of Criminal Psychopaths', in W. Sinnott-Armstrong (ed.), *Moral Psychology* (Cambridge, USA: The MIT Press, 2008), 119–149. See also S. Tassy, C. Deruelle, J. Mancini, S. Leistedt, and B. Wicker, 'High Levels of Psychopathic Traits Alters Moral Choice But Not Moral Judgment', *Front Hum Neurosci*. **7** (2013): https://doi.org/10.3389/fnhum.2013.00229.

[44] For an example see K. B. Francis, C. Howard, I. S. Howard, M. Gummerum, G. Ganis, G. Anderson, and S. Terbeck, 'Virtual Morality: Transitioning from Moral Judgment to Moral Action?', *PLoS One* **11**:10 (2016), 1–22.

[45] I. Patil, C. Cogoni, N. Zangrando, L. Chittaro, and G. Silani, 'Affective Basis of Judgment-Behavior Discrepancy in Virtual Experiences of Moral Dilemmas', *Soc Neurosci*. **9**:1 (2014), 95.

[46] See Navarrete, et al., 'Virtual Morality: Emotion and Action in a Simulated Three-Dimensional "Trolley Problem"', 364–370. See also Skulmowski, et al., 'Forced-Choice Decision-Making in Modified Trolley Dilemma Situations: A Virtual Reality and Eye Tracking Study', 1–16.

greater utilitarian endorsements observed in virtual dilemmas.[47] For example, in a recent study, we found that when individuals were required to simulate the harmful action of pushing the man off the bridge in a virtual simulation of the personal footbridge dilemma, the majority of people chose the utilitarian action.[48] When faced with the text-based version of the dilemma, on the other hand, the majority of people refused to endorse the utilitarian outcome. Arguably, the degree of contextual saliency and subsequent affective responses experienced in virtual moral dilemmas produces this discrepancy.

Virtual reality systems offer considerable advantages. Unlike other research domains in which actions can be examined both in the laboratory and in the field, the domain of morality presents unique challenges; participants cannot be placed in real-world precarious situations.[49] While economic paradigms have begun to shed light on non-harmful actions, studies investigating morality of harm have remained largely non-behavioural for the reason that ethically harmful behaviours prove difficult to test.[50] Although the incorporation of harm-based moral dilemmas, whether text-based or virtual, is a somewhat limited approach, helping us to investigate 'only a fragment of our moral psychology', it is a 'potentially significant one'.[51] The application of virtual reality to study harm-specific moral actions for example has significance for professions exposed to sensitive and emotionally arousing moral decision-making on a regular basis.[52] Emergency service professionals have begun to adopt virtual reality

[47]   See Francis, et al., 'Virtual Morality: Transitioning from Moral Judgment to Moral Action', 1–22. See also Patil, et al., 'Affective Basis of Judgment-Behavior Discrepancy in Virtual Experiences of Moral Dilemmas', 94–107. See also X. Pan and M. Slater, 'Confronting a Moral Dilemma in Virtual Reality: A Pilot Study', *Proceedings of the 25th BCS Conference on Human-Computer Interaction* (2011).
[48]   For a full description see Francis, et al., 'Virtual Morality: Transitioning from Moral Judgment to Moral Action', 1–22.
[49]   M. Slater, A. Antley, A. Davison, D. Swapp, C. Guger, C. Barker, and M. V. Sanchez-Vives, 'A Virtual Reprise of the Stanley Milgram Obedience Experiments', *PLoS One* **1**:1 (2006), 1–10.
[50]   A. Rovira, D. Swapp, B. Spanlang, and M. Slater, 'The Use of Virtual Reality in the Study of People's Responses to Violent Incidents', *Front Behav Neurosc.* **3**:59 (2009), 1–10.
[51]   M. Hauser, et al., 'A Dissociation Between Moral Judgments and Justifications', 4.
[52]   Francis, et al., 'Virtual Morality: Transitioning from Moral Judgment to Moral Action', 1–22.

systems for several reasons. Not only does it offer full immersion, but it is also both cost-effective and safe in contexts where there is little room for error.[53] This application of virtual reality demonstrates its broader value, investigating real-world moral decision-making beyond that of hypothetical scenarios centred round normative theories.

The level of "realism" available in virtual environments not only relies on visual saliency but also on "sensorimotor contingencies" or the congruence between motor actions and sensory simulation. Presently, virtual reality systems can only 'offer crude approxima-tions' of sensorimotor contingencies and subsequent plausibility.[54] Despite this shortcoming, research has shown that even basic virtual environments can elicit a range of realistic responses providing opportunities to bridge the "reality gap" in social domains. Essentially, if the virtual environment can deliver the subjective experience of "being there", life-like thoughts and emotions can be prompted.[55] Importantly, research demonstrates that virtual reality systems can offer successful collaboration between the experimental control available in laboratory settings and components of ecological validity in providing enhanced affective experiences.[56]

In fact, with regards to making virtual environments true to life, we face a paradox in research settings. Preserving the distinction between reality and virtual reality is essential for ethical reasons.[57] If the boundary were to break down, then the potentially hazardous reasons for not evaluating moral choices in the field in the first place would become of concern in virtual reality paradigms.[58] Despite the compromise here between bridging the reality gap and

[53] P. B. Andreatta, E. Maslowski, S. Petty, W. Shim, M. Marsh, T. Hall, and J. Frankel, 'Virtual Reality Triage Training Provides a Viable Solution for Disaster-Preparedness', *Academic Emergency Medicine* **17**:8 (2010), 870–876.

[54] Rovira, et al., 'The Use of Virtual Reality in the Study of People's Responses to Violent Incidents', 2, 9.

[55] A. Carassa, F. Morganti, and M. Tirassa, 'A Situated Cognition Perspective on Presence', *Proceedings of the Cognitive Science Society* **27** (2005), 384.

[56] See Parsons, 'Virtual Reality for Enhanced Ecological Validity and Experimental Control in the Clinical, Affective and Social Neurosciences', 1–14.

[57] Slater, et al., 'A Virtual Reprise of the Stanley Milgram Obedience Experiments', 1–10.

[58] Rovira, et al., 'The Use of Virtual Reality in the Study of People's Responses to Violent Incidents', 1–10.

preserving the technological boundary, virtual reality systems can generate experiences and trigger emotions that de-contextualised and impoverished text-based paradigms cannot.[59]

To date, existing models of moral decision-making have been shaped with moral judgements in mind,[60] offering little insight into moral actions. Although virtual research is in its infancy, by promoting "judicious use" of these virtual reality paradigms within moral psychology, we can begin to validate their potential in assessing morality. Crucially, the finding that moral judgements in text-based paradigms diverge from moral actions in virtual reality paradigms raises two key questions: (i) are moral judgement and moral action driven by at least partially distinct mechanisms and (ii) do immersive virtual environments reveal moral choices that are closer to real-life responses? In either stream, the incorporation and validation of both methods must continue to better our assessment of both moral judgements and actions; after all 'by examining only one blade of a pair of scissors, one will not understand how scissors cut'.[61] Only through adopting these multifaceted approaches to the study of morality can we begin to assess moral decision-making and, subsequently, begin to examine, understand, and assess the impact of moral enhancement.

4. Conclusion

In this chapter we have demonstrated that psychopharmacological manipulation can in fact alter moral judgements[62] as well as social

---

[59] Francis, et al., 'Virtual Morality: Transitioning from Moral Judgment to Moral Action', 1–22.

[60] For an example see Greene, et al., 'An fMRI Investigation of Emotional Engagement in Moral Judgment', 2105–2108.

See also F. Cushman, 'Action, Outcome, and Value: A Dual-System Framework for Morality', *Pers Soc Psychol Rev.* **17**:3 (2013), 273–292.

See also J. Moll, R. de Oliveira-Souza, and P. J. Eslinger, 'Morals and the Human Brain: A Working Model', *Neuroreport* **14**:3 (2003), 299–305.

[61] A. Bunge and A. Skulmowski, 'Descriptive and Pragmatic Levels of Empirical Ethics: Utilizing the Situated Character of Moral Concepts, Judgment, and Decision-Making', in C. Luetge, H. Rusch, and M. Uhl (eds), *Experimental Ethics: Toward an Empirical Moral Philosophy* (Basingstoke, UK: Palgrave Macmillan, 2014), 176.

[62] Terbeck, et al., 'Beta Adrenergic Blockade Reduces Utilitarian Judgement', 323–328.

behaviours and attitudes.[63] In this sense, "morality" does appear susceptible to alteration and enhancement. However, many of the studies that we review were originally designed to unearth the underlying neural mechanisms responsible for such moral judgements and social behaviours, placing little focus on the concept of moral enhancement and short and long-term effects of drug use outside of the lab. When considering moral enhancement in this practical and pragmatic framework, we highlight two key areas in need of advancement. Firstly, there will likely never be a drug without side-effects.[64] As such, without first establishing control over or abolishing such harmful side-effects, we cannot yet advocate psychopharmacological-based moral enhancement. Secondly, given the multifaceted nature of morality as a construct and debates concerning the reliability of its measurement,[65] we must first validate and refine its assessment prior to fully understanding the nature and extent of any such moral enhancement.

University of Plymouth
sylvia.terbeck@plymouth.ac.uk

---

[63] Terbeck, et al., 'Beta-Adrenoceptor Blockade Modulates Fusiform Gyrus Activity to Black versus White Faces', 2951–2958.

[64] Terbeck and Chesterman, 'Will There Ever Be a Drug With No or Negligible Side Effects? Evidence From Neuroscience', 189–194.

[65] Francis, et al., 'Virtual Morality: Transitioning from Moral Judgment to Moral Action', 1–22.

Drugs *and* Hugs: Stimulating Moral Dispositions as a Method of Moral Enhancement

MICHAŁ KLINCEWICZ,[1] LILY EVA FRANK, AND
MARTA SOKÓLSKA[2]

Abstract
Advocates of moral enhancement through pharmacological, genetic, or other direct interventions sometimes explicitly argue, or assume without argument, that traditional moral education and development is insufficient to bring about moral enhancement. Traditional moral education grounded in a Kohlbergian theory of moral development is indeed unsuitable for that task; however, the psychology of moral development and education has come a long way since then. Recent studies support the view that moral cognition is a higher-order process, unified at a functional level, and that a specific moral faculty does not exist. It is more likely that moral cognition involves a number of different mechanisms, each connected to other cognitive and affective processes. Taking this evidence into account, we propose a novel, empirically informed approach to moral development and education, in children and adults, which is based on a cognitive-affective approach to moral dispositions. This is an interpretative approach that derives from the cognitive-affective personality system (Mischel and Shoda, 1995). This conception individuates moral dispositions by reference to the cognitive and affective processes that realise them. Conceived of in this way, moral dispositions influence an agent's behaviour when they interact with situational factors, such as mood or social context. Understanding moral dispositions in this way lays the groundwork for proposing a range of indirect methods of moral enhancement, techniques that promise similar results as direct interventions whilst posing fewer risks.

1. Direct vs Indirect Methods of Moral Enhancement

The viability of the project of enhancing human morality by manipulating our brains with pharmaceuticals or direct brain stimulation (hereafter, "moral bioenhancement") is controversial among

[1] Work on this essay was financed by the Polish National Science Centre (NCN) SONATA 9 Grant, PSP: K/PBD/000139, under decision UMO-2015/17/D/HS1/01705.
[2] All three authors worked equally on this chapter. Parts of it are based on on Marta Sokólska's Master's thesis in cognitive science defended in 2016 at Jagiellonian University: 'Udoskonalenie moralne w świetle nauk kognitywnych' ('Moral Enhancement in the Light of Cognitive Science').

doi:10.1017/S1358246118000437   © The Royal Institute of Philosophy and the contributors 2018
Royal Institute of Philosophy Supplement **83** 2018

philosophers, neuroscientists, and psychologists. However, the motivations for widespread moral enhancement offered by its proponents remain persuasive. Our species may not be morally prepared to deal with rapid technological advance and a changing environment.[3] Traditional non-invasive forms of moral enhancement, such as moral education, but also more structural political and institutional changes, have not been given much attention in the moral enhancement debate, with some exceptions.[4] This is at least in part because the advocates of moral bioenhancement convincingly argue that moral education and other non-invasive means are not potent enough, do not act quickly enough, and have failed to work in the past. But pessimism about the efficacy of noninvasive means of moral enhancement is premature. We critically review promising methods and suggest new ones that take into account developmental psychology, neuroscience, and some themes from current debates in moral psychology.

In section 2 we review evidence that moral cognition[5] is multi-faceted and sketch some of the characteristics of that complexity. In section 3 we outline the cognitive-affective model of moral dispositions, recently articulated by Nancy Snow and Daniel C. Russell, among others. This model fits well with the complex picture of moral cognition discussed in section 2. If this model is plausible, we can then create non-invasive methods of moral enhancement that target moral dispositions of the individual. Section 4 presents recent insights into child development and gives examples of childrearing practices that can positively influence

---

[3] I. Persson and J. Savulescu, 'Unfit for the Future? Human Nature, Scientific Progress, and the Need for Moral Enhancement', in J. Savulescu, R. ter Meulen, and G. Kahane (eds), *Enhancing Human Capacities* (Oxford: Wiley-Blackwell, 2011), 486–500.

[4] See for example: O. Flanagan, *The Geography of Morals: Varieties of Moral Possibility* (Oxford: Oxford University Press, 2016); B. Fröding, *Virtue Ethics and Human Enhancement* (Cham: Springer Science & Business Media, 2012); B. Fröding and W. Osika, *Neuroenhancement: How Mental Training and Meditation Can Promote Epistemic Virtue* (Cham: Springer International Publishing, 2015); R. Powell and A. Buchanan, 'The Evolution of Moral Enhancement', in T. Coady, S. Sanyal, and A. Giubilini (eds), *The Ethics of Human Enhancement: Understanding the Debate* (Oxford: Oxford University Press, 2015).

[5] We use the term "moral cognition" as a shorthand for all the psychological mechanisms that underlie moral behaviour. These include the capacity to have beliefs, emotions, and other mental states or processes, which may but need not be connected to morality. It is important to note that we use these terms without making any commitment to a particular view of moral psychology as inherently cognitive as opposed to affective.

children's moral development. Section 5 gives examples of non-invasive practices for adults that can take advantage of the cognitive-affective model of moral dispositions. Section 6.1 and 6.2 consider objections to our view and our replies.

2. Moral Cognition is Multi-Faceted

There are, broadly speaking, two main contemporary theoretical positions on the nature of moral cognition: the domain-specific and the domain-general approach.[6] Simplifying greatly, the domain-specific approach assumes that there is a psychological mechanism dedicated to moral functioning. The domain-general approach assumes that a dedicated mechanism does not exist and that moral functioning is realised by a number of other mechanisms.

According to the domain-specific approach, the moral mechanism (or module) receives external inputs from, for example, the self, intentions, or predictions about consequences of actions. On the basis of these inputs, the moral mechanism generates a particular moral output: a judgement, a reaction, a behaviour, etc.[7,8] Arguably, the inspiration for this approach is the notion of universal grammar in linguistics and the module that implements it. According to that theory, people acquire and develop their linguistic abilities because they have innate linguistic competencies, which interact with their linguistic environment. The domain-specific approach predicts that there is a similar set of competencies or dispositions to acquire morality.

John Rawls first brought attention to the possibility of applying the sort of arguments one finds supporting the universal grammar approach in linguistics to moral functioning.[9] Mikhail and Hauser take up this idea and argue that an adequate theory of morality will include an account of a computational mechanisms responsible for

[6] L. Young and J. Dungan, 'Where in the Brain is Morality? Everywhere and Maybe Nowhere', *Social Neuroscience* **7**:1 (2012), 1–10.

[7] M. Hauser, F. Cushman, L. Young, R. Kang-Xing Jin, and J. Mikhail, 'A Dissociation Between Moral Judgments and Justifications', *Mind & Language* **22**:1 (2007), 1–21.

[8] J. Mikhail, 'Universal Moral Grammar: Theory, Evidence and the Future', *Trends in Cognitive Sciences* **11**:4 (2007), 143–152.

[9] J. Rawls, *A Theory of Justice* (Cambridge, MA: Harvard University, 1971), 46–47.

bridging the gap between one's perception of an act and one's emotional/cognitive reaction to it and eventual judgement about it.

However, numerous studies that concern moral cognition show that no specific neural structures or neural functions for morality exist.[10] This leads us to the alternative domain-general approach, which is the view that no specific mechanism or module for moral cognition exists. Instead, a number of other mechanisms, such as the mechanisms of reasoning or affect, realise what we characterise as moral cognition.[11,12] This approach is general in the sense that it assumes that moral cognition, moral development, and the process of making moral judgements are unified at a functional level, but not on a biological level.

On the domain-general approach, human morality is likely to be realised by a higher-order cognitive function. If so, then understanding the mechanisms of moral cognition demands an analysis of the relationship between lower-order mechanisms and how they interact to create moral judgements, dispositions, and behaviours at a higher level of psychological organisation.[13,14] Moral cognition on this view is multi-faceted because it is a higher-order domain-general function involving several lower-level functions.

The other relevant feature of moral cognition is that it is affected by many factors, some outside of the moral domain, and often without the individual's awareness.[15] One's social context can impact on one's hierarchy of values, as well as the way in which one orders the

---

[10] For a review see: J. D. Greene, 'The Cognitive Neuroscience of Moral Judgment and Decision Making', in M. S. Gazzaniga (ed.), *The Cognitive Neurosciences*, 5th edn (Cambridge, MA: MIT Press, 2014), 1013–1023. See also J. D. Greene, 'The Rise of Moral Cognition', *Cognition* **135**, 39–42.

[11] J. Moll, R. Zahn, R. de Oliveira-Souza, F. Krueger, and J. Grafman, 'The Neural Basis of Human Moral Cognition', *Nature Reviews Neuroscience* **6**:10 (2005), 799–809.

[12] J. Moll, D. Oliveira-Souza, and R. Zahn, 'The Neural Basis of Moral Cognition', *Annals of the New York Academy of Sciences* **1124**:1 (2008), 161–180.

[13] W. D. Casebeer and P. S. Churchland, 'The Neural Mechanisms of Moral Cognition: A Multiple-Aspect Approach to Moral Judgment and Decision-Making', *Biology and Philosophy* **18**:1 (2003), 169–194.

[14] J. Prinz, 'Is Morality Innate?', in W. Sinnott-Armstrong (ed.), *Moral Psychology*, Vol. 1 (Cambridge, MA: MIT Press, 2008), 367–406.

[15] J. J. Van Bavel, O. Feldman Hall, and P. Mende-Siedlecki, 'The Neuroscience of Moral Cognition: From Dual Processes to Dynamic Systems', *Current Opinion in Psychology* **6** (2015), 167–172.

needs of others and one's own needs.[16] Other experiments demonstrate that moral decisions preceded by conversations that are morally oriented are more likely to result in participants telling the truth than when the conversations are self-oriented.[17]

The third relevant feature of moral cognition is that it varies between individuals[18] and within individuals over time.[19,20] Furthermore, different cognitive mechanisms are crucial in the exercise of moral abilities at different times during human development. While affective structures are the most relevant in children, in adults structures connected to executive control and other higher order processes play a bigger role by integrating information about one's affective reactions with inferences about the mental states of others.[21]

This brief sketch of current empirical research and theoretical approaches to moral cognition and moral development strongly suggests that they involve many disparate mechanisms. Their complexity casts doubt on the idea that a specific pharmacological, neural, or genetic intervention will consistently yield moral enhancement on a wide scale.[22] This is because we cannot confidently state that each

[16] E. Sharma, N. Mazar, A. L. Alter, and D. Ariely, 'Financial Deprivation Selectively Shifts Moral Standards and Compromises Moral Decisions', *Organizational Behavior and Human Decision Processes* **123**:2 (2014), 90–100.
[17] B. C. Gunia, L. Wang, L. I. Huang, J. Wang, and J. K. Murnighan, 'Contemplation and Conversation: Subtle Influences on Moral Decision Making', *Academy of Management Journal* **55**:1 (2012), 13–33.
[18] K. Prehn, I. Wartenburger, K. Mériau, C. Scheibe, O. R. Goodenough, A. Villringer, and H. R. Heekeren, 'Individual Differences in Moral Judgment Competence Influence Neural Correlates of Socio-Normative Judgments', *Social Cognitive and Affective Neuroscience* **3**:1 (2008), 33–46.
[19] W. Edelstein, M. Keller, and E. Schröder, 'Child Development and Social Structure: A Longitudinal Study of Individual Differences', in Paul B. Baltes, David L. Featherman, Richard M. Lerner (eds), *Life-Span Development and Behavior*, Vol. 10 (London: Psychology Press, 2016), 151–185.
[20] R. Svensson, L. J. Pauwels, F. M. Weerman, and G. J. Bruinsma, 'Explaining Individual Changes in Moral Values and Moral Emotions Among Adolescent Boys and Girls: A Fixed-Effects Analysis', *European Journal of Criminology* **14**:3 (2017), 290–308.
[21] J. Decety and L. H. Howard, 'The Role of Affect in the Neurodevelopment of Morality', *Child Development Perspectives* **7**:1 (2013), 49–54, 49.
[22] H. Wiseman, *The Myth of the Moral Brain: The Limits of Moral Enhancement* (Cambridge, MA: MIT Press, 2016).

individual's cognitive and affective systems will be identically impacted by an intervention. The system that underlies moral cognition is unlike the serotonin reuptake system which can be predictably modulated by an appropriate intervention.

3. The Cognitive-Affective Conception of Moral Dispositions

If moral cognition is a domain-general, higher-order, dynamic faculty, influenced by a variety of non-moral factors, then it is also difficult to accept the existence of permanent moral traits. People are not morally good, morally bad, honest, or cowardly, and so on, except in particular situations. If that is true, then moral enhancement should not aim at improving moral traits, but other, more general faculties or at improving the environment itself. Limiting situational factors that contribute to immoral behaviour may be the best way towards moral enhancement.

This line of thinking is advanced in the situationist challenge to the existence of moral virtues.[23,24] Situationists rely on evidence from cognitive and social psychology, citing experiments that show our judgements and behaviours come under the influence of unconscious processes and situational factors.[25] Mark Alfano created a taxonomy of the kinds of factors that interfere with moral judgement and behaviour: 'bad reasons, situational non-reasons, and non-moral individual differences' and identifies situational non-reasons as the most troubling for the existence of moral character traits.[26] These are factors like ambient smells, sounds, and mood.[27] This evidence undermines the vision of a thoughtful moral reasoner weighing her options and also seems to undermine the classic virtue ethics picture of the individual's virtues responsible for consistent behaviour across a range of situations.

On the other hand, there is also a growing body of research critiquing situationism and the situationist interpretation of the relevant

[23] G. Harman, 'Skepticism About Character Traits', *The Journal of Ethics* **13**:2/3 (2009), 235–242.

[24] J. M. Doris, *Lack of Character: Personality and Moral Behaviour* (Cambridge: Cambridge University Press, 2002).

[25] C. A. Anderson, W. E. Deuser, and K. M. DeNeve, 'Hot Temperatures, Hostile Affect, Hostile Cognition, and Arousal: Tests of a General Model of Affective Aggression', *Personality and Social Psychology Bulletin* **21**:5 (1995), 434–448.

[26] M. Alfano, *Character as Moral Fiction* (Cambridge: Cambridge University Press, 2013), 40.

[27] Alfano, *Character as Moral Fiction*, 44–46.

experiments.[28] The upshot of this research can be simplified as follows. Firstly, some people, even under external pressure or conditions which tend to stimulate immoral acts, choose the action considered moral nonetheless. Secondly, moral dispositions should not be understood merely in behavioural terms, that is, as behaviour that is recurrent in a specific type of situation. Instead, moral dispositions should be understood as abilities that allow the individual to interpret and to adapt to situations in appropriate ways.

Drawing similar conclusions, Snow,[29] Russell,[30] and Natasza Szutta[31] advocate a theory of moral traits as a subset of personality traits in the cognitive-affective personality system (CAPS).[32] CAPS characterises personality traits as dispositions that are the effect of longitudinal interactions between endogenous factors (mood, beliefs, etc.) and exogenous factors (situation, context, etc.). On this view, dispositions are constitutive parts of one's personality and mediate interaction with exogenous factors. One's personality traits are expressed in the constant interaction of individual and situational factors, where that expression exhibits relatively stable patterns of behaviour across situations.

Szutta (2015) argues that CAPS accords with the observation that most people are relatively consistent in their behaviour, if we take into consideration their distinctive cognitive-affective system and the way

28   S. Arjoon, 'Ethical Decision-Making: A Case for the Triple Font Theory', *Journal of Business Ethics* **71**:4 (2007), 395–410; E. J. Wielenberg, 'Saving Character', *Ethical Theory and Moral Practice* **9**:4 (2006), 461–491; J. J. Kupperman, 'The Indispensability of Character', *Philosophy* **76**:2 (2001), 239–250; R. Kamtekar, 'Situationism and Virtue Ethics on the Content of Our Character', *Ethics* **114**:3 (2004), 458–491; E. S. Radcliffe, 'Moral Naturalism and the Possibility of Making Ourselves Better', in B. K. Wilburn (ed.), *Moral Cultivation: Essays on the Development of Character and Virtue* (London: Rowman & Littlefield, 2010), 101–24; J. Sabini and M. Silver, 'Lack of Character? Situationism Critiqued', *Ethics* **115**:3 (2005), 535–562; G. Sreenivasan, 'The Situationist Critique of Virtue Ethics', in D. C. Russell (ed.), *The Cambridge Companion to Virtue Ethics* (Cambridge: Cambridge University Press, 2013), 290–314.
29   N. E. Snow, *Virtue as Social Intelligence: An Empirically Grounded Theory* (Abingdon: Routledge, 2010).
30   Daniel C. Russell, *Practical Intelligence and the Virtues* (Oxford: Oxford University Press, 2009).
31   N. Szutta and A. Szutta (eds), *W poszukiwaniu moralnego charakteru*, Vol.1 (Lublin: Wydawnictwo Academicon, 2015).
32   W. Mischel and Y. Shoda, 'A Cognitive-Affective System Theory of Personality: Reconceptualizing Situations, Dispositions, Dynamics, and Invariance in Personality Structure', *Psychological Review* **102**:2 (1995), 246–268.

Michał Klincewicz, *et al.*

they construe their own situation. For example, consider the case of imposter syndrome.[33] Kate, a hypothetical woman suffering from it, is an intelligent person, but also extremely insecure. She was often criticised by her parents as a child and young adult, and her society discriminates against women. From the perspective of an external observer, it appears that Kate does not have much to say. But when we learn about her past and her fears, it becomes difficult to view her behaviour in the same way: now we know she suffers from imposter syndrome, which can be understood as a trait. Attributing this trait to Kate allows us to make better sense of her behaviour and make better predictions about her.

Generalising, personality traits can be characterised by "if... then..." profiles of behaviour, which are relatively stable, but situationally dependent. Just as we can say solubility in water is a property of salt, we can call the relatively stable patterns of human moral behaviour traits, without having to say much about what underlies them. When human behaviour is inconsistent (as it often is), the trait remains. This consistent with Snow who argues that 'social-cognitivists stress the importance that the meanings of situations have for people, and claim that evidence of personality coherence can be found by paying attention to those meanings'.[34]

Returning to Kate, consider the following generalisation about her: when she is around people who she thinks will criticise her and threaten her sense of security, her characteristic way of reacting in these situations will be activated, and she will stay silent. However, when she feels comfortable, for example, among her close friends, she is not afraid to give her opinion, because there is nothing that triggers her insecurity. Nonetheless, her imposter syndrome remains.

So much is suggested by the one of the original Mischel and Shoda experiments that grounds CAPS. The experiment, conducted at a residential summer camp for children, investigated, among other things, the situations in which specific behaviours occur. Their aim was to capture psychological features, such as the subject's attitude toward specific circumstances, that triggered the behaviour. They observed the children's behaviours 'on selected dimensions' (e.g., verbal aggression, withdrawal, friendly, prosocial behaviour) and then made predictions about patterns in children's behaviour,

---

[33]   John Kolligian, Jr and Robert J. Sternberg, 'Perceived Fraudulence in Young Adults: Is There an "Imposter Syndrome"?', *Journal of Personality Assessment* **56**:2 (1991), 308–326.
[34]   Snow, *Virtue as Social Intelligence: An Empirically Grounded Theory*, 38.

based on an individual 'profile of situation-behaviour relation-ships'.[35] These profiles were accurate predictors of the ways children reacted in various situations. Their behavioural responses depended on the child's interpretation of their situation and were consistent with their "if...then..." patterns of reacting.

These sorts of results demonstrate that making generalisations about patterns of behaviour by attributing traits has significant predictive power. In the same way, before we knew the chemical composition of salt, we could still predict how it would "behave" by attributing to it a certain trait. If salt is put into water and it does not dissolve, this does not mean that salt lacks the relevant trait. The situation may have changed and something may be preventing the trait from ex-pressing itself. If we know enough about the situation we may also be able to predict that salt will not dissolve, though we cannot explain why it will not in terms of the relevant chemical reaction.

In similar vein, Snow argues that CAPS captures local personality traits which can be characterised as "virtues" and "flaws". Further, she argues that personality traits can become more global and can be developed through individual conscious reflection. For example, when Kate realises that she feels very sorry for impoverished children in her town, she can ask herself why she does not have the same feel-ings toward children in other regions, who are significantly worse off. Resulting from this reflection, she decides to give more attention to the suffering of distant children. She may then notice the common, morally relevant features shared by all suffering children.

According to Snow, desirable traits can also be developed by limit-ing related vices. This is corroborated by Patricia Devine and Margo Monteith's research on methods for decreasing the influence of nega-tive stereotypes in the individual.[36,37] Their research on the Behavioural Inhibition System makes sense of cases in which it is possible to change stereotypical thinking through inhibition of inter-mediary processes, such as negative thoughts and emotions related to the stereotype. The goal is to stop stereotypical behaviour and let one act with more self-awareness in line with one's updated beliefs.

---

[35] Mischel and Shoda, 'A Cognitive-Affective System Theory of Personality', 249.

[36] M. J. Monteith, J. W. Sherman, and P. G. Devine, 'Suppression as a Stereotype Control Strategy', *Personality and Social Psychology Review* **2**:1 (1998), 63–82.

[37] P. G. Devine and M. J. Monteith, 'Automaticity and Control in Stereotyping', in Shelly Chaiken and Yaacov Trope (eds), *Dual-Process Theories in Social Psychology* (New York: Guildford Press, 1999), 339–360.

It is easy to generate examples of this practice. For instance, someone who was raised in an environment where one ethnic group was discriminated against will likely end up with the disposition to behaviourally express negative stereotypes about this group. However, if Snow is right, she can change her attitude, if she consciously aims to rid herself of stereotypical reactions.

Snow refers to these practices as cultivation of moral virtue. Bracketing the notion of virtue, understood as a moral quality of a person, we can treat cultivation as a method of enhancement of traits. Traits can be developed and improved over time with the sort of deliberate practices that Snow suggests, even if we completely abandon the idea of virtues as they feature in context of virtue ethics.

Snow also points out that it is possible to develop traits intentionally and automate moral behaviour though automatic goal-dependent actions; these actions are voluntarily initiated and lead to a definite goal. While the goal activation is unconscious, the reactions themselves are both intelligent and situationally sensitive. Snow connects this research to the concept of virtue, but it seems equally justified to connect it to the notion of moral dispositions, as we have used it here. Returning to to Kate, she feels compassion toward poor children and consciously decides to help them. Helping becomes her goal and over time whenever she sees an impoverished child she thinks about how best to help. In other words, she intentionally developed a context-sensitive disposition that eventually becomes automatic.

All of these presented ways are good examples of how to make local CAPS traits global, in the sense of expanding the contexts in which they manifest. This process will involve, if this research is right, at least some conscious reflection or deliberate choice of a goal. This is why Snow's proposal, for example, is likely to work best for adults in whom higher cognitive functions such as reasoning or cognitive control are more developed, but not for young children, whose abstract thinking ability is limited.

Snow and Russell use CAPS as a rebuttal to the situationist challenge to virtue ethics and as an example of a new and improved way of talking about moral personality traits, which is consistent with the empirical evidence marshalled by situationists. Their approach is a significant improvement on the classic virtue ethics approach at least in part because it has the benefit of making sense of people acting morally in relatively consistent ways across a variety of situations, while at the same capturing the insight that these traits are highly context sensitive.

Their view is also an improvement over the approaches to moral enhancement open to situationists. A situationist would argue that the way to improve morally would be to change the situations in which people find themselves. In other words, the focus should be on moral technologies that improve the environment and not technologies and interventions that target moral agents and their dispositions or traits. This approach intentionally ignores the idea of stable traits.

If CAPS is an improvement on the traditional conceptualisation of traits, we can take advantage of it to find strategies for improvement of the agent. But we take a more cautious approach than the virtue ethicists just mentioned and remain as neutral as possible in their debate with situationists. For us, CAPS is a good guide to the *mechanisms* that are potential candidates for targeted non-invasive methods of moral enhancement.

The key to our model is identification of traits (A, B, and C in Figure 1). It should be emphasised that on our view traits are not qualities of the person or virtues in the classical sense. Traits are characterisations of context-sensitive dispositions, which, in turn, are realised in particular individuals in particular ways. This means that, to some extent, they are useful fictions.

However, unlike mere fictions, understanding their complex relationships can tell us a lot about potential non-invasive strategies for individual moral enhancement. On our view, the best non-invasive strategies of enhancement are going to focus on components of moral cognition that are relevant to the realisation of dispositions. Interventions should start early, with child development. This is the first set of strategies we consider.

4. Child Development and Moral Cognition

There are significant differences in the processing of morally-laden stimuli in children and adults. Jean Decety and Lauren Howard's line of research sheds light on the relationship between particular emotions, motivations, and other types of neural activation in people exposed to morally laden stimuli.[38] Their results suggest that affect is key in early development and that higher order cognitive mechanisms, such as cognitive control and response inhibition, have greater influence in adults. This yields an important insight: higher-order cognitive abilities have a larger role in adults, whose patterns of processing emotions are different.

Supporting this view, Decety and Howard point to research on what may be described as precursors of moral dispositions in

[38] J. Decety and L. H. Howard, 'The Role of Affect in the Neurodevelopment of Morality', *Child Development Perspectives* 7:1 (2013), 49–54.

Cognitive-Affective Personality System (CAPS)

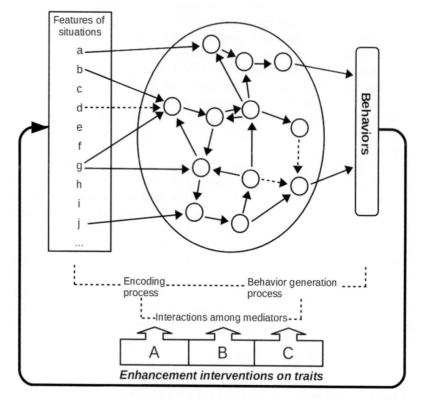

Figure 1. (Adopted from Mischel and Shoda, 1995.) Simplified illustration of types of cognitive-affective mediating processes that generate an individual's distinctive behaviour patterns. Non-invasive enhancement interventions on traits A, B, and C aim at strengthening or inhibiting interactions among mediating units, which together comprise a stable network of relations that characterise an individual.

infants. In early development affective mechanisms play a key role with relatively little involvement of cognitive mechanisms, which at that time, are under-developed. Bandstra, et al. demonstrate that young children display a much higher level of personal distress when witnessing someone's sadness than older children. Older children display higher levels of sympathy than personal distress.[39]

[39] N. F. Bandstra, C. T. Chambers, P. J. McGrath and C. Moore, 'The Behavioural Expression of Empathy to Others' Pain Versus Others' Sadness in Young Children', *Pain* **152**:5 (2011), 1074–1082.

This is one example, among many, of the ways that development of aspects of childrens' social cognition is connected to the rate of maturation of the prefrontal cortex. Again, it reinforces that moral cognition is not based on any morally-specific neural structures, but is rather an integrative cognitive function. It further shows that stimulating moral cognition in children should focus on mediating factors that are anatomically and functionally different from those that underlie moral abilities in adults.

Furthermore, in young children (4–8 years old) there is stronger (than in adults) functional connectivity between ventromedial prefrontal cortex (vmPFC) and the brainstem, whereas in 18–25 year-olds, functional connectivity is stronger between vmPFC and posterior superior temporal sulcus/amygdala. The idea that emotions play a key role in moral development in the early life is supported by evidence of greater activation of parts of brain regions responsible for affect at younger ages. This is corroborated by lesion studies, which show that early damage to the vmPFC and amygdala cause much more significant problems in processing morally-laden stimuli than similar damage later in life.[40,41] In sum, this research confirms the platitude that emotional development early in life is crucial for moral functioning later in life.

Caregivers and children's relation to them play also an important role in moral development.[42,43] For example, in families with a higher level of emotional warmth, children are more altruistic.[44] Inconsistent child-rearing strategies leads to depression, anxiety, lowered social abilities, or aggression.[45] Attitudes of the parents

[40] P. Shaw, E. J. Lawrence, C. Radbourne, J. Bramham, C. E. Polkey, and A. S. David, 'The Impact of Early and Late Damage to the Human Amygdala on "Theory of Mind" Reasoning', *Brain* **127**:7 (2004), 1535–1548.

[41] S. W. Anderson, A. Bechara, H. Damasio, D. Tranel, and A. R. Damasio, 'Impairment of Social and Moral Behaviour Related to Early Damage in Human Prefrontal Cortex', *Nature Neuroscience* **2**:11 (1999), 1032–1037.

[42] M. Christen and D. Narvaez, 'Moral Development in Early Childhood is Key for Moral Enhancement', *AJOB Neuroscience* **3**:4 (2012), 25–26.

[43] J. M. Cowell and J. Decety, 'Precursors to Morality in Development as a Complex Interplay Between Neural, Socioenvironmental, and Behavioural Facets', *Proceedings of the National Academy of Sciences* **112**: 41 (2015), 12657–12662.

[44] G. H. Brody and D. R. Shaffer, 'Contributions of Parents and Peers to Children's Moral Socialisation', *Developmental Review* **2**:1 (1982), 31–75.

[45] A. Schore, 'Bowlby's "Environment of Evolutionary Adaptedness": Recent Studies on the Interpersonal Neurobiology of Attachment and

and their engagement and reactivity to their child's behaviour, help develop a sense of conscience, and result in a higher likelihood of the child developing proper moral attitudes.

There are also practices that may help in the development of particular traits: breastfeeding for empathy, immediate response to the child's needs for conscience, touch for control of one's behaviour, letting the mother stay with the child right after birth for self-regulation, play for lowering aggression, and parental support for resistance to stress.[46] Additionally parental attitudes and values play an important role because of the attitudes they convey to the child. Overall, value transmission from parent to child seems to be the result of multifarious interactions.

None of the processes that have an effect on a child's personality development are likely to occur in isolation from others, and are probably best understood as biology and environment dynamically interacting. On the one hand, innate emotional and cognitive predispositions are important in some models of interaction between the parent and the child. On the other hand, the environment is equally important. Relevant work done on moral technologies, technologies for behaviour change, nudges, etc. is useful. In sum, unlike direct, biomedical methods of moral enhancement, those grounded in education and the early-life shaping of moral attitudes and their character allow for a more nuanced and individualised approach.

5. Non-Invasive Methods of Moral Enhancement in Adults and Older Children

Targeted moral improvement in adults by non-invasive means can take many forms.[47] One particularly promising method focusses on affective perspective taking, sometimes considered to be constitutive of empathy.[48] One strategy for improving affective perspective taking is reading fiction, which increases the ability to understand others'

Emotional Development', in D. Narvaez, J. Panksepp, A. Schore, and T. Gleason (eds), *Evolution, Early Experience and Human Development* (New York: Oxford University Press, 2013) 31–67.

[46] Christen and Narvaez, 'Moral Development in Early Childhood', 25.

[47] For example: D. Narvaez and T. Bock, 'Developing Ethical Expertise and Moral Personalities', *Handbook of Moral and Character Education* (Abingdon: Routledge, 2014), 140–158.

[48] J. Decety and J. M. Cowell, 'The Complex Relation Between Morality and Empathy', *Trends in Cognitive Sciences* **18**:7 (2014), 337–339.

Drugs *and* Hugs

mental states and increases empathic concern.[49] The mediating mechanism that underlies development of these traits is likely to be theory of mind (ToM).[50] Reading is an effective part of programmes aimed at promoting social skills, treating personality disorders, and increasing empathy among groups ranging from prisoners to medical students and physicians.[51] In prisons the role of books in improving ToM skills can have a significant impact on inmates' rehabilitation. At the same time other art-forms, such as films and theatre, may similarly facilitate empathy and identification with the experiences of others.[52,53]

Another possible non-invasive method of moral enhancement is Forum Theatre – a version of the Theatre of the Oppressed.[54] In Forum Theatre the play is always presented twice – the first time to show "anti-model", which embodies the morally, politically, or socially problematic and oppressive state of affairs and the second time to give the audience an opportunity to react and intervene. Audience members can stop the performance and present their own solution to the conflict presented on stage.

What is crucial in Forum Theatre is that the division between the audience and the performers is partially erased. The spectators can at

[49] D. Carr, 'On the Contribution of Literature and the Arts to the Educational Cultivation of Moral Virtue, Feeling and Emotion', *Journal of Moral Education* **34**:2 (2005), 137–151; D. R. Johnson, G. K. Cushman, L. A. Borden, and M. S. McCune, 'Potentiating Empathic Growth: Generating Imagery While Reading Fiction Increases Empathy and Prosocial Behaviour', *Psychology of Aesthetics, Creativity, and the Arts* **7**:3 (2013), 306–312.

[50] D. C. Kidd and E. Castano, 'Reading Literary Fiction Improves Theory of Mind', *Science* **342**:6156 (2013), 377–380.

[51] J. Billington, '"Reading for Life": Prison Reading Groups in Practice and Theory', *Critical Survey* **23**:3 (2011), 67–85; J. Billington, E. Longden, and J. Robinson, 'A Literature-Based Intervention for Women Prisoners: Preliminary Findings', *International Journal of Prisoner Health* **12**:4 (2016), 230–243; J. F. Shapiro, 'Using Literature and the Arts to Develop Empathy in Medical Students', in F. D. T. Farrow and P. Woodruff (eds), *Empathy in Mental Illness* (Cambridge: Cambridge University Press, 2007), 473–494.

[52] J. M. Reilly, J. Trial, D. E. Piver, and P. B. Schaff, 'Using Theater to Increase Empathy Training in Medical Students', *Journal for Learning Through the Arts: A Research Journal on Arts Integration in Schools and Communities* **8**:1 (2012): https://escholarship.org/uc/item/68x7949t.

[53] A. Eisenberg, S. Rosenthal, and Y. R. Schlussel, 'Medicine as a Performing Art: What We Can Learn About Empathic Communication from Theater Arts', *Academic Medicine* **90**:3 (2015), 272–276.

[54] Augusto Boal, 'Theatre of the Oppressed', trans. by Charles A. McBride and Maria-Odilia Leal McBride (New York: Theatre Communication Group, 1985), 144–45.

any point become the actors, replacing an actor currently on stage.[55] The audience is invited to engage in affective perspective-taking. They are asked to broaden their point of view and consequently their concern for other, sometimes very different, people.

Forum Theatre has been shown to be very effective in developing the relevant attitudes towards victims of sexual assault in an empirical study on 561 students, which

> showed that the participants exposed to [a Forum Theatre] performance, in comparison to a sexual assault lecture and a control group, reported greater perceived self-efficacy in: perspective taking, emotional contagion, empathic concern, and comforting behavior toward potential sexually assault survivors.[56]

Extensive evaluation studies in other domains are not available, but it seems reasonable to expect that being involved in a scene, and becoming an oppressed character on stage may trigger the relevant mechanism of perspective taking in general. This rate of success likely generalises to other domains from issues of sexual assault.

The other capacity that can be influenced through Forum Theatre is an ability to notice morally relevant problems in daily life and to react in the best possible ways. Again, it is important to emphasise that this method was not evaluated scientifically; however, its form suggests that it could be an appropriate tool for enhancement of particular components of moral cognition. It is also safe to assume that this method can be modified to focus on specific moral problems, such as environmental degradation or global poverty.

There is some reason to think that stimulating empathy inhibits aggressive behaviours and elicits altruism.[57] This idea has been successfully applied in childhood education[58] and in prison rehabilitation programmes.[59] In some classrooms, for instance, children care for

[55]   The Forum Project: http://theforumproject.org/whatistoforumtheatre/.
[56]   J. I. Rodríguez, et al. 'Assessing the Impact of Augusto Boal's "Proactive Performance": An Embodied Approach for Cultivating Prosocial Responses to Sexual Assault', *Text and Performance Quarterly* **26**:3 (2006), 229–252, 245.
[57]   C. Zahn-Waxler and M. Radke-Yarrow, 'The Origins of Empathic Concern', *Motivation and Emotion* **14**:2 (1990), 107–130.
[58]   B. Daly and S. Suggs, 'Teachers' Experiences with Humane Education and Animals in the Elementary Classroom: Implications for Empathy Development', *Journal of Moral Education* **39**:1 (2010), 101–112.
[59]   R. Kohl and A. Wenner, *State Comparison of Life Sentenced Inmates* (Milford, MA: Massachusetts Department of Correction, Office of Strategic Planning and Research, 2012).

and interact with a pet, encouraging them to develop a sense of responsibility for the creature's well-being. When pets are also subjects of discussion empathy for the animals is stimulated.[60]

In a growing number of prison programmes inmates have an opportunity to care for an animal: for example, service dog training.[61] In the Wild Horse Inmate Program,[62] supervised prisoners train and gently break wild horses. The bond this creates with a horse increases the inmates' empathic concern and sense of responsibility, in addition to giving them practical skills.[63]

One reason to think that animals are useful in moral development programmes is evidence that many overlapping brain-regions are activated while looking pictures of humans *and* animals in distress.[64] Creating and maintaining a relationship with an animal positively affects the development of empathy in children.[65] This confirms the link between aggressive behaviours toward animals in childhood and similar behaviours toward other people later in life.[66] Aggression levels are negatively correlated with empathy levels, so that a person with a higher level of empathy will be less inclined to hurt others.[67]

---

[60] Daly and Suggs, 'Teachers' Experiences with Humane Education', 105–106.

[61] C. Deaton, 'Humanizing Prisons with Animals: A Closer Look at "Cell Dogs" and Horse Programs in Correctional Institutions', *Journal of Correctional Education*, 46–62.

[62] Colorado Correctional Industries, 'Wild Horse Inmate Program': https://www.coloradoci.com/serviceproviders/whip/.

[63] Arizona Correctional Industries, 'Wild Horse Program': https://aci.az.gov/wild-horse-program/.

[64] R. G. Franklin, Jr, A. J. Nelson, M. Baker, J. E. Beeney, T. K. Vescio, A. Lenz-Watson, and R. B. Adams, Jr, 'Neural Responses to Perceiving Suffering in Humans and Animals', *Social Neuroscience* 8:3 (2013), 217–227.

[65] Thompson, Gullone, Daly, and Suggs refer to the project of *humane education* which focusses on issues such as social justice and citizenship and which is meant to encourage people to respect and be compassionate toward all beings, human and nonhuman, and to take into consideration the environment and its welfare. However, the benefits of using pets, presented by the mentioned authors, make it an interesting method also for moral education, which are not directly connected to *humane education* in its original presentation. See notes 68 and 69 for full citations.

[66] M. Robin and R. T. Bensel, 'Pets and the Socialization of Children', *Marriage & Family Review* 8:3/4 (1985), 63–78.

[67] P. A. Miller and N. Eisenberg, 'The Relation of Empathy to Aggressive and Externalizing/Antisocial Behaviour', *Psychological Bulletin* **103**:3 (1988), 324–344.

There is also evidence of the impact that interaction with an animal has on emotional development and empathic concern.[68] Most teachers who had classes incorporating animals observed higher levels of empathy and faster socio-emotional development.[69] However, there is no systematic research on the effectiveness of animal use in rehabilitation programmes.[70] What we have is anecdotal evidence from prison staff and inmates, who are overwhelmingly positive about using animals as components of rehabilitation.

6.1. Objections and Replies: Cognitive Demands

One should note that Russell, Szutta, and Snow's application of the CAPS system to moral traits has been subject to various criticisms,[71] to which virtue ethicists have responded.[72] The debate is by no means over. Since we do not adopt an interpretation of traits as moral virtues, but merely treat traits as guides to an individual's components of moral cognition, we will not address these objections here, save one concerning self-control and integrity, raised by Laura Papish.[73]

Papish points out that a central ingredient in Snow's account of the development of virtue is the claim that humans desire internal mental and emotional consistency in moral and non-moral matters,

[68] K. L. Thompson and E. Gullone, 'Promotion of Empathy and Prosocial Behaviour in Children Through Humane Education', *Australian Psychologist* **38**:3 (2003), 175–182.

[69] B. Daly and S. Suggs, 'Teachers' Experiences with Humane Education and Animals in the Elementary Classroom: Implications for Empathy Development', *Journal of Moral Education* **39**:1 (2010), 101–112.

[70] R. Kohl and A. Wenner, *State Comparison of Life Sentenced Inmates* (Milford, MA: Massachusetts Department of Correction, Office of Strategic Planning and Research, 2012).

[71] M. Alfano and D. Russell, 'Review of "Practical Intelligence and the Virtues"', *Ethical Theory and Moral Practice* **16**:3, 671–673; C. Miller, 'Does the CAPS Model Improve Our Understanding of Personality and Character?', in J. Webber and A. Masala (eds), *From Personality to Virtue* (Oxford: Oxford University Press, 2016), 155–185.

[72] R. West, 'Virtue Ethics is Empirically Adequate: A Defense of the CAPS Response to Situationism', *Pacific Philosophical Quarterly* **99**:S1 (2018), 79–111.

[73] L. Papish 'CAPS Psychology and the Empirical Adequacy of Aristotelian Virtue Ethics', *Ethical Theory and Moral Practice* **20**:3 (2017), 537–549.

yet it is not obvious that people actually have such a desire. Our ability to act in ways that are inconsistent with our values is evident even in participants of the Milgram experiment who report being very disturbed and distressed by their own behaviour as they shocked the learners. Our everyday experiences of inner moral conflict also suggest that we are actually fairly comfortable maintaining moral conflicts. If that is the case, then any theory that assumes that we aim at coherent moral integration in our moral lives depends on a questionable assumption about moral psychology.

Furthermore, suppose that we do value integration and that we are capable of achieving it, contrary to evidence that we do not and that we often cannot. If so, then we would move towards a morally praiseworthy personality trait (or virtue) only if we revise and integrate it in the right way. For example, we choose to try to rid ourselves of negative stereotypes rather than the egalitarian values with which they conflict. This also means, as Papish points out, that we have to count on people holding some set of morally right beliefs in the first place. Unfortunately, this may be an unreasonable assumption about anyone and difficult to verify, even if true.

This line of objection is relevant to our use of the CAPS model to inform indirect moral enhancement methods in the following ways: 1) if we do not strive for integrated moral personalities, then some of the methods suggested may not be effective, and 2) if we do strive for integrated moral personalities, then moral enhancement will depend on individuals holding at least some morally right beliefs to begin with and working towards an integration with those, which we cannot depend on happening.

Our first response is to concede to point (1). Conscious self-reflection and a motivation to have a consistent moral personality are prerequisites for strategies initiated by the individual, as in the case of Kate who holds stereotypes. These are unlikely to work without conscious self-reflection and the relevant motivation. However, we further point out that these methods explicitly endorsed by Snow and others are not a part of all the indirect methods we suggest.

Early childhood interventions, participatory theatre, reading fiction, and animal therapy do not demand conscious self-reflection on one's moral beliefs or a motivation to have an integrated moral personality. Instead, these methods focus on the mediating mechanisms that underlie moral dispositions. For example, on developing the capacity to take the perspective of others through enactment in Forum Theatre or on developing empathic concern by gently

347

breaking horses. Engaging in these practices morally enhances an individual indirectly, by improving capacities that underlie moral cognition in general.

This still leaves point (2) which suggests some limits to our proposal that Papish's objections bring into relief. Indirect methods are unlikely to be effective in changing moral dispositions of people with personalities constituted mostly by traits that dispose them to act immorally. This is perhaps also why it is good to be cautious about the standalone potential of indirect methods. The most successful moral enhancement programme would include the widest possible range of techniques, including indirect methods, but also potentially, pharmacological, neural, and genetic interventions.

6.2. Objections and Replies: Identifying Mediating Mechanisms

On our view, names of moral traits are understood to be useful shorthand labels for underlying moral dispositions realised by a complex interplay of cognitive and affective mechanisms. Indirect moral enhancement targets psychological and biological mechanisms that underlie those dispositions. This creates an epistemic problem for our view: it is not clear how to determine when and why particular mechanisms should be targeted.

The glib answer to this objection is: it depends. The serious answer is twofold. First, there are ways to categorise groups that can help determine the appropriate target for an indirect intervention. Second, there are also ways to account for relevant individual differences in moral cognition.

Some group selection criteria were already mentioned in this chapter. For example, children below a certain age will be ideal targets for interventions that focus on affect and processing of affective stimuli. Adults may be better suited for strategies that rely on conscious self-reflection. People with particular personalities are potential target groups.[74] Particularly useful here may be research into personality traits that compose the so-called Dark Triad, which underlies much of what is typically considered immoral

---

[74]   Avshalom Caspi, et al., 'Personality Differences Predict Health-Risk Behaviours in Young Adulthood', *Journal of Personality and Social Psychology* **73**:5 (1997), 1052–1063.

behaviour.[75] Individuals can also be distinguished from one another based on aspects of their personality, elements of their cognition, or even features of their learning styles.[76]

This goes some way toward answering the objection, but nowhere near fully. Group differences and individual differences in context of moral cognition, with an eye to biological and cognitive mechanisms, are not typically studied in the context of possible interventions. However, this information is not impossible to get in principle and nothing stands in the way of this research being carried out.

7. Conclusion

Advocates of moral bioenhancement via invasive means aim to find the best interventions, but as they are well aware, existing methods are on their own inadequate and offer only directions for future research. There is, for example, some evidence of selective serotonin reuptake inhibitors (SSRIs) reducing aggressive attitudes and increasing willingness to co-operate for common goals, and also evidence of oxytocin increasing in-group trust and competence in ToM tasks.[77] Such methods carry with them side-effects, which differ across individuals. SSRIs, for example, may weaken episodic and long-term memory performance and oxytocin may lower the performance of the amygdala and lower fear-responses to potentially dangerous stimuli.

It could turn out that indirect methods, such as those we discuss here, are more effective than moral bioenhancement. But if we are serious about moral enhancement, we should consider all possible interventions, even the direct ones. Whatever problems moral bioenhancement may have, it may become more effective if supplemented with indirect methods. Looking forward, the idea that we can morally improve and enhance individuals by indirect

---

[75] Bianca Bertl, et al., 'More or Less than the Sum of its Parts? Mapping the Dark Triad of Personality Onto a Single Dark Core', *Personality and Individual Differences* **114** (2017), 140–144.

[76] David F. Bjorklund and Kayla B. Causey, *Children's Thinking: Cognitive Development and Individual Differences* (Thousand Oaks, CA: SAGE Publications, 2017).

[77] R. De Jongh, I. Bolt, M. Schermer, and B. Olivier, 'Botox for the Brain: Enhancement of Cognition, Mood and Pro-Social Behaviour and Blunting of Unwanted Memories', *Neuroscience & Biobehavioral Reviews* **32**:4 (2008), 760–776.

methods with an eye to biological factors leaves much room for exploration and experimentation.

Institute of Philosophy, Cognitive Science, Jagiellonian University
michal.klincewicz@uj.edu.pl
Ethics and Philosophy, Technical University, Eindhoven
l.e.frank@tue.nl
Institute of Philosophy, Cognitive Science, Jagiellonian University
sokolska.marta@gmail.com

An Unfit Future: Moral Enhancement and Technological Harm

LEWIS COYNE

Abstract

This essay addresses two aspects of Persson and Savulescu's case for moral enhancement: 1) the precise technological nature of ultimate harm, particularly as it applies to the ecological crisis, and 2) what is at stake in the solution they propose. My claim is that Persson and Savulescu's treatment of both issues is inadequate: the ecological crisis is a more complex phenomenon than they suppose, and more is at stake in moral enhancement than they claim. To make my case I draw on the work of Hans Jonas, who presciently and insightfully dealt with related questions. Jonas' philosophy unites bioethical, technological, and environmental concerns and so offers a useful contrast to Persson and Savulescu's proposal. If my analysis is correct then we have both practical and principled reasons to be sceptical about the prospect of moral bioenhancement, which I assume, for the sake of argument, to be feasible.[1]

1. Introduction

I shall start with the question of technology. Persson and Savulescu argue that modern scientific technology poses the threat of 'Ultimate Harm', namely, 'forever destroying life on Earth' or at least 'making *worthwhile* life forever impossible on this planet'.[2] This discrepancy will become relevant later on. They identify nuclear warfare and anthropogenic climate change as the principal sources of this danger, but also mention a variety of other cases such as biological and chemical weapons.[3] Persson and Savulescu speculate that the mid-twentieth century represented a turning point in human history as we acquired the capacity through nuclear technology to cause ultimate harm, which until then would have been 'wildly implausible'.[4] Equally, they note that around the same

---

[1] I use "moral enhancement" and "moral bioenhancement" interchangeably throughout, as, for reasons that shall become apparent, I do not accept the claim that education can be understood as part of the former.

[2] Ingmar Persson and Julian Savulescu, *Unfit for the Future: The Need for Moral Enhancement* (Oxford: Oxford University Press, 2012), 133, 10, 46 (my emphasis).

[3] Persson and Savulescu, *Unfit for the Future*, 48–51.

[4] Persson and Savulescu, *Unfit for the Future*, 126.

doi:10.1017/S1358246118000449　　©The Royal Institute of Philosophy and the contributors 2018

Royal Institute of Philosophy Supplement **83** 2018　　　　　351

time 'catastrophic degradation of the environment had not yet gained momentum'.[5] For this reason they claim that technological development from that point on might be regarded as for the worse, all things considered.[6]

Of the two main cases I will focus on the ecological crisis, although much of what I have to say below about technology in that context also applies to nuclear warfare.[7] The key difference between the two is that nuclear harm does not necessarily follow from modern industrial civilisation: despite many nation states having the technological and economic capacity for nuclear armament, just nine are in possession of deployable warheads.[8] This is more than enough to bring about ultimate harm through nuclear warfare – a possibility encouraged by the particular designs of the weapons systems – but armament is not itself an inevitability. Persson and Savulescu's associated concern is that a suicidal terrorist group could either commandeer an existing nuclear weapons systems or develop their own.[9] But again, whilst this increases the chance of ultimate harm, it does not forge a necessary link between the development of modern technological civilisation and that harm coming about.

By contrast, the ultimate harm posed by the ecological crisis is *built in to industrial civilisation*. This difference reveals a curious oversight in Persson and Savulescu's argument: there is little analysis of what technology actually is, how it develops, or how it in turn influences society. Enough is said, however, to make an educated guess. Persson and Savulescu speak of the 'risks of misapplying' and 'misusing' technology, leading them to wonder whether 'human beings will waste most of the huge potential to do good that modern scientific technology offers'.[10] Such comments imply that the conception of technology at play here is an instrumental one: the idea that technology is a neutral means and that what matters, morally speaking, are the ends to which it is put to use. The remainder of the chapter

---

[5]   Persson and Savulescu, *Unfit for the Future*, 126.
[6]   Persson and Savulescu, *Unfit for the Future*, 127.
[7]   In particular that nuclear weapons cannot be understood in an 'instrumentalist' way, as the likelihood of their use is informed by the systems in which they are embedded (in this case primarily military).
[8]   This figure includes Israel, whose nuclear status is likely but unconfirmed. 'Nuclear Notebook', *Bulletin of the Atomic Scientists*: http://thebulletin.org/search/feature-type/nuclear-notebook.
[9]   Persson and Savulescu, *Unfit for the Future*, 47–48.
[10]   Persson and Savulescu, *Unfit for the Future*, 10, 52, 11.

therefore assumes Persson and Savulescu to be technological instrumentalists.

This position is no longer widely taken by philosophers of technology. The countervailing substantive conception of technology came to prominence through Martin Heidegger,[11] Jacques Ellul,[12] and Herbert Marcuse,[13] and was prefigured in the work of Lewis Mumford.[14] The basic idea is that technology is not just an instrument, a simple means to an end, but can also shape our behaviour and so inform the ends to which it is put. Albert Borgmann gives an example of this by contrasting a traditional household fireplace with a modern central heating system. He notes that the fireplace, as provider of warmth in the house, tended to physically and socially centre the inhabitants in one room. At the same time it was intimately tied to the local source of timber, and provided skilful routine tasks such as fire-lighting.[15] The central heating system, however, disperses warmth equally throughout the household and thus lacks a focal social point. Moreover, it is less intimately connected to the environment fuelling it, and any more work involved in using it than clicking a button is considered laborious. Finally, its complex workings are largely hidden from the view and understanding of the user and become the domain of an operational specialist. As a result the central heating system encourages different social, environmental, and economic relations, which in turn influence the sort of technology we want – i.e., technology which fits these new relations, such as the thermostat.

What this brief example shows is that in various ways – some subtle and unintentional, others obvious – technology changes us when we change it. There is, in other words, no simple means-end relation between technology and human goals, as I take Persson and Savulescu to suppose, but rather a dialectic of means and ends.[16]

[11]   Martin Heidegger, *The Question Concerning Technology and Other Essays*, trans. by William Lovitt (New York: Harper & Row, 1977).
[12]   Jacques Ellul, *The Technological Society*, trans. by John Wilkinson (New York: Vintage, 1964).
[13]   Herbert Marcuse, *One Dimensional Man: Studies in the Ideology of Advanced Industrial Society* (London: Abacus, 1972).
[14]   Lewis Mumford, *Technics and Civilization* (Chicago: University of Chicago Press, 2010).
[15]   Albert Borgmann, *Technology and the Character of Contemporary Life: A Philosophical Inquiry* (Chicago: University of Chicago Press, 1984), 41–42.
[16]   In the work of some technological substantivists, particularly Heidegger and Ellul, this aspect admittedly takes on an indefensibly deterministic character. However, this is by no means necessary. Marcuse, for

We shall see that in analysing the ecological crisis this conception of technology offers greater explanatory power.

2. The Dynamics of Modern Technology

Hans Jonas has explored the connection between the development of modern technology and the ecological crisis, tracing the origin of both to the Renaissance. At its core the Renaissance was a 'revolution of thought' entailing a 'change in theory, in world-view, in metaphysical outlook', the consequences of which have slowly played out over the last six centuries.[17] The old Aristotelian-Scholastic understanding of a teleological and hierarchical universe – the *scala naturae* – was decisively challenged by Copernicus' heliocentric model of the solar system. Newtonian physics then revealed the universe to be devoid of final causes, and was instead conceived of as matter in motion subject to causal laws – as Galileo famously stated, nature was an 'all-encompassing book [...] written in a mathematical language'.[18] At the same time the materialist revolution extended to the realm of living beings. In Descartes' mechanistic biology both animal and plant life were stripped of ends, and finally, in the nineteenth and twentieth centuries, the Darwinian revolution allowed the human being to undergo similar treatment. In both cases – living beings and the wider universe – nature became ever more homogenous, machine-like, and devoid of teleological significance.

According to Jonas this new mechanistic metaphysics facilitated an approach to nature involving 'actual manipulation in the investigative process'.[19] For this reason he claims modern science 'is technological by nature'.[20] By this I take Jonas to mean the following: whereas

---

instance, offers a critique of modern technology based on its interactions with capitalist society without recourse to fatalism. Even "posthumanist" philosophers of technology such as Tamar Sharon and Rosi Braidotti, both proponents of biotechnology and human enhancement, subscribe to a substantive conception of technology.

[17] Hans Jonas, *Philosophical Essays: From Ancient Creed to Technological Man* (New York: Atropos Press, 2010), 48.

[18] Galileo, *The Essential Galileo*, ed. and trans. by Maurice A. Finocchiaro (Indianapolis: Hackett, 2008), 183.

[19] Jonas, *Philosophical Essays*, 48.

[20] Hans Jonas, *The Phenomenon of Life: Toward a Philosophical Biology* (Illinois: Northwestern University Press, 1966), 198.

premodern science largely divorced contemplation of nature (*theoria*) from the realm of practical intervention (*praxis*), modern science's emphasis on mathematical quantification better lends itself to practical intervention. The distinction between theory and practice is then partially dissolved in experimentation by actively doing things to nature in the pursuit of empirical knowledge, and this practical bent allows actual instruments to take centre stage: from telescope, to microscope, to Large Hadron Collider, *technology increasingly becomes the means by which scientific advances are made.* With this fusion of theory and practice Jonas claims a merging takes place in the means-end relationship between them. Now, rather than scientific theory acting as the bedrock upon which technological innovation occurs, technological innovation is also at the heart of scientific discovery. Thus a circularity emerges: new scientific discoveries allow for technological advances, which in turn propel scientific research, which in turn generates novel technologies, and so on, *ad infinitum.* Jonas calls this forward thrust the 'formal automatics' of modern technology.[21]

The industrial revolution of the eighteenth and nineteenth centuries then saw scientific-technology put to the widespread use of capitalism. The fusion of research, innovation, and economic activity further dissolved the distinction between technological means and social ends and served to rapidly hasten development. In addition to market competition, technological advance was driven by the desire for greater production, efficiency, and safety from the new capital-intensive means of mass production. Finally military and political struggles between nations spurred on industrialisation. Initially this involved the market economies of Western Europe and North America (and later Japan), before the Cold War set them against the planned economies.[22] Market economies ultimately proved more efficient than their adversaries, and following the collapse of the Soviet Union the industrial capitalist mode of production spread worldwide. Although it has adapted to particular national institutions and circumstances, most countries can now be characterised

[21] Hans Jonas, 'Toward a Philosophy of Technology', *Hastings Center Report* **9**:1 (1979), 34–43, 36.
[22] Jonas notes that centralisation of the sort required by a state-led economy and its "five-year-plans" requires efficient infrastructure, communications, and bureaucracy, and speculates that this would act as a sufficient impetus for technological change (albeit at a slower pace) even in the absence of a Cold War.

Lewis Coyne

to some extent as part of a global 'scientific-technological-industrial civilization'.[23]

In market economies the dynamic of supply and demand informs both the sort of technology developed and its necessity. This accelerates the aforementioned forward momentum, as technology, intertwined with our social, economic, and political activity, 'suggests' and 'creates' new ends.[24] In other words, we are encouraged to consume novel technology because prior technology makes it desirable, on both an individual and social level. Here is Jonas again:

> Technology thus adds to the very objectives of human desires, including objectives *for technology itself*. The last point indicates the dialectics or circularity of the case: once incorporated into the socioeconomic demand diet, ends first [...] generated by technological invention become necessities of life and set technology the task of further perfecting the means of realizing them.[25]

Take the automobile as an example. Cars and trucks were not isolated technological inventions, but brought about tarmacked roads, motorways, petrol stations, speed cameras, traffic lights, new laws, taxes, and insurance, the driving instruction and mechanic professions, new opportunities for trade, and so on. All become desirable when accommodating the new technology into our socio-economic life, and any of *these* technologies or practices may serve to facilitate others. Langdon Winner, another substantivist philosopher of technology, has called this effect 'necessity through aimless drift', wherein 'possibilities widen, but so do the demands'.[26] This relation lies at the heart of an adequate philosophy of technology: the positive feedback loop of technological innovation and consumption strengthening our reliance upon ever more technology.

We come to realise that there is no single power directing technological development. It is rather a *mélange* of scientific technology on the one hand and industrial capitalism on the other, each containing 'a variety of currents of innovation', as Winner says, 'moving in a

---

[23] Hans Jonas, *The Imperative of Responsibility: In Search of an Ethics for the Technological Age*, trans. by Hans Jonas and David Herr (Chicago: Chicago University Press, 1984), 140.

[24] Jonas, 'Toward a Philosophy of Technology', 36.

[25] Jonas, 'Toward a Philosophy of Technology', 36 (my emphasis).

[26] Langdon Winner, *Autonomous Technology: Technics-out-of-Control as a Theme in Political Thought* (Cambridge, MA: MIT Press, 1977), 89, 102.

number of directions toward highly uncertain destinations'.[27] It has, however, a coherent ideological dimension in the notion of *progress*. This is essentially the idea that technological innovation as such is a good thing, and that problems encountered in its forward march will likely be solved by better technology. Progress has a more extreme counterpart in techno-utopianism: the belief held by Bacon,[28] Descartes, and contemporary transhumanists, that technology will make us 'masters and possessors of nature'.[29]

Successful ideologies, as Antonio Gramsci argued, 'modify the average opinion of a particular society' and obtain the status of common sense through a process he called 'cultural hegemony'.[30] Social structures such as the media, education, politics, art, and entertainment unintentionally serve to reproduce ideas beneficial to the general functioning of a particular system. These structures, widely available in contemporary capitalism, disperse appropriate ideas like progress throughout society. The ideology of progress is clearly not adhered to by all – no ideology is – but is prevalent enough to motivate consumer behaviour and further feed the dynamics outlined above.

3. The Systemic and Psychologistic Analyses of Technological Harm

Now, Persson and Savulescu explain the ecological crisis as at bottom a moral problem, citing 'the selfish and short-sighted behaviour of masses of people' that follows, they say, from the 'limitations of our altruism and sense of justice'.[31] Our moral psychology is 'designed for life in small communities with limited technology', and therefore not fit for purpose in light of the looming, self-created ultimate harm.[32] In short, the problem is not technology but those who use it. This appears, however, to be a partial misdiagnosis. Much of our behaviour may

[27]   Winner, *Autonomous Technology*, 88.
[28]   Francis Bacon, *The New Organon*, ed. by Lisa Jardine and Michael Silverthorne (Cambridge: Cambridge University Press, 2000).
[29]   René Descartes, *Discourse on Method and the Meditations*, trans. by F. E. Sutcliffe (London: Penguin, 1968), 78.
[30]   Antonio Gramsci, *Prison Notebooks*, Vol. 1, ed. by Joseph A. Buttigieg (New York: Columbia University Press, 1992), 173, 179.
[31]   Persson and Savulescu, *Unfit for the Future*, 68, 105.
[32]   Ingmar Persson and Julian Savulescu, 'The Art of Misunderstanding Moral Bioenhancement: Two Cases', *Cambridge Quarterly of Healthcare Ethics* 24:1 (2015), 48–57, 49.

very well be selfish and short-sighted, but the psychological 'limitations' invoked by Persson and Savulescu as the cause are questionable. Our senses of altruism and justice, while still felt most keenly toward those close to us in space and time, now extend both into the future and across the globe. As Michael Hauskeller points out, we need only think of the recent expansion of the circle of moral considerability to include not only other nations and races, but also future generations, non-human animals, and living beings as such.[33] This last is the most contentious, but even so finds international agreement in the 1982 UN World Charter for Nature (voted against only by the United States).[34] Each of these ethical positions, though certainly not universally held, are sufficiently common to challenge Persson and Savulescu's ahistorical claims about our inherently 'myopic' and 'parochial' moral purview.[35]

The question, then, is why we continue to act in short-sighted and ecologically deleterious ways in spite of our moral beliefs. Drawing on the substantive conception of technology, rooted in a historical and social critique, we are able to explain the ecological crisis as a predominantly *systemic* phenomenon. Individuals act within the framework described above which structures actions and their consequences. For this reason we cannot avoid the direct or indirect use of fossil fuels, production of unrecyclable waste, and consumption of resources from across the globe, simply because our social world is structured that way. As a banal example, consider the following: I wake up in the morning to the alarm on my mobile phone, a device made in China with materials including tantalum extracted in Africa. It is still dark so I turn on the light, running on electricity generated by nuclear power and burning coal, put on my dressing gown (made in Bangladesh), and go to the kitchen to make a coffee. The coffee beans were grown in Colombia and transported across the Atlantic before being packaged in an unrecyclable plastic wrapper somewhere in Europe. I turn on the stove, using gas extracted from the North Sea, to heat the coffee pot, before fetching some milk

---

[33] Michael Hauskeller, 'The Art of Misunderstanding Critics: The Case of Ingmar Persson and Julian Savulescu's Defense of Moral Bioenhancement', *Cambridge Quarterly of Healthcare Ethics* **25**:1 (2016), 151–161, 154.

[34] 'Every form of life is unique, warranting respect regardless of its worth to man, and, to accord other organisms such recognition, man must be guided by a moral code of action'. United Nations General Assembly, Resolution 37/7, 'World Charter for Nature', 28th October 1982: www.un.org/documents/ga/res/37/a37r007.htm.

[35] Persson and Savulescu, *Unfit for the Future*, 39.

from the fridge which has been running all night.[36] And so on. On an individual level my actions are innocuous, but they are of course only possible as part of a destructive socio-economic whole. Each act presupposes a chain of events which, on a large enough scale and over a long enough time, entail serious ecological harms.[37]

Such are the consequences of our collective patterns of behaviour. Of course, each of us has the ability to opt out of some ecologically harmful practices, from luxuries such as air travel to more prosaic activities like eating meat. Equally, we could choose to have no more than two children so as to arrest population growth. All these and more might be reasonable demands if we are serious about upholding our professed ecological, international, and intergenerational morals. But individuals can only opt out of certain harmful practices while remaining part of mainstream society, and here lies the crux of the matter: we have to live somewhere, work, travel, eat, drink, wash, clothe ourselves, and so on, and most of us can only do so in the society we already inhabit. "Dropping out" is simply not a reasonable option for the majority. As such, even well-meaning individuals, if they remain within industrial society, have only limited scope for lifestyle changes which would fully accord with their moral beliefs. The ecological threat of ultimate harm is therefore far more complex than Persson and Savulescu recognise, and the possible efficacy of moral enhancement more limited than they suppose. A further-reaching critique of technological harm reveals that the problem is more social and systemic than it is individual and moral.

4. Persson and Savulescu's Psycho-Politics

The neglect of social conditions at the expense of evolutionary psychology also serves to undermine Persson and Savulescu's analysis of liberal democracy, which they rightly identify as playing a role in the threat of ultimate harm. Liberal democracy is defined as a form

[36] The milk, at least, came from an organic farm in England.

[37] Moreover, I rarely actually see these harms, which are situated at a geographic or temporal remove: the pollution generated by manufacturing and shipping goods occurs elsewhere, the rubbish I dispose of is dumped in a remote landfill, nuclear waste is buried underground, and the climatic change caused by any greenhouse gas emissions does not yet affect me. For more on the social allocation of risk, see Ulrich Beck, *Risk Society: Towards a New Modernity*, trans. by Mark Ritter (London: SAGE Publications, 1992).

of elected government prioritising individual freedom, in which the state only interferes to uphold the equal freedoms of others.[38] The problem, as Persson and Savulescu see it, is that this liberty gives free reign to our moral psychology which is prone to selfishness and short-sightedness: 'climatic and environmental problems stem from the very heart of democracy – the behaviour of the majority'.[39] Despite the clear need to lower our levels of consumption, '[i]t seems unlikely that citizens of Western democracies will voluntarily consent to such restraint' and, moreover, 'governments in liberal democracies are likely to be disinclined to propose such regulations' for fear of un-popularity and therefore electoral unviability.[40] As our psychological shortcomings make such sacrifices unlikely, they believe 'individual liberty, which is a mark of these democracies, will have to be curtailed'.[41]

There is a sense in which Persson and Savulescu are correct whilst at the same time missing the mark. Liberalism (rather than democracy) is indeed part of the problem insofar as it grants excessive freedom in sci-entific research, technological innovation, and the marketplace, the amalgamation of which we have identified as the underlying cause of ul-timate harm. It follows that *this* component should be curtailed, as it already is to some degree in continental European countries and less so in the Anglophone nations. Given that liberal democracies already permit degrees of freedom facilitating technological harm, subject to political control, it seems we ought to demand greater political control so as to tackle the ecological crisis. But having framed the issue incorrectly this is not the conclusion reached by Persson and Savulescu. Viewing liberal democracy as the quintessential political ex-pression of our evolutionary psychology, rather than an ideological tradition forming part of a socio-economic system, they are led to underestimate the possibility of political transformation.

As indicated, much like the expansion of the moral circle, history tells us that liberal democracy is not immutable but rather open to change. Charles Taylor notes that to dispel any sense of political fatalism '[w]e need only think of the whole movement since the Romantic era [...] and of the offshoot of that movement today, which is challenging our ecological mismanagement'.[42] The classic case is the campaign,

---

[38] Persson and Savulescu, *Unfit for the Future*, 43.
[39] Persson and Savulescu, *Unfit for the Future*, 92.
[40] Persson and Savulescu, *Unfit for the Future*, 79, 80.
[41] Persson and Savulescu, *Unfit for the Future*, 77.
[42] Charles Taylor, *The Ethics of Authenticity* (Cambridge, MA: Harvard University Press, 1991), 99.

following the publication of Rachel Carson's *Silent Spring*, to ban agricultural usage of DDT which contributed to the establishment of the US Environmental Protection Agency.[43] For internationally-negotiated examples we could point to the apparently successful 1987 Montreal Protocol, banning substances contributing to the depletion of stratospheric ozone, or, more recently, the 2015 Paris Agreement on climate change which aims to limit the global mean temperature rise to 1.5–2°C above preindustrial levels. The point is that *some* real political changes have been demanded and made. Once again this should make us wary of Persson and Savulescu's strong claims for our selfish, short-termist psychology which supposedly drives liberal democracy.

The alternative critique of technological civilisation I have offered is better able to explain how such reforms come about. Following Gramsci, we saw that ideologies such as progress are hegemonically transmitted through social institutions. It should be noted, however, that hegemony is not deterministic since the social structures which entrench ideology as common sense only do so *via* individual agency. Anthony Giddens has described how this works in a process he calls 'structuration'. Whereas Gramsci explained how ideology becomes common sense on an abstract level, Giddens showed that con-crete social structures are reinforced and ideologically justified *through* agents: those who are able to 'exercise some sort of power'.[44] According to Giddens, social actors, though possessing little agency individually, are yet collectively responsible for the structural reproduction of ideol-ogy. He notes that structural conditions are dialectically 'both consti-tuted by human agency, and yet at the same time are the very medium of this constitution'.[45] That is to say: agents, who are to a great degree shaped by social structures, nevertheless possess the cap-acity to inform those structures in their reproduction of them. This is how seemingly monolithic structures are changed or even toppled – if enough agents challenge a particular structure, shifting collective opinion, that structure can be overturned.

Courtesy of Giddens we can explain how politically-driven changes to technological civilisation have come about and how they could continue to do so, provided they are sufficiently agitated for.

---

[43]   Rachel Carson, *Silent Spring* (London: Penguin Books, 1965).
[44]   Anthony Giddens, *The Constitution of Society: Outline of the Theory of Structuration* (Berkeley and Los Angeles: University of California Press, 1984), 14.
[45]   Anthony Giddens, *New Rules of Sociological Method: A Positive Critique of Interpretative Sociologies*, 2nd edn (Stanford: Stanford University Press, 1993), 129.

There is no imperative of evolutionary psychology preventing us from establishing more powerful regulatory bodies to oversee scientific research and development, or imposing heavy taxes on the worst polluting industries and using the proceeds to transfer to renewable energy sources. Such policies would challenge core aspects of technological civilisation – in particular the free market – and for *this* reason are hard, though not impossible, to achieve. The most plausible solution to ultimate harm would therefore be political action rather than moral enhancement.

Now, Persson and Savulescu would respond by saying that moral enhancement could help in motivating the political struggle for such reforms.[46] Perhaps it could: let us follow this train of thought. If changes to technological civilisation are driven by public will, as I suggest, then the current level must be insufficient to pose a fundamental challenge. If this is the case, and more people need to be engaged – numbering in the millions or perhaps even billions – moral enhancement would have to be comparably widespread in order to have the desired effect. However, there seems to be no reason for such uptake to occur voluntarily. Why would anyone not already agitating for action to tackle the ecological crisis be willing to undergo moral enhancement *in order to agitate for action to tackle the ecological crisis*? There seems to be a problem here in that those most in need of moral enhancement are those least likely to volunteer for it, and *vice versa*.

If voluntary moral enhancement is unlikely to work on the necessary scale it would presumably have to be compulsory, as Persson and Savulescu initially proposed.[47] This raises the following question: if Persson and Savulescu are willing in principle to countenance an authoritarian application of moral bioenhancement to address ultimate harm, why not just advocate authoritarian solutions to the ultimate harm itself? It seems unnecessary to take the detour through moral bioenhancement if one can, with Persson and Savulescu, accept authoritarian means in principle. After all, a government with the power to implement compulsory moral enhancement on the necessary scale would presumably also have the power to

---

[46]   Persson and Savulescu, 'The Art of Misunderstanding Moral Bioenhancement', 55.

[47]   Ingmar Persson and Julian Savulescu, 'The Perils of Cognitive Enhancement and the Urgent Imperative to Enhance the Moral Character of Humanity', *Journal of Applied Philosophy* **25**:3 (2008), 162–177, 174. This stipulation was apparently dropped by the publication of *Unfit for the Future*.

implement the sorts of policies to tackle the ecological crisis mentioned above. This would be a more straightforward approach, which, to be clear, is not one I am advocating – it simply seems strange, given their previous commitments, that Persson and Savulescu do not take this position.

Let us give them the benefit of the doubt, however, and assume that moral enhancement is a more efficacious solution to ultimate harm than political action alone. In this case, is there any reason why *in principle* we ought to be sceptical of moral enhancement – voluntary or otherwise – to assist the kind of political action I have suggested is necessary? I want to argue that there is such a reason, drawing once more on Jonas' work and that of Jürgen Habermas.[48]

5. Freedom and Dignity

Neither Jonas nor Habermas wrote about moral enhancement specifically, but both made important contributions to the ethical debates around genetic engineering which, as one of the methods envisioned, can be brought to bear on the topic. Jonas offers an 'existential critique' of genetic engineering, by which he means a reflection on what it would be like to be an engineered being, in order to reveal problems that would be raised by the practice.[49] This method leads him to make two observations: firstly that genetic engineering could undermine our existential freedom, and secondly that it would corrupt the relation between those who performed it and those who underwent it. These concerns pertain not to the physical consequences of manipulating the genome, which is not deterministic, but instead to the *significance* of such an intervention.

The first change Jonas points to is that the process of self-becoming is disrupted by the knowledge of having been manipulated in order to be a particular way. Regardless of whether that manipulation works as

[48]   John-Stewart Gordon has argued that Jonas' theory of responsibility can justify a state-sponsored programme of moral enhancement. However, he is only able to make this claim by overlooking Jonas' essays on bioethics which build on his theory of responsibility, and – as I show below – preclude the possibility. Furthermore, Gordon misconstrues Jonas' philosophy of technology as instrumentalist, e.g.: 'the real danger – also according to Jonas – is the *misuse* of modern technology'. John-Stewart Gordon, 'Refined Marxism and Moral Enhancement', in Holger Burckhart and John-Stewart Gordon (eds), *Global Ethics and Moral Responsibility: Hans Jonas and his Critics* (Farnham: Ashgate, 2014), 185–208, 206.
[49]   Jonas, *Philosophical Essays*, 165 (emphasis removed).

intended, *the intention itself* changes the person's self-understanding as they second-guess the authenticity of their physical or psychological being. As Jonas says, 'it does not matter one jot whether the [engineered] genotype is really, by its own force, a person's fate: it is *made* his fate'.[50] In knowing that I am intended to be a particular way I am bound to this intent, whether in conformity to it or rebellion against it. What is lost, in other words, is the spontaneity of becoming by instead measuring ourselves against a pre-established design:

> [T]he sexually produced genotype is a novum in itself, unknown to all to begin with and still to reveal itself to owners and fellow men alike. Ignorance is here the precondition of freedom: the new throw of the dice has to discover itself in the guideless efforts of living its life for the first and only time, i.e., to *become* itself in meeting a world as unprepared for the newcomer as [he] is for himself.[51]

Note that this freedom invoked by Jonas is not the same as the 'freedom to fall' defended by John Harris, which pertains to the possibility of agency and moral responsibility.[52] It is a different sort of freedom: the existential freedom to become oneself in the absence of an ingrained idea.

It might be objected that this would only hold in the case of persons who actually knew they were engineered. This much is true. Perhaps, then, we could morally enhance foetuses or infants; after all, if we never informed them it would thereby preserve their existential freedom through ignorance. This brings us to the second of Jonas' concerns: that genetic engineering corrupts the relation between the generations by becoming one of manipulator and manipulated. This is particularly apt given that Persson and Savulescu do in fact advocate the moral enhancement of children, with a view to taking advantage of their more malleable psychology.[53] Jonas' concern is that this creates an entirely one-sided control 'of present men over future men, who are the defenceless objects of antecedent choices by the planners of today. [...] [P]ower is here entirely unilateral and of the few, with no recourse to countervailing power open to its patients'.[54] Here the concern is not to do with self-understanding,

---

[50] Jonas, *Philosophical Essays*, 163.
[51] Jonas, *Philosophical Essays*, 161.
[52] John Harris, 'Moral Enhancement and Freedom', *Bioethics* **25**:2 (2011), 102–111, 104.
[53] Persson and Savulescu, *Unfit for the Future*, 113.
[54] Jonas, *Philosophical Essays*, 147.

but one's objective relation to others. In my being manipulated in a particular way – again, even if not deterministically – I become the object of someone else's design. The worry is that this one-sided power relation once more undercuts freedom, although this time not of the existential sort. As Robert Sparrow says, drawing on the work of Philip Pettit, this state of affairs threatens our freedom understood as non-domination by others.[55] This is not an implausible libertarian concern for maximum negative freedom, but a weaker desire to simply be free from arbitrary subordination.[56]

The proponent of moral enhancement could argue that we regularly engage in a practice which conforms to this type of power-relation, one that we not only tolerate but actively champion: education. In both education and moral enhancement one person seeks to inform the character and values of another, so if the former practice is permitted presumably the other should be also. Drawing this comparison, Persson and Savulescu say that '[t]here is no reason to assume that moral bioenhancement to which children are exposed without their consent would restrict their freedom and responsibility more than the traditional moral education to which they are also exposed without their consent'.[57] To challenge this equivalence I turn to Habermas, who addressed it by building on Jonas' insights.

Habermas notes that education and genetic engineering in fact embody fundamentally different principles: the former operates according to the discursive principles of communicative rationality, and the latter according to the technical principles of instrumental rationality.[58] What this means is as follows. Education, relying as it does on sensible communication, presupposes the *mutual capacity for reason*. Even if the pupil does not at the time understand the reasons behind a particular lesson, as a rational being in development they are in principle able to – and in time hopefully will – comprehend those reasons. When they do, they are then free to accept or reject those reasons. This shared ground allows for a fundamental equality between agents despite the asymmetry inherent in the practice of education. As

[55] Robert Sparrow, 'Better Living Through Chemistry? A Reply to Savulescu and Persson on "Moral Enhancement"', *Journal of Applied Philosophy* **31**:1 (2014), 23–32, 27.
[56] Philip Pettit, *Republicanism: A Theory of Freedom and Government* (Oxford: Oxford University Press, 1997), 21–27.
[57] Persson and Savulescu, *Unfit for the Future*, 113.
[58] Jürgen Habermas, *The Future of Human Nature*, trans. by Wilhelm Rehg, Max Pensky, and Hella Beister (Cambridge: Polity Press, 2003), 61–64.

Habermas says, 'expectations underlying the parents' efforts at character building are essentially "contestable" [...] the adolescents in principle still have the opportunity to respond to and retroactively break
away from it'.[59] Indeed, one might go so far as to say that developing
the ability to question what one has learned – to think for oneself – *is*
an objective of education. However, this is not required for the
present point. Even in instances where learning to think for oneself is
not an objective of the educator, the nature of education itself means
the content can always be subsequently contested, as Habermas' own
schooling in Nazi Germany starkly demonstrates.

By contrast, genetic engineering lacks the mutual ground of reason
which allows for equality between participants. Instead, as a technical
procedure carried out on the child as an object, the manipulation
makes retrospective disagreement impossible:

> With genetic enhancement, there is no communicative scope for
> the projected child to be addressed as a second person and to be
> involved in a communication process. [...] It does not permit the
> adolescent looking back on the prenatal intervention to engage in
> a *revisionary* learning process. *Being at odds with* the genetically
> fixed intention of a third person is hopeless.[60]

The difference in principle, therefore, is that the power-relation of
genetic engineering is not only unilateral but also incontestable: the
child is bound to an intent from which they cannot be released.
Habermas himself does not consider this a problem if the child subsequently 'affirms', or identifies with, the intent behind the intervention.[61] One could go further, however, and argue that whatever the
child's appraisal of the intervention turns out to be, the intervention
itself curtails freedom insofar as the child is aware that invasive and
domineering biotechnological means, rather than readily available re-
flexive and communicative ones, were chosen by their predecessors.[62]
There is, as Habermas says, no scope for autonomous contestation of
the former. By contrast, education, courtesy of its basis in rational

---

[59] Habermas, *The Future of Human Nature*, 62.
[60] Habermas, *The Future of Human Nature*, 62.
[61] Habermas, *The Future of Human Nature*, 61.
[62] Persson and Savulescu do not even think it likely that an enhanced
child would be at odds with the intervention: they speculate, outlandishly,
that '[i]t is quite unlikely that later in life the morally bioenhanced individuals will regret the fact that they have undergone this treatment, since
otherwise they might have been criminals who would have been punished
and condemned by society'. Persson and Savulescu, *Unfit for the Future*,
113.

communication, possesses an inherent reflexivity and thereby presupposes freedom as non-domination. Education is for this reason different in kind, and not simply degree, from cognitive or moral enhancement.

Here Persson and Savulescu fundamentally disagree. They claim 'common sense and science' tell us that 'it is surely evident that when small children are taught language, religion, basic moral rules, or whatever, this education is just as effective, irresistible, and irrevocable as biomedical intervention is likely to be'.[63] In fact common sense tells us no such thing, for the reasons provided by Habermas. Even education as fundamental to psychological development as religion, moral rules, or metaphysical beliefs can be questioned and rejected (although whether fundamental moral rules *should* be questioned and rejected is another matter). The reason, in short, is that critical reflection breaks the 'quasi-natural' status of educative content: even if it is subsequently accepted, one's relation to the content is altered through contestation.[64] The most obvious exception is language, which holds a unique status due to its hermeneutic centrality: it is the foremost ground on which understanding occurs, allowing subsequent learning to take place.[65] The first language learned, one's mother tongue, is incomparable even with additional languages which are learned on the basis of the first. Even so, in grammar language possesses an internal logic which allows its usage to be refined or mastered, including in opposition to the way one was taught, thus preserving the fundamental symmetry of a shared rational ground. Moral enhancement, as a unilateral and incontestable intervention, therefore remains qualitatively distinct.

6. Conclusion

What, then, is the scope of these objections raised by Jonas and Habermas? What do they rule out, if accepted? The threats to existential freedom and freedom as non-domination apply most obviously to compulsory moral enhancement, which would involve an alien intention almost by necessity. According to Michael Hauskeller the

---

[63] Persson and Savulescu, 'The Art of Misunderstanding Moral Bioenhancement', 52.

[64] Jürgen Habermas, *On the Logic of the Social Sciences*, trans. by Shierry Weber Nicholsen and Jerry A. Stark (Cambridge: Polity, 1988), 168.

[65] Hans-Georg Gadamer, *Truth and Method*, 2nd edn, trans. by Joel Weinsheimer and Donald G. Marshall (London: Continuum, 2004), 390.

latter could also apply to voluntary enhancement, or enhancement of oneself ("auto-enhancement"). Extending Habermas' argument he claims that the relation corrupted in voluntary enhancement would not be between self and other, but between one's past and present. The intention would belong to the past self and bind the present self, thus exerting a unilateral and incontestable control from which the latter cannot escape:

> The event would be similar to the case where someone voluntarily signed a contract that made them a slave for the rest of their lives. Although they would have freely chosen to be a slave, once a slave they would no longer have the choice not to be one, and it is not an uncommon intuition that *therefore* it is wrong (and should not be permitted) to make such a choice.[66]

The worry is not that one might regret the decision to have undergone moral enhancement, but that the individual is beholden to that decision whether they regretted it or not. In this way voluntary or self-enhancement appears to parallel the threat to freedom as non-domination.

However, the concern raised by Hauskeller regarding the domination of one's present by one's past applies most forcefully to genetic engineering, and less so to the other method envisioned by Persson and Savulescu, namely, pharmaceutical means.[67] Whereas in genetic engineering the intention is engraved in the genome for posterity, oxytocin or selective serotonin reuptake inhibitors (SSRIs) could conceivably be intended for merely short-term effect. To be sure, any *compulsory* moral enhancement via such drugs would still threaten freedom as non-domination, but their voluntary and temporary usage alone might evade the concerns raised about being incontestably beholden to one's past decision. Provided that the effects of this sort of moral enhancement were short-lived, it might be comparable less to voluntary enslavement and more to being under the influence of recreational drugs taken with an express purpose in mind, such as spiritual insight or artistic inspiration. This is clearly a vague suggestion (how short is an appropriately short length of time?), but given that in some nations and cultures the usage of hallucinogens is acceptable under such conditions, a moral enhancement of this sort might be also.

---

[66] Michael Hauskeller, 'Is it Desirable to Be Able to Do the Undesirable? Moral Bioenhancement and the Little Alex Problem', *Cambridge Quarterly of Healthcare Ethics* **26**:3 (2017), 365–376, 374.
[67] Persson and Savulescu, *Unfit for the Future*, 118–121.

Therefore if a version of moral enhancement is possible which by-passes the concerns raised by Jonas and Habermas it would be voluntary and short-term enhancement via pharmaceutical means.[68] Now, it may be that additional arguments motivated by other concerns, such as Michael Sandel's virtue-based case against the drive to mastery, would also rule out this form of moral enhancement – I here leave the possibility open.[69] More pertinent is that voluntary pharmaceutical moral enhancement, even if permissible, is likely to be woefully insufficient for the stated purpose of confronting the systemic threat of the ecological crisis. As explained above, generating the necessary will to politically challenge the relevant aspects of technological civilisation would require that moral enhancement was undertaken on a mass scale, which seems highly improbable on a voluntary basis.

The proponent of moral enhancement who was unsatisfied with this conclusion might yet endorse its application in spite of the objections discussed. They could bite the bullet and argue that the risk of ultimate harm is simply so great that by any measure it outweighs concerns about the threats to existential freedom and freedom as non-domination. However, doing so would come at a cost even on their own terms. Ultimate harm, we recall, was defined by Persson and Savulescu not simply as 'forever destroying life on Earth', but also 'making *worthwhile* life forever impossible on this planet' – thereby pertaining to a qualitative and not merely quantitative loss. Runaway climate change or nuclear war would almost certainly result in the impossibility of worthwhile life, and perhaps even the impossibility of life itself. But something of the former, qualitative loss might also hold true of compulsory moral enhancement, particularly if carried out through biotechnological manipulations of the human germline. There is a real harm done to our lives in any form of moral enhancement which restricted our existential freedom or freedom as non-domination. Not an ultimate harm, it is true, but a

---

[68]   I should emphasise that this judgement chiefly applies to the arguments presented by Habermas in *The Future of Human Nature*. According to Ehni and Aurenque, Habermas' wider body of work would appear to permit other forms of moral enhancement, specifically that proposed by Thomas Douglas. See Hans-Joerg Ehni and Diana Aurenque, 'On Moral Enhancement from a Habermasian Perspective', *Cambridge Quarterly of Healthcare Ethics* **21**:2 (2012), 223–234, 232.

[69]   Michael J. Sandel, *The Case Against Perfection: Ethics in the Age of Genetic Engineering* (Cambridge, MA: Harvard University Press, 2007) 27, 46.

significant one nonetheless, which even those who otherwise advocate moral enhancement may not wish to sacrifice.

Through Jonas' insights, supported by Habermas', we are first of all alerted to the precise nature of the ecological crisis as a technological harm, and secondly to the technological harm present in those forms of moral enhancement involving either genetic engineering or compulsory/long-term application through pharmaceutical means. On this basis we arrive at something like the reverse of Persson and Savulescu's conclusion: rather than being unfit for the future without moral enhancement to save us, moral enhancement could itself create a future unfit for ourselves. By this I mean that what is most valuable about human beings – our freedom and the dignity it bestows, perhaps – deserves a future which allows it to flourish. The prospect of moral enhancement, at least as envisioned by Persson and Savulescu, is by that measure an unfit future.

Acknowledgements

I am grateful to Michael Hauskeller and Cameron Hunter for comments on earlier drafts of this essay. This work was supported by the Economic and Social Research Council.

University of Exeter
lc453@exeter.ac.uk

Moral Enhancement and Climate Change: Might it Work?

ALEKSANDRA KULAWSKA AND
MICHAEL HAUSKELLER

Abstract

Climate change is one of the most urgent global problems that we face today. The causes are well understood and many solutions have been proposed; however, so far none have been successful. Ingmar Persson and Julian Savulescu have argued that this is because our moral psychology is ill-equipped to deal with global problems such as this. They propose that in order to successfully mitigate climate change we should morally enhance ourselves. In this chapter we look at their proposal to see whether moral enhancement is indeed a viable solution to the climate crisis, and conclude that due to various theoretical and practical problems it most likely is not.

1. Introduction

Climate change is one of the most urgent problems that humanity has to face in the 21st century. The threat of altering the atmospheric composition of our climate beyond safe levels necessary for maintaining life on Earth is real, with impacts of climate change already visible across the world.[1,2,3,4] Global temperatures are rising in an unprecedented way and, if nothing changes, will continue to rise even faster, leading to considerable sea-level rise, biodiversity loss, extreme weather, and increased mortality later in this century.[5] In order to

---

[1] Gian-Reto Walther, et al., 'Ecological Responses to Recent Climate Change', *Nature* **416**: 6879 (2002), 389–395.

[2] Camille Parmesan and Gary Yohe, 'A Globally Coherent Fingerprint of Climate Change Impacts Across Natural Systems', *Nature* **421**:6918 (2003), 37–42.

[3] Jonathan Patz, et al., 'Impact of Regional Climate Change on Human Health', *Nature* **438**:7066 (2005), 310–317.

[4] IPCC, *Climate Change 2014: Synthesis Report. Contribution of Working Groups I, II and III to the Fifth Assessment Report of the Intergovernmental Panel on Climate Change* (Cambridge: Cambridge University Press, 2014).

[5] IPCC, *Climate Change 2013: The Physical Science Basis. Contribution of Working Group I to the Fifth Assessment Report of the*

doi:10.1017/S1358246118000450

mitigate the worst consequences that climate change can impose on us, we desperately need to act now.[6]

This, however, is not an easy task. The first major scientific report on climate change was published by the Intergovernmental Panel on Climate Change (IPCC) in 1990, establishing that 'there is a natural greenhouse effect which already keeps the Earth warmer than it otherwise would be', and that 'emissions resulting from human activities are substantially increasing the atmospheric concentrations of greenhouse gases'.[7] The resulting international conferences in Rio de Janeiro in 1992, Kyoto in 1997, and, more recently, Paris in 2015, as well as the multiple newly established research institutes, environmental charities, and governmental organisations took climate change mitigation as their priority. Many reports on climate change have been published,[8,9,10,11] and novel solutions to the problem have been

---

Intergovernmental Panel on Climate Change (Cambridge: Cambridge University Press, 2013).

[6] Robert Henson, *The Rough Guide to Climate Change* (London: Rough Guides, 2008).

[7] J. T. Houghton, et al., *Climate Change: The IPCC Scientific Assessment. Report Prepared for Intergovernmental Panel on Climate Change by Working Group I* (Cambridge: Cambridge University Press, 1990), xi.

[8] IPCC, *Climate Change 2007: The Physical Science Basis. Contribution of Working Group I to the Fourth Assessment Report of the Intergovernmental Panel on Climate Change* (Cambridge: Cambridge University Press, 2007).

[9] IPCC, *Climate Change 2013: The Physical Science Basis. Contribution of Working Group I to the Fifth Assessment Report of the Intergovernmental Panel on Climate Change* (Cambridge: Cambridge University Press, 2013).

[10] William Chander, et al., *Climate Change Mitigation in Developing Countries: Brazil, China, India, Mexico, South Africa, and Turkey* (Arlington: Pew Center on Global Climate Change, 2002).

[11] EEA, *Climate Change, Impacts and Vulnerability in Europe 2016* (Luxembourg: European Environmental Agency, 2016).

widely researched.[12,13,14] Moreover, the knowledge of climate change amongst the public has risen,[15] with popular newspapers, television programmes, and even famous actors describing the dangers of climate change and the urgent need to mitigate from its worst consequences. And yet, amongst all this striving and publicity, the emissions of greenhouse gases (GHGs) from 2000 to 2010 were the highest so far in history.[16] Moreover, the average global temperature relative to 1884 rose from 0.44°C in 1990 to 0.99°C in 2016.[17] It seems, then, that the problem is much more complex than we previously thought and that the solution is not easily achievable by producing and publicising new knowledge. There is, then, an increased need to determine the causes of our inaction, and the possible ways in which we could change the situation, so that we can successfully mitigate climate change.

2. Persson and Savulescu's Proposal

So why have we not done so already? According to Ingmar Persson and Julian Savulescu, the reason we have so far been unable to tackle the problem is our ill-equipped moral psychology, which has not adapted to deal with complex, global problems. Supposedly our concerns are biologically limited to those around us and our immediate future. Climate change, however, is likely to have the biggest effect on the poorest people in distant countries, and perhaps not for some time. To successfully tackle climate change we would need to be able to entertain more far-reaching concerns, extending towards

---

12 Stephen Pacala and Robert Socolow, 'Stabilization Wedges: Solving the Climate Problem for the Next 50 Years with Current Technologies', *Science* **305**:5686 (2004), 968–972.

13 Rattan Lal, 'Soil Carbon Sequestration to Mitigate Climate Change', *Geoderma* **123**:1 (2004), 1–22.

14 R. E. H. Sims, 'Renewable Energy: A Response to Climate Change', *Solar Energy* **76**:1 (2004), 9–17.

15 Anthony Leiserowitz, 'International Public Opinion, Perception, and Understanding of Global Climate Change', *Human Development Report* (Human Development Report Office Occasional Paper, 2007).

16 IPCC, *Climate Change 2014: Mitigation of Climate Change. Contribution of Working Group III to the Fifth Assessment Report of the Intergovernmental Panel on Climate Change* (Cambridge: Cambridge University Press, 2014).

17 NASA, *Vital Signs*: https://climate.nasa.gov/.

future generations and those living in other parts of the globe. The key to mitigating climate change is, then, to change our moral psychology accordingly, i.e., to morally enhance ourselves. The moral enhancement that Persson and Savulescu have in mind is an intervention which aims to improve human moral capacities or dispositions beyond those occurring normally in human beings.[18,19] This does of course not necessarily mean that moral enhancement has to be radical, in that it would turn us into moral saints, unable to do the wrong thing. Rather, we could perhaps simply lift those with normal levels of moral capacities to the standard of those of us who by nature possess high levels.[20]

How could we achieve this? Persson and Savulescu propose that we enhance two features of our moral psychology: altruism and a sense of justice, both of which, they argue, have a biological basis and hence can be improved through biomedical means. Enhancing altruism would presumably help us to become more motivated to alleviate the suffering of those whose lives will be severely disrupted by climate change, as well as provide a motivation to co-operate with others in joint efforts to fight climate change. Enhancing our sense of justice would presumably help us to include future generations in our moral considerations by making us recognise that our inaction is not morally neutral, but, rather, morally wrong and unjust towards those in the distant future. That could perhaps also provide the necessary motivation to act against climate change. The proposed enhancement could be achieved through the administration of drugs that have morally-enhancing properties or through genetic engineering. Persson and Savulescu point to oxytocin and serotonin as the best candidates for moral enhancement. Oxytocin has been found to increase trust and sympathy towards others,[21,22] while serotonin has been shown to 'make subjects more fair-minded and willing to cooperate'.[23] Persson and Savulescu admit that there are some problems with the administration of some of

---

[18] Ingmar Persson and Julian Savulescu, *Unfit for the Future: The Need for Moral Enhancement* (Oxford: Oxford University Press, 2012).

[19] T. L. Beauchamp, 'Are We Unfit for the Future?', *Journal of Medical Ethics* **41**:4 (2015), 346–348.

[20] Ingmar Persson and Julian Savulescu, 'Reply to Commentators on "Unfit for the Future"', *Journal of Medical Ethics* **41**:4 (2015), 348–352.

[21] Michael Kosfeld, et al., 'Oxytocin Increases Trust in Humans', *Nature* **435**:7042 (2005), 673–676.

[22] P. J. Zak, et al., 'Oxytocin Increases Generosity in Humans', *PloS ONE* **2**:11 (2007), e1128.

[23] Persson and Savulescu, *Unfit for the Future*, 120.

these drugs, yet they are optimistic that fine-tuning the dosages and combinations of these chemicals could, after careful research and experimentation, lead us to achieve the desired moral states. Another option (although less likely) is genetic engineering, which could be used to overcome problems around the administration of these drugs to everyone on the globe and ensure that everyone is enhanced.

Moral enhancement is seen by Persson and Savulescu as a possible way out of the climate crisis. They are very much aware that the moral enhancement necessary to mitigate climate change is currently not possible and will perhaps not be possible in time to alleviate the problem. However, they claim that our current situation is so serious that we should at least consider their proposal seriously and put money into research and development of moral enhancement as soon as possible. Are they right?

3. Can Moral Enhancement Really Help?

Let us first look at the causes of climate change as we know them today. Our climate changes because of the greenhouse effect, which is a natural phenomenon responsible for keeping the planet warm. Energy comes from the Sun in the form of light, and is reflected by the Earth's surface. The so-called "greenhouse gases" (such as carbon dioxide or methane) act like a blanket, trapping some of the heat and keeping the planet warm. By increasing the concentrations of these gases in our atmosphere, we are artificially increasing the Earth's temperature.

How did we manage to do this? Over the last 150 years we have been adding enormous quantities of greenhouse gases into the atmosphere,[24] primarily through the burning of fossil fuels, such as coal, gas, and oil. It is estimated that we add around 30 billion metric tonnes of carbon dioxide alone into the atmosphere each year.[25] The more we add, the more dangerous the situation becomes, which means that our top priority right now should be trying to stabilise and reduce our emissions as soon as possible. Indeed, as Archer, et al. point out, 'avoiding climate change means limiting the emission of CO_2'.[26] This, of course, is not an easy task in a world that largely

---

[24] Henson, *The Rough Guide to Climate Change.*
[25] Henson, *The Rough Guide to Climate Change.*
[26] David Archer and Stefan Rahmstorf, *The Climate Crisis* (New York: Cambridge University Press, 2012), 22.

depends on burning fossil fuels to meet its needs. However, it is not an impossible task, as the strategies needed to stabilise our emissions already exist and have been widely researched.[27,28,29,30] The problem, then, is not that we do not know what to do, but, rather that we do not do it. The question is why.

Persson and Savulescu think our inability to deal effectively with climate change has something to do with our moral psychology, and they may well be right. A number of studies have concluded that our moral psychology is still at the level of the "tribe", which means that we are not well-equipped to cope with complex, global problems.[31,32] We are disposed to care more for our kin and prioritise their needs over the needs of distant others.[33,34] We also have a bias towards the near future and it is easy for us to ignore threats that are remote in time.[35] It seems, then, that correcting these biases, and hence improving our moral psychology, would make us better able to engage in co-operative action against climate change.

Persson and Savulescu also seem to be right to focus on the enhancement of altruism and a sense of justice because these have been found to be strong predictors of an individual's willingness to act on climate change.[36,37,38] Those individuals who rated 'high' on

[27]   Pacala and Socolow, 'Stabilization Wedges'.
[28]   Lal, 'Soil Carbon Sequestration to Mitigate Climate Change'.
[29]   Sims, 'Renewable Energy'.
[30]   T. M. Wigley, 'A Combined Mitigation/Geoengineering Approach to Climate Stabilization', *Science* **314**:5798 (2006), 452–454.
[31]   Robert Gifford, 'The Dragons of Inaction: Psychological Barriers that Limit Climate Change Mitigation and Adaptation', *American Psychologist* **66**:4 (2011), 290–302.
[32]   E. M. Markowitz and A. F. Shariff, 'Climate Change and Moral Judgement', *Nature Climate Change* **2**:4 (2012), 243–247.
[33]   Markowitz and Shariff, 'Climate Change and Moral Judgement'.
[34]   Helen Bernhard, et al., 'Parochial Altruism in Humans', *Nature* **442**:7105 (2006), 912–915.
[35]   George Loewenstein and Jon Elster, *Choice Over Time* (New York: Russell Sage Foundation, 1992).
[36]   J. L. Dickinson, et al., 'Which Moral Foundations Predict Willingness to Make Lifestyle Changes to Avert Climate Change in the USA?', *PloS ONE* **11**:10 (2016), e0163852.
[37]   Ignor Knez, 'How Concerned, Afraid and Hopeful Are We? Effects of Egoism and Altruism on Climate Change Related Issues', *Psychology* **4**:10 (2013), 744–752.
[38]   Igor Knez, 'Is Climate Change a Moral Issue? Effects of Egoism and Altruism on Pro-Environmental Behavior', *Current Urban Studies* **4**:2, 157–174.

altruism were willing to make bigger sacrifices and were more afraid of climate change.[39] Since altruism and a sense of justice seem to make us more willing to adopt climate-friendly behaviours, it seems that morally enhancing people in that way could have enormous benefits. Firstly, morally enhanced people would presumably be more motivated to adopt climate-friendly actions in their daily lives. These actions, such as e.g. driving a bike to work, purchasing solar panels, or refraining from eating meat would reduce individual household GHG emissions. Morally enhanced people would also presumably vote for politicians that promise climate action or create their own political parties with a strong agenda for mitigating climate change. This would undoubtedly lead to many social, political, and economic changes that could help lower our national and international GHG emissions. Moreover, morally enhanced people could also be more likely to agree to pay taxes for developing climate technologies. These technologies could play a key role in reducing the concentrations of GHG in the atmosphere.[40]

4. Problems with Persson and Savulescu's Proposal

There are, however, some problems with the proposal, the most serious of which is perhaps the fact that climate change is not entirely a moral problem. It is true that our moral psychology is not well-equipped to deal with global problems such as climate change, and it is also true that altruism and a sense of justice are strong predictors of willingness to act on climate change. However, there are other, non-moral factors that play an important part. For one thing, climate change is also a significant cognitive problem. It seems that understanding the causes of climate change is a powerful predictor of behavioural response to the problem.[41] Greater knowledge of climate change is correlated with greater corncern over its impacts, which in turn is associated with higher willingness to take action.[42]

[39] Knez, 'How Concerned, Afraid and Hopeful are We?'.

[40] Henson, *The Rough Guide to Climate Change*.

[41] R. E. O'Connor, et al., 'Risk Perceptions, General Environmental Beliefs, and Willingness to Address Climate Change', *Risk Analysis* **19**:3 (1999), 461–471.

[42] T. L. Milfont, 'The Interplay Between Knowledge, Perceived Efficacy, and Concern About Global Warming and Climate Change: A One-Year Longitudinal Study', *Risk Analysis* **32**:6 (2012), 1003–1020.

Moreover, those who perceive climate change as temporally and spatially distant as well as less serious than it is generally considered to be, are less willing to take action.[43,44] It becomes clear, then, that the understanding of the causes and risks of climate change significantly determines our willingness to act on climate change. However, there are also other cognitive factors that come into play. For example, a first-hand experience of a natural disaster, such as flooding, tends to increase concern over climate change and the willingness to adopt climate-friendly behaviours.[45] Those who have had a first-hand experience of a flood generally believed that their actions have more effect on climate change, and were observed to be significantly more motivated to save energy with the aim of climate change mitigation.[46]

Climate change is also a problem that concerns our values and beliefs. Different belief systems and personal values lead to different attitudes towards climate change, and, hence, different levels of motivation to engage in climate-friendly behaviour. For example, those of us who believe that humans are a part of nature and understand our position as interdependent on others and the natural world, are more concerned about environmental issues and more willing to engage in environmentally-friendly behaviour.[47,48] Those cultural groups that express biospheric values are more likely to behave pro-environmentally.[49] Interestingly, it has also been speculated that those who

[43] Anthony Leiserowitz, et al., *Climate Change in the American Mind: Americans' Global Warming Beliefs and Attitudes in November, 2013* (Yale University and George Mason University, New Haven: Yale Project on Climate Change Communication, 2014).

[44] A. S. Singh, et al., 'The Perceived Psychological Distance of Climate Change Impacts and its Influence on Support for Adaptation Policy', *Environmental Science and Policy* **73** (2017), 93–99.

[45] Alexa Spence, et al., 'Perceptions of Climate Change and Willingness to Save Energy Related to Flood Experience', *Nature Climate Change* **1**:1 (2011), 46–49.

[46] Alexa Spence, et al., 'Perceptions of Climate Change'.

[47] P. W. Schultz, et al., 'Implicit Connections With Nature', *Journal of Environmental Psychology* **24**:1 (2004), 31–42.

[48] Steven Arnocky, et al., 'Self-Construal Predicts Environmental Concern, Cooperation, and Conservation', *Journal of Environmental Psychology* **27**:4 (2007), 255–264.

[49] T. L. Milfont, et al., 'A Cross-Cultural Study of Environmental Motive Concerns and Their Implications for Proenvironmental Behavior', *Environment and Behavior* **38**:6 (2006), 745–767.

believe that the world is stable, orderly, and just are more likely to deny the existence of climate change or the extent of risks that it can impose on us, effectively lowering their willingness to act.[50] The differences can also be seen in terms of political values. Those who align their values and beliefs with right-wing parties are less likely to adopt high-cost climate-friendly behaviours and support policies which aim to mitigate climate change than those with other political beliefs.[51]

Last, but not least, climate change is also a social problem. This means that it is a problem that arises due to the ways in which our societies function; our social norms and habits, the infrastructure of our cities, the local economies and governments, as well as existing policies. For example, the infrastructure of our cities has an enormous effect on our work and travel habits, which, in turn, determine the amount of GHGs that a city will emit each year.[52] Those cities that have a well-developed public transport system allow citizens to reduce their individual GHG emissions by forgoing their car, and using public transport to commute to work each day. Those cities that cannot provide a well-developed transport system, for example because they are very spread-out, tacitly encourage their citizens to use cars each day in order to earn their living, effectively increasing GHG emissions. This means that our desire to adopt climate-friendly behaviours is often restricted by the type of society we live in, and the opportunities that such society can provide, given its geographical location, political and economic status, available finances, and so on.

This is of course not an exhaustive presentation of the aspects and causes of climate change inaction. For example, climate change can also be understood as an existential problem,[53] a problem that arises

---

[50]   Matthew Feinberg and Robb Willer, 'Apocalypse Soon? Dire Messages Reduce Belief in Global Warming by Contradicting Just-World Beliefs', *Psychological Science* 22:1 (2011), 34–38.

[51]   Christina Tobler, et al., 'Addressing Climate Change: Determinants of Consumers' Willingness to Act and to Support Policy Measures', *Journal of Environmental Psychology* 32:3 (2012), 197–207.

[52]   Dimitri Zenghelis and Nicholas Stern, 'Climate Change and Cities: a Prime Source of Problems, Yet Key to Solution', *The Guardian*, 17th November 2015: https://www.theguardian.com/cities/2015/nov/17/cities-climate-change-problems-solution.

[53]   J. L. Dickinson, 'The People Paradox: Self-Esteem Striving, Immortality Ideologies, and Human Response to Climate Change', *Ecology and Society* 14:1 (2009): http://www.ecologyandsociety.org/vol14/iss1/art34/.

Aleksandra Kulawska and Michael Hauskeller

due to our differing personalities,[54,55] or an economic problem.[56] The important point here, however, is that our ill-equipped moral psychology is not the only, or perhaps even the most important, cause of our inaction in the face of climate change. There are many other factors that come into play, which means that it is unlikely that moral enhancement alone could mitigate climate change.

5. The Unpredictability of Outcomes

However, even if moral enhancement were the sole factor in determining behavioural responses to climate change, it is unlikely that we could predict whether its outcome would be satisfactory. Persson and Savulescu are optimistic that research and experimentation in the field of moral enhancement can lead us to achieving moral states necessary for climate change mitigation. They acknowledge that developing such moral enhancement could take a long time, and that it would certainly be a complicated and costly endeavour, yet they are confident that such technology could eventually be realised. However, it is doubtful that moral enhancement could ever be fine-tuned in such a way that it leads to climate change mitigation, no matter how much money or effort we put into the research. Upon closer examination it becomes clear that there are many theoretical and practical difficulties with Persson's and Savulescu's claim, which ultimately render the outcome of moral enhancement uncertain.

Consider the two chemicals that Persson and Savulescu think are likely to play a role in moral enhancement. Oxytocin is a chemical responsible for creating and maintaining social bonds, promoting trust and altruism, and reducing anxiety.[57] Naturally, it seems that enhancing the levels of oxytocin in a person's brain will lead to more trusting, altruistic behaviours, and hence that oxytocin has "morally enhancing" properties. However, a significant number of studies

---

[54]   J. B. Hirsh, 'Personality and Environmental Concern', *Journal of Environmental Psychology* **30**:2 (2010), 245–248.
[55]   T. L. Milfont and C. G. Sibley, 'The Big Five Personality Traits and Environmental Engagement: Associations at the Individual and Societal Level', *Journal of Environmental Psychology* **32**:3 (2012), 187–195.
[56]   W. D. Nordhaus, *Managing the Global Commons: The Economics of Climate Change*, Vol. 31 (Cambridge: MIT Press, 1994).
[57]   Markus MacGill, 'Oxytocin: What Is it and What Does it Do?', *Medical News Today*: http://www.medicalnewstoday.com/articles/275795.php.

have found that artificially increasing the levels of oxytocin in a person's brain results in unexpected outcomes. Oxytocin has been found to decrease pro-social behaviour towards out-group individuals,[58] increase human ethnocentrism,[59] and promote group-serving dishonesty.[60] Moreover, participants with increased levels of oxytocin were less likely to adhere to fairness norms when dealing with out-group individuals and were less generous towards them.[61] Oxytocin has also been found to only increase altruism in the social, rather than environmental domain. Those participants who were treated with oxytocin were less willing to donate money to environmental causes.[62]

Serotonin, on the other hand, is responsible for modulating our emotions and increasing harm aversion. It has been speculated that increasing the levels of serotonin in the brain will lead to increased sense of fairness and decreased willingness to cause harm.[63] However, it has been found that individuals with increased levels of serotonin were more likely to tolerate behaviours that were unjust, in order to avoid having to punish others.[64]

These examples show that the outcomes of even such basic moral enhancements of small groups of people in controlled study environments are highly unexpected and uncertain, and, hence, that the situation is much more complex than Persson and Savulescu let on. Of

[58] C. K. De Dreu, et al., 'The Neuropeptide Oxytocin Regulates Parochial Altruism in Intergroup Conflict Among Humans', *Science* **328**:5984 (2010), 1408–1411.

[59] C. K. De Dreu, et al., 'Oxytocin Promotes Human Ethnocentrism', *Proceedings of the National Academy of Sciences* **108**:4 (2011), 1262–1266.

[60] Shaul Shalvi and C. K. De Dreu, 'Oxytocin Promotes Group-Serving Dishonesty', *Proceedings of the National Academy of Sciences* **111**:15 (2014), 5503–5507.

[61] Sina Radke and E. R. De Bruijn, 'The Other Side of Coin: Oxytocin Decreases the Adherence to Fairness Norms', *Frontiers in Human Neuroscience* **6** (2012): https://www.frontiersin.org/articles/10.3389/fnhum.2012.00193/full.

[62] Nina Marsh, et al., 'The Neuropeptide Oxytocin Induces a Social Altruism Bias', *Journal of Neuroscience* **35**:47 (2015), 15696–15701.

[63] J. Z. Siegel and M. J. Crockett, 'How Serotonin Shapes Moral Judgement and Behavior', *Annals of the New York Academy of Sciences* **111**:15 (2014), 5503–5507.

[64] M. J. Crockett, et al., 'Serotonin Selectively Influences Moral Judgement and Behavior Through Effects on Harm Aversion', *Proceedings of the National Academy of Sciences* **107**:40 (2010), 17433–17438.

course, it could be objected that just because oxytocin and serotonin are not good targets for moral enhancement, there may be other ways to bring about the necessary psychological states for climate change mitigation. This, however, seems unlikely for a couple of reasons.

Firstly, the brain is a very complex, fine-tuned mechanism which continuously processes and combines hundreds of different highly-specialised chemicals which all work together to maintain the cognitive, emotional, and moral processes of a person. Our understanding of the brain and even its basic processes is still very limited and it is not clear whether we can ever achieve that understanding, simply due to the sheer complexity of the multitude of processes that continuously work together to create a conscious being. For example, as Crockett explains, many of the brain's neurotransmitters, which would presumably play a key role in moral enhancement, serve multiple different functions and can be found in many different areas of the brain.[65] Serotonin, she argues, besides its key role in social behaviour, also regulates sleep, appetite, pain, memory, sexual behaviour, and vision. Moreover, there are many different types of serotonin, all of which have different effects on neurotransmission. The task of selecting the right type of serotonin and making sure that its effects will increase our willingness to lower our carbon emissions seems close to impossible. The issue would be complicated further by the fact that we would presumably need different chemicals to achieve the desired effect. The task of discerning how these chemicals would work together and what else they would influence in the brain seems daunting. And, most importantly, given our poor understanding of these processes, we would likely not know whether the enhancement could achieve its aims until after we have implemented it.

Secondly, Handfield, et al. argue that our altruistic and trusting behaviours are always accompanied by defensive behaviours, which means that if we enhance altruism or trust, we also need to account for change in our defense mechanisms.[66] It is, of course, not clear what change would be brought about, but the studies on the effects of oxytocin mentioned before could perhaps be a good indication of what we should expect. For example, consider the De Dreu study from 2011, where participants with increased altruism levels were much less trusting and more hostile towards out-group persons. It seems that in that study the enhanced participants "compensated"

---

[65] M. J. Crockett, 'Moral Bioenhancement: A Neuroscientific Perspective', *Journal of Medical Ethics* **40**:6 (2014), 370–371.
[66] Toby Handfield, et al., 'Climate Change, Cooperation and Moral Bioenhancement', *Journal of Medical Ethics* **42** (2016), 742–747.

for their increased levels of trust and empathy with increased levels of mistrust and hostility towards those not belonging to their group. Handfield, et al. argue that evolutionarily it would be an extremely dangerous situation if our altruistic, trusting behaviours were enhanced while our defensive mechanisms stayed the same.[67] That is why our defensive mechanisms, such as our cognitive bias towards immediate kin, will likely not disappear with moral enhancement, but rather get strengthened, as a part of the brain's natural defense mechanism. We do not know exactly what effects different kinds and doses of chemicals could have, but it is guaranteed to upset the balance between the altruistic and the defensive mechanisms embedded in our brains. Hence, the effect of moral enhancement will vary greatly, and it is not clear in what ways our brain will adapt to the new situation. This increases the uncertainty of the outcome.

Thirdly, the outcome of moral enhancement will likely be uncertain as there will still be room for us to make wrong decisions. This is because Persson and Savulescu, prompted by criticism, argue that they never meant moral enhancement to be so radical that it turns us all into "moral saints", unable to do the wrong thing. Rather, they now propose that we should enhance people with normal levels of altruism or sense of justice to the levels of those who by nature possess high levels. But of course, this does not guarantee that we will engage in actions that mitigate climate change. Many altruistic people do not care much for the environment, instead putting their priorities in social causes, for example. Moreover, altruistic people can also make mistakes, based on a misunderstanding of the problem or the ways in which it can be solved. Hence, given that our enhancement will not be radical, we could never predict the goals and behaviours of the enhanced person.

6. Cognitive Enhancement?

Persson and Savulescu mention that it would be beneficial to enhance more cognitive aspects of our moral psychology. However, they do not account for the fact that without cognitive enhancement their proposal could not get off the ground. This, however, complicates the project further as now two separate enhancements would have to be developed in order to make "moral enhancement" a viable solution to the climate crisis. Persson and Savulescu argue that increasing

---

[67]   Handfield, et al., 'Climate Change, Cooperation and Moral Bioenhancement'.

Aleksandra Kulawska and Michael Hauskeller

our levels of altruism would result in our being more altruistic towards distant others, the planet, and animals. In other words, they believe that enhancing our levels of altruism would increase the *scope* of our altruism, which would then make us better able to respond to global problems. This, however, seems unlikely. As we have seen in the previous section, altruism enhanced through bio-medical means did not result in the increased *scope* of altruism, but rather, in the increased *intensity* of altruism, which means that people felt more altruistic towards those with whom they were already socially bonded. This, in turn, led to a number of anti-social behaviours towards the out-group members. Hence, as one study concluded, 'although in humans OT [oxytocin] may strengthen existing social bonds (for example, between relatives/friends), [...] it does not create bonds de novo (for example, between strangers)'.[68] It seems that in order to get past this problem and realise Persson and Savulescu's proposal of enhancing the scope of our altruism, we will need to cognitively enhance ourselves. This is because a cognitive bias, parochialism, is responsible for our prioritising the interests of our immediate kin over the interests of the strangers.[69,70] Simply increasing levels of altruism does not get rid of cognitive bias, and, hence, is unlikely to impact on our concern for distant others and motivate us to join strangers in co-operative actions aiming to mitigate climate change. Rather, it is only through cognitive enhancement that we could forgo our bias towards family and friends and become more concerned for global issues and distant strangers.

However, enhancing altruism in scope would not be enough to achieve the desired effect of mitigating climate change. This is because we would still be biased towards our near future, and as such, we would prioritise issues that that require our immediate attention, rather than issues that seem more distant. Imagine that a person X is enhanced so that she is more altruistic towards strangers, and, hence, more motivated to alleviate their suffering. Given that she is still biased towards the near future, she will focus on the issues that will alleviate the suffering of the distant others in the present. For example, X may support charities that aim to feed the hungry or build new houses for the homeless. It is only when we cognitively enhance ourselves so that we can forgo our bias

---

[68]   Christian Grillon, et al., 'Oxytocin Increases Anxiety to Unpredictable Threat', *Molecular Psychiatry* **18**:9 (2013), 958–960.
[69]   Bernhard, 'Parochial Altruism in Humans'.
[70]   Gifford, 'The Dragons of Inaction'.

towards the near future, that we can become truly concerned and motivated to alleviate the suffering of future generations by acting in the present, and, hence, become more motivated to adopt climate-friendly behaviours. Otherwise we will continue to focus on the issues that require immediate attention – such as hunger, homelessness, direct injustice, etc. Of course, this is not to say that these issues are not important. The point we wish to make is simply that moral enhancement without cognitive enhancement is not likely to achieve the goals that Persson and Savulescu assume it will.

It also seems that cognitive enhancement of some sort would have to accompany moral enhancement in order to ensure that morally enhanced people know what actions they should engage in in order to mitigate climate change. This is because many of us do not understand the causes and drivers of climate change and, hence, do not know in what ways we can help to mitigate it.[71] They would not suddenly achieve that understanding following moral enhancement, which would mean that many of them would be motivated to fight climate change, but would not know how. Cognitive enhancement would fill that gap, ensuring that the morally enhanced would be able to take the right course of action for climate change mitigation.

Moral enhancement without cognitive enhancement could not achieve its aims. However, the current state of science of cognitive enhancement of this sort is still very much limited. We do not know in what ways, if any, it would be possible to engineer our brains so that we could get rid of something so specific as parochialism or bias towards the near future. This makes Persson's and Savulescu's proposal even more complicated, and, hence, less viable as a response to the ongoing climate crisis.

7. Implementation Problems

Finally, there are also some practical problems with Persson and Saculescu's proposal. Firstly, it seems that moral enhancement will have to be compulsory in order to have the potential of mitigating climate change. This is because the overwhelming majority of people on the globe will not voluntarily agree to moral enhancement. Moral enhancement will be perceived as dangerous and there will certainly be many misconceptions and conspiracy theories regarding its

---

[71] T. W. Reynolds, et al., 'Now What Do People Know About Climate Change? Survey Studies of Educated Laypeople', *Risk Analysis* **30**:10 (2010), 1520–1538.

implementation. Moreover, since the majority of us are not overly concerned about climate change and are not very willing to engage in climate-friendly behaviours, we will likely not have any motivation to undergo such risky biomedical intervention. Most Probably only those of us who are already concerned about climate change and highly motivated to mitigate it will choose to undergo moral enhancement. This of course will not lead to any satisfactory outcomes, as moral enhancement could only be successful in mitigating climate change if we enhanced those of us who are not highly motivated to adopt climate-friendly behaviours. Hence, in order to have the potential to mitigate climate change, moral enhancement would have to be compulsory.

However, it is not clear whether such moral enhancement could even be possible to implement. After all, the majority of us tend to consider freedom to be one of the most important rights. Those policies that propose to limit our freedom in some narrow social or economic domain are usually strictly opposed by the majority of citizens and often lead to violent protests. It is easy to imagine the uproar and hostility with which the proposal of forced moral enhancement would be met.

Hence, the only way in which we could implement forced moral enhancement would be to do it without the knowledge of the public. This proposal, however, raises further problems. Not only would it be morally wrong to enhance people without their knowledge and consent, such "hidden" enhancement could also easily lead to a situation where politicians, businessmen, or otherwise powerful people could avoid being enhanced either because they would be the ones implementing moral enhancement or because they could bribe those who would be in charge of implementing moral enhancement. Those people, however, are the ones that are probably in most urgent need of moral enhancement, as they hold an enormous power to implement climate-friendly policies and put money into research on climate technologies. It is also difficult to imagine how the public would not realise that there are being enhanced. After all, those people who were previously less altruistic would suddenly become much more altruistic than before. Moreover, we would also presumably notice the changes in our mental states.

This is of course just a brief sketch of the problems that we may encounter when planning forced or voluntary moral enhancement. However, it already tells us that the project will be incredibly difficult, if not impossible, to implement in a way which would not create social havoc and disorder yet still allow for successful climate change mitigation.

One last point: Persson and Savulescu argue that if we are able to develop satisfactory moral enhancement we should enhance everyone on the globe. This is presumably to avoid the issues of free-riding of the unenhanced on the enhanced and ensure that enough people co-operate in joint goals to mitigate climate change. Moreover, this also ensures that we enhance those who, if enhanced, could have a significant positive impact on the planet. These would include presidents, heads of environmental agencies, businessmen, and so on. However, once again this proposal raises many difficult problems. Some are moral, and they have been widely discussed already, which is why we will not discuss them here. Others are legal and administrative. The legal and administrative process required to ensure that 7 billion people on the planet are enhanced seems, frankly, impossible. A more plausible solution here could perhaps be to genetically engineer future populations so that they are more just and altruistic. However, as Persson and Savulescu admit, we are not anywhere near developing such complicated technology. Moreover, such technology would result in a world consisting of the younger, morally "better" people and the older, morally "worse" people. Such an unequal situation would be likely to have a detrimental effect on intergenerational relations and increase potential free-riding. Hence it seems that it is both problematic to enhance only some people and to enhance everyone.

8. Conclusion

To conclude: even if we could, somehow, overcome all these various problems, it is very unlikely that we would be able to develop moral enhancement necessary for mitigating climate change in time. The science of moral enhancement is still very much in its infancy,[72] while climate change is already having serious effects on the planet. If we proceed with the "business as usual" scenario, meaning that we fail to reduce our emissions of GHGs, and hence, the concentrations of GHGs in the atmosphere, then climate change will start becoming a serious problem very soon and potentially prove deadly in the second half of this century.[73] This would mean that our time

---

[72] Crockett, 'Moral Bioenhancement'.
[73] IPCC, *Climate Change 2007*.

Aleksandra Kulawska and Michael Hauskeller

for developing sufficient moral enhancement, proving its safety, establishing world-wide regulation and laws necessary for making sure that everyone is enhanced, and then distributing morally-enhancing pills and ensuring that everyone takes them, is very limited, and in all likelihood much too short.

University of Birmingham
aek851@student.bham.ac.uk
University of Liverpool
M.Hauskeller@liverpool.ac.uk

Should We Biochemically Enhance Sexual Fidelity?

ROBBIE ARRELL

Abstract

In certain corners of the moral enhancement debate, it has been suggested we ought to consider the prospect of supplementing conventional methods of enhancing sexual fidelity (e.g. relationship counselling, moral education, self-betterment, etc.) with biochemical fidelity enhancement methods. In surveying this argument, I begin from the conviction that generally-speaking moral enhancement ought to expectably attenuate (or at least not exacerbate) vulnerability. Assuming conventional methods of enhancing sexual fidelity are at least partially effective in this respect – e.g., that relationship counselling sometimes successfully attenuates the particular vulnerability victims of infidelity feel – then presumably the case for supplementing conventional methods with biochemical methods turns, in part, on the claim that doing so will better promote attenuation of victim vulnerability.

In this chapter I argue that on a sufficiently sophisticated conception of what this vulnerability consists in, biochemical methods of enhancing fidelity will not expectably attenuate victims' vulnerability. Moreover, when combined with conventional methods, biochemical methods will predictably tend to undermine whatever attenuation conventional methods expectably promote in that respect. Thus, I conclude that couples committed to saving their relationship following an instance of sexual infidelity have reason to prefer conventional methods of enhancing sexual fidelity *sans* biochemical methods to conventional methods *plus* biochemical methods.

1. Introduction

Sexual infidelity is bad.[1] Extra-pair sex is frequently cited as being amongst the most powerful predictors of relationship failure and/or

---

[1] I provide no real argument for this assertion here. I merely assume that if you value your partner's sexual fidelity, their being sexually unfaithful will constitute a harm to you. I also assume that being in a sexually open or otherwise non-monogamous relationship does not insulate against such harms; by the shared norms of even open or polygamous relationships there are still persons who are presumably deemed off-limits (e.g. partners' siblings, parents, friends, etc.), such that having sex with them would constitute a harmful sexual betrayal. For ease of exposition, I will also assume that sexual infidelity involves sexual intercourse. I do not as a matter of

doi:10.1017/S1358246118000462   ©The Royal Institute of Philosophy and the contributors 2018

Royal Institute of Philosophy Supplement **83** 2018

divorce.[2] Cross-culturally, affronts to 'male sexual proprietariness' resulting from sexual infidelities by women (actual or suspected) are a leading cause of spousal battering and spousal homicide.[3] And of course there are simply the painful experiences of anguish, psychological distress, depression, anger, betrayal, resentment, and humiliation that commonly afflict victims of infidelity. Given this list of harms, sexual betrayals are often not obstacles to be overcome, but reasons to part ways. Other times, though, couples desire nothing more than to rescue their relationships and are willing to go to great lengths to make that happen. However, whilst conventional methods of mending faltering relationships such as relationship counselling are commonplace, the statistics suggest that such methods are, at best, only partially effective. According to some research, approximately one third of couples fail to realise any significant gains as a result of counselling, whilst 30–60% report significant deterioration in their relationship in studies that track marital satisfaction for two years or longer after counselling ends, with as many as 35% of couples divorced within four years of termination.[4]

In an intriguing turn in the moral enhancement debate, Brian D. Earp, Anders Sandberg, Julian Savulescu, and Olga A. Wudarczyk have variously touted biochemical methods of enhancing sexual fidelity as a potential and even desirable solution to fidelity-related relationship woes.[5] Recent research in behavioural genetics and neuroscience

---

fact believe sexual infidelity requires intercourse, but the debate about what does constitute sexual infidelity is beyond the remit of this essay.

   [2]   Laura Betzig, 'Causes of Conjugal Dissolution: A Cross-Cultural Study', *Current Anthropology* **30**:5 (1989), 654–676; Paul R. Amato and Denise Previti, 'People's Reasons for Divorcing: Gender, Social Class, the Life Course, and Adjustment', *Journal of Family Issues* **24**:5 (2003), 602–626.

   [3]   Martin Daly and Margo Wilson, 'Evolutionary Social Psychology and Family Homicide', *Science* **242**:4878 (1988), 519–524, 521.

   [4]   Douglas K. Snyder, Angela M. Castellani, and Mark A. Whisman, 'Current Status and Future Directions in Couple Therapy', *Annual Review of Psychology* **57** (2006), 317–344.

   [5]   Julian Savulescu and Anders Sandberg, 'Neuroenhancement of Love and Marriage: The Chemicals Between Us', *Neuroethics* **1**:1 (2008), 31–44; Brian D. Earp, Anders Sandberg, and Julian Savulescu, 'Natural Selection, Childrearing, and the Ethics of Marriage (and Divorce): Building a Case for the Neuroenhancement of Human Relationships', *Philosophy & Technology* **25**:4 (2012), 561–587; Brian D. Earp, Olga A. Wudarczyk, Anders Sandberg, and Julian Savulescu, 'If I Could Just Stop Loving

Should We Biochemically Enhance Sexual Fidelity?

suggests that certain of the counter-moral impulses that commonly contribute to relationship breakdown – amongst them the proclivity for extra-pair sexual intimacy – are, in part, biologically or genetically determined.[6] On the back of this research, and the great value to us that comes of partaking in loving and lasting relationships (as well as the disvalue of squandered love), Earp, et al. have suggested 'it is time to move beyond merely *describing* the brain systems involved in love, attachment and commitment; we should begin to think about *intervening* in those systems directly, to give love a helping hand'.[7]

At first blush, the prospect of deploying 'love drugs'[8] to enhance relationships strikes many as worrisome, and reservations about their desirability abound. These include doubts about efficacy (could biotechnologies realise the intrinsic good of love at all?); concerns about restrictions of freedom (is the freedom to form and act upon morally suboptimal motives perhaps valuable in its own right, even if the bad motives and acts themselves are not?); fears surrounding authenticity (would a bioenhanced love be an "authentic" love of the kind we generally desire?); and worries about misuse (is there a risk love drugs will be forced on recalcitrant partners? Or perhaps even used to sustain bad relationships?). I mention these reservations only fleetingly here since they arguably all presuppose the success of a prior claim which is the concern of this essay: that biochemical methods of morally enhancing relationships expectably attenuate (or at least do not exacerbate) vulnerability. If this is not so, as I argue in the case of sexual fidelity bioenhancements, the independent objections these concerns foreground are superfluous.

In the opening section of this chapter, I motivate the claim that generally-speaking moral enhancement ought to expectably attenuate vulnerability. Assuming conventional methods of morally enhancing

---

You: Anti-Love Biotechnology and the Ethics of a Chemical Breakup', *The American Journal of Bioethics* **13**:11 (2013), 3–17.

[6] Justin R. Garcia, James MacKillop, Edward L. Aller, Ann M. Merriwether, David Sloan Wilson, and J. Koji Lum, 'Associations between Dopamine D4 Receptor Gene Variation with Both Infidelity and Sexual Promiscuity', *PLoS One* **5**:11 (2010), e14162; Brendan P. Zietsch, Lars Westberg, Pekka Santtila, and Patrick Jern, 'Genetic Analysis of Human Extrapair Mating: Heritability, Between-Sex Correlation, and Receptor Genes for Vasopressin and Oxytocin', *Evolution and Human Behaviour* **36**:2 (2015), 130–136.

[7] Earp, et al., 'Natural Selection, Childrearing, and the Ethics of Marriage (and Divorce)', 583. Emphasis in original.

[8] Savulescu and Sandberg, 'Neuroenhancement of Love and Marriage', 37.

Robbie Arrell

sexual fidelity are at least partially effective in this respect – e.g., that relationship counselling sometimes successfully attenuates the particular vulnerability victims of infidelity experience – then presumably the case for supplementing conventional methods with biochemical methods presupposes that doing so will better promote attenuation of victim vulnerability. In order to explore whether that is so or not, I go on in the next section to construct a hypothetical case of a couple committed to rescuing their relationship following an instance of sexual infidelity. In assessing that case, the question is not whether it is actually possible to biochemically modulate sexual fidelity (I assume it is); nor is it whether a "fidelity drug" of sorts would work (I assume it works precisely as intended); and nor is it whether it would be morally permissible for the couple in question to deploy fidelity drugs (I assume it is). Rather, the driving question is whether – even with these assumptions in place – the couple have good reason to introduce fidelity drugs into their relationship therapy regime. In section four, I suggest not, for on a sufficiently sophisticated conception of what vulnerability born of sexual infidelity consists in, fidelity drugs will not expectably attenuate victims' vulnerability. Moreover, when fidelity drugs are introduced into therapy regimes alongside conventional methods like counselling, they will predictably tend to undermine whatever attenuation conventional methods expectably promote in that respect. Thus, in section five, I conclude that couples committed to saving their relationship following an instance of sexual infidelity have presumptively decisive reason to prefer conventional methods of morally enhancing sexual fidelity *sans* biochemical methods to conventional methods *plus* biochemical methods. In the final section I canvas two objections.

2. Moral Enhancement and Vulnerability

Thomas Douglas defines moral enhancement thus: '[a] person morally enhances herself if she alters herself in a way that may reasonably be expected to result in her having morally better future motives, taken in sum, than she would otherwise have had'.[9] That usefully clarifies what moral enhancement consists in, but what, we may yet ask, is its end? David DeGrazia's model which distinguishes three mutually

---

[9] Thomas Douglas, 'Moral Enhancement', *Journal of Applied Philosophy* **25**:3 (2008), 228–245, 229.

supportive functions of moral enhancement suggests a response to that further question:

1. *Motivational improvement*: better motives, character traits and overall motivation to do what is right.
2. *Improved insight*: better understanding – accessible when decisions are needed – of what is right.
3. *Behavioural improvement*: greater conformity to appropriate moral norms and therefore a higher frequency of right action.[10]

DeGrazia proposes that motivational improvement and improved insight, whether promoted in conjunction or independently, conduce to behavioural improvement. And since '[b]*ehavioural improvement is highly desirable in the interest of making the world a better place and securing better lives for human beings and other sentient beings*', moral enhancement is therefore desirable.[11] Notably, neither improvements of motivation or insight, nor the behavioural improvements they conduce to, are themselves the ends. Rather, the end of moral enhancement is to make the world a better and safer place for human and non-human beings alike. Thus, motivational, epistemic, and behavioural improvements fostered by moral enhancement are desirable, in part, for the concomitant attenuation of vulnerability such improvements expectably promote.

This notion – that attenuation of vulnerability is a core end of moral enhancement – is oft-implied in the literature, though rarely made explicit. For example, Douglas's defence of moral bioenhancement against the 'Bioconservative Thesis' demonstrably lends itself to such an interpretation.[12] The Bioconservative Thesis posits that whilst bioenhancement of physical ability, intelligence, cognitive capacity, etc. might benefit enhanced individuals, such enhancements risk introducing a manifestly unjust social stratification of enhanced/unenhanced. A world in which an elite bioenhanced stratum are able to run faster and jump higher (both literally and metaphorically) would foreseeably disadvantage and exacerbate the vulnerability of those for whom bioenhancement is not within reach. Therefore, bioenhancement is morally impermissible. However, Douglas rejects this objection as indecisive *vis-à-vis* moral bioenhancement. He contends that, unlike

---

[10] David DeGrazia, 'Moral Enhancement, Freedom, and What We (Should) Value in Moral Behaviour', *Journal of Medical Ethics* **40**:6 (2014), 361–368, 362–363. Emphasis in original.
[11] DeGrazia, 'Moral Enhancement, Freedom, and What We (Should) Value in Moral Behaviour', 363. Emphasis in original.
[12] Douglas, 'Moral Enhancement', 229.

cognitive or physical bioenhancements, *moral* bioenhancements 'could not easily be criticised on the ground that their use by some would disadvantage others. On any plausible moral theory, a person's having morally better motives will tend to be to the advantage of others'.[13] If Douglas is right, then the Bioconservative Thesis – that bioenhancement generally is impermissible because it exacerbates the vulnerability of the unenhanced – is false.

If Douglas's negative argument saved moral bioenhancement from the charge that bioenhancements generally exacerbate vulnerability, it simultaneously paved the way for positive arguments in favour of moral bioenhancements. For if it is generally true of moral bioenhancements that what is good for the goose is good for the gaggle, their increased uptake is in principle concordant with promoting attenuation of vulnerability globally (i.e., amongst enhanced and unenhanced alike), or at least not in competition with that end. And nowhere is the pressing need to diminish our vulnerability to harm so pivotally deployed in defence of the moral enhancement project as in the works of Ingmar Persson and Julian Savulescu.[14] They observe that the *status quo* of moral behaviour is disconcertingly unsatisfactory, pointing out that conventional methods of moral enhancement such as moral education, socialisation, public policies and self-improvement have thus far proved, at best, modestly effective in averting pressing contemporary crises such as climate change and poverty. And things are only set to get worse, it seems. Given the increasing risk of catastrophic eventualities that accompanies exponential technological innovation and expansion, they worry that already off-the-pace conventional methods will fare even worse going forward. As the title of Persson and Savulescu's book suggests, our evolved social and psychobiological natures have, it would seem, left us *Unfit for the Future*.[15] Since conventional methods of moral enhancement have thus far proved so unequal to the task of attenuating or even abating vulnerability risks, they argue that moral bioenhancement deserves our serious consideration as a prospective (and perhaps the only) way out of the corner humanity has backed itself into.

---

[13] Douglas, 'Moral Enhancement', 230.

[14] Ingmar Persson and Julian Savulescu, *Unfit for the Future: The Need for Moral Enhancement* (Oxford: Oxford University Press, 2012); Ingmar Persson and Julian Savulescu, 'Moral Enhancement, Freedom and the God Machine', *Monist* **95**:3 (2012), 399–421; Ingmar Persson and Julian Savulescu, 'Getting Moral Enhancement Right: The Desirability of Moral Bioenhancement', *Bioethics* **27**:3 (2013), 124–131.

[15] Persson and Savulescu, *Unfit for the Future*.

Should We Biochemically Enhance Sexual Fidelity?

Whether civilisation can rescue itself from itself via moral bioenhancement is a question for another time, and the argument presented here cannot and should not be read as a jeremiad against moral bioenhancement generally. The purpose here is merely to motivate an end common to all modes of moral bioenhancement, not an objection that necessarily afflicts all modes of moral bioenhancement in common. If one such common end is, as I conjecture, attenuation of vulnerability, then plausibly one of the first questions we should ask when assessing any particular mode of moral bioenhancement is: will it expectably attenuate (or at least not exacerbate) vulnerability? If the answer is yes (as I believe it is with respect to the more general modes of moral bioenhancement Persson and Savulescu endorse), then proceeding to address further questions concerning authenticity, coercion, freedom, misappropriation, societal implications, etc. may be warranted; but if the answer is no, then however philosophically interesting such questions may be, that may be all they are.

Thus parsed, the question that informs the remainder of this essay is this: would supplementing conventional methods of enhancing sexual fidelity with biochemical methods – or "fidelity drugs" – expectably attenuate (or at least not exacerbate) the vulnerability victims typically experience in the wake of instances of sexual infidelity?

3. Fidelity Actually[16]

Biotechnologies designed to enhance sexual fidelity specifically have not received much focussed attention in the literature, but the potentiality of them is often invoked (most squarely by Earp, et al.) in a supporting role as part of a suite of possible relationship neuroenhancements:

> Just like fidelity, adultery appears to be heavily influenced by brain and even gene-level factors. Variations in a dopamine receptor gene have been found to correlate in humans with infidelity and sexual promiscuity (Garcia, et al. 2010). This outcome might be carried out through effects on libido, sensation-seeking, or impulsivity. Similar findings have been reported in rodents (Curtis, et al. 2006). Infidelity may also occur through less direct routes – stemming from asymmetrical sexual interests

[16] The Harry and Karen case introduced in this section is loosely adapted from the storyline involving those characters (played by Alan Rickman and Emma Thompson) in the 2003 Richard Curtis film *Love Actually*.

between partners, for instance. As relationships outlast their evolved scaffolding, disparities in sexual desire between men and women tend to expand (Klusmann 2002, 2006): in the typical pattern, men whose libido remains constant while their wives' begins to wane disproportionately seek sexual fulfilment outside the relationship (Buss 1994). By heightening sexual desire in the less aroused partner (by using testosterone, for instance, see Braunstein, et al. 2005; Sherwin 2002; Sherwin and Gelfand 1987; Sherwin, et al. 1985) or reducing it in the more aroused partner, the discrepancy could be minimized, possibly softening a major source of relationship strain. In fact, testosterone levels fall naturally in men upon marriage or the birth of a child and rise naturally at a relationship's end (to encourage novel mate-seeking behaviors, see Eastwick 2009): deliberately moderating these levels in the right way could promote male parenting and discourage a wandering eye.[17]

Given such advances in our understanding of the psychobiological underpinnings of monogamy, sexual fidelity, attraction, etc., the prospect of fidelity drugs is not a far-fetched one. Moreover, fidelity drugs are in certain respects arguably more appealing than love drugs. For whilst perhaps few would want their partner's love to be caused or sustained by drugs, if the partner's tendency to bestow loving care on their beloved is there but impaired by some psychobiological feature that may be biochemically manipulated into submission, then many of the standard objections to bioenhancing love *per se* lose much of their force. The fact is that even otherwise loving partners sometimes lie, and sometimes they cheat. If, as the neuroscientific research suggests, the proclivity for extra-pair sexual activity is in part biologically determined and we could attenuate it via biochemical manipulation, should we?

We can easily imagine cases in which we would (and should) say no, but it is equally plausible to construct more favourable cases. Suppose Harry and Karen have been married for 25 years and are still very much in love. However, whilst Karen's interest in sex has waned over the years, Harry's has remained relatively constant. Harry is the managing director of a design agency, and finds himself subject to increasingly overt sexual advances from his attractive young secretary Mia. Despite managing to resist the temptation initially, his resolve ultimately deserts him and he ends up embarking upon a sexual affair

---

[17]   Earp, et al., 'Natural Selection, Childrearing, and the Ethics of Marriage (and Divorce)', 583. Parenthetical references in original.

with Mia. Karen discovers the affair and is unsurprisingly devastated. However, upon confronting Harry about it, she sees that he is profoundly regretful of his indiscretion and believes him when he says he still loves her. After talking it through openly and honestly, they reach a joint decision that they do not want to give up on their marriage and both commit to doing their level best, whatever that may entail, to save it. The first thing they do is start seeing a relationship counsellor. After a number of sessions, the counsellor tells them about a new fidelity drug. She never mentioned it earlier because she only recommends this particular treatment to couples once she is convinced (a) that neither party is coercing the other to attend; and (b) that the love they share, though tarnished, is genuine and authentic in both directions. Having decreed that these criteria are satisfied, their counsellor proceeds to explain that all the drug will do is modulate Harry's psychobiology so as to diminish his proclivity for extra-pair sexual activity, and that there are no adverse side effects. In addition, she stresses to them that (c) the effect of the drug is merely to inhibit the impulse to engage in extra-pair copulation, not eliminate it. And finally, she assures them that (d) the drug will not immutably alter Harry's psychobiology, and he is free to unilaterally terminate the course of treatment at any time (as is Karen).

The hypothetical scenario is stylised so as to nullify a number of standard objections to the neuroenhancement of relationships. Firstly, (a) mitigates concerns surrounding coercion or offence against individual or marital autonomy. Secondly, (b) allows us to fence off concerns about preserving bad or damaging relationships, as well as authenticity issues. Harry and Karen's relationship is not unhealthy or oppressive, and whilst authenticity might be an issue if love drugs are used to cause or create love where none previously existed, it is less troublesome in cases like this where the authenticity is already there and not in question. Thirdly, (c) circumvents the objection that the virtue of fidelity requires the possibility of infidelity, since the possibility that Harry will be unfaithful remains live, just less probable. (c) also dilutes the objection that bioenhanced Harry would lack the freedom to form and act upon the motive to sleep with other women which might itself be valuable even if the bad motives and acts are not. Harry's freedom is perhaps restricted, but by no means vanquished, and it is difficult to see any problem with this kind of self-imposed voluntary restriction of freedom providing it is fully informed. Finally, whatever one might think about temporally restricted Ulysses pacts – e.g., the pact Ulysses himself made with his crew that they bind him to the ship's mast until out of earshot of the Sirens' songs (from which the term derives) – to metaphorically bind oneself to the mast once and for all time is apt to strike some as troublesome, hence the inclusion of (d).

With these conditions *in situ*, I think Earp, et al. might say (as they do of love drugs generally) that the couple should at least 'be at *liberty* to use love drugs, and that they may have several good *reasons* to do so as well'.[18] The first part of this statement need not detain us. I doubt there exist many methods (conventional or otherwise) of enhancing sexual fidelity that could be deemed morally impermissible, once the kinds of background conditions built into the Harry and Karen case are satisfied. It is the second part that interest me. Elsewhere, Earp, et al. similarly lay claim to establishing 'a reasonable initial case for the moral permissibility – even prudence – of attempting drug-based modification of love and love-related phenomena for at least some individuals and some couples'.[19] However, it is not always prudent to do that which is morally permissible. And so the question remains: do Harry and Karen have good reason to deploy the fidelity drug?

Suppose the only expectable consequences of taking the fidelity drug for Harry will be: (i) an alteration of his psychobiology in those (and only those) ways necessary to curtail his desire for extra-pair sexual activity; (ii) enhancement of his '"bigger picture" decision-making autonomy'[20] as his higher order goals are freed from the shackles of his lower order psychobiological urges; and (iii) promotion of the probability that he will be faithful. If the end of moral enhancement is moral improvement in motivations, insight, and behaviour, and (by hypothesis) the fidelity drug improves Harry in these respects, then it would seem the couple do indeed have good reason to introduce the fidelity drug into their relationship therapy regime.

But this is too quick. The consequences for Harry are surely not the only relevant (or perhaps even most important) consequential considerations in the vicinity. In order to reach a fully informed position on whether the couple have good reason to deploy the fidelity drug, we also need to consider the expected consequences of Harry's bioenhancement for Karen. Three candidate consequences in particular warrant detailed analysis.

---

[18] Earp, et al., 'Natural Selection, Childrearing, and the Ethics of Marriage (and Divorce)', 562. Emphasis in original.

[19] Brian D. Earp, Anders Sandberg, and Julian Savulescu, 'Brave New Love: The Threat of High-Tech "Conversion" Therapy and the Bio-Oppression of Sexual Minorities', *AJOB Neuroscience* 5:1 (2014), 4–12, 5.

[20] Earp, et al., 'Brave New Love', 4–5.

Should We Biochemically Enhance Sexual Fidelity?

3.1 The Promotion of the Probability of Fidelity

The first and most obvious expected consequence of Harry's bioenhancement for Karen would be promotion of the probability that he will in future be faithful. This would seem like a positive consequence for Karen. However, on refection, it is not clear that how probable it is that one's partner will comply with their duty to be faithful really matters. As Philip Pettit has argued, robustly demanding goods like fidelity tend by nature to be probabilistically insensitive.[21] Suppose Harry attends a work party where there are two women seeking a sexual encounter, and by the aesthetic standards of one – Mia – he is judged attractive, whilst by the standards of the other – Sarah – he is not. If the utility to Karen of Harry complying with his duty to be faithful is the same with respect to both women, and both are equally desirous of attractive men (despite their divergent subjective aesthetic standards), the probability of Karen's realising the utility of Harry's compliance with his duty to be faithful is lower with respect to Sarah who deems him unattractive, and higher with respect to Mia who deems him very attractive. Thus, assuming the expected utility to Karen of Harry's fidelity = utility x probability, and the probability of Harry having to comply with his duty to be faithful is higher with respect to Mia, then it should count for less with Karen if he buckles and sleeps with Sarah than if he buckles and sleeps with Mia. But this seems deeply counterintuitive (and, I suspect, deeply irrelevant to Karen).

Moreover, if ramping up the probability that Harry will not be unfaithful again were what really mattered to Karen, alternative more effective methods should surely be preferred to the fidelity drug (which, by hypothesis, merely reduces the likelihood that Harry will be unfaithful). For example, if Harry were instead to agree to don a male chastity device whenever out of Karen's sight from now on, the probability of his being faithful would presumably be 1. The fact that intuitively there seems something amiss in relying on such strategies suggests that, although fidelity drugs would reduce the likelihood of sexual indiscretions, this is not what really matters (or at least it is not all that matters). If there is good reason from Karen's perspective as the victim of infidelity to introduce the fidelity drug into their therapy programme, it seems the explanation of why that is must derive from something over and beyond the expectation that it will promote the probability that Harry will in future remain faithful.

---

[21] Philip Pettit, *The Robust Demands of the Good* (Oxford: Oxford University Press, 2015), 111–115.

3.2 The Reduced Likelihood of Exposure to Negative Reactive Emotions

A second predictable consequence of Harry's bioenhancement for Karen would be a decreased likelihood that she will experience a repeat of the kinds of negative reactive emotions the initial sexual betrayal provoked. Presuming Karen hopes to never again experience the betrayal, humiliation, and resentment Harry's sexual indiscretion sparked in her, this looks like another welcome consequence. But this cannot be the whole story either. Suppose upon discovering the affair Karen immediately presses Harry to reveal how long it has been going on, and he admits that it began six months ago. Karen might feel that, right there and then, at the moment of revelation, she is robbed of the good of Harry's fidelity. Or, she might feel that whatever good of Harry's fidelity she "thought" she enjoyed was dashed six months ago the moment he leapt into bed with Mia for the first time. Intuitively, the right conclusion is the latter. Yet, if what really mattered to Karen in desiring Harry's fidelity were the insulation against betrayal, humiliation, and resentment she enjoys as a result, and if it is only at the moment of revelation that those negative emotions "react" in her, then there would be no reason to think the second conclusion should follow more readily than the first. That it does suggests there must be more to the story of fidelity and why it matters than the fact that it insulates against negative reactive emotions. So, again, if it is a good idea from Karen's perspective to deploy the fidelity drug, the basis for that must be something more than the mere fact that Harry's bioenhancement would expectably decrease the likelihood that she will in future experience the negative emotions that go hand-in-hand with being a victim of sexual infidelity.

3.3 The Attenuation of Vulnerability

If the two expected consequences of fidelity bioenhancement just canvassed do not really matter (or at least they alone do not matter), what does? I propose there is a third expectable consequence of Harry's bioenhancement that Karen might desire above promotion of the probability that Harry will in future be faithful, and the decreased likelihood of being put through the emotional wringer again (though of course she desires these too). This third consequence of Harry's bioenhancement is attenuation of the heightened vulnerability Karen experiences in the wake of his sexual indiscretion.

Should We Biochemically Enhance Sexual Fidelity?

The relevant conception of vulnerability here is that of vulnerability to another's free will developed by Pettit.[22] The basic idea stems from what seems a truism of romantic relationships: that sharing a romantic relationship with someone typically renders you vulnerable to certain special kinds of wrongs and betrayals they are uniquely placed to inflict upon you.[23] After all, in virtue of being an agent to whom you ascribe free will, your partner is practically-speaking free to enact all kinds of options across choice-sets relevant to your welfare: they are free to be unfaithful should they so choose, or not; free to abuse you, or not; free to walk out on you, or not; and so on. Since in these kinds of choice-sets there is no practical barrier to prevent them from choosing one option or the other, you are in effect subject to their power to impose/withhold those harms. To be subject to the will of another in this way is to be vulnerable. Ordinarily, however, knowing with reasonable confidence that your partner is appropriately disposed to accord your interests special deliberative significance across choice sets relevant to your welfare provides you with valuable protection against the expansive exercise of their will. For in virtue of their being so disposed, the range of deliberative options that populate their choice sets are self-restricted in a way that attenuates your vulnerability to being hurt by them. Indeed, if all is well in this respect, many of the options your partner is practically free to enact – e.g., to sleep around, abuse you, or walk out on you without explanation – will not register as options at all, being ring-fenced outside of the range of your partner's relevant choice-sets properly restricted.

Having sketched the details of Pettit's conception of vulnerability, we begin to see more clearly the particular character of the harm

---

[22] Pettit, *The Robust Demands of the Good*, 120–137.

[23] More specifically, your partner is capable of inflicting certain wrongs on you or hurting you in ways that strangers are not; i.e., wrongs rendered "special" in virtue of facts about the special relationship you share. Strangers are of course perfectly capable of imposing on you all sorts of general harms or wrongs, but it would be bizarre to charge a stranger with the wrong of being sexually unfaithful to you in the absence of any kind of sexually exclusive relationship between you. Additionally, even when a stranger is capable of inflicting a wrong on you that is qualitatively similar to some wrong your partner might inflict on you, the partner-inflicted wrong will be special in a manner that the stranger-inflicted wrong cannot be, since in addition to the substantive wrong suffered the former also comprises a betrayal. This is why it feels worse if your partner steals money from your bank account than if an anonymous hacker steals from your account, even when the sum stolen is the same.

Harry's sexual infidelity wreaks on Karen and their marriage. At the time of embarking on his affair with Mia, Harry was practically free to enact either of two options: remain faithful, or be unfaithful. In choosing the latter, Harry opted to wrong Karen (the refrain "I didn't mean to hurt you – it just happened!" does not change the fact that he freely chose to cheat over the equally practically viable option of not cheating). As a result, Karen's confidence that Harry is appropriately disposed to be robustly faithful to her (of which she previously felt reasonably assured) is shattered. Importantly, what Karen loses confidence in is not Harry's disposition to be faithful *as such*. Rather, what she is stripped of is the confidence she had (pre-affair) that Harry's disposition to be faithful is sufficient to ensure he robustly refrains from engaging in extra-marital sex. In other words, what she previously believed – that Harry is sufficiently well disposed to refrain from sleeping with other women, not just across scenarios in which doing so comes easy (e.g., scenarios in which no-one sexually propositions him), but also across scenarios in which doing so does not (e.g., the scenario in which Mia sexually propositions him) – no longer holds.

Thus, what Karen doubts (post-affair) is not so much that Harry wants to be faithful to her, but that his wanting to be faithful is enough to ensure he actually will be (or to warrant confidence on her part that he will be). And it is this worry which reduces her to a state of vulnerability, stripped of the valuable protection from Harry's free will she once enjoyed. To give their marriage a fighting chance, then, it is imperative the couple alight on a therapy regime that not only promotes the probability that, in future, Harry will be faithful, but also (and crucially) restores Karen's confidence that he is appropriately disposed to be. For as long as Karen remains plagued by doubts about whether Harry is able to "keep it in his pants", not just when no-one is trying to get in his pants anyway, but also when attractive younger women like Mia are, attenuation of the heightened vulnerability to Harry's will she experiences in the wake of his affair will elude her. So, the question is: would introducing the fidelity drug into their therapy regime foster restoration of Karen's confidence in Harry's disposition to be robustly faithful?

4. The Problem with Fidelity Drugs

It seems to me highly unlikely that administering the fidelity drug to Harry would do much, if anything, to bolster Karen's confidence that he is sufficiently well disposed to robustly refrain from sleeping with other women. And that is so, even in this highly stylised case where, by hypothesis, the fidelity drug successfully: (i) promotes the probability that Harry will be faithful; (ii) enhances Harry's '"bigger picture" decision-making autonomy';[24] and (iii) decreases the likelihood of Karen experiencing painful emotions of resentment, humiliation, and betrayal. That is, even despite the fact that the drug has, for all intents and purposes, "morally enhanced" Harry precisely as intended. However, I think the reason the fidelity drug will not foster restoration of Karen's confidence in the sufficiency of Harry's disposition vis-à-vis fidelity (and thus will not attenuate the heightened vulnerability she experiences post-affair), has little to do with its being a drug. In fact, the biochemical/conventional distinction is perhaps not all that pertinent here at all. The more relevant distinction is that between "noncognitive" methods of enhancing fidelity – i.e., methods of inhibiting the proclivity or physical capacity for extra-pair sex that do not directly aim at correcting or preventing errors of moral cognition; and "cognitive" methods that do – i.e., methods that promote sexually faithful behaviour via cognition-improving means.[25] Relationship counselling is a species-type of the latter and fidelity drugs a species-type of the former, but the correspondence across the two distinctions here is merely contingent. That is, not all biochemical enhancement methods are "noncognitive", and nor are all conventional enhancement methods "cognitive".

A prosaic example of a conventional noncognitive method of enhancing sexual fidelity is the issuing of threats; e.g., if you cheat on me again I will leave you, take the kids, take your money, kill myself, kill you, etc. By imposing external constraints and/or high costs, such threats might more or less successfully promote the probability that your partner will be faithful and decrease the likelihood of you experiencing the emotional anguish of being cheated on. However, to the extent that you are reliant on threats for protection against being sexually betrayed by your partner, you are scarcely likely to feel much less vulnerable (in the sense previously outlined) to being sexually betrayed by them. And something similar, I think, would also hold for more technological noncognitive fidelity enhancers such as chastity devices voluntarily donned by philandering partners committed to mending their ways. For, again, if the only way your partner can prevent himself from cheating on you – despite being

---

[24] Earp, et al., 'Brave New Love', 4–5.
[25] For an illuminating discussion of noncognitive moral enhancements, see Douglas, 'Moral Enhancement via Direct Emotion Modulation: A Reply to John Harris', *Bioethics* **27**:3 (2013) 160–168.

generally (albeit apparently insufficiently) disposed not to – is to bind himself to the mast so to speak (or his mast to himself for that matter), it seems unlikely you would feel much less vulnerable for all that.

In any case, it may be that Earp, et al. would themselves reject deploying threats and chastity devices as methods of enhancing fidelity, since arguably neither satisfy the four criteria they posit as necessary and sufficient conditions in their ethical framework for the responsible use of anti-love biotechnologies:[26]

1. The love [or sexual desire for someone other than the person's spouse] would be clearly harmful and in need of dissolving one way or another.
2. The person would have to want to use the technology, so that there would be no problematic violations of consent.
3. The technology would help the person follow her higher order goals instead of her lower order feelings, thereby enhancing her "bigger picture" decision-making autonomy.
4. It might not be psychologically possible to overcome the perilous feelings without the help of anti-love biotechnology – or at least more "traditional" methods had already been tried or thoroughly considered.[27]

Threats would presumably fail to satisfy criteria 2 and 3; and since chastity devices merely prevent philanderers from doing what they want *in the moment* to do (i.e., have sex with someone who they should not) it might seem a stretch to think they would enhance the trussed-up philanderer's bigger picture decision-making autonomy (criterion 3). However, I think a strong case can be made to say that all four conditions are satisfied in the Harry and Karen scenario where the noncognitive biotechnology in question is the fidelity drug. Criteria 1 and 2 are straightforwardly satisfied. 4 is satisfied since "traditional" methods like self-control and will-power have evidently already failed Harry, and we can also assume the relationship counselling has thus far proven inadequate to allay his fears that he might stray again. And 3 looks to be satisfied too, for, unlike a chastity device, the fidelity drug would not merely prevent Harry from doing what he wants *in the moment* to do (i.e., have sex with someone else);

---

[26] This is straightforwardly true insofar as threats and chastity devices are not "biotechnologies", but plugging them into the authors' ethical framework for illustrative purposes should not, I hope, do them too great a disservice.

[27] Earp, et al., 'Brave New Love', 5. The text that appears in brackets in the first criterion conveys detail from a footnote found in the original.

rather it might prevent him from wanting to do it at all, thus unshackling his higher order goals.

It is hardly surprising, of course, that a biotechnology could meet Earp, et al.'s criteria for the responsible use of biotechnologies, but it is not insignificant that even a low level noncognitive biotechnology like the fidelity drug portrayed here gets through. On what we should say about neuroenhancing relationships via artificially boosting oxytocin, vasopressin, dopamine, etc. to promote pair-bonding, or even the theoretical possibility that we may one day be able to synthetically induce precise brain states characteristic of loving partners, I am somewhat undecided. Such possibilities are, to be sure, a worthwhile and important target of ethical enquiry, and Earp, Sandberg, Savulescu, and Wudarczyk deserve plaudits for paving the way in this regard. However, I believe the ethical issues surrounding low-level noncognitive biotechnologies are perhaps more pressing, if only for the fact some are already in existence (and in some cases already in use). Consider, for example, the noncognitive sexual fidelity bioenhancement *par excellence*: chemical castration. Treatment of sexual deviancy via administration of anti-androgen drugs and more recently Lupron (both of which block testosterone production) is typically associated with sex offenders. However, in a relatively recent turn of events, medical centres like The Institute for Sexual Wellness in Weymouth, MA, have begun offering Lupron to voluntary patients seeking to curb illicit sexual behaviours, including serial infidelity.[28] Chemical castration of voluntary patients clearly meets Earp, et al.'s four criteria. And, moreover, the fact that it does would apparently establish the 'strongest possible moral justification' for using chemical castration to dissolve 'what would seem to be "obviously" harmful forms of love or attraction', amongst which they list 'love that might lead to adultery'.[29]

And perhaps that is fine, as far as it goes, for in line with what I intimated earlier, I see no grounds for believing fidelity bioenhancement by chemical castration to be morally impermissible, providing reasonably strict background conditions are satisfied. Like all the noncognitive methods of enhancing sexual fidelity canvassed, chemical castration will expectably promote the probability that philanderers will be faithful. Moreover, being noncognitive does not render chemical

---

[28] Alexa Tsoulis-Reay, 'What It's Like to Be Chemically Castrated', *New York Magazine*, December 2015: http://nymag.com/scienceofus/2015/11/what-its-like-to-be-chemically-castrated.html.
[29] Earp, et al., 'If I Could Just Stop Loving You', 10.

castration incapable of promoting moral enhancement. This is straight-forwardly true if the bar for moral enhancement is set relatively low – if it merely has to make it less likely that philanderers will philander (i.e., act immorally). But it is also arguably true even if the bar sits somewhat higher – if it has to make philanderers "more moral". For it is not incon-ceivable that, despite not being directly aimed at correcting or prevent-ing errors of moral cognition, noncognitive biotechnologies might, over time, conduce (indirectly) to moral betterment. Furthermore, the fact that biotechnologies like chemical castration are noncogni-tive need not rule out their adoption being motivated by moral rea-soning. Thus, if philanderers are moved by moral considerations (pertaining to their partners, families, etc.) to undergo chemical cas-tration, and doing so does indeed result in their moral enhancement, then enhancing sexual fidelity via chemical castration looks like something they should be morally permitted to do.

The problem, however, is that it simply does not follow straight-forwardly from the fact that chemical castration or noncognitive fi-delity drugs generally are morally permissible that couples therefore have good reason to deploy them. That might follow if one accepts Douglas's claim quoted back in section 2: that '[o]n any plausible moral theory, a person's having morally better motives will tend to be to the advantage of others'.[30] But that is just not true of *all* forms of moral enhancement. Or, at least, it is untrue if we take ser-iously the claim that the end of moral enhancement is attenuation of vulnerability. That said, it perhaps is true of *most* forms of moral en-hancement (hence the earlier caveat that this argument cannot and should not to be read as an objection to moral enhancement gener-ally). If I take a drug that makes me more empathetic and thus less likely to act immorally towards you, *ipso facto* your vulnerability is attenuated. Or, if someone with a strong aversion to certain racial groups takes a drug that inhibits their racism, thus making them less likely to act immorally towards persons from those racial groups, *ipso facto* the vulnerability of those persons is attenuated.[31] But, if Harry takes a fidelity drug that inhibits his desire to sleep with other women, thus making him less likely to act immorally towards Karen, it simply does not follow that *ipso facto* Karen's vulnerability is attenuated. No doubt vulnerability to the kinds of special wrongs and betrayals that only those with whom you share special relation-ships (e.g., partners, friends, parents, children, siblings, etc.) are capable of inflicting upon you is quite unlike the vulnerability of

---

[30]   Douglas, 'Moral Enhancement', 230.
[31]   Douglas, 'Moral Enhancement', 231.

persons subject to racial discrimination, or indeed that of persons generally. But vulnerability it is, nonetheless.

Fidelity drugs might make it more likely that Harry will refrain from sleeping with other women; and they might make it less likely that Karen will again experience the negative reactive emotions Harry's affair with Mia wrought upon her. But a lessening of the probabilities of these harms will not necessarily entail a lessening of the heightened vulnerability she experiences as a victim of infidelity. If the end of moral enhancement is not merely moral improvement of the enhanced patient (which the fidelity drug successfully effects), but attenuation of the vulnerability of enhanced and unenhanced alike, and if bioenhancement of Harry's sexual fidelity does not expectably attenuate Karen's vulnerability, then I think we should not recommend fidelity drugs as a solution to the kinds of fidelity issues couples like Harry and Karen face. Generalising, then, the first substantive conclusion of this essay is this: couples seeking to rescue their relationships following instances of sexual infidelity have presumptively decisive reason not to deploy fidelity drugs. That is, they have decisive reason to reject fidelity drugs if one of the things they reasonably hope for from a relationship therapy regime is attenuation of the heightened vulnerability the victim experiences in the aftermath of their partner's sexual infidelity.

5. The Problem with Supplementing Conventional Fidelity Enhancement Methods with Fidelity Drugs

Whilst I think this first conclusion is right, it is also weak in two respects. Firstly, "the problem with fidelity drugs" exposed in the last section perhaps only establishes the fairly weak conclusion that couples have good reason not to deploy low level non-cognitive fidelity drugs *in lieu* of conventional methods. However, the role of biotechnologies is invariably depicted as one of supplementation rather than supplantation. In Earp, et al.'s words: 'while neuroenhancement would not replace marriage counselling and other self-help methods, it could certainly supplement and improve those well-worn measures to good effect'.[32] Translated into the terms employed here, the equivalent claim would be: counselling *plus* fidelity drugs will better restore infidelity victims' confidence that their partners are sufficiently well disposed to be robustly faithful

---

[32]   Earp, et al., 'Natural Selection, Childrearing, and the Ethics of Marriage (and Divorce)', 576.

to them (thus better attenuating their vulnerability), than counselling *sans* fidelity drugs. If so, then couples have good reason to prefer counselling *plus* fidelity drugs to counselling *sans* fidelity drugs.

However, this seems unlikely, at least with respect to noncognitive fidelity bioenhancements. Administering fidelity drugs to philanderers will predictably impair the ability of their partners to ascertain that they are faithful because they are appropriately disposed to be, rather than for merely contingent reasons (e.g., because they are fidelity-drugged). This is because supplementing counselling with fidelity drugs unavoidably introduces grounds for doubt otherwise absent in regimes comprised of counselling *sans* fidelity drugs. For example, if Harry and Karen opt for supplementing their counselling with the fidelity drug, Karen's epistemic position – her ability to ascertain with reasonable confidence that Harry's refraining from jumping into bed again with Mia or someone else is the result of his being appropriately disposed to be faithful to her – will be impaired relative to what it otherwise would have been.[33] Moreover, if they were to opt for counselling *plus* fidelity drugs, what the fact of the matter is about what stops Harry jumping into bed again with Mia or anyone else – e.g., the Lupron duping the hormone in his brain that tells the pituitary gland to produce testosterone directly; or his disposition to be faithful flawlessly restored as an indirect result of the Lupron duping the hormone in his brain – is largely immaterial. All that matters is that, merely in virtue of folding the Lupron into the causal mix of their relationship therapy regime, Karen's epistemic ability to ascertain that Harry's renewed fidelity stems from his being appropriately disposed to be faithful to her will be impaired relative to what it would be were the Lupron not in his system. Thus, counselling *plus* fidelity drugs would predictably not better attenuate Karen's vulnerability to Harry's will than counselling *sans* fidelity drugs expectably would.

The second weakness issue is this: even if it is true that a fidelity drug would not expectably *attenuate* the vulnerability a victim of infidelity experiences, providing it does not *exacerbate* their vulnerability, then the first conclusion may seem less than fatal. However, if the previous response is plausible, and counselling *sans* fidelity drugs fares better than counselling *plus* fidelity drugs in terms of expectably attenuating the heightened vulnerability infidelity victims typically

---

[33]   Indeed, not only might it never be as clear to Karen that bioenhanced Harry is faithful because he is appropriately and sufficiently disposed to be, and not for merely contingent reasons (e.g., because he is fidelity drugged), but what the truth of the matter is will perhaps never be as clear even to Harry himself.

experience, then the second weakness issue is overcome too. One way to see this is to speculate about whether, or in what circumstances, a relationship counsellor would or should recommend fidelity drugs as a supplement to counselling. What if relationship counselling alone has not proved effective at all (i.e., it has done nothing whatsoever to assuage the heightened vulnerability the infidelity victim experiences)? Presumably not. Fidelity drugs should not be recommended as a supplement to failed counselling for the same reason that we should not endorse supplanting counselling with fidelity drugs: deployed *in lieu* of counselling (whether tried and failed, or never tried at all) they will not expectably attenuate victims' vulnerability. But what if counselling *is* proving effective? Presumably the counsellor should not recommend supplementary fidelity drugs even then, since their interposition will predictably undermine whatever gains in terms of attenuation of victim vulnerability the counselling has already realised. For the introduction of fidelity drugs into a relationship therapy regime that has thus far proved at least partially effective will inevitably introduce previously absent grounds for the victim to question the moral calibre and sufficiency of their partner's restored disposition to be faithful. If this is correct – i.e., we should not recommend fidelity drugs either as supplements or substitutes – we should not recommend biochemically enhancing sexual fidelity, period.

In the end, then, I suspect that not only will introducing fidelity drugs alongside conventional counselling techniques *not* 'supplement and improve those well-worn measures to good effect';[34] I think folding fidelity drugs into the causal mix will actually tend to undermine whatever attenuation of vulnerability those 'well-worn measures' expectably promote (however imperfectly). If that is so, we can now reframe the initial "weak" conclusion so as to yield a somewhat stronger, second substantive conclusion: couples seeking to rescue their relationship following instances of sexual infidelity have presumptively decisive reason to prefer conventional methods of enhancing sexual fidelity *sans* fidelity drugs to conventional methods *plus* fidelity drugs.

6. Final Thoughts and Objections

If all that you care about is that your partner just stops having sex with other people, I suspect the arguments of this chapter will not reach you. Indeed, fidelity drugs like Lupron might be just what you are

---

[34] Earp, et al., 'Natural Selection, Childrearing, and the Ethics of Marriage (and Divorce)', 576.

looking for. It is with an eye to this that the reasons I have given for rejecting fidelity drugs are framed as "presumptively decisive". Yet I think the presumption therein – that what many of us desire in desiring the fidelity of our partners is something more than that they merely refraining from illicit sex – is a reasonable one. Not all desires are like this, of course; in many situations desiring agents are indifferent as to the manner in which their desires are satisfied. Suppose your partner is an alcoholic and that you ardently desire that they cease drinking alcohol (for the sake of their health, your relationship, your family, etc.). It seems plausible to assume that you would be utterly indifferent as to whether your desire is satisfied (i.e., they cease drinking) as a result of their taking disulfiram, or as a result of their getting counselling. However, I think that, typically, in desiring that your partner stops cheating on you with other persons, you would not be indifferent as to whether your desire is satisfied (i.e., they stop cheating on you) as a result of their taking Lupron, or as a result of counselling. Sometimes what we desire, in desiring certain types of goods, is not mere non-frustration of that desire, and for many of us I think fidelity is a good of that type. The fact is, most of us have considered preferences concerning the manner in which we realise the good of fidelity in our relationships, and I think that to deny this would be to deny a feature of the phenomenological experience of fidelity. And, for what it is worth, I think Earp, et al. would be no more willing to tread that path than I am, for they themselves see it as significant that 'most couples *as a matter of fact* value sexual fidelity'.[35] However, even if they are willing to come with me this far, I suspect there are (at least) two independent objections they might have.

6.1 Won't Somebody Think of the Children?!

In Earp, et al.'s paper on 'Natural Selection, Childrearing, and the Ethics of Marriage (and Divorce)', they argue that if troubled married couples have dependent children, their turning to biotechnologies to save their marriages might be not just permissible, but perhaps even morally obligatory.[36] Their argument begins from the premise that parents have a special obligation to protect their

[35]   Earp, et al., 'Natural Selection, Childrearing, and the Ethics of Marriage (and Divorce)', footnote 15, 572.
[36]   Earp, et al., 'Natural Selection, Childrearing, and the Ethics of Marriage (and Divorce)', 562–564.

children from harm. Marriage failure and/or divorce is, generally speaking, detrimental to children. Since marriage failure/divorce goes hand-in-hand with adultery (statistically speaking), and since parents have 'an obligation (all else being equal) to preserve and enhance their relationships for the sake of their offspring', they should therefore refrain from adulterous behaviour. 'In many cases', they go on, '*the only way to do this* is through pharmacological intervention, in conjunction with other more conventional strategies like couple's therapy'.[37] Thus, supplementing conventional strategies (e.g., couple's therapy) with pharmacological interventions (e.g., fidelity drugs) can 'be justified from the perspective of child welfare [...] since extramarital sex can lead to the formation of extramarital bonds that could drive resources away from existing offspring'.[38]

If Harry and Karen have children, they will of course have parental obligations, and considerations pertaining to their children's welfare will indeed provide them with additional weighty reasons to try to save their marriage. However, it is not clear why the fact that this is so should dictate which method(s) of therapy they have reason to prefer so as to maximise the prospects of preserving and enhancing their marriage. The relevant question, rather, is whether couple's therapy *plus* fidelity drugs better promotes that end than couple's therapy *sans* fidelity drugs. If what has been argued here is correct, then the latter will expectably promote attenuation of Karen's vulnerability better than the former. And so, assuming that in general the level of vulnerability in a marriage is inversely correlated with the prospects of preserving it, Harry and Karen still ought to prefer couple's therapy *sans* fidelity drugs, even when there are children involved.

6.2 The Depression Analogy

At another point in that same 2012 paper, Earp, et al. speak of administering love drugs to give couples the boost they need to get '"over the initial hump" of their marital difficulties'. Doing so, they contend, would really be no different (morally speaking) to prescribing antidepressants to a patient 'whose brain chemistry

---

[37] Earp, et al., 'Natural Selection, Childrearing, and the Ethics of Marriage (and Divorce)', 564. Emphasis in original.
[38] Earp, et al., 'Natural Selection, Childrearing, and the Ethics of Marriage (and Divorce)', footnote 15, 572.

Robbie Arrell

may be so out of order that she requires a dose of medication to "get over the initial hump of her depression"'.[39] A similar analogy with treating depression also appears in Sandberg and Savulescu's 2008 paper on 'Neuroenhancement of Love and Marriage' in which they ask us to imagine a hypothetical case in which Betty's loving partner

> John becomes prone to mild depression. This affects their relationship adversely. He starts to lose interest in Betty, becomes absorbed in himself, grumpy, withdrawn and painful to be around. He takes an antidepressant and their love is maintained. From the point of view of their relationship and his life, he has good reason to take the drug.[40]

Assuming the analogy between love drugs and antidepressants is as tight as the authors evidently believe it is, this might appear problematic for my account. For it might seem that John's taking antidepressants will predictably impair Betty's ability to ascertain with reasonable confidence that bioenhanced John treats her lovingly because he is appropriately disposed to do so, rather than for merely contingent reasons (e.g., because of the antidepressants in his system). If this is right, then supplementing psychotherapy with antidepressants in order to biochemically enhance John's moods will not expectably attenuate the heightened vulnerability to John's will to maltreat her that Betty experiences as a result of John's depression. Thus, consistency might require the following rather unintuitive conclusion: that, at least from the point of view of their relationship and love for each other, John and Betty have presumptively decisive reason to prefer psychotherapy *sans* antidepressants to psychotherapy *plus* antidepressants.

However, the depression and infidelity cases are disanalogous in a significant respect, for Betty's confidence that John treats her lovingly because he is appropriately disposed to do so is never at any point imperilled. During the period of John's depression – the period in which he treats Betty poorly – his disposition is offline (so to speak), such that his poor treatment of her is unanchored by his disposition. Thus, Betty has no reason whatsoever to doubt that John's disposition to treat her lovingly is perfectly sufficient, knowing that, were it not paralysed by the depression, he would

---

[39] Earp, et al., 'Natural Selection, Childrearing, and the Ethics of Marriage (and Divorce)', 564.

[40] Savulescu and Sandberg, 'Neuroenhancement of Love and Marriage', 38.

412

be moved to provide her with the good of his loving care robustly, just as he (presumably) always did (prior to the onset of depression). By contrast, since Harry's disposition was never offline in the infidelity case, Karen, unlike Betty, has perfectly good reason to doubt that he is appropriately and sufficiently well disposed to robustly refrain from hurting her, and that makes the fidelity case quite different. To put it another way, in the depression case, all that Betty requires is unblocking of John's disposition to provide her with love and care robustly, not convincing of its sufficiency (which she has never had reason to doubt). And so, the question of whether John's biochemical enhancement via antidepressants would expectably restore Betty's confidence in the sufficiency of his disposition (and thus attenuate her vulnerability to his will) is moot. In the infidelity case, by contrast, what Karen requires is not unblocking of Harry's disposition to robustly refrain from sleeping around (for his disposition was never offline at all), but restoration of her confidence in its sufficiency. Unlike in the depression case, then, the question of whether or not Harry's biochemical enhancement via fidelity drugs would expectably restore Karen's confidence in that respect (and the suggestion that it would not) remains very much live.[41]

7. Conclusion

I began this chapter pondering the question: what is the end of moral enhancement? The argument presented here supposes that the answer to that question is attenuation of vulnerability. If that is so, then I believe we should not recommend supplementing conventional methods of morally enhancing sexual fidelity with fidelity drugs for the reasons given. As we shuffle into an ever-more technologically advanced future, no-one can rule out the possibility that advances in neuroscience will yield new biotechnologies capable of making philanderers more faithful; more capable of seeing why it matters that they are faithful; and perhaps even more capable of being faithful for the right reasons. If what has been argued here is compelling, however, it may be that, in the end, none of that really matters. At least, however successfully fidelity drugs might promote behavioural, epistemic, and motivational improvement in philanderers – even to the point of making them "more moral", gains in those respects will

---

[41]   I am grateful to Andrew Komasinski for impressing upon me the need to deal with this objection.

not matter if, ultimately, they do little to assuage the heightened vulnerability victims of sexuality infidelity experience. And surely we should care about the victims, too.[42]

Wuhan University
robbiearrell@whu.edu.cn

---

[42] I thank Rob Sparrow for his extremely detailed and helpful comments; the audience at the 2016 'Australasian Association of Philosophy Conference' hosted by Monash University, Australia; and the audience at the 'International Conference on Applied Ethics: The Past, Present and Future of Applied Ethics' hosted by Hokkaido University, Japan. I would also like to thank Michael Selgelid, from whom I received helpful feedback on the seed of the argument that became this essay.

Psychedelic Moral Enhancement

BRIAN D. EARP

Abstract

The moral enhancement (or bioenhancement) debate seems stuck in a dilemma. On the one hand, the more radical proposals, while certainly novel and interesting, seem unlikely to be feasible in practice, or if technically feasible then most likely imprudent. But on the other hand, the more sensible proposals – sensible in the sense of being both practically achievable and more plausibly ethically justifiable – can be rather hard to distinguish from both traditional forms of moral enhancement, such as non-drug-mediated social or moral education, and non-moral forms of bioenhancement, such as smart-drug style cognitive enhancement. In this essay, I argue that bioethicists have paid insufficient attention to an alternative form of moral bioenhancement – or at least a likely candidate – that falls somewhere between these two extremes, namely the (appropriately qualified) use of certain psychedelic drugs.

1. Introduction[1]

The world would be a better place if the people in it were more moral than they are. If only there were a way we could enhance the moral character of humanity.[2] Violence would drop. Co-operation would climb. Global poverty might be ameliorated through a boost in charitable giving. And the danger of human-caused climate change could at last be mitigated through improved collective action.[3] Unfortunately, our current methods are not working – or at least, not well enough.

[1]   The author would like to thank Michael Hauskeller, Lewis Coyne, and Ole Martin Moen for helpful feedback on an earlier draft of this essay. Please note that a handful of sentences have been adapted from the earlier piece, 'Moral Neuroenhancement' by Brian D. Earp, Thomas Douglas, and Julian Savulescu – see reference below.

[2]   Ingmar Persson and Julian Savulescu, 'The Perils of Cognitive Enhancement and the Urgent Imperative to Enhance the Moral Character of Humanity', *Journal of Applied Philosophy* **25**:3 (2008), 162–77; Ingmar Persson and Julian Savulescu, 'Getting Moral Enhancement Right: The Desirability of Moral Bioenhancement', *Bioethics* **27**:3 (2013), 124–31.

[3]   Julian Savulescu and Ingmar Persson, 'Moral Enhancement', *Philosophy Now* **91** (2012), 6–8; Ingmar Persson and Julian Savulescu, 'Reply to Commentators on "Unfit for the Future"', *Journal of Medical Ethics* **41**:4 (2015), 338–39.

doi:10.1017/S1358246118000474   ©The Royal Institute of Philosophy and the contributors 2018

Royal Institute of Philosophy Supplement **83** 2018
                                                                                415

Brian D. Earp

Maybe it is time to think creatively and ponder new approaches to making morally better humans.

One proposal that has generated a lot of attention in recent years involves the deployment of modern neuroscience and its discoveries. Instead of relying solely on traditional, external means of moral improvement – childrearing, socialisation, political institutions, and the like – this approach suggests that we should try, or at least consider trying, "internal" methods as well.[4] For example, we could explore the use of gene therapies or brain-level neurotechnologies to expand our moral capacities, as it were, from the inside out – perhaps even transcending our presently inherent moral limitations.[5] Since what is at stake is no less than the preservation of the Earth and the welfare of its inhabitants both now and in the future, all options should be on the table.[6] Or should they?

2. Reasons for Scepticism

When I first dipped my toe into the moral bioenhancement literature,[7] I was sceptical. I presumed that the idea would turn out to be a dead-end or at best a side-show – a flashy fad set to go out of fashion. Since I had been writing over the years, more or less favourably, about the prospect of using biotechnology to enhance human romantic relationships,[8] and since I had been doing so in close

---

[4] Thomas Douglas, 'Moral Enhancement', *Journal of Applied Philosophy* **25**:3 (2008), 228–45.

[5] But see: Harris Wiseman, *The Myth of the Moral Brain: The Limits of Moral Enhancement* (Cambridge, MA: MIT Press, 2016).

[6] Ingmar Persson and Julian Savulescu, *Unfit for the Future: The Need for Moral Enhancement* (Oxford: Oxford University Press, 2012).

[7] For a recent review, see: Thomas Douglas, 'The Morality of Moral Neuroenhancement', in Jens Clausen and Neil Levy (eds), *Handbook of Neuroethics* (Dordrecht: Springer, 2015), 1227–49.

[8] The main contributions are: Brian D. Earp, Anders Sandberg, and Julian Savulescu, 'Natural Selection, Childrearing, and the Ethics of Marriage (and Divorce): Building a Case for the Neuroenhancement of Human Relationships', *Philosophy & Technology* **25**:4 (2012), 561–87; Brian D. Earp, et al., 'If I Could Just Stop Loving You: Anti-Love Biotechnology and the Ethics of a Chemical Breakup', *The American Journal of Bioethics* **13**:11 (2013), 3–17; Brian D. Earp, Anders Sandberg, and Julian Savulescu, 'Brave New Love: The Threat of High-Tech "Conversion" Therapy and the Bio-Oppression of Sexual Minorities', *AJOB Neuroscience* **5**:1 (2014), 4–12; Brian D. Earp, Anders Sandberg,

collaboration with one of the foremost architects of the moral enhancement movement, you might think that I would have been drawn to this other enhancement proposal with an air of optimism or even enthusiasm.

But I was not. For one thing, it was hard to pin down what the term "moral enhancement" was supposed to refer to, and the options for achieving it, however defined, seemed either plausible but uninteresting (primarily, those accounts that emphasised continuity with more traditional forms of moral education), or sexy and thought-provoking, but too much like science fiction (morally re-engineering the species to save the planet). In other words, the interventions that were being floated seemed either hopelessly far-fetched or, if more realistic, not worth writing home about.

Moreover, the general focus seemed to be on the potential modification of specific psychological capacities, such as the ability to empathise, rather than more global, flexible capacities that would allow one to respond appropriately to a wide range of situations (whatever those capacities or modifications turned out to be). A problem with the former approach is that the lower-level capacities, while clearly relevant to moral decision-making and behaviour, probably cannot – due to basic facts about neurochemistry – ever be successfully tweaked in isolation like so many dials in the brain.[9]

One reason for this likely impossibility is the delicate interconnectedness of many if not most neural processes and systems. In other words, due to the overlapping web of electrochemical interactions by which the brain carries out its business, any attempt to intervene in some specific low-level cognitive or emotional capacity (assuming that such a target could ever be discretely defined, whether conceptually or in terms of physical instantiation) would likely result in

---

and Julian Savulescu, 'The Medicalization of Love', *Cambridge Quarterly of Healthcare Ethics* **24**:3 (2015), 323–36; Julian Savulescu and Brian D. Earp, 'Neuroreductionism about Sex and Love', *Think* **13**:38 (2014), 7–12; Brian D. Earp, et al., 'Addicted to Love: What Is Love Addiction and When Should It Be Treated?', *Philosophy, Psychiatry, & Psychology* **24**:1 (2017), 77–92; Brian D. Earp and Julian Savulescu, 'Love Drugs: Why Scientists Should Study the Effects of Pharmaceuticals on Human Romantic Relationships', *Technology in Society* **52**:2 (2018), 10–16.

[9] Harris Wiseman, 'SSRIs Moral Enhancement Interventions: A Practical Dead End', *AJOB Neuroscience* **5**:3 (2014), 21–30; Molly Crockett, 'Moral Enhancement? Evidence and Challenges' (Presentation at the "The Moral Brain", New York University, New York, March 2012).

undesirable side-effects, at best, and at worst, the disruption or impairment of other important functions.[10]

But even if such capacities *could* be otherwise harmlessly fine-tuned,[11] what then? I did not see how this approach would guarantee, much less amount to, moral improvement in any reliable sense. Imagine that you could take a drug that made you feel more empathy (without incurring other serious problems). Would that make you morally enhanced? Not necessarily, because the "right" amount of empathy you should feel is not a question with a stable, universal answer. Rather, it depends on the circumstances you are in, the social role you occupy, the specifics of the moral predicament you are facing, and many other factors, all of which might change over time or be different for different people.[12] Biochemically fiddling with dials, then, in an attempt to land on the right "settings" – I hope

---

[10]   Molly J. Crockett, 'Moral Bioenhancement: A Neuroscientific Perspective', *Journal of Medical Ethics* **40**:6 (2014), 370–71; Hannah Maslen, et al., 'Brain Stimulation for Treatment and Enhancement in Children: An Ethical Analysis', *Frontiers in Human Neuroscience* **8**:953 (2014), 1–5.

[11]   Tom Douglas has pointed out that, even if such side-effect-free fine-tuning is not likely to be possible any time soon, or even ever, we do not normally require that brain-level pharmaceutical interventions be quite so precise in their effects for us to find their use (for, e.g., medical purposes) appropriate. He writes, 'most medical interventions are rather blunt, and it is thus difficult to prevent them from having overall negative effects in some cases (this is perhaps particularly true of psychiatric interventions)'. However, 'we do not, and should not, regard this as providing us with decisive reasons to abstain from medical treatments. Rather, we take it as giving us reasons to exercise caution in using such treatments, and to try to reduce the risks posed by the treatments over time, for example, by making them more precise'. Thomas Douglas, 'Moral Enhancement via Direct Emotion Modulation: A Reply to John Harris', *Bioethics* **27**:3 (2013), 160–68, 166–167.

[12]   Robert Sparrow illustrates the problem: '[e]ncouraging empathy and a sense of justice in individuals may usually be a good thing, but enhancing either of these faculties may make individuals more likely to behave unethically in various situations, as when, for instance, a judge declares a person "not guilty" as a result of empathic concern for them, despite the presence of overwhelming evidence that they are in fact guilty of the crime with which they are charged, or when a parent neglects a child out of an excessive concern for duties of justice toward strangers'. Robert Sparrow, 'Egalitarianism and Moral Bioenhancement', *The American Journal of Bioethics* **14**:4 (2014), 20–28, 20–21.

this metaphor is not too strained to serve its purpose – seemed to me to be a non-starter.

In response to this kind of concern, which I stress is in no way original to me,[13] some writers have shifted away from a focus on low-level psychological capacities and their attempted biochemical modification, to thinking of moral enhancement in more general terms. G. Owen Schaefer,[14] for example, recommends what he calls indirect moral enhancements centered on improving the capacity to reason and strengthening willpower; while Harris Wiseman has recently advanced a "soft" understanding of moral enhancement that encompasses everything from 'social control', to 'paternalism, law-making, medicine, and mental health, all of whose institutions involve intervening in behavior [...] to prevent and punish activities that are not explicitly immoral, but that have morally related dimensions'.[15]

But that strikes me as changing the conversation. In this respect, I agree with Robert Sparrow, who writes:

Debate about moral bioenhancement is shaped, at least in part, by hopes and fears about the impacts of scientific research into the human brain, especially its anatomy and neurochemistry, into human genetics, and into technologies that might leverage the insights offered by both sorts of research to make people "more moral". Such interventions would alter human biology and not just human behavior. That is to say, the "bio" is essential to the philosophical and cultural buzz around moral bioenhancement. If every revision of social mores, or attempt at institutional design directed toward getting people to behave in particular desirable ways, counts as moral bioenhancement, the category dissolves into meaninglessness.[16]

---

[13]   Inmaculada de Melo-Martín and Arleen Salles, 'Moral Bioenhancement: Much Ado About Nothing?', *Bioethics* **29**:4 (2015), 223–32; Wiseman, *The Myth of the Moral Brain*; John Harris, 'Moral Enhancement and Freedom', *Bioethics* **25**:2 (2011), 102–11.

[14]   G. Owen Schaefer, 'Direct vs. Indirect Moral Enhancement', *Kennedy Institute of Ethics Journal* **25**:3 (2015), 261–89.

[15]   Harris Wiseman, 'Would We Even Know Moral Bioenhancement If We Saw it?', *Cambridge Quarterly of Healthcare Ethics* **26**:3 (2017), 398–410, 405.

[16]   Robert Sparrow, 'Commentary: Moral Bioenhancement Worthy of the Name', *Cambridge Quarterly of Healthcare Ethics* **26**:3 (2017), 411–14, 412.

Brian D. Earp

So we seem to be stuck with a dilemma. Either we talk about brain-level "bio" interventions that are probably neurologically impossible, or if possible, either too risky to be desirable or unlikely to be reliable moral enhancers; or we stretch out the concept of moral enhancement – and even moral bioenhancement – to the point that we sacrifice the very thing about the idea that made it seem new and exciting and thus worth talking about in the first place. That is, we sacrifice the aspect of moral enhancement that made it distinguishable from the more mundane, traditional methods of moral improvement that have been written about since the dawn of history. John Harris has described the quandary like this:

> so far from being susceptible to new forms of high tech manipulation, either genetic, chemical, surgical or neurological, the only reliable methods of moral enhancement, either now or for the foreseeable future are either those that have been in human and animal use for millennia, namely socialization, education and parental supervision or those high tech methods that are general in their application. By that is meant those forms of cognitive enhancement that operate across a wide range of cognitive abilities and do not target specifically "ethical" capacities.[17]

In other words, according to Harris, while high-tech enhancers might plausibly improve our ability to think clearly, concentrate, or rationally pick apart complex scenarios (which in turn could potentially help us identify and respond to moral reasons more efficiently or effectively than we would have done otherwise), there would not be anything distinctively *moral* about either the enhancers themselves or the capacities they would target in the brain. If Harris is correct, then it seems as though the conversation should go back to the somewhat older and more established "cognitive" enhancement debate[18] – concerning the use of "smart drugs" like methylphenidate (Ritalin),

[17] John Harris, 'Moral Enhancement and Freedom', 102.
[18] Nick Bostrom and Anders Sandberg, 'Cognitive Enhancement: Methods, Ethics, Regulatory Challenges', *Science and Engineering Ethics* **15**:3 (2009), 311–41; Simon M. Outram, 'Ethical Considerations in the Framing of the Cognitive Enhancement Debate', *Neuroethics* **5**:2 (2012), 173–84; Hannah Maslen, Nadira Faulmüller, and Julian Savulescu, 'Pharmacological Cognitive Enhancement – How Neuroscientific Research Could Advance Ethical Debate', *Frontiers in Systems Neuroscience* **8**:107 (2014), 1–12; Brian D. Earp, et al., 'When Is Diminishment a Form of Enhancement? Rethinking the Enhancement Debate in Biomedical Ethics', *Frontiers in Systems Neuroscience* **8**:12 (2014), 1–8.

or gene therapy to improve IQ[19] – which, while certainly important and perhaps indirectly relevant to moral enhancement, also feels like changing the topic.

Is there any way to have our cake and eat it too? In other words, is there any possible or actual intervention that is both practically achievable and likely to be ethically justifiable (under the right conditions), while also being radical enough to merit the flood of ink that continues to be spilled in this area? Something that would:

(1) keep the "bio" in moral bioenhancement, which Sparrow argues is essential to the current philosophical and cultural buzz surrounding the concept (thus ruling out "purely" social, environmental, or psycho-behavioural interventions);

(2) avoid the pitfalls associated with low-level "dial adjustment" (that is, attempts to biochemically intervene in, or fine-tune, particular cognitive or emotional capacities involved in moral decision-making, behaviour, and the like);

(3) exert a more general or wide-ranging effect on the moral agent that would contribute to her moral improvement in a robust, sustainable, flexible-across-contexts sort of way, without simply collapsing into Ritalin-style cognitive enhancement.

I believe that there is. In this essay,[20] I offer a tentative account of moral (bio) enhancement that sits between the prevailing extremes of boring-but-possible and interesting-but-not-going-to-happen. Indeed, I will suggest that such enhancement is not merely hypothetical or a likely prospect for the future, but is already taking place in some communities today. And by looking at such practices and communities – which, as my title prevents me from mining for suspense, involve the use of psychedelic substances – I claim that bioethicists can gain practical insights to help focus the moral enhancement debate.

---

[19] Cynthia Forlini and Eric Racine, 'Autonomy and Coercion in Academic "Cognitive Enhancement" Using Methylphenidate: Perspectives of Key Stakeholders', *Neuroethics* 2:3 (2009), 163–77; Ole Martin Moen, 'Bright New World', *Cambridge Quarterly of Healthcare Ethics* 25:2 (2016), 282–87; Jim Kozubek, 'Can CRISPR–Cas9 Boost Intelligence?', *Scientific American Blog Network*, 2016: https://blogs.scientificamerican.com/guest-blog/can-crispr-cas9-boost-intelligence/.

[20] I mean essay in its original sense of trying something out – I am only planting a seed here, which others may water if they wish.

3. Defining the Phenomenon

Before I turn to specific interventions, I need to define my terms. In a recent essay,[21] my co-authors and I proposed a novel definition for what we call *agential moral neuroenhancement*, which is a subclass of moral bioenhancement that focusses specifically on durable changes to a moral agent, as effectuated (at least in part) by direct interventions into the central nervous system (CNS). We chose this focus because the CNS is the part of human biology most likely to be modified by any actual intended moral bioenhancer; but if you prefer the more general "bioenhancement" you can make the necessary adjustments to the following:

Agential moral neuroenhancement: Any change in a moral agent – effected or facilitated in some significant way by the application of a neurotechnology [i.e., a technology that works directly on the CNS] – that results, or is reasonably expected to result, in the agent being a morally better (i.e., more moral) agent.

You will notice that this definition, by itself, is agnostic about what counts as 'morally better' or 'more moral'. In principle, therefore, one and the same neurointervention could be considered a moral enhancer by one person or moral theory, and a moral diminisher, or something more neutral, by another person or theory; but this should not cause us too much concern. Reasonable people disagree about what constitutes moral improvement compared to baseline, not only in the realm of potential high tech bioenhancers, but also in the realm of more traditional methods of moral education or spiritual practice.

So, you might raise your children to believe such-and-so about ethics and morality, and encourage them to be and behave accordingly, while I might raise mine to believe so-and-such, but this does not mean that moral improvement is impossible or that we should not try to better our children – and ourselves – to the best of our abilities. For one thing, not only is there likely to be a great deal of overlap between our respective sos and suches (there are wide pockets of concurrence across societies and moral systems),[22] but insofar as

---

[21] Brian D. Earp, Thomas Douglas, and Julian Savulescu, 'Moral Neuroenhancement', in Syd Johnson and Karen Rommelfanger (eds), *Routledge Handbook of Neuroethics* (New York: Routledge, 2017), 166–84.
[22] Tom L. Beauchamp, 'A Defense of the Common Morality', *Kennedy Institute of Ethics Journal* **13**:3 (2003), 259–74.

there *is* a genuine clash between our views or approaches to morality, this is often beneficial from a moral perspective. As Schaefer notes, 'moral disagreement – while potentially inhibiting consensus-building – is actually an important feature of society'.[23] Among other reasons, it is important because

> Without dissent, conventional wisdom will go unchallenged and moral progress becomes essentially impossible. This might not be a problem if we were infallible (i.e., already knew all the relevant moral truths), but because we are not, [suppression of disagreement] will prevent the revision of morally odious policies that, at the time of suppression, seemed perfectly sound. Dissent is instrumentally valuable, then, as a constant check on the validity of the conventional moral wisdom of our time.[24]

There is more that could be said about such moral disagreement. But let us set that issue aside: for our purposes, it should be enough for you to fill in whatever account of moral betterness you prefer as needed over the course of what follows. Now that we have a definition of moral enhancement – or moral neuroenhancement – in hand, we can ask ourselves the central question of this essay: Are there any real-life technologies that could facilitate the sort of change described in that definition (again, granting that some people will disagree about what counts as moral improvement in certain cases), while also meeting the three desiderata listed in the introduction? I have already alluded to the idea that certain psychedelic drugs might plausibly play such a role. I will now explore this suggestion more directly.

4. Drugs, Spirituality, and Religion

Writing in the *Journal of Philosophy* in 1964, the scholar of religions Huston Smith observed that 'in his trial-and-error life explorations, man almost everywhere has stumbled upon connections between vegetables (eaten or brewed) and actions (yogic breathing exercises, whirling dervish dances, flagellations) which altered states of consciousness'. From a neuroscientific perspective, Smith continues, 'we now understand these states to be the products of changes in brain chemistry. From the sociological perspective we see that they tended to be connected in some way with religion'.[25]

---

[23] Schaefer, 'Direct vs. Indirect Moral Enhancement', 262–263.
[24] Schaefer, 'Direct vs. Indirect Moral Enhancement', 265.
[25] Huston Smith, 'Do Drugs Have Religious Import?', *The Journal of Philosophy* **61**:18 (1964), 517–30, 518.

More recently, the theologian Ron Cole-Turner – referring to what he calls 'technologies of spiritual enhancement' – similarly notes that drugs and religion have been linked in human societies for millennia.[26] As he sees it, the most readily (bio)enhanceable human trait is in fact 'our capacity for spiritual experience'. Compared to cosmetic surgeries aimed at bodily enhancement,[27] he writes, 'spiritual enhancement is inexpensive and painless'. Compared to cognitive enhancement with drugs like methylphenidate, 'spiritual enhancement is highly effective and enduring'. Compared to lifespan extension, 'compelling evidence indicates that spiritual enhancement actually works in a highly positive and predictable way'.[28]

Our topic is moral enhancement, of course, not spirituality or religion. In quoting Cole-Turner and Smith, therefore, I do not mean to suggest that there is a straightforward, much less affirmative relationship between either of the latter notions and agential moral neuroenhancement as I have defined it: indeed religions in particular, as well as perceived religious commitments, often encourage immoral behaviour.[29] I am only setting the stage for the idea that altered states of consciousness, brought about in part or in whole by the ingestion of certain biochemical substances, have long been considered to yield (whether on their own or in conjunction with other teachings or practices) important insights into the nature of reality and human existence, often with transformative implications for how we should live from a moral perspective.[30]

In *The Doors of Perception*, Aldous Huxley writes of his experience taking mescaline, a cactus-derived drug most commonly used today

[26] Ron Cole-Turner, 'Spiritual Enhancement', in Calvin Mercer and Tracy J. Trothen (eds), *Religion and Transhumanism: The Unknown Future of Human Enhancement* (Denver: Praeger, 2015), 369–83, 369.

[27] For critical discussion, see: Arianne Shahvisi and Brian D. Earp, 'The Law and Ethics of Female Genital Cutting', in Sarah Creighton and Lih-Mei Liao (eds), *Female Genital Cosmetic Surgery: Solution to What Problem?* (Cambridge: Cambridge University Press, forthcoming).

[28] Cole-Turner, 'Spiritual Enhancement', 369.

[29] Sam Harris, *The End of Faith: Religion, Terror, and the Future of Reason* (New York: W. W. Norton & Company, 2005); but see Cecil Anthony John Coady, 'Violence and Religion', *Revue Internationale de Philosophie* **3** (2013), 237–57.

[30] Graham Harvey, *Shamanism: A Reader* (New York: Psychology Press, 2003).

by members of the Native American Church.[31] The 'mescaline experience', Huxley writes,

> is what Catholic theologians call "a gratuitous grace", not necessary to salvation but potentially helpful and to be accepted thankfully, if made available. To be shaken out of the ruts of ordinary perception, to be shown for a few timeless hours the outer and the inner world, not as they appear to an animal obsessed with survival or to a human being obsessed with words and notions, but as they are apprehended, directly and unconditionally, by Mind at Large – this is an experience of inestimable value.[32]

Notice the 'helpful' rather than 'necessary' effect of the drug in bringing about the experience that was, to Huxley, of inestimable value. I will say more about this issue in a later section, but for now I wish to simply raise the suggestion that if psychedelic substances are ever to feature in a prudent plan for personal moral bioenhancement,[33] they should probably serve a *facilitating* or *adjunctive* role, rather than *determinative* one, in the overall enhancement

---

[31]   Peter N. Jones, 'The Native American Church, Peyote, and Health: Expanding Consciousness for Healing Purposes', *Contemporary Justice Review* **10**:4 (2007), 411–25; John H. Halpern, et al., 'Psychological and Cognitive Effects of Long-Term Peyote Use among Native Americans', *Biological Psychiatry* **58**:8 (2005), 624–31.

[32]   The quote finishes with 'to everyone, but especially intellectuals'. Aldous Huxley, *The Doors of Perception* (London: Chatto and Windus, 1954): http://nacr.us/media/text/the_doors_of_perception.pdf. See page 53 of the version available online at the preceding link.

[33]   I am just flagging my use of the word 'personal' in this sentence. In this essay, I am concerned only with mature individuals' voluntary attempts to morally self-enhance, which is *prima facie* not only morally permissible, but desirable. Top-down or coerced moral enhancement of others – particularly if psychedelics were involved – would be much harder to justify from a moral perspective and I will make no attempt to do so here. Still, you might ask, what about drug-mediated moral enhancement of children by their parents or guardians? In some contexts, such enhancement may indeed be appropriate – the careful administration of methylphenidate to children with severe conduct disorders, for example, may be consistent with moral neuroenhancement as I have defined it, and in some cases is presumably justified – but a full discussion of the ethics of such interventions is beyond the scope of this essay. See: Rachel G. Klein, et al., 'Clinical Efficacy of Methylphenidate in Conduct Disorder with and without Attention Deficit Hyperactivity Disorder', *Archives of General Psychiatry* **54**:11 (1997), 1073–80.

process.[34] In other words, they should not be taken "in a vacuum" – that is, by oneself or with unprepared others, without adequate mental or emotional groundwork, stripped of all cultural context – with the expectation that they will somehow *cause* moral improvement all on their own. Writing about psilocybin, the active ingredient in "magic mushrooms", Johns Hopkins psychologist William Richards highlights the need for realistic expectations:

> It is clear that [the drug] never can be responsibly administered as a medication to be taken independent of preparation and careful attention to the powerful variables of [one's mindset] and [physical] setting. One cannot take psilocybin as a pill to cure one's alienation, neurosis, addiction, or fear of death in the same way one takes aspirin to banish a headache. What psilocybin does is provide an opportunity to explore a range of non-ordinary states. It unlocks a door; how far one ventures through the doorway and what awaits one [...] largely is dependent on non-drug variables.[35]

Over a century earlier, a more famous William advanced a similar perspective in reference to the altered states of consciousness occasioned by his use of nitrous oxide.[36] In his 1902 masterpiece, *The Varieties of Religious Experience*, William James writes that such drug-induced subjective changes 'may determine attitudes though they cannot furnish formulas, and open a region though they fail to give a map'.[37] Elsewhere in the same passage, he presages

---

[34]   I have made similar arguments using the example of "love drugs" in greater depth elsewhere: Brian D. Earp, Anders Sandberg, and Julian Savulescu, 'The Medicalization of Love: Response to Critics', *Cambridge Quarterly of Healthcare Ethics* **25**:4 (2016), 759–71; Brian D. Earp and Julian Savulescu, 'Is There Such a Thing as a Love Drug? Reply to McGee', *Philosophy, Psychiatry, & Psychology* **23**:2 (2016), 93–96; Olga A. Wudarczyk, et al., 'Could Intranasal Oxytocin Be Used to Enhance Relationships? Research Imperatives, Clinical Policy, and Ethical Considerations', *Current Opinion in Psychiatry* **26**:5 (2013), 474–84.

[35]   William A. Richards, 'Understanding the Religious Import of Mystical States of Consciousness Facilitated by Psilocybin', in J. H. Ellens and B. Roberts (eds), *The Psychedelic Policy Quagmire: Health, Law, Freedom, and Society* (Denver: Praeger, 2015), 139–44, 140.

[36]   William James, 'Subjective Effects of Nitrous Oxide', *Mind* **7**:1 (1882), 186–208.

[37]   William James, *The Varieties of Religious Experience* (Mineola, New York: Dover Publications, 1902).

Huxley's point about the potential value of non-rational aspects of mental life:

> One conclusion was forced upon my mind at that time, and my impression of its truth has ever since remained unshaken. It is that our normal waking consciousness, rational consciousness as we call it, is but one special type of consciousness, whilst all about it, parted from it by the filmiest of screens, there lie potential forms of consciousness entirely different. We may go through life without suspecting their existence; but apply the requisite stimulus, and at a touch they are there in all their completeness, definite types of mentality which probably somewhere have their field of application and adaptation.[38]

Might one of those fields of application be moral neuroenhancement? To answer this question, let us zoom out from the specific examples we have so far been discussing and consider the class of relevant substances all together.

5. Psychedelics and Moral Neuroenhancement

In their study of spirituality in psychedelic drugs users, Levente Móró and colleagues write that the class of psychoactive substances most closely associated with transpersonal and spiritual domains is psychedelics.[39] The word psychedelic, coined in the 1950s, is a mashup of the Ancient Greek words *psychē* (ψυχή, "soul") and *dēloun* (δηλοῦν, "to make visible, to reveal"), roughly translatable as "mind-revealing". Some psychedelics may be found in nature; others are produced in the lab. The most prominent examples include lysergic acid diethylamide (LSD); psilocybin and psilocin from the mushroom *Psilocybe* ("magic" mushrooms); mescaline from cacti, such as *peyote* (*Lophophora williamsii*); and N,N-dimethyltryptamine (DMT), along with ingestible preparations containing that molecule plus MAOI inhibitors, such as the plant-based brew *ayahuasca*.[40] On some classifications, 3,4-Methylenedioxymethamphetamine (MDMA), commonly known as ecstasy, also counts as a psychedelic substance, although it has a

---

[38] James, *The Varieties of Religious Experience*, 388.

[39] Levente Móró, et al., 'Voice of the Psychonauts: Coping, Life Purpose, and Spirituality in Psychedelic Drug Users', *Journal of Psychoactive Drugs*, **43**:3 (2011), 188–98, 189.

[40] Móró, et al., 'Voice of the Psychonauts'. Paraphrased.

Brian D. Earp

different risk profile and mechanism of action compared to the others; it will therefore be treated separately in this chapter.[41]

Primarily acting on serotonin receptors in neocortical pyramidal cells, psychedelics may induce 'temporary and reversible altered states of consciousness by destabilizing and repatterning several psychological subsystems, such as perception, attention, cognition, memory, and sense of self'. Such changes may result in marked shifts in subjective experience, sometimes involving hallucinations across multiple modalities, synesthesia (blending of senses), 'strong emotions varying from terror to awe, encounters and communication with seemingly autonomous entities, space and time distortions, and feelings of oneness, understanding, or insight'.[42]

Generally considered physiologically safe and nonaddictive, psychedelics are characterised by much lower acute toxicity than other drugs such as alcohol.[43] In carefully structured research or therapeutic settings with appropriate supervision, the above-mentioned mental states can typically be reached in a controlled way, reducing the risk for negative long-term physiological and psychological aftereffects to a minimum.[44]

---

[41] There is some debate about whether MDMA should be counted as a psychedelic (for an interesting discussion, see the YouTube video, 'Is MDMA a Psychedelic?': https://www.youtube.com/watch?v=yuXWDV LaRzQ). Psychedelic drugs are typically serotonin receptor agonists: they mimic serotonin and tie to serotonin receptors in serotonin's place. MDMA, on the other hand, causes a very significant release of serotonin, as well as dopamine and norepinephrine, and it has a higher potential for abuse and neurotoxic effects. See: David E. Nichols, 'Differences Between the Mechanism of Action of MDMA, MDBD, and the Classic Hallucinogens: Identification of a New Therapeutic Class: Entactogens', *Journal of Psychoactive Drugs* **18**:4 (1986), 305–13; Erika Check, 'Psychedelic Drugs: The Ups and Downs of Ecstasy', *Nature* **429**:6988 (2004), 126–28; Una D. McCann, et al., 'Serotonin Neurotoxicity after (±)3,4-Methylenedioxymethamphetamine (MDMA; "Ecstasy"): A Controlled Study in Humans', *Neuropsychopharmacology* **10**:2 (1994), 129–38. I thank Ole Martin Moen for calling my attention to these distinctions.

[42] Móró, et al., 'Voice of the Psychonauts', 190.

[43] David E. Nichols, 'Hallucinogens', *Pharmacology & Therapeutics* **101**:2 (2004), 131–81.

[44] Matthew W. Johnson, William A. Richards, and Roland R. Griffiths, 'Human Hallucinogen Research: Guidelines for Safety', *Journal of Psychopharmacology* **22**:6 (2008), 603–20.

Adverse reactions, including persisting hallucinations[45] and 'bad trips',[46] do sometimes occur. Generally these are associated with 'unintentional or unattended usage, a disturbing or overstimulating environment, inadequate preparedness and a careless attitude toward drug use, pre-existing or dormant psychiatric conditions, and earlier or recent unprocessed traumas of the psyche'.[47] Moreover, too-frequent or highly repeated use may increase the risk of neurotoxic effects, especially in the case of MDMA, and even more especially when combined with other drugs such as the stimulants cocaine or methamphetamine.[48] More moderate or occasional use, by contrast, particularly in a supportive environment and with 'proper conceptual and ideological background',[49] can trigger

---

[45]   See, e.g., Leo Hermle, Martin Ruchsow, and K. L. Täschner, 'Hallucinogen Persisting Perception Disorder (HPPD) and Flashback Phenomena – Differential Diagnosis and Explanation Models', *Fortschritte der Neurologie-Psychiatrie* **83**:9 (2015), 506–15; and John H. Halpern and Harrison G. Pope, 'Hallucinogen Persisting Perception Disorder: What Do We Know After 50 Years?', *Drug and Alcohol Dependence* **69**:2 (2003), 109–19. Hermle, et al. note in their abstract that persisting hallucinations can occur in the form of 'flashbacks', which refer to 'brief visual perceptual, mood, and altered states of consciousness effects reminiscent of acute hallucinogen intoxication effects', and that 'many users regard flashback phenomena as benign and even pleasant'. If altered perception persists for months or years, however, and causes severe individual distress, then Hallucinogen Persisting Perception Disorder (HPPD) may be diagnosed. According to Halpern and Pope (see second reference), HPPD is uncommon and is associated mostly with the unmonitored, recreational use of LSD.

[46]   Robert L. Taylor, John I. Maurer, and Jared R. Tinklenberg, 'Management of Bad Trips in an Evolving Drug Scene', *JAMA* **213**:3 (1970), 422–25.

[47]   Móró, et al., 'Voice of the Psychonauts', 190; see also: R. J. Strassman, 'Adverse Reactions to Psychedelic Drugs: A Review of the Literature', *The Journal of Nervous and Mental Disease* **172**:10 (1984), 577–95.

[48]   Edmund Silins, Jan Copeland, and Paul Dillon, 'Qualitative Review of Serotonin Syndrome, Ecstasy (MDMA) and the Use of Other Serotonergic Substances: Hierarchy of Risk', *Australian & New Zealand Journal of Psychiatry* **41**:8 (2007), 649–55.

[49]   Móró, et al., 'Voice of the Psychonauts', 190. As with the issue of moral disagreement discussed above, it is likely that people will also disagree about what constitutes the 'proper conceptual and ideological background' for a successful drug-mediated experience, as well as the appropriate setting in which the experience should take place. Following Foucault, for

Brian D. Earp

subjective experiences that may be interpreted by the drug-user as including – or fostering the development of – profound moral insights,[50] 'deeply meaningful religious revelations', and even 'spiritual awakenings'.[51]

For example, in a recent double-blind clinical study, Roland R. Griffiths and colleagues reported that psilocybin, when administered to carefully pre-screened volunteers, 'occasioned experiences which had marked similarities to classic mystical experiences and which were rated by volunteers as having substantial personal meaning and spiritual significance'. Moreover, 'the volunteers attributed to the experience sustained positive changes in attitudes and behavior that were consistent with changes rated by friends and family', including increased patience, good-natured humour and playfulness,

---

example, one might worry that, rather than psychologically emancipating people, an institutionalised or clinical setting could perform an ideological function in terms of producing people who better conform to societal expectations (I thank Lewis Coyne for bringing this possibility to my attention). That certainly may turn out to be the case – however, the deeper question is whether or when societal expectations are consistent with one's moral enhancement aims as opposed to in conflict with them, and this is something that will have a different answer depending on the individual. There are no simple solutions here. Any person who seeks to improve herself as a moral agent, whether with the adjunctive use of drugs or through more conventional means, will have to grapple with such contextual matters. Should one attend church services, and follow the teachings of a particular religious leader? If so, which one? Should one embed in this spiritual community or that one? And so on. Needless to say, there are many institutions in place already to try to get people to conform to (potentially problematic) societal expectations, even setting drug use aside. If anything, the voluntary use of psychedelic substances as part of a carefully considered programme of moral self-development seems more likely to bring such institutions into a sceptical light than to blindly reinforce them or compel conformity. Nevertheless, the basic point Coyne raises is right: the social, physical, and ideological setting of the drug experience could undoubtedly influence which of those outcomes was more likely, and a "clinical" atmosphere in particular may very well pose special risks.

[50] Sam Harris, *Waking Up: A Guide to Spirituality Without Religion* (New York: Simon and Schuster, 2014); Thomas B. Roberts, *The Psychedelic Future of the Mind: How Entheogens Are Enhancing Cognition, Boosting Intelligence, and Raising Values* (New York: Simon and Schuster, 2013).

[51] Móró, et al., 'Voice of the Psychonauts', 190.

mental flexibility, optimism, interpersonal perceptiveness and caring, and compassion or social concern.[52]

Similar effects have been reported for ayahuasca, the above-mentioned brew containing DMT and MAOI inhibitors. Although less-well studied in a scientific context, ayahuasca has been used in traditional shamanic ceremonies across the Amazon basin and elsewhere for hundreds of years.[53] The medical anthropologist Michael Winkelman argues that the active ingredients in ayahuasca, in combination with an appropriate diet, facilitate altered states of consciousness in the initiate that allow him or her to better appreciate the teachings of the shaman:

> Ayahuasca is often seen as opening the heart, expanding love for others, and leading to healing of both self and relationships. Ingesting the brew is seen as expanding awareness, healing the personality, and providing the insight and energies to restore personal relations. The effects also enable people to better deal with personal death and dying, as well as that of their loved ones and the grieving process. [...] Some spoke of ayahuasca as [...] enabling [them] to control their own spiritual energies.[54]

It is not entirely clear what it means to be able to control one's 'spiritual energies', but some insight into the matter may be gained from observational studies looking at the positive effects of ayahuasca on mindfulness,[55] which preliminary research suggests may augment one's ability to resist powerful urges (thereby allowing one to act less impulsively), reduce a person's susceptibility to acting in response to addictive drug cues, and increase one's capacity to maintain perspective in response to strong emotional states.[56]

---

[52] Roland R. Griffiths, et al., 'Psilocybin Can Occasion Mystical-Type Experiences Having Substantial and Sustained Personal Meaning and Spiritual Significance', *Psychopharmacology* **187**:3 (2006), 268–83, 280.

[53] Dennis J. McKenna, 'Clinical Investigations of the Therapeutic Potential of Ayahuasca: Rationale and Regulatory Challenges', *Pharmacology & Therapeutics* **102**:2 (2004), 111–29.

[54] Michael J. Winkelman, 'Psychedelic Medicines', in J. H. Ellens and B. Roberts (eds), *The Psychedelic Policy Quagmire: Health, Law, Freedom, and Society* (Denver: Praeger, 2015), 93–117, 108.

[55] G. Thomas, et al., 'Ayahuasca-Assisted Therapy for Addiction: Results from a Preliminary Observational Study in Canada', *Current Drug Abuse Reviews* **6**:1 (2013), 30–42.

[56] J. Soler, et al., 'Exploring the Therapeutic Potential of Ayahuasca: Acute Intake Increases Mindfulness-Related Capacities.', *Psychopharmacology* **233**:5 (2016), 823–29; Katie Witkiewitz, G. Alan Marlatt, and Denise Walker, 'Mindfulness-Based Relapse Prevention for

Brian D. Earp

If such findings turn out to be robust and replicable,[57] they would appear to support the existence of a biochemically assisted means of improving a higher-level, flexible capacity to modulate one's moral and emotional responses across a range of settings – akin to what was described in the third desideratum for a plausible real-life moral neuroenhancer (see Introduction). Given such suggestive findings, as well as many others that could be cited, it is curious that bioethicists engaged in the current moral enhancement debate, with few exceptions,[58] have written hardly a word about psychedelic drugs.[59] How might this apparent blind spot be explained?

In his recent book on the revival of hallucinogen research since the "decade of the brain" – the 1990s – Nicolas Langlitz argues that the idea of using biotechnology for moral enhancement, in roughly the sense intended by current advocates, had already been raised in earnest in the second half of the last century. Among others, Timothy Leary and his followers, as well as the wider hippie movement, actively hoped that psychedelic drugs (in concert with other factors including changes to prevailing social norms and institutions) 'would turn us into a more virtuous, more creative, and happier species'.[60]

Alcohol and Substance Use Disorders', *Journal of Cognitive Psychotherapy* **19**:3 (2005), 211–28.

[57] This caveat is important to highlight as there are now serious concerns about the reproducibility of many published findings across medicine and social psychology. See: Brian D. Earp and David Trafimow, 'Replication, Falsification, and the Crisis of Confidence in Social Psychology', *Frontiers in Psychology* **6**:621 (2015), 1–11.

[58] E.g., Rafael Ahlskog, 'Moral Enhancement Should Target Self-Interest and Cognitive Capacity', *Neuroethics* **10**:3 (2017), 1–11; Michael N. Tennison, 'Moral Transhumanism: The Next Step', *The Journal of Medicine and Philosophy: A Forum for Bioethics and Philosophy of Medicine* **37**:4 (2012), 405–16.

[59] That is not to say that philosophers or ethicists generally have not written about psychedelic drugs and the moral implications of their use; rather, it is the ethicists involved in the moral bioenhancement debate specifically who seem not to have noticed the potential relevance of these substances to their arguments. For good introductions, see: S. Luper-Foy and C. Brown (eds), *Drugs, Morality, and the Law* (New York: Garland Publishing, 1994); Douglas N. Husak, *Drugs and Rights* (Cambridge: Cambridge University Press, 1992); Rob Lovering, *A Moral Defense of Recreational Drug Use* (New York: Springer, 2015).

[60] Nicolas Langlitz, *Neuropsychedelia: The Revival of Hallucinogen Research Since the Decade of the Brain* (University of California Press,

Continuing into the 1970s, many academic researchers besides Leary were convinced that their investigations into psychedelic experiences 'would contribute to propelling human consciousness toward unheard of capacities'. But by the 1990s, following a conservative shift in the culture, research into mind-altering substances had taken an entirely different turn: 'utopian dreams gave way to a less fanciful conception of enhancement as optimization of already known human capacities'. In contrast to the earlier 'psychedelic explorations of human potential', Langlitz notes, 'this one-dimensional notion of enhancement lent itself to an experimental operationalization', consistent with the increasingly reductionist approach of contemporary science.[61]

Thus, while we do see research into psychedelic substances being conducted today, it is almost exclusively within a highly medicalised context that has not had much bearing on the moral enhancement literature.[62] In the meantime, as noted earlier, advocates of moral bioenhancement have focussed their attention primarily on "one-dimensional" interventions into specific capacities (relying on oxytocin sprays, brain stimulation devices, and the like), or on more global drug-based interventions that are confined to the "cognitive" realm. To see how a psychotropic drug, by contrast, might be used in practice to foster apparent moral improvement (without reducing to the augmentation of purely "cognitive" capacities like attention or reasoning ability), consider the case of MDMA.

6. How Would it Work? A Case Study With MDMA

In the 1980s, before it was made illegal, MDMA – popularly known as "ecstasy" due to the feelings of euphoria it can induce – was

---

2013), 233. Following up on this idea, Ole Martin Moen (personal correspondence) suggested to me that 'one possible path from psychedelics to moral enhancement might be that, used in the right way, psychedelics can help make people become more happy and satisfied. Of course, happy and satisfied people might do pretty bad things (vote for bad parties, support practices that are cruel toward animals, etc.), but it is presumably uncommon that happy and satisfied people commit atrocities'.

[61] Langlitz, *Neuropsychedelia*, 233.
[62] Attila Szabo, 'Psychedelics and Immunomodulation: Novel Approaches and Therapeutic Opportunities', *Frontiers in Immunology* 6:358 (2015), 1–11.

being used as an aid in couple's therapy by professional counselors.[63] Writing in the *Journal of Psychoactive Drugs* in 1998, George Greer and Requa Tolbert described a method of conducting MDMA-enhanced therapeutic sessions based on their experience with roughly 80 clients between 1980–1985.[64] After careful pre-screening and obtaining informed consent, Greer and Tolbert met with the clients in their homes, believing that a more personal setting would be best for 'facilitating comfort and trust'.[65] Consistent with the caveat raised by William Richards concerning psilocybin that I quoted earlier, they emphasised the importance of non-drug variables, such as the person's mindset, intentions, and expectations, in shaping the drug-mediated experience:

> We never recommended an MDMA session to anyone seeking to be a passive participant who would be "cured" of [a] psychological problem. We believed that the person treated or cured themselves, with the assistance of MDMA and their relationship to us.[66]

Depending on client preference, they started the session with meditation or prayer. Then, they administered a controlled dose of 75 to 150 mg, adjusting for the client's sex or body mass, with a 50 mg booster if requested later on. Clients wore eyeshades to shut out visual distractions and reduce the risk of overstimulation. While waiting for the drug to take effect, they listened to classical music, usually through a pair of headphones – Mahler and Beethoven were among the more popular choices. Then, when they felt ready, clients spoke with their romantic partner. Often, they would speak for hours.

Not everyone had a major breakthrough. But some did. Three years after her treatment, one client, the thirty-something daughter of Holocaust survivors, wrote: 'I still am a different person. I'm not prone to getting caught up in the negative dark influences in my character. I have more choice over how I feel'. Previously prone

---

[63] Julie Holland, *Ecstasy: The Complete Guide: A Comprehensive Look at the Risks and Benefits of MDMA* (Rochester, VT: Inner Traditions / Bear & Co, 2001).

[64] George R. Greer and Requa Tolbert, 'A Method of Conducting Therapeutic Sessions with MDMA', *Journal of Psychoactive Drugs* **30**:4 (1998), 371–79.

[65] Greer and Tolbert, 'A Method of Conducting Therapeutic Sessions with MDMA', 365.

[66] Greer and Tolbert, 'A Method of Conducting Therapeutic Sessions with MDMA', 372.

to 'anxiety attacks' and intrusive thoughts about concentration camps, she now said: 'I can handle my emotions [...] I understand how they work more'.[67]

Through their own research and that of other pioneers, Greer and Tolbert came to argue that MDMA – administered in the right way, and with the careful oversight of an appropriately qualified guide – could help some individuals achieve 'a more healthy and accurate perspective of who and what they [are] psychologically', by decreasing irrational fear responses to perceived emotional threats.[68] Their clients seemed to agree. According to Greer and Tolbert, 'roughly 90%' of their clients 'had generally positive and useful experiences' after participating in MDMA-assisted therapy, with some reporting that they felt more love toward their partners and were better able to 'forgive the pain of the past'.[69]

Some of these outcomes seem consistent with moral improvement; others seem to apply to other domains such as mental health. Nevertheless, the immediate effects of MDMA wear off after a few hours. Especially at lower doses, the drug does not seem to 'significantly distort perception, thinking, or memory'.[70] Greer and Tolbert speculate that the 'learning that took place during the session often became consolidated and applied to clients' everyday lives long after the session had ended'. For example, couples who experienced a session together 'frequently reported basing their relationships much more on love and trust than on fear and suspicion'.[71] But these

---

[67] Greer and Tolbert, 'A Method of Conducting Therapeutic Sessions with MDMA', 377.
[68] Greer and Tolbert, 'A Method of Conducting Therapeutic Sessions with MDMA', 371.
[69] Greer and Tolbert, 'A Method of Conducting Therapeutic Sessions with MDMA', 372.
[70] Greer and Tolbert, 'A Method of Conducting Therapeutic Sessions with MDMA', 378.
[71] Greer and Tolbert, 'A Method of Conducting Therapeutic Sessions with MDMA', 378. Generally this sort of outcome is a good thing, but it is obviously possible to be "too trusting" toward one's partner, particularly if the partner habitually takes advantage of one's trust. This consideration highlights how important it will be, if drugs ever are to be used in a context such as the one illustrated here, to ensure that they are used thoughtfully and that their personal and interpersonal effects are monitored and reflected upon both during the drug-mediated experience and after the effects of the drug have worn off. That said, insofar as psychedelics do allow one to gain deeper insights into one's mind and situation, as is often claimed by those who use them, then it is quite possible that (to pursue the present

results were not simply *caused* by MDMA – or so it seemed to Greer and Tolbert. Rather, they were 'achieved by the clients making decisions based on what they learned during their MDMA sessions, and [by] remembering and applying those decisions for as long as they were able and willing after the session was over'.[72]

What practical lessons might bioethicists take from the historical example of MDMA-assisted marital therapy for the debate about moral bioenhancement? To my mind, at least two main points stand out:

(1)   If drugs are to be used for moral enhancement, they should be administered in a carefully controlled setting to willing volunteers who have been properly prepared for the experience, ideally under the guidance of an appropriately qualified person or persons (i.e., someone with requisite experience with the drug, its likely effects, means for addressing any problems, etc.).

(2)   Moral neuroenhancers would likely not function by simply causing moral improvement in the agent, nor should they be expected to work in such a way. Instead, they would most likely foster states of mind that that allowed one to engage with the moral domain in a more productive or insightful way, storing away any lessons learned for application in the "real world" once the effects of the drug had worn off.

The second point is important to emphasise. Some people might be concerned that "popping a pill" to achieve deep moral insights would be in some sense too easy, superficial, or unsustainable – the sort of thing that, quickly obtained, could just as quickly be lost. As Huston Smith has put it: 'what promised to be a shortcut will

---

example) the partner's tendency to betray one's trust would become more, rather than less, apparent to the user while under the influence of the drug, thereby allowing her to make a better informed decision about whether the relationship should continue. In other words, at least anecdotally, psychedelics such as MDMA do not seem to have a context-insensitive or generalised "trust-enhancing" (or other similar) effect, whereby one simply becomes *more* trusting (etc.), regardless of the dynamic between oneself and the other people in one's life. Rather, the idea is precisely that greater genuine insight into the nature of what is really going on can be facilitated by the use of psychedelics (under the right circumstances), at least in many cases.

[72]   Greer and Tolbert, 'A Method of Conducting Therapeutic Sessions with MDMA', 378.

prove to be a short circuit; what began as a religion will end as a religion surrogate'.[73]

Thinking of the "pill" as an *adjunct* to moral development, however, leaves plenty of room for active, non-superficial engagement and intentional moral learning. As Smith wrote, the evidence concerning psychedelics that was available to him as early as the 1960s

> would seem to [suggest] that chemicals can aid the religious life, but only where set within a context of faith (meaning by this the conviction that what they disclose is true) and discipline (meaning diligent exercise of the will in the attempt to work out the implications of the disclosures for the living of life in the every day, common sense world).[74]

Again, Smith is focussing on 'religion', but the word "moral" could be swapped in and the sentence remain just as plausible. The point is that the drug should not be doing all the work. Rather, it should be used, if at all, as an aid to moral enhancement – and on an "as needed" rather than routine basis. Moreover, whatever insights are gained through such use should be combined with 'diligent exercise of the will' to be properly understood, much less productively applied to the agent's normal waking world.

James Hughes has given a helpful illustration of this approach in his essay, 'Using Neurotechnologies to Develop Virtues: A Buddhist Approach to Cognitive Enhancement'. According to Hughes, 'a distinctively Buddhist approach to the use of neurotechnologies' would seek to 'avoid being stuck in any one set of moods or mental states' by constantly turning to biotechnologies to elicit the desired states of mind. Thus, 'using a drug or nanoneural device that created an addiction to a blessed out state of pleasure would [be] unwholesome' and morally problematic.[75]

In other words, there is an important difference between 'a dynamic *eudaemonic* happiness grounded in [genuine] self-awareness', and 'the constant stimulation of dopamine [or other brain chemicals] on a hedonic treadmill'. So, while some Western Buddhists 'credit their experimentation with psychedelics with catalyzing their interest in meditation, and providing an initial glimpse of their inner lives that they would not otherwise have had', few such Buddhists believe that the

[73]   Smith, 'Do Drugs Have Religious Import?', 529.
[74]   Smith, 'Do Drugs Have Religious Import?', 529.
[75]   James Hughes, 'Using Neurotechnologies to Develop Virtues: A Buddhist Approach to Cognitive Enhancement', *Accountability in Research* **20**:1 (2013), 27–41, 32, internal citations omitted.

psychedelics, on their own, were responsible for effectuating the positive changes to their personality over the long-term, further recognising that 'habitual use of psychedelics would be very unhealthy'.[76]

The approach advocated by Smith and Hughes seems sensible. Psychedelic moral enhancers should not be regarded as a panacea, or as something that magically overrides all conscious, rational thought to directly instill the desired moral changes in the agent. Instead, they should be seen as potentially contributing to an opportunity for moral growth, in part by providing or fostering the recognition of insights into oneself and one's inner workings, as well as the world around one, that might not otherwise be so readily obtained. Then, it is up to the agent to make good use of those insights in her process of moral development.

7. Conclusion

I would like to conclude with a note of caution. Because I have been interested to explore the potentially positive role of psychedelics in moral self-development, I have primarily focussed on "successful" anecdotes – that is, cases in which people seem genuinely to have benefitted, morally or otherwise, from their drug-enhanced experiences. But more negative experiences are certainly possible, as mentioned earlier. As the prominent drug researcher Ben Sessa argues, we are right to adopt a stance of healthy scepticism toward any proposal that, 'in the eyes of the general public, is associated with recreational drug abuse'.[77]

Indeed, psychedelic drugs – just like other drugs such as alcohol or prescription medication – can, when used irresponsibly, cause 'physical, psychological and social harm, and even deaths'. So we must be cautious, and take seriously the concerns of those people who fear that the use of such drugs may cause 'greater social and health problems than it may solve'.[78] Even so, Sessa suggests that there is more than enough evidence already from recent, controlled studies to render plausible the folk knowledge – accumulated over centuries – that psychedelics can also be beneficial. At a minimum, he concludes, the

---

[76] Hughes, 'Using Neurotechnologies to Develop Virtues', 32, internal citations ommitted.

[77] Ben Sessa, 'Is There a Case for MDMA-Assisted Psychotherapy in the UK?', *Journal of Psychopharmacology* **21**:2 (2007), 220–24, 223.

[78] Sessa, 'Is There a Case for MDMA-Assisted Psychotherapy in the UK?', 223.

'evidence against at least researching' psychedelics for therapeutic or enhancement purposes 'appears to be very scant indeed'.[79] That is my position as well. While others may wish to argue that people should be free to ingest whatever substances they like toward whatever ends they choose, my offering here is only to suggest that careful research – both empirical and ethical – into the potential use of psychedelic drugs as moral bioenhancers should be carried out. Armed with better data about the likely effects of different drugs on different people at different dosages and in different settings, and drawing inspiration from earlier periods of history (or from contemporary communities where such drugs are used in a richly contextualised way), it may then be possible to outline the ideal conditions for voluntary moral neuroenhancement with the aid of psychedelics.

Yale University
brian.earp@yale.edu

---

[79] Sessa, 'Is There a Case for MDMA-Assisted Psychotherapy in the UK?', 223. See also Ben Sessa and David J. Nutt, 'MDMA, Politics and Medical Research: Have We Thrown the Baby Out With the Bathwater?', *Journal of Psychopharmacology* **21**:8 (2007), 787–91.

Index of Names

Alfano, Mark 334, 346n.
Arendt, Hannah 111, 188n.
Aristotle 11–12, 110, 115, 120, 125, 190, 193n., 199–201, 205–7

Bacon, Francis 357
Beauchamp, Tom 134, 168, 169, 170, 374n., 422n.
Berofsky, Bernard 134
Borgmann, Albert 353
Bostrom, Nick 45n., 52, 137n., 420n.
Brown, W. S. 49n.
Buchanan, Allen 84, 130n., 191n., 235n., 330n.

Childress, James 134, 168, 169, 170
Churchland, Patricia S. 69n., 136n., 332n.
Cohen, G. A., 97–8, 100
Coyne, Lewis 415n., 430
Curtis, B. L. 275

Dancy, Jonathan 170, 171, 194, 199, 202n.–3n.
DeGrazia, David 19n.–20n., 23, 28n.,

29n., 81n., 88n.– 90n., 128–9, 167n., 202n., 274n., 275, 392–3
de Lazari-Radek, Katarzyna 168n.
de Melo-Martín, Inmaculada 235n., 287, 287n., 419n.
Descartes, René 99, 354, 357
Dewey, John 293, 294, 300–7
Donagan, Alan 168
Doris, John 97n., 197n., 320n., 334n.
Douglas, Thomas 19n., 23n., 27n., 28n., 29n., 63, 84, 88n., 101n., 128n., 131n., 132n., 165n., 191n., 192n., 202n., 212n., 276n., 319n., 369n., 392–4, 403n., 406n., 415n., 416n., 418n.

Earp, Brian D. 390–1, 395, 396n., 398, 403–12ff.
Ellul, Jacques 353–4
Eysenck, Hans 37

Feinberg, Joel 122n.
Fischer, John Martin 62, 245n.
Foot, Philippa 10, 74, 110ff., 116, 313n., 321n.

Frankfurt, Harry 134, 245n.

Gadamer, Hans-Georg 367n.
Galilei, Galileo 354
Garshin, Rodion 118n.
Gert, Bernard 168
Gilligan, Carol 146n., 150
Glannon, Walter 252n.
Gordon, John-Stewart 363n.
Gramsci, Antonio 357, 361
Greene, Joshua 45, 74n., 75n., 313n., 315n., 316, 320n., 321n., 327n.

Habermas, Jürgen 247, 363, 365–70
Handfield, Toby 191n., 382–3
Harman, Gilbert 97n., 197n., 334n.
Harris, John 2, 28n., 39, 63, 80n.–2n., 92n., 106, 114, 115n., 132n., 133n., 152n., 192n., 212n., 227n., 233n.–5n., 274n., 287n., 299n., 364n., 403n., 418n., 419n., 420
Harris, Sam 424n., 430n.

441

Index of Names

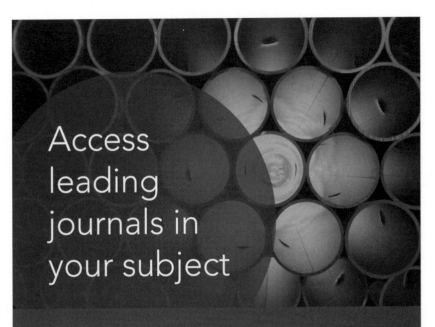